Additional praise for *The Wiley Handbook of Positive Clinical Psychology*

The purpose of this edited volume is to relate issues, concepts, and ideas emerging from the field of positive psychology to the domain of clinical psychology. The book accomplishes this goal in a much more than satisfactory way.

Michael F. Scheier,
Professor and Departmental Head of Psychology, Carnegie Mellon University,
former President and Outstanding Scientific Contribution Award winner
(Division 38, Health Psychology), American Psychological Association

An excellent and thought-provoking book that encourages us to understand the duality of our nature. This book extends the boundaries of both positive psychology and clinical psychology, whilst at the same showing how the two can be integrated in meaningful and actionable ways.

Lea Waters,
Gerry Higgins Chair in Positive Psychology, Director, Centre for Positive Psychology,
Melbourne Graduate School of Education, University of Melbourne

Anybody who has seen Alex Wood and I spar intellectually will not be not surprised that I'm giving this very balanced book as an enthusiastic endorsement as a Negateer can muster. Alex and I disagree on whether positive psychology can be integrated with the rest of the field, but if he is proved right and I am proved wrong, it will be because the committed scientists in positive psychology, not the salesforce, heed his excellent suggestions.

James C. Coyne,
Director Behavioural Oncology Programme, Professor of Psychology, Department of
Psychiatry, University of Pennsylvania School of Medicine

The Wiley Handbook of Positive Clinical Psychology

Edited by

Alex M. Wood and Judith Johnson

WILEY Blackwell

This edition first published 2016
© 2016 John Wiley & Sons, Ltd.

Registered Office
John Wiley & Sons, Ltd, The Atrium, Southern Gate, Chichester, West Sussex, PO19 8SQ, UK

Editorial Offices
350 Main Street, Malden, MA 02148-5020, USA
9600 Garsington Road, Oxford, OX4 2DQ, UK
The Atrium, Southern Gate, Chichester, West Sussex, PO19 8SQ, UK

For details of our global editorial offices, for customer services, and for information about how to apply for permission to reuse the copyright material in this book please see our website at www.wiley.com/wiley-blackwell.

The right of Alex M. Wood and Judith Johnson to be identified as the authors of the editorial material in this work has been asserted in accordance with the UK Copyright, Designs and Patents Act 1988.

Library of Congress Cataloging-in-Publication data applied for

Hardback ISBN: 9781118468241

A catalogue record for this book is available from the British Library.

Cover image: Getty/Comstock

Set in 9.5/11.5pt Galliard by SPi Global, Pondicherry, India
Printed and bound in Malaysia by Vivar Printing Sdn Bhd

1   2016

"To Ms Flacke, an English teacher who always believed in me. As I promised when aged 11, my first book is dedicated to you.".

Alex Wood

"To Mum and Dad, thank you for letting me monopolise the desktop computer and dial-up modem for long periods. I told you I was working on something good!"

Jude Johnson

Contents

List of Contributors

Elizabeth L. Addington is completing her doctoral training in the Health Psychology Ph.D. Program, Clinical Concentration, at the University of North Carolina, Charlotte, and at VA Connecticut Healthcare System, West Haven campus. Her clinical and research interests involve psycho-oncology, positive psychology, and responses to trauma or other major stressors, including post-traumatic growth.

Sara B. Algoe is an Assistant Professor in the Department of Psychology and Neuroscience at the University of North Carolina, Chapel Hill. She received her Ph.D. in Psychology from the University of Virginia, and completed a postdoctoral fellowship in Health Psychology at the University of California, Los Angeles, and another at the University of North Carolina, Chapel Hill, in psychophysiology. Algoe's expertise spans emotions, interpersonal relationships, and health psychology. Specifically, her research focuses on understanding the basic emotional and interpersonal mechanisms through which people capitalize on opportunities from the social environment; she uses this information to guide predictions about how and why these moments can have cumulative impact on intrapersonal and interpersonal functioning.

Arnoud Arntz, Ph.D., is a Professor of Clinical Psychology at the University of Amsterdam. He is also active as a clinician, mainly in the area of personality disorders. His research focuses on psychological processes in and treatment of PTSD, depression, and personality disorders. More specifically, he contributed to the development and tests of schema therapy as a treatment for a range of personality disorders and chronic depression. As part of this, he also studies the effects of psychological treatment on happiness, quality of life, social and societal functioning. He has co-authored books on schema therapy, including *Schema Therapy for Borderline Personality Disorder* (with van Genderen, Wiley, 2009); *Schema Therapy in Practice* (with Jacob, Wiley, 2012), and was senior author of the main publications on the (cost)-effectiveness of Schema Therapy, published in the *Archives of General Psychiatry*, *British Journal of Psychiatry*, *American Journal of Psychiatry*, and *Journal of Clinical Psychiatry*.

Lawrence G. Calhoun lived during his formative years in Brazil, moved to the United States to attend college, and has remained there since. A licensed psychologist, he has maintained a part-time clinical practice for many years. Together with Richard Tedeschi he is one of the pioneers in the research and theory on post-traumatic growth. He is co-editor or co-author of nine books, including *Posttraumatic Growth in Clinical Practice*. He is a recipient of the Bank of America Award for Teaching Excellence, the University of North Carolina Board of Governor's Award for Teaching Excellence, and of the First Citizens Bank Scholar's Medal (with Richard Tedeschi). Although he is no longer engaged in classroom teaching, he continues his research work and he continues to mentor doctoral students at the University of North Carolina, Charlotte.

Adam Davidson is currently completing his MSc. in Positive Psychology at the University of East London. He holds a MSc in Physics from the University of Bristol and works as a researcher for Happiness Works, making workplaces great. Adam was the lead researcher for Dr. Sir Anthony Seldon's "Beyond Happiness," and he is currently working with Olympic athletes to investigate the topic of passion. His passion is for martial arts and it was his role as a teacher and coach that lead him to study positive psychology.

Barnaby D. Dunn is a research and clinical psychologist, currently employed as an Associate Professor at the University of Exeter Mood Disorders Centre (http://psychology.exeter.ac.uk/staff/index.php?web_id=Barney_Dunn). He leads a research program developing new ways to treat reduced positive mood and lowered well-being in clinical depression. He co-directs the AccEPT clinic at the Mood Disorders Centre, where he treats individuals suffering from depression with cognitive-behavioral therapy or novel treatment approaches.

Robert A. Emmons, Ph.D., is the world's leading scientific expert on gratitude. He is a professor of psychology at the University of California, Davis, and the founding editor-in-chief of the *Journal of Positive Psychology*. He is also the author of the books *Gratitude Works!: A 21-Day Program for Creating Emotional Prosperity* and *Thanks! How the New Science of Gratitude Can Make You Happier*.

Giovanni A. Fava is currently Professor of Clinical Psychology at the University of Bologna and Clinical Professor of Psychiatry at the State University of New York at Buffalo. He holds a medical degree from the University of Padova, 1977, with electives at McMaster University, Rochester, NY (Engel) and Dartmouth (Lipowski). In Padova, he also completed his residency training in psychiatry in 1981. After working for several years in the United States (Albuquerque and Buffalo, NY), he returned to Italy in 1988, where he established an Affective Disorders Program in the Department of Psychology of the University of Bologna. He is editor-in-chief of *Psychotherapy and Psychosomatics*.

Timothy K. Feeney is a fourth-year graduate student in the Clinical Psychology Doctoral Program at the University of Nevada. He holds a bachelor's degree in psychology from San José State University. His previous work focused on the development of a functional assessment device oriented toward body image disturbance. His current research pertains to assessment procedures for interpersonal functioning and mechanisms of change in acceptance and commitment therapy and functional analytic psychotherapy.

Eamonn Ferguson is Professor of Health Psychology at Nottingham University. He is a chartered health and occupational psychologist, a Fellow of the Royal Society for Public Health, an Associate Fellow of the British Psychological Society, and co-founding president of the British Society for the Psychology of Individual Differences (www.bspid.org.uk). He was recently made a "Distinguished International Affiliate" of the division of Health Psychology of the American Psychological Association. His current theoretical work focuses on the integration of theory and models from psychology, in particular personality theory, with behavioral economics, to address questions focusing on (1) the overlap of personality and pro-social preferences, (2) the understanding of blood and organ donor behavior, and (3) subjective wellbeing and emotion processing. He has published 150 peer reviewed journal articles to date (including in the *BMJ*, *Annals of Behavioral Medicine*, *Health Psychology*, *BMC Medicine*, *Psychosomatic Medicine*) with his work funded by the HSE, ESRC, and DEFRA, amongst others.

Michael B. Frisch, Ph.D., studies and practices positive psychology and clinical psychology in the Department of Psychology and Neuroscience at Baylor University where he is a full professor of psychology. He is the author of Pearson Assessments' well-being test, the *Quality of Life Inventory* or *QOLI*, and the books, *Quality of Life Therapy*, and *Creating Your Best Life* (with Caroline Adams Miller). Dr. Frisch is a Research Fellow in the International Society for Quality of Life Studies. He is a Founding Fellow in Aaron T. Beck's Academy of Cognitive Therapy. He is also a past Director of Clinical Training in Baylor's APA-approved doctoral program in clinical psychology, and he is the youngest member in history to serve on the National Board of Governors of the American Red Cross.

Jeffrey J. Froh, Psy.D., is an Associate Professor of Psychology at Hofstra University and associate editor of the *Journal of Positive Psychology*. His research focuses on the assessment, development, and enhancement of gratitude in youth, as well as positive education. He is co-editor of *Activities for Teaching Positive Psychology: A Guide for Instructors*, published by the American Psychological Association, and co-author of *Making Grateful Kids: The Science of Building Character*.

Chelsea L. Greer, Ph.D., is an Assistant Professor of Psychology at Spring Hill College. She earned her Ph.D. from Virginia Commonwealth University and completed her clinical internship at Thomas E. Cook Counseling Center at Virginia Tech University. She studies forgiveness of offenders within religious communities and self-directed forgiveness interventions.

Brandon J. Griffin, M.S., is a doctoral student in the APA-accredited Counseling Psychology program at Virginia Commonwealth University (VCU). He specializes in developing and evaluating positive psychological interventions for administration to individuals, groups, and communities. His current interests include conducting basic and applied research on people's experiences of self-forgiveness in the aftermath of perpetrating interpersonal wrongdoing.

Carley Hauck is the founder of Intuitive Wellness and works as an integrative life coach, instructor, writer, and consultant in research and with worksite organizations, such as LinkedIn and Pixar. Carley holds a Master's Degree in health psychology and specializes in creating curriculum, training programs, and teaching on the intersection of mindfulness and well-being at home, at work, and in our relationships. She has been a lead consultant in several research studies observing the long-term benefits of mindfulness as it relates to health, stress resiliency, and the prevention of disease. She teaches on the subjects of Becoming a Better You, Mindful Nourishment and Food as Medicine at Stanford University and Stanford's Center for Integrative Medicine. Carley has written several articles on mindfulness and well-being. Her writing is regularly featured in *My Fitness Pal*, *Tricycle & Paleo* magazine, and on www.intuitivelywell.com.

Steven C. Hayes, Ph.D., is Nevada Foundation Professor at the Department of Psychology at the University of Nevada. An author of 39 books and more than 550 scientific articles, he has shown in his research how language and thought leads to human suffering. He is the developer of Relational Frame Theory, an account of human cognition, and has guided its extension to acceptance and commitment therapy (ACT), an evidence-based psychotherapy. Dr. Hayes has been president of several scientific and professional societies, including the Association for Behavioral and Cognitive Therapy, and the Association for Contextual Behavioral Science. His work has been recognized by several awards, including the Exemplary Contributions to Basic Behavioral Research and Its Applications from Division 25 of APA, the Impact of Science on Application award from the Society for the Advancement of Behavior Analysis, and the Lifetime Achievement Award from the Association for Behavioral and Cognitive Therapy.

Barbara S. Held is the Barry N. Wish Research Professor of Psychology and Social Studies at Bowdoin College in Maine. She is the 2012 recipient of the American Psychological Foundation Joseph B. Gittler Award for "scholarly contributions to the philosophical foundations of psychological knowledge," and she served as the 2008–2009 president of the Society for Theoretical and Philosophical Psychology of the American Psychological Association. Her work focuses on the ontological and epistemological underpinnings of psychological inquiry, especially as manifested in postmodern, hermeneutic, and positive psychology movements. Her books include *Back to Reality: A Critique of Postmodern Theory in Psychotherapy*, *Psychology's Interpretive Turn: The Search for Truth and Agency in Theoretical and Philosophical Psychology*, and *Stop Smiling, Start Kvetching: A 5-Step Guide to Creative Complaining*. She has appeared on NPR's "All Things Considered" and "Talk of the Nation," NBC's "Today" show, ABC News, the BBC, and the CBC.

Ryan N. Howes is a graduate of the University of Toronto Scarborough. His primary research interests concern narrative processing, cybernetic systems, identity, and common factors of psychotherapeutic change. He currently works at the University of Toronto Scarborough as a project coordinator, lab manager, and teaching assistant, and is involved in research programs exploring positive interventions among secondary and post-secondary students, self-knowledge among emerging adults, integrative functioning in life-story narratives, and narrative identity.

Chelsea M. Hughes, M.S., is a doctoral student in the APA-accredited Counseling Psychology program at Virginia Commonwealth University (VCU). She is a member of the Positive Psychology Research Group. Chelsea's research focuses on communication, specifically social interaction in online gaming and the promotion of prosocial behavior therein.

Paul Hutton, Clin.Psy.D., is a clinical psychologist and Chancellor's Fellow at the University of Edinburgh. He is interested in the development and evaluation of psychological treatments for psychosis, having been involved in a number of clinical trials and meta-analyses in this area. He has a particular interest in understanding treatment decision-making capacity in psychosis, and developing effective interventions to improve both this and service user autonomy.

Judith Johnson, Ph.D., Clin.Psy.D., is a Clinical Psychologist and Lecturer at the University of Leeds and the Bradford Institute of Health Research. She completed a Ph.D. in Clinical Psychology at the University of Manchester in 2010, and a Clinical Psychology Doctorate (Clin. Psy.D.) at the University of Birmingham in 2013. Her research is focused upon understanding and supporting the development of well-being and resilience, and how this can be applied in healthcare settings to improve treatments and service delivery.

Stephen Joseph is a professor in the School of Education at the University of Nottingham, where he is convener of the counselling and psychotherapy group. Stephen is a registered psychotherapist and coaching psychologist with interests in positive psychology. He has written, co-written, and edited numerous books, chapters, and papers on many aspects of positive psychology, psychotherapy, and psychological trauma, including *What Doesn't Kill Us: The New Psychology of Posttraumatic Growth* (2011) and, most recently, *Positive Psychology in Practice: Promoting Human Flourishing in Work, Health, Education and Everyday Life* (Wiley-Blackwell, 2015).

Evan M. Kleiman, Ph.D., is College Fellow in Psychology at Harvard University. He earned his Ph.D. from George Mason University, Fairfax, VA, and completed his clinical internship at Temple University, Philadelphia, PA. He studies cognitive and interpersonal suicide risk and resilience factors through the lens of positive clinical psychology.

Nathanial M. Lambert, Ph.D., is a psychologist, professor, author, and public speaker. He is the author of over 70 research articles and book chapters on the topic of thriving in life and served as an editor of the *Journal of Positive Psychology*. He has presented his research across the United States and on four continents. His research has been featured in *Today, Men's Health, America Online News, Woman's Health, Good Housekeeping Magazine, Radio Rhema New Zealand, Canadian Broadcasting Corporation, Encyclopedia Britannica, Health Day, MSN Healthy Living, Examiner, Science Daily*, and *The Economist*. Dr. Lambert is also the author of the book *See the World on Any Budget*, as well as the books *Publish and Prosper, Standing Up for Standing Out: Making the Most of Being Different*, and *Four Truths about Weight Loss that Nobody Tells You*.

Caroline R. Lavelock, M.S., is a doctoral candidate in the APA-accredited Counseling Psychology program at Virginia Commonwealth University (VCU). She studies positive psychology and is particularly interested in how virtues work and can be cultivated. Her current research focuses on the development and evaluation of interventions for promoting virtues including patience, humility, and forgiveness.

Sonja Lyubomirsky, Ph.D., is Professor of Psychology at the University of California, Riverside and author of *The How of Happiness* and *The Myths of Happiness*. She received her B.A. summa cum laude from Harvard University, and her Ph.D. in social psychology from Stanford University. Lyubomirsky's teaching and mentoring of students have been recognized with the Faculty of the Year and Faculty Mentor of the Year Awards. Her research – on the possibility of lastingly increasing happiness – have been the recipients of many honors, including the Templeton Positive Psychology Prize, a Science of Generosity grant, and a Character Lab grant. Lyubomirsky lives in Santa Monica, California, with her family.

Andrew K. MacLeod is Professor of Clinical Psychology at Royal Holloway University of London, where he is also Director of Clinical Psychology Training. He received a 1st class degree in Psychology from the University of Aberdeen, and his Ph.D. from the University of Cambridge, where he also trained as a clinician. He was an early advocate for the importance of deficits in positive aspects of experience in psychological disorders, especially suicidal behavior, and has pioneered research on the role that thinking about the future plays in well-being and mental health. He has published widely on these topics and has received support from the Medical Research Council, the Economic Research Council, the Wellcome Trust, and the Department of Health (all UK). He is the author of a forthcoming book, *Prospection, Well-being and Mental Health.*

James E. Maddux, Ph.D., is University Professor Emeritus in the Department of Psychology and Senior Scholar at the Center for the Advancement of Well-Being at George Mason University (Fairfax, VA). He is the former editor of the *Journal of Social and Clinical Psychology* and former director of the clinical psychology doctoral program at George Mason University. He is the co-editor (with June Tangney) of *Social Psychological Foundations of Clinical Psychology* and (with Barbara Winstead) *Psychopathology: Foundations for a Contemporary Understanding*, now in its fourth edition. Maddux is a Fellow of the American Psychological Association's Divisions of General, Clinical, and Health Psychology, and a Fellow of the Association for Psychological Science. His recent activities have included extensive international travel that has involved giving lectures, teaching graduate students, and organizing workshops on evidence-based clinical interventions, primarily in the former communist bloc countries of Eastern Europe.

Warren Mansell, D.Phil., D.Clin.Psy., is a Reader in Clinical Psychology at the University of Manchester. He completed a Ph.D. at the University of Oxford, and a Doctorate in Clinical Psychology at the Institute of Psychiatry, Kings College, London. The focus of his work is psychological approaches to bipolar disorder, transdiagnostic interventions for mental health problems (e.g., a transdiagnostic approach to CBT using method of levels therapy), and perceptual control theory. He has produced over a hundred peer-reviewed publications, as well as a popular science book, a self-help book, and two therapy manuals. In 2011, he was awarded the May Davidson Award by the British Psychological Society, marking an outstanding contribution to clinical psychology in the first 10 years since qualifying as a clinical psychologist.

Acacia Parks, Ph.D., is an Associate Professor of Psychology at Hiram College and Chief Scientist at Happify, a start-up company that spreads the science of happiness to the general public. Her research focuses on self-help methods for increasing happiness via books, smart-phones, and the World Wide Web. She also studies factors that impact on whether a person can successfully make themselves happier. Acacia regularly publishes articles in scientific journals and has edited three books. She is also associate editor at the *Journal of Positive Psychology*. She is an active teacher, offering courses on positive psychology, as well as health psychology, abnormal and clinical psychology, research methods, and critical writing.

Tom G. Patterson is currently Academic Director of the Clinical Psychology Doctoral Training Programme at Coventry University and the University of Warwick. His clinical interests lie principally in the applications of psychology to clinical work with older people and to people with dementia. He has research interests in the experiences of people living with dementia, positive aspects of caregiving in dementia, person-centered theory, positive psychology, and mindfulness.

Andrew Pereira is a McNair Fellow and graduate researcher at University of North Texas in the Counseling Psychology doctoral program, with an emphasis on minority well-being. He has worked with Dr. Philip Watkins during his baccalaureate education at Eastern Washington University for over four years on research projects related to the psychology of gratitude, and he has attended various symposia and conferences to present findings in the field. Andrew is currently collecting data on gratitude and well-being within disadvantaged populations and is interested in protective factors associated with resilience to minority stress.

Tayyab Rashid, Ph.D., is a licensed clinical and school psychologist at the Health & Wellness Centre, University of Toronto Scarborough (UTSC), Canada. Trained under Dr. Martin Seligman, one of the leading experts in optimism and well-being, Dr. Rashid's expertise includes strength-based resilience interventions in clinical and educational settings, personal and professional growth, search for meaning, and how to succeed doing the right thing, both individually and collectively. Dr. Rashid has trained clinicians and educators internationally and is the current co-chair of national community of practice for campus mental health, and also chairs the International Positive Psychology Association's (IPPA) Clinical Division's launch steering committee. He has worked with the families of 9/11 survivors, the Asian tsunami, and flood relief workers in Pakistan. Published in peer-reviewed journals, an invited keynote speaker, Rashid's work has also been featured in the *Wall Street Journal*, Canadian Broadcasting Corporation and at the TEDx. Dr. Rashid leads Flourish, a preventative mental health initiative at UTSC, which has recently won two awards.

Henrietta Roberts, Ph.D., completed her Ph.D. at the University of Exeter's Mood Disorders Centre, and holds research interests in motivation, depression, repetitive negative thinking (rumination and worry), and executive functioning. Research projects Henrietta has been involved in include examining the associations between reward system function and mood disorders; investigating the role of goal discrepancies in rumination and emotional regulation; and developing and evaluating a working memory training intervention to reduce repetitive negative thinking. Henrietta is currently undertaking doctoral training in Clinical Psychology (D.Clin. Psy.) at Exeter.

Chiara Ruini, Ph.D., is Associate Professor of Clinical Psychology at the University of Bologna, Department of Psychology. Since 2006 she has been teaching the course "Clinical Applications of Positive Psychology" for students attending the Master's Program in Clinical Psychology. Chiara Ruini has authored more than sixty articles published in peer-reviewed international journals, has edited a book titled *Increasing Psychological Well-being Across Cultures* for the series "Positive Psychology across Cultures" and serves on the editorial boards for international journals such as Psychotherapy and Psychosomatics, *Psychology of Well-being, Theories Research and Practice*, and *Journal of Happiness and Wellbeing*. Her research interests are concerned with positive psychology, clinical psychology, positive youth development, and psychotherapy.

Mark S. Rye, Ph.D., is Professor of Psychology at Skidmore College in Saratoga Springs, NY. He received his Ph.D. in clinical psychology from Bowling Green State University in Bowling Green, OH, and is a licensed clinical psychologist. His positive psychology research, which focuses on how forgiveness and gratitude impact mental health, has been funded by the John Templeton Foundation and the Fetzer Institute. He co-authored *The Divorce Recovery Workbook* (2015), which promotes evidence-based positive psychology strategies for coping with divorce.

Carol D. Ryff is Director of the Institute on Aging and Hilldale Professor of Psychology at the University of Wisconsin-Madison. Her research has examined how psychological well-being varies by age, gender, socioeconomic status, ethnic/minority status, and cultural context, as well as by the experiences, challenges, and transitions individuals confront as they age. Whether well-being is protective of good physical health is major interest, with ongoing studies probing biological and brain-based pathways. A guiding theme is resilience – how some are able to maintain, or regain, well-being in the face of adversity. More than 500 publications have used her scales of well-being, which have been translated to over thirty languages. Dr. Ryff currently directs the Midlife in the US (MIDUS) longitudinal study, a large national sample of Americans, including twins. Funded by the National Institute on Aging, MIDUS has become a major forum for studying health and aging as an integrated biopsychosocial process. She also leads the Midlife in Japan (MIDJA) study, a parallel to the MIDUS, for which she received an NIH Merit Award.

Steven J. Sandage, Ph.D., LP, is the Albert and Jessie Danielsen Professor of Psychology of Religion and Theology at Boston University and Research Director and Senior Staff Psychologist at the Danielsen Institute. He also has appointments in the Department of Psychological and Brain Sciences and the Graduate Division of Religious Studies. His books include *To Forgive is Human*, *The Faces of Forgiveness*, *Transforming Spirituality*, *The Skillful Soul of the Psychotherapist*, and *Forgiveness and Spirituality: A Relational Approach*. His clinical specializations include couple and family therapy, multicultural therapy, and spiritually-integrative therapy.

Pete Sanders spent over 30 years practicing as a counselor, educator, and clinical supervisor. He has written, co-written, and edited numerous books, chapters, and papers on many aspects of counseling, psychotherapy, and mental health. He continues to have an active interest in developing person-centered theory, the politics of counseling and psychotherapy, and the demedicalization of distress. He has given keynote addresses at several UK and European conferences and also offers workshops in a few areas that continue to interest him. He is a pre-therapy/contact work trainer and trustee of the Soteria Network UK.

Constantine Sedikides' research is on self and identity and their interplay with emotion (especially nostalgia) and motivation (especially self-evaluation motives). He has published twelve volumes and over 250 articles in journals such as *Advances in Experimental Social Psychology*, *Journal of Experimental Social Psychology*, *Journal of Personality*, *Journal of Personality and Social Psychology*, and *Personality and Social Psychology Bulletin*. He has received several awards, such as the Kurt Lewin Medal for Outstanding Scientific Contribution from the European Association of Social Psychology, and the Presidents' Award for Distinguished Contributions to Psychological Knowledge, the British Psychological Society (2012). Before coming to the University of Southampton, where he presently teaches, Constantine taught at the University of Wisconsin-Madison, USA, and the University of North Carolina at Chapel Hill, USA. He also holds an honorary appointment at Aalborg University, Denmark. He has a BA from the Aristotle University of Thessaloniki, Greece, and a Ph.D. from the Ohio State University, USA.

Shauna L. Shapiro, Ph.D., is a Professor at Santa Clara University, a clinical psychologist, and an internationally recognized expert in mindfulness. Dr. Shapiro is the recipient of the American Council of Learned Societies teaching award, acknowledging her outstanding contributions to education in the area of mindfulness, and was awarded a Contemplative Practice fellowship by the Mind and Life Institute, co-founded by the Dalai Lama. Dr. Shapiro lectures and leads mindfulness training programs internationally, and has been invited to present for the king of Thailand, the Danish Government, and the World Council for Psychotherapy, Beijing, China. She has published over 100 articles and book chapters, and is co-author of the critically acclaimed text, *The Art and Science of Mindfulness* and the recent book, *Mindful Discipline: A Loving Approach to Raising an Emotionally Intelligent Child*. Dr. Shapiro's work has been featured in *Wired Magazine*, *USA Today*, *The Yoga Journal*, and the *American Psychologist*.

Lilian J. Shin is a Ph.D. student in the Social/Personality Psychology program at the University of California, Riverside. She completed her B.A. in psychology at Northwestern University and her M.A.T. in social studies education at Georgia State University. Lilian's research interests include both the factors that protect against mental health conditions and those that promote well-being, particularly in minority populations.

Sarah de Sousa holds a B.A. in modern thought and literature from Stanford University and is a master's candidate in counseling psychology at Santa Clara University. She has co-authored several academic publications on topics related to mindfulness and positive psychology. Sarah is a dedicated student of contemplative practices, a published poet, competitive dancer, and educational consultant. Her academic publications include contributions to the *Handbook of Mindfulness in Education* and the *Oxford Handbook of Positive Psychology*. Her poetry most recently appeared in the online journal *2River View*.

Christopher D. J. Taylor, Clin.Psy.D., is a clinical psychologist and an NIHR Clinical Research Fellow based in the Early Intervention Psychosis Service, Lancashire Care NHS Foundation Trust. He is also an Honorary Lecturer in Clinical Psychology in the School of Psychological Sciences at the University of Manchester and an Associate Fellow of the British Psychological Society (AFBPsS). His research interests are in the development of psychological therapies for severe mental health experiences, with a focus on beliefs, schemas, and imagery. His current work is funded by the National Institute for Health Research (NIHR) supported through a personal fellowship grant award.

Peter J. Taylor, Ph.D., Clin.Psy.D., is a Clinical Psychologist and lecturer based at the University of Liverpool, where he acts as a research tutor on the doctorate of Clinical Psychology program. His research interests are varied, but have focused on understanding psychological processes surrounding self-injury, and understanding distress and suicidal feelings in those with experiences of psychosis. His research has included a focus on the difficulties faced by young people and adolescents, including work around those at risk of psychosis, and more generally in those who experience emotional difficulties like depression and anxiety.

Richard Tedeschi, Ph.D., is a licensed psychologist and Professor of Psychology at the University of North Carolina, Charlotte, where he is core faculty for the Health Psychology Doctoral Program. He teaches Ethics and Professional Issues, Psychological Treatment, and supervises doctoral students in their clinical practicum work. He has published numerous articles and books on the concept of post-traumatic growth that he helped to develop. He serves as media consultant on trauma for the American Psychological Association, is a Fellow of the Division of Trauma Psychology, and has provided presentations and training on trauma for the US Army, and many professional organizations, clinics, and educational institutions.

Liudmila Titova received her B.A. in Psychology from Hiram College, Hiram, Ohio. Currently she is a Ph.D. student at University of Missouri, Columbia. She is specifically interested in cross-cultural and positive psychology. The projects she has worked on have examined cross-cultural differences connected to well-being, attitudes toward happiness, and positive psychology interventions. She has presented her research at a number of regional, national, and international conferences. She is also an editorial assistant at the *Journal of Positive Psychology*. Overall, she would like to continue to study cross-cultural differences and similarities connected to emotions.

George E. Vaillant, MD, is a Professor of Psychiatry at Harvard Medical School and the Department of Psychiatry, Massachusetts General Hospital. From 1970 to 2005 he was Director of the Study of Adult Development at the Harvard University Health Service. The study is arguably the longest (75 years) prospective psychosocial *and* medical study of males in the world. In 2000, he became a founding member of Positive Psychology. More recently, Vaillant has been interested in positive emotions and their relationship to Positive Psychology. His published works include *Adaptation to Life* (1977), *The Natural History of Alcoholism-Revisited* (1995), *Aging Well* (2002), *Spiritual Evolution* (2008), and *Triumphs of Experience* (2012).

Philip Watkins is Professor of Psychology at Eastern Washington University, where he has taught since 1990. He received his Ph.D. at Louisiana State University, where his work focused on implicit memory biases in depression. He began investigating gratitude around 1996, but has focused on gratitude and subjective well-being since 2000. His research now investigates questions related to how gratitude enhances well-being.

David Watson, University of Notre Dame, is a personality psychologist with particular expertise in personality assessment. His work investigates the structure and measurement of personality, emotion, and psychopathology, as well as examining how personality traits and emotional characteristics relate to clinical disorders. He works in a variety of substantive areas within psychopathology, including the emotional disorders (e.g., major depression, social anxiety disorder, the bipolar disorders, post-traumatic stress disorder, and obsessive-compulsive disorder), the personality disorders, schizotypy, and the sleep and dissociative disorders. The long-term goal of this work is to develop comprehensive taxonomic models that integrate normal range and pathological processes into a single overarching scheme. He served as an advisor to the DSM-IV Anxiety Disorders Workgroup and to the DSM-5 Personality and Personality Disorders Workgroup. He also served as the editor-in-chief of the *Journal of Abnormal Psychology* from 2006 through 2011.

Thomas A. Widiger, Ph.D., is the T. Marshal Hahn Professor of Psychology at the University of Kentucky. He has published extensively with respect to dimensional trait models of personality disorder, as well as diagnosis and classification more generally. He is the editor or co-editor of a variety of texts, including most recently, *Personality Disorders and the Five-Factor Model of Personality*, and the *Oxford Handbook of Personality Disorders*. He served as the research coordinator for the fourth edition of the American Psychiatric Association's *Diagnostic and Statistical Manual of Mental Disorders*, and currently serves as a co-editor of the *Annual Review of Clinical Psychology* as well as the editor of *Personality Disorders: Theory, Research, and Treatment*.

Tim Wildschut is an Associate Professor of Psychology at the University of Southampton. He received his Ph.D. from the University of North Carolina at Chapel Hill. His main research interest is in self-conscious emotions, in particular nostalgia, and he has published extensively in this area. He is a recipient of the Gordon Allport Intergroup Relations Prize and the Jaspars Medal for Early Career Scientific Achievement in Social Psychology from the European Association of Social Psychology. He has served as associate editor for *Self and Identity* and currently serves as associate editor for *Personality and Social Psychology Bulletin*.

Alex M. Wood is Professor and Director of the Behavioural Science Centre, University of Stirling, Scotland. His interdisciplinary research spans the full range of well-being topics, including clinical psychology and happiness. One of the youngest full professors in UK history, Alex gained his first Chair in 2012 aged 29, having completing his Ph.D. in 2008 at the University of Warwick and worked in the University of Manchester whom awarded him an honorary Chair in 2013. Over his first 10 years Alex published over 100 academic papers, was cited over 5,000 times in academic texts, attracted over US$1.5 million in research funding, gave over 50 presentations, reviewed for over 70 journals, edited a special issue of *Clinical Psychology Review*, and featured in over 50 news outlets, including *Time Magazine*, *Financial Times*, and *BBC Radio*. He divides his time between working and hanging out with his musician friends in Glasgow, traveling, hiking, wild swimming, and reading literature and philosophy.

Everett L. Worthington, Jr., Ph.D., is Commonwealth Professor of Psychology at Virginia Commonwealth University (VCU). He is also a licensed clinical psychologist in Virginia. He has published 35 books and about 400 articles and scholarly chapters, mostly on forgiveness, marriage, and family topics. He is a former president of the American Psychological Association (APA) Division 36 (Society for the Psychology of Religion and Spirituality), and a fellow of the Association for Psychological Science and two divisions of the American Psychological Association. He won VCU's annual top award for teaching, research, and service – VCU's Award for Excellence – in 2009 and several organizations' top awards. In the last 30 years, he has studied a variety of topics relevant to positive psychology that include forgiveness, altruism, love, humility, mercy, marriage enrichment, and religion and spirituality. For more information and free resources on promoting forgiveness, visit www.EvWorthington-forgiveness.com.

Part I
Developing a Positive Clinical Psychology

1

Positive Clinical Psychology
An Introduction
Alex M. Wood and Judith Johnson

Positive Clinical Psychology (PCP) is not new. As shown in chapters throughout this book, clinical psychology has a long history of incorporating the positive into clinical practice. From Maslow (1954) onward there have been calls to change clinical psychology to focus more on the positive in life, and even the term "positive clinical psychology" has been used in the past (see, e.g., Duckworth, Steen, & Seligman, 2005; Maddux, Chapter 2, this volume). What is new is the movement from wise but isolated calls, often from outside clinical psychology, to a real impetus for change from within. PCP is built around a clearly defined shared set of aims that are increasingly considered mainstream within the field. We set out our mission statement in a special issue of *Clinical Psychology Review* (Wood & Tarrier, 2010, as clarified in Johnson & Wood, in press). This has proved seminal to the acceptance in mainstream clinical psychology of calls to increase a focus on the "positive" alongside the "negative." PCP, as we envision it, aims to change the discipline of clinical psychology into one "which has an integrated and equally weighted focus on both positive and negative functioning in all areas of research and practice" (Wood & Tarrier, 2010, p. 819). The distinctive feature of PCP is the emphasis on integration; PCP points out the illogicality and impossibility of studying only the "positive" or the "negative" in clinical psychology (or for that matter, in any discipline), and it seeks to better integrate research and practice toward a joint focus on both. We are staggered by how much this message has resonated amongst clinical psychologists in the last six years, including the expert contributors for this book, to whom we are very grateful for enthusiastically contributing outstanding chapters. This *Handbook*, the first of its kind, represents the culmination of six years of increasing acceptance of PCP. It is built on decades of scholarship from the contributors to this book and others, without whom the development of PCP would not be possible.

The purpose of this chapter is to provide an overview of the development of PCP and to overview the empirical and theoretical evidence as to why the movement is needed. This burgeoning area seeks to draw together the two fields of Positive Psychology and Clinical Psychology, which have generally developed independently of each other despite many convergences in research foci and aims. We suggest that further integration between positive and clinical psychologies could serve to advance the research, knowledge, goals, and practice of both. Our hope is that this book can contribute to this endeavor. We have been overawed by the responses we received from authors we approached to write on this topic for the book, each leaders in their field. As such, the book represents a bringing together of expert clinical psychologists, keen to consider how a recognition of the positive relates to their work, and the expert positive psychologists, keen to integrate their research with the wider clinical research base and move towards a PCP.

The Wiley Handbook of Positive Clinical Psychology, First Edition. Edited by Alex M. Wood and Judith Johnson.
© 2016 John Wiley & Sons, Ltd. Published 2016 by John Wiley & Sons, Ltd.

The Historical Development of Positive Clinical Psychology

Prior to the Second World War, psychology had the key aim of curing distress and fostering optimal functioning (see Linley, Joseph, Harrington, & Wood, 2006). In the immediate aftermath of the war, there was an urgent need within war-torn countries to explain and address the psychological distress and trauma that the war had created. Within clinical psychology, there was a renewed focus on curing distress, particularly that related to trauma (later known as post-traumatic stress disorder). Within social psychology, there was a focus on such topics as conformity that aimed to explain why the atrocities associated with the war had occurred. This was all valuable, and much needed, but it had two undesired side effects. First, it led to an over-focusing of psychology on distress and dysfunction. Second, and potentially more seriously, it led to distress and dysfunction becoming viewed as a discrete subject of enquiry, rather than as part of a broader enquiry into the full continuum of human functioning. In the United States, this process was accelerated by the development of the National Institute of Mental Health in 1947 (which exclusively focused on *ill* health) and the Veterans' Administration in 1949. Both organizations funded excellent research and treatment, but by providing financial incentives (e.g., research grants) to study the dysfunctional side of the mental ill-health continuum, there was perhaps too much encouragement for researchers to focus on these topics. Furthermore, the tendency of academics to teach in their areas of research is likely to have led this focus upon poor mental health and distress to be transferred to their students. As such, it can be seen how well-meaning and valuable funding into distress led to new generations of psychologists viewing the discipline of psychology as one focused upon maladaptive, rather than adaptive, functioning. As Abraham Maslow warned over half a century ago:

> The science of psychology has been far more successful on the negative than on the positive side. It has revealed to us much about man's shortcomings, his illness, his sins, but little about his potentialities, his virtues, his achievable aspirations, or his full psychological height. It is as if psychology has voluntarily restricted itself to only half its rightful jurisdiction, and that, the darker, meaner half. (Maslow, 1954, p. 354)

This situation largely persisted throughout the latter half of twentieth century. A concerted attempt to reintroduce the "positive" into psychology arose from the positive psychology movement initiated by the American Psychological Association (APA) President Martin Seligman, with his joint special issue and the accompanying influential editorial (Seligman & Csikszentmihalyi, 2000). This, and the ensuing movement, had a huge impact on psychology in a very short space of time, with millions of dollars in funding, the development of new psychotherapeutic techniques, specialist masters courses across the world, and several special issues of journals and handbooks (see Linley et al., 2006). A quantitative bibliometric analysis (Rusk & Waters, 2013) charted the growth of positive psychology, showing that 18,000 papers linked to positive psychology topics have been published, and that there has been a steady year-on-year increase in the number of publications. In their 2011 census year, there were 2,300 papers published, representing 4% of those indexed by the representative *PsychInfo®* database. If these papers were classed together as a field, they would be at the median of disciplines indexed in the *Journal Citation Reports®*, and the 2011 impact factor would be 2.64, showing that the number of citations to the papers would respectably rank amongst other academic fields. The increase in number of papers was seen in each field in which the papers were published, including psychology (and all sub-areas), psychiatry, sports science, business, and management. This quantitative analysis showed that positive psychology can no longer be considered a minority or fringe endeavor.

The uncontroversial message from positive psychology was that psychology (and other fields) must consider the positive as well as the negative. The movement can be credited with raising the profile of topics that are considered "positive," and making them as likely to receive funding and to be published as those considered "negative." However, in the intervening years since the initial rush of enthusiasm, and despite the ever-growing impact of the field, the wider field of psychology has arguably become somewhat ambivalent about positive psychology (see Wood, et al., in press), and many critical pieces have been written against the movement (e.g., Bohart, 2002; Lazarus, 2003; Tennen & Affleck, 2003; Held, 2004; Coyne & Tennen, 2010; Coyne, Tennen, & Ranchor, 2010).

Perhaps one reason for this ambivalence within wider psychology relates to the movement's lack of clear aims. The most distinguishable goal of the movement was that psychology should focus more upon the positive, a message which most psychologists endorsed. However, this perhaps led to a growing tension between those who wanted to integrate the study of the positive and the negative, and those who wanted to create a separatist field of positive psychology. Notably, Rusk's and Water's (2013) bibliometric analysis focused on papers on positive psychology topics, but many of these would not have been self-identified as "positive psychology"; they were just seen by the authors as "psychology." The growth of the study of positive psychology topics is undeniable. The nature of the "movement," whether there is even still a movement, the aims of this movement, and its consequences are more controversial. A separation (not often made by critics) needs to be clearly made between the research on topics associated with positive psychology (which, other than isolated examples, attract no more criticism than other areas of psychology) and a possible straw man of a positive psychology movement. It is on the latter most criticisms have been leveled.

The critical narrative around the positive psychology movement often seems to be dominated by concerns of separatism, with "positive" research and interventions sometimes seen to be developing in isolation from the wider literature. It could be argued that this branding of positive approaches within "positive psychology" helped to raise their profile and served to highlight the importance of their study. However, we would suggest that any separation between positive psychology and other fields – particularly from clinical psychology – comes at the cost of the advancement of each. Both positive and clinical psychology research psychological treatments, often in similar groups (e.g., those with depression), but sometimes independently and without either fully recognizing or utilizing the findings of the other. In failing to acknowledge the full influence *from* clinical psychology research, the positive psychology movement has failed to fulfil its full potential to influence clinical psychology in return. PCP aims to address these concerns through transforming the discipline of clinical psychology into one that equally studies and intervenes in topics branded as "positive" or "negative." It is designed to utilize the great scholarship within positive psychology to the full effect within clinical psychology by making it inseparably a part of the fabric of the field.

The development of PCP is also aimed to help positive psychology research more broadly by making it accessible to new audiences and addressing some of the previous criticisms. Perhaps if there had been a greater focus on the message of those within positive psychology movement seeking to integrate positive with the negative (e.g., Joseph & Linley, 2006a,b), then greater advances would already have been made toward building a more holistic psychology. The danger that the positive psychology movement faces is that it will be dominated by a different separatist message, the content of which seems to be leading to a growing consternation in wider psychology, including clinical psychology, where it is in some quarters seen as being a research-lite "happiology." Whether or not this characterization is appropriate is moot; the perception itself is hampering attempts to focus clinical psychology more on the positive.

Through promoting a fundamentally integrative message between positive and clinical psychologies, between the focus on maladaptive and adaptive functioning, this *Handbook* aims to help positive psychology regain its true vision of a holistic and balanced psychology, through showing common ground between different approaches and fundamentally challenging any separatist message with conceptual, evidential, and pragmatic arguments. We also seek to address the (often unfair) criticisms of positive psychology that have been raised.

Criticisms of Positive Psychology

Several concerns were raised about positive psychology, in addition to the increasingly perceived separatist message. First, the original paper (Seligman & Csikszentmihalyi, 2000) included factually untrue statements about humanistic psychology lacking an evidence base. This was particularly unfortunate considering the similarities in the goals of both fields (see the Maslow quote above). This avoided the opportunity to engage with the very community that may have been most supportive to the integrative aim of positive psychology (see Sanders and Joseph, Chapter 28, this volume, for the fit between positive and humanistic approaches). With PCP we aim to rebuild bridges between communities, and some of the chapters in this book are dedicated to showing how many areas are already incorporating what may be classed otherwise as positive psychology.

Second, the quality of the research in the field was questioned from inception (e.g., Lazarus, 2003). This was probably an unfair criticism as: (a) the complaints often overgeneralized from isolated examples of research in the field; (b) many of the criticisms (e.g., a reliance on self-report) apply to psychology as a whole; and (c) the critiques did not recognize that the research methods that were being criticized were often commensurate with the developmental stage of research into new topics (e.g., showing correlation before causation). Nevertheless, PCP needs to hold itself to the highest level of methodological account, building on the increasing refinement within positive psychology and the best clinical psychology practice.

Third, there are concerns that there has perhaps been an overwillingness to put positive psychology research into practice before interventions are tested to the same level as clinical interventions. In our opinion, the flaws highlighted in the second and third criticisms may have been due to the foundations of the movement in personality psychology. Indeed, most positive psychologists had begun as personality psychologists, and the studies that they designed to test interventions were based on common designs for proof of concept studies published in top rated personality journals. Here, the interest is in showing a potentially causal impact of a characteristic rather than providing a full interventional trial. Whilst this was often appropriate for the research questions in the original publications, this strategy became problematic and potentially dangerous when this evidence base (and not a clinical trial) was used to make recommendations for interventions. In part, this reflected a poor tendency amongst psychology researchers in general, reinforced by journal reviewers, to make "practical recommendations" as part of the discussion in a research study. From a proof of concept study, such recommendations should not go beyond suggesting that a clinical trial be conducted. However, the claim is that the tendency has instead been to overspeculate about the implications of the findings. In some cases this has involved claiming that a study with undergraduate participants, and no follow-up, was a basis for recommending a therapeutic approach. There has also been more general concern about how the media reporting of scientific studies make claims that go beyond the evidence base, which seems to originate from the press release of the institution (Sumner et al., 2014). The early proof of concept studies within positive psychology have been seminal in suggesting what might work (analogous to the early stages of a drug trial), and there now needs to be more full clinical trials that completely test interventions using the clinical psychology methods that have emerged from the best practice within medicine. The increased linkage that this *Handbook* seeks to provide between positive and clinical psychologists is hoped to help build the multidisciplinary teams that this kind of work will require.

Possibly these three criticisms of positive psychology culminated in the attraction to the field of untrained, unaccredited, and unregulated "positive psychology coaches." This development has been particularly harmful to the field of psychology, as whilst such a title is unprotected, and essentially meaningless, it seems to infer that psychology has leant its credibility and regulatory procedures to this "profession." Claimants of this approach have been keen to stress the "scientific basis" of their studies (which have usually been the proof of concept studies within personality psychology journals, at best). As might have been predicted, there has been a backlash against this approach, and this backlash has not been confined simply to positive psychology. To the wider population not familiar with the distinction between "positive psychology" and "clinical psychology," both psychologies have been at risk of being discredited. Unsurprisingly, it seems that this has led to some resentment amongst clinical psychologists of their positive psychology colleagues. PCP aims to utilize the existing regulatory frameworks within clinical psychology to provide public assurance of safety of interventions and thus increase their acceptability and usability amongst many communities, including amongst those who are most vulnerable.

We stress that many of these criticisms are concerns for psychology at large, and that they are perhaps unfair characterizations of positive psychology. However, irrespective of whether one accepts them with regard to positive psychology, it seems apt to raise them here as PCP must avoid these pitfalls and characterizations. We stress that we *are* positive psychologists, in the sense of promoting an integrative message between studying both the positive and the negative, and that we both work and publish within both positive and clinical psychology. Our emphasis here on criticisms of positive psychology is simply based on our desire to be aware of the (real or imagined) pitfalls of the movement and to ensure that these do not reoccur with PCP.

The PCP Solution

PCP aims to address the separatist criticism of positive psychology and redress any imbalanced focus on either the "positive" or "negative" in both positive and clinical psychologies in order to promote a more fully integrative field of psychology. Incorporating the strengths of positive psychology, and responding to the criticisms, PCP aims to develop a field where adaptive and maladaptive functioning are considered holistically, as inseparable, and as deserving of an equal amount of attention in both research and practice. It aims, at least within a clinical setting, to reset the positive psychology movement, having it originate from within clinical psychology. PCPs aim is that positive psychology will not be (or be seen to be) a separatist endeavor, but would instead both influence and work with the existing field of clinical psychology. The potential benefits of this approach are considerable and bidirectional between positive and clinical psychology. These benefits include:

1 The attraction of a new population of researchers and practitioners to work on the integration of maladaptive and adaptive functioning.
2 The likely attraction of those with a healthy degree of skepticism about the value of studying adaptive functioning. Having such critics on board will help maintain credibility and the focus on trying to *disprove* the importance of the "positive," in line with how positivistic science should be conducted. Where such attempts to disprove the hypotheses fail, we can have more confidence in the research base.
3 The influence on positive psychology of clinical psychology standards of what is deemed optimum interventional research. As clinical psychology standards have arisen in part from medicine, they tend to be of a higher standard than the proof of concept studies within personality psychology. For example, clinical journals are moving towards requiring that trials involve: (a) pre-trial registration; (b) a sample from the population to which the authors generalize; (c) use of best practice CONSORT guidelines for the conduct of clinical trials; (d) adequately powered designs; (e) proper and active control groups; (f) avoidance of demand characteristics with steps in place to prevent selection effects (e.g., where those interested in positive psychology are most likely to take part); (g) replication; and (h) conclusions that do not go beyond the data. Positive psychology has much to offer such trials, including highly novel ways of viewing mental health, its correlates, antecedents, and consequences. As such, an integration of both these fields is likely to lead to a raising of research standards in both, and more generally we do strongly encourage researchers in all fields to adopt these best practice approaches.

4   The well-established accreditation and regulation procedures to safeguard client well-being within clinical psychology, which can be used to ensure that positive psychology interventions are given to the most vulnerable people by the most appropriately trained and accountable practitioners.

5   Overall, the key aim of PCP is to engender a change within clinical psychology, so that the field examines functioning holistically, at both the adaptive and maladaptive end, and makes use of a full range of treatment techniques – including those from traditional and positive psychology – in a balanced manner to individual client need.

Why Do We Need a Positive Clinical Psychology?

In many ways, all chapters within this *Handbook* are focused on stating the need for PCP. Each author was asked – interpreting the question and issues as they chose – to consider whether the "positive" and "negative" should be considered together by clinical psychologists with respect to their expert topic area. Although a selected and self-selecting group, it notable that not a single author concluded that they should not. The book is organized into five parts, which largely correspond to the topics forming the argument for PCP: "Developing a Positive Clinical Psychology," "Personality and Individual Differences," "Disorders," "Positive Psychology Interventions in Clinical Practice," and "Reinterpreting Existing Therapies." We highlight and integrate the core arguments for PCP from across the book here.

Characteristics Are on a Continuum from Low to High

As we have previously argued (Joseph & Wood, 2010; Johnson, Wood, Gooding, & Tarrier, 2011; Johnson & Wood, in press) and discussed by Joseph and Patterson (Chapter 4, this volume), a simple fact that has been ignored by both the positive and clinical psychology communities is that all characteristics range from low to high. Consider the traits that Peterson and Seligman (2004) highlight in the "Values in Action" (VIA) project, which they consider "virtues." These included humility, fairness, kindness, integrity, gratitude, optimism, open-mindedness, and (one assumes high) social intelligence. A moment's reflection shows that each of these is on continua from arrogance to humility, unfairness to fairness, unkindness to kindness, dishonesty to integrity, ingratitude to gratitude, pessimism to optimism, closed- to open-mindedness, low to high social intelligence. Obviously, one cannot say the whole continuum is positive; rather, researchers seem to simply be referring to the "high end." It then becomes theoretically nonsensical for a field to focus only on the high end of a continuum, and even more so to write papers as if the other half of the continuum did not exist. It is no less a mistake to focus on only the low end of a continuum and write papers as if the high end does not exist.

To claim that positive psychologists are normally studying anything other than the high end of a bipolar continuum would be inconsistent with both the methods and the findings of the field. Normally the characteristics are studied with self-report scales that include items that are reverse coded prior to analysis. Thus, for example, the GQ6 measure of gratitude includes items measuring ingratitude, and the scale has been shown to be a single continuum (McCullough, Emmons, & Tsang, 2002). The same can be said for most of the measures in positive psychology. Indeed, when the "positive psychology" scales were developed, given that there was generally a balance of positively and negatively worded items (or should have been with normal psychometric practice), it was an arbitrary choice which of the items to reverse code. The gratitude scales, for example, could equally be called ingratitude scales if the arbitrary decision to recode the ingratitude items had not been made in favor of the equally arbitrary decision to recode the gratitude items.

In such a case, it would be called the ingratitude scale, although *it would be the same scale*. At the moment we have the absurd situation where if one codes the scales in one direction it can go to a positive psychology journal, and if one codes it the other it can go to a clinical psychology journal.

Johnson (Chapter 6) considers the implications of not realizing that constructs are on a continuum from high to low with respect to the literature on resilience, where it has been typical to take the same characteristic (such as social support) and call low levels risk and high levels resilience (Johnson, Gooding, Wood, and Tarrier, 2010). With these definitions, the construct of resilience is meaningless as it is just a word for low risk. Instead, this chapter proposes that resilience lies in the particular interaction between two characteristics. Each characteristic (the resilience variable and the risk variable) goes from low to high, but the interaction between the two contributes more than the sum of its parts (e.g., the presence of high levels of one mitigates low levels of another). This model has previously been used to explain resilience to suicide in both non-clinical populations (where coping self-efficacy moderates the impact of negative life events; Johnson et al., 2010) and clinical populations (where coping self-efficacy moderates the effect of hopelessness; Johnson, Gooding, Wood, Taylor, Pratt, and Tarrier, 2010).

It seems, then, that some positive psychologists have failed to recognize that factors fall on a continuum from high to low, and as such, they have failed to recognize where their research studies the "negative." However, clinical psychologists have also fallen into this trap. For example, assessment of global functioning is often included as part of a diagnostic assessment of clinical disorders, and functioning ranges from highly impaired to superior. As such, clinical psychologists are in fact already measuring the "positive," often without fully acknowledging this. Furthermore, given concerns about the scientific basis and usefulness of the diagnostic categories in general, there have been calls to replace these with a greater focus on global functioning. James Maddux (Chapter 2) makes a powerful argument as to how the focus on continua of functioning within PCP can help depathologize and destigmatize mental illness, by moving the focus away from "mental illness" and instead toward "wellness," a continuum upon which we all exist.

Some measures of global functioning might include "subjective well-being" (SWB) and "psychological well-being" (PWB). As discussed by Joseph and Patterson (Chapter 4), SWB is a higher-order factor comprising positive affect, negative affect, and satisfaction with life. Ruini and Ryff provide a chapter on PWB (Chapter 11), which they see as comprising self-acceptance, positive relationships with others, purpose in life, environmental mastery, and autonomy. It is important to realize that the higher-order constructs of both SWB and PWB are continua ranging from low to high. Specifically, SWB ranges from low positive effect, high negative effect, and low life satisfaction to high positive effect, low negative effect, and high life satisfaction. PWB ranges from self-rejection, impaired relationship with others, purposelessness, environmental incompetence, and subjugation to self-acceptance, positive relationships with others, purpose in life, environmental mastery, and autonomy. Clearly, neither SWB nor PWB are inherently positive, but rather two very different ways of conceptualizing continua of functioning (and in the measurement of both, commonly positively and negatively worded items are used to measure both sides of the continuum). As they measure different conceptions of well-being, each as full continua, they will be somewhat factorially distinct not because one is positive and the other negative, but simply because they are assessing different forms of functioning. The factorial distinctiveness is shown in a large body of work (e.g., Linley Maltby, Wood, Osborn, and Hurling, 2009). Interestingly, these two higher-order factors are very highly correlated (at around $r = .76$; Linley et al., 2009), which fits in with what Joseph and Patterson (Chapter 4) present as a humanistic meta-theory. This theory suggests that people do not generally feel good (high SWB) whilst behaving in a personally and socially destructive manner (low PWB; as expanded upon by Pete Sanders and Stephen Joseph in Chapter 28), although these factors are still factorially distinct.

The factorial distinctiveness between SWB and PWB has caused much confusion in the field and has worked against the integration that PCP proposes. For example, Westerhof and Keyes

(2010) influentially argue for a dual-continuum model of mental health, consisting of ill-being and positive functioning. This is based on SWB and PWB being two (highly correlated but) separate factors. As discussed in Johnson and Wood (in press), their interpretation misses the point that both SWB and PWB are bipolar continua from high to low, and that they are simply measuring different concepts. Thus, one may talk about dual-continua in the sense of our need to assess more than one kind of functioning, but one *cannot* claim one is positive and the other negative, and to do so directly goes against the integration that we are trying to promote. This obvious although influential error of interpretation has hindered the development of PCP (although we value the author's contributions to the popularization of the important PWB concept). With Westerhof and Keyes (and Maddux, Chapter 2), we would support a shift away from a sole focus on diagnostic categories toward a larger focus on global assessment, and we agree that SWB and PWB are a good starting point. However, it is critical to have a balanced, holistic, and accurate field that recognizes the fact that each factor ranges from high to low.

Global functioning is one area in which clinical psychologists are already intuitively implementing the core PCP recommendation to focus on full continua from maladaptive to adaptive functioning (even if the implications of this are not normally considered). However, there is a second area in which this is already occurring which is more subtle and even less acknowledged. Almost all clinical disorders, or the processes that underlie them, range from maladaptive to adaptive. Wood, Taylor and Joseph (2010) have shown this directly with respect to depression. This was based on the observation that the Center for Epidemiological Studies Depression (CES-D) scale (one of the five most used) includes both normal depression items as well as reverse coded ones such as "I am happy." Clearly, then, on the logic above, this can be said to measure a continuum from depression to "happiness." The factor analyses reported in that paper support the view that these items comprise a single continuum. Similarly, Siddaway, Taylor, and Wood (2016) have investigated the State-Trait Anxiety Inventory (STAI), which again has items measuring both anxiety and reverse coded items measuring calmness, and which also we find form a single continuum. As highlighted by Wood and Joseph (2010), work on depression or anxiety that has used these measures is probably already in line with PCP, as a full continuum of well-being has already been measured. It is simply an error of interpretation that has led to this not being recognized.

Despite our work having shown that the CES-D measures a continuum from depression to happiness, and the STAI from anxiety to calmness, we prefer not to see the constructs in such simplistic terms (and the use of the word "happiness" is particularly problematic, as this is a deep philosophical issue, and what defines happiness is possibly the choice of the individual). Instead, we would suggest that the findings emerge as it is the forms of functioning underlying the diagnostic criteria for mental disorders that range from adaptive to maladaptive. For example, most diagnostic criteria for depression involves high negative affect, low positive affect (anhedonia), lack of engagement, poor sleep, impaired appetite, and poor social relationships. Each of these is clearly on continua from maladaptive to adaptive; respectively, low negative affect, high positive affect, engagement, good sleep, appropriate eating, and good social relationships. Thus, irrespective of our results of studies analyzing depression questionnaires, the criteria on which the construct of depression is based can be said to logically range from maladaptive to adaptive. The same can be said of nearly all mental disorders.

The approach of focusing on the full continuum of the process underlying mental disorders allows for even the most categorical appearing disorders to be seen as existing on a maladaptive to adaptive continuum, consistent with PCP. Thomas Widger (Chapter 18) makes this argument with respect to personality disorders. These disorders are amongst those most frequently viewed as dichotomously "present" or "absent" in the mental health literature (indeed, they are often referred to as "categorical disorders"). In contrast, Widger shows that they arise from particular extreme "normal" personality continua, each of which range from high to low. His model of personality is the Five Factor model, which focuses on the observable psychological differences between people. It arose from factor analyzing responses to sets of person adjectives sourced from representative dictionaries (excluding skills or not-psychological differences), and thus represents the basic differences in behavioral propensities between people. Treatment, from a PCP perspective, should not then focus on removing the categorical disorder (which turns out to be epiphenomena of the personality process), but rather helping the individual change their levels of behavioral propensities toward what is most adaptive in their lives. Quite how this may be done is shown by Christopher Taylor and Arnoud Arntz (Chapter 30) who make the same argument, but focus on another definition of personality; the particular schematic beliefs about the world which lead to these behavioral propensities. Referring to the work of Lockwood and Perris (2012), they argue that parenting and early life conditions (ranging from traumatic to optimum) lead to needs being met to varying degrees, which in turn leads to eighteen schematic ways of viewing the world (each of which ranges from maladaptive to adaptive). With these additions to Schema Therapy there is an approach with the potential to be an ideal PCP therapy, with the aim of helping all clients move toward the adaptive end of each of the core schemas. The theory would predict that in such a case not only would personality disorders be removed (which arise from certain constellation of schemas), but rather all other psychopathology, and indeed this would foster full psychological development.

Central to our argument for the need for a PCP are the observations that (a) most of the concepts studied by positive psychologists range from low to high, and (b) most of the topics of study for clinical psychologists are equally on continua from maladaptive to adaptive. It is not logical, and perhaps not even possible, to study only half of a continuum. If we have seemed critical here, it is only in order to promote a joining of clinical and positive psychologies into one holistic discipline to better understand and help people.

No Characteristic is "Positive" or "Negative"

In her inimitable style, Barbara Held (Chapter 3) has chosen as her focus a critique of one of our own papers, the editorial paper of the special issue on PCP (Wood & Tarrier, 2010). A prominent "positive psychology critic," she shows her trademark authenticity, and her critique is much needed and welcome. Whilst endorsing the rationale above that all characteristics range from low to high, Held thinks that we should go further in our criticism of a sole focus on the "positive" or "negative."

Held highlights a core reason of why PCP is needed, namely, that neither the low or high end of any characteristic is inherently "positive" or "negative," as nothing is good for everyone all of the time. She suggests that we should instead consider where something is adaptive for individual clients in individual situations. Optimism, for example, is considered a "positive psychology" characteristic, and it is generally positively linked to well-being, although it can also lead to overly risky behavior. Conversely, for some individuals "defensive pessimism" is constructive. In previous work, Boyce, Wood, and Brown (2010) focused on how conscientiousness, a trait generally seen as adaptive for everything from well-being to team performance, becomes maladaptive and leads to greater decreases in life satisfaction following unemployment. Wood, Emmons, Algoe, Froh, Lambert, and Watkins, Chapter 10, this volume, argue that "gratitude" can in some situations be maladaptive, as when it is inappropriately placed (such as toward an abuser, or when it is being used by a power elite to keep a population subjugated). Warren Mansell explores these issues with respect to bipolar disorder in Chapter 16, arguing that there is nothing inherently negative about any level of the positive or negative moods that characterize the disorder, but rather that problems emerge with how these conflict with each other and the other goals of the individual. Eamonn Ferguson (Chapter 8) shows how high levels of empathy are not indiscriminately desirable, noting that psychopaths have high levels of some kinds of empathy whilst being notably deficient in others. Furthermore, Sedikides and Wildschut (Chapter 9) explore the bittersweet nuances of nostalgia, also a factor, they argue, which is not wholly "positive" at either the high or low end.

Thus, even accepting the point above, that most characteristics range from low to high, we cannot then say that the high (or for that matter, the low), are desirable, as this would be an overgeneralization. Indeed, Aristotle (350 BC/1999) wrote the most conclusive work on virtues, which was based around culturally valued characteristics, and he was very explicit that (a) the behavior associated with the characteristic ranged from low to high, and (b) both too high and too low levels of the characteristics are unvirtuous (lit. vicious). Rather, the virtue (and desirability) lies within situationally appropriate displays of the correct level between these two extremes. Thus, views about the future may be said to range from dysfunctionally strong pessimism, to an appropriate point, to a Pollyanna-like dysfunctional expectation of constant positive outcomes. Deviations from the situationally appropriate point in either direction may lead to inappropriate actions. Where this appropriate point lies will depend on the situation and other characteristics of the person, and where the point lies on the continuum would vary between the two extreme poles between individuals or in different situations. This wisdom is consistent with Held's account.

To Held's points, we would like to make a brief response, as we believe that the issues she raises need to be prominently and directly considered by PCP. First, in response to her suggestion that talking about *when* something is adaptive or maladaptive is of the utmost importance, we agree, but suggest that to make this claim there first needs to be a wider acceptance of the PCP premise that all factors exist on a continuum (from high to low). Only with this in place can it be considered in what situations and for whom different points along the continuum are most adaptive. Second, she correctly chastises errors in our earlier paper (Wood & Tarrier, 2010) in which we, on the one hand, suggested that all factors exist on a continuum from high to low, and, on the other hand, referred to constructs popularized by positive psychology (like gratitude) as "positive," in direct opposition to the former point. We correct and discuss this extensively in Johnson and Wood (in press). Essentially, the point we raise here is that whilst the constructs studied by positive psychologists cannot be described as "positive" (or those by clinical psychologists described as "negative"), the characteristics studied by positive psychologists are qualitatively *different* traits than those typically studied by clinical psychologists. That is, where positive psychology research has often investigated personality characteristics such as gratitude, optimism or self-efficacy, traditional clinical psychology has tended to focus more upon cognitive and symptom-related variables. As such, there may be value in considering both sets of characteristics. We hope that these responses address some of Held's criticisms of PCP, and look forward to future dialogue with critics of PCP. We suggest that it is only through welcoming contributions like Held's that PCP can be ultimately be successful, useful, and accurate, and avoid the allegations of isolationist and unscientific practice sometimes leveled at certain parts of the positive psychology movement.

If we accept the argument that high (or low) levels of characteristics are not always adaptive for all people, then there are three implications as to why we need PCP. First, it is meaningless for one field to study some characteristics and another field to study others on the basis that some are "positive" and the others "negative," as whether any variable is "positive" or "negative" will depend upon the individual and the context. The designation of what is positive and negative is also sometimes more of a value judgment of the researchers than being rooted in science, philosophy, or objective reality.

Second, individual case conceptualizations should consider an individual's life holistically – examining characteristics that are generally seen as "good" or "bad" – whilst keeping an open mind as to the role of these in the particular client's life, given their biology, early experiences, life history, current environment, and constellations of traits, attitudes, and functioning levels. Only through a PCP approach, where the need for such a holistic approach is emphasized, does this true integration become possible.

Third, interventional techniques – from both traditional and positive psychology – that may be helpful to one client may be harmful for another. Again, we draw on our recent work in personality psychology showing that personality interacts with situation (e.g., Boyce and Wood, 2011a,b), so one cannot just promote any one thing out of context. This shows the need for PCP in that clinicians need to be aware of the full range of techniques, in order to match the best technique with the individual client. Geraghty, Wood, and Hyland (2010a,b), for example, show that in one specific situation (online interventions where drop-out is expected to be high) a technique based on increasing gratitude is as effective on the presenting problem, and results in lower drop-out than automatic thought monitoring and changing. However, as argued by Wood et al., Chapter 10, this volume, on gratitude, there is the potential for carelessly administered gratitude techniques in some situations to be harmful (as where a person is already excessively subjugating their needs to an abusive other, and incorrectly uses the intervention to deepen this problem). The key message is that we have to move away from talking about characteristics as positive or negative, even if this is their impact on average, and rather consider the role of – and advisability of fostering – any characteristic for the specific client. And to do this, we have to stop arbitrarily focusing on one or other, and certainly stop situating the two in separate fields of study, based more on history and value judgments than reality.

Much more work is needed to establish the optimum point on various characteristics. Statistically, Aristotle's argument implies an inverted "U" relationship between the behaviors underlying virtuous characteristics and their outcomes, where high and low levels are maladaptive and some point in the middle is optimum. Whilst the assumption of linear relationships is tested as a matter of course in fields like economics, this is very rarely seen in psychology. In contrast, it rarely seems to occur to psychological researchers to check that linear regression is appropriate, except in the unusual cases when this is the whole hypothesis under consideration, even though there are very well-known cases of non-linearity effects in the well-being literature (such as adaptation: Boyce and Wood, 2011b). A prominent counterexample to our case here is Park, Peterson, and Seligman (2004), who show that there is a linear relationship between the VIA characteristics and life satisfaction (ruling out inverted "U"s or other nonlinearities appropriately). There are, however, three answers to this.

First, the predictors themselves must actually measure the full continuum of the characteristic. Self-report of highly socially desirable characteristics (that they call virtues) will likely share high method variance with life satisfaction as outcome, so it is perhaps not surprising that people who say they are extremely high on modesty might also say they are very satisfied with their lives.

Second, by accident or by design the predictors may not be intended to ask about a full continuum of behavior, but rather the extent to which those behaviors are displayed in a moderate or situationally appropriate manner. In this case, we would expect a linear relationship between the measure and healthy functioning, as the focus on the moderation and situational appropriateness avoids the high end of the measure picking up dysfunctionally immoderate and excessive displays of the underlying behavior. This type of measurement may well be appropriate for many a usage, but precludes an Aristotelean-influenced test of nonlinearities, which would require a measurement of the full continuum of the underlying behaviors. Also, the outcomes must be the appropriate ones. For example, it is quite possible that increasing levels of a characteristic are related to a sense of smugness that is captured by life satisfaction, but that the individual is still not living a good life (under various socially held definitions of the "good life"). Analogically, it has been observed clinically that part of the problem with treating personality disorders is that a sense of entitlement feels good and individuals are not motivated to change until they see how it is destructive to other areas of their lives (i.e., until they change their outcome measure from life satisfaction to something else). Future work in PCP will have to address this directly.

Third, we believe that some characteristics are by their nature always more positive as one moves up the continuum (which is why, after considering Held's points, we retain the language "maladaptive" and "adaptive" in places within this chapter). If one accepts certain humanistic assumptions about human nature (described by Sanders and Joseph in Chapter 28), then movement toward core nature may always be seen as positive. To the extent that Taylor and Arntz (Chapter 30) correctly identify these, movement from maladaptive to adaptive ends of schemas will always be positive. Here, however, we show our core assumptions of humanity and with which, whilst unavoidable in clinical practice (Wood & Joseph, 2007), readers are free to disagree.

Positive Psychology Characteristics have Incremental Validity in Predicting Clinical Distress

With the qualification above that the characteristics studied by positive psychologists are not inherently positive, there remains huge evidence that the characteristics that they highlight are novel to psychology, and the topics of study of positive psychologists have incremental validity in predicting clinical outcomes beyond what has previously been studied. Taking gratitude (Wood, Froh, & Geraghty, 2010; Wood et al., Chapter 10, this volume) as an example, it substantially predicts both life satisfaction (Wood, Joseph, & Maltby, 2008) and PWB (Wood, Joseph, & Maltby, 2009) above each of the thirty facets of the NEO-PI R measure of the Big Five, which incorporate the most commonly studied traits in psychology as a whole and are meant to be an exhaustive compilation. Notably, the NEO includes individual trait measurement of trait levels of the clinical characteristics of anxiety, stress, depression, vulnerability, and impulsivity. Gratitude also longitudinally predicts decreases in depression (and concomitant increases in happiness), decreases in stress, and increases in perceptions of social support, again beyond the Big Five (Wood, Maltby, Gillett, Linley, & Joseph, 2008). Finally, gratitude predicts improved quality of sleep, also beyond the Big Five (Wood, Joseph, Lloyd, and Atkins, 2009). Whilst there is nothing inherently positive about a characteristic that ranges from ingratitude to gratitude (but see our language clarifications in Chapter 10), it is clearly a measure originating from the field of positive psychology that is capturing something new to psychology and that has considerable clinical relevance. Much of Parts II and III of this book on individual differences and disorders, respectively, are dedicated to making these arguments, including contributions from David Watson on positive affect (Chapter 5), James Maddux and Evan Kleiman on self-efficacy (Chapter 7), Adam Davidson and George Valliant on understudied characteristics in positive ageing (Chapter 12), and Chiara Ruini and Carol Ryff on PWB (Chapter 11). Philip Watkins and Andrew Pereira discuss the role of positive psychological characteristics in anxiety (Chapter 14), and Peter Taylor in the context of childhood disorders (Chapter 19). The absence of positive mood and expectations are explored by Barney Dunn and Henrietta Roberts in relation to depression (Chapter 13), and in relation to suicide by Andrew MacLeod (Chapter 20). Finally, Elizabeth Addington, Richard Tedeschi, and Lawrence Calhoun (Chapter 15) consider the importance of focusing on growth in response to trauma rather than just suffering. Although we do not see the characteristics studied by positive psychologists as always wholly "positive," we do see them as highly understudied and of great utility to clinical psychology theory and practice (Johnson & Wood, in press), as each of these chapters highlight.

Positive Psychology Techniques have Potential to be Used in Clinical Practice

Part IV considers specific techniques that have developed from, or are associated with, positive psychology and their application to clinical psychology. Five are deigned to be fully-fledged therapies: positive psychotherapy (Tayyab Rashid, Chapter 22); forgiveness therapy (Everett Worthington et al., Chapter 24); mindfulness (Shauna Shapiro, Sarah de Sousa and Carley Hauck, Chapter 25); well-being therapy (Giovanni Fava, Chapter 26); and quality of life therapy (Michael Frisch, Chapter 27). Each has the potential to be a positive clinical therapy, as although they developed based on the learnings of positive psychology, they remain grounded in traditional therapeutic approaches, keeping a holistic core. As the authors acknowledge, with the exception of mindfulness, the evidence base is still preliminary for these relative to traditional approaches. Nevertheless, each shows promise and has early supportive evidence. It is hoped that their inclusion here will encourage attention to these highly novel approaches and motivate (and help fund) more multicenter randomized control trials, conducted to the highest standards. In future these therapies may routinely replace more traditional approaches, although further research studies will need to assess which, if any, will amass that evidence base. We hope that they will. For now, they are promising and interesting therapies raising issues that all therapists should consider. Finally, two chapters provide excellent overviews of the specific techniques to have emerged from positive psychology (positive psychological approaches, Acacia Parks and Liudmila Titova, Chapter 21, and positive activities and interventions, Lilian Shin and Sonja Lyubomirsky, Chapter 23). We believe that these positive activities have particular potential to be incorporated into existing clinical psychology therapies. For example, in our previous work we explored the effectiveness of the Broad Minded Affective Coping procedure (BMAC) protocol (Johnson, Gooding, Wood, Fair, & Tarrier, 2013). The BMAC is a positive mood induction technique based on the client's own memories, and is suitable for use in clinical therapy sessions to boost positively valenced affect. This is consistent with how we generally see the use of positive psychology techniques in clinical psychology. Not as replacements for existing therapies, but rather as specific techniques that can be applied based on individual clinical judgment in collaborative dialogue with the client. These chapters provide a wealth of novel suggestions and discuss the variable evidence base for these. We hope that the next few years will see more rigorous trials in clinical settings testing the relative benefits of adding these positive activities to well-validated therapies.

Many Existing Therapies are Already PCP if Viewed Through this Lens

Finally, PCP is first and foremost intended to be a new way of viewing the fields of positive psychology and clinical psychology. We are delighted that for our Part V, leading experts from major therapeutic approaches have considered how their therapies, as currently practiced, are already working with a full continuum of well-being (or simultaneously working on reducing maladaptive aspects whilst improving adaptive ones). Pete Sanders and Stephen Joseph (Chapter 28) consider person-centered therapy, Timothy Feeney and Steve Hayes (Chapter 29) consider acceptance and commitment therapy, and Christopher Taylor and Arnold Arntz (Chapter 30) consider schema therapy. We hope that the next few years will see wider consideration within other therapies of how they too may already be focusing on the full spectrum of well-being.

Conclusion

Thomas Kuhn (1962), in *The Structure of Scientific Revolutions*, describes the progress of science as distinctly nonlinear and as influenced by the existing zeitgeist. A paradigm develops encapsulating the standard interpretation of the evidence base at the time. This paradigm is strengthened by new evidence, which is generally interpreted as consistent with this paradigm if such an interpretation is possible. Eventually, however, sufficient disconfirming evidence emerges that topples the paradigm, creating a period of healthy crisis. Out of this crisis arises a new paradigm, around which a new critical mass of evidence emerges, until this in turn is toppled; it is such that human knowledge progresses. Until positive psychology came along, the paradigm was based around only understanding and reducing what was seen as the negative within clinical research and practice. Positive psychology successfully provided enough disconfirming evidence to topple this paradigm and create a crisis in the field. Whilst some expected positive psychology to be the next paradigm, arguably this has not happened, possibly due to divisive isolationist factions, lack of acknowledgment of previous approaches, some (isolated) research quality problems, and a lack of openness to criticism. Rather, some might see positive psychology as causing and epitomizing the crisis. This is a massive contribution to psychology, as knowledge progresses only through the toppling of paradigms and no greater compliment can be made than to have toppled a paradigm. We do not know yet if PCP is the next paradigm for clinical psychology, as history shows that only years after the event can this be judged. PCP may very well be simply a refinement of the criticisms that are contributing to the fall of an untenable paradigm. In that case, it will have provided an invaluable service and we hope to live to see the next paradigm emerge. We are grateful to all our contributors for being a part of this landmark development of PCP, representing a step change in clinical psychology research and practice. The involvement of so many prominent people in the present volume evidences that the PCP approach is now part of the mainstream. We hope that readers will be provoked by the chapters and, even if they disagree with what they read here, that they will leave with more reflections upon assumptions about their work and a new determination to improve the quality of clinical psychology research and practice.

References

Aristotle (1999 [350 BC]). *Nicomachean Ethics.* Trans. T. Irwine. Indianapolis, Indiana: Hackett.

Bohart, A. C. (2002). Focusing on the positive. *Focusing on the negative: Implications for psychotherapy. Journal of Clinical Psychology, 58*, 1037–1043.

Boyce, C. J. & Wood, A. M. (2011a). Personality and the marginal utility of income: Personality interacts with increases in household income to determine life satisfaction. *Journal of Economic Behavior & Organization, 78*, 183–191.

Boyce, C. J. & Wood, A. M. (2011b). Personality prior to disability determines adaptation: Agreeable individuals recover lost life satisfaction faster and more completely. *Psychological Science, 22*, 1397–1402.

Boyce, C. J., Wood, A. M., & Brown, G. D. A. (2010). The dark side of conscientiousness: Conscientious people experience greater drops in life satisfaction following unemployment. *Journal of Research in Personality, 44*, 535–539.

Coyne, J. C. & Tennen, H. (2010). Positive psychology in cancer care: Bad science, exaggerated claims, and unproven medicine. *Annals of Behavioral Medicine, 39*, 16–26.

Coyne, J. C., Tennen, H., & Ranchor, A. V. (2010). Positive psychology in cancer care: a story line resistant to evidence. *Annals of Behavioral Medicine, 39*, 35–42.

Duckworth, A. L., Steen, T. A., & Seligman, M. E. P. (2005). Positive psychology in clinical practice. *Annual Review of Clinical Psychology, 1*, 629–651.

Geraghty, A. W. A., Wood, A. M., & Hyland, M. E. (2010a). Attrition from self-directed interventions: Investigating the relationship between psychological predictors, intervention content and dropout from a body dissatisfaction intervention. *Social Science & Medicine, 71*, 31–37.

Geraghty, A. W. A., Wood, A. M., & Hyland, M. E. (2010b). Dissociating the facets of hope: Agency and pathways predict dropout from unguided self-help therapy in opposite directions. *Journal of Research in Personality, 44*, 155–158.

Held, B. S. (2004). The negative side of positive psychology. *Journal of Humanistic Psychology, 44*, 9–46.

Johnson, J., Gooding, P. A., Wood, A. M., & Tarrier, N. (2010). Resilience as positive coping appraisals: Testing the schematic appraisals model of suicide. *Behavior Research and Therapy, 48*, 179–186.

Johnson, J., Gooding, P. A., Wood, A. M., Fair, K. L., & Tarrier, N. (2013). A therapeutic tool for boosting mood: The broad-minded affective coping procedure (BMAC). *Cognitive Therapy and Research, 37*, 61–70.

Johnson, J., Gooding, P. A., Wood, A. M., Taylor, P. J., Pratt, D., & Tarrier, N. (2010). Resilience to suicidal ideation in psychosis: Positive self-appraisals buffer the impact of hopelessness. *Behavior Research and Therapy, 48*, 883–889.

Johnson, J., Wood, A. M., Gooding, P., & Tarrier, N. (2011). Resilience to suicidality: The buffering hypothesis. *Clinical Psychology Review, 31*, 563–591.

Johnson, J. & Wood, A. M (in press). Integrating positive and clinical psychology: Viewing human functioning as continua from positive to negative can benefit clinical assessment, interventions and understandings of resilience. *Cognitive Therapy and Research.*

Joseph, S. & Linley, P. A. (2006a). *Positive therapy: A meta-theory for positive psychological practice.* London: Taylor & Francis.

Joseph, S. & Linley, P. A. (2006b). Positive psychology versus the medical model? *American Psychologist, 61,* 332–333.

Kuhn, Thomas S. (1962). *The structure of scientific revolutions.* Chicago: University of Chicago Press.

Lazarus, R. S. (2003). Does the positive psychology movement have legs? *Psychological Inquiry, 14,* 93–109.

Linley, P. A., Joseph, S., Harrington, S., & Wood, A. M. (2006). Positive psychology: Past, present, and (possible) future. *Journal of Positive Psychology, 1,* 3–16.

Linley, P. A, Maltby, J., Wood, A. M., Osborne, G., & Hurling, R. (2009). Measuring happiness: The higher order factor structure of subjective and psychological well-being measures. *Personality and Individual Differences, 47,* 878–884.

Lockwood, G. & Perris, P. (2012). A new look at core emotional needs. In: J. B. M. van Vreeswijk & M. Nadort (Eds.), *The Wiley-Blackwell handbook of schema therapy: Theory research and practice* (pp. 41–66). Chichester: Wiley-Blackwell.

Maslow, A. H. (1954). *Motivation and personality.* New York: Harper.

McCullough, M. E., Emmons, R. A., & Tsang, J. (2002). The grateful disposition: A conceptual and empirical topography. *Journal of Personality and Social Psychology, 82,* 112–127.

Park, N., Petterson, C., & Seligman, M. E. P. (2004). Strengths of character and well being. *Journal of Social and Clinical Psychology, 23,* 603–619.

Rusk, R. D, & Waters, L. E. (2013). Tracing the size, reach, impact, and breadth of positive psychology. *Journal of Positive Psychology, 8,* 207–221.

Seligman, M. E. P. & Csikszentmihalyi, M. (2000). Positive psychology: An introduction. *American Psychologist, 55,* 5–14.

Siddaway, A. P., Taylor, P. J., & Wood, A. M. (2016). The State-Trait Anxiety Inventory (STAI) measures a linear continuum from anxiety to calmness: Potential implications for the professional "agenda" of mental health services [working title], unpublished manuscript, available at: www.alexwoodpsychology.com.

Sumner, P., Vivian-Griffiths, S., Boivin, J., Williams, A., Venetis, C. A., Davies, A. Ogden, A., Whelan, L., Hughes, B., Dalton, B., Boy, F., & Chambers, C. D. (2014). The association between exaggeration in health related science news and academic press releases: Retrospective observational study. *British Medical Journal, 349,* g701.

Tennen, H. & Affleck, G. (2003). When accentuating the positive, don't forget the negative or Mr. In-between. *Psychological Inquiry, 14,* 163–169.

Westerhof, G. J. & Keyes, C. L. M. (2010). Mental illness and mental health: The two continua model across the lifespan. *Journal of Adult Development, 17,* 110–119.

Wood, A. M., Froh, J. J., & Geraghty, A. W. A. (2010). Gratitude and well-being: A review and theoretical integration. *Clinical Psychology Review, 30,* 890–905.

Wood, A. M. & Joseph, S. (2007). Grand theories of personality cannot be integrated. *American Psychologist, 62,* 57–58.

Wood, A. M. & Joseph S. (2010). The absence of positive psychological (eudemonic) well-being as a risk factor for depression: A ten year cohort study. *Journal of Affective Disorders, 122,* 213–217.

Wood, A. M., Joseph, S., Lloyd, J., & Atkins, S. (2009). Gratitude influences sleep through the mechanism of pre-sleep cognitions. *Journal of Psychosomatic Research, 66,* 43–48.

Wood, A. M., Joseph, S., & Maltby, J. (2008). Gratitude uniquely predicts satisfaction with life: Incremental validity above the domains and facets of the five factor model. *Personality and Individual Differences, 45,* 49–54.

Wood, A. M, Joseph, S., & Maltby, J. (2009). Gratitude predicts psychological well-being above the Big Five facets. *Personality and Individual Differences, 46,* 443–447.

Wood, A. M., Maltby, J., Gillett, R., Linley, P. A., & Joseph, S. (2008). The role of gratitude in the development of social support, stress, and depression: Two longitudinal studies. *Journal of Research in Personality, 42,* 854–871.

Wood, A. M., Taylor, P. T., & Joseph, S. (2010). Does the CES-D measure a continuum from depression to happiness? Comparing substantive and artifactual models. *Psychiatry Research, 177,* 120–123.

Wood, A. M. & Tarrier, N. (2010). Positive Clinical Psychology: A new vision and strategy for integrated research and practice. *Clinical Psychology Review, 30,* 819–829.

Wood et al. (in press). Applications of Positive Psychology. *The Oxford Handbook of Positive Psychology.*

2

Toward a More Positive Clinical Psychology

Deconstructing the Illness Ideology and Psychiatric Diagnosis

James E. Maddux

This chapter is concerned with how clinical psychologists traditionally have conceived the difference between psychological illness and wellness and how they *should* conceive this difference. Thus, the major purpose of this chapter is to challenge traditional conceptions of psychological wellness and illness and to offer a new conception a corresponding new *vision* of and *mission* for clinical psychology. We will do this by offering a "deconstruction" of what we refer to as the *illness ideology* in general and psychiatric diagnosis in particular.

A *conception* of the difference between wellness and illness is not a *theory* of either wellness or illness (Wakefield, 1992). Conceptions of wellness and illness attempt to define these terms – to delineate which human experiences are to be considered "well" or "ill." A *theory* of wellness and illness, however, is an attempt to explain those psychological phenomena and experiences that have been identified by the conceptions as well and ill (see also Maddux, Gosselin, & Winstead, 2016).

As medical philosopher Lawrie Reznek (1987) has said in writing about the elusiveness and arbitrariness of the word *disease*: "Concepts carry consequences – classifying things one way rather than another has important implications for the way we behave towards such things" (p. 1). How we conceive psychological illness and wellness has wide-ranging implications for individuals, medical and mental health professionals, government agencies and programs, and society at large. It determines what behaviors we consider it necessary to explain with our theories, thus determining the direction and scope of our research efforts. It also determines how we conceive the subject matter of clinical psychology, the roles and functions of clinical psychologists, and the people with whom they work.

Conceptions of psychological wellness and illness cannot be subjected to tests of empirical validation. They are *social constructions* grounded in values, not science, and socially constructed values cannot be proven true or false by science, as we will later discuss. Because this chapter deals with socially constructed conceptions, it offers no new "facts" or "research findings" intended to persuade the reader of the greater value of one conception of psychological wellness and illness over another or one view of clinical psychology over another. Instead, this chapter offers a different perspective based on a different set of values.

The Wiley Handbook of Positive Clinical Psychology, First Edition. Edited by Alex M. Wood and Judith Johnson.
© 2016 John Wiley & Sons, Ltd. Published 2016 by John Wiley & Sons, Ltd.

The Illness Ideology and Clinical Psychology

Words can exert a powerful influence over thought. Long after the ancient roots of the term *clinical psychology* have been forgotten, they continue to influence our thinking about the discipline. *Clinical* derives from the Greek *klinike* or "medical practice at the sickbed," and *psychology* derives from *psyche*, meaning "soul" or "mind." (*Webster's Seventh New Collegiate Dictionary*, 1976). Many practitioners and most of the public still view clinical psychology as a kind of "medical practice" for people with "sick souls" or "sick minds." The discipline is still steeped not only in an *illness metaphor*, but also an *illness ideology*. Although the illness metaphor (sometimes referred to as the *medical model*) prescribes a certain way of thinking about psychological problems (e.g., a psychological problem is *like* a biological disease), the illness *ideology* goes beyond this and tells us to what aspects of human behavior we should pay attention. It dictates that the focus of our attention should be disorder, dysfunction, and disease rather than health. It emphasizes abnormality over normality, poor adjustment over healthy adjustment, and sickness over health. It promotes dichotomies between normal and abnormal behaviors, between clinical and nonclinical problems, and between clinical and nonclinical populations. Thus, it narrows our focus on what is weak and defective about people to the exclusion of what is strong and healthy. It also locates human adjustment and maladjustment *inside* the person rather than in the person's interactions with the environment and encounters with sociocultural values and societal institutions. Finally, it views people who seek help for problems in living as passive victims of intrapsychic and biological forces beyond their direct control. As a result, people who seek help for distress are relegated to the role of passive recipient of an expert's care as opposed to an active participant in solving their own problems and taking control of their own lives.

Ideologies are captured by language, and the language of clinical psychology remains the language of medicine and pathology. Terms such as *symptom, disorder, pathology, illness, diagnosis, treatment, doctor, patient, clinic, clinical*, and *clinician* are all consistent with both a metaphor and an ideology of illness and disease (Maddux, 2008). The more we use these words when talking about clinical psychology and the work of clinical psychologists, the more we indoctrinate ourselves to the illness ideology.

The illness ideology has outlived its usefulness for clinical psychology. Decades ago, the field of medicine began to shift its emphasis from the treatment of illness to the prevention of illness and then moved from the prevention of illness to the enhancement of health. Furthermore, over three decades ago, the field of health psychology acknowledged the need to emphasize illness prevention and health promotion. Unless clinical psychology embraces a similar change in emphasis, it will struggle for identity and purpose in much the same manner as psychiatry has for the last several decades (Wilson, 1993; Francis, 2013). In fact, it already is. For example, over half a century ago in the United States, clinical psychologists overtook psychiatrists as the major providers of psychotherapy. Now, social workers have overtaken clinical psychologists in the provision of these same services. Clinical psychology needs to redefine itself as a science and a profession, and expand its roles and opportunities in order to survive and thrive in the rapidly changing marketplace of mental health services. The best way to do this is to abandon the illness ideology and replace it with a *more positive clinical psychology* grounded in positive psychology's ideology of health, happiness, and human strengths. We do not have to change the name of the discipline to "positive clinical psychology," but we do have to change its scope and its mission.

Historical Roots of the Illness Ideology in Clinical Psychology

Clinical psychology was not steeped in the illness ideology at its start. Some historians of psychology trace the beginnings of clinical psychology in the United States back to the 1886 founding of the first "psychological clinic" at the University of Pennsylvania by Lightner Witmer

(Reisman, 1991; Benjamin & Baker, 2004). Witmer and the other early clinical psychologists worked primarily with children who had learning or school problems – not with "patients" with "mental disorders" (Reisman, 1991; Routh, 2000; Benjamin & Baker, 2004). Thus, they were more influenced by psychometric theory and its emphasis on careful measurement than by psychoanalytic theory and its emphasis on psychopathology and illness. Following Freud's 1909 visit to Clark University, however, psychoanalysis and its derivatives came to dominate both psychiatry and clinical psychology (Korchin, 1976; Barone Maddux, & Snyder, 1997; Benjamin & Baker, 2004). Psychoanalytic theory, with its emphasis on hidden intrapsychic processes and sexual and aggressive urges, provided a fertile soil into which the illness ideology deeply sank its roots.

Several other factors encouraged clinical psychologists to devote their attention to psychopathology and thereby strengthened the hold of the illness ideology on the field. First, although clinical psychologists were trained academically in universities, their practitioner training occurred primarily in psychiatric hospitals and clinics where they worked primarily as psycho-diagnosticians under the direction of psychiatrists trained in medicine and psychoanalysis (Morrow, 1946; Benjamin & Baker, 2004). Second, the US Veterans Administration (VA) was founded after the Second World War, and soon joined the American Psychological Association in developing standards for training clinical psychologists and centers for training them in VA hospitals. Thus, the training of clinical psychologists continued to occur primarily in psychiatric settings steeped in both biological and psychoanalytic models. Third, the US National Institute of Mental Health (NIMH) was founded in 1947. Very soon "thousands of psychologists found out that they could make a living treating mental illness" (Seligman & Csikszentmihalyi, 2000, p. 6). By the 1950s, clinical psychologists in the United States had come "to see themselves as part of a mere subfield of the health professions" (Seligman & Csikszentmihalyi, 2000, p. 6), and the practice of clinical psychology was grounded firmly in the illness ideology.

This ideology is characterized by four basic assumptions about the scope and nature of psychological adjustment and maladjustment (Barone, Maddux, & Snyder, 1997). First, clinical psychology is concerned with alleviating mental illness or psychopathology: deviant, abnormal, and maladaptive behavioral and emotional conditions. Thus, its focus is not on the everyday problems in living experienced by millions or on increasing the well-being of the relatively well adjusted, but on severe conditions experienced by a relatively small number of people. Common problems in living, instead, became the purview of counseling psychology, social work, and child guidance.

Second, psychopathology, clinical problems, and clinical populations differ in kind, not just in degree, from normal problems in living, nonclinical problems, and nonclinical populations. Psychopathologies are *disorders*, not merely extreme variants of common problems in living and expected human difficulties and imperfections. As such, understanding psychopathology requires theories different from those theories that explain normal problems in living and effective psychological functioning. Wellness and illness demand separate explanatory processes.

Third, psychological disorders are analogous to biological or medical diseases in that they reflect distinct conditions *inside* the individual that cause the individual to think, feel, and behave maladaptively. This principle does not necessarily imply that psychological disorders directly caused by biological dysfunctions, but it does hold that the causes of emotional and behavioral problems are located inside the person, rather than in the person's interactions with his or her environment, including his or her relationships with other people and society at large.

Fourth, the psychological clinician's task, similar to the medical clinician's task, is to identify (diagnose) the disorder (disease) that resides inside the person (patient), to prescribe an intervention (treatment) to eliminate (cure) the internal disorder (disease), either biological or psychological, that is responsible for the symptoms. Even if the attempt to alleviate the problem is a purely verbal attempt to educate or persuade, it is still referred to as *treatment* or *therapy*, unlike often equally beneficial attempts to educate or persuade on the part of teachers, ministers, friends, and family (see Szasz, 1978). In addition, these "psychotherapeutic" interactions between clinicians and their "patients" differ in quality from helpful and distress-reducing interactions between the "patient" and other people in his or her life, as understanding these "psychotherapeutic" interactions requires special theories (see Maddux, 2010).

Albee (2000) suggests that "the uncritical acceptance of the medical model, the organic explanation of mental disorders, with psychiatric hegemony, medical concepts, and language" (p. 247) was the "fatal flaw" of the standards for clinical psychology training in the United States that were established in 1950 by the American Psychological Association at a conference in Boulder, Colorado. Albee argues that this fatal flaw "has distorted and damaged the development of clinical psychology ever since" (p. 247). Little has changed since 1950. The basic assumptions of the illness ideology continue as implicit guides to clinical psychologists' activities, and they permeate the view of clinical psychology held by the public and policy makers.

The Illness Ideology and the DSM

The influence of the illness ideology has increased over the past three-and-a-half decades as clinical psychologists have acquiesced to the influence of the American Psychiatric Association's (APA) *Diagnostic and Statistical Manual of Mental Disorders* (*DSM*) (APA, 2013). First published in the early 1950s (APA, 1952), the *DSM* is now in its fifth edition, and its size and influence have increased with each revision, especially beginning with the greatly expanded third edition in 1980.

The influence of the *DSM* has increased with the increasing size and scope of the subsequent revisions. The first edition (including all appendices) ran to 130 pages; the fifth edition runs just over 900 pages. The number of official mental disorders recognized by the APA has increased from six in the mid-nineteenth century to close to 300 in the *DSM-5* (Francis & Widiger, 2012). The growth in the role of third-party funding for mental health services in the United States during this same period fueled the growth of the influence of the *DSM* as these third parties began requiring a DSM diagnostic label as a condition for payment or reimbursement for mental health services.

Although most of the previously noted assumptions of the illness ideology are disavowed in the *DSM*-5 introduction (APA, 2013), most of the manual is inconsistent with this disavowal. For example, still included in the revised definition of *mental disorder* is the notion that a mental disorder is "a dysfunction in the individual" (p. 20). Numerous common problems in living are viewed as mental disorders (Francis, 2013), and several others are listed as "conditions for further study" (e.g., Persistent Complex Bereavement Disorder, Caffeine Use Disorder, Internet Gaming Disorder), and therefore likely to find their way into *DSM-6*. *DSM-5* does pay greater attention to alternative dimensional models for conceptualizing psychological problems and to the importance of cultural considerations in determining whether or not a problematic pattern should be viewed as a "mental disorder," and these are steps in the right direction. Yet it remains steeped in the illness ideology for most of its 900 pages.

So closely aligned are the illness ideology and the *DSM*, and so powerful is the influence of the *DSM* over clinical psychology (at least in the United States) that clinical psychology's rejection of the illness ideology must go hand in hand with its rejection of the *DSM* and other categorical schemes such as the *ICD* as the best way to conceive of psychological difficulties. This must begin with the acknowledgment that the DSM is not a scientific document, but a social and political document – a topic we next address.

The Social Construction of Conceptions of Psychological Wellness and Illness

A more positive clinical psychology rejects the illness ideology as the most accurate or effective approach for conceiving of the psychologically problematic aspects of human life. As such, a more positive clinical psychology refutes the basic premise of the illness ideology and the *DSM* that normal problems in living are symptoms of "psychopathologies" – that is, psychological illnesses, diseases, or disorders – and that giving a person a formal diagnosis for a problem in living contributes to the understanding to that person and his or her problem. This refutation is based on the assumption that the illness ideology is not a scientific theory or set of facts but rather a *socially constructed ideology*. Social constructionism is concerned with "examining ways in which people understand the world, the social and political processes that influence how people define words and explain events, and the implications of these definitions and explanations – who benefits and who loses because of how we describe and understand the world" (Muehlenhard & Kimes, 1999, p. 234). The process of social construction involves "elucidating the process by which people come to describe, explain, or otherwise account for the world in which they live" (Gergen, 1985, pp. 3–4; 1999). Because the prevailing views depend on who has the power to determine them, universal or "true" conceptions and perspectives do not exist. The people who are privileged to define such views usually are people with power, and their conceptions reflect and promote their interests and values (Muehlenhard & Kimes, 1999). Because the interests of people and institutions are based on their values, debates over the definition of concepts often become clashes between deeply and implicitly held beliefs about the way people should live their lives and differences in moral values.

The social constructionist perspective can be contrasted to the *essentialist* perspective that is inherent in the illness ideology and the *DSM*. Essentialism assumes that there are natural categories and that all members of a given category share important characteristics (Rosenblum & Travis, 1996). For example, the essentialist perspective views our categories of race, sexual orientation, and social class as objective categories that are independent of social, cultural, and political processes and that represent "empirically verifiable similarities among and differences between people" (Rosenblum & Travis, 1996, p. 2). In the social constructionist view, such categories represent not what people *are*, but rather the ways that people think about and attempt to make sense of differences among people. Social, cultural, and political processes also determine what differences among people are more important than other differences (Rosenblum & Travis, 1996).

From the essentialist perspective, the distinctions between psychological wellness and illness and among various so-called psychopathologies and mental disorders, such as those described in the *DSM* (and the *ICD*) are natural distinctions that can be discovered and described. From the social constructionist perspective, however, these distinctions are not scientifically verifiable "facts" or even scientifically testable theories. Instead, they are abstract ideas that have been constructed by people with particular personal, professional, and cultural values. The meanings of these and other concepts are not *revealed* by the methods of science, but are *negotiated* among the people and institutions of society who have an interest in their definitions. They reflect shared world views that were developed and agreed upon collaboratively over time by the members of society, including theorists, researchers, professionals, clients and patients, the media, business and finance, and the culture in which all are embedded.

For this reason, the illness ideology, its conception of "mental disorder," and the various specific categories of mental disorders found in traditional psychiatric diagnostic schemes (such as the *DSM* and *ICD*) are not psychological facts about people, nor are they testable scientific theories. Instead, they are social artifacts that serve the same sociocultural goals as do our constructions of race, gender, social class, and sexual orientation – maintaining and expanding the power of certain individuals and institutions, as well as maintaining social order as defined by those in power

(Becker, 1963; Beall, 1993; Parker, Georgaca, Harper, McLaughlin, & Stowell-Smith, 1995; Rosenblum & Travis, 1996). As are these other social constructions, our concepts of psychological normality and abnormality are tied ultimately to social values – in particular, the values of society's most powerful individuals, groups, and institutions – and the contextual rules for behavior derived from these values (Becker, 1963; Parker et al., 1995; Rosenblum & Travis, 1996).

Reznek (1987) has demonstrated that even our definition of physical disease "is a normative or evaluative concept" (p. 211) because to call a condition a disease "is to judge that the person with that condition is less able to lead a good or worthwhile life" as defined by the person's society and culture (p. 211). If this is true of physical disease, it certainly is true of psychological "disease."

Given these precursors, it comes as no surprise that a highly *negative* clinical psychology evolved during the twentieth century. The socially constructed illness ideology and associated traditional psychiatric diagnostics schemes, also socially constructed, have led to the *pathologization* of normal psychological phenomena and thus the proliferation of "mental illnesses" (Francis, 2013; Greenberg, 2013). Sociologists view this as an aspect of an even more general *medicalization* of a wide range of normal human problems and ailments, whereby "a problem is defined in medical terms, described using medical language, understood through the adoption of a medical framework, or 'treated' with a medical intervention" (Conrad, 2007, p. 5). As the socially constructed boundaries of "mental disorder" have expanded with each *DSM* revision, more and more relatively common human problems and frailties human have become pathologized and medicalized. Mental health professionals have not been content to label only the obviously and blatantly dysfunctional patterns of behaving, thinking, and feeling as "mental disorders." As a result, the number of people with a diagnosable "mental disorder" has continued to grow. If this continues, eventually everything that human beings think, feel, do, and desire that is not perfectly logical, adaptive, or efficient, or that "creates trouble in human life" (Paris, 2013, p. 43) will become a mental disorder (Francis, 2013; Paris, 2013). *DSM-5* has made normality "an endangered species," partly because we live in a society that is "perfectionistic in its expectations and intolerant of what were previously considered to be normal and expectable distress and individual differences" (Francis & Widiger, 2012, p. 116), but also partly because pharmaceutical companies are constantly trying to increase the market for their drugs by encouraging the loosening and expanding of the boundaries of mental disorders described in the *DSM* and encouraging the creation of new disorders, often through direct-to-consumers advertising (Conrad, 2007; Horwitz & Wakefield, 2007; Francis, 2013; Greenberg, 2013; Paris, 2013). The APA also has a strong financial interest in the marketing of psychopathology given that sales of the *DSM* account for about 10% of its annual income (Greenberg, 2013). (The World Health Organization's *ICD*, on the other hand, can be downloaded for free from its website.)

The powerful sociocultural, political, professional, and economic forces that constructed the illness ideology now continue to sustain it. The debate over the conception of psychological wellness and illness is not a search for "truth." Rather, it is a struggle over the definition of a socially constructed abstraction and over the personal, political, and economic benefits that flow from determining what and whom society views as normal and abnormal. This struggle is played out in the continual debates involved in revision of the *DSM* (Kirk & Kutchins, 1992; Kutchins & Kirk, 1997; Conrad, 2007; Horwitz & Wakefield; 2007; Francis, 2013; Greenfield; 2013).

The Illness Ideology and the Categories versus Dimensions Debate

Embedded in the illness ideology's conception of psychological wellness and illness is a *categorical model* in which individuals are determined to either have or not have a disorder – that is, to be either psychologically well or psychologically ill – and, if they do have a disorder, that it is a specific type of disorder. This view is embodied in the *DSM* and the *ICD*. An alternative model is the *dimensional model*, which assumes that normality and abnormality, wellness and illness, and effective and ineffective psychological functioning lie along a continuum. In this dimensional approach, so-called psychological "disorders" are simply extreme variants of normal psychological phenomena and ordinary problems in living (Keyes & Lopez, 2002; Widiger, 2016). Great differences among individuals on the dimensions of interest are expected, such as the differences we find on formal tests of intelligence. As with intelligence, divisions made between normality and abnormality may be demarcated for convenience or efficiency, but they are *not* to be viewed as reflecting a true discontinuity among "types" of phenomena or "types" of people. Inherent in the dimensional view is the assumption that these distinctions are not natural demarcations that can be "discovered"; instead, they are created or constructed "by accretion and practical necessity, not because they [meet] some independent set of abstract and operationalized definitional criteria" (Francis & Widiger, 2012, p. 111).

Understanding the research supporting the dimensional approach is important because the vast majority of this research undermines the illness ideology's assumption that we can make clear, scientifically-based distinctions between the psychologically well or healthy and the psychological ill or disordered. The empirical evidence for the validity of a dimensional approach to psychological adjustment is formidable and can be found in research on personality disorders (Costello, 1996; Maddux & Mundell, 2005; Trull & Durrett, 2005; Crego & Widiger, 2016); the variations in normal emotional experiences (e.g., Oatley & Jenkins, 1992); adult attachment patterns in relationships (Fraley & Waller, 1998); self-defeating behaviors (Baumeister & Scher, 1988); children's reading problems or "dyslexia"; (Shaywitz, Escobar, Shaywitz, Fletcher, & Makuch, 1992); attention deficit/hyperactivity disorder (Barkeley, 1997); post-traumatic stress disorder (Anthony, Lonigan, & Hecht, 1999); depression (Costello, 1993a); somatoform disorders (or somatic symptom disorders) (Zovlensky, Eifert, & Garey, 2016); anxiety disorders (Williams, 2016); sexual dysfunctions and disorders (Gosselin, 2016); and of the symptoms of schizophrenia and affective psychoses (Costello, 1993b; Claridge, 1995; Nettle, 2001). To ignore this research and continue to cling to categories is to ignore science and reason.

Social Constructionism and the Role of Science in Clinical Psychology

A social constructionist perspective is not "anti-science." To say that conceptions of psychological wellness and illness are socially constructed rather than scientifically constructed is not to say that the patterns of thinking, feeling, and behaving that society decides to label as "ill" – including their causes and treatments – cannot be studied objectively and scientifically. Instead, it is to acknowledge that science can no more determine the "proper" or "correct" conceptions of psychological wellness and illness than it can determine the "proper" and "correct" conception of other social constructions such as beauty, justice, race, and social class.

We nonetheless can use the methods of science to study the psychological phenomena that our culture refers to as "well" or "ill." We can use them to understand a culture's conception of psychological wellness and illness, how this conception has evolved, and how it affects individuals and society. We also can use them to understand the origins of the patterns of thinking, feeling, and behaving that a culture considers psychopathological and to develop and test ways of modifying those patterns.

The science of medicine is not diminished by the acknowledgment that the notions of *health* and *illness* are socially constructed (Reznek, 1987). The science of economics is not diminished by the acknowledgment that the notions of *poverty* and *wealth* are socially constructed. Likewise, the science of clinical psychology will not be diminished by the acknowledgment that its basic concepts are socially constructed and not scientifically constructed (Lilienfeld and Marino, 1995).

Beyond the Illness Ideology: Toward a More Positive Clinical Psychology

The viability and survival of clinical psychology depends on its ability to build a more positive clinical psychology that breaks with its "pathological" past. In building a more positive clinical psychology, we must adopt not only a new ideology, but also a new language for talking about human behavior that reflects this ideology. In this new language, ineffective patterns of behaviors, cognitions, and emotions are construed as problems in living, not as disorders or diseases. Likewise, these problems in living are construed not as located inside individuals, but in the interactions between the individual and other people that are embedded in situations that include rules for behavior that are, in turn, embedded in the larger culture. Also, those who seek assistance in enhancing the quality of their lives are clients or students, not patients. The professionals who specialize in facilitating psychological health are teachers, counselors, consultants, coaches, or even social activists, not clinicians or doctors. Strategies and techniques for enhancing the quality of lives are educational, relational, social, and political interventions, not medical treatments. Finally, the facilities to which people will go for assistance with problems in living are centers, schools, or resorts, not clinics or hospitals. Such assistance might even take place in community centers, public and private schools, churches, and people's homes rather than in specialized facilities.

A more positive clinical psychology would emphasize goals, well-being, satisfaction, happiness, interpersonal skills, perseverance, talent, wisdom, and personal responsibility. It would be concerned with understanding what makes life worth living, with helping people become more self-organizing and self-directed, and with recognizing that "people and experiences are embedded in a social context" (Seligman & Csikszentmihalyi, 2000, p. 8).

These principles offer a conception of psychological functioning that gives at least as much emphasis to mental health as to mental illness and that gives at least as much emphasis to identifying and understanding human strengths and assets as to human weaknesses and deficits (see Lopez & Snyder, 2003). A more positive clinical psychology would be as much concerned with understanding and enhancing subjective well-being and effective functioning as with alleviating subjective distress and maladaptive functioning. This does not entail a shift away from relieving suffering, but rather "an integrated and equally weighted focus on both positive and negative functioning in all areas of research and practice" (Wood & Tarrier, 2010, p. 819).

Consistent with our social constructionist perspective, we are not arguing that the positive psychology ideology is more "true" than the illness ideology. Both ideologies are socially constructed views of the world, not scientific theories or bodies of facts. We do argue, however, that positive psychology offers an ideology that is more useful to clinical psychology than the obsolete illness ideology. As Bandura (1978) has observed: "Relatively few people seek cures for neuroses, but vast numbers of them are desirous of psychological services that can help them function more effectively in their everyday lives" (p. 99).

Unlike a traditional negative clinical psychology based on the illness ideology, a positive clinical psychology is concerned not just with identifying weaknesses and treating or preventing "disorders," but also with identifying human strengths and promoting "mental health." It is concerned not just with alleviating or preventing "suffering, death, pain, disability, or an important loss of freedom" (APA, 2000, p. xxxi), but also with promoting health, happiness, physical fitness, pleasure, and personal fulfillment through the free pursuit of chosen and valued goals.

A clinical psychology that is grounded not in the illness ideology, but in a positive psychology ideology rejects: (1) the pathologization and categorization of humans and normal human experiences, problems, and frailties; (2) the assumption that so-called mental disorders exist in individuals rather than in the relationships between the individual and other individuals and the culture at large; and (3) the notion that understanding what is worst and weakest about us is more important than understanding what is best and bravest.

A more positive psychological assessment will emphasize the evaluations of people's strengths and assets along with their weaknesses and deficiencies (Keyes & Lopez, 2002; Wright & Lopez, 2002; Lopez, Snyder, & Rasmussen, 2003; Joseph & Wood, 2010; Wood & Tarrier, 2010). More often than not, strategies and tactics for assessing strengths and assets will borrow from the strategies and tactics that have proven useful in assessing human weaknesses and deficiencies (Lopez, Synder, & Rasmussen, 2003; Wood & Tarrier, 2010). Positive psychological interventions will emphasize the enhancement of people's strengths and assets in addition to, and at times instead of, the amelioration of their weaknesses and deficiencies, secure in the belief that strengthening the strengths will weaken the weaknesses. The interventions most often will derive their strategies and tactics from traditional "treatments" of traditional psychological "disorders" (Wood & Tarrier, 2010).

One can argue about whether or not what is now called "positive psychology" is really anything new, but it is difficult to deny that it has sparked a healthy dose of "soul searching" among many clinical psychologists. The greater utility of a more positive clinical psychology is found in its expanded view of what is important about human behavior and what we need to understand about human behavior to enhance people's quality of life, which results in an expanded view of what clinical psychology has to offer society.

References

Albee, G. W. (2000). The Boulder model's fatal flaw. *American Psychologist, 55*, 247–248.

American Psychiatric Association. (1952). *Diagnostic and statistical manual of mental disorders.* Washington, DC: APA.

American Psychiatric Association. (1980). *Diagnostic and statistical manual of mental disorders*, 3rd edn. Washington, DC: APA.

American Psychiatric Association. (2000). *Diagnostic and statistical manual of mental disorders*, 4th edn. text revision. Washington, DC: APA.

American Psychiatric Association (2013). *Diagnostic and statistical manual of mental disorders*, 5th edn. Washington, DC: APA.

Anthony, J. L., Lonigan, C. J., & Hecht, S. A. (1999). Dimensionality of post-traumatic stress disorder symptoms in children exposed to disaster: Results from a confirmatory factor analysis. *Journal of Abnormal Psychology, 108*, 315–325.

Bandura, A. (1978). On paradigms and recycled ideologies. *Cognitive Therapy and Research, 2*, 79–103.

Barkeley, R. A. (1997). *ADHD and the nature of self-control*. New York: Guilford.

Barone, D. F., Maddux, J. E., & Snyder, C. R. (1997). *Social cognitive psychology: History and current domains*. New York: Plenum.

Baumeister, R. F. & Scher, S. J. (1988). Self-defeating behavior patterns among normal individuals: Review and analysis of common self-destructive tendencies. *Psychological Bulletin, 104*, 3–22.

Beall, A. E. (1993). A social constructionist view of gender. In: A. E. Beall & R. J. Sternberg (Eds.), *The psychology of gender* (pp. 127–147). New York: Guilford.

Becker, H. S. (1963). *Outsiders*. New York: Free Press.

Benjamin, L. T. & Baker, D. B. (2004). *From séance to science: A history of the profession of psychology in America*. Belmont, CA: Wadsworth.

Crego, C. & Widiger, T. A. (2016). Personality disorders. In: J. E. Maddux & B. A. Winstead (Eds.), *Psychopathology: Foundations for a contemporary understanding* (pp. 218–236). New York: Routledge.

Claridge, G. (1995). *Origins of mental illness*. Cambridge, MA: Malor Books/ISHK.

Conrad, P. (2007). *The medicalization of society: On the transformation of human conditions into treatable disorders*. Baltimore: Johns Hopkins University Press.

Costello, C. G. (1993a). *Symptoms of depression*. New York: Wiley.

Costello, C. G. (1993b). *Symptoms of schizophrenia*. New York: Wiley.

Costello, C. G. (1996). *Personality characteristics of the personality disordered*. New York: Wiley.

Fraley, R. C. & Waller, N. G. (1998). Adult attachment patterns: A test of the typological model. In: J. A. Simpson & W. S. Rholes (Eds.), *Attachment theory and close relationships* (pp. 77–114). New York: Guilford.

Francis, A. (2013). *Saving normal: An insider's revolt against out-of-control psychiatric diagnosis, DSM-5, big pharma, and the medicalization of everyday life.* New York: HarperCollins.

Francis, A. J. & Widiger, T. (2012). Psychiatric diagnosis: Lessons from the DSM-IV past and cautions for the DSM-5 future. *Annual Review of Clinical Psychology, 8,* 109–130.

Gergen, K. J. (1985). The social constructionist movement in modern psychology. *American Psychologist, 40,* 266–275.

Gergen, K. J. (1999). *An invitation to social construction.* Thousand Oaks, CA: Sage.

Gosselin, J. T. (2016). Sexual dysfunctions and paraphilic disorders. In: J. E. Maddux & B. A. Winstead (Eds.), *Psychopathology: Foundations for a contemporary understanding* (pp. 00–00). New York: Routledge.

Greenberg, G. (2013). *The book of woe: The DSM and the unmaking of psychiatry.* New York: Plume/Penguin.

Horwitz, A. V. & Wakefield, J. C. (2007). *The loss of sadness: How psychiatry transformed normal sorrow into depressive disorder.* New York: Oxford University Press.

Joseph, S. & Wood., A. (2010). Assessment of positive functioning in clinical psychology: Theoretical and practical issues. *Clinical Psychology Review, 30,* 830–838.

Keyes, C. L. & Lopez, S. J. (2002). Toward a science of mental health: Positive directions in diagnosis and interventions. In: C. R. Snyder & S. J. Lopez (Eds.), *Handbook of positive psychology* (pp. 45–59). New York: Oxford University Press.

Kirk, S. A. & Kutchins, H. (1992). *The selling of DSM: The rhetoric of science in psychiatry.* New York: Aldine de Gruyter.

Korchin, S. J. (1976). *Modern clinical psychology.* New York: Basic Books.

Kutchins, H. & Kirk, S. A. (1997). *Making us crazy: DSM: The psychiatric bible and the creation of mental disorder.* New York: Free Press.

Lilienfeld, S. O. & Marino, L. (1995). Mental disorder as a Roschian concept: A critique of Wakefield's "harmful dysfunction" analysis. *Journal of Abnormal Psychology, 104,* 411–420.

Lopez, S. J. & Snyder, C. R. (Eds.). (2003). *Positive psychological assessment: A handbook of models and measures.* Washington, DC: American Psychological Association.

Lopez, S. J., Snyder, C. R., & Rasmussen, H. N. (2003). Striking a vital balance: Developing a complementary focus on human weakness and strength through positive psychological treatment. In: S. J. Lopez & C. R. Snyder (Eds.), *Positive psychological assessment: A handbook of models and measures* (pp. 3–20). Washington, DC: American Psychological Association.

Maddux, J. E. (2008). Positive psychology and the illness ideology: Toward a positive clinical psychology. *Applied Psychology: An International Review, 57,* 54–70.

Maddux, J. E. (2010). Social-cognitive theories of behavior change. In: J. E. Maddux & J. P. Tangney (Eds.), *Social psychological foundations of clinical psychology* (pp. 416–430). New York: Guilford.

Maddux, J. E., Gosselin, J. T., & Winstead, B. A. (2016). Conceptions of psychopathology: A social constructionist perspective. In: J. E. Maddux & B. Winstead (Eds.), *Psychopathology: Foundations for a contemporary understanding.* New York: Routledge.

Maddux, J. E. & Mundell, C. E. (2004). Disorders of personality: Diseases or individual differences? In: V. J. Derlega, B. A. Winstead, & W. H. Jones (Eds.), *Personality: Contemporary theory and research,* 2nd edn. (pp. 541–571). Chicago: Nelson-Hall.

Morrow, W. R. (1946). The development of psychological internship training. *Journal of Consulting Psychology, 10,* 165–183.

Muehlenhard, C. L. & Kimes, L. A. (1999). The social construction of violence: The case of sexual and domestic violence. *Personality and Social Psychology Review, 3,* 234–245.

Nettle, D. (2001). *Strong imagination: Madness, creativity, and human nature.* New York: Oxford University Press.

Oatley, K. & Jenkins, J. M. (1992). Human emotions: Function and dysfunction. *Annual Review of Psychology, 43,* 55–85.

Parker, I., Georgaca, E., Harper, D., McLaughlin, T., & Stowell-Smith, M. (1995). *Deconstructing psychopathology.* London: Sage.

Paris, J. (2013). *The intelligent clinician's guide to the DSM-5.* New York: Oxford University Press.

Reisman, J. M. (1991). *A history of clinical psychology*. New York: Hemisphere.

Reznek, L. (1987). *The nature of disease*. London: Routledge & Kegan Paul.

Rosenblum, K. E. & Travis, T. C. (1996). Constructing categories of difference: Framework essay. In: K. E. Rosenblum & T. C. Travis (Eds.), *The meaning of difference: American constructions of race, sex and gender, social class, and sexual orientation* (pp. 1–34). New York: McGraw-Hill.

Routh, D. K. (2000). Clinical psychology training: A history of ideas and practices prior to 1946. *American Psychologist, 55*, 236–240.

Seligman, M. E. P. & Csikszentmihalyi, M. (2000). Positive psychology: An introduction. *American Psychologist, 55*, 5–14.

Shaywitz, S. E., Escobar, M. D., Shaywitz, B. A., Fletcher, J. M., & Makuch, R. (1992). Evidence that dyslexia may represent the lower tail of a normal distribution of reading ability. *New England Journal of Medicine, 326*, 145–150.

Szasz, T. (1978). *The myth of psychotherapy*. Syracuse, NY: Syracuse University Press.

Trull, T. J. & Durrett, C. A. (2005). Categorical and dimensional models of personality disorders. *Annual Review of Clinical Psychology, 1*, 355–380.

Wakefield, J. C. (1992). The concept of mental disorder. On the boundary between biological facts and social values. *American Psychologist, 47*, 373–388.

Widiger, T. A. (2016). Classification and diagnosis: Historical development and contemporary issues. In: J. E. Maddux & B. A. Winstead (Eds.), *Psychopathology: Foundations for a contemporary understanding* (pp. 97–110). New York: Routledge.

Williams, S. L. (2016). Anxiety disorders and obsessive-compulsive disorder. In: J. E. Maddux & B. A. Winstead (Eds.), *Psychopathology: Foundations for a contemporary understanding*. New York: Routledge.

Wilson, M. (1993). DSM-III and the transformation of American psychiatry: A history. *American Journal of Psychiatry, 150*, 399–410.

Wood, A. M. & Tarrier, N. (2010). Positive clinical psychology: A new vision and strategy for integrated research and practice. *Clinical Psychology Review, 30*, 819–829.

World Health Organisation. (1992). *The ICD-10 classification of mental and behavioural disorders: Clinical descriptions and diagnostic guidelines*. Geneva: WHO.

Wright, B. A. & Lopez, S. J. (2002). Widening the diagnostic focus: A case for including human strengths and environmental resources. In: C. R. Snyder & S. J. Lopez (Eds.), *Handbook of positive psychology* (pp. 26–44). New York: Oxford University Press.

Zovlensky, M. J., Eifert, G. H., & Garey, L. (2016). Somatic symptom and related disorders. In: J. E. Maddux & B. A. Winstead (Eds.), *Psychopathology: Foundations for a contemporary understanding*. New York: Routledge.

3

Why Clinical Psychology Should Not Go "Positive" – and/or "Negative"

Barbara S. Held[1]

Many years ago, Aldo Llorente, MD, my friend and colleague who directed a small community-hospital inpatient psychiatric unit, offhandedly remarked, "You know, even psychiatric patients have problems." Although I initially thought that Aldo was stating the obvious, I should have known better. He meant that life confronts us all with many problems, independently of whether any of us is diagnosed with a mental illness. In one way or another, we all must come to terms with our individual particularities – our temperaments, personality traits, relational/interpersonal styles, cognitive capacities and styles, physical health/characteristics, as well as our many social contexts, such as family environment, employment/socioeconomic situation, geographic location, to name just a few.

To be clear, Aldo was not a fan of Thomas Szasz's (1960) (in)famous position that mental illness is a myth. Contra Szasz, Aldo did not deny the existence of bona fide mental illness, nor did he accept Szasz's replacement of the term "mental illness" with the term "problems in living," to emphasize the historical and sociocultural relativity of the former term and thus to dismiss its (realist) ontological status. Instead, Aldo meant that those who suffer from mental illness are also burdened with everyday life problems, just like those who do not so suffer. He humanized those who suffer from mental illness in his own unique way, that is, without even a nod to the depathologizing and growth fundamentals of humanistic psychologists, to whom editors Alex Wood and Nicholas Tarrier (2010) sometimes appeal in their call for a "Positive Clinical Psychology" in a special issue of the *Clinical Psychology Review*.

Aldo developed a unique group format that reflected his philosophy of inpatient treatment. Each evening, every patient on the twelve-bed unit (with an average stay of five days) who was able to participate in the group did so. The group had three rules: (1) the group members selected the topic of discussion each evening; (2) when a patient was to be discharged the next day, he or she said goodbye to the group; and (3) there was no discussion of personal details. What?! Right, no personal details. Aldo believed that patients had been trained by the mental health system to focus so much on their symptoms, on their illness, on their status *as* mental patients, that they forgot how to be persons in an ordinary sense, that is, in a non-(psychiatric) patient sense (cf. Sarbin, 1969).

Each evening, Aldo asked the group to settle on a topic that everyone could discuss, rather than discuss the unique problems of members' personal lives, past and present, for example, their individual histories and attributions of blame. This forced the group members to discuss

The Wiley Handbook of Positive Clinical Psychology, First Edition. Edited by Alex M. Wood and Judith Johnson.

the universal themes of personhood, such as phenomenal experiences of hurt and anger, fear, anxiety, shame, confusion, contentment, love, loss of relationships, physical illness, the weather, politics, sports – you name it. When patients inevitably started to mention the details of their own personal problems or deviated from that night's chosen theme, Aldo reminded them of the rules and got them back on track. He insisted that the point of the group was to make it possible for discharged patients "to go downtown and sit at the counter of the local doughnut shop, have a cup of coffee, and talk to the guy sitting next to them about the weather instead of their mental illness, just like any regular person." Although there were no formal outcome studies, the group enjoyed much success, so much so that others who worked on the unit at the time learned this format from Aldo and taught it to their students. The group is no longer practiced on that unit, nor any others to my knowledge, and Aldo died in 1995. Yet his legacy lives on informally, and his philosophy of treatment struck me as a good way to begin my chapter in this volume. What could be more positive in a clinical (inpatient) setting than Aldo's group, with its aim to (re)establish the personhood of its members!

The title of my chapter is meant to give away the punch line. In their special issue of the *Clinical Psychology Review*, Wood and Tarrier (2010) make a thoughtfully nuanced case on behalf of their "Positive Clinical Psychology," with all due awareness of the profound problems created for the entire discipline of psychology by the positive psychology movement. Nonetheless, I cannot tumble to the concept of a positive clinical psychology, at least as it was made there, if not in this follow-up volume, in progress as I write. In this chapter, I cite instances from that special issue, to help "concretize" my analysis.

To make my case, I begin with the conceptual problems that arise when positive psychologists use the terms "positive" and "negative,"[2] which problems lead us into the very dualist traps that Wood and Tarrier, in their integrationist spirit, seek to avoid. Next, I challenge the claim that clinical practice itself can be understood as either "positive" or "negative" in any sense, owing not only to conceptual problems but also to the highly idiographic/circumstantial nature of practice (even in applying the nomothetic findings of science). Of special import is the considerable body of research by psychologists who for three decades have consistently found functional coping value in "negative" emotions and thoughts. In short, eliminating or reducing "negative" emotions, thoughts, and coping strategies can, in many circumstances, be detrimental to constructive/adaptive, or even optimal, functioning.

Throughout this chapter I return repeatedly and critically to the positive psychology distinction between "negative" and "positive" *interventions* – those in which therapists aim to decrease "negative" states and functioning *directly*, with "negative" or traditional clinical interventions,[3] and those in which therapists aim to increase "positive" states and functioning *directly*, with "positive" clinical interventions (Linley & Joseph, 2004a; Seligman, Rashid, & Parks, 2006; Joseph & Wood, 2010; Wood & Tarrier, 2010; Schueller & Parks, 2014).[4] Especially problematic, as I shall explain, is the application of positive/negative terminology to different domains – for example, in the domains of psychological states and interventions versus the domain of goal-directed functioning, where, as it turns out, "positivity" in the former two can erode functionality, and "negativity" in the former two can enhance functionality.

In my conclusion, I return to Aldo Llorente's worry about the loss of personhood status by those treated in inpatient settings. This loss may be reformulated as a loss of agency in ordinary terms, so much so that I am inclined to see an overarching goal for most, if not all, psychological interventions as the restoration of agency to those whose agency has been diminished owing to psychological problems and their treatment. By agency I mean the universal human rational capacity to deliberate about goals and thus act with good reason(s) on the products of those deliberations (Fulford, 1994; Martin, Sugarman, & Thompson, 2003; Evnine, 2008; Held, 2010). And so I conclude with just that issue – rational agency – as it pertains to psychological interventions of any sort.

The Conceptual Quagmire of the Positive/Negative Distinction

I make no quarrel with the positive/negative distinction as it appears in mathematics, where negative numbers hold their own, nor in medical pathology, where negative results indicate the absence of pathology and so are to be celebrated. In positive psychology, by contrast, "negative" characteristics should be diminished and replaced with "positive" characteristics. And so we see the polysemantic (or polysemous) nature of the terms "positive" and "negative," each of which can mean either good or bad (or neutral) depending on their domain of application. Yet positive psychologists tend to make *a priori*[5] designations of positivity and negativity in reference to psychological states, functioning, and interventions, which creates considerable conceptual muddles that defy elimination logically within their conceptual framework of positivity and negativity.

And so, with ambiguity built into the meanings of the terms "positive" and "negative" themselves, the very concept of a positive (or negative) psychology, clinical or otherwise, is dubious at best. Even Wood's and Tarrier's (2010) circumspect, repeated call for a thoroughgoing integration of the "positive" and "negative" within (clinical) psychology, "based on a balanced and equally weighted focus on the positive and negative aspects of life"[6] (p. 820), opens a Pandora's box of questions. Not least, we may ask why they seek integration. After all, if no positive/negative compartmentalization of psychological reality had been imposed by positive psychologists in the first place, then need for such integration would not exist. Moreover, their own retention of the positive/negative distinction destines them to perpetuate the very dualism that they seek to integrate/synthesize – or so I shall argue.[7]

Consistent with their call for integration, Wood and Tarrier (2010) propose a dimensional approach, in which, for example, happiness and depression constitute two opposite anchors of a single bipolar dimension rather than two categories:

> There are strong conceptual and empirical arguments that no emotion or characteristic can be uniformly positive or negative.... A more fundamental and less considered issue [is] a lack of appreciation that most characteristics have both positive and negative poles. For many characteristics, presumably due to historical or zeitgeist reasons, focus is predominantly on only one pole, with the other becoming forgotten or ignored, and a lack of appreciation of the polarity of the construct. (p. 825)

Fair enough. But what about appreciation of the possible benefits of the designated negative pole? These presumably cannot be seen by positive psychologists, owing perhaps to their adherence to their *a priori* designation of what is "positive" (i.e., good) and "negative" (i.e., bad, or at least not *as* good as what is "positive").

Wood and Tarrier rightly expand their concerns about dimensionality to encompass the arbitrary nature of what is considered positive versus negative, in two distinct respects:

> [a] The designation of the characteristic [humility, kindness, open-mindedness, integrity, fairness, high social intelligence] and their [polar] opposites [arrogance, unkindness, closed-mindedness, dishonesty, unfairness, and low social intelligence] as either positive or negative is totally arbitrary, depending on which pole is focused on (or which way a scale is coded). Indeed, had the authors not been working within positive psychology, they could have easily reverse coded their scales, named them after the opposite pole, and conducted mainstream clinical work.... [b] Any designation of a characteristic as positive or negative is simplistic and inaccurate, as any trait or emotion can be "positive or negative" depending on the situation and concomitant goals and motivations. (pp. 826–827)

Regarding "a,"[8] since one of the meanings of positivity and negativity is the dimensional feature described by Wood and Tarrier, the applications of these terms to relevant domains are, as they say, "totally arbitrary" – that is, which pole is considered "positive" and which "negative" is just what any researcher or group of researchers decides them to be. In that case, positive and negative states, functioning, and interventions do not exist ontologically prior to (and so independently of) our designations of them *as* positive or negative; they are not just out there "waiting" to be discovered by us, as in a standard view of realist ontologies (Held, 2007, ch. 5). This may suggest an antirealist ontological underpinning of the psychological science of positivity and negativity, about which most positive psychologists would, I suspect, be less than pleased (Held, 2002, 2004, 2005). Moreover, if the distinction between positive and negative *characteristics* is arbitrary, simplistic, and inaccurate, then it follows that the distinction between positive and negative *interventions* (both in "mainstream clinical work" and otherwise), which distinction depends logically on the positive/negative characteristic distinction, is also arbitrary, simplistic, and inaccurate. And yet, the positive/negative dualism obtains for interventions too.

"Positive" versus "Negative" Interventions

Retention of positive/negative terminology was surely destined to beget positive clinical psychologists, those who use, in addition to the negative/clinical interventions that directly target the decrease of negative/pathological states and functioning, the positive interventions that directly target the increase of positive/healthy states and functioning. And so we move with apparent ease from positive versus negative states and functioning to positive versus negative interventions, despite this shift in the domains of application of the positive/negative distinction. As Wood and Tarrier (2010) proclaimed: "It is not logical to study either negative or positive *functioning* in isolation [of each other], as ... this prevents *interventions* being designed to *both decrease the negative and promote the positive*" (p. 827; emphasis added). Thus, the solution to the problem of integration remains dualistic: retain the negative-intervention/positive-intervention dichotomy, and develop a positive clinical psychology composed of both kinds of interventions, rather than adhere to a (negative) clinical psychology, *allegedly* composed of only negative interventions. Dropping the positive/negative distinction does not seem to be an option, especially since it was "institutionalized" by Seligman's movement.

Positive interventions and negative interventions, then, are cast as two distinct kinds of interventions, each of which expressly targets two distinct kinds of states and two distinct kinds of functioning. However, this conceptualization may be more apparent than real. For example, Joseph and Wood (2010) believe that existing (pre-positive clinical psychology and thus presumably negative/clinical) interventions increase positive functioning if they are theoretically compatible with a "growth" view (as in client-centered therapy) (p. 836). And Kashdan and Rottenberg (2010) go further, stating that "even when psychological interventions do not explicitly discuss flexibility as an aim of treatment ... flexibility is such an integral part of psychological functioning that it is almost inevitable that it will in some way be impacted" (p. 874). In this the inviolate positive/negative intervention divide begins to blur, since even certain negative interventions can in principle (i.e., logically) impact certain positive states/functioning, such as flexibility, at least indirectly.

As Kashdan and Rottenberg (2010, pp. 866–867) appreciate, an underlying problem is the arbitrary designation of mental states and functioning as positive or negative *a priori* – that is, independent of circumstantial particularity (see n. 5, below). I prefer the terms "constructive" and "destructive" (or "adaptive" and "maladaptive") because they at least hint at the necessity of case-specific empirical observation and evidence, to determine whether any *one* state or process is helpful or harmful in the pursuit of a particular goal by a particular person facing particular circumstantial demands, both interpersonal and intrapersonal (e.g., McNulty & Fincham, 2012). And let us be clear that interventions designed to (a) build up what we deem adaptive and to (b) tear down what we deem maladaptive are both not only circumstance dependent but also constructive, even though we tear down in the latter case. This way of thinking entails obstacles for Barbara Fredrickson's "broaden-and-build theory of positive emotions," which strongly limits the value of negative emotions in constructive endeavors. The problem is, this limiting is also a profound limitation; it flies in the face of extensive empirical evidence that supports the constructive value of "negativity," a value that transcends the limitations imposed by Fredrickson.

The Broaden-and-Build Theory of Positive Emotions

Garland, Fredrickson, Kroing, Johnson, Meyer, and Penn (2010) succinctly summarize the broaden-and-build theory of positive emotions, which is promoted enthusiastically in the positive psychology literature, not least in such canonical texts as the *Oxford Handbook of Positive Psychology* (Lopez & Snyder, 2009) and *The Encyclopedia of Positive Psychology* (Lopez, 2009):

> Negative emotions have long been held to narrow the scope of people's attention and thinking.... The broaden-and-build theory ... holds that positive emotions broaden individuals' thought–action repertoires, enabling them to draw flexibly on higher-level connections and wider-than-usual ranges of percepts, ideas, and action urges; broadened cognition in turn creates behavioral flexibility that over time builds personal resources, such as mindfulness, resilience, social closeness, and even physical health.... Importantly, unlike the transient nature of positive emotions, these resources are durable.... Thus, according to the theory and data, pleasurable positive emotions, although fleeting, can have a long-lasting impact on functional outcomes, leading to enhanced well-being and social connectedness. (Garland et al., 2010, p. 850)

This theory and the evidence gathered on its behalf have now been challenged extensively in a debate between Fredrickson and Losada, on the one side, and Brown, Sokal, and Friedman, on the other.[9] Yet it continues to stick with positive psychologists. In the next section, I present extensive research that demonstrates the "positive power" of negative emotions, thinking, and coping.

Just here I make the obvious point that *all* clinical interventions are designed to help people function better, whether they target positive *or* negative states/functioning directly. And so they are designed to be "positive" by being constructive in just *that* way, even if they consist in "tearing down" what is destructive to adaptive functioning. The crucial corollary that seems to get lost in the rush to positivity is this: improving coping/functioning is not always compatible with *feeling* happy, with positive *affect*, and thus with interventions that are positive in virtue of aiming to increase positive emotional states directly, which is one component of standard definitions of "positive interventions."

Practice and Nomothetic versus Idiographic Principles

Both the research and the rhetoric of the positive psychology movement are nomothetic in their promotion of generalizations, though they are generalizations of different sorts. Wood and Tarrier (2010) rightly criticize the generalizations made in the rhetoric of the movement, which, they maintain, overpromote the movement's research findings, findings which, they note, are not themselves without problems.

Here I contrast the generalities of positive psychology research with the particularities that necessarily inhere in any kind of psychotherapy practice. That is, whereas science entails nomotheticity in its search for law-like if not lawful generalizations, practice entails individualized particularity. As I once put it: "No two schizophrenics are alike for *all* therapeutic purposes" (Held, 1995, p. 19). To be clear, I do not deny the logic of subjecting (clinical) psychological questions (about human/mental kinds) to scientific scrutiny (Held, 2007) – after all, all scientists study particular instantiations of kinds to arrive at generalities of some sort, if not the universal laws of physics.

My point about the idiographic nature of practice is twofold. First, the old adage about working *with* the client's (temperamental etc.) tendencies, not against them. Second, to do this, we need to appreciate each client as a unique individual with unique features, including strengths *and* weaknesses, as well as a member of some categorical set, or even a point on a dimension. These do not readily reduce to the attributes that positive psychologists have designated positive or negative. Thus, as with any clinical intervention, even positive interventions can cause negative/deterioration effects.[10] For example, J. Wood, Perunovic, and Lee (2009) found that repeating positive self-statements (such as "I accept myself completely") or focusing on ways in which the statement was true caused those with low self-esteem to feel worse and boosted those with high self-esteem only mildly. They speculate that positive self-statements may backfire for those with low self-esteem because the attempt to "avoid negative thoughts [unsuccessfully] ... may have signified that the positive self-statement was not true of them ... the very people they are designed for" (p. 865). And McNulty and Fincham (2012) challenge the positive/negative labeling of traits and processes altogether, on conceptual as well as empirical/circumstantial grounds: "the psychological characteristics that benefit people experiencing optimal circumstances may not only fail to help people experiencing suboptimal circumstances, but may harm them" (p. 106).[11] The *a priori* positive/negative dichotomy in psychology, then, is arguably a false dichotomy.

Returning to practice, how to guide the idiographics of practice with the nomothetics of science continues to elude us. Still, we must have some general principles, even if only at the highest level of generality (Held, 1995). For example, I agree with Kashdan's and Rottenberg's (2010) view of "Psychological Flexibility as a Fundamental Aspect of Health," if for no other reason than the semantic fact that health (physical or mental) entails flexibility, whereas pathology constricts. Although this may sound like the broaden-and-build theory of positive emotions, in which only positive emotions increase options for living, that is not the case. Positive and negative emotions (and thoughts) do not determine adaptive and maladaptive functioning, respectively, certainly not as robustly as positive psychologists often suppose: adaptive functioning can in some cases entail feeling bad, and maladaptive functioning can in some cases entail feeling good, as I now explain.

When "Negative" Interventions are Constructive/"Positive": The Case of Defensive Pessimism

Recall that those who promote a positive clinical psychology call for, in addition to the use of negative/clinical interventions, the use of positive interventions, those that *directly* target building up the states and processes that are alleged to be conducive to more adaptive/constructive, even optimal,[12] functioning (Wood & Tarrier, 2010; Schueller & Parks, 2014). But what about the wealth of research that demonstrates how negative coping strategies, including the negative emotions and thinking that constitute such strategies, can be highly advantageous to adaptive/constructive functioning? That is, what about the cases in which negative states are crucial for adaptive/constructive functioning?

The coping strategy of defensive pessimism, so studied for some three decades by Julie Norem, provides the most prominent case in point, not least in her popular book, *The Positive Power of Negative Thinking* (2001). Despite the consistent finding of the adaptive functional value of defensive pessimism for those whose functioning is impaired by debilitating anxiety, there is scant attention to Norem's findings about the value of defensive pessimism in the positive psychology literature.

Let us begin with Norem's (2008) own recent definition and description of defensive pessimism, namely, a "motivated cognitive strategy" that entails (a) "setting low expectations (being pessimistic) and then thinking through, in concrete and vivid detail, all the things that might go wrong as one prepares for an upcoming situation or task" (p. 123) and that (b) "helps people manage their anxiety and pursue their goals" (abstract, p. 121). Like Joseph and Wood (2010) and Kashdan and Rottenberg (2010), Norem examines executive functioning or self-regulation/control/determination (even in regard to some clinical issues), although she also emphasizes the complexities (in enhancing such self-regulation) that implicate a role for "negative" coping:

> Research on a variety of phenomena, from self-handicapping to stereotype threat, demonstrates the potential effectiveness of defensive pessimism as a self-regulation strategy.... Understanding how and why defensive pessimism works requires an integrated understanding [of] the role of traits, motivations, and self structures within the individual, the resultant goals toward which strategies are directed, and the particular constraints of different situations and cultural contexts. (abstract, p. 121)

Norem (2008) explains how defensive pessimism works by means of *certain kinds* of negativity, kinds which she later (Norem, 2014) calls "the right tool for the job." Thus, negative affect effect and thinking "function as positive motivation for defensive pessimists," in that in distinction to, for example, rumination and catastrophizing, defensive pessimists' "negative reflections are directed toward the future, and focus on potential negative scenarios that are directly relevant to the situation or goal he or she wants to approach" (p. 126). The point is that what seemingly begins as a "negative" process in fact functions as a definite "positive" process, that is, functions adaptively or constructively: "The defensive pessimist is able to shift emphasis from anxious feelings to thoughts about possible specific problems, and then to actions to prevent those problems from derailing progress [see Norem & Cantor, 1986]" (p. 126).

Norem (2008) also explains how "different personalities" require the use of "different strategies" for adaptive functioning: compared to those who deploy strategic optimism,[13] defensive pessimists report greater degrees of trait anxiety, neuroticism, lower self-esteem, and negative affect in general; they also "generate more negative potential outcomes and plans" (p. 124). And it is those crucial findings that tend to be under (or un)appreciated:

> By themselves, those results do little to demonstrate that defensive pessimism is more than a generally negative view of self and the world; this raises the question of why those using the strategy cannot just "lighten up," especially given that they typically perform as well as the strategic optimists.... Yet, just as saying "hey, relax" to an anxious person rarely helps, the research evidence makes clear that simply trying to be more optimistic will not work for defensive pessimists. (pp. 124–125)

Of equal importance, Norem delineates the effects of positive versus negative manipulations – that is, *interventions* – with defensive pessimists:

> Attempts to disrupt or make more optimistic any component of their strategy seem to interfere with the defensive pessimists' performance, *and* lower their satisfaction after the fact.... (Further analyses showed that anxiety indeed mediated these results.). (p. 125)

And so it should come as no surprise that Norem's extensive findings point to a familiar punch line, namely, one size does not fit all. Surely this is as true of coping as it is of clothing: "Both defensive pessimists and strategic optimists perform best when allowed to pursue (or avoid) mental simulation according to their preferences" (p. 126). This conclusion hardly shocks. Yet that circumstance-dependent message is lost on those committed to "accentuating the positive." Referring expressly to mood, Norem (2008) warns of the dangers of "cheering up" defensive pessimists:

While it is possible to put defensive pessimists in a better mood, doing so leads to poorer performance (Sanna, 1998; Norem & Illingworth, 2004).... Defensive pessimists appear to use their negative feelings as a cue to work harder, which then typically leads to better performance. (p. 126)

With their determination to enhance adaptive functioning, one might think that positive psychologists would happily embrace Norem's extensive findings about defensive pessimism. Instead, her findings are most commonly ignored (e.g., Linley & Joseph, 2004a; Parks & Schueller, 2014), especially in positive psychology's aforementioned canonical texts, or when mentioned, they tend to be dismissed as "negative" and thus problematic.[14] For example, early on Scheier and Carver (1993) certainly conceded that "defensive pessimism does seem to work," in that defensive pessimists perform better than "real [i.e., dispositional] pessimists." But they also said that "people who use defensive pessimism in the short run report more psychological symptoms and a lower quality of life in the long run than do optimists. Such findings call into serious question the adaptive value of defensive pessimism" (p. 29). And more recently, Peterson and Seligman (2004) weighed in critically.[15] The problem is, the evidence does not support Scheier and Carver's and Peterson and Seligman's claims. For example, Norem and Chang (2002), in comparing anxious people who used defensive pessimism to those who did not, found that

defensive pessimists show significant increases in self-esteem and satisfaction over time, perform better academically, form more supportive friendship networks, and make more progress on their personal goals than equally anxious students who do not use defensive pessimism.... Taking away their defensive pessimism is not the way to help anxious individuals. (p. 997)

Norem readily concedes precise benefits and costs of both strategic optimism and defensive pessimism. We may therefore ask why the negatives of defensive pessimism are typically considered "true negatives" by positive psychologists who discuss Norem's findings, whereas the negatives of strategic optimism tend to be ignored by positive psychologists who compare defensive pessimism, a *context-dependent* coping strategy, to *dispositional/traitlike* optimism instead of to strategic optimism or to the functioning of anxious persons who do not use defensive pessimism (see Scheier & Carver, 1993, p. 29 and Held, 2004, pp. 23–24).

Norem (2014) reminds us that an important question for adaptive functioning is what negative thoughts and affects *do*, what kind of functioning they motivate, not simply how they *feel*. Thus, we should consider functionality itself to be an important outcome category, distinct from affect. In particular, Norem (2014, p. 259) acknowledges the "hedonic failure" of defensive pessimism, but asks us to consider how it improves adaptive functioning nonetheless. Of interest is that this distinction between hedonic and functionality variables permeates the positive psychology literature as well, in the distinction between "subjective well-being" and "psychological well-being," respectively (e.g., Ryan & Deci, 2001).

Not surprisingly, Norem (2014) now wishes that she had not used the term "defensive pessimism," because "defensive" is too negative:

If I could go back in time, I would change the name *defensive pessimism* to *reflective pessimism*, as opposed to *non-reflective optimism*.... By choosing *defensive* to label the pessimistic strategy we were studying, but *strategic* to label the optimistic counterpart, we inadvertently implied that there was something better (i.e., more "strategic") about strategic optimism compared to defensive pessimism before we had gathered any data. (pp. 265–266, n. 4)

I would add to this that the term "pessimism" can be poison to positive psychologists who cannot get past their toxic reaction, even when confronted with the undeniable positives of defensive pessimism.[16]

And so we see that terminology matters. Norem is surely most prominent among those who study the "positive power of negativity." And the failure of positive psychologists to integrate, or better still to synthesize, Norem's consistent findings across three decades of research into their own research is the single most glaring example of how what is deemed negative *a priori* by them cannot possibly contribute to bona fide positive functioning. That is because positive functioning for them logically entails enhancing, via "positive" interventions, what they deem to be in "positive" territory, and anything less remains in "negative" territory, even if that territory becomes significantly less "negative."[17] Put differently, if allegedly "negative" interventions and states can be demonstrated to enhance adaptive/constructive – dare I say positive – outcomes/functioning, then the entire positive psychology enterprise collapses.

A More "Integrative" Research Program

Earlier I asked what positive (clinical) psychologists mean by integration, and why they seek integration. Recall that Wood and Tarrier (2010, p. 280) express a common-sense view of integration, namely, "a balanced and equally weighted focus on the positive and negative aspects of life," so that we should use both "positive" and "negative" interventions in practice. But just what are the "positive and negative aspects of life"? As Norem demonstrates, what is positive/functional for some, may be negative/dysfunctional for others, even within any given situation. Again, the assumption that positivity and negativity have stable meanings/referents independent of circumstantial particularity does not hold in psychology. And as I said earlier, the need for this integration, or combined use, would not press if positive psychologists had not made the ontologically dubious move of carving psychological reality *a priori* into positive and negative components, which components then must be put back together again, much like Humpty Dumpty, alas.

One possible reason for seeking integration besides putting psychological reality back together again is the desire to be comprehensive or complete, as an empirical precondition not to disregard or exclude, on ideological grounds, any aspect of reality, as any legitimate science should strive to do. But scrapping the divisive and dubious positive/negative distinction altogether does not seem to be an option or even to occur to those who seek a more complete clinical science via such integration.

As an antidote to all this, what if psychologists seeking to integrate negative/clinical interventions with positive interventions studied how clinicians might work with, not against, "negative" thinking, moods/emotions, and coping styles? Could this prescription have the potential to ground a more comprehensive research program?

In *The Positive Side of Negative Emotions*, editor Gerrod Parrott (2014) compiled twelve chapters written by psychologists who, taken collectively, have conducted three decades of research in which they demonstrate how various negative emotions – including sadness; anxiety; such social emotions as embarrassment, shame, guilt, jealousy; and negative coping styles such as defensive pessimism – can be functional/adaptive.[18] Since people seeking treatment often experience emotions and thoughts (and behave in ways) that are bothersome (to someone), it seems obvious that this line of research would be a prime candidate for integration into a positive clinical psychology, to work with each patient's tendencies (both positive and negative) as well as against them. But as with Norem's findings, to my knowledge this has not yet come to pass, at least not in any sustained, thoroughgoing way.

In his preface, Parrott begins conceptually by examining what is meant by positive versus negative emotions. He notes that there is agreement historically about which emotions are negative and which are positive (Colombetti, 2005).[19] However, there is disagreement about "what makes an emotion positive or negative" (p. x). Regarding the criteria or boundary conditions for the use of these two terms, he cites Solomon and Stone (2002), who listed 18 ways in which positive and negative emotions have been distinguished. Some of the distinctions are ethical: virtue versus vice, right versus wrong, socially approved versus socially unacceptable. Other distinctions … focus more on the emotions' effects: healthy or unhealthy, calming or upsetting, strengthening or weakening, satisfying or dissatisfying, motivating approach or motivating avoidance. Yet other interpretations focus on the various appraisals and judgments that are attached to the emotions: is the situation in accord with one's wishes or not.… Positive and negative have also been taken to refer to qualities of phenomenal experience: perhaps the former emotions are pleasant whereas the latter are painful. (Parrott, 2014, p. x)

Of prime empirical importance, Parrott adds, "One commonality is that both positive and negative emotions can be either functional or dysfunctional," and so he is keen to study the "factors that help determine when an emotion will work adaptively in a particular context" (p. xiii).

Parrott does not reject the distinction between positive and negative emotions, and so some may charge him with perpetuating the dubious dualism. However, he and his contributors do not use it *a priori*, but rather in regard to circumstantial demands, both interpersonal and intrapersonal, thereby allowing negative emotions to have positive consequences. The retention of this non-*a priori* use of positivity and negativity can be seen as a corrective step along the way to a more complete (and objective) psychological science, just as Wood's and Tarrier's (2010) call for integration can be seen as a corrective step, albeit one that is less radical. In any case, in addressing what psychologists might mean when they expressly categorize emotions as either positive or negative, Parrott says that the aforementioned eighteen senses of positive and negative are problematic because they "do not categorize the same emotion consistently. For example, anger can be painful or pleasurable or both, depending on the circumstances, so phenomenal experience does not explain why anger is considered a negative emotion" (p. x).

What is needed is of course a "consistent basis for justifying why each emotion is classified as positive or negative," and Parrott finds "the most useful criterion [to be] the situation's perceived compatibility with a person's needs, goals, and values: negative emotions generally involve interpreting something as being against one's wishes" (p. xi). Needs, goals, values, and wishes are all highly pertinent to agency, the enhancement or restoration of which, I said at the outset, may arguably be seen as an overarching goal of all (clinical) psychological interventions. If this is so, then perhaps yet another answer to the "why" question of integration is to enhance agency as robustly as possible, in which case, I submit, the muddled positive/negative distinction hinders rather than helps. Put differently, if the overarching goal of clinical psychological interventions is agency, then that goal should reflect the aspect of reality to which that goal is applied. And the ontologically dubious conceptualization that carves reality into positive and negative domains, in which, as we have seen, "negativity" can enhance "positivity" and vice versa (Norem, 2008; Parrott, 2014), is, I again submit, not a conceptualization of reality that clearly or rationally serves that goal. With this in mind, I turn to consideration of rational agency in clinical psychology.

Agency and Psychological Interventions

Parrott's preferred criterion for classifying an emotion as positive or negative resides in agency's neighborhood, if not in the same house. As I have been using the term, agency consists in the ability to deliberate about one's goals (usually based on one's desires) and then act on the products of those deliberations. In deliberating about and acting on a goal *rationally*, one's beliefs about how best to fulfill (or not to fulfill) a desire should be in accord with reality and each other and with what action (or nonaction) is realistic, given the circumstances.[20] Rational agency may thus be said to entail self-control/autonomy, which is surely a component of the executive functioning and psychological flexibility on which psychological well-being necessarily depends (Joseph & Wood, 2010, pp. 834–835; Kashdan & Rottenberg, 2010, pp. 870–873).

If this is so, restoration of agency, to whatever degree, must be at the conceptual core of a positive clinical psychology – or, in my parlance, of most if not all kinds of psychological interventions, whether they are considered positive or negative *by anyone*.

Being an agent, one who acts with intention/self-control/autonomy, may now be said to depend on one's rational agency. The inability to act rationally, then, means that one cannot be an agent, in which case one cannot act at all. To clarify, K. W. M. Fulford (1994) proposed that delusions, which, he asserts, are "the paradigm symptoms of mental illness" (p. 205), reflect a lack of agency, in that the delusional person lacks good reasons for his or her actions (at least in the delusional domain), and in so lacking lacks action itself (in the delusional domain). This is so because for Fulford (and other philosophers) bona fide action (logically) entails good/rational reasons for that action. So, no (rational) reason for an "action," no action – period. (In which case the term "rational agency" or "rational action/acts" is redundant; agency/action entails reason/rationality.) Indeed, loss of agency as broadly defined here may be thought of as a superordinate characteristic of mental illness and psychological distress, in their diverse mani festations. Put differently, loss of agency entails loss of personhood, which depends on agency (Evnine, 2008; Held, 2010), to return to Aldo Llorente, with whom we began.

Since Parrott's contributors demonstrate how various negative emotions may, in their relevant circumstances, contribute to adaptive functioning and thus to rational action/agency, we may again wonder why positive psychologists of all stripes have not been happily inclined to integrate this large body of research into their research programs rigorously. One reason may be the blinders worn by many of them owing to their *a priori* understanding of the terms "positive" and "negative." Alternatively, if most positive psychologists have been aware of this research and have deliberately chosen not to entertain it seriously, then they may not be quite as integrative/inclusive as they may suppose.

Conclusion

To advance a comprehensive science of clinical psychology in which agency gets top billing, it is just as important to study the adaptive/constructive enhancement of "negativity" as it is to study the adaptive/constructive enhancement of "positivity." I would therefore broaden Wood's and Tarrier's conceptualization of integration: in addition to their proposed use of both "positive" interventions, those that directly target enhancing "positive" states, and "negative"/clinical interventions, those that directly target diminishing "negative" states, I propose the use of what I will now call "positive–negative" interventions, those that directly target enhancing "negative" states that benefit adaptive/constructive/rational or "positive" functioning, as in the case of defensive pessimism interventions for anxious people.

All of these I prefer to call "psychological interventions," in a synthesizing semantic/conceptual move that allows what has been labeled "negative" to be construed as "positive" (and vice versa) where warranted – if we absolutely must continue to use the misleading terminology of "positivity" and "negativity" in psychology.

Notes

1   The author thanks Michael Katzko, Robert Sheehan, Lisa Osbeck, and William Meehan for their helpful comments on earlier drafts of this manuscript. Thanks also to Emily Martin for her help in the preparation of the manuscript itself.
2   Accordingly, I sometimes place the terms "positive" and "negative" and their variants in scare quotes, especially when I want to emphasize the misleading and dubious meanings given to them by positive psychologists.

3   The term "positive clinical psychology" suggests that "clinical psychology" is actually "negative clinical psychology," meaning it does not employ positive psychology interventions, as defined above.

4   Seligman, Rashid, and Parks (2006) state, "Positive Psychotherapy (PPT) contrasts with standard interventions for depression by increasing positive emotion, engagement, and meaning rather than directly targeting depressive symptoms" (abstract, p. 774). Smith, Harrison, Kurtz, and Bryant (2014) state, "By *positive intervention*, we mean a structured activity 'aimed at cultivating positive feelings, positive behaviors, or positive cognitions' (Sin & Lubomirsky, 2009, p. 467)" (p. 45).

5   By "*a priori*," I do not mean that designations of positivity and negativity in positive psychology were themselves *derived* independently of *all* experience, as in a strict definition of *a priori*. Instead, I mean that these designations, having been determined, are certainly *used* independently of the experiential/circumstantial particularities of any and all individuals to whom those designations are then applied by positive psychologists.

6   Wood and Tarrier state, "Positive psychology research can best impact on the scientific knowledge base of psychology, and be utilized to improve people's lives, if it avoids becoming embroiled in a movement and rather becomes fully integrated with the daily research and practice of mainstream disciplines (so that positive functioning is included alongside negative functioning in research designs, and increasing the positive is as important a focus of therapy as decreasing the negative)" (p. 820). In *Authentic Happiness*, positive psychology movement founder Seligman (2002) himself calls for integration and balance: "Positive Psychology aims for the optimal balance between positive and negative thinking.... Positive psychology is a supplement to negative psychology, not a substitute" (pp. 288–289, n. 96).

7   Vella-Brodrick (2014) challenges the "positive and negative divide" and calls for its removal: "The divide between positive and negative is not helpful or representative of best practice and more work is needed to remove this dichotomy and create a more blended and inclusive concept of mental health" (p. 421). But then she reinstates that very dualism by "emphasizing the need for positive processes" (p. 421).

8   I return to "b" in my discussion of the relation of goals and motivations to what is considered positive and negative.

9   Fredrickson (2009) and Fredrickson and Losada (2005) touted the evidence for this theory repeatedly in the now-famous 3:1 and 12:1 ratios of positive to negative emotions (i.e., "tipping points"), in which only scores within those ranges allegedly predict "flourishing." In their debate, Fredrickson's and Losada's (2005) "nonlinear dynamic model" of positive emotions was challenged convincingly by Brown, Sokal, and Friedman (2013). As Brown and colleagues (2014) summarize, "Fredrickson and Losada (2013) withdrew [that] model, but Fredrickson (December 2013) reaffirmed some claims concerning positivity ratios on the basis of empirical studies" (p. 629), which "evidential" basis they also challenge clearly and dismiss convincingly.

10 Barlow (2010) said, "Greater emphasis on more *individual idiographic* approaches to studying the effects of psychological interventions would seem necessary if psychologists are to avoid harming their patients" (abstract, p. 13; emphasis added).

11 McNulty and Fincham (2012) demonstrate how forgiveness, optimism, benevolent attributions, and kindness – favorite "positives" of positive psychologists – have backfired. Also see Held (2013).

12 Linley and Joseph (2004b) designate "optimal functioning" the "desired outcomes of positive psychology" (p. 5).

13   Norem (2008) defines strategic optimism as a strategy used by people who "do not feel anxious or out of control in performance situations,... set high expectations, and ... avoid thinking very much about what might happen, whether good or ill. They do what they need to do, without the effort of mentally simulating various possible outcomes (*but ...* they also begin without the defensive pessimists' anxiety)" (p. 124).

14   See Held (2005, pp. 9–10) for quotation of positive psychologists (e.g., Aspinwall & Staudinger, 2003; Gable & Haidt, 2005) who speak of defensive pessimism with unqualified approbation.

15   Peterson and Seligman (2004) said, "We do not deny that defensive pessimism can prove useful in some circumstances, but the relevant research also shows that defensive pessimists annoy others" (p. 528). They evidently miss the point of defensive pessimism, which is to decrease debilitating anxiety so as to improve functioning. And need it be said that optimists can be annoying?

16   Seligman (2002) said, "Pessimism is maladaptive in most endeavors.... Thus, pessimists are losers on many fronts" (p. 178).

17   As Seligman (2002) put it, "Lying awake at night, you probably ponder, as I have, how to go from plus two to plus seven in your life, not just how to go from minus seven to minus three and feel a little less miserable every day" (p. xi).

18   For earlier research on the benefits of negative emotions conducted by contributors to Parrott (2014), see, for example, Forgas (2007) on sadness, Perkins & Corr (2005) on anxiety, Van Kleef and Côté (2007) on anger, and Tamir and Ford (2009) on fear.

19   Typically, negative emotions include "fear, anxiety, loneliness, guilt, shame, embarrassment, regret, disappointment, sadness, envy, jealousy, disgust, scorn, anger, frustration, and irritability," and positive emotions include "pride, contentment, relief, hope, exhilaration, delight, eagerness, amusement, cheerfulness, happiness, wonderment, desire, admiration, infatuation, and love" (Parrott, 2014, p. x).

20   One can have defective desires, which are by definition irrational and so should not be pursued. See Erwin (2011) for a detailed exposition of defective desires, especially in psychotherapy.

References

Aspinwall, L. G. & Staudinger, U. M. (2003). A psychology of human strengths: Some central issues of an emerging field. In: L. G. Aspinwall & U. M. Staudinger (Eds.), *A psychology of human strengths: Fundamental questions and future directions for a positive psychology* (pp. 9–22). Washington, DC: American Psychological Association.

Barlow, D. H. (2010). Negative effects from psychological treatments: A perspective. *American Psychologist, 65,* 13–20.

Brown, N. J. L., Sokal, A. D., & Friedman, H. L. (2013). The complex dynamics of wishful thinking: The critical positivity ratio. *American Psychologist, 68,* 801–813.

Brown, N. J. L., Sokal, A. D., & Friedman, H. L. (2014). The persistence of wishful thinking: Response to "Updated Thinking on Positivity Ratios." *American Psychologist, 69,* 629–632.

Colombetti, G. (2005). Appraising valence. *Journal of Consciousness Studies, 12,* 103–126.

Erwin, E. (2011). Evidence-based psychotherapy: Values and the a priori. In: M. J. Shaffer & M. L. Veber (Eds.), *What place for the a priori?* (pp. 33–60). Chicago: Open Court.

Evnine, S. (2008). *Epistemic dimensions of personhood.* Oxford: Oxford University Press.

Forgas, J. P. (2007). When sad is better than happy: Negative affect can improve the quality and effectiveness of persuasive messages and social influence strategies. *Journal of Experimental Social Psychology, 43,* 513–528.

Fredrickson, B. L. (2009). *Positivity: Top-notch research reveals the 3 to 1 ratio that will change your life.* New York: Crown.

Fredrickson, B. L. (2013). Updated thinking on positivity ratios. *American Psychologist, 68*, 814–822.

Fredrickson, B. L. & Losada, M. F. (2005). Positive affect and the complex dynamics of human flourishing. *American Psychologist, 60*, 678–686.

Fredrickson, B. L. & Losada, M. F. (2013). Correction to Fredrickson and Losada. *American Psychologist, 68*, 822.

Fulford, K. W. M. (1994). Value, illness, and failure of action: Framework for a philosophical psychopathology of delusions. In: G. Graham & G. L. Stephens (Eds.), *Philosophical psychopathology* (pp. 205–233). Cambridge, MA: MIT Press.

Gable, S. L. & Haidt, J. (2005). What (and why) is positive psychology? *Review of General Psychology, 9*, 103–110.

Garland, E. L., Fredrickson, B. L., Kroing, A. M., Johnson, D. P., Meyer, P. S., & Penn, D. L. (2010). Upward spirals of positive emotions counter downward spirals of negativity: Insights from the broaden-and-build theory and affective neuroscience on the treatment of emotion dysfunctions and deficits in psychopathology. *Clinical Psychology Review, 39*, 849–864.

Held, B. S. (1995). *Back to reality: A critique of postmodern theory in psychotherapy.* New York: Norton.

Held, B. S. (2002). The tyranny of the positive attitude in America: Observation and speculation. *Journal of Clinical Psychology, 58*, 965–991.

Held, B. S. (2004). The negative side of positive psychology. *Journal of Humanistic Psychology, 44*, 9–46.

Held, B. S. (2005). The "virtues" of positive psychology. *Journal of Theoretical and Philosophical Psychology, 25*, 1–34.

Held, B. S. (2007). *Psychology's interpretive turn: The search for truth and agency in theoretical and philosophical psychology.* Washington, DC: American Psychological Association.

Held, B. S. (2010). Why there is universality in rationality. *Journal of Theoretical and Philosophical Psychology, 30*, 1–16.

Held, B. S. (2013). Feeling bad, being bad, and the perils of personhood. In A. C. Bohart, B. S. Held, E. Mendelowitz, & K. Schneider (Eds.), *Humanity's dark side: Evil, destructive experience, and psychotherapy* (pp. 259–272). Washington, DC: American Psychological Association.

Joseph, S. & Wood, A. (2010). Assessment of positive functioning in clinical psychology. *Clinical Psychology Review, 30*, 830–838.

Kashdan, T. B. & Rottenberg, J. (2010). Psychological flexibility as a fundamental aspect of health. *Clinical Psychology Review, 30*, 865–878.

Linley, P. A. & Joseph, S. (2004a). *Positive psychology in practice.* Hoboken, NJ: John Wiley.

Linley, P. A., & Joseph, S. (2004b). Applied positive psychology: A new perspective for professional practice. In P. A. Linley & S. Joseph (Eds.), *Positive psychology in practice* (pp. 3–12). Hoboken, NJ: John Wiley.

Lopez, S. J. (2009). *The encyclopedia of positive psychology.* Malden, MA: Wiley-Blackwell.

Lopez, S. J. & Snyder, C. R. (Eds.). (2009). *Oxford handbook of positive psychology*, 2nd edn. New York: Oxford University Press.

Martin, J., Sugarman, J., & Thompson, J. (2003). *Psychology and the question of agency.* Albany, NY: SUNY Press.

McNulty, J. K. & Fincham, F. D. (2012). Beyond positive psychology? Toward a contextual view of psychological processes and well-being. *American Psychologist, 67*, 101–110.

Norem, J. K. (2001). *The positive power of negative thinking.* New York: Basic Books.

Norem, J. K. (2008). Defensive pessimism, anxiety, and the complexity of evaluating self-regulation. *Social and Personality Psychology Compass, 2*, 121–134.

Norem, J. K. (2014). The right tool for the job: Functional analysis and evaluating positivity/negativity. In: W. G. Parrott (Ed.), *The positive side of negative emotions.* New York: Guilford.

Norem, J. K. & Cantor, N. (1986). Defensive pessimism: Harnessing anxiety as motivation. *Journal of Personality and Social Psychology, 51*, 1208–1217.

Norem, J. K. & Chang, E. C. (2002). The positive psychology of negative thinking. *Journal of Clinical Psychology, 58*, 993–1001.

Norem, J. K. & Illingworth, K. S. (2004). Mood and performance among defensive pessimists and strategic optimists. *Journal of Research in Personality, 38*, 351–366.

Parks, A. C. & Schueller, S. (Eds.). (2014). *The Wiley-Blackwell handbook of positive psychological interventions.* Malden, MA: Wiley-Blackwell.

Parrott, W. G. (2014). Preface. In: W. G. Parrott (Ed.), *The positive side of negative emotions* (pp. ix–xiv). New York: Guilford.

Perkins, A. M. & Corr, P. J. (2005). Can worriers be winners? The association between worrying and job performance. *Personality and Individual Differences, 38*, 25–31.

Peterson, C. & Seligman, M. E. P. (2004). *Character strengths and virtues: A handbook and classification.* New York: American Psychological Association/Oxford University Press.

Ryan, R. M. & Deci, E. L. (2001). On happiness and human potentials: A review of research on hedonic and eudaimonic well-being. *Annual Review of Psychology, 52*, 141–166.

Sanna, L. J. (1998). Defensive pessimism and optimism: The bitter-sweet influence of mood on performance and prefactual and counterfactual thinking. *Cognition and Emotion, 12*, 635–665.

Sarbin, T. R. (1969). Schizophrenic thinking: A role theoretical analysis. *Journal of Personality, 37*, 190–206.

Scheier, M. F. & Carver, C. S. (1993). On the power of positive thinking: The benefits of being optimistic. *Current Directions in Psychological Science, 2*, 26–30.

Seligman, M. E. P. (2002). *Authentic happiness: Using the new positive psychology to realize your potential for lasting fulfillment.* New York: Simon & Schuster.

Seligman, M. E. P., Rashid, T., & Parks, A. C. (2006). Positive psychotherapy. *American Psychologist, 61*, 774–788.

Sin, N. L. & Lubomirsky, S. (2009). Enhancing well-being and alleviating depressive Symptoms with positive psychology interventions: A practice-friendly meta-analysis. *Journal of Clinical Psychology: In Session, 65*, 467–487.

Smith, J. L., Harrison, P. R., Kurtz, J. L., & Bryant, F. B. (2014). Nurturing the capacity to savor: Interventions to enhance the enjoyment of positive experiences. In: A. C. Parks & S. M. Schueller (Eds.), *The Wiley-Blackwell handbook of positive psychological interventions* (pp. 42–65). Malden, MA: Wiley-Blackwell.

Solomon, R. C. & Stone, L. D. (2002). On "positive" and "negative" emotions. *Journal for the Theory of Social Behaviour, 32*, 417–435.

Szasz, T. S. (1960). The myth of mental illness. *American Psychologist, 15*, 113–118.

Tamir, M. & Ford, B. Q. (2009). Choosing to be afraid: Preferences for fear as a function of goal pursuit. *Emotion, 9*, 488–497.

Van Kleef, G. A. & Côté, S. (2007). Expressing anger in conflict: When it helps and when it hurts. *Journal of Applied Psychology, 92*, 557–569.

Vella-Brodrick, D. A. (2014). Dovetailing ethical practice and positive psychology to promote integrity, industriousness, innovation, and impact. In: A. C. Parks & S. M. Schueller (Eds.), *The Wiley-Blackwell handbook of positive psychological interventions* (pp. 416–432). Malden, MA: Wiley-Blackwell.

Wood, A. M. & Tarrier, N. (2010). Positive clinical psychology: A new vision and strategy for integrated research and practice. *Clinical Psychology Review, 30*, 819–829.

Wood, J. V., Perunovic, W. Q., & Lee, J. W. (2009). Positive self-statements: Power for some, peril for others. *Psychological Science, 20*, 860–866.

4

A Practical Guide to Positive Functioning Assessment in Clinical Psychology

Stephen Joseph and Tom G. Patterson

For the past 30 years clinical psychology research and practice has largely been driven by the psychiatric terminology of the *Diagnostic and Statistical Manual*, now in its fifth edition (American Psychiatric Association, 2013). What this has meant is that clinical psychologists have traditionally not been concerned with the promotion of well-being, but with the alleviation of disorder, leading to a call for clinicians to go beyond the zero point in their assessment of psychopathology (Joseph & Lewis, 1998). Since the introduction of the positive psychology perspective (Seligman, 1999; Seligman & Csikszentmihalyi, 2000), there has been an increasing emphasis in psychology on the promotion of optimal functioning defined by the presence of certain emotions, cognitions, and behaviors.

At first glance, the study of positive psychology would seem not to be of concern to clinical psychologists, but indications are that the positive psychology perspective can add value to clinical practice (Duckworth, Steen, & Seligman, 2005). It may be that interventions to increase positive functioning can help to alleviate disorder in some patients where traditional methods have not worked, or where an increase in well-being may help to prevent future relapse. But it is not only in the pursuit of the traditional goals of clinical psychology to alleviate disorder or prevent relapse that the positive psychology perspective promises to be useful; the promotion of well-being may also be a goal of value in itself to clinical psychology (Joseph & Linley, 2006a). As such, the agenda of clinical psychology has begun to change as the ideas of positive psychology permeate practice and research.

There is a need for clinical psychologists to introduce the measurement of optimal functioning. As straightforward as this may sound, it requires consideration of the theories underpinning clinical psychology practice and research. Our approach to this task is influenced by humanistic psychology, which allows us to step back from the medical model assumptions of traditional clinical psychology and consider alternative meta-theoretical views that may be better suited to the development of a positive clinical psychology.

In this chapter we will: (1) discuss the place of meta-theory in clinical psychology, followed by (2) an examination of the three different ways in which clinical psychologists can introduce measures and assessment procedures into their research and practice, and, finally, (3) a discussion of the implications for professional identity.

The Wiley Handbook of Positive Clinical Psychology, First Edition. Edited by Alex M. Wood and Judith Johnson.
© 2016 John Wiley & Sons, Ltd. Published 2016 by John Wiley & Sons, Ltd.

The Place of Meta-Theory

By meta-theory what we mean are the deep-seated core assumptions underpinning practice and research. In this respect, clinical psychology has traditionally been grounded in the medical model (Joseph & Linley, 2006a). As familiar as the term "medical model" is, it is worth spending some time describing what we mean by the medical model as in our view it is often misunderstood.

In short, the medical model is the idea that problems in living are akin to physical disorders. When we suffer from physical disorders we visit a practitioner who, because of their expert status, is able to identify the nature of our disorder and prescribe the appropriate treatment. If, for example, we have a stomach complaint we might be given indigestion tablets. If we have a broken leg we need to have it set in plaster so that the bone can heal. When we apply the medical model as a metaphor to psychology we do exactly the same – the practitioner must be expert in the different ways in which people experience problems in living so that they are able to dispense the correct treatment. So it is that textbooks lay out their contents according to psychiatric categories of disorder with summaries of research into the causes and treatments of those specific disorders.

It is true that recent debate within the clinical psychology profession has led to challenges to the medical model (e.g., Bentall, 2003; Marzillier, 2004; Johnstone, 2014). However, typically, leading texts on clinical and abnormal psychology, including the present volume, continue to be arranged according to clinical disorders: anxiety disorders, somatoform and dissociative disorders, mood disorders, personality disorders, substance-related disorders, psychotic disorders, and so on. Within such textbooks, it is a taken for granted assumption that it is only through understanding the causes and treatments for each specific disorder that we can conduct research and find the most helpful treatments. Thus, even in a volume such as the present one, which proposes that we seek new positive psychological approaches, there remains an implicit medical ideology at the core.

The fact that the medical model became the dominant way of thinking about psychological problems is not surprising given the important historical role of psychiatry as a branch of medicine and its gatekeeper function over healthcare. Clinical psychology in its early history was servant to psychiatry and, as such, it is understandable that as it developed professionally over the years it took the metaphor of the medical model forward. By doing so, it may have served its own interests well in helping to establish itself as a mainstream profession alongside psychiatry. In contrast, counseling psychology with its roots in the humanistic tradition and its explicit rejection of the medical model struggled to find a similar status (Vossler, Steffan, & Joseph, 2015). Ironically, as clinical psychology moves toward challenging the medical model assumptions at its core and looks to positive psychology to provide a new vision for its practice, it now follows in the footsteps of counseling psychology several decades earlier.

However, after several decades of adopting the medical model, clinical psychology is well established internationally as a profession in its own right and no longer servant to psychiatry. Even so, the medical model remains a pervasive influence in clinical psychology. This last statement might surprise many readers who would see clinical psychology as having moved beyond the medical model, but what they often tend to mean is the biomedical model.

The biomedical model applies the same logic as the medical model, but additionally assumes a biological cause. The medical model as we have described it does not necessarily imply a biological cause. What is medical is that the approach taken is metaphorically a medical one requiring diagnosis and prescription. For example, an approach to depression and anxiety based on viewing them as distinct disorders requiring disorder-specific psychological treatments is a medical model approach.

It is also true that the current context of the clinical psychology profession in the United Kingdom, which practices predominantly within the National Health Service (NHS), may serve to promote the continuation of medical-model informed approaches to mental health difficulties. For example, NHS services and professionals are expected to follow the National Institute for Health and Clinical Excellence (NICE) guidelines on the therapies or "treatments" considered effective for mental health difficulties, and these in turn are often based on evidence from randomized control trial (RCT) research designs that can often reinforce medical model conceptualization of mental health difficulties.

Diagnosis and prescription are terms that many clinical psychologists will not identify with and as such may not view themselves as medical model practitioners, and certainly there has been much criticism from within clinical psychology of the limitations of narrow diagnostic approaches over recent years (e.g., Bentall, 2003; Marzillier, 2004; Johnstone, 2014). However, clinical psychology does concern itself with formulation, an approach to making sense of the client's distress and mental health difficulties.

Formulation is a broad concept, perhaps best considered as a continuum. At one extreme it is akin to person-centered practice insofar as the client takes the lead in understanding their situation and the therapist offers no intervention as the client's understanding is sufficient to drive the therapeutic process forward (see Sanders & Joseph, Chapter 28, this volume). At the other extreme, it is akin to medical model practice as the therapist takes the lead in formulating the problem and offering the solution. It is important to acknowledge that, between these two extremes, there are many different approaches to formulation and also that the importance of collaborative development of a formulation and of respecting service users' views about accuracy and helpfulness of the formulation has been increasingly emphasized in recent years (Johnstone & Dallos, 2006; Division of Clinical Psychology, 2011) and underpins many clinical psychologists' approach to formulation.

Formulation in clinical psychology increasingly attempts to value clients' perspectives in making sense of difficulties. For example, clinical psychologists adopting a social constructionist informed perspective such as in systemic formulation do not assume that a position of certainty can be reached, but will instead strive to collaboratively develop working hypotheses that are constantly open to revision, drawing upon social and relational factors while also recognizing that the therapist's assumptions and values are inherently present in any hypothesis (Johnstone & Dallos, 2006). However, it is important to emphasize that whenever guided by a professional-as-expert stance, formulation simply becomes another form of medical model practice, insofar as it requires the practitioner to apply his or her expert knowledge to understand a client's problems in such a way as to recommend the best course of treatment.

By turning our attention to well-being we have the opportunity to rethink our adherence to the medical model, but a further misunderstanding is that positive psychology is by definition not a medical model approach (Joseph & Linley, 2006b). Insofar as we seek to find ways to prescribe interventions for people to increase certain aspects of well-being, positive psychology is also grounded in the medical model. Instructing people to use gratitude exercises, for example, to overcome depression may make use of positive psychology, but it does so within a medical model framework.

As already noted, even this book on positive clinical psychology continues to propagate the notion of the medical model insofar as it, like traditional texts, is structured in terms of psychiatric categories. An alternative meta-theoretical framework to the medical model is the humanistic person-centered approach that posits that people are intrinsically and naturally motivated toward their full potential and optimal functioning unless this tendency is usurped and thwarted by social environmental conditions leading to incongruence between self and experience (Joseph & Worsley, 2005a). As such, the person-centered approach is a nonmedical model as there is no need for specific diagnosis and prescription of specific treatments as all psychological problems result from this same underlying cause – incongruence between self and experience or self-alienation (Joseph, 2015).

It may be that how problems in living manifest are different from person to person in the ways described in the typical clinical psychology text book, but this is an irrelevant observation for person-centered therapists insofar as the problems are always at root caused by alienation between self and experience. For those that adopted the humanistic approach, diagnosis was often rejected because the medical model was rejected. If, as in the person-centered tradition, all problems in living stem from inauthenticity there is no need for diagnosis because there is no need to determine specific treatments for specific problems. In person-centered psychology this is known as the specificity myth as it is understood that all psychological problems can be helped through accepting, empathic, and genuine relationships that foster the client's agency (Bozarth & Motomasa, 2005). This approach, which has been at the core of person-centered psychology for over 50 years, emphasizes the therapeutic relationship over and above the use of techniques (Sanders & Joseph, Chapter 28, this volume).

The point is that the core issue when considering measurement is always first and foremost a consideration of underpinning theoretical frameworks and thus the selection of theory consistent instruments and assessment procedures (Patterson & Joseph, 2007; Joseph, 2015). As such, clinical psychologists have traditionally tended to work within the medical model framework and use diagnostically based measurement, whereas counseling psychologists when they have used measurement have tended to prefer those that emphasize growthful functioning, authenticity, and the ways in which people find meaning and purpose.

Next we will offer the reader a practical framework for the selection and use of various measurement tools. We will summarize what we see as the most important theoretical issue confronting the positive clinical psychologist: whether the positive psychology perspective adds value to the existing business of clinical psychology, but does not change its essential medical model nature, or whether the positive psychology perspective revolutionizes the way clinical psychologists conceptualize people's problems.

Three Forms of Measurement

First, the most obvious approach is to introduce new measures of positive functioning alongside existing clinical scales. For example, there are several measures of well-being and life satisfaction available that have proved popular among positive psychologists (e.g., Diener, Suh, Lucas, & Smith, 1999; Lyubomirsky & Lepper, 1999; Tennant, Hillier, Fishwick, Platt, Joseph, Weich, Parkinson, Secker, & Stewart-Brown, 2007). This would seem to be an obvious way forward, but it can be problematic. The needs of the positive psychologist are different to those of the positive clinical psychologist. Positive psychologists may choose these new measures without necessarily having to consider their conceptual relationship to psychopathology. For the positive clinical psychologist, however, this consideration should be uppermost in their mind. Otherwise, the danger is that measures are selected that are derived from incompatible theoretical frameworks. For example, in recent years the study of post-traumatic growth has gained attention as researchers and clinicians seek to understand how people may thrive in the aftermath of adversity. It is relatively easy to select both measures of post-traumatic stress disorder and post-traumatic growth for inclusion in the same study. No alarm bells ring if you do this. It is relatively easy to administer paper-and-pencil tests and then conduct statistical analysis on the association between measures. It is not unusual to see such studies. But this is to misunderstand that the concepts themselves can be understood from mutually exclusive paradigms such as the medical model and humanistic psychology, respectively, and as such it is like mixing oil and water (Joseph & Linley, 2005, 2006b).

What does it mean to say that a medical model construct such as post-traumatic stress disorder is correlated with a humanistic construct of posttraumatic growth? Such data can be interpreted only from one of these mutually exclusive paradigms. Either post-traumatic growth is viewed through the lens of the medical model, or post-traumatic stress is seen through a humanistic lens. This can be seen most clearly in the evidence wars for the effectiveness of therapies for specific treatments when outcomes are defined in terms of medical model categories regardless of their meta-theoretical assumptions. However, reliance on symptom reduction as the key indicator of effectiveness in research into therapeutic effectiveness implies an assumption that symptom reduction is a neutral concept that is shared by all the different therapeutic approaches. This assumption of neutral objectivity is erroneous in the same way that claims that a neutral language of scientific observation exists have been shown to be erroneous (Popper, [1959] 1980). For example, how do humanistic therapies compare with cognitive therapies in the treatment of depression? Traditionally, the answer to this question would be determined on that basis of comparison of "treatments" using RCT studies with symptoms of depression as the measured outcome. This approach was developed within a biomedical model paradigm, initially to compare treatments for physical illnesses and later extended to study effectiveness of treatments for mental health difficulties. The choice of depression as the outcome is, however, not theoretically compatible with those humanistic therapies that do not conceptualize problems as symptoms of disorder, but as problems of self-alienation and lack of authenticity (Joseph & Wood, 2010).

Despite the fact that humanistic therapies do not focus on symptom reduction as the key indicator of therapeutic effectiveness, approaches such as client-centered therapy still perform relatively well in RCT studies (see, e.g., Elliott, 1996; Friedli, King, Lloyd, & Horder, 1997; King, Sibbald, Ward, Bower, Lloyd, Gabbay, & Byford, 2000; Sanders & Joseph, Chapter 28, this volume). However, that does not mean we should ignore the fact that the basis for comparison in such studies is a conceptualization of mental distress and an indicator of recovery that is not congruent with nonmedicalized approaches. A more balanced question, one that respects the different paradigms within which each of these therapeutic approaches has evolved, would be how do these therapies compare in the facilitation of authenticity and the treatment of depression? In this latter way, each therapy is evaluated on the basis of its own epistemological framework and that of the other therapy.

The second way in which clinical psychologists can introduce positive psychology into their practice is to re-evaluate their existing tools. Some existing clinical measures may already be inadvertently assessing positive functioning. An example of such a measure would be the Center for Epidemiological Studies Depression Scale (CES-D, Radloff, 1977). The CES-D is one of the most widely used tools to measure depression. The CES-D consists of twenty items, sixteen of which are negatively worded (e.g., "I felt sad"; "I felt I could not shake the blues even with help from my family or friends"; "I thought my life had been a failure"), and four of which are positively worded items ("I felt happy"; "I enjoyed life"; "I felt that I was just as good as other people"; "I felt hopeful about the future"). Scoring of the CES-D involves reverse coding the positive items and totaling all items to form a single score ranging from 0 to 60. A score of zero means that the respondent has rated all negative items as "rarely or none of the time" and all the positive items as "most or all of the time." As such, it is evident that a score of zero does not simply indicate the absence of depression, but also the presence of happiness. Researchers have traditionally used the CES-D to measure levels of depression, but have not paid attention to the fact that it can equally be conceptualized as a measure of happiness (Joseph, 2006, 2007), a fact supported by a factor analysis conducted during the initial development of the measure that identified "positive affect" as one of four underlying factors that together account for 48% of the total variance in the scale (Radloff, 1977; see also Wood, Taylor, & Joseph, 2010). Thus, one can imagine how by a re-evaluation of existing instruments in light of positive psychology it will be possible to select instruments that serve a dual purpose. By selecting such instruments it is possible to accommodate the ideas of positive psychology. However, the challenge of this approach is that it requires us to reconceptualize what it is that we are measuring in the first place.

Depression in psychiatric terms is a categorical variable, but it is not unusual for psychologists to assess depression dimensionally. An example of this is the use of the Beck Depression Inventory (BDI; Beck, Ward, Mendelson, Mock, & Erbaugh, 1961), a widely used measure of depression. Originally developed as a taxonomic tool, it has since been used in many studies to provide a dimensional score of depressive experiences. Scores on the BDI have a potential range of 0 to 63. A score of 63 indicates intense depressive experience, whereas a score of 0 indicates the absence of depression. But a score of zero on the BDI does not imply positive functioning (Joseph & Lewis, 1998). What does it imply if we think of depression dimensionally and more importantly what is the nature of that dimensional construct? As discussed, the CES-D goes beyond the zero point of the absence of depression to the presence of happiness. At a practical level such an approach has its uses as it allows clinicians to seemingly maintain their business as usual approach while incorporating positive psychology, but at a theoretical level such an approach is more complex as it challenges the original conceptualization of the measure. In the case of the CES-D, the implication is that the constructs of depression and happiness are essentially synonymous, representing opposite end-points of a single continuum (Wood, Taylor, & Joseph, 2010). As such it may be that one rejects the traditional psychiatric system for its neglect of the positive aspects of living, and for painting an incomplete and skewed portrayal of clients, but nonetheless adopts the medical model (Joseph & Linley, 2006b). The medical model need not be a deficit-based approach. Positive clinical assessment within the medical model can explore strengths as well as weaknesses.

The idea that depression and anxiety can be studied dimensionally in this way offers a useful positive clinical psychology perspective (Joseph & Wood, 2010). Such a measure is the twelve-item Positive Functioning Inventory (Joseph & Maltby, 2014), which addresses the traditional needs of clinical psychologists to assess levels of depression and anxiety, but within a framework of positive psychology that recognizes that when assessed dimensionally, these are statistically bipolar continuous states with happiness and contentment.

Going beyond the specific categories of depression and anxiety, one groundbreaking example of a comprehensive nondeficit strengths-based approach to the medical model is presented by Rashid (2015), who conceptualizes symptoms of major psychological disorders in terms of lack or excess of strengths. For example, depression can result, in part, because of lack of hope, optimism, and zest, among other variables; likewise, a lack of grit and patience can explain some aspects of anxiety, and a lack of fairness, equity, and justice might underscore conduct disorders. The above are approaches that are consistent with the language of the medical model, but extend thinking to new forms of continuous assessment with a positive psychology focus.

The third way is to use measures developed specifically for positive clinical psychology, which move away from diagnostic terminology and the medical model and are developed on the basis of new understandings of well-being. The humanistic approach is one such example, particularly person-centered psychology with its meta-theoretical perspective of actualization as the core motivation underpinning psychological development (Joseph & Linley, 2006a). Specifically, there is an important philosophical distinction to be made between hedonic well-being and eudaimonic well-being, or subjective well-being (SWB) and psychological well-being (PWB), respectively, in the contemporary language of positive psychology. As illustrated in the section above, the traditional focus of clinical psychology has been on SWB, which has been conceptualized as decreasing negative affective states such as depression and anxiety, and, more recently, drawing upon positive psychology to also increase positive states such as happiness and contentment.

In contrast, PWB reflects engagement with the existential challenges of life (see Ryan & Deci, 2001), and is often operationalized as involving autonomy, self-acceptance, environmental mastery, purpose in life, positive relationships with others, and personal growth (Ryff & Keyes, 1995). Although SWB and PWB are related, philosophically (Ryff & Keyes, 1995; Ryff & Singer, 1996) and empirically, they can be considered separable (Waterman, 1993; Compton, Smith, Cornish, & Qualls, 1996; Keyes, Shmotkin, & Ryff, 2002).

Previously, while SWB has been the focus of clinical psychology, PWB has been the focus of humanistic and existential psychology (e.g., Rogers, 1959; Joseph, 2015). But with the emergence of positive psychology and now positive clinical psychology, in conjunction with challenges to the illness ideology, clinical psychologists are beginning to rediscover the ideas of humanistic and existential psychology. For example, above we considered the difficulties in bringing together post-traumatic stress and post-traumatic growth as they can represent competing meta-theoretical systems. Viewing post-traumatic growth as an expression of the humanistic orientation we can begin to reconceptualize post-traumatic stress as a process rather than as an outcome variable. Another example of measures based on nonmedical model frameworks is the Authenticity Scale (Wood, Linley, Maltby, Baliousis, & Joseph, 2008), which was designed to be consistent with person-centered psychology (Rogers, 1959). Absence of authenticity is viewed as arising through a lack of congruence between conscious awareness, inner emotional and cognitive states, and the social environment, and is the cornerstone of all expressions of psychopathology that are not biological in origin (Joseph & Worsley, 2005b).

Similarly consistent with the person-centered goal of facilitating a loosening of the client's rigid internalized rules and values, resulting in less constrained and less contingent self-relating, the Unconditional Positive Self-Regard Scale (Patterson & Joseph, 2006, 2013) provides a brief and theoretically congruent measure of therapeutic change within a humanistic paradigm. As such, although humanistic psychologists such as Rogers have discussed fully-functioning authenticity and unconditional positive self-regard, these notions did not evolve in an organized system of clinical assessment and intervention, as in that approach there is no need for such an organized system. Indeed, such a system is contrary to the aim of therapy which is to foster agency in the client.

Professional Issues

Described above are the three ways in which positive psychology measurement can be introduced into clinical psychology. Each in its own way demands reflection on the rationale for the choice of measures and assumptions about how the negative and the positive relate to each other. These are also issues of professional concern, as in their different ways they redefine clinical psychology. The first approach would simply involve introducing measures of positive functioning alongside existing clinical measures. The second approach emphasizes the promotion of positive functioning within a strengths-based approach that continues to adopt the medical model. The third approach challenges the medical model and looks to alternatives such as the humanistic approach. The latter approach is the most controversial because it challenges the nature of the clinical psychology profession and puts it into alignment with the traditional aims of counseling psychology. Historically, counseling psychology was aligned with the humanistic tradition of psychology and its emphasis on self-actualization and fully functioning behavior.

Conclusion

While traditionally, clinical psychology has largely adopted psychiatric terminology, it has more recently started to question the medical model of mental distress, and it is now important that practitioners begin to introduce positive functioning into their practice. In this chapter we have discussed ways in which clinical psychologists can engage with this new agenda by using measures that are based on alternative conceptualizations of functioning. We find that humanistic psychology offers new ideas that can inform how to conceptualize the relationship between negative and positive functioning. Each tool offers a conceptualization of well-being, either explicitly or implicitly. It is becoming ever more important to build evidence for positive change over the course of therapy. It is reasonable to expect that funders should want to see evidence for effectiveness. But how effectiveness is defined is not straightforward. Traditionally, it has been based on quite specific diagnostic criteria and the psychiatric terminology of symptom reduction, which has suited some forms of clinical practice but not all. However, we can now expect to see how outcomes are defined begin to change to include newer constructs drawn from positive clinical psychology.

In changing the outcomes that we are interested in, we also change the parameters of therapeutic engagement. Typically, clients perceive therapy as a time to talk about their distress and dysfunction and to seek ways to find relief. But in changing the discourse to be about the absence of positive functioning or authenticity, for example, expectations for therapy may change to include seeking positive changes, and to learn to value oneself unconditionally or to grow from adversity. As such, not only are such measures of positive functioning useful in tracking change, but they can also play a valuable therapeutic role if used skillfully and in the client's interests. As clinical psychologists increasingly adopt the ideas of positive psychology we hope our discussion will prove helpful to practitioners and researchers in choosing their assessment tools.

References

American Psychiatric Association (2013). *Diagnostic and statistical manual of mental disorders*, 5th edn. Washington, DC: American Psychiatric Press.

Beck, A. T., Ward, C. H., Mendelson, M., Mock, J. E., & Erbaugh, J. K. (1961). An inventory for measuring depression. *Archives of General Psychiatry, 4*, 561–571.

Bentall, R. (2003). *Madness explained: Psychosis and human nature*. London: Allen Lane.

Bozarth, J. D. & Motomasa, N, (2005). Searching for the core: The interface of client-centered principles with other therapies. In S. Joseph & R. Worsley (Eds.), *Person-centered psychopathology: A positive psychology of mental health* (pp. 293–309). Ross-on-Wye: PCCS Books.

Compton, W. C., Smith, M. L., Cornish, K. A., & Qualls, D. L. (1996). Factor structure of mental health measures. *Journal of Personality and Social Psychology, 71*, 406–413. doi/10.1037/0022-3514.71.2.406.

Diener, E., Suh, E. M., Lucas, R. E., & Smith, H. (1999). Subjective well-being: Three decades of progress. *Psychological Bulletin, 125*, 276–302. doi.org/10.1037//0033-2909.125.2.276.

Division of Clinical Psychology (2011). *Good practice guidelines on the use of psychological formulation*. Leicester: British Psychological Society.

Duckworth, A. L., Steen, T. A., & Seligman, M. E. P. (2005). Positive psychology in clinical practice. *Annual Review of Clinical Psychology, 2005*, 629–651.

Elliott, R. (1996). Are client-centred/experiential therapies effective? A meta-analysis of outcome research. In: U. Esser, H. Pbast, & G-W Speierer (Eds.), *The power of the person-centred approach: New challenges–perspectives–answers* (pp. 125–138). Cologne: GwG Verlag.

Friedli, K., King, M., Lloyd, M., & Horder, J. (1997). Randomised controlled assessment of non-directive psychotherapy versus routine general practitioner care. *The Lancet, 350*, 1662–1665. doi.org/10.1016/S0140-6736(97)05298-7.

King, M., Sibbald, B., Ward, E., Bower, P., Lloyd, M., Gabbay, M., & Byford, S. (2000). Randomised controlled trial of non-directive counselling cognitive behaviour therapy and usual general practitioner care in the management of depression as well as mixed anxiety and depression in primary care. *British Medical Journal, 321*, 1383–1388.

Johnstone, L. & Dallos, R. (2006). Introduction to formulation. In: L. Johnstone and R. Dallos (Eds.). *Formulation in psychology and psychotherapy: Making sense of people's problems* (pp. 1–16). Hove: Routledge.

Johnstone, L. (2014). *A straight talking introduction to psychiatric diagnosis*. Ross-on-Wye: PCCS Books.

Joseph, S. (2006). Measurement in depression: Positive psychology and the statistical bipolarity of depression and happiness. *Measurement: Interdisciplinary Research and Perspectives, 4*, 156–160.

Joseph, S. (2007). Is the CES-D a measure of happiness? *Psychotherapy and Psychosomatics, 76,* 60. doi.org/10.1159/000096368.

Joseph, S. (2015). *Positive therapy: Building bridges between positive psychology and person-centred psychotherapy,* 2nd edn. London: Routledge.

Joseph, S. & Lewis, C. A. (1998). The depression–happiness scale: reliability and validity of a bipolar self-report scale. *Journal of Clinical Psychology, 54,* 537–544.

Joseph, S. & Linley, P. A. (2005). Positive adjustment to threatening events: An organismic valuing theory of growth through adversity. *Review of General Psychology, 9,* 262–280. doi.org/10.1037/1089-2680.9.3.262.

Joseph, S. & Linley, P. A. (2006a). *Positive therapy: A meta theory for positive psychological practice.* London: Routledge.

Joseph, S. & Linley, P. A. (2006b). Positive psychology versus the medical model. *American Psychologist, 61,* 332–333. doi/10.1037/0003-066X.60.4.332.

Joseph, S. & Maltby, J. (2014). Positive functioning inventory: Initial validation of a 12-item self-report measure of well-being. *Psychology of Well-being, 4,* 15.

Joseph, S. & Worsley, R. (2005a). A positive psychology of mental health: The person-centered perspective. In: S. Joseph & R. Worsley (Eds.), *Person-centered psychopathology: A positive psychology of mental health* (pp. 348–357). Ross-on-Wye: PCCS Books.

Joseph, S. & Worsley, R. (Eds.). (2005b). *Person-centered psychopathology: A positive psychology of mental health.* Ross-on-Wye: PCCS Books.

Keyes, C. L. M., Shmotkin, D., & Ryff, C. D. (2002). Optimizing well-being: The empirical encounter of two traditions. *Journal of Personality and Social Psychology, 82,* 1007–1022. doi.org/10.1037//0022-3514.82.6.1007.

Lyubomirsky, S. & Lepper, H. S. (1999). A measure of subjective happiness: Preliminary reliability and construct validation. *Social Indicators Research, 46,* 137–155.

Marzillier, J. (2004). The myth of evidence-based psychotherapy. *The Psychologist, 17,* 392–395.

Patterson, T. G. & Joseph, S. (2006). Development of a self-report measure of unconditional positive self-regard. *Psychology and Psychotherapy: Theory, Research, and Practice, 79,* 557–570. doi.org/10.1348/147608305X89414.

Patterson, T. G. & Joseph, S. (2007). Outcome measurement in person-centered practice. In: S. Joseph & R. Worsley (Eds.), *Person-centered practice: Case studies in positive psychology* (pp. 200–215). Ross-on-Wye: PCCS Books.

Patterson, T. G. & Joseph, S. (2013). Unconditional Positive Self-Regard. In: M. Bernard (Ed.), *The strength of self-acceptance: Theory, research and practice* (pp. 93–106). New York: Springer.

Popper, K. ([1959] 1980). *The logic of scientific discovery.* London: Hutchinson.

Radloff, L. S. (1977). The CES-D scale: A self-report depression scale for research in the general population. *Applied Psychological Measurement, 1,* 385–401. doi.org/10.1177/014662167700100306.

Rashid, T. (2015). Strength-based assessment. In: S. Joseph (Ed.), *Positive psychology in practice: Promoting human flourishing in work, health, education and everyday life,* 2nd edn. (pp. 519–542). Hoeboken, NJ: Wiley-Blackwell.

Rogers, C. R. (1959). A theory of therapy, personality, and interpersonal relationships as developed in the client-centered framework. In: S. Koch (Ed.) *Psychology: A study of a Science, vol. 3: Formulations of the person and the social context* (pp.184–256). New York: McGraw-Hill.

Ryan, R. M. & Deci, E. L. (2001). On happiness and human potentials: A review of research on hedonic and eudaimonic well-being. *Annual Review of Psychology, 52,* 141–166. doi: 10.1146/annurev.psych.52.1.141.

Ryff, C. D. & Keyes, C. L. M. (1995). The structure of psychological well-being revisited. *Journal of Personality and Social Psychology, 69,* 719–727.

Ryff, C. D. & Singer, B. H. (1996). Psychological well-being: Meaning, measurement, and implications for psychotherapy research. *Psychotherapy and Psychosomatics, 65,* 14–23. doi.org/10.1037//0022-3514.69.4.719.

Seligman, M. E. P. (1999). The president's address. *American Psychologist, 54,* 559–562.

Seligman, M. E. P. & Csikszentmihalyi, M. (2000). Positive psychology: An introduction. *American Psychologist, 55,* 5–14. doi.org/10.1037/0003-066X.55.1.5.

Tennant, R., Hillier, L., Fishwick, R., Platt, S., Joseph, S., Weich, S., Parkinson, J., Secker, J., & Stewart-Brown, S. (2007). The Warwick–Edinburgh Mental Well Being Scale (WEMWBS): Development and UK validation. *Health and Quality of Life Outcomes, 5,* 63. doi.org/10.1186/1477-7525-5-63.

Vossler, A., Steffan, E., & Joseph, S. (2015). The relationship between counseling psychology and positive psychology. In: S. Joseph (Ed.), *Positive psychology in practice: Promoting human flourishing in work, health, education and everyday life*, 2nd edn. (pp. 429–441).Hoeboken, NJ: Wiley-Blackwell.

Waterman, A. S. (1993). Two conceptions of happiness: Contrasts of personal expressiveness (eudaimonia) and hedonic enjoyment. *Journal of Personality and Social Psychology, 64*, 678–691. doi.org/10.1037/0022-3514.64.4.678.

Wood, A. M., Linley, P. A., Maltby, J., Baliousis, M., & Joseph, S. (2008). The authentic personality: A theoretical and empirical conceptualization and the development of the authenticity scale. *Journal of Counselling Psychology, 55*, 385–399. doi: 10.1037/0022-0167.55.3.385.

Wood, A. M., Taylor, P. J., & Joseph, S. (2010). Does the CES-D measure a continuum from depression to happiness? Comparing substantive and artifactual models. *Psychiatry Research, 177*, 120–123. doi.org/10.1016/j.psychres.2010.02.003.

Part II
Personality and Individual Differences

5

Positive Mood Dysfunction in Psychopathology
A Structural Perspective
David Watson

Introduction

The goal of this chapter is to examine the associations between positive emotional experience and major forms of psychopathology. In reviewing this evidence, I will use the hierarchical structure of affect as an organizing framework. Starting in the 1980s, extensive evidence has established the existence of two dominant dimensions of emotional experience: Negative Affect (or Activation) and Positive Affect (or Activation) (Watson & Tellegen, 1985; Watson, Wiese, Vaidya, & Tellegen, 1999). Negative Affect is a general dimension of subjective distress and dissatisfaction. It subsumes a broad range of specific negative emotional states, including fear, anger, sadness, guilt, and disgust. Its emergence in analyses of affect ratings indicates that these various negative emotions significantly co-occur both within and across individuals. Thus, an individual who reports feeling anxious and fearful is also likely to report substantial levels of anger, guilt, sadness, and so on. In parallel fashion, the general Positive Affect dimension reflects important co-occurrences among positive mood states; for instance, an individual who reports feeling happy and joyful will also report feeling interested, excited, confident and alert. These two higher-order factors emerge consistently across diverse sets of descriptors, time frames, response formats, and languages (Watson & Clark, 1997b; Watson et al., 1999).

Both of these dimensions have important links to psychopathology (Clark & Watson, 1991; Mineka, Watson, & Clark, 1998; Kotov, Gamez, Schmidt, & Watson, 2010; Watson & Naragon-Gainey, 2010; Watson, Clark, & Stasik, 2011).To date, however, research in this area has focused primarily on dysfunctional manifestations of negative affect. This focus is understandable, given that elevated levels of negative affect are associated with a wide array of syndromes, including anxiety disorders, depressive disorders, substance use disorders, somatoform disorders, eating disorders, personality and conduct disorders, and schizophrenia/schizotypy (Mineka et al., 1998; Kotov et al., 2010). Kotov et al. (2010) reported particularly striking meta-analytic evidence for neuroticism, a personality trait that essentially reflects individual differences in negative affectivity (Watson et al., 1999). Kotov and colleagues compared the mean neuroticism scores of individuals without and without unipolar mood, anxiety, and substance use disorders. Neuroticism displayed medium to large effect sizes (expressed as Cohen's *d*; J. Cohen, 1992) with every analyzed disorder; for example, *d*s (corrected for unreliability) ranged from 1.33 to

The Wiley Handbook of Positive Clinical Psychology, First Edition. Edited by Alex M. Wood and Judith Johnson.
© 2016 John Wiley & Sons, Ltd. Published 2016 by John Wiley & Sons, Ltd.

2.25 for major depression, generalized anxiety disorder (GAD), post-traumatic stress disorder (PTSD), panic disorder, social phobia, and obsessive compulsive disorder (OCD). More generally, based on an extensive literature review, Widiger and Costa (1994) concluded that "neuroticism is an almost ubiquitously elevated trait within clinical populations" (p. 81).

In order to get a complete and balanced picture, however, it also is important to explicate the nature of positive mood dysfunction in psychopathology. As I will show, the evidence here differs from that reviewed earlier for Negative Affect in two important ways. First, in contrast to the pervasiveness of negative emotional disturbance in psychopathology, positive mood dysfunction shows much greater specificity: that is, although many syndromes show substantial links to positive affect, others do not, such that individuals with these disorders report relatively normal levels of positive mood. Second, unlike negative affect – which is consistently elevated in clinical populations – positive affect does not display a consistent directional trend: whereas many syndromes are associated with anhedonia and low levels of positive mood, other disorders have been linked to excessive positive affect.

In the following sections, I review evidence for positive mood dysfunction in psychopathology. I begin by examining three types of psychopathology that are clearly associated with anhedonia and deficits in positive affect: (a) depression, (b) social anxiety/social phobia, and (c) schizophrenia/schizotypy. I then conclude by examining data related to the bipolar disorders, which are associated with elevated levels of positive affect.

Depression

Basic Mood Evidence

Basic data   Findings from the mood literature have established that positive affect has stronger and more consistent (negative) associations with sad, depressed mood than with other types of negative affect. For example, Watson and Naragon-Gainey (2010, table 1) reported data based on the eight-item Well-Being scale from the Inventory of Depression and Anxiety Symptoms (IDAS; Watson et al., 2007), which contains items tapping high energy and positive mood (e.g., *I felt cheerful, I looked forward to things with enjoyment*). Across large samples of psychiatric outpatients ($N = 1,006$) and college students ($N = 980$), Well-Being had significantly stronger correlations with a measure of depressed mood ($r = -.49$ and $-.46$) than with scales assessing anxious mood and anger (rs ranged from $-.19$ to $-.37$). Watson (2005) reported similar findings based on the Sadness (e.g., *sad, lonely*), Fear (e.g., *scared, nervous*), and Joviality (e.g., *happy, enthusiastic*) scales of the Expanded Form of the Positive and Negative Affect Schedule (PANAS-X; Watson & Clark, 1999). Across fourteen samples (overall $N = 9,663$), Joviality was consistently more strongly related to Sadness (mean $r = -.36$) than to Fear (mean $r = -.10$).

Two-factor model   On the basis of similar data, Watson, Clark and Carey (1988) proposed a two-factor model of depression and anxiety. In this model, negative affect represents a nonspecific factor that is common to depression and anxiety, whereas low positive affect is a specific factor that is primarily related to depression. With one noteworthy exception, this model has received extensive support (e.g., Jolly, Dyck, Kramer, & Wherry, 1994; Watson, 2005). For example, Watson et al. (1988) found that a negative affect scale was broadly related to measures of both depression and anxiety (including indicators of panic disorder, phobias, and OCD), whereas low positive emotionality was related primarily to depressive symptoms and diagnoses. The one contrary finding is that positive affect also shows consistent negative associations with social anxiety/social phobia (e.g., Brown, Chorpita, & Barlow, 1998; Watson, Gamez, & Simms, 2005; Kashdan, 2007; Naragon-Gainey, Watson, & Markon, 2009); I return to this issue subsequently.

IDAS-based Evidence

Overview Our ongoing work with the original IDAS (Watson et al., 2007) and the expanded second version of the IDAS (IDAS-II; Watson et al., 2012) has helped to clarify the nature of positive mood dysfunction in the mood and anxiety disorders. This research has yielded two key conclusions. First, although positive affect measures are significantly negatively related to many indicators of anxiety (including social anxiety/social phobia), they are most strongly and systematically associated with depression. Second, low positive affect actually shows greater specificity than traditional indicators of depression, including some of the formal symptom criteria for a *DSM-IV* (American Psychiatric Association, 2000) major depressive episode. Our data therefore demonstrates that the assessment and differential diagnosis of major depression can be enhanced by focusing more on this positive mood deficit and deemphasizing nonspecific aspects of the disorder.

Relations with the Beck Inventories Three types of evidence support these conclusions. First, the IDAS contains six scales that jointly capture all of the important symptom content included in the nine *DSM-IV* diagnostic criteria for a major depressive episode (see Watson, 2009): dysphoria (which contains items assessing depressed mood – Criterion 1, anhedonia/loss of interest Criterion 2, psychomotor disturbance – Criterion 5, worthlessness/guilt – Criterion 7, and cognitive problems – Criterion 8); Lassitude (which captures both fatigue/anergia – Criterion 6, and the hypersomnia portion of Criterion 4), Suicidality (which measures Criterion 9), Insomnia (which taps the corresponding portion of Criterion 4), and Appetite Loss and Appetite Gain (which jointly capture Criterion 3).

Watson (2009) examined how the IDAS scales correlated with the Beck Depression Inventory-II (BDI-II; Beck, Steer, & Brown, 1996) and the Beck Anxiety Inventory (BAI; Beck & Steer, 1990) in two large samples (combined $N = 2,783$). Well-Being – which, as noted earlier, is a measure of positive emotional experience – showed the most impressive specificity in these data, correlating much more strongly with the BDI-II (mean $r = -.56$) than with the BAI (mean $r = -.32$). Lassitude (mean $rs = .62$ and .50, respectively), Suicidality (mean $rs = .58$ and .47, respectively), and Dysphoria (mean $rs = .81$ and .71, respectively) also displayed a reasonable level of specificity in these data (for an expanded version of these results, see Watson & Naragon-Gainey, 2010).

In contrast, the three remaining scales – Insomnia, Appetite Loss, and Appetite Gain – showed much poorer specificity (see Watson, 2009, table 7). Indeed, Insomnia (mean $rs = .50$ and .47, respectively) and Appetite Loss (mean $rs = .39$ and .39, respectively) had virtually identical correlations with the two instruments. These results are particularly striking when one considers that these IDAS scales actually share overlapping item content with the BDI-II, but not the BAI.

Relations with DSM-IV Diagnoses Second, Well-Being shows impressive specificity in relation to formal *DSM-IV* mood and anxiety disorder diagnoses (Watson & Naragon-Gainey, 2010). Watson and Stasik (2014) reported six analyses of diagnostic specificity that enabled them to evaluate the robustness of these patterns across methods, measures, and populations. To obtain current *DSM-IV* diagnoses, all participants were interviewed using the SCID-IV (for inter-rater reliability data, see Watson et al., 2008). To examine diagnostic specificity, Watson and Stasik (2014) computed polychoric correlations between depression symptom measures and various *DSM-IV* mood and anxiety disorder diagnoses. Polychoric correlations estimate the associations between normally distributed latent continuous variables that are presumed to underlie observed scores (Watson & Tellegen, 1999; Flora & Curran, 2004; Schmukle & Egloff, 2009). They retain the relative rank order information provided by Pearson correlations (i.e., the same scales will be relatively strong – or weak – predictors of particular diagnoses), but are unaffected by differences in prevalence rates, thereby facilitating cross-diagnosis comparisons. Diagnoses were scored as 0 = *absent*, 1 = *present*, so that positive correlations indicate that higher scores on a scale are associated with an increased likelihood of receiving the diagnosis.

Consistent with the BDI-II/BAI results, indicators of positive mood/well-being showed impressive diagnostic specificity in these data. Across the six analyses, they had a weighted mean correlation of –.50 with diagnoses of major depression; in contrast, their average associations with specific anxiety disorder diagnoses ranged from only –.05 (specific phobia) to –.30 (agoraphobia). Once again, measures of dysphoria, lassitude, and suicidality also showed good specificity in these data. Indicators of dysphoria had a mean correlation of .69 with major depression; their average correlations with specific anxiety disorder diagnoses ranged from .18 (specific phobia) to .44 (GAD). Lassitude symptoms had a mean correlation of .55 with major depression, whereas their average correlations with specific anxiety diagnoses ranged from only .14 (specific phobia) to .32 (panic disorder). Similarly, suicidality symptoms had a mean correlation of .49 with diagnoses of major depression, whereas their average correlations with anxiety diagnoses ranged from only .11 (specific phobia) to .25 (PTSD).

In contrast, the remaining depression symptoms again displayed poor specificity. Insomnia symptoms had very similar mean correlations with major depression (.36), PTSD (.34), panic disorder (.31), and GAD (.28). Similarly, symptoms of appetite loss had a mean correlation of only .35 with major depression; they correlated very similarly with panic disorder (average $r = .32$) and actually had a slightly stronger association with PTSD (mean $r = .38$). Finally, the appetite gain scales displayed weak associations with both depression (mean $r = .17$) and anxiety (rs ranged from only –.09 to .09) diagnoses.

Incremental predictive power   Third, Watson et al. (2008, table 7) reported a series of logistic regression analyses that established the unique, incremental predictive power of individual IDAS scales in relation to *DSM-IV* mood and anxiety disorders. The IDAS scales were the predictors in these analyses; each of six individual *DSM-IV* mood and anxiety disorder diagnoses (major depression, GAD, PTSD, panic disorder, social phobia, OCD) served as criteria in separate analyses. Well-Being contributed significantly to the prediction of major depression (odds ratio = 0.60; 95% confidence interval = 0.45 to 0.80), but did not add to the prediction of any of the anxiety disorders. Among the IDAS depression scales, only Dysphoria added significantly to the prediction of major depression; in contrast to Well-Being, however, Dysphoria also was significantly related to GAD and panic disorder. Thus, Well-Being again showed diagnostic specificity to depression and, in fact, showed greater specificity than formal symptoms of depression.

Social Anxiety/Social Phobia

Associations with Extraversion versus Positive Affect

As stated previously, low positive affect also is consistently related to social anxiety, although the magnitude is weaker than its association with depression. When examining these data, it is helpful to include extraversion, one of the Big Five personality traits that is particularly relevant to social anxiety and that is closely linked to the experience of positive affect. Numerous studies have shown that although extraversion and positive emotionality are clearly related, they are not identical, with most correlations ranging from about .50 to .70 (Watson & Clark, 1992; Watson et al., 1999; Burger & Caldwell, 2000; Lucas & Fujita, 2000). Broadly speaking, extraversion is a multidimensional higher-order trait that includes both positive affectivity and interpersonal facets (Watson & Clark, 1997a). More specifically, Naragon-Gainey, Watson, and Markon (2009) examined the lower-order structure of extraversion in two samples (students and psychiatric patients), and identified four related but distinguishable facets: sociability, positive affectivity, ascendance, and fun-seeking.

Whereas depression tends to be more strongly correlated with positive affect than with extraversion, social anxiety shows the reverse pattern (e.g., Watson, Gamez, & Simms, 2005). Among the mood and anxiety disorders, social phobia consistently has the strongest negative association with extraversion, with correlations typically in the $-.35$ to $-.55$ range (e.g., Trull & Sher, 1994; Bienvenu, Samuels, Costa, Reti, Eaton, & Nestadt, 2004; Watson et al., 2005). The negative relation between social anxiety and positive affect is weaker but still significant: Kashdan (2007) reported a weighted mean correlation of $-.36$ in a meta-analysis of nineteen studies.

Similarly, Watson and Naragon-Gainey (2010, table 3) compared the extraversion scores of individuals with and without major depression and various anxiety disorder diagnoses. As expected, extraversion had its strongest effect size with social phobia ($d = -0.84$). Moreover, extraversion had a stronger association with social phobia than with major depression ($d = -0.52$), GAD ($d = -0.44$), PTSD ($d = -0.30$), and panic disorder ($d = -0.28$). The IDAS Well-Being scale showed the opposite pattern in these data, exhibiting a much stronger association with depression ($d = -0.89$) than with social phobia ($d = -0.31$). Overall, the available data indicate that positive affect and extraversion have relatively specific associations with depression and social anxiety, respectively.

Clarifying the Relation between Social Anxiety and Positive Affect

Given that social phobia is highly comorbid with depression (Watson, 2005, 2009), it is important to examine whether the association between social anxiety and positive affect is largely due to this shared variance. The available evidence indicates that although the magnitude of the association is somewhat weakened, social anxiety remains significantly correlated with positive affect independent of depressive symptoms. Kashdan (2007) analyzed thirteen studies that reported partial correlations between social anxiety symptoms and positive affect, after controlling for depression or related constructs (e.g., negative affect; eleven of these studies controlled specifically for depressive symptoms). The weighted mean partial correlation was $-.21$; although this is weaker than the zero-order meta-analytic correlation ($r = -.36$), it is substantial enough to establish an independent association between social anxiety and positive affect.

To tease apart the unique and shared components of these constructs, Naragon-Gainey et al. (2009) used structural equation modeling to examine each of the four facets of extraversion (including positive affectivity) in relation to social anxiety and depressive symptoms. After controlling for shared variance among these constructs, positive affectivity remained significantly related to social anxiety in two independent samples. Thus, the social anxiety-positive affect association appears to extend beyond comorbidity with depression and beyond shared variance with the interpersonal components of extraversion. Taken together, these results suggest that social anxiety is specifically associated with a positive affect deficit.

Most of the research in this area is based on concurrent reports of social anxiety and positive affect. Two studies by Kashdan and colleagues help to shed light on temporal issues and causal directions, while also controlling for negative affect and depression. In an experience sampling study, Kashdan and Steger (2006) found that socially anxious people reported lower levels of daily positive affect and fewer daily positive events than nonanxious individuals. Furthermore, both socially anxious and nonanxious participants reported lower positive affect on those days they experienced greater social anxiety. In a prospective, three-month longitudinal study, those with high levels of social anxiety subsequently endorsed stable, low levels of positive affect. However, the reverse causal pattern was not supported, in that changes in positive emotions did not predict changes in social anxiety (Kashdan & Breen, 2008).

Finally, there is evidence that the subtypes of social phobia may be differentially related to positive affect. Generalized social phobia consists of anxiety during most or all social interactions, whereas the performance subtype is limited to the fear of being observed by others while performing an action (APA, 2000). Hughes, Heimberg, Coles, Gibb, Liebowitz, & Schneier (2006) found that, after partialing out negative affect, the generalized subtype was associated with low levels of positive affect; in contrast, performance anxiety was unrelated to positive affect. Similarly, Kashdan (2002) reported that positive subjective experiences (a factor on which positive affect loaded highly) continued to be moderately correlated with generalized social anxiety after removing shared variance with the performance subtype; in contrast, the association with performance anxiety became nonsignificant after partialing out generalized social anxiety.

Watson and Naragon-Gainey (2010) presented further data supporting this differential pattern. Specifically, they reported that generalized social anxiety correlated significantly more strongly with positive affect ($r = -.44$) than did performance anxiety ($r = -.31$) in a sample of 204 psychiatric patients. After controlling for negative affect, the partial correlation with generalized social anxiety remained significant ($r = -.26$), whereas the partial correlation with performance anxiety did not ($r = -.08$). Additional studies of these subtypes may provide further insight into the nature of the relation between social anxiety and positive affect.

Schizophrenia/Schizotypy

The Hedonic Deficit in Schizophrenia/Schizotypy

Overview   There has been extensive research on emotional dysfunction in schizophrenia and related disorders (including schizotypy and schizotypal personality), as well as several integrative reviews. The accumulating evidence yields two broad conclusions (Watson & Naragon-Gainey, 2010). First, schizophrenia and schizotypy clearly are associated with a marked deficit in positive affect, although the nature of this deficit differs somewhat from that observed in depression and social anxiety. Second, more limited evidence suggests that this deficit is not as great as that observed in depression. Thus, these data further suggest that low positive affect shows relative specificity to depression.

The expressive deficit   One striking aspect of schizophrenia – which distinguishes it from depression and other disorders – is that it is associated with a specific deficit in emotional expression. That is, individuals with schizophrenia display a reduced capacity to communicate their feelings both facially and vocally. Kring and Moran (2008) reviewed twenty-three studies and concluded:

> Compared to individuals without schizophrenia, individuals with schizophrenia display fewer positive and negative emotional expressions in response to emotionally evocative film clips, foods, and social interactions. Moreover, schizophrenia patients' diminished facial and vocal expression distinguishes them from other patient groups, including individuals with depression. (p. 821)

The experiential deficit   This expressive deficit partly accounts for clinical reports of anhedonia in the disorder (i.e., inexpressiveness can be misinterpreted as flat, constricted affect). Clearly, however, there is an experiential deficit as well. Horan, Blanchard, Clark, and Green (2008) reviewed thirteen studies that compared schizophrenia patients and nonclinical controls on trait measures of neuroticism/negative affectivity and extraversion/positive affectivity. Compared with the nonclinical controls, the schizophrenia patients showed a consistent pattern of higher neuroticism/negative affectivity and lower extraversion/positive affectivity. Nine of the reviewed studies used measures of extraversion, but the remaining four were based on direct indicators of positive affectivity. These four studies reported standardized group differences (Cohen's d) ranging from -0.68 to -0.78 (median $= -0.72$), which reflects a medium effect size. Similarly, Barch, Yodkovik, Sypher-Locke, and Hanewickel (2008) reported a medium-sized difference ($d = -0.61$) in positive affectivity between individuals with schizophrenia and healthy controls.

Positive versus negative symptoms   Multiple studies have shown that self-report measures of schizotypy and schizotypal personality are associated with higher neuroticism/negative affectivity and lower extraversion/positive emotionality (Ross, Lutz, & Bailley, 2002; Kerns, 2006; Chmielewski & Watson, 2008; for a review, see Horan et al., 2008). It is noteworthy, moreover, that neuroticism/negative affectivity is broadly related to both the negative (e.g., constricted affect, social aloofness) and positive (e.g., magical thinking, perceptual aberrations, suspiciousness) symptoms of schizotypy, whereas extraversion/positive emotionality shows greater specificity: it is consistently associated with the former but only weakly related to the latter. For example, Chmielewski and Watson (2008) examined relations between extraversion and five symptom factors derived from the Schizotypal Personality Questionnaire (Raine, 1991); Extraversion correlated strongly with Social Anxiety ($r = -.60$ and $-.62$ at Time 1 and Time 2, respectively), moderately with Social Anhedonia ($r = -.29$ and $-.31$, respectively), and weakly with Eccentricity/Oddity, Mistrust, and Unusual Beliefs and Experiences (rs ranged from only $-.07$ to $.10$).

The anticipatory deficit   Surprisingly, however, individuals with schizophrenia have an undiminished *capacity* to experience pleasure; that is, they show no impairment in positive affect following a pleasant mood induction (interestingly, however, schizotypy scores *are* associated with an hedonic deficit in this paradigm; for discussions of this issue, see Kring & Moran, 2008; A. S. Cohen & Minor, 2010; A. S. Cohen, Callaway, Najolia, Larsen, & Strauss, 2012; Strauss & Gold, 2012). A. S. Cohen and Minor (2010) conducted a meta-analysis of fourteen studies that compared the positive affect levels of (a) patients with schizophrenia versus (b) nonclinical controls in response to positive stimuli. The group difference was small (Hedges $D = -0.16$) and nonsignificant, leading them to conclude that "there was little evidence to suggest that patients were anhedonic in response to laboratory stimuli" (p. 147).

   Why, then, do schizophrenia patients consistently report anhedonia/low positive affect on trait measures (Horan et al., 2008)? There is growing evidence that schizophrenia is associated with an anticipatory pleasure deficit, such that individuals with the disorder do not expect to experience positive affect when engaging in future goal-directed activities (Kring & Moran, 2008; A. S. Cohen & Minor, 2010). For example, Gard, Kring, Gard, Horan, and Green (2007) found that schizophrenia patients anticipated less pleasure from future activities than did healthy controls, particularly in relation to goal-directed activities. Furthermore, this anticipatory deficit was associated with a reduction in goal-directed activity in the schizophrenia group. These results suggest that although individuals with schizophrenia experience normal levels of pleasure in response to rewarding activities, this anticipatory deficit causes them to engage in these activities less frequently, thereby leading to lower overall levels of positive affect.

   In support of this argument, experience-sampling studies suggest that individuals with schizophrenia do report lower levels of positive affect in their everyday lives (Kimhy, Delespaul, Corcoran, Ahn, Yale, & Malaspina, 2006; Gard et al., 2007). Kimhy et al. (2006), for instance, collected repeated mood ratings from ten hospitalized schizophrenia patients and ten healthy controls over the course of a single day. Compared with the controls, the patients reported elevated levels of sadness/depression and loneliness and lower levels of cheerfulness.

Specificity of the Deficit in Relation to Depression

To examine the specificity of this hedonic deficit, however, one must compare (a) patients with schizophrenia versus (b) those with other disorders. Myin-Germeys et al. (2003) reported the best available evidence to date. They obtained experience sampling data from 42 patients with non-affective psychosis (a total of 1,890 momentary assessments), 46 patients with current major depression (2,070 assessments), and 49 healthy controls (2,499 assessments); analyses were based on a three-item measure of positive affect (*happy, cheerful, satisfied*). As would be expected, the schizophrenia group reported substantially lower levels of positive affect (overall mean = 4.4) than the healthy controls (mean = 5.5); using the standard deviation of the psychosis patients, this translates into a *d* of –1.10.

It is important to note, however, that the schizophrenia patients also reported substantially *higher* positive affect than the depressed patients (mean = 2.2; again using the standard deviation of the psychotic patients, this translates into a *d* = 2.20). These results suggest that although schizophrenia is associated with a reduction in positive affect, this hedonic deficit is not as great as that observed in depression. It should be noted, however, that whereas all the depressed patients currently were experiencing an acute episode, most of the schizophrenia patients were (a) in remission and (b) on medication. Thus, these findings very likely exaggerate the true magnitude of the difference between these groups.

Joiner, Brown and Metalsky (2003) compared the BDI scores of 50 patients with major depression and 52 patients with schizophrenia. They created two scales from the BDI, one using three items assessing anhedonic symptoms and the other based on the eighteen remaining items. It is noteworthy that the two groups did not differ significantly on the nonanhedonic items or on the BDI total score. Consistent with the results of Myin-Germeys et al. (2003), however, patients with major depression obtained significantly higher scores on the anhedonia scale than the patients with schizophrenia. Overall, the available data suggest that anhedonia/low positive affect is more strongly linked to depression than to schizophrenia.

Mania

State Associations

Until now, I have examined disorders that are associated with positive mood deficits. I conclude with an examination of the bipolar disorders, which show a very different relation to positive affect (Watson & Naragon-Gainey, 2010). Heightened positive affect is clearly relevant to mania, in that the definition of manic episodes includes "abnormally and persistently elevated, expansive, [or irritable] mood" (APA, 2000, p. 362). Manic symptoms are, in fact, associated with the experience of elevated positive mood, with one daily diary study reporting a strong positive correlation between mean levels of manic symptoms and positive affect over a period of several weeks (r = .54; Meyer & Hofmann, 2005).

Related to this, the expanded IDAS-II (Watson et al., 2012) contains two bipolar symptom scales: Mania (e.g., *It felt like my mind was moving "a mile a minute", I kept racing from one activity to the next*) and Euphoria (e.g., *I felt like I was "on top of the world", I had so much energy it was hard for me to sit still*). Although it clearly has a pathological component, Euphoria is associated with elevated positive affect and correlates strongly with the Well-Being scale that was described earlier (Watson et al., 2012, report an overall correlation of .51 in a large combined sample); thus, it essentially represents a pathological form of positive affect. Euphoria also demonstrates impressive criterion validity (Watson et al., 2012): among the IDAS-II scales, it had the strongest individual associations with both (a) SCID diagnoses of current manic episodes (polychoric r = .47) and (b) the Mania scale (r = .64) from the Interview of Mood and Anxiety Symptoms (IMAS; Gamez, Kotov, & Watson, 2010; Watson et al., 2007, 2012).

Current manic episodes are clearly associated with elevated levels of positive affect, a fact that distinguishes them from most types of psychopathology. Because current mania also is likely to impact ratings of trait positive affect (see Johnson, Gruber, & Eisner, 2007), I emphasize findings in remitted patients or analogues in the following section.

Trait Associations

Self-report data based on trait positive affect scales have yielded mixed results for those at risk for mania. Studies have found that trait positive affect levels among currently remitted individuals diagnosed with bipolar I disorder do not differ from those of normal controls (e.g., Bagby et al., 1996, 1997). Likewise, in a daily diary study, mean levels of daily positive affect over 28 days among those with a lifetime diagnosis of cyclothymia were similar to levels reported by normal controls (Lovejoy & Steuerwald, 1995). However, other results suggest atypical levels of trait positive affect among those with a bipolar disorder or who are at risk for developing a bipolar disorder. For instance, when shown positive, neutral, and negative film clips, those at high risk for mania (as identified using a self-report measure) reported greater levels of positive mood than those at low risk for mania, regardless of the valence of the clip (Gruber, Johnson, Oveis, & Keltner, 2008). In contrast, Gruber, Culver, Johnson, Nam, Keller, & Ketter (2009) reported unexpectedly low levels of positive affect among individuals in recovery from bipolar I or a bipolar spectrum disorder, as compared with normal controls ($d = -1.5$). In interpreting these conflicting results, it should be noted that because individuals with bipolar disorders experience extreme levels of positive affect during mania and depression, their subjective scale for rating positive affect might differ from those who have never been manic (Johnson et al., 2007).

Conclusion

Positive affect shows impressive specificity in its associations with psychopathology. That is, the reviewed data establish that low levels of positive affect are a distinguishing feature of depression, social anxiety, and schizophrenia/schizotypy. Moreover, a more limited range of evidence suggests that indicators of positive affect are more strongly and systematically linked to depression than to these other syndromes. Finally, in marked contrast to these other disorders, indicators of mania tend to be associated with *elevated* levels of positive affect.

However, my review of the literature also reveals some significant limitations of the current evidence. I conclude this chapter by highlighting three basic considerations that should inform future work in this area. First, specificity evidence still is limited in a number of key areas. For instance, very few studies have directly compared the magnitude of the affective deficits in depression and schizophrenia. Although the limited evidence tentatively suggests a greater positive mood deficit in the former compared with the latter, more work is needed before any firm conclusions can be drawn.

Second, this review demonstrates the importance of distinguishing carefully between strongly related – but separable – constructs. For instance, the evidence indicates that depression is more strongly negatively correlated with measures of positive affect than with scales assessing extraversion, whereas social anxiety shows the reverse pattern. Future work in this area will benefit from a more intensive assessment strategy that targets several related constructs within this domain. Moreover, as is demonstrated by the results of Naragon-Gainey et al. (2009), it can be very informative to assess multiple subcomponents within each of these basic constructs (e.g., different facets within extraversion; specific types of positive affect).

Third, future studies should clarify the nature and source of these observed deficits. One particularly crucial issue is the extent to which observed deficits reflect (a) reduced exposure to rewarding activities versus (b) a diminished capacity to experience pleasure in response to such activities. For example, the reviewed evidence suggests that individuals with schizophrenia retain a normal capacity to experience pleasure, but engage in rewarding activities less frequently because of an anticipatory deficit that leads them to underestimate the hedonic value of these activities. How do these processes compare/contrast with those experienced in depression and other disorders? This is a critical question for future research.

Acknowledgments

I thank Kristin Naragon-Gainey for her help in the preparation of this chapter. This research was supported by NIMH Grant R01-MH068472 to David Watson.

References

American Psychiatric Association. (2000). *Diagnostic and statistical manual of mental disorders*, 4th edn., text revision. Washington, DC: APA.

Bagby, R. M., Bindseil, K. D., Schuller, D. R., Rector, N. A., Young, L. T., Cooke, R. G., & Joffe, R. T. (1997). Relationship between the five-factor model of personality and unipolar, bipolar and schizo-phrenic patients. *Psychiatry Research, 70*, 83–94. doi.org/10.1016/S0165-1781(97)03096-5.

Bagby, R. M., Young, L. T., Schuller, D. R., Bindseil, K. D., Cooke, R. G., Dickens, S. E., & Joffe, R. T. (1996). Bipolar disorder, unipolar depression and the five factor model of personality. *Journal of Affective Disorders, 41*, 25–32. doi.org/10.1016/0165-0327(96).00060-2.

Barch, D. M., Yodkovik, N., Sypher-Locke, H., & Hanewickel, M. (2008). Intrinsic motivation in schizo-phrenia: Relationships to cognitive function, depression, anxiety and personality. *Journal of Abnormal Psychology, 117*, 776–787. doi.org/10.1037/a0013944.

Beck, A. T. & Steer, R. A. (1990). *Beck Anxiety Inventory manual*. San Antonio, TX: Psychological Corporation.

Beck, A. T., Steer, R. A., & Brown, G. K. (1996). *Beck Depression Inventory manual*, 2nd edn. San Antonio, TX: Psychological Corporation.

Bienvenu, O. J., Samuels, J. F., Costa, P. T., Reti, I. M., Eaton, W. W., & Nestadt, G. (2004). Anxiety and depressive disorders and the five-factor model of personality: A higher- and lower-order person-ality trait investigation in a community sample. *Depression and Anxiety, 20*, 92–97. doi.org/10.1002/da.20026.

Brown, T. A., Chorpita, B. F., & Barlow, D. H. (1998). Structured relationships among dimensions of the *DSM-IV* anxiety and mood disorders and dimensions of negative affect, positive affect, and autonomic arousal. *Journal of Abnormal Psychology, 107*, 179–192. doi.org/10.1037/0021-843X.107.2.179.

Burger, J. M. & Caldwell, D. F. (2000). Personality, social activities, job-search behavior and interview success: Distinguishing between PANAS trait positive affect and NEO extraversion. *Motivation and Emotion, 24*, 51–62. doi.org/10.1023/A:1005539609679.

Chmielewski, M. & Watson, D. (2008). The heterogeneous structure of schizotypal personality disorder: Item-level factors of the Schizotypal Personality Questionnaire and their associations with obsessive-compulsive disorder symptoms, dissociative tendencies, and norma personality. *Journal of Abnormal Psychology, 117*, 364–376. doi.org/10.1037/0021-843X.117.2.364.

Clark, L. A. & Watson, D. (1991). Tripartite model of anxiety and depression: Psychometric evidence and taxonomic implications. *Journal of Abnormal Psychology, 100*, 316–336. doi.org/10.1037/0021-843X.100.3/316.

Cohen, A. S. & Minor, K. S. (2010). Emotional experience in patients with schizophrenia revisited: Meta-analysis of laboratory studies. *Schizophrenia Bulletin, 36*, 143–150. doi.org/10.1093/schbul/sbn061.

Cohen, A. S., Callaway, D. A., Najolia, G. M., Larsen, J. T., & Strauss, G. P. (2012). On "risk" and reward: Investigating state anhedonia in psychometrically defined schizotypy and schizophrenia. *Journal of Abnormal Psychology, 121*, 407–415. doi.org/10.1037/a0026155.

Cohen, J. (1992). A power primer. *Psychological Bulletin, 112*, 155–159. doi.org/10.1037/0033-2909.112.1.155.

Flora, D. B. & Curran, P. J. (2004). An empirical evaluation of alternative methods of estimation for confirmatory factor analysis with ordinal data. *Psychological Methods, 9*, 466–491. doi.org/10.1037/1082-989X.9.4.466.

Gamez, W., Kotov, R., & Watson, D. (2010). The validity of self-report assessment of avoidance and distress. *Anxiety, Stress & Coping: An International Journal, 23*, 87–99. doi.org/10.1080/10615800802699198.

Gard, D. E., Kring, A. M., Gard, M. G., Horan, W. P., & Green, M. F. (2007). Anhedonia in schizophrenia: Distinctions between anticipatory and consummatory pleasure. *Schizophrenia Research, 93*, 253–260. doi.org/10.1016/schres.2007.03.008.

Gruber, J., Culver, J. L., Johnson, S. L., Nam, J. Y., Keller, K. L., & Ketter, T. A. (2009). Do positive emotions predict symptomatic change in in bipolar disorder? *Bipolar Disorders, 11*, 330 336. doi. org/10 1111/j.1399 5618.2009.00679.x.

Gruber, J., Johnson. S. L., Oveis, C., & Keltner, D. (2008). Risk for mania and positive emotional responding: Too much of a good thing? *Emotion, 8*, 23–33. doi.org/10.1037/1528-3542.8.1.23.

Horan, W. P., Blanchard, J. J., Clark, L. A., & Green, M. F. (2008). Affective traits in schizophrenia and schizotypy. *Schizophrenia Bulletin, 34*, 856–874. doi.org/10.1093/schbul/sbn083.

Hughes, A. A., Heimberg, R. G., Coles, M. E., Gibb, B. E., Liebowitz, M. R., & Schneier, F. R. (2006). Relations of the factors of the tripartite model of anxiety and depression to types of social anxiety. *Behaviour Research and Therapy, 44*, 1629–1641. doi.org/10.1016/j.brat.2005.10.015.

Johnson, S. L., Gruber, J., & Eisner, L. R. (2007). Emotion and bipolar disorder. In: J. Rottenberg & S. L. Johnson (Eds.), *Emotion and psychopathology: Bridging affective and clinical science* (pp. 123–150). Washington, DC: American Psychological Association.

Joiner, T. E., Brown, J. S., & Metalsky, G. I. (2003). A test of the tripartite model's prediction of anhedonia's specificity to depression: Patients with major depression versus patients with schizophrenia. *Psychiatry Research, 119*, 243–250. doi.org/10.1016/S0165 1781(03)00131 8.

Jolly, J. B., Dyck, M. J., Kramer, T. A., & Wherry, J. N. (1994). Integration of positive and negative affectivity and cognitive content-specificity: Improved discrimination of anxious and depressive symptoms. *Journal of Abnormal Psychology, 103*, 544–552. doi.org/10.1037/0021-843X.103.3.544.

Kashdan, T. B. (2002). Social anxiety dimensions, neuroticism, and the contours of positive psychological functioning. *Cognitive Therapy and Research, 26*, 789–810. doi.org/10.1023/A:1021293501345.

Kashdan, T. B. (2007). Social anxiety spectrum and diminished positive experiences: Theoretical synthesis and meta-analysis. *Clinical Psychology Review, 27*, 348–365. doi.org/10.1016/j.cpr.2006.12.003.

Kashdan, T. B. & Breen, W. E. (2008). Social anxiety and positive emotions: A prospective examination of a self-regulatory model with tendencies to suppress or express emotions as a moderating variable. *Behavior Therapy, 39*, 1–12. doi.org/10.1016/j.beth.2007.02.003.

Kashdan, T. B. & Steger, M. F. (2006). Expanding the topography of social anxiety: An experience-sampling assessment of positive emotions, positive events, and emotion suppression. *Psychological Science, 17*, 120–128. doi.org/10.1111/j.1467-9280.2006 01674.x.

Kerns, J. G. (2006). Schizotypy facets, cognitive control, and emotion. *Journal of Abnormal Psychology, 115*, 418–427. doi.org/10.1037/0021-843X.115.3.418.

Kimhy, D., Delespaul, P., Corcoran, C., Ahn, H., Yale, S., & Malaspina, D. (2006). Computerized experience sampling method (ESMc): Assessing feasibility and validity among individuals with schizophrenia. *Journal of Psychiatric Research, 40*, 221–230. doi.org/10.1016/j.jpsychires.2005.09.007.

Kotov, R., Gamez, W., Schmidt, F., & Watson, D. (2010). Linking "big" personality traits to anxiety, depressive, and substance use disorders: A meta-analysis. *Psychological Bulletin, 136*, 768–821. doi.org/10.1037/a0020327.

Kring, A. M. & Moran, E. K. (2008). Emotional response deficits in schizophrenia: Insights from affective science. *Schizophrenia Bulletin, 34*, 819–834. doi.org/10.1093/schbul/sbn071.

Lovejoy, M. C. & Steuerwald, B. L. (1995). Subsyndromal unipolar and bipolar disorders: Comparisons on positive and negative affect. *Journal of Abnormal Psychology, 104*, 381–384. doi.org/10.1037/0021-843X.104.2.381.

Lucas, R. E. & Fujita, F. (2000). Factors influencing the relation between extraversion and positive affect. *Journal of Personality and Social Psychology, 79*, 1039–1056. doi.org/10.1037/0022-3514.79.6.1039.

Meyer, T. D. & Hofmann, B. U. (2005). Assessing the dysregulation of the behavioral activation system: The Hypomanic Personality Scale and the BIS-BAS Scales. *Journal of Personality Assessment, 85*, 318–324. doi.org/10.1207/s15327752jpa8503_08.

Mineka, S., Watson, D., & Clark, L. A. (1998). Comorbidity of anxiety and unipolar mood disorders. *Annual Review of Psychology, 49*, 377–412. doi.org/10.1146/annurev.psych.49.1.377.

Myin-Germeys, I., Peeters, F., Havermans, R., Nicolson, N. A. deVries, M. W., Delespaul, P., & van Os, J. (2003). Emotional reactivity to daily life stress in psychosis and affective disorder: An experience sampling study. *Acta Psychiatrica Scandinavica, 107*, 124–131. doi.org/10.1034/j.1600-0447.2003.02025.x.

Naragon-Gainey, K., Watson, D., & Markon, K. (2009). Differential relations of depression and social anxiety symptoms to the facets of extraversion/positive emotionality. *Journal of Abnormal Psychology, 118*, 299–310. doi.org/10.1037/a0015637.

Raine, A. (1991). The SPQ: A scale for the assessment of schizotypal personality based on *DSM-III-R* criteria. *Schizophrenia Bulletin, 17*, 555–564. doi.org/10.1093/schbul/17.4.555.

Ross, S. R., Lutz, C. J., & Bailley, S. E. (2002). Positive and negative symptoms of schizotypy and the five-factor model: A domain and facet-level analysis. *Journal of Personality Assessment, 79*, 53–72. doi.org/10.1207/S15327752JPA7901_04.

Schmukle, S. C. & Egloff, B. (2009). Exploring bipolarity of affect ratings by using polychoric correlations. *Cognition and Emotion, 23*, 272–295. doi.org/10.1080/02699930801987330.

Strauss, G. P. & Gold, J. M. (2012). A new perspective on anhedonia in schizophrenia. *American Journal of Psychiatry, 169*, 364–373. doi.org/10.1176/appi.ajp.2011.11030447.

Trull, T. J. & Sher, K. J. (1994). Relationship between the five-factor model of personality and Axis I disorders in a nonclinical sample. *Journal of Abnormal Psychology, 103*, 350–360. doi.org/10.1037/0021-843X.103.2.350.

Watson, D. (2005). Rethinking the mood and anxiety disorders: A quantitative hierarchical model for *DSM-V*. *Journal of Abnormal Psychology, 114*, 522–536. doi.org/10.1037/0021-843X.114.4.522.

Watson, D. (2009). Differentiating the mood and anxiety disorders: A quadripartite model. *Annual Review of Clinical Psychology, 5*, 221–247.

Watson, D. & Clark, L. A. (1992). On traits and temperament: General and specific factors of emotional experience and their relation to the five-factor model. *Journal of Personality, 60*, 441–476.

Watson, D. & Clark, L. A. (1997a). Extraversion and its positive emotional core. In: R. Hogan, J. Johnson, & S. Briggs (Eds.), *Handbook of personality psychology* (pp. 767–793). San Diego, CA: Academic Press.

Watson, D. & Clark, L. A. (1997b). Measurement and mismeasurement of mood: Recurrent and emergent issues. *Journal of Personality Assessment, 68*, 267–296.

Watson, D. & Clark, L. A. (1999). *The PANAS-X: Manual for the Positive and Negative Affect Schedule-Expanded Form*, retrieved from University of Iowa, Department of Psychology, available at: http://www.psychology.uiowa.edu/Faculty/Watson/Watson.html.

Watson, D., Clark, L. A., & Carey, G. (1988). Positive and negative affectivity and their relation to anxiety and depressive disorders. *Journal of Abnormal Psychology, 97*, 346–353. doi.org/10.1037/0021-843X.97.3.346.

Watson, D., Clark, L. A., & Stasik, S. M. (2011). Emotions and the emotional disorders: A quantitative hierarchical perspective. *International Journal of Clinical and Health Psychology, 11*, 429–442.

Watson, D., Gamez, W., & Simms, L. J. (2005). Basic dimensions of temperament and their relation to anxiety and depression: A symptom-based perspective. *Journal of Research in Personality, 39*, 46–66.

Watson, D. & Naragon-Gainey, K. (2010). On the specificity of positive emotional dysfunction in psycho-pathology: Evidence from the mood and anxiety disorders and schizophrenia/schizotypy. *Clinical Psychology Review, 30*, 839–848.

Watson, D., O'Hara, M. W., Chmielewski, M., McDade-Montez, E. A., Koffel, E., Naragon, K., & Stuart, S. (2008). Further validation of the IDAS: Evidence of convergent, discriminant, criterion, and incremental validity. *Psychological Assessment, 20*, 248–259. doi.org/10.1037/a0012570.

Watson, D., O'Hara, M. W., Naragon-Gainey, K., Koffel, E., Chmielewski, M., Kotov, R., Ruggero, C. J. (2012). Development and validation of new anxiety and bipolar symptom scales for an expanded version of the IDAS (the IDAS-II). *Assessment, 19*, 399–420.

Watson, D., O'Hara, M. W., Simms, L. J., Kotov, R., Chmielewski, M., McDade-Montez, E., Gamez, W., & Stuart, S. (2007). Development and validation of the Inventory of Depression and Anxiety Symptoms (IDAS). *Psychological Assessment, 19*, 253–268. doi.org/10.1037/1040-3590.19.3.253.

Watson, D. & Stasik, S. M. (2014). Examining the comorbidity between depression and the anxiety disorders from the perspective of the quadripartite model. In: C. S. Richards & M. W. O'Hara (Eds.), *The Oxford handbook of depression and comorbidity* (pp. 46–65). New York: Oxford University Press.

Watson, D. & Tellegen, A. (1985). Toward a consensual structure of mood. *Psychological Bulletin, 98*, 219–235.

Watson, D. & Tellegen, A. (1999). Issues in the dimensional structure of affect – effects of descriptors, measurement error, and response formats: Comment on Russell and Carroll (1999). *Psychological Bulletin, 125,* 601–610. doi.org/10.1037/0033-2909.125.5.601.

Watson, D., Wiese, D., Vaidya, J., & Tellegen, A. (1999). The two general activation systems of affect: Structural findings, evolutionary considerations, and psychobiological evidence. *Journal of Personality and Social Psychology, 76,* 820–838. doi.org/10.1037/0022-3514.76.5.820.

Widiger, T. A. & Costa, P. T., Jr. (1994). Personality and the personality disorders. *Journal of Abnormal Psychology, 103,* 78–91.

6

Resilience
The Bi-Dimensional Framework
Judith Johnson

Introduction

Positive clinical psychology is a new area of research that aims to integrate findings from positive psychology and clinical psychology in order to move both these fields forward (Wood & Tarrier, 2010; Johnson & Wood, 2016). This chapter will consider the topic of resilience, which is a popular term and concept in each of these areas, but one that has been poorly defined and understood. Indeed, although a range of terms have been used to describe it, including "psychological resilience," "emotional resilience," "mental toughness," and "hardiness," conclusive definitions have been elusive. In general, there seems to be a consensus that resilience refers to an ability of an individual to show reduced evidence of negative outcomes, or maintained evidence of positive outcomes, in the face of difficult circumstances or experiences. However, there are no clear criteria that a proposed resilience variable must meet in order to be recognized as conferring resilience. The impact of this has been that different concepts of resilience have been investigated using a wide range of methodologies, and have therefore been difficult to compare and review. Because of this, different strands of resilience research have remained largely disparate, preventing the field from moving forward toward more developed and refined concepts of resilience.

The present chapter aims to (1) provide a brief overview of the development of two influential areas of resilience research, and (2) to then contribute to this field by presenting a framework for investigating resilience, the Bi-Dimensional Framework (Johnson, Wood, Gooding, Taylor, & Tarrier, 2011b; Johnson & Wood, 2016). The Bi-Dimensional Framework outlines a set of criteria by which to test whether psychological variables confer resilience.

First, it is suggested that in order to understand resilience, we must also measure risk. This view has been proposed by previous researchers in the field (e.g., Masten & Powell, 2003) and is widely accepted. However, the current framework extends this view by proposing that resilience must be understood as a construct that arises out of the *interaction* of resilience factors and risk factors. That is, resilience factors must be those that act to moderate or buffer the impact of risk upon the development of negative outcomes.

Second, this framework suggests that previous resilience research has been limited by a need to define resilience as a positive variable. Based on the observation that all positive variables have an inverse that is negative, and vice versa, it is proposed that this criterion for defining resilience is redundant. Instead, it is suggested resilience can best be understood as a spectrum with both negative and positive poles, and a lack of a positive resilience factor is likely to have negative implications for an individual. This definition of resilience was utilized by a review of research into resilience to suicidality (Johnson, Wood, Gooding, Taylor, & Tarrier, 2011b), where it was

The Wiley Handbook of Positive Clinical Psychology, First Edition. Edited by Alex M. Wood and Judith Johnson.
© 2016 John Wiley & Sons, Ltd. Published 2016 by John Wiley & Sons, Ltd.

found to enable a new perspective on suicide resilience and to generate new suggestions for future research in the area. It seems that a view of resilience which incorporates both positive and negative poles may represent a more accurate and promising perspective.

By providing a set of standards against which to test proposed resilience variables, the Bi-Dimensional Framework provides a means by which to compare and review proposed resilience variables. By enabling the comparison of proposed and tested resilience variables, it is hoped that this framework will help the field of resilience research move toward more refined and developed concepts of resilience.

Origins

The importance of resilience is now widely appreciated. Despite this, it is a relatively new area of psychological research which has largely developed within the past 50 years. Here, a brief overview will be provided of two of the most influential areas of resilience research.

Resilience in Development

One strand of early resilience research focused on populations of children considered to be facing high levels of risk. This area of research began to flourish in the 1970s, at a time when developmental theories emphasizing the importance of early experiences (e.g., Bowlby, 1958) were dominant. In contrast to these ideas, resilience research highlighted the prevalent capacity of individuals to overcome stressors experienced in early life and show healthy patterns of development. Several researchers have been credited as being "pioneers" in this area, including Lois Murphy, Michael Rutter, Emmy Werner and Norman Garmezy (Vernon, 2004).

Researchers investigating resilience from this perspective were interested in identifying the factors that enabled individuals to show this ability to adapt and adjust. The dominant approach taken by these researchers was to identify groups of children considered to be at high risk, and to measure factors that predicted healthy patterns of development. For example, in one seminal study Emmy Werner and Ruth Smith followed a cohort of 698 children growing up in the Hawaiian Island of Kauai from before birth and at ages 1, 2, 10, 18, 32 and 40 (Werner & Smith, 2001). Around a third of this cohort was identified as being at high risk due to exposure to multiple risk factors before the age of 2. Of this subgroup, it was noted that a third showed evidence of healthy development at age 18 despite their high-risk status. These children were distinguished from the remaining two-thirds of the subgroup by having an "easy" temperament, higher self-confidence, and higher levels of social play (Werner, 1990, 1995). Similarly, in a highly influential series of studies conducted entitled "Project Competence," Norman Garmezy, together with colleagues such as Ann Masten and Auke Tellegen, investigated those factors that were associated with positive outcomes in the face of risk. For example, one Project Competence study focused on a community sample of 200 children (Garmezy, Masten, & Tellegen, 1984). Although these children were not considered high risk per se, risk was estimated by asking parents for information regarding each child's exposure to a range of risk factors such as life stress. Analyses investigated whether proposed resilience variables could predict behavioral outcomes in addition to, and in interaction with, reported risk measures. Results suggested that high IQ and high socioeconomic status were predictive of one of the outcomes of interest, although no factors appeared to interact with measures of stress (Garmezy et al., 1984).

In general, researchers in this area have tended to stress that resilience should be viewed as a process involving the individual and their surrounding context, rather than a personality construct or fixed individual trait (e.g., Rutter, 1985; Masten, Best, & Garmezy, 1990). Because of this premise, much research in this area has focused on the impact of family and community-level variables, as well as psychological variables. For example, work by Michael Rutter investigated the development of women raised in the care of social services and found that a positive school environment could be an important protective factor (Rutter & Quinton, 1984). The social focus of this research, combined with the long follow-up periods of several studies (e.g., Rutter & Quinton, 1984; Werner & Smith, 2001), has led this area of resilience to have a high level of external validity, and relevance for the fields of politics, social work, and education. For the field of mental health, this research provided evidence to suggest that mental health disorders were not genetically or biologically predetermined, but that the causality of such disorders was complex, and likely to be social and psychological as well as biological in origin. At the time this research was being conducted such views were not widely accepted, and these studies can be credited with helping the field of mental health move toward its current, more holistic understanding of mental and emotional disorders.

However, despite this influence, findings from this area of research suffer from limitations. One of these is the variation and lack of clarity regarding the criteria for what represents a "resilient" outcome. Researchers in this area have used a wide range of both risk and outcome measures which vary in quality, and challenge the internal validity of studies. Another considerable limitation is the lack of a framework for the investigation of resilience. Research in this area has generally understood resilience to be the capacity to produce good outcomes in the face of risk or adversity, which would suggest the need to investigate resilience using a "buffering" model, where proposed resilience factors would be expected to moderate the likelihood that risk will lead to a negative outcome. However, the methodologies used by many of the studies in this area have not demonstrated this, and theoretical thinking in this area has viewed this as only one of several possible approaches to investigating resilience (Garmezy et al., 1984; Masten, 2001).

Hardiness

As resilience research from a developmental perspective became more established in the 1980s, an alternative approach to resilience research also began to emerge. This focused on resilience in relation to stress and health and centered on the concept of "Hardiness," proposed by Suzanne Kobasa (1979). The research into Hardiness can be viewed as an investigation into a personality-based concept of resilience. In particular, the construct of Hardiness was based on existential personality theory, and defined as a set of characteristics that enable individuals to resist the negative impact of stressors (Kobasa, Maddi, & Kahn, 1982). Hardiness has generally been viewed as consisting of three subfacets, Commitment, Control, and Challenge (Kobasa, 1979; Maddi, 2002). Commitment refers to a predisposition to be engaged and involved with others and the surrounding environment; Control describes a tendency to try and take control of the surrounding environment and events; and Challenge refers to a propensity to view potentially difficult events as challenges rather than threats (Maddi, 2002). There has been contention surrounding the Challenge subfacet, with some research suggesting it may have poor predictive validity in relation to health outcomes, and weak psychometric properties (Funk & Houston, 1987; Hull, Van Treuren, & Virnelli, 1987). Although more recent measures of Hardiness were designed to address these issues (e.g., Maddi & Khoshaba, 2001) it still seems to be the weakest predictor of a range of outcomes of the three subfacets (e.g., Eschleman, Bowling, & Alarcon, 2010).

Early studies set out to test whether Hardiness was protective against stress. For example, in the first study in the area, Kobasa (1979) compared a group of executives who had experienced high levels of stress and fallen ill with a group of executives who had experienced high levels of stress but maintained health. Results suggested that the group who had maintained health reported holding a greater degree of hardy attitudes (Kobasa, 1979). Later studies sought to examine Hardiness in relation to a wider range of outcomes such as occupational performance (e.g., Rich & Rich, 1987), and mental health (e.g., Florian, Mikulincer, &

Taubman, 1995; Harrisson, Loiselle, Duquette, & Semenic, 2002), and to explore associations between hardiness and coping styles (e.g., Williams, Wiebe, & Smith, 1992; Crowley, Hayslip, & Hobdy, 2003). These studies have found Hardiness to be positively associated with reduced levels of burnout at work (Rich & Rich, 1987), reduced mental distress in the face of stressors (Florian et al., 1995; Harrisson et al., 2002), and more adaptive use of coping strategies (Williams et al., 1992; Crowley et al., 2003).

Research into Hardiness can be credited with helping to advance understanding in the areas of stress and health. As Maddi (2002) describes, when the concept of Hardiness was first introduced, there was a burgeoning appreciation for the negative impact of stress, but a confusion surrounding how to approach and manage this. The research conducted into Hardiness has confirmed this association between stress and health, but explained that this relationship varies according to psychological factors, in particular those attitudes described as Hardiness. This has led to both an understanding that stress can be managed, and the development of interventions designed to improve Hardiness and well-being (Maddi, Kahn, & Maddi, 1998).

Thus, the Hardiness literature has advanced understanding of resilience in relation to the fields of occupational and health psychology. However, this literature suffers from two main limitations. The first limitation concerns the lack of development surrounding the concept of Hardiness. This concept was based on existential personality theory and initially proposed by Kobasa (1979) over 30 years ago. Since this time, there has been a dramatic increase in knowledge regarding the cognitions, coping strategies, appraisal styles, and other psychological factors which support well-being and stress management. Despite this, the concept of Hardiness has been relatively static and has not sought to incorporate this wide range of research findings.

The second limitation is shared with the literature investigating resilience from a developmental perspective, and refers to the lack of a framework for testing Hardiness. Similar to the concept of resilience in the developmental literature, Hardiness is viewed as a factor or set of factors which enable individuals to resist the negative impact of stress (Maddi, 2002), and, as such, would be expected to be a buffer or moderator of the association between stress and negative outcomes. However, much research into Hardiness has failed to recognize the need to investigate and establish the presence of moderation effects. Indeed, some studies have instead either tested for direct associations between Hardiness and the outcome or tested Hardiness as a mediator of the association between stress and outcome (e.g., Kobasa, Maddi, & Courington, 1981; Garmezy et al., 1984). Mediators do not impact the relationship between two variables, but rather provide an explanation for the relationship. As such, studies of mediation provide no evidence that a variable confers resilience or acts as a buffer. Furthermore, amongst those studies which have investigated Hardiness as a moderator of stress, findings have been equivocal. Whereas some studies have found evidence that Hardiness buffers the association between risk and outcomes (Waysman, Schwarzwald, & Solomon, 2001; Klag & Bradley, 2004), others have not supported this (Tang & Hammontree, 1992; Heckman & Clay, 2005). This challenges the view that Hardiness does indeed provide resistance to stress, but this has not been recognized by many researchers in the field.

Limitations in the Current Literature

These areas of resilience research have generated a large amount of interest in the topic, and there is now a considerable body of literature describing factors and processes which appear to have a positive impact on the well-being of individuals exposed to risk or difficult circumstances. However, these areas of resilience research have suffered from limitations, most notably from the lack of a framework for testing whether a proposed variable confers resilience.

This lack of a guiding framework has led to confusion concerning the criteria that need to be met in order to establish that a factor confers resilience. Because of this there has been a wide range of analytical approaches taken to investigating potential resilience factors. Much of this research has investigated resilience as a direct correlate of outcome scores. This has been based on the view that resilience is a positive factor or constellation of positive factors, and an inverse association with a negative outcome provides evidence of resilience. However, this has led to a difficulty distinguishing how resilience factors differ from risk factors. This is because every factor has an inverse or opposite and, when using this approach, low levels of a proposed risk factor could be described as resilience. For example, whereas some researchers have described higher levels of substance use as a risk factor for violent behavior (Dahlberg, 1998), others have described abstaining from substance use as a resilience factor (McKnight & Loper, 2002).

One way to resolve this difficulty could be to suggest that resilience factors are internal characteristics and risk factors are those factors that are external. This resolution would be consistent with the research into Hardiness, which has viewed resilience as a personality construct and has tended to research this in relation to stressors that are viewed as external (e.g., Kobasa, 1979; Kobasa et al., 1981; Florian et al., 1995). However, research suggests that many factors that are considered to be external, such as life events, are to some extent influenced by qualities of the individual, and cannot be assumed to have occurred entirely randomly (Eschleman et al., 2010). Furthermore, some of the strongest risk factors for negative outcomes are known to be internal, for example, depression and hopelessness are known to be some of the most consistent and reliable predictors of suicidality (e.g., Beck, Steer, Kovacs, & Garrison, 1985; Beck, Brown, Berchick, Stewart, & Steer, 1990; Hawton, Sutton, Haw, Sinclair, & Harriss, 2005). It could be suggested that individuals may have other psychological constructs which could prevent feelings of hopelessness or depression from leading to suicidality. However, when a framework for resilience requires risk factors to be external, it is not possible to investigate such research questions.

In summary then, it is suggested that: (1) correlational research cannot provide evidence of resilience, but instead can only suggest whether a proposed factor increases or decreases risk; and (2) distinguishing risk and resilience factors based solely on the criterion that resilience is internal and risk is external is both inaccurate and limiting. Here, we will present the Bi-Dimensional Framework for resilience (Johnson et al., 2011b), which aims to outline criteria for resilience that can overcome these limitations. The framework was first introduced for the study of resilience to suicide. Here, it will be presented and adapted for the study of resilience research more generally.

The Bi-Dimensional Framework for Resilience

The Bi-Dimensional Framework outlines three main criteria for variables to be viewed as conferring resilience. First, it suggests that resilience must be viewed as constituting a separate dimension to risk, which acts to moderate or buffer the impact of risk on negative outcomes. Second, both risk and resilience should be understood as bipolar dimensions. That is, each risk factor also has an inverse that can be viewed as positive and protective, and each resilience factor has an inverse that can be understood as negative, amplifying the effect of risk. For this reason, concepts of resilience should not view it as a purely positive factor, but understand it as a spectrum incorporating both positive and negative possibilities. Third, the Bi-Dimensional Framework suggests that resilience factors need to be understood as internal characteristics.

Resilience and Risk as Separate Dimensions

The first and most integral part of the framework concerns the need to distinguish resilience factors from risk factors. In order to make this distinction, it is suggested that research needs to go beyond the investigation of basic bivariate associations and examine interactions between variables. This is because evidence of direct associations between proposed resilience factors and outcome variables can only demonstrate whether the factor increases or decreases risk of the outcome. For example, abstaining from substance misuse could be described as a resilience factor for developing antisocial behavior (McKnight & Loper, 2002), but this could simply be because it represents low levels of a risk factor, namely, substance misuse. If this is the case, substance abstinence does not represent resilience as such, but simply reduced risk. In order to be understood as conferring resilience, the Bi-Dimensional Framework suggests that a factor needs to demonstrate evidence of *attenuating, moderating,* or *buffering* the strength of the association between risk and outcome.

In many ways, this suggestion is consistent with the direction in which resilience research appears to be moving, as it is becoming increasingly common in the literature to investigate interactions when researching potential resilience variables. However, there is a lack of clarity surrounding the extent to which it should be considered *necessary* to establish an interaction effect to demonstrate the presence of resilience, and some researchers have viewed this as one of several approaches to investigating resilience, rather than a required criterion (e.g., Masten, 2001). Furthermore, it is unclear whether any form of interaction can be considered to demonstrate resilience, or whether a particular pattern of interaction is necessary to show a buffering effect. The Bi-Dimensional Framework provides clarity on this issue by suggesting that a resilience factor should become active when individuals are experiencing increased high risk, and act to reduce the likelihood of negative outcomes. Conversely, when levels of risk are low, resilience could be expected to be dormant. Thus, for individuals experiencing low levels of risk, there should be minimal difference in reported distress (or other negative outcome) between those reporting high versus low resilience. However, for individuals facing high risk, there should be a marked difference in distress dependent upon level of resilience (see Figure 6.1).

The Bi-Dimensional Framework suggests that resilience can be understood as a separate dimension to risk which interacts with it to reduce its negative impact (see Figure 6.2). For individuals experiencing low levels of risk, there is no causal factor driving the likelihood of negative outcomes, so resilience factors may be dormant. However, for individuals experiencing increased exposure to adversity, high levels of resilience may act as a barrier, rendering the relationship between risk and negative outcomes weak. Conversely, for individuals exposed to increased risk with lower levels of resilience, the barrier protecting from the impact of risk is

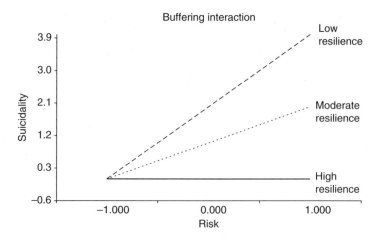

Figure 6.1 Hypothetical resilience interaction. For individuals with high levels of resilience, the association between risk and suicidality is reduced. Reprinted from Johnson, Wood, Gooding, Taylor, & Tarrier, "Resilience to suicidality: The buffering hypothesis," *Clinical Psychology Review* (2011), vol. *31*(4), pp. 563–591, with permission from Elsevier.

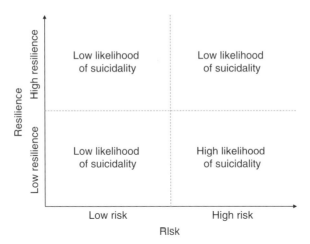

Figure 6.2 Risk and resilience as separate dimensions. Reprinted from Johnson, Wood, Gooding, Taylor, & Tarrier, "Resilience to suicidality: The buffering hypothesis," *Clinical Psychology Review* (2011), vol. 31(4), pp. 563–591, with permission from Elsevier.

lower, and the likelihood of negative outcomes could be expected to be increased. In this way, the bi-dimensional view of resilience and risk proposes that individuals can be understood as occupying one of four basic quadrants dependent upon their levels of risk and resilience (depicted by Figure 6.2).

This suggests that it is necessary to measure three parameters in order to ascertain presence of resilience: (1) risk or adversity, (2) the proposed resilience variable, and (3) the outcome variable. Again, to some extent this is consistent with previous thinking in this area. For example, Masten and Powell (2003) suggest that two judgments are necessary to ascertain resilience. The first of these is evidence that an individual is coping or "doing okay," and the second is that the individual is facing adversity. However, the Bi-Dimensional Framework extends this by suggesting that the first of these judgments should be viewed as containing two parameters. The first parameter is the evidence of coping defined by outcome, for example, a reduction in the likelihood of a negative outcome. The second parameter is what we would understand as resilience, and this is the buffering or moderating factor that attenuates the impact of the risk factor to lead to the outcome.

Resilience and Risk as Bipolar Dimensions

To sum up, the first proposal of the Bi-Dimensional Framework is that risk and resilience are separate dimensions. Extending this, the second proposal is that both these dimensions are bipolar. This is based on the observation that each risk factor has an inverse or opposite that can be understood as being positive or reducing risk, and each resilience factor has an inverse that can be understood as negative, amplifying risk. For example, loneliness could be described as a risk factor that *increases* the likelihood of suicidality, or social support could be described as a protective factor that *reduces* the likelihood of suicidality (e.g., Bonner & Rich, 1990; Stravynski & Boyer, 2001; Jeglic, Pepper, Vanderhoff, & Ryabchenko, 2007). Whether these dimensions are viewed as positive or negative is essentially arbitrary as both dimensions have positive and negative poles (see Figure 6.3). This suggests that concepts of resilience should instead view it as a spectrum, recognizing that low levels of proposed positive resilience factors are likely to have a negative impact for an individual experiencing stress, and low levels of negative risk factors are

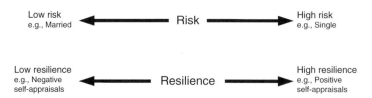

Figure 6.3   Risk and resilience as separate bipolar dimensions. Reprinted from Johnson, Wood, Gooding, Taylor, & Tarrier, "Resilience to suicidality: The buffering hypothesis," *Clinical Psychology Review* (2011), vol. *31*(4), pp. 563–591, with permission from Elsevier.

likely to lead to more positive outcomes. The Bi-Dimensional Framework suggests that individuals considered to be high on risk factors can also be described as being low on protective factors, and individuals considered to be high on resilience factors can also be described as having low levels of amplifying factors (see Figure 6.3).

This proposal deviates from the implicit, underlying assumption of much previous resilience research which has viewed risk factors as primarily negative factors, and resilience factors as primarily positive factors. Indeed, the fact that a variable is considered to be "positive" or to reflect positive processes has previously appeared to be the main defining quality of factors considered to constitute resilience. However, as Masten, Best and Garmezy (1990) note, this has led to a problem in distinguishing between studies of resilience and studies of cumulative risk. To return to the example above, a study could examine the predictive value of a variable called "social support" in addition to risk variables, and describe the research as investigating resilience. Alternatively, the same study could instead call the same variable "loneliness" and describe the study as investigating cumulative risk.

The Bi-Dimensional Framework suggests, then, that resilience variables should be identified by their ability to buffer the impact of other variables which increase likelihood of negative outcomes. Previous views of resilience and risk have been limited by suggesting that resilience factors need to be positive, and risk factors need to be negative. By understanding that all risk and resilience factors are spectrums with both positive and negative poles, the Bi-Dimensional Framework may lead to more accurate and comprehensive views of resilience. However, by proposing that both resilience and risk factors have positive and negative poles, it may become unclear which variables in an interaction constitute risk and which constitute resilience. Because of this, it is necessary to outline additional criteria by which to determine whether a factor can be viewed as resilience or risk.

Resilience as an Internal Characteristic

The Bi-Dimensional Framework suggests that risk factors can be any factor, either internal or external, that directly increase or decrease the likelihood of a particular outcome. Risk is a broad category, then, and any negative outcome is likely to have many risk factors. By contrast, the framework suggests that resilience factors are much narrower in scope. First, as discussed above, they are factors that must moderate or buffer the impact of a risk factor or risk factors upon the negative outcome of interest. Furthermore, the framework suggests that these factors need to be internal characteristics of the unit under study. For example, if you are interested in the resilience of families, resilience factors must be internal characteristics of the family unit, rather than the family's context or setting. Where the "unit" is an individual, resilience must be understood as a psychological construct. This framework takes this view for three main reasons. First, it is consistent with much previous research; second, it is consistent with the generally held understanding of resilience amongst psychologists (Cohen, Pooley, Ferguson, &

Harms, 2011); and, third, it is consistent with wider definitions of resilience in other areas of research (e.g., Seybold, Herrick, & Brejda, 1999; Brand & Jax, 2007; Haimes, 2009). In general, resilience is a term used to refer to the quality of an entity or object which enables it to withstand or quickly recover from the impact of negative external forces. Most research into resilience has focused on the individual, and in this case, it would be congruent to define resilience as a psychological capability or construct.

It should be noted that some previous researchers have preferred to describe resilience as a process between internal characteristics and the setting or context (Rutter, 1987; Masten et al., 1990). However, the Bi-Dimensional Framework seeks to extend these views by suggesting that although external factors are likely to influence resilience, they cannot be viewed as constituting resilience. That is, it is possible that external factors may support or denigrate the development of resilience (Almeida, 2005), but they are influences upon resilience rather than resilience itself.

Strengths of the Framework

The Bi-Dimensional Framework does not describe or support any particular concept of resilience, but instead outlines a method by which to (a) investigate new concepts of resilience, and (b) evaluate existing research into resilience. This approach has three main strengths.

1. It is inductive and bottom-up When investigating the concept of resilience, the framework requires the researcher to first identify the outcome or risk factor of interest, and then to work from this towards identifying particular buffers. Previously, resilience research has often taken a more top-down approach, proposing a resilience concept and then investigating the range of situations in which this seems to confer resilience. Because it begins with the proposed resilience concept and seeks to apply this to risk factors and outcomes, this prevents the concept itself from being refined. By contrast, the Bi-Dimensional Framework provides a method by which to aggregate research into resilience in relation to particular negative outcomes or risk factors. By facilitating this review process, the Bi-Dimensional Framework could enable evidence-based, more refined concepts of resilience to be developed.

2. It is flexible The Bi-Dimensional Framework is flexible and able to adapt to a range of potential risk and resilience factors. Because of this, it can be applied to a range of situations and used to develop broad, comprehensive views of risk and resilience factors relevant for particular outcomes.

3. It overcomes jargon The criteria outlined by the framework enable the identification of resilience variables based on their nature (e.g., psychological) and their function (i.e., their ability to moderate or buffer the impact of risk on outcome), rather than the terminology used to describe them. That is, these criteria transcend the various terms that have been used in the literature to describe resilience, such as "hardiness," "adaptive coping," and "mental toughness," and provide researchers with a common framework for interpreting studies from each of these literatures. This is useful when (a) aggregating and reviewing studies of resilience against a particular risk factor or negative outcome, and (b) developing new concepts of resilience.

Research using the Bi-Dimensional Framework

The Bi-Dimensional Framework was originally developed to guide research investigating resilience to suicidality. One of the benefits of this approach is its flexibility, and it has been used to guide both questionnaire research and experimental studies in this area. Studies that have applied this framework to questionnaire research have now found evidence to suggest that an individual's positive self-beliefs regarding their ability to solve problems, cope with emotions, and gain social support may moderate the association between risk factors and suicidality (Johnson, Gooding, Wood, & Tarrier, 2010a; Johnson et al., 2010b). In particular, these types of positive belief have been found to buffer the association between negative life events and suicidality in a nonclinical population (Johnson et al., 2010a), and to buffer the association between hopelessness and suicidality amongst individuals with a diagnosis of schizophrenia (Johnson et al., 2010b).

Two studies have applied this framework to experimental research investigating trait reappraisal, which refers to a tendency to try to control emotions by controlling thought processes (Johnson, Gooding, Wood, Taylor, & Tarrier, 2011a). This research was interested in investigating whether trait reappraisal acted to buffer or to amplify the impact of an experience of failure on subsequent feelings of defeat, an emotion linked to suicidality. All participants completed a measure of trait reappraisal and subjective defeat at baseline before taking part in a task. Half of the participants were allocated to the "success" condition, where the task was easy and they gained a high score, but the other half were allocated to a "failure" condition, where the task was extremely difficult and the score they gained was extremely low. Results suggested that all participants in the "failure" condition felt more defeated than participants in the "success" condition following the task. However, there was an interaction which suggested that participants with higher levels of trait reappraisal were particularly vulnerable to the effects of the fixed failure task. This pattern was found amongst both clinical and nonclinical participants. According to the Bi-Dimensional Framework, these results can be viewed as suggesting that a reduced tendency to control emotions by controlling thoughts may confer resilience upon individuals. Previously, the value of this research for exploring resilience may not have been recognized, but when resilience variables are viewed as bipolar, it becomes clear how factors which moderate risk – either by buffering or amplifying risk – can further our understanding of resilience.

More recent work has applied the framework to investigate resilience in relation to paranoia, a prevalent and important symptom of psychosis (Johnson, Jones, Lin, Wood, Heinze, & Jackson, 2014). This research was conducted amongst young adults using mental health services, and found that the extent to which individuals experienced shame moderated the association between stressful life events and paranoia. High shame amplified the association, and low shame was a buffer, suggesting that individuals who are not prone to feeling shame are likely to be resilient to experiencing paranoia when under stress (Johnson et al., 2014).

The Bi-Dimensional Framework as a Tool to Interpret Existing Studies

One of the strengths of the Bi-Dimensional Framework is that it is not limited to being a guide for new research, it can also be used as a tool for interpreting, aggregating, and reviewing existing studies. For example, one review has used this approach to investigate resilience to suicidality (Johnson et al., 2011b). This review found that when the criteria outlined by the framework were used to identify relevant studies for review, studies that had claimed to investigate resilience had in fact only investigated direct associations, and could not be included. Conversely, studies that had investigated interactions involving at least one psychological variable had not viewed themselves as investigating resilience, although their findings had implications for understandings of resilience. Any search that included only relevant labels for resilience, such as "resilience," "hardiness," or "coping" would have missed these studies. By using criteria to define resilience which concern the methodological approach taken rather than the researchers' interpretation of their study and findings, the Bi-Dimensional Framework was able to identify and review psychological variables that conferred resilience, but had not necessarily been viewed as relevant to resilience research. For example, the review found evidence suggesting that more positive attributional styles and a higher sense of agency buffered the impact of risk on suicidality.

Furthermore, there was evidence that higher levels of hopelessness and perfectionism were both amplifiers of risk, suggesting that lower levels of these psychological constructs can confer resilience. By taking an approach that incorporated both positive and negative factors, it was possible to move toward a more comprehensive understanding of resilience in the area of suicidality.

Resilience and Positive Clinical Psychology

The study of resilience is the study of factors that seem to buffer individuals from negative outcomes in the face of stress; it is the investigation of what people do that means they carry on when others are unable to cope. As such, it is clear why this topic is so popular amongst both positive psychologists, who want to focus on what people do "right," and clinical psychologists, who want to know how they can help to stop things going "wrong" for their clients. It is the very heart of resilience to look at both the "positive" and the "negative" in tandem; to recognize that there is a complex interplay between stressors, risk factors, and individual qualities. Resilience, then, is likely to be a key concept in the developing field of Positive Clinical Psychology, which is focused upon drawing together research findings from these two fields (Wood & Tarrier, 2010; Johnson & Wood, 2016). The Bi-Dimensional Framework may be a useful tool in this endeavor, particularly as it can be used to identify and aggregate studies which have tested resilience factors, even if they have not been described in this way by the researchers. Indeed, a range of so-called "positive" psychological variables have been tested as resilience variables in relation to mental health outcomes, according to the framework. For example, both hope and optimism have been found to reduce the likelihood that rumination, a known risk factor for a range of psychological disorders, will lead to suicidal ideation (Tucker et al., 2013). Similarly, gratitude has been found to buffer against the development of depression in response to financial strain (Krause, 2009), and authenticity has been found to buffer against the development of depression in response to low social support. Self-compassion, a construct that comprises self-kindness, feelings of common humanity, and mindfulness, has been found to confer resilience against depression in response to burn-out (Woo Kyeong, 2013) and against loss of functioning in response to stressful menopausal symptoms (Brown, Bryant, Brown, Bei, & Judd, 2014).

One of the observations underpinning both Positive Clinical Psychology and the Bi-Dimensional Framework for resilience is that no variable is purely positive, or purely negative, and that all variables exist on a continuum from positive and negative. When this is considered, it is interesting to note that some studies from a clinical perspective have investigated similar concepts as resilience factors, albeit at the other end of the continuum. For example, shame, which can be viewed as the inverse of self-compassion (i.e., rejection of the self rather than acceptance) has been found to amplify mental health problems in response to abuse (Beck et al., 2011; Shorey et al., 2011), and hopelessness, the inverse of hope, is one of the most consistent amplifiers of suicidality in response to risk factors (Johnson et al., 2011b). This suggests that the two fields may have more in common than initial appearances would suggest, and that an integrative, positive clinical psychology approach would be beneficial for researchers developing concepts of resilience.

Resilience in Clinical Practice

The Bi-Dimensional Framework may initially appear to be a research-oriented, technical approach to understanding resilience, but it could have some important implications for psychological formulation, intervention, and risk assessment. In line with the literature, recent years have seen a growing emphasis on the discussion of "resilience" factors amongst psychological therapists, which have generally been viewed as being simply "positive variables," for example, the presence of social support or evidence of past coping ability. These factors tend to be viewed as optional add-ons to psychological formulations, as a way of recognizing client strengths and offering a more positive slant to things. However, as has been outlined in this chapter, the Bi-Dimensional Framework instead suggests that rather than being "positive" or "negative" factors (as, indeed, every factor exists on a continuum from positive to negative), resilience factors are *buffers of risk*. That is, compared with factors with an additive effect on the outcome variable, for every unit level of change, resilience factors should have a greater impact. Another way to describe this, is that resilience factors can be viewed as "switches" that "turn down" the impact of risk. Rather than being an optional add-on to a psychological formulation, then, resilience factors could unlock both the reasons why a client may be vulnerable to life stressors or other risk factors, and also to indicate the point at which to target interventions aimed at preventing relapse. For example, evidence that positive self-appraisals buffer the association between life stress and suicidal ideation (Johnson et al., 2010a) would suggest that low levels of positive self-appraisal would put an individual at higher risk of suicidal ideation, and that developing more positive self-appraisals with these clients could help to prevent suicidal ideation occurring in the face of future stressful events. Knowledge of buffers and amplifiers of risk may be particularly important when working with clients with risk factors that are difficult or impossible to change. For example, those that are related to gender, age, socioeconomic, or relationship status. For these clients, working to develop resilience factors may be an important route for reducing the risk of negative outcomes (or, indeed, increasing the likelihood of things "going well").

This research may also have implications for clinical risk assessments, which are notoriously difficult, particularly when the negative outcome the assessment is focused upon is rarer (such as suicide) (Gangwisch, 2011). For example, when risk assessing with a client currently experiencing low levels of stress, it can be difficult to estimate how they will respond should their situation change. An assessment of relevant resilience factors could be used to inform this prediction, as this should indicate the extent to which a person is likely to be "buffered" or resilient to subsequent stressful events.

Where Next? The Bi-Dimensional Framework for Studying Team Resilience

To date, the Bi-Dimensional Framework has been used as an approach for investigating resilience at the level of the individual (i.e., psychological resilience). However, it could also be applied to research investigating resilience at the group level, such as families or teams. Here, rather than looking at psychological resilience, the research would focus on internal characteristics of the group, for example, if the group of interest were teams, this might be team communication, cohesion or functioning.

Healthcare Teams

This possibility is particularly interesting in relation to healthcare. In the United Kingdom, for example, the healthcare system is facing growing demands from an ageing, sicker population (National Health Service, 2014), and it is likely to become increasingly more important that healthcare teams are able to deliver high quality, safe care when under pressure. However, it is currently unclear which factors lead a team to be "resilient," or able to deliver high quality care when demands vary, and how this "resilience" might be developed. A burgeoning area of research has begun to consider these questions, and propose qualities and factors that resilient healthcare teams, systems, and organizations demonstrate (Hollnagel, Braithwaite, & Wears, 2013), but there is a need for more empirical research in this area. The Bi-Dimensional Framework could be used to test some of these proposed resilience variables. For example, Hollnagel (2010) suggests that resilient healthcare organizations are those with the ability to (1) respond to variation in demands, (2) monitor what is happening, (3) anticipate future events, and (4) learn from experience. Using the framework, it would be possible to test one or more of these variables using a multilevel modelling design. For example, staff across a range of comparable teams (e.g., inpatient ward teams) could be asked to complete measures of (a) stressors (e.g., staffing ratios, complexity of patients' healthcare needs, increases in demand), and (b) proposed team resilience variables (e.g., team learning and ability to adapt). Outcome variables could then be sought at the team level, such as the occurrence of adverse events on the ward, or the patient perceived quality of care. This data could then be analyzed to investigate whether the proposed resilience variables moderate the association between reported stressors and the outcome variables at team level. Such research could help to identify which factors enable teams to withstand stress, and the ways in which teams could be supported to provide a high level of care both in ideal circumstances, and also when demands vary.

Conclusion

This chapter has aimed to give a brief overview of the development of resilience research and some of its achievements to date. It has highlighted some of the limitations of the existing literature and outlined the need for a set of criteria by which to test whether a proposed factor confers resilience. The Bi-Dimensional Framework offers such a set of criteria. These criteria overcome limitations in the existing literature, and importantly, they highlight the importance of viewing resilience factors as existing on a continuum with both positive and negative poles. All positive factors have an inverse that is negative, and vice versa: A lack of a positive factor is likely to have negative implications, and a lack of a negative factor is likely to have positive implications. The Bi-Dimensional Framework offers a way to integrate findings from both positive psychology and clinical psychology research when building concept of resilience, and in this way may be a useful tool for the emerging field of Positive Clinical Psychology.

Acknowledgments

I would like to thank Christopher Jackson and Christopher Jones for their feedback on an earlier draft of this chapter.

References

Almeida, D. M. (2005). Resilience and vulnerability to daily stressors assessed via diary methods. *Current Directions in Psychological Science, 14,* 64–68.

Beck, A. T., Brown, G., Berchick, R. J., Stewart, B. L., & Steer, R. A. (1990). Relationship between hopelessness and ultimate suicide: a replication with psychiatric outpatients. *American Journal of Psychiatry, 147,* 190–195.

Beck, A. T., Steer, R. A., Kovacs, M., & Garrison, B. (1985). Hopelessness and eventual suicide: A 10-year prospective study of patients hospitalized with suicidal ideation. *American Journal of Psychiatry, 142,* 559–563.

Beck, J. G., McNiff, J., Clapp, J. D., Olsen, S. A., Avery, M. L., & Hagewood, J. H. (2011). Exploring negative emotion in women experiencing intimate partner violence: shame, –Bonner, R. L. & Rich, A. R. (1990). Psychosocial vulnerability, life stress, and suicide ideation in a jail population: A cross-validation study. *Suicide and Life Threatening Behavior, 20*, 213–224.

Bowlby, J. (1958). The nature of the child's tie to his mother. *International Journal of Psychoanalysis, 39*, 350–373.

Brand, F. S. & Jax, K. (2007). Focusing the meaning(s) of resilience: Resilience as a descriptive concept and a boundary object. *Ecology and Society, 12*(1), 23.

Brown, L., Bryant, C., Brown, V. M., Bei, B., & Judd, F. K. (2014). Self-compassion weakens the association between hot flushes and night sweats and daily life functioning and depression. *Maturitas, 78*, 298–303.

Cohen, L., Pooley, J. A., Ferguson, C., & Harms, C. (2011). Psychologists' understandings of resilience: Implications for the discipline of psychology and psychology practice. *Australian Community Psychology, 23*, 7–22.

Crowley, B. J., Hayslip, B., Jr., & Hobdy, J. (2003). Psychological hardiness and adjustment to life events in adulthood. *Journal of Adult Development, 10*, 237–248.

Dahlberg, L. L. (1998). Youth violence in the United States: Major trends, risk factors, and prevention approaches. *American Journal of Preventive Medicine, 14*, 259–272.

Eschleman, K. J., Bowling, N. A., & Alarcon, G. M. (2010). A meta-analytic examination of hardiness. *International Journal of Stress Management, 17*, 277–307.

Florian, V., Mikulincer, M., & Taubman, O. (1995). Does hardiness contribute to mental health during a stressful real-life situation? The roles of appraisal and coping. *Journal of Personality and Social Psychology, 68*, 687–695.

Funk, S. C. & Houston, B. (1987). A critical analysis of the Hardiness Scale's validity and utility. *Journal of Personality and Social Psychology, 53*, 572–578.

Gangwisch, J. E. (2011). Suicide risk assessment. *International Journal of Clinical Review, 1*, 04.

Garmezy, N., Masten, A. S., & Tellegen, A. (1984). The study of stress and competence in children: A building block for developmental psychopathology. *Child Development, 55*, 97–111.

Haimes, Y. Y. (2009). On the definition of resilience in systems. *Risk Analysis, 29*, 498–501.

Harrisson, M., Loiselle, C. G., Duquette, A., & Semenic, S. E. (2002). Hardiness, work support and psychological distress among nursing assistants and registered nurses in Quebec. *Journal of Advanced Nursing, 38*, 584–591.

Hawton, K., Sutton, L., Haw, C., Sinclair, J., & Harriss, L. (2005). Suicide and attempted suicide in bipolar disorder: A systematic review of risk factors. *Journal of Clinical Psychiatry, 66*, 693–704.

Heckman, C. J. & Clay, D. L. (2005). Hardiness, history of abuse and women's health. *Journal of Health Psychology, 10*, 767–777.

Hollnagel, E. (2010). *How resilient is your organisation? An introduction to the Resilience Analysis Grid (RAG)*. Toronto, Canada.

Hollnagel, E., Braithwaite, J., & Wears, R. L. (2013). *Resilient health care*. Farnham: Ashgate.

Hull, J. G., Van Treuren, R. R., & Virnelli, S. (1987). Hardiness and health: A critique and alternative approach. *Journal of Personality and Social Psychology, 53*, 518–530.

Jeglic, E. L., Pepper, C. M., Vanderhoff, H. A., & Ryabchenko, K. A. (2007). An analysis of suicidal ideation in a college sample. *Archives of Suicide Research, 11*, 41–56.

Johnson, J., Gooding, P. A., Wood, A. M., & Tarrier, N. (2010a). Resilience as positive coping appraisals: Testing the schematic appraisals model of suicide (SAMS). *Behaviour Research and Therapy, 48*, 179–186.

Johnson, J., Gooding, P. A., Wood, A. M., Taylor, P. J., Pratt, D., & Tarrier, N. (2010b). Resilience to suicidal ideation in psychosis: Positive self-appraisals buffer the impact of hopelessness. *Behaviour Research and Therapy, 48*, 883–889.

Johnson, J., Gooding, P. A., Wood, A. M., Taylor, P. J., & Tarrier, N. (2011a). Trait reappraisal amplifies subjective defeat, sadness, and negative affect in response to failure versus success in nonclinical and psychosis populations. *Journal of Abnormal Psychology, 120*, 922–934.

Johnson, J., Jones, C., Lin, A., Wood, S., Heinze, K., & Jackson, C. (2014). Shame amplifies the association between stressful life events and paranoia amongst young adults using mental health services: Implications for understanding risk and psychological resilience. *Psychiatry Research, 220*, 217–225.

Johnson, J. & Wood, A. M. (2016). Integrating positive and clinical psychology: Viewing human functioning as continua from positive to negative can benefit clinical assessment, interventions and understandings of resilience. *Cognitive Therapy and Research.*

Johnson, J., Wood, A. M., Gooding, P., Taylor, P. J., & Tarrier, N. (2011b). Resilience to suicidality: The buffering hypothesis. *Clinical Psychology Review, 31*, 563–591.

Klag, S. & Bradley, G. (2004). The role of hardiness in stress and illness: An exploration of the effect of negative affectivity and gender. *British Journal of Health Psychology, 9*, 137–161.

Kobasa, S. C. (1979). Stressful life events, personality, and health: An inquiry into hardiness. *Journal of Personality and Social Psychology, 37*, 1–11.

Kobasa, S. C., Maddi, S. R., & Courington, S. (1981). Personality and constitution as mediators in the stress–illness relationship. *Journal of Health and Social Behavior, 22*, 368–378.

Kobasa, S. C., Maddi, S. R., & Kahn, S. (1982). Hardiness and health: A prospective study. *Journal of Personality and Social Psychology, 42*, 168–177.

Krause, N. (2009). Religious involvement, gratitude, and change in depressive symptoms over time. *International Journal for the Psychology of Religion, 19*, 155–172.

Maddi, S. R. (2002). The story of hardiness: Twenty years of theorizing, research, and practice. *Consulting Psychology Journal: Practice and Research, 54*, 173–185.

Maddi, S. R., Kahn, S., & Maddi, K. L. (1998). The effectiveness of hardiness training. *Consulting Psychology Journal: Practice and Research, 50*, 78–86.

Maddi, S. R. & Khoshaba, D. M. (2001). *Personal views survey*, 3rd edn., rev. Newport Beach, CA: The Hardiness Institute.

Masten, A. S. (2001). Ordinary magic: Resilience processes in development. *American Psychologist, 56*, 227–238.

Masten, A. S., Best, K. M., & Garmezy, N. (1990). Resilience and development: Contributions from the study of children who overcome adversity. *Development and Psychopathology, 2*, 425–444.

Masten, A. S. & Powell, J. L. (2003). A resilience framework for research, policy, and practice. In: S. S. Luthar (Ed.), *Resilience and vulnerability: Adaptation in the context of childhood adversities* (pp. 1–25). New York: Cambridge University Press.

McKnight, L. R. & Loper, A. B. (2002). The effect of risk and resilience factors on the prediction of delinquency in adolescent girls. *School Psychology International, 23*, 186–198.

National Health Service. (2014). *Five year forward view.* London: HM Government.

Rich, V. L. & Rich, A. R. (1987). Personality hardiness and burnout in female staff nurses. *Journal of Nursing Scholarship, 19*, 63–66.

Rutter, M. (1985). Resilience in the face of adversity: Protective factors and resistance to psychiatric disorder. *British Journal of Psychiatry, 147*, 598–611.

Rutter, M. (1987). Psychological resilience and protective mechanisms. *American Journal of Orthopsychiatry, 57*, 316–331.

Rutter, M. & Quinton, D. (1984). Long-term follow-up of women institutionalized in childhood: Factors promoting good functioning in adult life. *British Journal of Developmental Psychology, 2*, 191–204.

Seybold, C. A., Herrick, J. E., & Brejda, J. J. (1999). Soil resilience: A fundamental component of soil quality. *Soil Science, 164*, 224–234.

Shorey, R. C., Sherman, A. E., Kivisto, A. J., Elkins, S. R., Rhatigan, D. L., & Moore, T. M. (2011). Gender differences in depression and anxiety among victims of intimate partner violence: The moderating effect of shame proneness. *Journal of Interpersonal Violence, 26*, 1834–1850.

Stravynski, A. & Boyer, R. (2001). Loneliness in relation to suicide ideation and parasuicide: A population-wide study. *Suicide and Life-Threatening Behavior, 31*, 32–40.

Tang, T. L. & Hammontree, M. L. (1992). The effects of hardiness, police stress, and life stress on police officers' illness and absenteeism. *Public Personnel Management, 21*, 493–510.

Tucker, R. P., Wingate, L. R., O'Keefe, V. M., Mills, A. C., Rasmussen, K., Davidson, C. L., & Grant, D. M. (2013). Rumination and suicidal ideation: The moderating roles of hope and optimism. *Personality and Individual Differences, 55*, 606–611.

Vernon, R. F. (2004). A brief history of resilience: From early beginnings to current constructions. In: C. S. Clauss-Ehlers & M. D. Weist (Eds.), *Community planning to foster resilience in children* (pp. 13–26). New York: Kluwer Academic/Plenum.

Waysman, M., Schwarzwald, J., & Solomon, Z. (2001). Hardiness: An examination of its relationship with positive and negative long term changes following trauma. *Journal of Traumatic Stress, 14,* 531–548.

Werner, E. E. (1990). Protective factors and individual resilience. In: S. J. Meisels (Ed.), *Handbook of early childhood intervention* (pp. 97–116). New York: Cambridge University Press.

Werner, E. E. (1995). Resilience in development. *Current Directions in Psychological Science, 4,* 81–85.

Werner, E. E. & Smith, R. S. (2001). *Journeys from childhood to midlife: Risk, resilience, and recovery.* New York: Cornell University Press.

Williams, P. G., Wiebe, D. J., & Smith, T. W. (1992). Coping processes as mediators of the relationship between hardiness and health. *Journal of Behavioral Medicine, 15,* 237–255.

Woo Kyeong, L. (2013). Self-compassion as a moderator of the relationship between academic burn-out and psychological health in Korean cyber university students. *Personality and Individual Differences, 54,* 899–902.

Wood, A. M. & Tarrier, N. (2010). Positive clinical psychology: A new vision and strategy for integrated research and practice. *Clinical Psychology Review, 30,* 819–829.

7

Self-Efficacy

A Foundational Concept for Positive Clinical Psychology

James E. Maddux and Evan M. Kleiman

What is Self-Efficacy?

A Very Brief History

Although the term "self-efficacy" is of relatively recent origin, interest in beliefs about personal control has a long history in philosophy and psychology. Spinoza, David Hume, John Locke, William James, and (more recently) Gilbert Ryle have all struggled with understanding the role of "volition" and "the will" in human behavior (Russell, 1945; Vessey, 1967). The theories of effectance motivation (White, 1959), achievement motivation (McClelland, Atkinson, Clark, & Lowell, 1953), social learning (Rotter, 1966), and helplessness (Abramson, Seligman, & Teasdale, 1978) are just a few of the many theories that have sought to explore relationships between perceptions of personal competence and human behavior and psychological well-being (see also Skinner, 1995; Molden & Dweck, 2006). Bandura's 1977 article, however, formalized the notion of perceived competence as "self-efficacy," defined it clearly, and embedded it in a theory of how it develops and influences human behavior.

Defining Self-Efficacy

A good way to understand self-efficacy is to distinguish it from related concepts. Self-efficacy is not perceived skill, but rather perceptions of what can be done with one's skill. It is not concerned with beliefs about the ability to perform specific and trivial motor acts, but rather with the beliefs that one can coordinate and orchestrate skills and abilities in changing and challenging situations. Self-efficacy is not concerned with what someone believes they *will* do, but about what someone believes they *can* do. Self-efficacy beliefs are not casual attributions. Casual attributions involve explanations for behavior that caused an event; self-efficacy involves the belief of capability for behavior. Self-efficacy beliefs are not intentions to behave or intentions to attain a particular goal. An intention is what you say you will probably do; and research has shown that intentions are influenced by a number of factors, including, but not limited to, self-efficacy beliefs (Maddux, 1999a).

Self-efficacy is not self-esteem. Self-esteem involves beliefs about other's ratings of self-worth. Efficacy beliefs contribute to self-esteem only in direct proportion to the importance placed on that domain. Self-efficacy is not a motive, drive, or need for control. An individual may have a

The Wiley Handbook of Positive Clinical Psychology, First Edition. Edited by Alex M. Wood and Judith Johnson.
© 2016 John Wiley & Sons, Ltd. Published 2016 by John Wiley & Sons, Ltd.

strong need for control in a particular domain and still hold weak beliefs about their efficacy for that domain. Self-efficacy beliefs are not outcome expectancies (Bandura, 1997) or behavior–outcome expectancies (Maddux, 1999b). A behavior–outcome expectancy is the belief that a specific behavior may lead to a specific outcome in a specific situation. A self-efficacy belief is the belief about the ability to perform the behavior or behaviors that produce the outcome. Self-efficacy is not a personality trait. It is a set of beliefs about the ability to coordinate skills and abilities to attain desired goals in specific domains. Measures of "general" self-efficacy have been developed (e.g., Sherer, Maddux, Mercandante, Prentice-Dunn, Jacobs, & Rogers, 1982; Tipton & Worthington, 1984; Chen, Gully, & Eden, 2001) and are used frequently in research, but they have not been as useful as more specific self-efficacy measures in predicting what people will do under more specific circumstances (Bandura, 1997; Maddux, 1995).

Are Self-Efficacy Beliefs Causes of Behavior?

Because the importance of self-efficacy beliefs depends on the assumption that they have some causal impact, this issue will be addressed first. Bandura and Locke (2003) summarized the findings of nine large meta-analyses conducted on work-related performances in both laboratory and field studies, psychosocial functioning in children and adolescents, academic achievement and persistence, health functioning, athletic performance, laboratory studies in which self-efficacy beliefs were altered experimentally, and collective efficacy in groups. According to Bandura and Locke (2003), "the evidence from these meta-analyses is consistent in showing that efficacy beliefs contribute significantly to the level of motivation and performance" (p. 87) (See Bandura & Locke, 2003, for a more in-depth discussion of this research.)

Where do Self-Efficacy Beliefs come From?

Understanding how self-efficacy beliefs develop requires understanding a the broader theoretical of social cognitive theory – an approach to understanding human cognition, action, motivation, and emotion that assumes that we are active shapers of rather than simply passive reactors to our environments (Barone, Maddux, & Snyder, 1997; Bandura, 2001, 2006; Molden & Dweck, 2006). Social cognitive theory's four basic premises, shortened and simplified, are:

1 We have powerful cognitive capabilities that allow for the creation of internal models of experience, the development of innovative courses of action, the hypothetical testing of such courses of action through the prediction of outcomes, and the communication of complex ideas and experiences to others. We also can engage in self-observation and can analyze and evaluate our own behavior, thoughts, and emotions. These self-reflective activities set the stage for self-regulation.
2 Environmental events, inner personal factors (cognition, emotion, and biological events), and behaviors are interactive influences. We respond cognitively, effectively, and behaviorally to environmental events. Also, through cognition we exercise control over our own behavior, which then influences not only the environment but also our cognitive, affective, and biological states.
3 "Self" and "personality" are socially embedded. They are perceptions (accurate or not) of our own and others' patterns of social cognition, emotion, and action as they occur in patterns of situations. Thus, self and personality are not simply what we bring to our inter-actions with others; they are created in these interactions, and they change through these interactions.

4 We are capable of self-regulation. We choose goals and regulate our behavior in the pursuit of these goals. At the heart of self-regulation is our ability to anticipate or develop expectancies – to use past knowledge and experience to form beliefs about future events and states and beliefs about our abilities and behavior.

These assumptions suggest that the early development of self-efficacy beliefs is influenced primarily by two interacting factors. First, it is influenced by the development of the capacity for symbolic thought, understanding cause–effect relationships, self-observation, and self-reflection. The development of a sense of personal agency begins in infancy and moves from the perception of the causal relationship between events, to an understanding that actions produce results, to the recognition that they can be the origin of actions that effect their environments. As children's understanding of language increases, so do their capacity for symbolic thought and, therefore, their capacity for self-awareness and a sense of personal agency (Bandura, 1997).

Second, the development of efficacy beliefs is influenced by the responsiveness of environments to the infant's or child's attempts at manipulation and control. Environments that are responsive to the child's actions facilitate the development of efficacy beliefs, whereas nonresponsive environments retard this development. The development of efficacy beliefs encourages exploration, which in turn enhances the infant's sense of agency. The child's social environment (especially parents) is usually the most important part of his or her environment. Thus, children usually develop a sense of efficacy from engaging in actions that influence the behavior of other people, which then generalizes to the nonsocial environment (Bandura, 1997).

Efficacy beliefs and a sense of agency continue to develop throughout the life span as we continually integrate information from five primary sources: performance experiences, vicarious experiences, imagined experiences, verbal persuasion, and physiological/emotional states.

Performance Experiences

Our own attempts to control our environments are the most powerful source of self-efficacy information (Bandura, 1997). Successful attempts at control that you attribute to your own efforts will strengthen self-efficacy for that behavior or domain. For example, if a professor gets strong ratings of teaching effectiveness from their students, and if they attribute those ratings to their abilities as a teacher (versus luck or easily pleased students), then their self-efficacy beliefs for teaching will probably be strengthened. Likewise, perceptions of failure that they attribute to lack of ability usually weaken self-efficacy beliefs.

Vicarious Experiences

Self-efficacy beliefs are influenced by our observations of the behavior of others and the consequences of those behaviors. We use this information to form expectancies about our own behavior and its consequences, depending on the extent to which we believe that we are similar to the person we are observing. Vicarious experiences generally have weaker effects on self-efficacy expectancy than do performance experiences (Bandura, 1997).

Imagined Experiences

We can influence self-efficacy beliefs by imagining ourselves or others behaving effectively or ineffectively in hypothetical situations. Such images may be derived from actual or vicarious experiences with situations similar to the one anticipated, or they may be induced by verbal persuasion, as when a psychotherapist guides a client through interventions, such as systematic desensitization and covert modeling (Williams, 1995). Simply imagining yourself doing something well, however, is not likely to have as strong an influence on your self-efficacy as will an actual experience (Williams, 1995).

Verbal Persuasion

Efficacy beliefs are influenced by what others say to us about what they believe we can or cannot do. The potency of verbal persuasion as a source of self-efficacy expectancies will be influenced by such factors as the expertness, trustworthiness, and attractiveness of the source, as suggested by decades of research on verbal persuasion and attitude change (e.g., Eagly & Chaiken, 1993). Verbal persuasion is a less potent source of enduring change in self-efficacy expectancy than performance experiences and vicarious experiences.

Physiological and Emotional States

Physiological and emotional states influence self-efficacy when we learn to associate poor performance or perceived failure with aversive physiological arousal and success with pleasant feeling states. When you become aware of unpleasant physiological arousal, you are more likely to doubt your competence than if your physiological state were pleasant or neutral. Likewise, comfortable physiological sensations are likely to lead me to feel confident in my ability in the situation at hand. Physiological indicants of self-efficacy expectancy, however, extend beyond autonomic arousal. For example, in activities involving strength and stamina, such as exercise and athletic performances, perceived efficacy is influenced by such experiences as fatigue and pain (e.g., Brown, Joscelyne, Dorfman, Marmar, & Bryant, 2012.)

Why is Self-Efficacy Important to Positive Clinical Psychology?

Fully describing the many ways that self-efficacy beliefs are important to positive clinical psychology would take hundreds of pages. We will focus on four areas: self-efficacy and self-regulation; self-efficacy and psychological adjustment; self-efficacy and physical health; self-efficacy and psychological interventions.

Self-Efficacy and Self-Regulation

All the effects of self-efficacy flow from its role in self-regulation, including the role that self-efficacy plays in psychological problems and successful psychological interventions. Almost all psychological problems can be conceived in terms of self-regulatory difficulties of breakdowns: behavioral, cognitive, and emotional. In addition, regardless of what happens during a psychotherapy session, the success of the intervention depends on the clients capacity to implement cognitive, emotional, and behavioral changes strategies in his or her everyday life – which requires good self-regulation skills.

Because self-regulation refers to a set of "processes by which people control their thoughts, feelings, and behaviors" (Hoyle, 2006, p. 1507), understanding self-regulation consists of not just understanding who self-regulates well and who does not: "stable tendencies to self-regulate in particular ways or with characteristic levels of success or failure" (Hoyle, 2006, p. 1508). It consists also of understanding the process of self-regulation or how people self-regulate. A social cognitive approach to self-regulation is concerned specifically with understanding this process, not simply measuring individual differences in general self-regulatory ability (Cervone, Shadel, Smirth, &

Fiori, 2006; Karoly, 2010). A social cognitive approach assumes that self-regulation consists of a set of skills that can be learned and improved with practice, while recognizing that people differ in the capacity for mastering these skills because of differences in personality and to some extent biology (e.g., effortful control, Eisenberg, Valiente, & Eggum, 2010; conscientiousness, McCrae & Löckenhoff, 2010).

Social cognitive theory views self-regulation as consisting largely of "proactive discrepancy production by adoption of goal challenges working in concert with reactive discrepancy reduction in realizing them" (Bandura & Locke, 2003, p. 87). By setting goals, people produce discrepancies between where they are and where they would like to be, and then work to reduce these discrepancies by striving to attain their goals. They then mobilize their resources and efforts based on what they believe is needed to accomplish those goals (Bandura & Locke, 2003).

Self-efficacy beliefs influence self-regulation in several ways (Locke & Latham, 1990; Bandura, 1997; Bandura & Locke, 2003). First, they influence the goals people choose and the tasks they decide to tackle. The higher one's self-efficacy in a specific domain, the loftier the goals that one sets in that domain (e.g., Tabernero & Wood, 2009).

Second, self-efficacy beliefs influence people's choices of goal-directed activities, allocation of resources, effort, persistence in the face of challenge and obstacles, and reactions to perceived discrepancies between goals and current performance (Bandura, 1997; Bandura & Locke, 2003; Vancouver, More, & Yoder, 2008). In the face of difficulties, people with weak self-efficacy beliefs easily develop doubts about their ability to accomplish the task at hand, whereas those with strong efficacy beliefs are more likely to continue their efforts to master a task when difficulties arise. Perseverance usually produces desired results, and this success then strengthens the individual's self-efficacy beliefs.

Third, self-efficacy for solving problems and making decisions influences the efficiency and effectiveness of problem solving and decision-making. When faced with complex decisions, people who have confidence in their ability to solve problems are able to think more clearly and make better decisions than do people who doubt their cognitive skills (e.g., Bandura, 1997). Such efficacy usually leads to better solutions and greater achievement. In the face of difficulty, people with high self-efficacy are more likely to remain task-diagnostic and to search for solutions to problems. Those with low self-efficacy, however, are more likely to become self-diagnostic and reflect on their inadequacies, which distract them from their efforts to assess and solve the problem (Bandura, 1997).

Most of the research on the effect of self-efficacy on self-regulation suggests that "more is better" – that is, the higher one's self-efficacy, the more effective one's self-regulation in pursuit of a goal. But can self-efficacy be "too high"? Perhaps so, in at least three ways. First, as Bandura (1986) suggested, "a reasonable accurate appraisal of one's capabilities is … of considerable value in effective functioning," and that people who overestimate their abilities may "undertake activities that are clearly beyond their reach" (p. 393). Certainly, an important feature of effective self-regulation is to know when to disengage from a goal because one's efforts are not paying off. Although strong self-efficacy beliefs usually contribute to adaptive tenacity, if these beliefs are unrealistically high, they may result in the relentless pursuit of an unattainable goal. Thus, high self-efficacy beliefs that are not supported by past experience or rewarded by positive goal-related feedback can result in wasted effort and resources that might be better directed elsewhere. As of yet, however, we have no way of determining when self-efficacy is "too high" and at what point people should give up trying to achieve their goals. Many successful individuals throughout history have a long record of failure and/or rejection before reaching success (Pajares, 2005).

Second, the way in which strong self-efficacy beliefs develop can affect their impact on behavior. Inflated self-efficacy beliefs (positive illusions) can lead to complacency and diminished effort and performance over time (Yang, Chuang, & Chiou, 2009), as well as an increased willingness to engage in potentially dangerous behaviors, such as using a cell phone while driving

(Schlehofer, Thompson, Ting, Ostermann, Nierman, & Skenderian, 2010). Further, people who develop high levels of self-efficacy without effort and struggle may set lower goals and may be satisfied with lower performance, compared with those who attain strong efficacy beliefs through hard work (Bandura & Jourdan, 1991). As a result, progress toward a goal may be hindered.

Third, help-seeking behaviors may be lower when self-efficacy is greater than actual abilities. For example, smokers with an inflated sense of self-efficacy to quit smoking are less inclined to enroll in programs to quit smoking and may have lower success in quitting smoking (Duffy, Scheumann, Fowler, Darling-Fisher, & Terrell, 2010). This potential disadvantage of unrealistically high self-efficacy and decreased help-seeking may apply to other domains, including one's ability to regulate alcohol and other substance use, diet, exercise, and many other behaviors that involve self-regulation.

Self-Efficacy and Psychological Well-Being

Most philosophers and psychological theorists agree that a sense of control over our behavior, our environment, and our own thoughts and feelings is essential for happiness and a sense of psychological well-being. Feelings of loss of control are common among people who seek the help of psychotherapists and counselors. This sense of a lack of control is a major factor in the self-regulation disruptions and failures that, as noted previously, are apparent in almost all psychological problems.

Self-efficacy beliefs play a major role in a number of common psychological problems. Low self-efficacy expectancies are an important feature of depression in adolescents (Flett, Panico, & Hewitt, 2011) and adults (Grembowski et al., 1993). Depressed people usually believe they are less capable than other people of behaving effectively in many important areas of life. Dysfunctional anxiety and avoidant behavior are the direct result of low-self-efficacy beliefs for managing threatening situations (Williams, 1995; Bandura, 1997). Self-efficacy beliefs also play a powerful role in substance abuse problems (DiClemente, Fairhurst, & Piotrowski, 1995), eating disorders (Lobera, Estébanez, Fernández, Bautista, & Garrido, 2009), post-traumatic stress (Lambert, Benight, Wong, & Johnson, 2013) and suicidal behaviors (Thompson, Kaslow, Short, & Wyckoff, 2002).

Self-Efficacy and Physical Well-Being

As research on *embodied emotions* (Niedenthal, 2007) has demonstrated, brain events, bodily feeling states, and felt and expressed emotions are interacting forces (see also Kagan, 2007). Therefore, a positive clinical psychology must also be a *holistic* clinical psychology that address the body as well as the mind. The growing research, for example on the effect of exercise on emotions and mood (Howarter, Bennett, Barber, Gessner, & Clark, 2014), suggests that positive clinical psychologists would be wise to include physical exercise as an interventions for clients with difficulty managing anxiety and depression. Thinking more broadly, positive clinical psychologists should also be concerned with what their clients eat and drink because poor nutrition can diminish overall physical and psychological well-being. For this reason, positive clinical psychologists should become familiar with the theory and research from health psychology that offers suggestions for motivating clients to make positive lifestyle changes that will enhance their health. Most strategies for preventing health problems, enhancing health, and hastening recovery from illness and injury involve changing behavior. Research on self-efficacy has greatly enhanced our understanding of how and why people adopt healthy and unhealthy behaviors and of how to change behaviors that affect health (Maddux, Brawley, & Boykin, 1995; O'Leary & Brown, 1995; Bandura, 1997). Beliefs about self-efficacy influence health in two ways.

First, self-efficacy beliefs influence the adoption of healthy behaviors, the cessation of unhealthy behaviors, and the maintenance of behavioral changes in the face of challenge and difficulty. All the major theories of health behavior, such as protection motivation theory (Maddux & Rogers, 1983; Rogers & Prentice-Dunn, 1997), the health belief model (Strecher, Champion, & Rosenstock, 1997), and the theory of reasoned action/ planned behavior (Fishbein & Ajzen, 1975; Ajzen, 1988; Maddux & DuCharme, 1997), include self-efficacy as a key component (see also Maddux, 1993; Weinstein, 1993). In addition, enhancing self-efficacy beliefs is crucial to successful change and maintenance of virtually every behavior crucial to health, including exercise (Kassavou, Turner, Kamborg, & French, 2014), diet (Berman, 2005), dental hygiene (Buglar, White, & Robinson, 2010), pain management (Costa, Maher, McAuley, Hancock, & Smeets, 2011), safe sex (Widman, Golin, Grodensky, & Suchindran, 2013), smoking cessation (Gwaltner, Metrik, Kahler, & Shiffman, 2009), overcoming alcohol abuse (Kelly & Greene, 2014), compliance with treatment and prevention regimens (Chan, Zalilah, & Hii, 2012), and disease detection behaviors such as skin cancer self-examination (Robinson et al., 2014).

Second, self-efficacy beliefs influence a number of biological processes, which, in turn, influence health and disease (Bandura, 1997). Self-efficacy beliefs affect how the immune system responds to stress (O'Leary & Brown, 1995; Bandura, 1997; Caserta, Wyman, Wang, Moynihan, & O'Connor, 2011). Lack of perceived control over environmental demands can increase susceptibility to infections and hasten the progression of disease (Gomez, Zimmermann, Froehlich, & Knop, 1994; Bandura, 1997). Self-efficacy beliefs also influence the activation of catecholamines, a family of neurotransmitters important to the management of stress and perceived threat, along with the endogenous painkillers referred to as endorphins (Bandura, Taylor, Williams, Mefford, & Barchas, 1985; O'Leary & Brown, 1995).

Self-Efficacy and Psychotherapy

We use the term "psychotherapy" to refer broadly to professionally guided interventions based on psychological theory and research that are designed to enhance psychological well-being, while acknowledging, again, that self-regulation plays an important role in all such interventions. Different interventions, or different components of an intervention, may be equally effective because they equally enhance self-efficacy for crucial behavioral and cognitive skills (Maddux & Lewis, 1995; Bandura, 1997; Goldin et al., 2012; Warren & Salazar, 2015) and help individuals cope with inevitable "backslides" in therapeutic progress (Kadden & Litt, 2011).

In therapy, enhancing self-efficacy for overcoming psychological difficulties and for implementing self-control strategies in specific challenging situations is essential to the success of therapeutic interventions (Maddux, 1995; Bandura, 1997). Self-efficacy is so important in treatment because a large amount of therapeutic progress occurs outside the therapy session when the client does homework (e.g., practicing therapy skills, exposure to feared stimuli, etc.). If clients do not believe in their ability to do work outside of session, they may be less likely to engage in homework activities, thus reducing the effectiveness of the treatment. Thus, it is important to assess, and if necessary, address, self-efficacy in regard to a client's ability to complete homework assignments in therapy. Indeed, increases in self-efficacy are key mechanisms of change in treatments for issues such as depression (Nash, Ponto, Townsend, Nelson, & Bretz, 2013), anxiety (Goldin et al., 2012; Brown et al., 2014), drug addiction (Kadden & Litt, 2011), and tobacco use (Hendricks, Delucchi, & Hall, 2010; Alessi & Petry, 2014).

Self-efficacy theory emphasizes the importance of arranging experiences designed to increase the person's sense of efficacy for specific behaviors in specific problematic and challenging situations. Self-efficacy theory suggests that formal interventions should not simply resolve specific problems, but should provide people with the skills and sense of efficacy for solving problems themselves. Some basic strategies for enhancing self-efficacy are based on the five sources of self-efficacy previously noted.

Performance experience The phrase "seeing is believing" underscores the importance of providing people with tangible evidence of their success. When people actually can see themselves coping effectively with difficult situations, their sense of mastery is likely to be heightened (Saemi, Porter, Ghotbi-Varzaneh, Zarghami, & Maleki, 2012). These experiences are likely to be most successful when both goals and strategies are specific. Goals that are concrete, specific, and proximal (short range) provide greater incentive, motivation, and evidence of efficacy than goals that are abstract, vague, and set in the distant future. Specific goals allow people to identify the specific behaviors needed for successful achievement and to know when they have succeeded. For example, the most effective interventions for phobias and fears involve "guided mastery" – in vivo experience with the feared object or situation during therapy sessions, or between sessions as "homework" assignments (Williams, 1995; Gallagher et al., 2013). Recent technological advances now allow for the use of "virtual reality" experiences in the treatment of phobias and fears (e.g., Rothbaum, Anderson, Zimand, Hodges, Lang, & Wilson, 2006). In cognitive treatments of depression, clients are provided structured guidance in arranging success experiences that will counteract low-self-efficacy expectancies (Maddux & Lewis, 1995).

Vicarious experience Vicarious learning and imagination can be used to teach new skills and enhance self-efficacy for those skills. For example, modeling films and videotapes have been used successfully to encourage socially withdrawn children to interact with other children. The child viewing the film sees the model child, someone much like him- or herself, experience success and comes to believe that he or she too can do the same thing (Conger & Keane, 1981). In vivo modeling has been used successfully in the treatment of phobic individuals. This research has shown that changes in self-efficacy beliefs for approach behaviors mediate adaptive behavioral changes (Bandura, 1986; Williams 1995; Ollendick, Öst, Reuterskiöld, & Costa, 2010). Common everyday (nonprofessional) examples of the use of vicarious experiences to enhance self-efficacy include advertisements for weight loss and smoking cessation programs that feature testimonials from successful people with whom an individual can identify. The clear message from these testimonials is that the listener or reader also can accomplish this difficult task. Formal and informal support groups – people sharing their personal experiences in overcoming a common adversity, such as addiction, obesity, or illness – also provide forums for the enhancement of self-efficacy.

Imagined experience Live or filmed models may be difficult to obtain, but the imagination is an easily harnessed resource. Imagining ourselves engaging in feared behaviors or overcoming difficulties can be used to enhance self-efficacy. For example, cognitive therapy of anxiety and fear often involves modifying visual images of danger and anxiety, including images of coping effectively with the feared situation. Imaginal (covert) modeling has been used successfully in interventions to increase assertive behavior and self-efficacy for assertiveness (Kazdin, 1979). Systematic desensitization and implosion are traditional behavioral therapy techniques that rely on the ability to imagine coping effectively with a difficult situation (Emmelkamp, 1994; Wiederhold & Bouchard, 2014). Because maladaptive distorted imagery is an important component of anxiety and depression, various techniques have been developed to help clients modify distortions and maladaptive assumptions contained in their visual images of danger and anxiety (e.g., Ng, Abbott, & Hunt, 2014). A client can gain a sense of control over a feared situation by imagining a future self that can deal effectively with the situation.

Verbal persuasion Most formal psychological interventions rely strongly on verbal persuasion to enhance a client's self-efficacy and encouraging small risks that may lead to small successes. In cognitive and cognitive-behavioral therapies (Holland, Stewart, & Strunk, 2006; Goldin et al., 2012), the therapist engages the client in a discussion of the client's dysfunctional beliefs, attitudes, and expectancies and helps the client to see the irrationality and self-defeating nature of such beliefs. The therapist encourages the client to adopt new, more adaptive beliefs and to act on these new beliefs and expectancies. As a result, the client experiences the successes that can lead to more enduring changes in self-efficacy beliefs and adaptive behavior. People also rely daily on verbal persuasion as a self-efficacy facilitator by seeking the support of others when attempting to lose weight, quit smoking, maintain an exercise program, or summon up the courage to confront a difficult boss or loved one.

Physiological and emotional states   We usually feel more self-efficacious when we are calm than when we are aroused and distressed. Thus, strategies for controlling and reducing emotional arousal (specifically anxiety) while attempting new behaviors should enhance self-efficacy beliefs and increase the likelihood of successful implementation. Hypnosis, biofeedback, relaxation training, meditation, and medication are the most common strategies for reducing the physiological arousal typically associated with low self-efficacy and poor performance. Relatedly, cognitive behavior therapy for Social Anxiety Disorder aims to reduce anxious emotional arousal by teaching individuals to reappraise the cognitions that lead to anxiety. Studies find that cognitive reappraisal self-efficacy is one of the paths through which cognitive behavior therapy functions (Goldin et al., 2012).

Summary

In the past three decades, we have learned much about the role of self-efficacy beliefs and psychological adjustment and maladjustment, physical health, and self-guided and professionally guided behavior change. Positive clinical psychology emphasizes the development of positive human qualities and the facilitation of psychological health and happiness in addition to the prevention of or remediation of negative human qualities and human misery. It also embraces the notion that individuals can be self-initiating agents for change in their own lives and the lives of others. The emphasis of social cognitive theory and self-efficacy theory on the development of "enablement" – providing people with skills for selecting and attaining the life goals they desire – over prevention and risk reduction is consonant with both of these emphases. Self-efficacy research concerned with enhancing our understanding of self-regulation will enhance our understanding of how to provide people with these enablement skills.

In the past few years, there has been growing research in this area; however, the majority of studies have been within the context of education (Ramdass & Zimmermann, 2011; Piperopoulos, & Dimov, 2014). Although research in education is strongly warranted, in agreement with others (e.g., Sitzmann & Ely, 2011), we note that it is also important to examine self-efficacy and self-regulation outside of education. Future studies on goal attainment in work, hobbies, and other areas of life are needed.

Second, positive clinical psychology emphasizes the social embeddedness of the individual and acknowledges that my individual success and happiness depends to a large degree on my ability to cooperate, collaborate, negotiate, and otherwise live in harmony with other people. In addition, the ability of businesses, organizations, communities, and governments (local, state, and national) to achieve their goals will increasingly depend on their ability to coordinate their efforts, particularly because these goals often conflict. For this reason, collective efficacy – including collective efficacy in organizations and schools (see Goddard, 2001), and efficacy for social and political change – provides numerous important questions for future research. In a world in which communication across the globe often is faster than communication across the street, and in which cooperation and collaboration in commerce and government is becoming increasingly common and increasingly crucial, understanding collective efficacy will become increasingly important.

The simple yet powerful truth that children learn from *The Little Engine That Could* ("I think I can! I think I can!") has been amply supported by over three decades of self-efficacy research: namely, that when equipped with an unshakable belief in one's ideas, goals, and capacity for achievement, there are few limits to what one can accomplish. As Bandura (1997) has stated: "People see the extraordinary feats of others but not the unwavering commitment and countless hours of perseverant effort that produced them" (p. 119). They then overestimate the role of "talent" in these accomplishments, while underestimating the role of self-regulation. The timeless message of research on self-efficacy is the simple, powerful truth that confidence, effort, and persistence are more potent than innate ability. In this sense, self-efficacy is concerned with human potential and possibilities, not limitations, thus making it an essential concept for a truly "positive" clinical psychology.

References

Abramson, L. Y., Seligman, M. E. P., & Teasdale, J. D. (1978). Learned helplessness in humans: Critique and reformulation. *Journal of Abnormal Psychology, 87*, 49–74.

Alessi, S. M. & Petry, N. M. (2014). Smoking reductions and increased self-efficacy in a randomized controlled trial of smoking abstinence: Contingent incentives in residential substance abuse treatment patients. *Nicotine & Tobacco Research, 16*, 1436–1445.

Ajzen, I. (1988). *Attitudes, personality, and behavior*. Chicago: Dorsey Press.

Bandura, A. (1977). Self-efficacy: Toward a unifying theory of behavioral change. *Psychological Review, 84*, 191–215.

Bandura, A. (1986). *Social foundations of thought and action*. New York: Prentice-Hall.

Bandura, A. (1997). *Self-efficacy: The exercise of control*. New York: Freeman.

Bandura. A. (2001). Social cognitive theory: An agentic perspective. *Annual Review of Psychology, 52*, 1–26.

Bandura, A. (2006). Toward a psychology of human agency. *Perspectives on Psychological Science, 1*, 164–180.

Bandura, A. & Locke, E. A. (2003). Negative self-efficacy and goal effects revisited. *Journal of Applied Psychology, 88*(1), 87–99.

Bandura, A. & Jourdan, F.J. (1991). Self-regulatory mechanisms governing the motivational effects of goal system. *Journal of Personality and Social Psychology, 60*, 941–951.

Bandura, A., Taylor, C. B., Williams, S. L., Mefford, I. N., & Barchas, J. D. (1985). Catecholamine secretion as a function of perceived coping self-efficacy. *Journal of Consulting and Clinical Psychology, 53*, 406–414.

Barone, D., Maddux, J. E., & Snyder, C. R. (1997). *Social cognitive psychology: History and current domains*. New York: Plenum.

Berman, E. S. (2005). The relationship between eating self-efficacy and eating disorder symptoms in a non-clinical sample. *Eating Behaviors, 7*, 79–90.

Brown, A. D., Joscelyne, A., Dorfman, M. L., Marmar, C. R., & Bryant, R. A. (2012). The impact of perceived self-efficacy on memory for aversive experiences. *Memory, 20*(4), 374–383.

Brown, L. A., Wiley, J. F., Wolitzky-Taylor, K., Roy-Byrne, P., Sherbourne, C., Stein, M. B., & Craske, M. G. (2014). Changes in self-efficacy and outcome expectancy as predictors of anxiety outcomes from the CALM study. *Depression and Anxiety*. Online before print publication.

Buglar, M. E., White, K. M., & Robinson, N. G. (2010). The role of self-efficacy in dental patients' brushing and flossing: testing an extended Health Belief Model. *Patient Education and Counseling, 78*(2), 269–272.

Caserta, M. T., Wyman, P. A., Wang, H., Moynihan, J., & O'Connor, T. G. (2011). Associations among depression, perceived self-efficacy, and immune function and health in preadolescent children. *Development and Psychopathology, 23*, 1139–1147.

Cervone, D., Shadel, W. G., Smith, R. E., & Fiori, M. (2006). Self-regulation: Reminders and suggestions from personality science. *Applied Psychology, 55*(3), 333–385.

Chan, Y. M., Zalilah, M. S., & Hii, S. Z. (2012). Determinants of compliance behaviours among patients undergoing hemodialysis in Malaysia. *Plos ONE, 7*.

Chen, G., Gully, S. M., & Eden, D. (2001). Validation of a new general self-efficacy scale. *Organizational Research Methods, 4*, 62–83.

Conger, J. C. & Keane, S. P. (1981). Social skills intervention in the treatment of isolated or withdrawn children. *Psychological Bulletin, 90*, 478–495.

Costa, L. D. C. M., Maher, C. G., McAuley, J. H., Hancock, M. J., & Smeets, R. J (2011). Self-efficacy is more important than fear of movement in mediating the relationship between pain and disability in chronic low back pain. *European Journal of Pain, 15*, 213–219.

DiClemente, C. C., Fairhurst, S. K., & Piotrowski, N. A. (1995). Self-efficacy and addictive behaviors. In: J. E. Maddux (Ed.), *Self-efficacy, adaptation, and adjustment: Theory, research, and application* (pp. 109–142). New York: Plenum.

Duffy, S. A., Scheumann, A. L., Fowler, K. E., Darling-Fisher, C., & Terrell, J. E. (2010). Perceived difficulty quitting predicts enrollment in a smoking-cessation program for patients with head and neck cancer. *Oncology Nursing Forum, 37*(3), 349–356.

Eagly, A. H. & Chaiken, S. (1993). *The psychology of attitudes*. New York: Harcourt, Brace, Jovanovitch.

Eisenberg, N., Valiente, C., & Eggum, N. D. (2010). Self-regulation and school readiness. *Early Education and Development, 21*(5), 681–698.

Emmelkamp, P. M. G. (1994). Behavior therapy with adults. In: A. E. Bergin & S. L. Garfield (Eds.), *Handbook of psychotherapy and behavior change*, 4th edn. (pp. 379–427). New York: John Wiley.

Fishbein, M. & Ajzen, I. (1975). *Belief, attitude, intention, and behavior: An introduction to theory and research*. Reading, MA: Addison-Wesley.

Flett, G. L., Panico, T., & Hewitt, P. L. (2011). Perfectionism, type A behavior, and self-efficacy in depression and health symptoms among adolescents. *Current Psychology, 30*, 105–116.

Gallagher, M. W., Payne, L. A., White, K. S., Shear, K. M., Woods, S. W., Gorman, J. M., & Barlow, D. H. (2013). Mechanisms of change in cognitive behavioral therapy for panic disorder: The unique effects of self-efficacy and anxiety sensitivity. *Behaviour Research and Therapy, 51*(11), 767–777.

Goddard, R. D. (2001). Collective efficacy: A neglected construct in the study of schools and student achievement. *Journal of Educational Psychology, 93*, 467.

Goldin, P. R., Ziv, M., Jazaieri, H., Werner, K., Kraemer, H., Heimberg, R. G., & Gross, J. J. (2012). Cognitive reappraisal self-efficacy mediates the effects of individual cognitive-behavioral therapy for social anxiety disorder. *Journal of Consulting and Clinical Psychology, 80*, 1034.

Gomez, V., Zimmermann, G., Froehlich, W. D., & Knop, J. (1994). Stress, control experience, acute hormonal and immune reactions. *Psychologische Beitrage, 36*, 71–81.

Grembowski, D., Patrick, D., Diehr, P., Durham, M., Beresford, S., Kay, E., & Hecht, J. (1993). Self-efficacy and health behavior among older adults. *Journal of Health and Social Behavior, 34*(2), 89–104.

Gwaltner, C. J. J., Metrik, C. W., Kahler, & Shiffman, S. (2009). Self-efficacy and smoking cessation: A meta-analysis. *Psychology of Addictive Behaviors, 23*, 56–66.

Hendricks, P. S., Delucchi, K. L., & Hall, S. M. (2010). Mechanisms of change in extended cognitive behavioral treatment for tobacco dependence. *Drug and Alcohol Dependence, 109*, 114–119.

Holland, S. D., Stewart, M. O., & Strunk, D. (2006). Enduring effects for cognitive behavior therapy in the treatment of depression and anxiety. *Annual Review of Psychology, 57*, 285–315.

Howarter, A. D., Bennett, K. K., Barber, C. E., Gessner, S. N., & Clark, J. M. (2014). Exercise self-efficacy and symptoms of depression after cardiac rehabilitation: Predicting changes over time using a piecewise growth curve analysis. *Journal of Cardiovascular Nursing, 29*(2), 168–177.

Hoyle, R. H. (2006). Personality and self-regulation: Trait and information-processing perspectives. *Journal of Personality, 74*(6), 1507–1526.

Kadden, R. M. & Litt, M. D. (2011). The role of self-efficacy in the treatment of substance use disorders. *Addictive Behaviors, 36*, 1120–1126.

Kagan, J. (2007). *What is emotion?* New Haven, CT: Yale University Press.

Kaplan, M. & Maddux, J. E. (2002). Goals and marital satisfaction: Perceived support for personal goals and collective efficacy for collective goals. *Journal of Social and Clinical Psychology, 21*, 157–164.

Karoly, P. (2010). Goal systems and self-regulation. *Handbook of Personality and Self-regulation*, 218–242.

Kassavou, A., Turner, A., Hamborg, T., & French, D. P. (2014). Predicting maintenance of attendance at walking groups: Testing constructs from three leading maintenance theories. *Health Psychology, 33*, 752–756.

Kazdin, A. E. (1979). Imagery elaboration and self-efficacy in the covert modeling treatment of unassertive behavior. *Journal of Consulting and Clinical Psychology, 47*, 725–733.

Kelly, J. F. & Greene, M. C. (2014). Where there's a will there's a way: A longitudinal investigation of the interplay between recovery motivation and self-efficacy in predicting treatment outcome. *Psychology of Addictive Behaviors, 28*, 928–934.

Lambert, J. E., Benight, C. C., Wong, T., & Johnson, L. E. (2013). Cognitive bias in the interpretation of physiological sensations, coping self-efficacy, and psychological distress after intimate partner violence. *Psychological Trauma: Theory, Research, Practice, and Policy, 5*, 494–500.

Lobera, I. J., Estébanez, S., Fernández, M. J., Bautista, E. Á., & Garrido, O. (2009). Coping strategies in eating disorders. *European Eating Disorders Review, 17*, 220–226.

Locke, E. A. & Latham, G. P. (1990). *A theory of goal setting & task performance.* Upper Saddle River, NJ: Prentice-Hall.

McClelland, D. C., Atkinson, J. W., Clark, R. W., & Lowell, E. L. (1953). *The achievement motive.* New York: Appleton-Century-Croft.

McCrae, R. R. & Löckenhoff, C. E. (2010). Self-regulation and the five-factor model of personality traits. *Handbook of Personality and Self-regulation*, 145–168.

Maddux, J. E. (1993). Social cognitive models of heath and exercise behavior: An introduction and review of conceptual issues. *Journal of Applied Sport Psychology, 5*, 116–140.

Maddux, J. E. (1995). Self-efficacy theory: An introduction. In: J. E. Maddux (Ed.), *Self-efficacy, adaptation, and adjustment: Theory, research, and application* (pp. 3–36). New York: Plenum.

Maddux, J. E. (1999a). Expectancies and the social-cognitive perspective: Basic principles, processes, and variables. In: I. Kirsch (Ed.), *How expectancies shape behavior* (pp. 17–40). Washington, DC: American Psychological Association.

Maddux, J. E. (1999b). The collective construction of collective efficacy. *Group Dynamics: Theory, Research, and Practice, 3*, 1–4.

Maddux, J. E., Brawley, L., & Boykin, A. (1995). Self-efficacy and healthy decision-making: Protection, promotion, and detection. In: J. E. Maddux (Ed.), *Self-efficacy, adaptation, and adjustment: Theory, research, and application* (pp. 173–202). New York: Plenum.

Maddux, J. E. & DuCharme, K. A. (1997). Behavioral intentions in theories of health behavior. In: D. Gochman (Ed.), *Handbook of health behavior research, vol. I: Personal and social determinants* (pp. 133–152). New York: Plenum.

Maddux, J. E. & Lewis, J. (1995). Self-efficacy and adjustment: Basic principles and issues. In: J. E. Maddux (Ed.), *Self-efficacy, adaptation, and adjustment: Theory, research, and application* (pp. 37–68). New York: Plenum.

Maddux, J. E. & Meier, L. J. (1995). Self-efficacy and depression. In: J. E. Maddux (Ed.), *Self-efficacy, adaptation, and adjustment: Theory, research, and application* (pp. 143–169). New York: Plenum.

Maddux, J. E. & Rogers, R. W. (1983). Protection motivation and self-efficacy: A revised theory of fear appeals and attitude change. *Journal of Experimental Social Psychology, 19*, 469–479.

Molden, D. C. & Dweck, C. S. (2006). Finding "meaning" in psychology: Alay theories approach to self-regulation, social perception, and social development. *American Psychologist, 61*, 192–203.

Nash, V. R., Ponto, J., Townsend, C., Nelson, P., & Bretz, M. N. (2013). Cognitive behavioral therapy, self-efficacy, and depression in persons with chronic pain. *Pain Management Nursing, 14*(4), e236–e243.

Niedenthal, P. M. (2007). Embodying emotion. *Science, 316*(5827), 1002–1005.

Ng, A. S., Abbott, M. J., & Hunt, C. (2014). The effect of self-imagery on symptoms and processes in social anxiety: A systematic review. *Clinical Psychology Review, 34*(8), 620–633.

O'Leary, A. & Brown, S. (1995). Self-efficacy and the physiological stress response. In: J. E. Maddux (Ed.), *Self-efficacy, adaptation, and adjustment: Theory, research, and application* (pp. 227–248). New York: Plenum.

Ollendick, T. H., Öst, L-G., Reuterskiöld, L., & Costa, N. (2010). Comorbidity in youth with specific phobias: Impact of comorbidity on treatment outcome and the impact of treatment on comorbid disorders. *Behaviour Research and Therapy, 48*, 827–831.

Pajares, F. (2005). *Gender differences in mathematics self-efficacy beliefs.* Cambridge: Cambridge University Press.

Piperopoulos, P. & Dimov, D. (2014). Burst bubbles or build steam? Entrepreneurship education, entrepreneurial self-efficacy, and entrepreneurial intentions. *Journal of Small Business Management.* Online before print publication.

Piper, W. (1930/1989). *The little engine that could.* New York: Platt & Monk.

Prussia, G. E. & Kinicki, A. J. (1996). A motivational investigation of group effectiveness using social cognitive theory. *Journal of Applied Psychology, 81*, 187–198.

Ramdass, D. & Zimmerman, B. J. (2011). Developing self-regulation skills: The important role of homework. *Journal of Advanced Academics, 22,* 194–218.

Robinson, J. K., Gaber, R., Hultgren, B., Eilers, S., Blatt, H., Stapleton, J., & Wayne, J. (2014). Skin self-examination education for early detection of melanoma: A randomized controlled trial of internet, workbook, and in-person interventions. *Journal of Medical Internet Research, 16,* 4–14

Rogers, R. W. & Prentice-Dunn, S. (1997). Protection motivation theory. In: D. Gochman (Ed.), *Handbook of health behavior research, vol. I: Personal and social determinants* (pp. 113–132). New York: Plenum.

Rothbaum, B. O., Anderson, P., Zimand, E., Hodges, L., Lang, D., & Wilson, J. (2006). Virtual reality exposure therapy and standard (in vivo) exposure therapy in the treatment for the fear of flying. *Behavior Therapy, 1*(37), 80–90.

Rotter, J. B. (1966). Generalized expectancies for internal versus external control of reinforcement. *Psychological Monographs, 80*(1, Whole No. 609).

Russell, B. (1945). *A history of Western philosophy.* New York: Simon & Schuster.

Saemi, E., Porter, J. M., Ghotbi-Varzaneh, A., Zarghami, M., & Maleki, F. (2012). Knowledge of results after relatively good trials enhances self-efficacy and motor learning. *Psychology of Sport and Exercise, 13*(4), 378–382.

Schlehofer, M. M., Thompson, S. C., Ting, S., Ostermann, S., Nierman, A., & Skenderian, J. (2010). Psychological predictors of college students' cell phone use while driving. *Accident Analysis & Prevention, 42*(4), 1107–1112.

Sherer, M., Maddux, J. E., Mercandante, B., Prentice-Dunn, S., Jacobs, B., & Rogers, R. W. (1982). The self-efficacy scale: Construction and validation. *Psychological Reports, 51,* 633–671.

Skinner, E. A. (1995). *Perceived control, motivation, and coping.* Thousand Oaks, CA: Sage.

Strecher, V. J., Champion, V. L., & Rosenstock, I. M. (1997). The health belief model and health behavior. In: D. Gochman (Ed.), *Handbook of health behavior research, vol. I: Personal and social determinants* (pp. 71–92). New York: Plenum.

Sitzmann, T. & Ely, K. (2011). A meta-analysis of self-regulated learning in work-related training and educational attainment: what we know and where we need to go. *Psychological Bulletin, 137,* 421.

Tabernero, C. & Wood, R. E. (2009). Interaction between self-efficacy and initial performance in predicting the complexity of task chosen. *Psychological Reports, 105*(3) (Pt 2), 1167.

Thompson, M. P., Kaslow, N. J., Short, L. M., & Wyckoff, S. (2002). The mediating roles of perceived social support and resources in the self-efficacy–suicide attempts relation among African American abused women. *Journal of Consulting and Clinical Psychology, 70,* 942.

Tipton, R. M. & Worthington, E. L. (1984). The measurement of generalized self-efficacy: A study of construct validity. *Journal of Personality Assessment, 48,* 545–548.

Vancouver, J. B., More, K. M., & Yoder, R. J. (2008). Self-efficacy and resource allocation: support for a nonmonotonic, discontinuous model. *Journal of Applied Psychology, 93*(1), 35.

Vessey, G. N. A. (1967). Volition. In: P. Edwards (Ed.), *Encyclopedia of philosophy*, vol. 8 (pp. 258–260). New York: Macmillan.

Warren, J. S. & Salazar, B. C. (2015). Youth self-efficacy domains as predictors of change in routine community mental health services. *Psychotherapy Research, 25*(5), 583–594.

Weinstein, N. D. (1993). Testing four competing theories of health-protective behavior. *Health Psychology, 12,* 324–333.

White, R. W. (1959). Motivation reconsidered: The concept of competence. *Psychological Review, 66,* 297–333.

Wiederhold, B. K. & Bouchard, S. (2014). Fear of flying (aviophobia): Efficacy and methodological lessons learned from outcome trials. In: *Advances in virtual reality and anxiety disorders* (pp. 65–89). New York: Springer.

Widman, L., Golin, C. E., Grodensky, C. A., & Suchindran, C. (2013). Do safer sex self-efficacy, attitudes toward condoms, and HIV transmission risk beliefs differ among men who have sex with men, heterosexual men, and women living with HIV. *AIDS and Behavior, 17,* 1873–1882.

Williams, D. M. (2010). Outcome expectancy and self-efficacy: Theoretical implications of an unresolved contradiction. *Personality and Social Psychology Review, 14,* 417–425.

Williams, S. L. (1995). Self-efficacy, anxiety, and phobic disorders. In: J. E. Maddux (Ed.), *Self-efficacy, adaptation, and adjustment: Theory, research, and application* (pp. 69–107). New York: Plenum.

Yang, M. L., Chuang, H. H., & Chiou, W. B. (2009). Long-term costs of inflated self-estimate on academic performance among adolescent students: a case of second-language achievements. *Psychological Reports, 105*(3) (Pt 1), 727.

8

Empathy
"The Good, The Bad and The Ugly"
Eamonn Ferguson

If you see someone in distress you may try to imagine how they feel, you may feel concern or sympathy for them, or imagine how you would feel if you were in the same situation. You may also experience distress from seeing them suffer. These types of experience are variously described in the scientific and philosophical literatures as empathy and empathy-related constructs (Batson, 2009). These resonate well with people's lay understandings of empathy (Kerem, Fishman, & Josselson, 2001; Hakansson & Montgomery, 2003). Empathy is an important construct as it is not only key for successful social interactions, but may also result in benefits to both the target of empathy and the empathizer themselves in terms of reputation building, positive well-being, and even longevity (Brown, Nesse, Vinokur, & Smith, 2003; Hakansson & Montgomery, 2003; Weinstein & Ryan, 2010). Based on these benefits, empathy is starting to take a more central role in applied psychology. For example, it is viewed as desirable trait for care providers (Ferguson, James, & Madely, 2002; Kim, Kaplowitz, & Johnston, 2004; Silvester, Patterson, Koczwara, & Ferguson, 2007) and as such a trait to be actively selected for (Patterson, Ferguson, Lane, Farrell, Martlew, & Wells, 2000).

While wholeheartedly acknowledging the benefits of empathy, the existence of variability in trait empathy in the population, implies that empathy also has a "dark side" (Nettle, 2006; Ferguson, 2013; Ferguson, Semper, Yates, Fitzgerald, Skatova, & James, 2014). One account – amongst others – to explain variation in trait expression is based on a trade-off between costs and benefits exhibited by the trait (Nettle, 2006). For example, neuroticism carries benefits, in terms of directing attentional resources toward danger, but carries a cost of increased susceptibility to psychiatric illness (Nettle, 2006). Motivated by this reasoning this chapter examines the evidence for the dark side of empathy, and examines potential implications for applied psychology practice.

Defining Empathy in a Costs and Benefits Models

Before exploring the dark side of empathy it is necessary to define empathy in terms of its constituent component and processes. These components and processes provide the basis of understanding when empathy will results in benefits (e.g., helping others, reputation building) or costs (e.g., increased pain sensitivity).

The Wiley Handbook of Positive Clinical Psychology, First Edition. Edited by Alex M. Wood and Judith Johnson.
© 2016 John Wiley & Sons, Ltd. Published 2016 by John Wiley & Sons, Ltd.

General Theoretical Frameworks

Broad theoretical models of empathic processes fall into three classes (Rameson & Lieberman, 2009): (1) Theory–Theories, (2) Simulation Theory, and (3) Dual-Process Theories.

Theory–Theories These models suggest that empathic representations arise from cognitive *mentalizing*, based on the application of "lay models" of the mind, to infer others' emotions (Batson, 2009; Rameson & Lieberman, 2009). This requires conscious and controlled processing, reflecting appraisals of the target and the situation in which the target is acting.

Simulation theories These theories require that we "put ourselves in the 'mental shoes' of another ..." (Rameson & Lieberman, 2009: p. 95) and use our own representation to simulate how the other is feeling (Decety & Jackson, 2004; Keysers & Gazzola, 2007). These processes are generally viewed as automatic and not requiring conscious awareness (Decety & Jackson, 2004). However, the automatic representations of another's emotions will, very probably, reflect basic emotions (e.g., fear) with more complex social emotions, such as sympathy requiring active cognitive processing (Decety & Jackson, 2004).

Dual-process These models acknowledge that both processes are important for the empathic responses with automatic processes feeding into conscious ones (Decety & Jackson, 2004; Shamay-Tsoory et al., 2005; Singer, 2006; Keysers & Gazzola, 2007; de Wall, 2008). There are a number of excellent reviews of this literature (e.g., Decety & Jackson, 2004; de Vignemont & Singer, 2006; Singer & Lamm, 2009).

Definition

The definition of empathy adopted here is based on a dual-process model, and in what follows the person who is in distress and to whom the empathic processes are directed will be called the "target" and the person who is empathizing the "empathizer."

The empathy process is defined here as follows:

1   The process that results in the formation of a representation and understanding of the targets emotional state, which forms the basis of the empathizer's responses.
2   This representation can occur without necessarily having direct emotional stimulation (Singer, 2006).
3   The empathizer knows that the target is the source of the empathizer's emotional experience – there is a self–other differentiation (Decety & Jackson, 2004; de Vignemont & Singer, 2006).
4   The emotional representation of the empathizer does not have to be isomorphic (i.e., the same) with that of the target, but can be (see Batson & Shaw, 1991). This is a departure from other theorists, especially those working in the neuroscience of empathy who view empathy as occurring only when the target's and empathizer's emotions are isomorphic (de Vignemont & Singer, 2006; Singer & Lamm, 2009; Bird & Viding, 2014). The approach adopted here does not require that the emotions experienced by the target and empathizer are the same and thus includes sympathy (Batson & Shaw, 1991; Batson, 2009). Sympathy is part of the experiential response to another's distress (Batson, 2009). The empathizers response to the target – helping, avoiding or harming – (Point 1 of the definition above) will depend, in part, on whether the empathizer emotional experiences are isomorphic (see "Benefits to Target" section below).

The Main and Subcomponents of Empathy

Three main components of empathy – (1) cognitive (i.e., understanding the targets' emotional states), (2) emotional (i.e., feeling the others' emotional state in some way), and (3) motor (i.e., automatic process that allow action–perception synchronization) – are traditionally recognized in the literature (Decety & Jackson, 2004, Blair, 2005). As an analogy, these three components can be thought of as moons orbiting the planet "Empathy" (Figure 8.1). The terrain of the moons can be explored to identify their different continents or subcomponents. Batson (2009) identified eight different concepts used in the literature to refer to empathy. I will use these to define the subcomponents of empathy that constitute the main cognitive, emotional, and motor components. I will also be drawing on the work of authors such as Singer and colleagues (Singer, 2006, Singer & Lamm, 2009) and Blair (2005, 2008).

First, two subcomponents linked to automatic processes can be identified that define the terrain of the moon "*Automatic (Motor) Empathy.*" These are: (1) Motor Mimicry (i.e., automatically synchronizing the posture, emotions, and expression of others: Singer & Lamm, 2009; Batson's 2nd Concept); and (2) Emotional Contagion (i.e., the automatic tendency to catch another's emotions: Singer & Lamm, 2009: Batson's 3rd Concept). Singer and Lamm (2009) suggest that motor mimicry and emotional contagion are linked, and Decety and Jackson (2004) include mimicry in their definition of emotional contagion.

However, many authors clearly state that both mimicry and emotional contagion do not equate to empathy, as these perception–action processes lack self–other differentiation (e.g., Bernhardt & Singer, 2012). They are, however, included here for two reasons. First, mimicry can be conscious – we may choose to deliberately mimic others (Decety & Jackson, 2004). Second, within a dual-process framework these represent the primitive processes that form a basis of

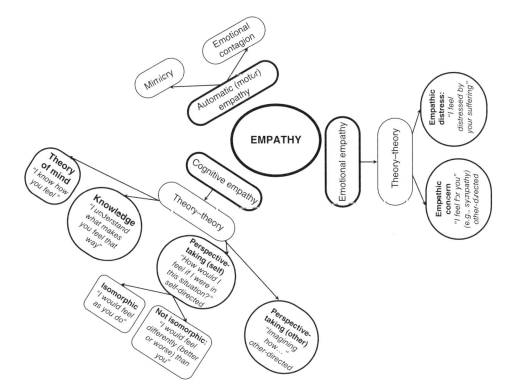

Figure 8.1   Components of empathy.

more complex processes (e.g., perspective-taking) that introduce mental flexibility (Decety & Jackson, 2004). Recent neuroimaging data supports this contention (Morelli, Rameson, & Lieberman, 2014) and thus from a process-oriented perspective these are the basic building blocks for higher-order empathic processes (e.g., de Wall 2008; see also Lamm, Nurbaum, Meltzoff, & Decety, 2007). While, it is acknowledged that, in some clinical cases, higher-order empathic processes can be adopted without these primitive processes (Danziger, Faillenot, & Peyron, 2009), it is argued that the ability to mimic and catch emotions is needed for higher-order empathic processes. Indeed, for most normal development they are likely to be the basis of empathic ability (de Wall, 2008). To be clear, if just emotional contagion is experienced this is not empathy, but the ability for this to occur is needed for empathy to be experienced.

The terrain of *Cognitive Empathy* has four subcomponents that primarily reflect Theory–Theory processes: "Theory of Mind," "Knowledge," "Perspective-Taking (other)" [$PT_{(o)}$], and "Perspective-Taking (self)" [$PT_{(s)}$].

"Theory of Mind" reflects an understanding that others have a mind and have emotions, desires, beliefs, etc. "Knowledge" refers to (1) memory, (2) appraisals of the situation the target is in, and (3) knowledge about the target. All three of these may be used to infer the target's emotions (see de Wall, 2008: Batson's 1st Concept). Thus "Knowledge" is a key part of the empathic process, as the strength of the empathic response varies as a function of appraisals of: (1) *similarity* between the empathizer's appraisals of the target's situation, emotions, and personality and their own; (2) *familiarity* with the target; (3) *fairness* of the targets actions; (4) *group* membership; and (5) *kinship* (see de Vignemont & Singer, 2006; Engen & Singer, 2013, for reviews).

The two perspective-taking components ([$PT_{(o)}$], and [$PT_{(s)}$]) differ with respect to how the empathizer represents their emotions relative to the target's emotions. $PT_{(o)}$ refers to *imagining how the other person might feel* (Batson, 2009: Batson's 5th Concept). $PT_{(s)}$ reflects *how the empathizer imagines they would feel if they were in the target's position*: Batson's 4th and 6th Concepts). Research shows that $PT_{(o)}$ and $PT_{(s)}$ are related but distinct processes: $PT_{(s)}$ has been shown to be distinct from $PT_{(o)}$ at both a neurological level (Lamm, Batson, & Decety, 2007), and psychometrically (Lockwood, Seara-Cardoso, & Viding, 2014), as well as in terms of emotional responses, with $PT_{(o)}$ resulting in sympathy and compassion (Empathic Concern) and $PT_{(s)}$ resulting also in personal distress (Batson, Early, & Salvarini, 1997).

While defined here as an example of theory–theory processes, there is some degree of *active simulation* in $PT_{(s)}$. $PT_{(s)}$ contains aspects *simulation* as the empathizer has to imagine, not only what the target is experiencing, but also simulate how they would feel in that situation themselves. Thus, $PT_{(s)}$ may be better envisaged as perspective-taking that is a mixture or theory–theory and simulation theory approaches.

$PT_{(s)}$ can be either "isomorphic" (imaging you would feel the same negative emotion as the target does), or "nonisomorphic" (imagining you would feel something different). In its weakest sense, nonisomorphic $PT_{(s)}$ may entail imagining you would feel the same emotion but in a more or less intense manner. This may represent a *self–other empathy gap* (Loewenstein, 2005). In its truest sense, nonisomorphic $PT_{(s)}$ may also result from the empathizer imagining that they would feel a different emotion to the target if they were in the same situation (the target is sad, but the empathizer would feel angry or even happy). For example, if someone adopts a $PT_{(s)}$ with respect to a target's bereavement, while the target may feel relief that the person's suffering is over (as well as sadness), the $PT_{(s)}$ empathizer may imagine that they would feel just sadness, or may even feel anger in the same situation as the target. There also may be contexts where the $PT_{(s)}$ empathizer would feel positive emotions if they were in the same situation. For example, if a target's romantic relationship ends, but the empathizer feels the target's partner was overly controlling and aggressive, the $PT_{(s)}$ empathizer may think that they would feel glad if they were in the target's position.

The terrain of *Emotional Empathy* can be divided into two subcomponents: Empathic Concern and Empathic Distress. Empathic Concern refers to feeling emotions such as sympathy and compassion *for* the target (Batson's 8th Concept). Sympathy is *feeling for* and, as such, the emotion felt by the empathizer is not isomorphic with the target (cf. Singer & Lamm, 2009). Empathic Distress refers to the distress someone feels when seeing the target distressed (Batson's 7th Concept). This may arise via PT$_{(s)}$.

A Dual-Process Account of the Components of Empathy

The main and subcomponents detailed in Figure 8.1 can be rearranged to provide a dual-process model (Figure 8.2), whereby earlier primitive process are the basis for later more complex empathic representations and processes (see also de Wall, 2008).

There are two primary processes: (1) Automatic (Motor) Empathy (mimicry and emotional contagion), and (2) Primary Cognitive Processes (ToM and knowledge). The former represents automatic representational processes and the later conscious cognitive processes that form the basis of subsequent cognitive and emotional empathic processes and responses. ToM is hypothesized to build from mirror neurones (see Gallese & Goldman, 1998) that underlie basic mimicry/imitation (Lieberman, 2007; Iacoboni, 2009). The combination of ToM and knowledge allows the person to know that another has emotions, provide self–other differentiation (which is key for empathic processes) and provides the contextual knowledge to start the appraisal process of identifying more complex emotions. This is a conscious theory–theory-driven process, but one that builds from the automatic simulation that underlies mimicry. Once this process begins, the empathizer can then actively "empathize" using one of four core empathic processes: (1) PT$_{(o)}$, (2) "Empathic Concern," (3) PT$_{(s)}$, or (4) "Empathic Distress."

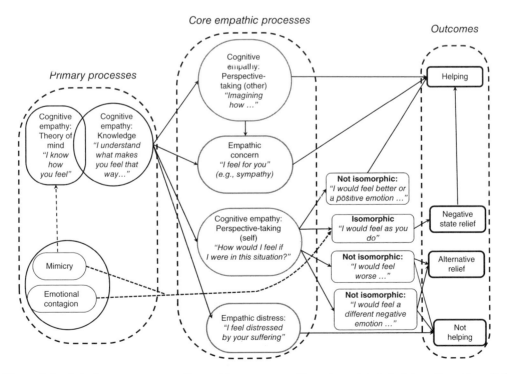

Figure 8.2 A dual-process account of empathic processes and how they relate to helping, alternative relief (drugs, entertainment, etc. as a mood regulator) and not helping.

Note that the automatic (motor) empathy components can feed directly to $PT_{(s)}$ isomorphic. This is because when the $PT_{(s)}$ process is isomorphic the representation will likely be consistent with activation of mirror neuron/emotional contagion systems. We will return to these later to explore how these core empathic processes may differentially influence prosocial and antisocial behavior.

Evolution of Traits: Cost and Benefits

It is recognized that empathic ability can be expressed as a heritable trait (Knafo, Zahn-Waxler, Hulle, Robinson, & Rhee, 2008) that shows variation in the population (Davis, 1983; Hein & Singer, 2008; Baron-Cohen, 2012; Georgi, Petermann, & Schipper, 2014). Trait empathy is correlated with many of the same brain areas involved empathic processes (Singer, Seymour, O'Doherty, Kaube, Dolan, & Frith, 2004), indicating that trait empathy taps the same basic empathic processes as described in the developmental, social, cognitive, and neuroscience literatures. Trait empathy also serves to enhance these empathic processes (Singer et al., 2004).

From an evolutionary perspective it is necessary to explain why this variability exists. Natural selection should select against variability and select the aspect of the trait that is best adapted to increasing fitness. One solution to the puzzle is offered in terms of a cost–benefit trade-off model (Nettle, 2006). The basic tenet of this approach is that traits evolved to meet the adaptive needs of changing environments, for which there is no optimal value, and as such traits carry both cost and benefits, the mixture of which will determine the optimal fitness level depending on the current context. By the same reasoning empathy, as an evolved trait showing variability in the population, will likewise have associated costs and benefits (Nettle, 2006; Ferguson, 2013). These costs and benefits are detailed in the following sections.

"The Good, the Bad and the Ugly"©

We can draw an analogy with Sergio Leone's film *The Good, The Bad and The Ugly*© to classify the relative costs and benefits of empathy. The "good" represents the benefits (automatic or intended) to the empathizer, target, and society; the "bad" represents unpleasant outcomes to all parties both automatic and intended; while the "ugly" represents the nasty and malevolent intended outcomes linked to empathy.

The Good

The benefits of empathy reflect benefits to the empathizer, the target, and society. The benefits of empathy of these parties are briefly detailed below.

Benefits to the Empathizer   The main benefits to the empathizer concern warm-glow and reputation building as well as longevity.

Reputation Building and Warm-Glow   The act of helping is likely to engender feelings of "warm-glow" in the helper (Andreoni, 1990), and those who express greater empathy (via trait empathy or perspective-taking manipulation) are more likely to help others (Batson & Shaw, 1991; Batson, 2002). Therefore, these feelings should be more likely to be experienced by those with high empathic traits. Thus, there are benefits for personal psychological well-being.

If the offer of help is made public, or the helper is known to be a "good person," the helper will gain utility in terms of reputation (Pfeiffer, Tran, Krumme, & Rand, 2012), with good reputation resulting in an increased likelihood of being helped by others (Milinski, Semmann, & Krambeck, 2002).[1] However, reputation can be faked and loses its value when it becomes a less reliable indicator of an individual's previous helping (Pfeiffer et al., 2012). Thus, people are more likely to offer help to another when the good deeds are observed (Milinski et al., 2002) or reliably signaled (Zahavi & Zahavi, 1997; Zollman, Bergstrom, & Huttegger, 2013).

Longevity   Empathy may also be indirectly linked to longevity. Helping others has been linked to increased longevity (Brown et al., 2003). With respect to empathy, emotional empathy has been linked to increased volunteering (Mitani, 2014), with other oriented motives (akin to empathy), and with autonomous motives for volunteering linked to increased longevity (Konrath, Fuhrel-Forbis, Lou, & Brown, 2012). Thus, empathy may have survival benefits. Studies directly linking empathy to longevity need to be conducted, with the hypothesis that empathy is linked to longevity via the degree of helping behavior it engenders.

Benefits to the Target   The empathy–altruism model of Batson (see Batson & Shaw, 1991; Batson, 2002), proposes that helping is motivated primarily to relieve the target's distress, and has generated a large body of work linking $PT_{(o)}$ and "Empathic Concern" to increased helping (Batson, 2002). "Empathic Distress," on the other hand, as a self-oriented subcomponent of empathy, tends to result in avoiding situations likely to result witnessing others' distress (Davis, Mitchell, Hall, Lothert, Snapp, & Meyer, 1999).

However, the relationship between $PT_{(s)}$ and behavior is more complex as $PT_{(s)}$ can result in helping, mood self-regulation, or not helping (see Figure 8.2), depending on whether the emotional representation experienced by the $PT_{(s)}$ empathizer and target are isomorphic or not. This is predicated on the idea that that those who adopt a $PT_{(s)}$ empathic process come to "feel," to some extent, the emotion they are imagining they would feel if they were in the target position. This may occur via two, interlinked routes: (1) affective priming (Fazio, 2001), and/or (2) vividness of the representation as the "vividness" to which an emotional state is represented (Loewenstein, Weber, Hsee, & Welch, 2001; Loewenstein & Small, 2007). Indeed, there is evidence to show that $PT_{(s)}$ results in reporting greater personal distress (Batson, Early, & Salvarini, 1997). Attribution processes may also lead to social comparison processes whereby the $PT_{(s)}$ empathizer views the target as being weaker or stronger (e.g., less or more able to cope) than they would be in the same situation.

If the $PT_{(s)}$ empathizer imagines that they would feel isomorphic emotions with the distressed target, they may direct their behavior to relieve any negative emotions that arise from taking a $PT_{(s)}$ position. One way to archive this is by *helping* the target, as relieving the target's distress reduces any isomorphic negative mood the $PT_{(s)}$ process generates for the empathizer. This is akin to the negative-state-relief (NSR) model of Cialdini and colleagues (Cialdini & Kenrick, 1976; Cialdini, Schaller, Houlihan, Arps, Fultz, & Beaman, 1987), whereby the empathizer helps the target, but is motivated primarily to relive his or her own negative state rather than the target's distress.

If the $PT_{(s)}$ empathizer feels they would experience a different negative emotion to the target, their representation is nonisomorphic, and their choice of action may be driven by a number of processes. In this case, relieving the target's distress is unlikely to relieve any emotional distress the empathizer feels as a function of the $PT_{(s)}$ process and therefore may instead result in *emotional regulation* by other means, such as drugs, exercise, watching a film, etc. (see Cialdini et al., 1987). If the empathizer believes that they would feel a more intense negative emotion (depression rather than sadness) or a different negative emotion, the empathizer may try to find ways to relieve any personal distress via mood regulation strategies (Cialdini et al., 1987). The $PT_{(s)}$ empathizer's choice of behavior to regulate their own mood may be linked to the specific action patterns of that emotion (Lazarus, 1993; Raghunathan & Pham, 1999). Thus, this personal mood regulation will result indirectly in *not helping* the target as the "empathizer" seeks relief for their negative emotions by means other than by helping. Social comparison processes may also result in *not offering help*. For example, if the target is sad and withdrawn but the empathizer feels they would be angry and would try to get even in the same context, the empathizer may *not help* as they see the target as passive. Similarly, blaming the target may result in reduced helping. Alternatively, if the empathizer feels that he or she would not cope as well as the target, he or she may adopt other mood regulation strategies and, again, not help. Finally, if the $PT_{(s)}$ empathizer imagines that they would feel better than the target and experience a positive emotion (e.g., happy), this positive affect felt by the empathizer may result in an increased probability of *helping* the target (Eisenberg, 1991).

The basic association between empathy ($PT_{(o)}$ and Empathic Concern) and helping is influenced by a number of contextual factors. For example, $PT_{(o)}$ is more likely to result in helping kin (Maner & Gaillior, 2007), and both $PT_{(o)}$ and Empathic Concern seems to be specifically important for low-cost helping (Neuberg, Cialdini, Brown, Luce, Sagarin, & Lewis, 1997; Ferguson, Farrell, & Lawrence, 2008) and unrelated to high-cost helping like blood donation (Ferguson, Lawrence, & Farrell, 2008; Schlumpf et al., 2008; Steele et al., 2008; Ferguson, Taylor, Keatley, Flynn, & Lawrence, 2012). Indeed, Batson, O'Quin, Fultz, Vanderplas, and Isen (1983: study 3) showed that when they increased the cost of helping, the impact of empathy was reduced and the pattern of responses conformed to a pattern more consistent with egoistic motives. Furthermore, empathy is also likely to be unrelated to planned helping behaviors where the target is not present: blood donation, charitable giving (Einolf, 2008).

The above evidence indicates a robust link between self-reported and manipulated (perspective-taking) empathy with helping (especially low-cost helping). Similar links have also been reported using physiological assessments of empathy (see Eisenberg & Miller, 1987). For example, Hein, Lamm, Brodbeck, and Singer (2011) examined the extent to which a match between people's skin conductance response (SCR), when feeling pain themselves, and observing another's pain predicted subsequent helping – willingness to take the place of another about to receive an electric shock. The electric shock was defined at tolerable but painful. The results showed an increased likelihood of helping when the match was greatest. Furthermore, Morelli, Rameson, and Lieberman (2014) showed that brain activation linked to empathic responses predicted daily prosocial behavior. All of which were low-cost (e.g., gave directions, picked up a fallen object for someone, held open a door).

Thus, consistent with all other reviews there is strong evidence that empathy in terms of $PT_{(o)}$ and Empathic Concern influences helping (mainly low-cost helping), the only deviation is Empathic Distress and $PT_{(s)}$ under certain conditions.[2]

A recent interesting development in this area has been to see the target not just as a passive recipient of empathy, but to examine the target's belief that another is actively taking their perspective. Goldstein, Vezich, and Shapiro (2014) refer to this as "perceived perspective-taking," and explore the consequences of believing another is taking the target's perspective. These authors show that when a target feels others are taking their perspective that this infers many of the same benefits as empathizing, including helping the empathizer.

Benefits to Society   The benefits of empathy to society reflect better, wider social interactions and reduced prejudice.

Simple Cooperation and Bargaining   As well as helping others, empathic processes may also promote better social interaction via beneficial mutual cooperation. In terms of social dilemmas, such as the prisoner's dilemma game, evidence shows that $PT_{(o)}$ with the co-player induces greater cooperation (Batson & Moran, 1999; Batson & Ahmad, 2001). Similarly, in dictator games,[3] processes akin to empathic concern induce greater offers of help (Andreoni & Rao, 2011). Thus, empathy promotes cooperation and this may have additional benefits in terms of wider helping via "upstream indirect reciprocity" (Nowak & Sigmund, 2005); that is, the target helped (shown cooperation) may feel gratitude and go on to help someone else.

Reducing Out-Group Bias and Prejudice   A final way in which empathy can help wider society is through the reduction of prejudice. There is evidence that $PT_{(o)}$ for out-group members can result in increased helping toward wider social groups such as charities (Batson, Chang, Orr, & Rowland, 2002), as well as less prejudicial behavior (Batson et al., 2011).

The Bad

The short review above supports the general consensus that empathy has benefits for the empathizer, the target, and society. This section details the potentially negative effects for the empathizer and wider society.

Costs to the Empathizer   There are costs of empathy to the empathizer in terms of pain perception, Empathic Distress, and psychiatric disorder.

Pain   If I empathize with another's physical pain will that affect my experience of pain? Theories that suggest that empathy has an automatic component where the same neural substrates are activated while observing pain, suggesting that observing pain will activate a pain representation. Indeed, there is a growing body of neuroimaging studies showing that observing another's pain activates that same "pain matrix" in the observer as is activated when they feel the pain themselves (Singer et al., 2004; see Singer & Frith 2005; Frith & Singer 2008; Lamm, Decety, & Singer, 2011; Bernhardt & Singer, 2012; Engen & Singer, 2013; Singer & Kimecki, 2014, for reviews). This pattern is seen whether the target is a loved one or a stranger, but is stronger for loved ones (Cheng, Chen, Lin, Chou, & Decety, 2010), and even when the target has an unusual pain response to the norm – showing pain to a Q-tip but not to a needle (Lamm, Meltzoff, & Decety, 2010). Furthermore, this effect is observed for both a $PT_{(o)}$ and $PT_{(s)}$, resulting in both similar (the anterior insula (AI)) as well as separate (the right temperoparietal junction) patterns of activation (Jackson, Brunet, Meltzoff, & Decety, 2006). These neural responses are stronger in those who score higher in trait Empathic Concern (Singer et al., 2004).

These studies also show that when the empathizer rates a target's pain, they rate it as being as painful as the pain they experienced themselves (see Singer et al., 2004; Loggia, Mogil, & Bushnell, 2008). They also indicate increased Empathic Distress as well as Empathic Concern for the target (Lamm, Meltzoff, & Decety, 2010), with $PT_{(s)}$ resulting in more intense pain ratings than $PT_{(o)}$ (Jackson et al., 2006). These laboratory-based results resonate well with epidemiological survey data showing that high trait empathy (cf. $PT_{(o)}$) is related to increased reported pain (Schieman & van Gundy, 2000).

Hyper-Empathy   When someone's empathy scores are very extreme they may care so much for others that they neglect themselves (Baron-Cohen, 2012) or be more likely to follow the group (Pessin, 2012). Both are potentially harmful to the individual as negating one's own needs (e.g., food, emotional support, etc.) can result in physical and psychological distress. Such pathological caring may also be distressing to others who do not want to be helped.

Empathic Distress   The experience of Empathic Distress, that is, the experience of negative feelings associated with another's distress, is not only linked to avoidance of highly emotionally charged helping situations (Davis, 1983; Davis et al., 1999), but is an obvious personal negative outcome of empathy.

Psychiatric Illness   Empathic responses also have a role to play in understanding psychiatric illness. Here I examine depression and obsessive-compulsive disorder.

Depression   The role of empathy in depression may be considered in terms of (1) a simple *deficit* model, (2) a *toxic combination* of empathic traits, or (3) a *risk* factor.

It has been suggested that the increased focus on the self in depression should result in *deficits* in empathic processing in depression (Preston, 2007).

A recent meta-analysis revealed, however, that not all components of empathy are in deficit in depression. Instead, there may be a *toxic combination* of empathic traits in depression (Schreiter, Pijnenborg, & ann het Rot, 2013). Specifically, Schreiter and colleagues (2013) show that in depression, while emotional empathy (Empathic Concern) was intact, there were deficits in Cognitive Empathy (ToM, perspective-taking), but increased levels of Empathic Distress. Thus, depression reflects an increased self-oriented distress ($PT_{(s)}$) at others' suffering, which may lead to avoiding social interactions, coupled with an intact Empathic Concern linked to a desire to help others. Therefore, it appears that depressed individuals are torn between avoiding social interactions and wanting to help. This intrapsychic conflict will inevitably be distressing and one that therapy may need to address.

Zahn-Waxler and Van Hule (2012) suggest that high levels of empathy may be a *risk* factor for depression when there is either (1) a predisposition to sadness or (2) when empathy leads to pathogenic guilt. They argue that pathogenic guilt may occur, for example, when a child has to care for an emotionally distressed parent and then begins to attribute a causal role to themselves for the parent's distress. Indeed, there is evidence linking high empathy to pathogenic guilt (O'Connor, Berry, Lewis, & Stiver, 2012). Thus, the caring context in which the empathic response is embedded is crucial to determining if empathy will act as a risk factor for depression or not. Consistent with this, there is evidence that when people develop empathy, as part of benefit seeking, while helping a target in a highly emotionally charged context, this empathy is linked to subsequent increased depression (Kim et al., 2007).

Obsessive-Compulsive Disorder (OCD)   Empathic traits also have a potential role to play in understanding OCD (Fontenelle et al., 2009). This is based on two observations by Fontenelle and colleagues (2009). First, those with OCD are more likely to be overly emotionally attached to items, which can take on symbolic meaning, representing significant others and sentiments of the past. The possessions are a way to "empathize" with (feeling for) loved ones. Second, higher levels of oxytocin are linked to both empathic responses and OCD. Consistent with this, Fontenelle et al. (2009) provide evidence that those with OCD show heightened levels of both Empathic Concern and Empathic Distress. This is a pattern similar to that described above for depression, except here both Empathic Concern and Empathic Distress are increased. Furthermore, both Empathic Concern and Empathic Distress were shown to be positively associated with greater reported levels of (1) checking, (2) ordering, (3) washing, and (4) hoarding.

Costs to Society   Empathy has costs to society in terms of reducing contributions to the public good and increasing in-group favoritism.

Contributing to the public good   Most psychology experiments on empathy (and many in neuroscience) have focused on helping a single targeted individual (either present or hypothetical). Fewer studies on empathy have examined the situation when there is a tension between helping either (1) a targeted individual, (2) the wider group, or (3) redirecting resources to the self.[4] If empathy benefits individuals, then it may be a potential threat to helping the wider community and the public good, as empathizers may direct resources toward specific individuals rather than resources being aggregated and used to help many (Batson, 2011).

It may be argued that society would be better off if we all contributed to the public good, as there are resources for all to use. If we all pay higher tax, then services such as street lights, healthcare, law enforcement, education, etc. can be provided for all. The problem here is one of free-riding, whereby people benefit from the resources without contributing.[5] Free-riding is seen as motivated by self-interest. These effects can be modeled in the laboratory in terms of public good games (PGG) – whereby, for example, people play in a group of four anonymous players. Everyone has an initial and equivalent endowment (private account) and can contribute some, none, or all to the public account. Whatever is contributed it is summed and doubled and paid back equally to all members of the group regardless of their level of initial contribution. So each person gets to keep for themselves what they had kept back in their public account, plus what is returned to them from the public account. If everyone contributes maximally, and equally, the group benefits as each individual gains the most. However, as individuals are unsure what others will do, then not contributing (free-riding) or contributing a small amount (cheap-riding) will most likely maximize the individual's payoff, but not the group's. What is the effect of empathic responses here? In more complex social exchanges, such as in a PGG, evidence indicates that empathizing with a target in the group results in resources being diverted to that target and away from the group (Batson, Batson, Todd, Brummett, Shaw, & Aldeguer, 1995; Batson, Klien, Highberger, & Shaw, 1995; Batson et al., 1999). Thus, while the targeted individual benefits, the wider group resource diminishes.

These findings may seem at odds with work cited earlier saying that empathizing with a target can reduce prejudice. As Batson (2011) points out, whether or not empathy is "friend or foe" of public goods depend on the target. It is a "friend" if empathy is targeted in such a way as to increase compassion for the wider group, and a "foe" when this is not the case and empathy is targeted at particular individuals in a group. Indeed, there is some support for the contention that empathizing with a wider group enhances the public good (Oceja, Heerdink, Stocks, Ambrona, Lopez-Perez, & Salagado, 2104). Thus, not only can self-oriented motivations (e.g., self-interest), as traditional theory states, be threats to the public good, but so also can other-oriented motivations (e.g., empathic concern and $PT_{(o)}$ for an individual) under very specific conditions.

In-Group Favoritism Parochial altruism and nepotism (Bernhard, Fischbacher & Fehr, 2006) arise when kin or in-groups are preferentially favored and receive beneficial treatment. While, kin selection is one key model for explaining the survival of altruism (Griffin & West, 2002), this may become a dark side of altruism as helping is not always directed at the most needy or deserving. There is also evidence that such in-group favoritism is enhanced by empathy toward in-group members (Sturmer, Snyder, & Omoto, 2005). This, again, may lead to social disadvantage and enhanced stereotyping. Also it is possible to help your in-group by harming the out-group (see also Griffin & West, 2002).

The Ugly

Finally, the darkest side of empathy – psychopathy/antisocial behavior and torture and exploitation – are explored

Psychopathy Blair (2005, 2008) has proposed a model of psychopathy (see also Shamay-Tsoory, Harari, Aharon-Peretz, & Levkovitz, 2010) whereby psychopathy is characterized by intact cognitive empathy (ToM) and motor empathy, but reduced emotional empathy. Smith (2006) proposes a similar model to explain Antisocial Personality Disorder (ASPD). Following Smith (2006), the psychopathic individual and the person with ASPD are able to understand the emotions and feelings of others (good and intact cognitive empathy) and thus be able to manipulate them, but are less likely to feel "for," or "as," or "with" the target, thus removing the motivation not to harm. Thus, it is the relative strength of cognitive and emotional empathy that motivates the behavior of these individuals, and there is evidence that high levels of psychopathic traits are associated with lower emotional empathy (Mahmut, Homewood, & Stevenson, 2008), but intact for cognitive perspective-taking (Jones, Happe, Gilbert, Burnett, & Viding, 2010). In nonclinical populations there is evidence that perspective-taking ability is advantageous in bargaining situations, enabling people to identify hidden agreements, whereas empathic concern is either not advantageous or disadvantageous (Galinsky, Massux, Gilin. & White, 2008). This pattern suggests that a combination of perspective-taking and reduced empathic concern is advantageous with respect to finding useful information to manipulate negotiations in one's favor.

Drawing on the subcomponents of empathy described above (see Figures 8.1 and 8.2), psychopathic traits should be linked to good Theory of Mind, Knowledge, and $PT_{(o)}$. That is, understanding that others have emotions, understanding how context influences those emotions, and be able to image what the other is feeling. They would also have low Empathic Distress, Empathic Concern, and deficits in $PT_{(s)}$. Thus, they are less likely to feel distress at the target suffering, feel sympathy for the target, or imagine how they would feel in the context of the target.

Recently, Bird and Viding (2014) have described a model of empathy – *the Self to Other Model of Empathy* (*SOME*) – which focuses on the mechanisms (cognitive and affective) that underlie the experience of empathy and use this to explain some of the darker aspects of empathy, including psychopathy. Five systems comprise the SOME. There are two input systems: (1) the Situational Understanding System, and (2) the Affective Cue Classification System. The Situational Understanding System is domain general and represents the system for understanding the emotions of a target based on the context in which the target is found. The Affective Cue Classification System provides an initial classification of a target's emotions based on cues such as facial expression. These systems feed bi-directionally into each other and feed into two representational systems: (1) the Affective Representation System, and (2) the Theory of Mind System (ToM). The Affective Representation System provides the emotional state of the empathizers toward the target. These two representational systems feed bi-directionally into each other and also feed back to the Situational Understanding System. The final system is a Mirror Neuron System that mediates the link between the Affective Cue Classification System and the Affective Representation System. The final component of the SOME is a Self/ Other Switch, which is necessary for the experience of empathy as opposed to emotional contagion.

The SOME model describes psychopaths as having the ability to conceptualize another's distress, via the Theory of Mind System, but to have impairments in the Affective Cue Classification System. This is similar to the description above. However, they extend this to argue that normally developing individuals use their Theory of Mind System to resolve conflicts that arise when the emotion expressed (Affective Cue Classification System) is at odds with the context in which it is expressed (Situational Understanding System); for example, being upset when the context affords being happy. Psychopathic individuals, it is argued, do not use the Theory of Mind System to resolve such issues.

Exploitation   Empathy has two roles to play in exploitation. First, some people may be more likely to be exploited, such as those high in emotional empathy (Buss & Duntley, 2008; Widiger & Presnall, 2012) or those who are hyper-empathic (Baron-Cohen, 2012), as they may be more easily talked into things, are overly trusting, and go along with the group (Pessin, 2012). Second, these "exploitative" actions are more likely to be taken by those high on cognitive empathy (Singer & Lamm, 2009), who may also be low in the subcomponent of emotional empathy – the psychopath described above.

Torture   It is often assumed that torturers tend to lack empathy so as to be able to torture effectively (Reeder, 2010). However, Reeder (2010) points out that there are "sadistic" torturers who are motivated to torture to enjoy the victim's suffering. As such, they need to empathize with the victim's suffering.

With respect to subcomponents of empathy the "sadistic" torturers should be low in emotional distress, $PT_{(s)}$ and Empathic Concern, but have intact Theory of Mind, Knowledge, $PT_{(o)}$. That is, this type of torturer will not be inhibited from action in terms of feeling for the victim, feeling pain via $PT_{(s)}$ processes, and trying to avoid their distress. They will, however, need to be able to understand the victim's pain in the context of torture (Theory of Mind, Knowledge, and $PT_{(o)}$). This pattern is the same as that proposed for psychopathy.

Related Constructs

Before concluding it is necessary to acknowledge and discuss two very recent developments that relate directly to the argument presented above. Specifically, the concept of "pathological altruism" (Oakley et al., 2012; Oakley, 2013) and "Self to other model of empathy" (SOME) described by Bird and Viding (2014).

Pathological Altruism

The concept of the dark side of empathy resonates with aspects of the notion of "pathological altruism" (Oakley et al., 2012; Oakley, 2013), whereby altruistic behavior can result in harm to the self, others, and society. Oakley (2013) defines "Pathological Altruism" as occurring when "the attempted altruism … results in objectively foreseeable and unreasonable harm to self, to the target of the altruism, or to others beyond the target" (p. 10408). The key issue for pathological altruism is that the harm is "objectively foreseeable and unreasonable." With respect to potential harm to self and others arising from the costs associated with empathy, some can be subsumed under the Pathological Altruism definition (i.e., directing public goods to in-group members), but others do not (such as increased pain sensitivity).

Self to Other Model of Empathy (SOME)

The components or systems of the SOME model of Bird and Viding (2014) have a degree of conceptual overlap with the subcomponents described above (see Figure 8.1).

The Situational Understanding System as a system for understanding the emotions of a target in context is similar to the "Knowledge" subcomponent. The Affective Cue Classification System as an initial emotion classification system is based on cues such as facial expression, and is similar to the Mimicry and Emotional Contagion subcomponents as well as perhaps to the "Knowledge" subcomponent. The Affective Representation System, which provides the emotional state of the empathizers, is most similar to the roles played by $PT_{(o)}$ and $PT_{(s)}$. The Theory of Mind System equates to the Theory of Mind subcomponent. The Mirror Neuron System is similar to the mimicry subcomponent detailed above. The emotional empathy component from Figure 8.1 is missing in the SOME, but this is not surprising as in the SOME model empathic responses are only isomorphic. As detailed above, nonisomorphic responses are included in the model of empathy in this chapter as (1) they are part of people's response to others' distress within a dual-process model, and (2) to they help us to understand a wider set of the benefits and costs of the empathic process, including, among others, pain perception, depression, OCD.

Future Directions

The brief overview above shows clearly that empathy has a bright side ("the good") in terms of helping others, reducing prejudice, and increasing the empathizer's well-being and reputation. But it also carries a dark side ("the bad") in terms of increased pain perceptions, reduced giving to the public good, a risk factor for psychiatric illness. Finally, the darkest side ("the Ugly") of empathy emerges in terms of psychopathy, torture, and exploitation. These have implications for the field in terms of (1) theory and research, as well as (2) practice.

Theoretical and Methodological Implication

There are four main theoretical/methodological conclusions.

Acknowledge the Dark Side   First, there is a need to acknowledge the dark and darkest sides of empathy, as has been done for other traits previously held to be "always beneficial," such as conscientiousness (Boyce, Wood, & Brown 2010; Ferguson et al., 2014). Traits like empathy should therefore be considered carefully not only in terms of the relative interplay between components of empathy, but also with respect to contexts, as negative effects may emerge only in specific contexts (see Kim et al., 2007).

Two Research Traditions as One   To date, work on empathy has generally fallen into two distinct camps: (1) the prosocial researchers, and the (2) dark-side researchers. If the cost–benefit model is valid then a single paradigm that combines both the dark side and prosocial side of research on empathy within a single design is needed. If the cost–benefit trade-off model has validity, then manipulation of empathy and assessment of trait empathy, should, in the same individuals, lead to both prosocial and dark-side behavior. The following basic multistage design would be fruitful in this context. In Stage 1, empathy can be manipulated using a perspective-taking paradigm developed by Batson and colleagues to explore the relationship to helping, with the simple prediction that $PT_{(o)}$ and Empathic Concern will result in greater helping. The perspective-taking manipulation would be with respect to someone suffering from pain, so that in later stages of the experiment association with pain could be assessed. In Stage 2, a pain threshold test (e.g., Cold Pressor) could be used to explore basic pain thresholds and perceptions of pain. The prediction would be that reported pain should be greater and pain thresholds reduced for those higher in trait empathy or exposed to a $PT_{(o)}$ manipulation. In a final stage, Stage 3, an economic game could be used, whereby tension is produced between giving money to the self, a larger group, or the target empathized with in Stage 1 could be explored. The hypothesis here is that the target will receive some of the money even if the money has been raised for the wider group.

Empathic Accuracy   It is important that, where possible, researchers assess the accuracy of the empathizer's emotional judgments of the targets emotions. This is important for $PT_{(s)}$, as here the target imagines how they would feel if they were the target. To judge whether this is isomorphic or not requires knowing how accurately the empathizer judges the target's emotions. As detailed above, there are different implications for helping depending on whether the emotion "felt" by the empathizer is isomorphic or not (see Figure 8.2). Crucially, however, the majority of the work on $PT_{(o)}$ and $PT_{(s)}$ has not assessed "empathic accuracy" and this needs to be done.

Other "Empathy"-Related Phenomena   There are a series of emotions that share some neuronal circuitry with empathic systems. These include shame, guilt, envy, and "Schadenfreude."

Such feelings may arise through perspective-taking and social comparison processes as described above. The empathizer may perceive that they would feel guilt or shame in a particular context, this could be that same as the target does (isomorphic) or they could feel shame when the target does not (nonisomorphic). Finally, envy occurs when we have a negative emotional response to perceiving another's good fortune and "Schadenfreude" when we feel a positive emotional response to another's perceived bad fortune. Again, these are important social emotions that arise via the perspective-taking process in a specific context and will influence bright- and dark-side behaviors. Shame and guilt may lead to helping behavior, for example, as a way of repairing relationships and mood (see Jankowski & Takahashi, 2104, for an excellent review).

Practical Implications

With respect to practice there are enormous implications for the professional psychology disciplines, especially occupational and clinical psychology. If empathy is identified as a key trait for a job (e.g., medicine, law enforcement), then care is needed to examine the relative balance of cognitive and emotional empathy in potential candidates. Also, there is a need to examine how empathy will interact with the nature of the work environment. For example, in some contexts it may be a risk factor for depression, specifically in jobs that involve social interactions that are highly emotionally charged. In such contexts, it may be better to (1) not select high empathy candidates, or (2) to make sure that appropriate training and monitoring are in place. Compassion training may be beneficial here. Compassion training aims to foster attitudes and feelings of loving kindness, friendliness, benevolence, and emotional positivity (Leiberg, Klimecki, & Singer, 2011). Evidence shows that compassion training leads to greater prosociality (Leiberg et al., 2011; Weng et al., 2013). Importantly, however, compassion training, compared with empathy training, reduced negative affect and enhanced positive affect in response to suffering (Klimecki, Lweiberg, Ricard, & Singer, 2014).

Finally, clinical psychology needs to consider the subtle interplay of the components of empathy when developing therapies for illness like depression. Specifically if illnesses like depression are function of tension between wanting to help, but feeling too distressed by others distress, then techniques that allow the patient to understand and deal with their responses to other distress may be beneficial. Again, compassion training may be beneficial here.

Conclusion

The aim of this chapter has been to show that there is a dark side to empathy, and that this needs to be both acknowledged and considered in both research and applications in applied psychology. I hope that this aim has been achieved and the reader is convinced that the dark side of empathy is out there and needs to be explored.

Notes

1   This represents indirect reciprocity (Nowak & Sigmund, 2005).
2   While the data suggest that empathy may be more important for predicting low-cost helping, some recent work suggests that this may depend on beliefs about empathic malleability. Schumann, Zaki, and Dweck (2014) show that people vary in their mental models of empathy from one that is malleable (believe it can be developed) to one that is fixed (empathy cannot be developed). Those who have a malleable model are more likely to exert effort in challenging contexts. Thus, empathy may be associated with helping in high-cost situation, but only for those with a malleable model of empathy.

3   In a dictator game there are two players – a dictator and a recipient. The dictator has a financial endowment and can choose to transfer some, none, or all of it to the recipient. Whatever the dictator decides is what both parties get. The rational position is for the dictator to give nothing.

4   There are examples of simple bargaining games like the Prisoner's Dilemma game, but in these cases empathy is still direct at a single target – the other player (Batson & Moran, 1999; Batson & Ahmad, 2001).

5   There is, of course, the possibility of legitimate "free-riding," whereby people do not contribute because they cannot (Ferguson & Corr, 2012; Ferguson et al., 2012); also referred to as phenotypic defectors (Lotem, Fishman, & Stone, 1999). These tend to be treated by other the same as co-operators and not like free-riders (Ferguson et al., 2012).

References

Andreoni, J. (1990). Impure altruism and donations to public goods: A theory of warm glow giving. *Economic Journal, 100*, 464–487. doi.10.2307/2234133.

Andreoni, J. & Rao, J. M. (2011). The power of asking: how communication affects selfishness, empathy and altruism. *Journal of Public Economics, 95*, 513–520. doi.0.1016/j.jpubeco.2010.12.008.

Baron-Cohen, S. (2012). Autism, empathizing–systematizing (E–S) theory, and pathological altruism. In: B. Oakley, A. Knafo, G. Madhava, & D. S. Wilson (Eds.), *Pathological Altruism* (pp. 345–348). Oxford: Oxford University Press.

Batson, C. D. (2002). Addressing the altruism question empirically. In: S. G. Post, L. G. Underwood, J. P. Schloss, & W. B. Huribut (Eds.), *Altruism and altruistic love: Science, philosophy and religion in dialogue* (pp. 89–105). Oxford: Oxford University Press.

Batson, C. D. (2009). These things called empathy: Eight related but distinct phenomena. In: J. Decety and W. Ickes (Eds.), *Social neuroscience of empathy* (pp. 3–16). Cambridge, MA: MIT Press.

Batson, C. D. (2011). Empathy induced altruism: Friend or foe of the common good? In: R. Donelson, C. Forsyth, & L. Hoyt (Eds.), *For the greater good of all: Perspectives on individualism, society, and leadership* (pp. 29–47). Basingstoke: Palgrave.

Batson, C. D. & Ahmad, N. (2001). Empathy-induced altruism in a prisoner's dilemma II: What if the target of empathy has defected? *European Journal of Social Psychology, 31*, 25–36. doi.0.1002/ejsp.26.

Batson, C. D. & Moran, T. (1999). Empathy-induced altruism in a prisoner's dilemma. *European Journal of Social Psychology, 29*, 909–92. doi.10.1002/(SICI)1099-0992(199911)29:7<909::AID-EJSP965>3.0.CO;2-L.

Batson, C. D. & Shaw, L L. (1991). Evidence for altruism: Towards a pluralism of prosocial motives. *Psychological Inquiry, 2*, 107–122.

Batson, C. D., Ahmad, N., Yin, J., Bedell, S. J., Johnson, J. W., Templin, C. M., & Whiteside, A. (1999). Two threats to the common good: self-interested egoism and empathy-induced altruism. *Personality and Social Psychology Bulletin, 25*, 3–16. doi.10.1177/0146167299025001001.

Batson, C. D., Batson, J. G., Todd, R. M., Brummett, B. H., Shaw, L. L., & Aldeguer, C. M. R. (1995). Empathy and the collective good: Caring for one of the others in a social dilemma. *Journal of Personality and Social Psychology, 68*, 619–631. doi.10.1037/0022-3514.68.4.619.

Batson, C. D., Chang, J., Orr, R., & Rowland, J. (2002). Empathy, attitudes and action: Can feeling for a member of a stigmatized group motivate one to help the group? *Personality and Social Psychology Bulletin, 28*, 1656–1666. doi.0.1177/014616702237647.

Batson, C. D., Early, S., & Salvarini. G.(1997). Perspective-taking: imagining how another feels versus imagining how you would feel. *Personality and Social Psychological Bulletin, 23*, 751–758. doi.10.1177/0146167297237008.

Batson, C. D., Klien, T. R., Highberger, L., & Shaw, L. L. (1995). Immorality from empathy-induced altruism: When compassion and justice conflict. *Journal of Personality and Social Psychology, 68*, 1042–1054. doi.10.1037//0022-3514.68.6.1042.

Batson, C. D., O'Quin, K., Fultz, J., Vanderplas, M., & Isen, A. M. (1983). Influence of self-reported distress and empathy on egoistic versus altruistic motivation to help. *Journal of Personality and Social Psychology, 45*, 706–718. doi.10.1037//0022-3514.45.3.706.

Batson, C. D., Polycarpou, M. P., Harmon-Jones, E., Imhoff, H. J., Mitchener, E. C., Bednar, L. L., Klien, T. R., & Highberger, L. (1997). Empathy and attitudes: Can feeling for a member of a stigmatized group improve feelings toward the group. *Journal of Personality and Social Psychology, 72*, 105–118. doi.10.1037/0022-3514.72.1.105.

Bernhard, H., Fischbacher, U., & Fehr, E. (2006). Parochial altruism in humans. *Nature, 442*, 912–915. doi.10.1038/nature04981.

Bernhardt, B. C. & Singer, T. (2012). The neural basis of empathy. *Annual Review of Neuroscience, 35*, 1–23. doi.10.1146/annurev-neuro-062111-150536.

Bird, G. & Viding, E. (2014). The self to other model of empathy: Proving a new framework for understanding empathy impairments in psychopathy, autism and alexithymia. *Neuroscience and Biobehavioral Reviews, 47*, 520–532.

Blair, R. J. P. (2005). Responding to the emotions of others: Dissociating form of empathy through the study of typical and psychiatric populations. *Consciousness and Cognition, 14*, 698–718. doi.10.1016/jconcog.2005.06.004.

Blair, R. J. P. (2008). Fine cuts of empathy and the amygdale: Dissociable deficits in psychopathy and autism. *Quarterly Journal of Experimental Psychology, 61*, 157–170. doi.10.1080/1740210701508855.

Boyce, C., Wood, A. M., & Brown, G. D. A. (2010). The dark side of conscientiousness: Conscientious people experience greater drops in life satisfaction following unemployment. *Journal of Research in Personality, 44*, 535–539. doi.10.1016/j jrp 2010.05.001.

Brown, S. L., Nesse, R. M., Vinokur, A. D., & Smith, D. M. (2003). Providing social support may be more beneficial than receiving it: Results from a perspective study of mortality. *Psychological Science, 14*, 320–327. doi 10.1111/1467-9280.14461.

Buss, D. M. & Duntley, J. D. (2008). Adaptations for exploitation. *Group Dynamics, 12*, 53–62. doi.10.1037/1089-2699.12.1.53.

Cheng, Y., Chen, C., Lin, C. P., Chou, K. H., & Decety, J. (2010). Love hurts: An fMRI study. *Neuroimage, 51*, 923–929. doi.1016/j.neuroimage.2010.02.047.

Cialdini, R. B. & Kenrick, D. T. (1976). Altruism as hedonism: A social development perspective on the relationship of negative mood state and helping. *Journal of Personality and Social Psychology, 34*, 907–914. doi.10.1037/0022-3514.34.5.907.

Cialdini, R. B., Schaller, M., Houlihan, D., Arps, K., Fultz, J., & Beaman, A. L. (1987). Empathy-based helping: Is it selflessly or selfishly motivated? *Journal of Personality and Social Psychology, 52*, 749–758. doi.10.1037/0022-3514.52.4.749.

Danziger, N., Faillenot, I., & Peyron, R. (2008). Can we share pain we never felt? Neural correlates of empathy in patients with congenital insensitivity to pain. *Neuron, 61*, 203–212. doi.10.1016/j.neuron.2008.11.023.

Davis, M. H. (1983). Measuring individual differences in empathy: Evidence for a multidimensional approach. *Journal of Personality and Social Psychology, 44*, 113–126. doi.10.1037//0022-3514.44.1.113.

Davis, M. H., Mitchell, K. W., Hall, J. A., Lothert, J., Snapp, T., & Meyer, M. (1999). Empathy, expectations and situational preferences: Personality influences on the decision to participate in volunteer helping behavior. *Journal of Personality, 67*, 469–503. doi.10.1111/1467-6494.00062.

de Vignemont, F. & Singer, T. (2006). The empathic brain: how, when and why? *Trends in Cognitive Science, 10*, 435–441. doi.10.1016/j.tics.2006.08.008.

de Wall, F. B. M. (2008). Putting the altruism back into altruism: The evolution of empathy. *Annual Review of Psychology, 59*, 279–300. doi.0066-4308/08/0203-0279$20.00.

Decety, J. & Jackson, P. L. (2004). The functional architecture of human empathy. *Behavioral and Cognitive Neuroscience Reviews, 3*, 71–100. doi.10.1177/153458230426187.

Drwecki, B. B., Moore, C. F., Ward, S. E., & Prkachin, K. M. (2011). Reducing racial disparities in pain treatment: The role of empathy and perspective-taking, *Pain, 152*, 1001-1006. Doi. 10.1016/j.pain.2010.12.005

Einolf. C. J. (2008). Empathic concern and prosocial behaviors: A test of experimental results using survey data. *Social Science Research, 37*, 1267–1279. doi.10.1016/j.ssresearch.2007.06.003.

Eisenberg, N. (1991). Meta-analytic contributions to the literature of prosocial behaviour. *Personality and Social Psychology Bulletin, 17*, 273–282. doi.10.1177/0146167291173007.

Eisenberg, N. & Miller, P. A. (1987). The relation of empathy to prosocial and related behaviors. *Psychological Bulletin, 101*, 91–119. doi.10.1037/0033-2909.101.1.91.

Engen, H. G. & Singer, T. (2013). Empathy circuits. *Current Opinion in Neurobiology, 23,* 275–282. doi.10.1016/j.conb.2012.11.003.

Fazio, R. H. (2001). On the automatic activation of associated evaluations: An overview. *Cognition and Emotion, 15,* 115–141. doi.10.1080/0269993004200024.

Ferguson, E. (2013). Personality is of central concern to understand health: Towards a theoretical model for health psychology. *Health Psychology Review, 7,* S32–S70. doi.10.1080/17437199.2010.547985.

Ferguson, E. & Corr P. (2012). Blood, sex, personality, power and altruism. *Behavior and Brain Sciences, 35,* 25–26. doi.10.1017/S0140525X11001245.

Ferguson, E., Farrell, K., & Lawrence, C. (2008). Blood donation is an act of benevolence rather than altruism. *Health Psychology, 27,* 327–336. doi.10.1037/0278-6133.27.3.327.

Ferguson, E., James, D., & Madely, L. (2002). Factors associated with success in medical school: systematic review of the literature. *British Medical Journal, 324,* 952–957. doi. 10.1136/bmj.324.7343.952.

Ferguson, E., Lawrence, C., & Farrell, K. (2008). High cost helping behavior is driven by benevolence rather than altruism. *International Journal of Psychology, 43,* 254–254.

Ferguson, E., Semper, H., Yates, J., Fitzgerald, J. E., Skatova, A., & James, D. (2014). The "dark side" and "bright side" of personality: When too much conscientiousness and too little anxiety are detrimental to the acquisition of medical knowledge and skill. *PLoS One, 9,* 2 e8860. doi.10.1371/journal.pone.0088606.

Ferguson, E., Taylor, M., Keatley, D., Flynn, N., & Lawrence, C. (2012). Blood donors' helping behavior is driven by warm glow more evidence for the blood donor benevolence hypothesis. *Transfusion, 52,* 2189–2200. doi.10.1111/j.1537-2995.2011.03557.x.

Fontenelle, L. F., Soares, I. D., Miele, F., Borges, M. C., Prazeres, A. M., Range, B. P., & Moll, J. (2009). Empathy and symptoms dimensions of patients with obsessive-compulsive disorder. *Journal of Psychiatric Research, 43,* 455–463. doi.10.1016/j.psychires.2008.05.007.

Frith, C. D. & Singer, T. (2008). The role of social cognition in decision making. *Philosophical Transactions of the Royal Society, 363,* 3875–3886. doi.10.1098/rstb.2008.0156.

Galinsky, A. D., Massux, W. W., Gilin, D., & White, J. B. (2008). Why it pays to get inside the head of your opponent: The differential effects of perspective taking and empathy in negotiations. *Psychological Science, 19,* 378–384. doi.10.1111/j.1467-9280.2008.02096.x.

Gallese, V. & Goldman, A. (1998). Mirror neurons and the simulation theory of mind-reading. *Trends in Cognitive Science, 2,* 493–501. doi.10.1016/S1364-6613(98)01262-5.

Georgi, E., Petermann, F., & Schipper, M. (2014). Are empathic abilities learnable? Implications for social neuroscientific research from psychometric assessments. *Social Neuroscience, 9,* 74–81. doi.10.1080/17470919.2013.855253.

Goldstein, N. J., Vezich, S. I., & Shapiro, J. R. (2014). Perceived perspective taking: When other walk in our shoes. *Journal of Personality and Social Psychology, 106,* 941–960. doi.10.1037/a0036395.

Griffin, A. S. & West, S. A. (2002), Kin selection: Fact and fiction. *Trends in Ecology and Evolution, 17,* 15–21. doi.10.1016/S0169-5347(01)02355-2.

Hakansson, J. & Montgomery, H. (2003). Empathy as an interpersonal phenomena. *Journal of Social and Personal Relationships, 20,* 267–284. doi. 10.1177/0265407503020003001.

Hein, G. & Singer, T. (2008). I feel how you feel but not always: the empathic brain and its modulation. *Current Opinion in Neurobiology, 18,* 153–158. doi.10.1016/j.conb.2008.07.012.

Hein, G., Lamm, C., Brodbeck, C., & Singer, T. (2011). Skin conductance responses to the pain of others predicts later costly helping. *PLos One, 6,* 8, e22759. doi.10.1016/j.conb.2008.07.012.

Iacoboni, M. (2009) Imitation, empathy and mirror neurons. *Annual Review of Psychology, 60,* 653–670. doi.10.1146/annrev.psych.60.110707.163604.

Jackson, P. L., Brunet, E., Meltzoff, A. N., & Decety, J. (2006). Empathy examined through the neural mechanisms involved in imaging how I feel versus how you feel pain. *Neuropsychologia, 44,* 752–761. doi.10.1016/j.neuropsychologia.2005.07.015.

Jankowski, K. F. & Takahashi, H. (2104). Cognitive neuroscience of social emotions and implications for psychopathology: Examining embarrassment, guilt, envy and schadenfreude. *Psychiatric and Clinical Neurosciences Frontier Review, 68,* 319–336. doi.10.1111/pcn.12182.

Jones, A. P., Happe, F. G. E., Gilbert, F., Burnett, S., & Viding E. (2010). Feeling, caring, knowing: Different types of empathy deficit in boys with psychotic tendencies and autistic spectrum disorder. *Journal of Child Psychology and Psychiatry, 51,* 1188–1197. doi.10.1111/j.1469-7610.2010.02280.x.

Kerem, E., Fishman, N., & Josselson, R. (2001). The experience of empathy in everyday relationships: Cognitive and affective elements. *Journal of Social and Personal Relationships, 18,* 709–729. doi. 10.1177/0265407501185008.

Keysers, C. & Gazzola, V. (2007). Integrating simulation and theory of mind: From self to social cognition. *Trends in Cognitive Science, 11,* 194–196. doi.10.1016/j.tics.2007.02.002.

Kim, S. S., Kaplowitz, S., & Johnston, MV. (2004). The effects of physician empathy on patient satisfaction and compliance. *Evaluation and the Health Professions, 27,* 237–251. doi. 10.1177/0163278704267037.

Kim, Y., Schulz, R., & Carver, C. S. (2007). Benefit finding in the cancer caregiving experience. *Psychosomatic Medicine, 69,* 283–291. doi.10.1097/PSY.0b013e3180417cf4.

Klimecki, O., Lweiberg, S., Ricar, M., & Singer, T. (2014). Differential pattern of functional brain plasticity after compassion and empathy training. *Social Cognitive and Affective Neuroscience, 9,* 873–879. doi.10.1093/scan/nst060.

Knafo, A., Zahn-Waxler, C., Hulle, C. V., Robinson, J. J., & Rhee, S. H. (2008). The developmental origins of a disposition towards empathy: Genetic and environmental contributions. *Emotion, 8,* 737–752. doi.10.1037/a0014179.

Konrath, S., Fuhrel-Forbis, A., Lou, A., & Brown, S. (2012). Motives for volunteering are associated with mortality risk in older adults. *Health Psychology, 31,* 87–96. doi.10.1037/a0025226.

Lamm, C., Decety, J., & Singer, T. (2011). Meta analytic evidence for common and distinct neural networks associated with directly experiencing pain and empathy for pain. *Neuroimage, 54,* 2492–2502. doi.10.1016/j.neuroimage.2010.10.014.

Lamm, C., Meltzoff, A. N., & Decety, J. (2010). How do we empathize with someone who is not like us? A functional magnetic resonance imaging study. *Journal of Cognitive Neuroscience, 22,* 362–376. doi.0.1162/jocn.2009.21186.

Lamm, C., Nurbaum, H. C., Meltzoff, A. N., & Decety, J. (2007). What are you feeling? Using functional magnetic resonance imaging to assess the modulation of sensory and affective responses during empathy for pain. *Plos One, 12,* e1292. doi.10.1371/journal.pone.0001292.

Lamm. C., Batson. C. D., & Decety, J. (2007). The neural substrate of human empathy: Effects of perspective-taking and cognitive appraisal. *Journal of Cognitive Neuroscience, 19,* 42–58. doi.10.1162/jocn.2007.19.1.42.

Lazarus, R. (1993). From psychological stress to the emotions: A history of changing outlooks. *Annual Review of Psychology, 44,* 1–22. doi.10.1146/annurev.ps.44.020193.000245.

Leiberg, S., Klimecki, O., & Singer, T. (2011). Short-term compassion training increases prosocial behaviour in a newly developed prosocial game. *PLoS One, 6,* e17798. doi.0.1371/journal.pone.0017798.

Lieberman, M. D. (2007). Social cognitive neuroscience: A review of core processes. *Annual Review of Psychology, 58,* 529–589. doi.10.1146/annrev-psych.58.110405.085654.

Lockwood, P. L., Seara-Cardoso, A., & Viding, E. (2014). Emotion regulation moderates the association between empathy and prosocial behaviour. *PLoS One, 9,* e96555. doi.10.1371/journal.pone.0096555

Loewenstein, G. F. (2005). Hot–cold empathy gaps in medical decision making. *Health Psychology, 24,* S49–S56. doi.10.1037/0278-6133.24.4.S49.

Loewenstein, G. & Small, D. A. (2007). The scarecrow and the tin man: The vicissitudes of human sympathy and caring. *Review of General Psychology, 11,* 112–126. doi.10.1037/1089-2680.11.1.112.

Loewenstein, G. F., Weber, E. U., Hsee, C. K., & Welch, N. (2001). Risk as feelings. *Psychological Bulletin, 127,* 267–286. doi.0.1037//0033-2909.127.2.267.

Loggia, M. L., Mogil, J. S., & Bushnell, M. C. (2008). Empathy hurts: Compassion for another increases both sensory and effective components of pain perception. *Pain, 136,* 168–176. doi.10.1016/j.pain.2007.07.017.

Lotem, A., Fishman, M. A., & Stone, L. (1999). Evolution of cooperation between individuals. *Nature, 400,* 226–227. doi.10.1038/22247.

Mahmut, M. K., Homewood, J., & Stevenson, R. J. (2008). The characteristics of non-criminals with high psychopathy traits: Are they similar to criminal psychopaths? *Journal of Research in Personality, 42,* 679–692. doi.10.1016/j.jrp.2007.09.002.

Maner, J. K. & Gailliot, M. T. (2007). Altruism and egoism: Prosocial motivations of helping depend on relationship context. *European Journal of Social Psychology, 37,* 347–358. doi.10.1002/ejsp.364.

Milinski, M., Semmann, M. M., & Krambeck, H. J. (2002). Donor to charity gain in both indirect reciprocity and political reputation. *Proceedings of the Royal Society of London, B, 269,* 881–883. doi.10.1098/rspb.2002.1964.

Mitani, H. (2014). Influences of resources and subjective dispositions on formal and informal volunteering. *Voluntas, 25*, 1022–1040. doi.10.1007/s11266-013-9384-3.

Morelli, S. A., Rameson, L. T., Lieberman, M. D. (2014). The neural components of empathy: Predicting daily prosocial behaviour. *Social Cognitive and Affective Neuroscience, 9*, 39–47. doi.10.1093/scan/nss088.

Nettle, D. (2006). The evolution of personality variation in humans and other animals. *American Psychologist, 61*, 622–631. doi.10.1037/0003-066X.61.6.622.

Neuberg, S. L., Cialdini, R. B., Brown, S. L., Luce, C., Sagarin, B. J., & Lewis, B. P. (1997). Does empathy lead to anything more than superficial helping? Comment on Batson et al (1997). *Journal of Personality and Social Psychology, 73*, 510–516.

Nowak. M. & Sigmund, K. (2005). Evolution of indirect reciprocity. *Nature, 437*, 1291–1298. doi.0.1038/nature04131.

O'Connor, L. E., Berry, J. W., Lewis, T. B., & Stiver, D. J. (2012). Empathy-based pathogenic guilt, pathological altruism, and psychopathology. In: B. Oakley, A. Knafo, G. Madhava, & D. S. Wilson (Eds.), *Pathological altruism* (pp. 10–30). Oxford: Oxford University Press.

Oakley, B. A. (2013). Concepts and implications of altruism bias and pathological altruism. *Proceedings of the National Academy of Science, 110*, 10405–10415. doi.10.1073/pnas.1302547110.

Oakley, B., Knafo, A., Madhava, G., & Wilson, D. S. (Eds.). (2012). *Pathological altruism*. Oxford: Oxford University Press.

Oceja, L. V., Heerdink, M. W., Stocks, E. L. Ambrona, T., Lopez-Perez, B., & Salagado, S. (2014). Awareness of others, and action: How feeling empathy for one-among-others motivates helping the others. *Basic and Applied Social Psychology, 36*, 111–124. doi.10.1080/01973533.2013.856787.

Patterson, F., Ferguson, E., Lane, P., Farrell, K., Martlew, J., & Wells, A. (2000). A competency model of general practice: Implications for selection, training and development. *British Journal of General Practice, 50*, 188–193.

Pessin, K. M. (2012). Seduction super-responders and hyper-trust: The biology of affective behaviour. In: B. Oakley, A. Knafo, G. Madhava, & D. S. Wilson (Eds.), *Pathological altruism* (pp. 349–367). Oxford: Oxford University Press.

Pfeiffer, T., Tran, L., Krumme, C., & Rand, D. G. (2012). The value of reputation. *Journal of the Royal Society Interface, 9*, 2791–2797. doi.1098/rsif.2012.0332.

Preston, S. D. (2007). A perception-action model of empathy. In: T. F. D. Farrow and P. W. R. Woodruff (Eds.), *Empathy in mental illness* (pp. 428–447). Cambridge: Cambridge University Press.

Raghunathan, R. & Phun, M. T. (1999). All negative moods are not equal: Motivational influences of anxiety and sadness on decision making. *Organizational Behavior and Human Decision Processes, 79*, 56–77. doi.10.1006/obhd.1999.2838.

Rameson. L. T. & Lieberman, M. D. (2009). Empathy: A social cognitive neuroscience approach. *Personality and Social Psychology Compass, 3*, 94–110. doi.10.111141751-9004.2008.00154x

Reeder, J. P., Jr. (2010). What kind of person could be a torturer. *Journal of Religious Ethics, 38*, 67–92.

Schieman, S. & van Gundy. (2000). The personal and social links between age and self-reported empathy. *Social Psychology Quarterly, 63*, 152–174. doi.10.2307/2695889.

Schlumpf, K. S., Glynn, S. A., Schreiber, G. B., Wright, D. J., Steele, W. R., Tu, Y., Hermansen, S., Higgins, M. J., Garratty, G., & Murphy, E. L. (2008). Factors influencing donor return. *Transfusion, 48*, 264–272. doi.10.1111/j.1537-2995.2007.01519.x.

Schreiter, S., Pijnenborg, G. H. M., & ann het Rot, M. (2013). Empathy in adults with clinical or subclinical depressive symptoms. *Journal of Affective Disorders, 150*, 1–16. doi.10.1016/j.jad.2013.03.009.

Schumann, K., Zaki, J., & Dweck, C. S. (2014). Addressing the empathy deficit: Beliefs about the malleability of empathy predict effortful responses when empathy is challenging. *Journal of Personality and Social Psychology, 107*, 475–493. doi.10.1037/a0036738.

Shamay-Tsoory, S. G., Lester, H., Chisin, R., Israel, O., Bar-Shalom, R., Pertez, A., Tomer, R., Tsitrinbaum, Z., & Aharon-Peretz, J. (2005). The neural correlates of understanding the other's distress: A positron emission tomography investigation of accurate empathy. *Neuroimage, 27*, 568–472. doi.10.1016j.nueoimage.2005.05.012.

Shamay-Tsoory, S., Harari, H., Aharon-Peretz, J., & Levkovitz, Y. (2010). The role of orbitofrontal cortex in affective theory of mind deficits in criminal offenders with psychopathic tendencies. *Cortex, 46*, 668–677. doi.10.1016/jcortex.2009.04.008.

Silvester, J., Patterson, F., Koczwara A., & Ferguson, E. (2007). "Trust me ...": Psychological and behavioral predictors of perceived physician empathy. *Journal of Applied Psychology, 92*, 519–527. doi.10.1037/0021-9010.92.2.519.

Singer, T. (2006). The neuronal basis and ontogeny of empathy and mind reading: Review of the literature and implications for future research. *Neuroscience and Biobehavioral Reviews, 30*, 855–863. doi.10.1016/j.neubiorev.2006.06.011.

Singer, T. & Frith, C. (2005). The painful side of empathy. *Nature Neuroscience, 8*, 845–846. doi.10.1038/nn0705-845.

Singer. T. & Kimecki, O. M. (2014). Empathy and compassion. *Current Biology, 24*, R875–R878.

Singer, T. & Lamm, (2009). The social neuroscience of empathy. *Annals of the New York Academy of Science, 1156*, 81–96. doi.10.1111/j.1749-6632.2009.04418x.

Singer, T., Seymour, B., O'Doherty, J., Kaube, H., Dolan, R. J., & Frith, C. (2004). Empathy for pain involves the affective but not sensory components of pain. *Science, 303*, 1157–1161. doi.10.1038/narure04271.

Smith, A. (2006). Cognitive empathy and emotional empathy in human behavior and evolution. *The Psychological Record, 56*, 3–21.

Steele, W. R., Schreiber, G. B., Guiltinan, A., Nass, C., Glynn, S. A., Wright, D. J., Kessler, D., Schlumpf, K. S., Tu, Y., Smith, J. W., & Garratty, G. (2008). The role of altruistic behaviour, empathic concern, and social responsibility motivation in blood donation behaviour. *Transfusion, 48*, 43–54. doi.10.1111/j.1537-2995.2007.01481.x.

Sturmer, S., Snyder, M., & Omoto, A. M. (2005). Prosocial emotions and helping: The moderating role of group membership. *Journal of Personality and Social Psychology, 88*, 532–546. doi.10.1037/0022-3514.88.3.532.

Weinstein, N. & Ryan, R. M. (2010). When helping helps: Autonomous motivation for prosocial behaviour and its influence on well-being for helper and recipient. *Journal of Personality and Social Psychology, 98*, 222–244. doi.10.1037/a0016984

Weng, H. Y., Fox, A. S., Shackman, A. J., Stodola, D. E., Caldwell, J. Z. K., Olson, M. C., Rogers, G. M., & Davidson, R. D. (2013). Compassion training alters altruism and neural responses to suffering. *Psychological Science, 24*, 1171–1180. doi.10/1177/0956797612469537.

Widiger, T. A. & Presnall, J. R. (2012). Pathological altruism and personality disorders. In: B. Oakley, A. Knafo, G. Madhava, & D. S. Wilson (Eds.), *Pathological altruism* (pp. 85–93). Oxford: Oxford University Press.

Zahavi, A. & Zahavi, A. (1997). *The handicap principle*. New York: Oxford University Press.

Zahn-Waxler, C. & Van Hule, C. (2012). Empathy, guilt and depression: When caring for others becomes costly to children. In: B. Oakley, A. Knafo, G. Madhava, & D. S. Wilson (Eds.), *Pathological altruism* (pp. 321–344). Oxford: Oxford University Press.

Zollman, K. J. S., Bergstrom, C. T., & Huttegger, S. M. (2013). Between cheap and costly signals: The evolution of partially honest communications. *Proceedings of the Royal Society, B, 280*, 20121878. doi.10.1098/rspb.2012.1878.

9

Nostalgia

A Bittersweet Emotion that Confers Psychological Health Benefits

Constantine Sedikides and Tim Wildschut

Nostalgia is, by its very nature, bittersweet, the happiest memories laced with melancholy. It's that combination, that opposition of forces, that makes it so compelling. People, places, events, times we miss them, and there's a pleasure in the missing and a sadness in the love.
Walk Like a Man: Coming of Age with the Music of Bruce Springstein,
Robert J. Wiersema

Positive Clinical Psychology is concerned with balancing positivity and negativity in human experience and clinical treatment (Wood & Tarrier, 2010). We are focusing in this chapter on the emotion of nostalgia, which is inherently positive and negative, and its implications for psychological health. We discuss depictions of bittersweetness or ambivalence in lay definitions of nostalgia, in narrations of nostalgic experiences, and in its affective signature. Further, we consider nostalgia's psychological health benefits: social, self-related, and existential. We conclude with a speculative link between nostalgic ambivalence and the health benefits that the emotion confers.

The Ambivalence of Nostalgia

The *New Oxford Dictionary of English* (1998) defines the emotion of nostalgia as "a sentimental longing or wistful affection for the past" (p. 1266). This definition implies bittersweetness or ambivalence. The nostalgizer feels both good and bad.

Speculations on Nostalgic Ambivalence

Speculative quests depict nostalgia as an ambivalent emotion. Although Davis (1979) argued that nostalgia "is infused with imputations of past beauty, pleasure, joy, satisfaction, goodness, happiness, love" (p. 18), other authors (Best & Nelson, 1985; Johnson-Laird & Oatley, 1989; Hertz, 1990) maintained that it is filled with sadness, as the nostalgizer comes to the realization that the past is irrevocably lost. Although Kaplan (1987) regarded nostalgia a "warm feeling about the past … one of joyousness, producing an air of infatuation

The Wiley Handbook of Positive Clinical Psychology, First Edition. Edited by Alex M. Wood and Judith Johnson.
© 2016 John Wiley & Sons, Ltd. Published 2016 by John Wiley & Sons, Ltd.

and a feeling of elation" (p. 465), Peters (1985) asserted that it ranges from "a fleeting sadness and yearning to an overwhelming craving that persists and profoundly interferes with the individual's attempts to cope with his present circumstances" (p. 135). And although Chaplin (2000) claimed that nostalgia reflects appreciation and re-enjoyment of past experiences, other authors (Fodor, 1950; Socarides, 1977) added that it involves psychological pain. Nostalgia, Werman (1977) stated, is "wistful pleasure, a joy tinged with sadness" (p. 393).

The nostalgizer, then, is presumed to feel negatively for a bygone way of life, for the passing of treasured moments, and for the current absence of persons significant to them. At the same time, the nostalgizer feels positively for having had the opportunity to share defining life events with those significant others. Davis (1979) mused extensively, if not poetically, on the ambivalence entailed in yearning for an experience while conceding to its irredeemable loss.

Empirical Support for Nostalgic Ambivalence

We will capitalize on four sources of empirical support for ambivalence: lay conceptions of nostalgia, content analysis of nostalgic narratives, comparisons of experimentally-induced nostalgic and ordinary autobiographical memories, and juxtaposition of positive and negative events in nostalgic narratives.

Lay conceptions of nostalgia We (Hepper, Ritchie, Sedikides, & Wildschut, 2012) examined lay conceptions of nostalgia by adopting a prototype approach, according to which nostalgia is regarded as a fuzzy category with more representative members (i.e., features) labeled as central and less representative members labeled as peripheral. Participants listed all descriptors that came to mind while thinking about nostalgia, and then two judges coded these descriptors into thirty-five features (Study 1). Another set of participants rated each feature for centrality or peripherality, that is, for level of semantic proximity to their view of nostalgia (Study 2). Central nostalgia features were positive (fond, rose-colored, and personally important recollections of childhood or relationships) and negative (missing, wanting to return to the past). Likewise, peripheral features were positive (warmth, calm, success) and negative (regret, lethargy). In both cases, though, the positive features outweighed the negative ones. We (Hepper et al., 2014) obtained similar findings in eighteen countries spanning five continents. In all, lay conceptions of nostalgia are characterized by a degree of ambivalence.

Content analysis of nostalgic narratives Ambivalence can also studied by asking participants to narrate a nostalgic event from their lives, and then coding the narratives for the extent to which they express positive or negative emotions. As a case in point, Holak and Havlena (1998) instructed participants to describe their feelings concerning, and circumstances surrounding, three nostalgic occasions that referred to persons, events, or objects. Judges rated the ensuing descriptions on several emotions. The narratives reflected both positive (warmth, joy, elation, tenderness, gratitude) and negative (sadness, irritation, fear) emotions, although the former outnumbered the latter.

We (Wildschut, Sedikides, Arndt, & Routledge, 2006, Studies 1–2) used a similar methodology. Study 1 relied on forty-two nostalgic essays (1,000–1,500 words) published in the periodical *Nostalgia* between 1998 and 1999. Two judges rated the extent to which the essays reflected each of the twenty adjectives of the Positive and Negative Affect Schedule (PANAS) (Watson, Clark, & Tellegen, 1988). The essays reflected both positive and negative affect, albeit more positive than negative. We established the replicability of these findings in Study 2, in which participants generated nostalgic narratives in the laboratory in response to the prompt "Please try to think of an important part of your past (e.g., event or episode) that makes you feel *most nostalgic*."

Comparisons of experimentally-induced nostalgic and ordinary autobiographical narratives Another approach to examining nostalgic ambivalence entails experimental manipulations of nostalgia and ratings of the produced narratives. Abeyta, Routledge, Sedikides, and Wildschut (2014) used the event reflection task (ERT) (Sedikides, Wildschut, Routledge, Arndt, Hepper, & Zhou, 2015), pioneered by Wildschut et al. (2006, Study 5), to manipulate nostalgia. Participants in the experimental condition were instructed to bring to mind "a nostalgic event in your life. Specifically, try to think of a past event that makes you feel most nostalgic. Bring this nostalgic experience to mind. Immerse yourself in the nostalgic experience. How does it make you feel?" Participants in the control condition were asked to bring to mind "an ordinary event in your life. Specifically, try to think of a past event that is ordinary. Bring this ordinary experience to mind. Immerse yourself in the ordinary experience. How does it make you feel?" In both conditions, participants contemplated briefly how the experience made them feel and then listed four keywords relevant to it. Finally, they spent a few minutes writing a narrative. Judges rated the nostalgic (relative to the ordinary) narratives as reflecting more feelings in general, and also more positive than negative feelings.

Juxtaposition of positive and negative events in nostalgic narratives Is the structure of nostalgic narratives indicative of ambivalence? Davis (1977) emphasized the juxtaposition of positive and negative affective states in nostalgic accounts. He maintained that, when nostalgic episodes comprise negative elements, these "hurts, annoyances, disappointments, and irritations ... are filtered forgivingly through an 'it was all for the best' attitude" (p. 418). Work by McAdams, Reynolds, Lewis, Patten, and Bowman (2001) is relevant to this point. These authors articulated two narrative sequences: redemption and contamination. In a redemption sequence, the narrative progresses from affectively unpleasant stages to affectively pleasant ones. As McAdams et al. put it: "The bad is redeemed, salvaged, mitigated, or made better in light of the ensuing good" (p. 474). In a contamination sequence, the narrative follows a reverse trajectory. As McAdams et al. put it: "The good is spoiled, ruined, contaminated, or undermined by what follows it" (p. 474).

We wondered whether redemption versus classification is more typical of nostalgic narrative structure. To answer this question, Wildschut et al. (2006) subjected the stories that readers had submitted to the periodical *Nostalgia* (Study 1) and the events that participants had generated in the laboratory under a nostalgia writing prompt (Study 2) to content analyses. In both studies, nostalgic narratives manifested a predominantly redemptive (rather than contaminative) trajectory. The structure of nostalgic narratives is characterized by redemption, a pattern that Shakespeare (1996) captured sublimely in Sonnet 30 (p. 47):

> When to the sessions of sweet silent thought
> I summon up remembrance of things past,
> I sigh the lack of many a thing I sought,
> And with old woes new wail my dear time's waste; ...
> But if the while I think on thee, dear friend,
> All losses are restor'd and sorrows end.

The Psychological Health Benefits of Nostalgia

Based on four sources of empirical evidence (lay conceptions of nostalgia, content analysis of nostalgic narratives, comparisons of experimentally-induced nostalgic and ordinary autobiographical narratives, juxtaposition of positive and negative events in nostalgic narratives), we have concluded that nostalgia is an ambivalent, yet predominantly positive, emotion. Below, we review research on the psychological health benefits of nostalgia. We then return to the possible implications of ambivalence for nostalgia's health benefits.

We conceptualize nostalgia as a resource that can be implemented to cope with distress. At the very least, this conceptualization requires evidence of an association between nostalgia and the fundamental approach-oriented action tendency. We have obtained such evidence (Stephan et al., 2014). Nostalgia (induced through the ERT) instigates approach motivation, as assessed by the Behavioral Activation System (BAS) subscale of the BIS/BAS Scales (Carver & White, 1994). Nostalgia is an approach-oriented emotion. Below, we engage in a more detailed discussion of nostalgia's health benefits.

Social, Self-Related, and Existential Benefits

We will consider three classes of health benefits that nostalgia bestows: social, self-related, and existential.

Social health benefits Nostalgic evocation refers to momentous events (e.g., family traditions, graduations, wedding anniversaries) or significant persons from one's past (e.g., relatives, friends, romantic partners) (Wildschut et al., 2006, Studies 1–2; Abeyta et al., 2014). Nostalgic experiences, then, are replete with social themes. In nostalgic reverie, "the mind is 'peopled'" (Hertz, 1990, p. 195), and one reinstates symbolic connections with figures of the past who are brought to life and become part of one's present (Batcho, 1998; Wildschut, Sedikides, Routledge, Arndt, & Cordaro, 2010). It follows that nostalgizing may entail social health benefits.

We have provided empirical evidence for this proposition. Nostalgia (induced via a prototype-based manipulation, scents, or the ERT) boosts social connectedness, that is, feelings of being loved, protected, connected to loved ones, and trustful of others (Wildschut et al., 2006, Study 5; Hepper et al., 2012, Study 7; Reid, Green, Wildschut, & Sedikides, 2014;) compared with corresponding control conditions. Likewise, nostalgia (induced via the ERT) fosters stronger perceptions of social support (e.g., "I can count on my friends when things go wrong," "I can talk about my problems with my friends") (Zimet, Dahlem, Zimet, & Farley, 1988) than control (Zhou, Sedikides, Wildschut, & Gao, 2008, Studies 2–3). Finally, ERT-induced nostalgia (versus control) reinforces the security of the attachment system by decreasing attachment anxiety (e.g., "I worry that romantic partners won't care about me as much as I care about them") and attachment avoidance (e.g., "I am very uncomfortable with being close to romantic partners") (Fraley, Waller, & Brennan, 2000; (Wildschut et al., 2006, Study 6).

Self-related health benefits The self occupies a prominent place in nostalgic narratives. Put differently, the self is invariably the protagonist of the event (Wildschut et al., 2006, Studies 1–2). It follows that nostalgizing may have implications for the self. We tested this idea by focusing on two classes of self-related health benefits, self-esteem and optimism.

Nostalgia augments self-esteem; that is, nostalgic participants report higher levels of self-esteem than control participants. This finding emerges regardless of whether nostalgia is induced via the ERT (Wildschut et al., 2006, Studies 5–6), by asking participants to compose stories that rely on central (versus peripheral) prototypical features (Hepper et al., 2012, Study 7), by requesting participants to listen to a nostalgic (versus control) song (Cheung, Wildschut, Sedikides, Hepper, Arndt, & Vingerhoets, 2013, Study 3), or by instructing participants to smell various scents (e.g., Chanel No. 5, apple pie, fresh-cut roses) (Reid et al., 2014). This finding also emerges regardless of whether self-esteem is assessed with validated scales (e.g., the Rosenberg [1965] Self-Esteem Scale; Wildschut et al., 2006, Study 6) or with preselected, face-valid items (e.g., "value myself," "feel good about myself") (Wildschut et al., 2006, Study 5; Cheung et al., 2013; Hepper et al., 2012, Study 7).

In addition, nostalgia raises optimism. Nostalgic narratives (resulting from the ERT) contain more references to optimism than control narratives (Cheung et al., 2013, Study 1). Scent-induced nostalgia increases optimism (e.g., "optimistic about my future") (Reid et al., 2014). Moreover, nostalgic participants report being more optimistic (e.g., "feel like the sky is the limit") than their control counterparts (Cheung et al., 2013, Study 2). Importantly, self-esteem mediates the effect of nostalgia on optimism: nostalgia raises optimism by lifting self-esteem (Cheung et al., 2013, Study 3).

But where does self-esteem come from? Theories converge on social connectedness as a key source of self-esteem. These theories include attachment (Mikulincer & Shaver, 2004), contingencies of self-worth (Crocker & Wolfe, 2001), sociometer (Leary, 2005), and terror management (Pyszczynski, Greenberg, Solomon, Arndt, & Schimel, 2004). On that basis, we hypothesized an extended causal sequence, according to which nostalgia nurtures social connectedness, which elevates self-esteem, which in turn raises optimism. The results were consistent with the hypothesis (Cheung et al., 2013, Study 4).

Existential health benefits As stated above, nostalgic memories pertain to momentous events or significant persons from one's past (Wildschut et al., 2006, Studies 1–2; Abeyta et al., 2014). Such memories may serve to reassure the individual of life's meaningfulness (Lambert, Stillman, Baumeister, Fincham, Hicks, & Graham, 2010). Nostalgia may "keep the wolf of insignificance from the door" (Bellow, 1970, p. 190) or "quiet our fears of the abyss" (Davis, 1979, p. 41). Nostalgia, then, is likely to serve as a reservoir of meaning in life. We have tested and supported the hypothesis that nostalgia amplifies perceptions of life as meaningful.

Scent-evoked nostalgia breeds meaning in life (e.g., "life has a purpose") (Reid et al., 2014). Following the ERT, nostalgic participant regard life as more meaningful (e.g., "sense of meaning," "sense of purpose") than control participants (Van Tilburg, Igou, & Sedikides, 2013, Study 5). After a prototype-based induction, nostalgizers report higher meaning (e.g., "life is worth living," "there is greater purpose to life") than controls (Hepper et al., 2012, Study 7). Finally, a nostalgic-event condition renders life more meaningful than an ordinary-event condition or a desired-future-event condition (Routledge, Wildschut, Sedikides, Juhl, & Arndt, 2012, Experiment 1), and decreases the quest for meaning – presumably because meaning has been found – relative to a positive-past condition (Routledge et al., 2012, Experiment 2).

Given the prevalence of social themes in nostalgic narratives, it is likely that the sociality of nostalgia undergirds its existential health benefits. Social themes (e.g., family, relationship partners, friends) are key sources of meaning in life (Hicks, Schlegel, & King, 2010; Lambert et al., 2010). In addition, experimental evidence indicates that, when individuals confront existential threat, social connectedness strengthens well-being and promotes adaptive functioning (Arndt, Routledge, Greenberg, & Sheldon, 2005). In all, the literature points to social connectedness as a mechanism through which nostalgia elevates meaning. We proceeded to test this idea. In particular, we (Routledge et al., 2012, Study 2) induced nostalgia (via song lyrics), measured sociality with the Social Provisions Scale (Cutrona & Russell, 1987; sample items: "There is someone I could talk to about important decisions in my life" "I feel part of a group of people who share my attitudes and beliefs"), and then assessed meaning with the Presence of Meaning in Life subscale of the Meaning in Life Questionnaire (Steger, Frazier, Oishi, & Kaler, 2006; sample item: "I have a good sense of what makes my life meaningful"). Sociality mediated the effect of nostalgia on meaning; that its, nostalgia cultivated meaning through its capacity to foster sociality. We replicated these finding with a song-based induction of nostalgia (Routledge et al., 2012, Study 1).

The Buffering Role of Nostalgia

Nostalgia not only grants psychological health benefits, but it may also buffer against psychological threat. We conceptualize the regulatory role of nostalgia as follows. Threat (e.g., noxious stimulus or aversive psychological state) impacts negatively on the social, self-related, or existential aspects of psychological functioning. However, threat also triggers nostalgia. In turn, nostalgia alleviates or counteracts this negative impact. Stated otherwise, the negative direct impact of the noxious stimulus or aversive state is attenuated or offset by its positive indirect impact through nostalgia.

We (Stephan et al., 2014, Study 2) tested a general version of this regulatory model in the domain of avoidance and approach motivation. First, we induced avoidance motivation (*noxious stimulus or aversive psychological state*). In the experimental condition, participants wrote down five events they wanted to avoid in the future, whereas, in the control condition, they wrote down five ordinary and likely future events. Next, we measured nostalgia. Participants filled out a state version of the Nostalgia Inventory (Batcho, 1995): they rated the extent to which they missed twenty aspects of their past (e.g., "my family house," "my childhood toys," "the way people were"). Lastly, we assessed approach motivation. Participants completed the BAS (Carver & White, 1994). Avoidance (versus control) motivation tended to decrease approach motivation. However, avoidance motivation also triggered nostalgia. In turn, avoidance-triggered nostalgia strengthened approach motivation. We discuss next specific tests of the regulatory model as they pertain to nostalgia's capacity to buffer assorted psychological threats.

Buffering against social threat   We examined whether nostalgia buffers against the social threat of loneliness, a discrete emotion defined in terms of negative thoughts or feelings (e.g., pessimism, unhappiness, self-blame, depression, lack of desired relationships) (Cacioppo et al., 2006). We hypothesized that loneliness (aversive state) would decrease sociality (i.e., perceptions of social support), but also trigger nostalgia. In turn, nostalgia would combat loneliness through its social health benefits, that is, by increasing perceived social support.

We (Zhou et al., 2008, Study 2) obtained support for this hypothesis. We induced loneliness with a procedure developed by Wildschut et al. (2006, Study 4). All participants read statements drawn from the UCLA Loneliness Scale (Russell, Peplau, & Cutrona, 1980). However, the response options to these statements varied depending on condition. In the experimental condition (high loneliness), we rigged the response options to maximize agreement (e.g., "I *sometimes* feel isolated from others") and, hence, engender in participants the sense of high loneliness. In the control condition (low loneliness), we rigged the response options to maximize disagreement (e.g., "I *always* feel isolated from others") and, hence, foster the sense low loneliness. On the ostensible basis of their responses to the UCLA Loneliness Scale, participants received feedback indicating that, compared with their peers, they were either high on loneliness (experimental condition) or low on loneliness (control condition). A manipulation check confirmed that participants in the experimental condition felt lonelier than those in the control condition.

Following the successful induction of loneliness, we assessed nostalgia and social support. For nostalgia, we used the state version of the Southampton Nostalgia Scale (Routledge, Arndt, Sedikides, & Wildschut, 2008; Barrett, Grimm, Robins, Wildschut, Sedikides, & Janata, 2010), which comprises items referring to the proneness, frequency, and personal relevance of nostalgia. For social support, we used the state version of the Multidimensional Scale of Perceived Social Support (e.g., "I can count on my friends when things go wrong") (Zimet et al., 1988). We found, as hypothesized, directionally opposite causal effects of loneliness on nostalgia and social support. Lonely participants felt socially unsupported but also nostalgic. In turn, their feelings of nostalgia combated loneliness by fostering a sense of social support.

Buffering against self-threat   We asked whether nostalgia buffers the self-threat inherent to negative performance feedback (Sedikides, 2012). Nostalgia increases self-esteem and optimism (Wildschut et al., 2006, Study 5; Hepper et al., 2012, Study 7; Cheung et al., 2013), and we hypothesized that these self-related health benefits act as barricades that deflect self-threat. Our findings were consistent with this hypothesis (Vess, Arndt, Routledge, Sedikides, & Wildschut, 2012, Experiment 2). We instructed participants to complete the Remote Associates Test (Mednick, 1962), an alleged assessment of analytic reasoning, and then gave them false feedback (negative versus positive). Subsequently, we induced nostalgia with the ERT. Lastly, we collected the dependent measure: Participants indicated the extent to which they attributed their test performance to their ability. Prior research shows that people respond defensively on this measure. That is, they deny that failure was due to their low ability (Campbell & Sedikides, 1999). In replication of this past research, participants were more likely to assume reduced personal responsibility (i.e., denied lack of ability) in the case of failure feedback than success feedback. However, their responses were contingent on how nostalgic they were. Nostalgic participants took more responsibility for their failure than control participants did, although the two groups did not differ in their assumed responsibility for success. Nostalgia lowered defensiveness to self-threat, which implies that nostalgia fortifies the self (Sedikides, 2012).

Buffering against existential threat   Being told that life is meaningless communicates threat (Becker, 1971). We wondered whether nostalgia buffers against this existential threat, and we hypothesized that it does so through its existential health benefits, that is by increasing meaningfulness. We (Routledge et al., 2011, Study 3) manipulated meaninglessness in the laboratory. In the experimental (meaning-threat) condition, participants read an essay, written allegedly by a philosophy professor at the University of Oxford, which argued that life has no meaning. An excerpt read as follows: "There are approximately 7 billion people living on this planet … The Earth is 5 billion years old and the average human life span across the globe is 68 years. What is 68 years of one person's rat-race compared with 5 billion years of history? We are no more significant than any other form of life in the universe." Participants in the control condition (no meaning-threat) read an essay arguing that computers had limitations. An excerpt read as follows: "the computer never understood a word of this text. A computer does not comprehend what is stored in its 'memory' any more than a book in the library understands what it contains." The essays were equal in length and rated similarly on interest, engagement, and originality. Following the manipulation of meaninglessness, we measured state nostalgia with a three-item scale (e.g., "I feel nostalgic at the moment"). Participants in the meaning-threat condition reported feeling more nostalgic than those in the control condition. Meaninglessness spontaneously evoked nostalgia.

Our regulatory model stipulates that, following threat (i.e., meaninglessness), nostalgia will surge to diffuse it. But how so? According to existential psychologists, one of the most common strategies to diffuse threat involves derogation of the message and its source (Berger & Luckman, 1967; Greenberg et al., 1990). We relied, once again, on the principle that if a psychological resource protects against threat, then strengthening this resource will lower defensiveness toward the threat (Pyszczynski et al., 2004; Sherman & Hartson, 2011). We proposed that nostalgia is a psychological resource that can protect against threat. If so, nostalgic engagement will lower defensiveness toward meaning threat. Following the ERT, we (Routledge et al., 2011, Study 4) exposed participants to the same meaningless manipulation as above (i.e., life has no meaning versus limitations of computers). Next, we assessed defensiveness through participants' responses to items that referred to the quality of the essay (e.g., "The essay is convincing in its points") and the competence of its author (e.g., "The author is a reliable source"). In the meaning-threat condition, nostalgic participants derogated the essay and its author to a lesser extent than control participants. The two groups did not differ in the control condition. Thus, an infusion of nostalgia curbed the intensity of defensive responding to meaning threat.

Meaning can be conceptualized as "presence of meaning in life" or as "search for meaning in life," but also as understanding the world in terms of basic relations between events or objects (Arndt, Landau, Vail, & Vess, 2013). Surrealist art is an example (Proulx, Heine, & Vohs, 2010). This kind of art violates accepted links between objects and events, thus imposing a threat to meaning. Surrealist art is structure-threatening in contrast to representational art, which is structure-preserving. We (Routledge et al., 2012, Study 3) used Surrealist versus representational art to manipulate meaning. In the experimental (meaning-threat) condition, we presented participants with a Surrealist painting (*The Son of Man* by René Magritte). In the control (no meaning-threat) condition, we presented them with a representational painting (*Landscape With a Double Rainbow* by John Constable). Next, we induced nostalgia with the ERT. Finally, we assessed meaning in life. Participants in the Surrealist (compared with representational) art condition reported lower meaning in life. However, nostalgia moderated this effect. In the Surrealist art condition, nostalgic participants evinced higher meaning in life than controls, whereas, in the representational art condition, the two groups did not differ in their perceptions of meaning in life. Once again, nostalgia buffered against reductions in life meaningfulness.

Buffering against well-being threat   We consider the regulatory role of nostalgia in respect to two domains of well-being threat: stress and boredom.

People vary at the dispositional level in their perceptions of meaning in life. Those with meaning deficits are especially vulnerable to experiencing stress in demanding circumstances (Park & Folkman, 1997). We (Routledge et al., 2011, Study 6) hypothesized that induced nostalgia would exert a palliative influence by assuaging their stress. First, we assessed dispositional levels of meaningfulness (e.g., "My life has meaning"). Then, we manipulated nostalgia via the ERT. Subsequently, we induced stress with the Trier Social Stress Test (TSST) (Kirschbaum, Pirke, & Hellhammer, 1993). This is validated stress-induction procedure that includes the impromptu delivery of a speech. Lastly, we measured stress (e.g., "jittery," "fearful") immediately following the TSST. In general, and in replication of past research (Park & Folkman, 1997), participants with meaning deficits reported higher levels of stress than their counterparts. However, this finding was qualified by nostalgia. In particular, nostalgia reduced the level of stress among participants with low dispositional meaning in life, but not among those with high dispositional meaning in life. Nostalgia buffered against stress.

We asked whether nostalgia also buffers against boredom. This unpleasant state is characterized by negative affect, dissatisfaction and, importantly, lack of meaningful engagement (Van Tilburg & Igou, 2012). As such, boredom is likely to prompt a search for meaning in life. Nostalgia may come to the rescue. Our findings lent support to these notions (Van Tilburg et al., 2013). First, we showed that boredom leads to nostalgia. We induced boredom by having participants copy ten (high-boredom) versus two (low-boredom) references about concrete mixtures (Study 1), or trace a line across either nine (high-boredom) or three (low-boredom) large spirals (Studies 2–3). In both cases, participants in the high-boredom condition reported greater levels of nostalgia (e.g., "Right now, I am feeling quite nostalgic") than those in the low-boredom condition. Next, we (Van Tilburg et al., 2013, Study 4) examined the meaning-regulation function of nostalgia. We manipulated boredom (with the reference-copying task), measured search for meaning (by asking participants if they were intended to engage in something meaningful or purposeful), and then measured nostalgia (through the retrieval and self-rating of nostalgic recollections). Boredom intensified the search for meaning and also triggered nostalgia. Further, search for meaning mediated the effect of boredom on nostalgia.

Does Ambivalence Account (Partially) for the Psychological Health Benefits of Nostalgia?

The ambivalence of nostalgia may, at least in part, be responsible for its psychological health benefits. The rationale for this proposition derives from the literature on mixed, that is, positive and negative, emotions ("taking the good with the bad"). Larsen, Hemenover, Norris, and Cacioppo (2003) took a favorable view on the experience of mixed emotions. They argued that the presence of positive emotions thwarts the influence of negative emotions in making meaning out of challenging or distressing life events, a process beneficial to well-being. If their reasoning is correct, then individuals who experience mixed emotions ought to show improved well-being over time (Zautra, Reich, Davis, Potter, & Nicolson, 2000). Empirical evidence has been consistent with this idea. For example, bereaved adults who display positive emotions during their grieving period report lower grief over time (Bonanno & Keltner, 1997). Individuals who visualize a stressful event along with their emotional responses to it manifest improved coping (e.g., greater acceptance of the event, more positive reinterpretations of it) (Rivkin & Taylor, 1999). Widows who report more positive emotions on stressful days show more successful adaptation later in life (Ong, Bergeman, Bisconti, and Wallace (2006). And the concurrent experience of positive and negative emotions among persons undergoing psychotherapy predicts higher well-being above and beyond other potential predictors (e.g., unique effects of positive and negative emotions, personality traits, the passage of time) (Adler & Hershfield, 2012). Nostalgia, with its signature affective ambivalence, may also be related to better adaptation and higher well-being in the long run.

We argued that the narrative structure of nostalgic episodes is also ambivalent. Past research has demonstrated that redemption (as opposed to contamination) is associated with well-being and improved health. For example, redemption-oriented life stories are positively associated with psychological maturity (Bauer, McAdams, & Sakaeda, 2005) and identity maturity (McLean & Pratt, 2006). Moreover, redemptive life stories are positively related to well-being both concurrently (Lilgendahl & McAdams, 2011) and longitudinally (Tavernier & Willoughby, 2012). Further, more-improved (compared with less-improved) psychotherapy patients are particularly likely to remember their therapeutic sessions in a redemptive manner (Adler, Skalina, & McAdams, 2008). Nostalgia, given its redemptive narrative structure, may also be associated positively with these indices of psychological adjustment. Future research will do well to focus on whether nostalgic ambivalence underlies, at least partially, the emotion's health benefits.

Coda

Nostalgia has long been considered a brain disease, a psychiatric illness, or a clinical disorder (for a review, see Sedikides, Wildschut, & Baden, 2004). Contemporary research has rehabilitated the image of nostalgia (Sedikides et al., 2015). It is now regarded a self-conscious and social emotion that is prevalent and universal. Nostalgia is a psychological resource with implications for psychological health. More relevant for the objectives of this chapter, nostalgia is an ambivalent (albeit predominantly positive) emotion, and this ambivalence may be partially responsible for nostalgia's health benefits. Consistent with the agenda of Positive Clinical Psychology (Wood & Tarrier, 2010), nostalgia showcases how "taking the good with the bad" in human experience can be advantageous for psychological health.

References

Abeyta, A., Routledge, C., Sedikides, C., & Wildschut, R. T. (2014). Attachment-related avoidance and the social content of nostalgic memories. *Journal of Social and Personal Relationships*. Advance online publication. doi.10.1177/0265407514533770.

Adler, J. & Hershfield, H. E. (2012). Mixed emotional experience is associated with and precedes improvements in psychological well-being. *PLoS ONE, 7,* 1–10. doi.10.1371/journal.pone.0035633.

Adler, J. M., Skalina, L., & McAdams, D. P. (2008). The narrative reconstruction of psychotherapy and psychological health. *Psychotherapy Research, 18,* 719–734. doi.10.1080/10503300802326020.

Arndt, J., Landau, M. J., Vail, K. E., Vess, M. (2013). An edifice for enduring personal value: A terror management perspective on the human quest for multilevel meaning. In: K. D. Markman, T. Proulx, & M. J. Lindberg (Eds.), *The psychology of meaning* (pp. 49–69). New York: APA Books.

Arndt, J., Routledge, C., Greenberg, J., & Sheldon, K. M. (2005). Illuminating the dark side of creative expression: Assimilation needs and the consequences of creative action following mortality salience. *Personality and Social Psychology Bulletin, 31,* 1327–1339. doi.10.1177/0146167205274690.

Barrett, F. S., Grimm, K. J., Robins, R. W., Wildschut, T., Sedikides, C., & Janata, P. (2010). Music-evoked nostalgia: Affect, memory, and personality. *Emotion, 10,* 390–403. doi.10.1037/a0019006.

Batcho, K. I. (1995). Nostalgia: A psychological perspective. *Perceptual and Motor Skills, 80,* 131–143. doi.10.2466/pms.1995.80.1.131.

Batcho, K. I. (1998). Personal nostalgia, world view, memory, and emotionality. *Perceptual & Motor Skills, 87,* 411–432. doi.10.2466/pms.1998.87.2.411.

Bauer, J. J., McAdams, D. P., & Sakaeda, A. (2005). Interpreting the good life: Growth memories in the lives of mature, happy people. *Journal of Personality and Social Psychology, 88,* 203–217. doi.10.1037/0022-3514.88.1.203.

Becker, E. (1971). *The birth and death of meaning.* New York: Free Press.

Bellow, S. (1970). *Mr. Sammler's planet.* New York: Viking Press.

Berger, P. L. & Luckmann, T. (1967). *The social construction of reality.* Garden City, NY: Anchor.

Best, J. & Nelson, E. E. (1985). Nostalgia and discontinuity: A test of the Davis hypothesis. *Sociology and Social Research, 69,* 221–233.

Bonanno, G. A. & Keltner, D. (1997). Facial expressions of emotion and the course of conjugal bereavement. *Journal of Abnormal Psychology, 106,* 126–137. doi.10.1037/0021-843X.106.1.126.

Cacioppo, J. T., Hawkley, L. C., Ernst, J. M., Burleson, M., Berntson, G. G., Nouriani, B., & Spiegel, D. (2006). Loneliness within a nomological net: An evolutionary perspective. *Journal of Research in Personality, 40,* 1054–1085. doi.10.1016/j.jrp.2005.11.007.

Campbell, W. K. & Sedikides, C. (1999). Self-threat magnifies the self-serving bias: A meta-analytic integration. *Review of General Psychology, 3,* 23–43. doi.10.1037/1089-2680.3.1.23.

Carver, C. S. & White, T. L. (1994). Behavioral inhibition, behavioral activation and affective responses to impending reward and punishment: The BIS/BAS scales. *Journal of Personality and Social Psychology, 67,* 319–333. doi.10.1037/0022-3514.67.2.319.

Chaplin, S. (2000). *The psychology of time and death.* Ashland, OH: Sonnet Press.

Cheung, W. Y., Wildschut, T., Sedikides, C., Hepper, E. G., Arndt, J., & Vingerhoets, A. J. J. M. (2013). Back to the future: Nostalgia increases optimism. *Personality and Social Psychology Bulletin, 39,* 1484–1496. doi.10.1177/0146167213499187.

Crocker, J. & Wolfe, C. T. (2001). Contingencies of self-worth. *Psychological Review, 108,* 593–623. doi.10.1037/0033-295X.108.3.593.

Cutrona, C. E. & Russell, D. (1987). The provisions of social relationships and adaptation to stress. In: W. H. Jones & D. Perlman (Eds.), *Advances in personal relationships,* vol. *1* (pp. 37–67). Greenwich, CT: JAI Press.

Davis, F. (1977). Nostalgia, identity, and the current nostalgia wave. *Journal of Popular Culture, 11,* 414–425.

Davis, F. (1979). *Yearning for yesterday: A sociology of nostalgia.* New York: Free Press.

Fodor, N. (1950). Varieties of nostalgia. *Psychoanalytic Review, 37,* 25–38.

Fraley, R. C., Waller, N. G., & Brennan, K. A. (2000). An item response theory analysis of self-report measures of adult attachment. *Journal of Personality and Social Psychology, 78,* 350–365. doi.10.1037//0022.3514.78.2.350.

Greenberg, J., Pyszczynski, T., Solomon, S., Rosenblatt, A., Veeder, M., Kirkland, S., & Lyon, D. (1990). Evidence for terror management II: The effects of mortality salience on reactions to those who threaten or bolster the cultural worldview. *Journal of Personality and Social Psychology, 58,* 308–318. doi.10.1177/01461672952111010.

Hepper, E. G., Ritchie, T. D., Sedikides, C., & Wildschut, T. (2012). Odyssey's end: Lay conceptions of nostalgia reflect its original Homeric meaning. *Emotion, 12,* 102–119. doi.10.1037/a0025167.

Hepper, E. G., Wildschut, T., Sedikides, C., Ritchie, T. D., Yung, Y.-F., Hansen, N., & Zhou, X. (2014). Pancultural nostalgia: Prototypical conceptions across cultures. *Emotion, 14*, 733–747. doi.10.1037/a0036790.

Hertz, D. G. (1990). Trauma and nostalgia: New aspects of the coping of aging holocaust survivors. *Israeli Journal of Psychiatry and Related Sciences, 27*, 189–198.

Hicks, J. A., Schlegel, R. J., & King, L. A. (2010). Social threats, happiness, and the dynamics of meaning in life judgments. *Personality and Social Psychology Bulletin, 36*, 1305–1317. doi.10.1177/0146167210381650.

Holak, S. L. & Havlena, W. J. (1998). Feelings, fantasies, and memories: An examination of the emotional components of nostalgia. *Journal of Business Research, 42*, 217–226.

Johnson-Laird, P. N. & Oatley, K. (1989). The language of emotions: An analysis of semantic field. *Cognition and Emotion, 3*, 81–123. doi.10.1080/02699938908408075.

Kaplan, H. A. (1987). The psychopathology of nostalgia. *Psychoanalytic Review, 74*, 465–486.

Kirschbaum, C., Pirke, K-M., & Hellhammer, D. H. (1993). The "Trier Social Stress Test": A tool for investigating psychobiological stress responses in a laboratory setting. *Neuropsychobiology, 28*, 76–81.

Lambert, N. M., Stillman, T. F., Baumeister, R. F., Fincham, F. D., Hicks, J. A., & Graham, S. M. (2010). Family as a salient source of meaning in young adulthood. *Journal of Positive Psychology, 5*, 367–376.

Larsen, J. T., Hemenover, S. H., Norris, C. J., & Cacioppo, J. T. (2003). Turning adversity to advantage: On the virtues of the coactivation of positive and negative emotions. In: L. G. Aspinwall & U. M. Staudinger (Eds.), *A psychology of human strengths: Perspectives on an emerging field* (pp. 211–216). Washington, DC: American Psychological Association.

Leary, M. R. (2005). Sociometer theory and the pursuit of relational value: Getting to the root of self-esteem. *European Review of Social Psychology, 16*, 75–111. doi.10.1080/10463280540000007.

Lilgendahl, J. P. & McAdams, D. P. (2011). Constructing stories of self-growth: How individual differences in patterns of autobiographical reasoning relate to well-being in midlife. *Journal of Personality, 79*, 391–428. doi.10.1111/j.1467-6494.2010.00688.x.

McAdams, D. P., Reynolds, J., Lewis, M., Patten, A. H., & Bowman, P. J. (2001). When bad things turn good and good things turn bad: Sequences of redemption and contamination in life narratives and their relation to psychosocial adaptation in midlife adults and in students. *Personality and Social Psychology Bulletin, 27*, 474–485. doi.10.1177/0146167201274008.

McLean, K. C. & Pratt, M. W. (2006). Life's little (and big) lessons: Identity status and meaning-making in the turning point narratives of emerging adults. *Developmental Psychology, 42*, 714–722. doi.10.1037/0012-1649.42.4.714.

Mednick, S. (1962). The associative basis of the creative process. *Psychological Review, 69*, 220–232.

Mikulincer, M. & Shaver, P. R. (2004). Security-based self-representations in adulthood: Contents and processes. In: W. S. Rholes & J. A. Simpson (Eds.), *Adult attachment: Theory, research, and clinical implications* (pp. 159–195). New York: Guilford Press.

Ong, A. D., Bergeman, C. S., Bisconti, T. L., & Wallace, K. A. (2006). Psychological resilience, positive emotions, and successful adaptation to stress in later life. *Journal of Personality and Social Psychology, 91*, 730–749. doi.10.1037/0022-3514.91.4.730.

Park, C. L. & Folkman, S. (1997). Meaning in the context of stress and coping. *Review of General Psychology, 1*, 115–144. doi.10.1037/1089-2680.1.2.115.

Peters, R. (1985). Reflections on the origin and aim of nostalgia. *Journal of Analytical Psychology, 30*, 135–148.

Proulx, T., Heine, S. J., & Vohs, K. D. (2010). When is the unfamiliar the uncanny? Meaning affirmative after exposure to absurdist literature, humor, and art. *Personality and Social Psychology Bulletin, 36*, 817–829. doi.10.1080/09658211.2012.677452.

Pyszczynski, T., Greenberg, J., Solomon, S., Arndt, J., & Schimel, J. (2004). Why do people need self-esteem? A theoretical and empirical review. *Psychological Bulletin, 130*, 435–468. doi.10.1037/0033-2909.130.3.469.

Reid, C. A., Green, J. D., Wildschut, T., & Sedikides, C. (2014). Scent-evoked nostalgia. *Memory. Advance online publication*. doi.10.1080/09658211.2013.876048.

Rivkin, I. D. & Taylor, S. E. (1999). The effects of mental simulation on coping with controllable stressful events. *Personality and Social Psychology Bulletin, 25*, 1451–1462. doi.10.1177/01461672992510002.

Rosenberg, M. (1965). *Society and the adolescent self-image*. Princeton, NJ: Princeton University Press.

Routledge, C., Arndt, J., Sedikides, C., & Wildschut, T. (2008). A blast from the past: The terror management function of nostalgia. *Journal of Experimental Social Psychology, 44*, 132–140. doi.10.1016/j.jesp.2006.11.001.

Routledge, C., Wildschut, T., Sedikides, C., Juhl, J., & Arndt, J. (2012). The power of the past: Nostalgia as a meaning-making resource. *Memory, 20*, 452–460. doi.10.1080/09658211.2012.677452.

Russell, D., Peplau, L. A., & Cutrona, C. E. (1980). The revised UCLA Loneliness Scale: Concurrent and discriminant validity evidence. *Journal of Personality and Social Psychology, 39*, 472–480.

The New Oxford Dictionary of English. (1998). Ed. J. Pearsall. Oxford: Oxford University Press.

Sedikides, C. (2012). Self-protection. In: M. R. Leary & J. P. Tangney (Eds.), *Handbook of self and identity*, 2nd edn. (pp. 327–353). New York: Guilford Press.

Sedikides, C., Wildschut, T., & Baden, D. (2004). Nostalgia: Conceptual issues and existential functions. In: J. Greenberg, S. Koole, & T. Pyszczynski (Eds.), *Handbook of experimental existential psychology* (pp. 200–214). New York: Guilford Press.

Sedikides, C., Wildschut, T., Routledge, C., Arndt, J., Hepper, E. G., & Zhou, X. (2015). To nostalgize: Mixing memory with affect and desire. *Advances in Experimental Social Psychology, 51*, 189–273. doi.10.1016/bs.aesp.2014.10.001.

Shakespeare, W. ([1609] 1996). *The sonnets.* Cambridge: Cambridge University Press.

Sherman, D. K. & Hartson, K. A. (2011). Reconciling self-protection with self-improvement: Self-affirmation theory. In: M. Alicke & C. Sedikides (Eds.), *Handbook of self-enhancement and self-protection* (pp. 128–151). New York: Guilford Press.

Socarides, C. W. (1977). (Ed.). *The world of emotions: Clinical studies of affects and their expression.* New York: International University Press.

Steger, M. F., Frazier, P., Oishi, S., & Kaler, M. (2006). The Meaning in Life Questionnaire: Assessing the presence of and search for meaning in life. *Journal of Counseling Psychology, 53*, 80–93. doi.10.5502/ijw.v2.i3.2.

Stephan, E., Wildschut, T., Sedikides, C., Zhou, X., He, W., Routledge, C., Cheung, W. Y., & Vingerhoets, A. J. J. M. (2014). The mnemonic mover: Nostalgia regulates avoidance and approach motivation. *Emotion, 14*, 545–561. doi.10.1037/a0035673,

Tavernier, R. & Willoughby, T. (2012). Adolescent turning points: The association between meaning-making and psychological well-being. *Developmental Psychology, 48*, 1058–1068. doi.10.1037/a0026326.

Van Tilburg, W. A. P. & Igou, E. R. (2012). On boredom: Lack of challenge and meaning as distinct boredom experiences. *Motivation and Emotion, 36*, 181–194. doi.10.1007/s11031-011-9234-9.

Van Tilburg, W. A. P., Igou, E. R., & Sedikides, C. (2013). In search of meaningfulness: Nostalgia as an antidote to boredom. *Emotion, 13*, 450–461. doi.10.1037/a0030442.

Vess, M., Arndt, J., Routledge, C., Sedikides, C., & Wildschut, T. (2012). Nostalgia as a resource for the self. *Self and Identity, 3*, 273–284. doi.10.1080/15298868.2010.521452.

Watson, D. Clark, L. A., & Tellegen, A. (1988). Development and validation of brief measures of positive and negative affect: The PANAS scales. *Journal of Personality and Social Psychology, 55*, 1063–1070.

Werman, D. S. (1977). Normal and pathological nostalgia. *Journal of the American Psychoanalytic Association, 25*, 387–398.

Wiersema, R. J. *Walk like a man: Coming of age with the music of Bruce Springstein.* Available at: http://www.goodreads.com/work/quotes/16071366-walk-like-a-man-coming-of-age-with-the-music-of-bruce-springsteen, last accessed October 31, 2014.

Wildschut, T., Sedikides, C., Arndt, J., & Routledge, C. (2006). Nostalgia: Content, triggers, functions. *Journal of Personality and Social Psychology, 91*, 975–993. doi.10.1037/0022-3514.91.5.975.

Wildschut, T., Sedikides, C., Routledge, C., Arndt, J., & Cordaro, F. (2010). Nostalgia as a repository of social connectedness: The role of attachment-related avoidance. *Journal of Personality and Social Psychology, 98*, 573–586. doi.10.1037/a0017597.

Wood, A. M. & Tarrier, N. (2010). Positive Clinical Psychology: A new vision and strategy for integrated research and practice. *Clinical Psychology Review, 30*, 819–829. doi.10.1016/j.cpr.2010.06.003.

Zautra, A. J., Reich, J. W., Davis, M. C., Potter, P. T., & Nicolson, N. A. (2000). The role of stressful events in the relationship between positive and negative affects: Evidence from field and experimental studies. *Journal of Personality, 68*, 927–951.

Zhou, X., Sedikides, C., Wildschut, C., & Gao, D-G. (2008). Counteracting loneliness: On the restorative function of nostalgia. *Psychological Science, 19*, 1023–1029. doi.10.1111/j.1467-9280.2008.02194.x.

Zimet, G. D., Dahlem, N. W., Zimet, S. G., & Farley, G. K. (1988). The multidimensional scale of perceived social support. *Journal of Personality Assessment, 52*, 30–41. doi.10.1207/s15327752jpa5201_2.

10

A Dark Side of Gratitude?
Distinguishing between Beneficial Gratitude and its Harmful Impostors for the Positive Clinical Psychology of Gratitude and Well-Being

Alex M. Wood, Robert A. Emmons, Sara B. Algoe,
Jeffrey J. Froh, Nathanial M. Lambert,
and Philip Watkins

Gratitude is not only a virtue but the parent of all others

Cicero

Gratitude is an illness suffered by dogs

Joseph Stalin

Throughout history, the concept of gratitude has been seen as central to the understanding of well-being and the smooth running of society, being a mainstay of philosophical and religious accounts of living (Emmons & Crumpler, 2000). However, it was not until research adopted by (although predating) the positive psychology movement was conducted (beginning with McCullough, Kilpatrick, Emmons, & Larson, 2001) that it became a mainstream area of research within personality (McCullough, Emmons, & Tsang, 2001) and then clinical psychology (Wood, Froh, & Geraghty, 2010). Research has exploded over the last 15 years, with studies on gratitude being amongst the most quickly accruing within psychology. Our recent review (Wood, Froh, & Geraghty, 2010) summarizes this literature, which shows that low gratitude is strongly, uniquely, and possibly causally related to clinical impaired functioning and impaired clinically relevant processes. Our review also outlines the interventions that can be used to increase gratitude in order to improve well-being.

Gratitude has very much been adopted by the positive psychology movement and in many ways is the emblematic poster child (Bono, Emmons, & McCullough, 2004). However, particularly from philosophy (Carr, in press), there have been concerns raised about a potential dark side of gratitude. This has not been extensively discussed in the psychological literature, and yet understanding any possible "side effects" of gratitude is particularly important as interventions to promote gratitude move to into clinical practice. The aim of this chapter is to attempt to clarify when and where gratitude is apparently negative, with the aim of building a more

The Wiley Handbook of Positive Clinical Psychology, First Edition. Edited by Alex M. Wood and Judith Johnson.
© 2016 John Wiley & Sons, Ltd. Published 2016 by John Wiley & Sons, Ltd.

balanced study of gratitude within psychology. Our vision is for a field of gratitude research in which the potential negative side of gratitude is given as much consideration as the positive side. Specifically, we take the view that there are both beneficial and harmful forms of gratitude. Whilst the beneficial form may always be positive for the individual, it is easily confused (by both individuals and scholars) with the maladaptive forms. We call for more research to distinguish the two and caution that any use of gratitude interventions within clinical practice has to take care to promote the beneficial rather than harmful kinds of gratitude. Our aim with this chapter is in keeping with the positive clinical psychology (PCP) (Wood & Tarrier, 2010; Chapter 1, this volume), which aims to transform the discipline into one where the understanding and fostering the positive is given equal attention as understanding and reducing the negative. We aim to extend this approach to gratitude through clarifying the distinctions between the beneficial form of gratitude and its harmful imposter.

This chapter is aimed to be seminal to the field of gratitude research through beginning a new phase that moves beyond just showing that higher levels of gratitude are generally beneficial toward showing *how*, *when*, and *for whom* gratitude is beneficial. In doing so the area will develop a more balanced view of when trait and state levels of gratitude are and are not helpful to an individual's life, consistent with the general cognitive approach to emotions taken within psychology. This more balanced approach will be much more able to inform clinical practice as to when and how to promote gratitude within a given client. Such developments are also more likely to engage scholars who are skeptical about gratitude and gratitude research through perceiving an over-focus on only beneficial gratitude within the current research. Were it to emerge that most experiences of gratitude were beneficial (apart from specific cases) then the ensuing research literature would be a lot more convincing for the communities, cultures, and research and practitioner groups for whom gratitude does not immediately seem like an important concept, perhaps as the harmful kinds of gratitude more readily come to mind. A more balanced field of gratitude research and practice would be better able to answer the ready challenges that gratitude critics can make about a straw man of gratitude research in which all forms of gratitude are considered to be beneficial. We believe that only through engaging in the search for the "dark side" of gratitude can the field progress toward a full understanding of the concept and its roles in people's lives, be safely used in clinical practice, and be convincing to those who remain skeptical about engaging with gratitude research and practice.

The Beneficial Consequences of Gratitude

The psychological research into gratitude over the last 15 years has overwhelmingly focused on the benefits of higher levels of gratitude (Wood, Froh, & Geraghty, 2010). People who feel more gratitude in life are more generally appreciative of the positive in the self and world (Wood, Maltby, Stewart, & Joseph, 2008) as well as the future (McCullough et al., 2001). This suggests a possible key role for gratitude in determining mental health, given Beck et al.'s (1979) model of depression as involving a "negative triad" comprising negative views about the self, world, and future. Gratitude may form a "positive triad" comprising positive views about the self, world, and (due to its shared variance with optimism) (Emmons & McCullough, 2003; Froh, Yurkewicz, & Kashdan, 2009) future. In keeping with this book, we see gratitude and optimism as forming the "missing half" of Beck's triad, rather than as some separate entity; if mental health is seen as arising in part from a three continua (negative to positive views about the world, negative to positive views about the self, and negative to positive views about the future) then it would seem that gratitude is intimately linked to this process. The empirical evidence showing strong relationships between gratitude and mental health is consistent with this view (Wood, Froh, & Geraghty, 2010).

There are four factors that suggest that higher levels of gratitude may be clinically important in addition to the strong cross-sectional relationships between gratitude and well-being. First, higher levels of gratitude protect from stress and depression over time (Wood, Maltby, Gillett, Linley, & Joseph, 2008; Lambert, Fincham, & Stillman, 2012). This suggests a possible role of gratitude in the resilience to clinical levels of symptomatology during life transitions, and the findings further suggest that the role of gratitude in well-being may be causal.

Second, higher levels of gratitude predict a wide range of clinically relevant processes, including less impaired sleep (Wood, Joseph, Lloyd, & Atkins, 2009), more social support seeking and active coping, combined with less disengagement coping (Wood, Joseph, & Linley, 2007a,b), the greater development of social support (Wood et al., 2008), better quality relationships (Algoe, Haidt, & Gable, 2008; Lambert, Clarke, Durtschi, Fincham, & Graham, 2010; Lambert & Fincham, 2011; Algoe, 2012; Algoe & Stanton, 2012), and more generous interpretation of social transactions (through interpreting gifts received as more costly [to their benefactor], valuable [to them], and altruistically intended) (Wood, Maltby, Stewart, Linley, & Joseph, 2008). Impaired sleep, insufficient social support, and impaired relationship dynamics are implicated in a wide variety of variety of psychological and health problems (Rodriguez & Cohen, 1998; Cohen, Gottlieb, & Underwood, 2000; American Psychiatric Association, 2013) and coping determines psychological and behavioral reactions to stress (Lazarus, 1993). If gratitude is affecting these processes, then it may have a downstream consequence on mental health conditions.

Third, the relationship between gratitude and well-being seems to be unique, existing above the 30 facets of the NEO PI-R operationalization of the full breadth and depth of personality traits within the Five Factor model (Wood, Joseph, & Maltby, 2008, 2009). This is important as, whilst many traits within personality psychology predict well-being, there is a lot of conceptual and empirical overlap between the different traits, and newly conceptualized traits are often later shown to relate only to well-being due to their shared variance with other, already known predictors. Gratitude shows an exceptional degree of incremental validity in predicting well-being above the traits most studied in psychology.

Fourth, simple exercises have been developed to increase levels of gratitude (see Wood, Froh, & Geraghty, 2010; Shin and Lyubomirsky, Chapter 23, this volume), the most common of which is to simply write three things for which one is grateful at night before bed (Emmons & McCullough, 2002). In the first randomized controlled trials to compare this technique to one commonly used in clinical therapy (Geraghty, Wood, & Hyland, 2010a,b), "counting blessings" was found to be as effective as automatic thought monitoring and challenging in decreasing worry (in a population largely clinically high on anxiety) and improving body image (in a population largely clinically low on this appraisal). A notable feature of these studies was the use of an unguided self-help internet intervention; anyone could access and do these exercises. Such online interventions have the benefit of reaching greater numbers of people than conventional therapies, although they are hampered by very high drop-out rates, and those who do drop out cannot benefit fully from the intervention. Notably, the gratitude intervention had lower levels of drop-out whilst still (in intention to treat analysis) being as efficacious on the presenting problem. This would suggest that clinicians may sometimes wish to use these techniques preferentially as part of a therapy package for certain clients, such as those particularly at risk of disengaging from therapy.

Anecdotally, some participants reported that they initially did not think they could do the exercise at all, as they saw nothing in the world for which to be grateful. However, as the day passed they noticed things (specifically so that the observation could be recorded in the diary) that otherwise they would not have noticed. Seen in such a way, the intervention is not simply a five-minute daily exercise, but rather a continual attempt to reappraise events more accurately throughout the day by noticing the positive in addition to the negative. If this was an important factor then it would suggest that participant engagement is critical to success. Lack of engagement may explain why many studies into this technique show differences between the gratitude condition and a negative induction "hassles conditions" (to be interpreted as the hassles decreasing well-being, not a benefit of the gratitude condition), but not between the gratitude condition and a neutral control condition (see Wood, Froh, & Geraghty, 2010, for a general critique of control groups in gratitude research). Many of the null results seem to arise from samples who might be less enthusiastic about participating (e.g., undergraduates participating as a course requirement). Notably, some of the strongest supporting results for gratitude interventions emerge from our two studies (where participants volunteered for an experimental treatment for worry or body image, respectively): Seligman, Steen, Park, & Peterson (2005), who studied participants who had self-selected for a positive psychology intervention; and Study 3 of McCullough et al. (2002), which found significant results verses neutral controls in participants with rheumatoid arthritis (Study 3), but not undergraduate samples (Studies 1 and 2; although arguably the controls were more active than neutral). There is also a second intervention involving writing letters to people to whom one is grateful and have not properly thanked. Ongoing research is examining the relative efficacy of these two interventional types (see Wood, Froh, & Geraghty, 2010; Shin and Lyubomirsky, Chapter 23, this volume).

A third more experimental interventional technique has been developed for children (Froh et al., in press) which involves teaching them (in an age appropriate manner) to accurately read the appraisals of a gift-giving situation in order to feel appropriate levels of gratitude. Specifically, following the social cognitive model of Wood, Maltby, Stewart, Linley, & Joseph (2008), children were taught (in an age-appropriate manner) to more accurately identify the help they received from others in terms of how costly it was to provide (to their benefactor), how valuable it is them, and how altruistically intended was benefactor's help (the appraisals which in the social cognitive model cause transactional gratitude). The early evidence reported showed indication that the intervention was effective in improving both the children's self- and teacher-rated well-being, as well as motivating behavioral tendencies to express gratitude in different settings. Theoretically, this approach could be extended to adults. Part of the novelty in this approach is that its focus is specifically on *accurately* interpreting the situation. This approach may be more likely in certain client groups to promote beneficial gratitude rather than the harmful kinds discussed below; the focus is very specifically on the accurate reading of the situation rather than generally increasing gratitude without specific guidance as to how to ensure this is a good reflection of reality.

Gratitude interventions seem to work for some people some of the time. However, much more research is needed, and some of the enthusiasm seen within positive psychology communities to focus on the immediate implementation of these interventions in a wide variety of settings may be premature. Indeed, in one study (Sin, Della Porta, & Lyubomirsky, 2011) a gratitude intervention was found to decrease well-being, contrary to the general pattern in the literature. Important questions for future research (see also Watkins, 2013) are:

1   How do gratitude interventions work, what are the active mechanisms?
2   For whom do they work (do individual characteristics interact with whether the person is allocated to the gratitude or control group to determine outcome)?
3   What is the participant experience and what exactly do participants actually do?
4   For which groups of people (e.g., those with extrinsic versus intrinsic motivation to do gratitude exercises) do gratitude interventions work better or worse?
5   What is the optimum delivery of the intervention, for example: (a) how often should the exercise be performed (dose responsiveness)?; (b) how many things for which they are grateful should people list?; (c) what is the optimum length of the intervention?; (d) should people be guided to think of different categories of things for which to be grateful, such as people, life in general, etc. (see Wood, Maltby, Steward, & Joseph, 2008, for a list of the domains of gratitude)?

6   Do apparent null results emerge because of ceiling effects due to both the gratitude and control group being high in gratitude well-being prior to the intervention?
7   When and for whom might gratitude interventions be harmful?

Answers to these questions would likely explain some of the null results alluded to above (and discussed in Wood, Froh, & Geraghty, 2010); it may be that there are distinct "boundary conditions" or moderators that explain when and for whom gratitude interventions are helpful. Some emerging work is beginning to answer these questions, such as through showing that baseline levels of positive affect may moderate the effectiveness of the intervention (Froh, Kashdan, Ozimkowski, & Miller, 2009), and that people falling prey to "gratitude fatigue," with the usefulness of the intervention being dose responsive (Froh, Sefick, & Emmons, 2008); see also the work out of Sonja Lyubomirsky's laboratory and her chapter (Chapter 23) in this volume.

Gratitude interventions are quick and simple to deliver, apparently have client acceptability (as seen in the drop-out rates in Geraghty, Wood, & Hyland 2010a,b), and seem to work well for some people. These factors make gratitude interventions attractive to clinicians and can be a simple way of making existing therapeutic intervention more consistent with PCP through the inclusion of an additional gratitude task at low cost. However, as noted by Wood, Froh, and Geraghty (2010), and considering the challenges discussed throughout this chapter, this should be considered an "off-label" use of an intervention based on individual clinical judgment and with informed consent, as the evidence base is not yet sufficient to definitively recommend the technique under standard clinical guidelines for the amount of evidence needed for this purpose. We encourage the development of that evidence base. However, for the research questions we highlight to be answered, there needs to be a greater engagement in the question of whether there is a negative side to gratitude, and much greater awareness – and research into – related issues, resulting in movement from the occasional framing of all forms of gratitude as positive for everyone all of the time, toward a more balanced PCP view that recognizes that different forms of gratitude can be beneficial or harmful depending on the person and the situation that they are in.

Toward a Balanced View of Gratitude: Philosophical Considerations

As noted by Held (Chapter 3, this volume), it is complex to talk about the "positive" or "negative" characteristics, as these words have various meanings and it is often the case that different people are using the terms to connote different meanings. Positive and negative may refer to: (1) the valance of the emotional experience, (2) the general impact of something, or (3) the specific role of the experience for a given individual in a given context (whether it is beneficial to them or harmful). For example, anger may be negative in the sense of emotional valance, but positive in a given situation if it helps an individual behave more appropriately (as, e.g., in righting a genuine wrong). Such variable usage may be leading to unnecessary disagreements between scholars who are simply unaware that they are using the words "positive" and "negative" to mean different things. To clarify: it is to the third meaning of positive and negative that we mean to speak of in this chapter. In an attempt to avoid confusion, we refer to this "positive" and "negative" as beneficial and harmful, respectively. We are aware that these words may themselves be confusing but they are perhaps closest to our intended meaning. Clinical psychologists may talk about "adaptive" and "maladaptive" with the same meaning, although we prefer to avoid these terms to prevent confusion with evolutionary adaptation.

The question of what is beneficial or harmful for an individual may be seen from a prescriptive perspective (e.g., what is almost universally considered beneficial both within and across cultures), or an idiosyncratic perspective (e.g., what is positive for the life of the individual on their own terms). A useful starting point for considering when gratitude is beneficial or harmful is to consider the question: "is gratitude a virtue?" The word "virtue" is much used within positive psychology to refer to gratitude, although the meaning of this is not normally spelled out. A comprehensive view of virtue was provided by Aristotle (1999). In the Aristotelean view, virtue is the situationally appropriate use of several characteristics, when such appropriate use is near universally considered to be amongst the most excellent expressions of humanity (a generally prescriptive account of virtue). However, thoughts and behaviors associated with the use of potentially socially excellent characteristics are seen as existing on a continuum from high to low, with both the extreme high and low levels ends seen as equally nonvirtuous (lit. "vicious," the expression of vice). The socially excellent characteristic exists only at the "golden mean," where its use is situationally appropriate and displayed to the right degree. For example, modesty is the situationally appropriate occurrence of thoughts and behaviors that can range from self-effacement to arrogance. Behaviors at either side of this golden mean "sweet point" are harmful to the person or others, and only behaviors that occur at the situationally appropriate mid-point are considered beneficial. Modesty, as the situationally appropriate expression of behaviors that lie on a continuum from low (self-effacement) to high (arrogance), is by definition always beneficial. Behaviors, thoughts, and feelings on the self-effacement to arrogance continuum may however be harmful in that they are situationally inappropriate; in such cases they are not the virtue of modesty, which exists only at the appropriate point, but rather behaviors (such as self-effacement) that are incorrectly labeled as such.

Through applying this framework to gratitude,[1] the use of the word "gratitude" becomes complex, and it is likely that advocates and critics of gratitude research are using the term in somewhat different ways. In the virtues usage, gratitude can only be beneficial by definition, as it is a state comprising thoughts, emotions, and behaviors that are being situationally appropriately displayed in a way that is considered socially excellent. With the same usage one can refer to trait levels of gratitude ("grateful people") based on the frequency and intensity with which they experience state gratitude in this manner. However, a given state of thoughts, emotions, and behaviors that an individual or others may label (in a nonvirtue ethics usage) as gratitude may be situationally inappropriate and be harmful ("negative"), both in terms of what would be considered socially excellent, and in terms of the impact on the individual's life. Thus, inappropriately thanking an abuser would not be considered gratitude, in the virtues usage of the term, as the behavior is excessive for the situation. Thus, in a virtues usage, it would be a near truism to say that gratitude is always beneficial, as the word would refer exclusively to the situationally appropriate display of state gratitude, not its lack or excess.

The practical importance of this discussion is in interpreting the recommendations of gratitude researchers in the consulting room. Gratitude research can often be misunderstood if the author is using the word gratitude to refer to (virtuous) situationally appropriate displays, in which case it is entirely logical to say that we should always promote gratitude, whereas such claims would be nonsense if they were interpreted to mean that people should display an excess of gratitude. Appreciation of this point will also allow the development of a more advanced field of gratitude research and practice, where the focus becomes explicitly on when the thoughts, emotions, and behaviors associated with gratitude are appropriate, and thus meet the definition of "virtuous" gratitude, to which many authors have been implicitly but not explicitly referring.

In a related vein, Peterson and Seligman (2004), from a broadly virtue ethic position, refer to the golden mean as "gratitude," too low levels as entitlement, its absence is rudeness or forgetfulness, and its excess as ingratiation. Similarly, Shelton (2010) presents a taxonomy of seven types of quasi-gratitude (when qualities of goodness are negligible or absent) and three types of what he terms harmful gratitude (when gratitude is corrupted by behavior intended to hurt). The seven forms of quasi-gratitude are shallow gratitude, reluctant gratitude, self-serving gratitude, defensive gratitude, mixed gratitude, misperceived gratitude, and misplaced gratitude. The three types of harmful gratitude are more pathological: hurtful gratitude, deviant gratitude, and malignant gratitude.

From a virtue ethics position, none of Shelton's (2010) "false" gratitudes would be termed gratitude as, although they may share similar behaviors (e.g., expressing thanks), appraisals, and experienced emotion, each represent deviations from what would be considered culturally excellent situationally appropriate displays of these behavior, appraisals, and emotions. All would also be considered harmful, at least in the sense that they are not optimum reactions to the situation. To the extent that a person is characterized by these inappropriate forms of gratitude, they and others may describe themselves as high on trait gratitude, but from a virtues perspective they would be incorrect, based on mislabeling of the states that they are commonly experiencing. The field of gratitude research must engage more consciously in making these distinctions through more careful language usage, in order to avoid confusion and spend more time researching the specific situations under which these different forms of "gratitude" occur. We refer here to "beneficial" gratitude in the sense of an Aristotelean virtue, and "harmful" to refer to all other cases.

It seems that the word gratitude is being used in different ways by different scholars, leading to much disagreement and confusion. This may be due to a nonshared use of language rather than disagreement about the core concept. The subtlety in the types of gratitude should be critically important to clinical psychologists seeking to improve mental health through gratitude interventions, as their focus should be on promoting appropriate gratitude rather than its maladaptive or quasi forms.

This subtlety between beneficial and harmful gratitude may also not be being picked up by most psychological research into gratitude, which often relies on participant's understanding of the word gratitude. Even if they do understand it to refer exclusively to beneficial gratitude, as much of the research is based on self-report it will rely on participant's ability to correctly label what they are experiencing as beneficial rather than as harmful gratitude (for issues with the self-report of gratitude, see Davidson and Wood, in press). Similarly, some of the null results of gratitude interventions may result from a minority of participants misinterpreting the exercise and it promoting harmful forms of gratitude in them. We take the view that gratitude is by definition always positive, if in the virtues usage, but that similar experiences can easily masquerade as gratitude, and that this is both causing confusion in scholarly discussions as to whether gratitude is always positive and causing confusion for some individuals in their attempts to build gratitude into their own lives. It will be the job of the clinical psychologist to help the individual develop beneficial gratitude rather than the harmful forms, through appreciating these subtleties, whether through specific gratitude exercises or other aspects of the therapeutic encounter. On the academic side, there needs to be a new phase of gratitude research that separates out the antecedents, correlates, and consequences of beneficial verses harmful gratitude, as well as how these types of gratitude differentially interact with situations and are differentially fostered by variants of gratitude interventions.

Despite the above considerations it should be emphasized that the empirical research (see Wood, Froh, and Geraghty, 2010) overwhelmingly shows that trait gratitude measures are strongly, uniquely, and causally relate to well-being, and there is good evidence that gratitude interventions in general increase well-being. However, as with all such psychological work, this is a pattern based on statistics, forming a generality about the particular populations from which the sample was drawn. Even within these samples the variance in people's responses will incorporate some people who have higher gratitude and lower well-being (in trait research) or who get worse in an intervention. Whether this is random error or a systematic difference that could be picked up with moderation analysis remains to be seen. Also, as gratitude research and practice increasingly moves into clinical domains, the statistically rarer cases may be seen more frequently. It is important to understand when and for whom research is accidently picking up harmful gratitude and this is an important avenue for future research. What we are arguing for is the "emotionally intelligent" use of gratitude, and research and practice to become more subtle in picking this up. However, given the strong links shown in the empirical work between gratitude and well-being it seems that in general gratitude research is managing to pick up beneficial rather than harmful gratitude, and it is important to not be overcritical here, but rather to aim for ever increasing refinement as befits a growing field of research.

The distinction between beneficial and harmful gratitude also avoids a potential problem for gratitude research where gratitude is seen to be good all the time. Proponents of such views seem to be arguing that gratitude is the elixir for all that ails us. Then, they move to redefining gratitude: all that is good becomes gratitude. This is dangerous, because when we do this, gratitude paradoxically loses its power. Gratitude is an important trait to the good life because it is something meaningful and specific, and when we make it into everything good, we lose a clear conception of gratitude, and then gratitude pretty much becomes anything, or nothing. A clearer distinction between beneficial and harmful gratitude helps avoid this trap.

Harmful Gratitude

The proceeding discussion highlights examples of where harmful gratitude may occur, including in settings that clinical psychologists are particularly likely to encounter when they are aiming to increase gratitude with certain clients. Some of these examples are based on contributions to Carr (in press), and arise more from the philosophical than psychological literature. As such, they as yet lack an empirical basis, and must not overshadow the empirical findings that generally gratitude has been shown to be beneficial, at least with the outcomes and samples studied. However, much more research is needed into these areas whilst distinguishing between beneficial and harmful types of gratitude.

Gratitude Within Abusive Relationships

A harmful gratitude may occur within a context of an objectively abusive relationship, with the victim feeling what they experience as gratitude to the abuser (cf., Card, in press). In this case such feelings are extremely negative, not least as it will motivate the person to remain in the relationship and continue to tolerate the abuser. Indeed, this ingratiation may partially explain why people remain in clearly abusive relationships when those around them (including in extreme cases, the police and social services) say that they should leave. Consistent with the opening quote from Stalin, the abuser may also foster ingratiation in their victim in several ways with this express intent. For example, the abuser may encourage a false dependence from your victim (e.g., "you're nothing without me", "you could not survive without me", "no one else would put up with you, and then where would you be?"). Further, an abuser may normally provide such a low level of provision than any act (unworthy of gratitude and still unreasonable) would attract substantial gratitude as it would be *relatively* higher than what is normally given. This would be consistent with research by Wood, Brown, & Maltby (2011) that shows what determines transactional gratitude is not the act itself, but rather how that act ranks amongst what the person is used to receiving and how it falls on the overall range of the least to most help that they normally receive (see also Algoe et al., 2008).

In the virtues model, such feelings toward an abuser would not be seen as gratitude as the response is far beyond the virtuous, situationally appropriate mid-point (which here would be at the extreme poll of ungrateful behavior, at least toward the specific act of the abuser). There would certainly not be a widely held view in most modern societies that a wife feeling gratitude toward her husband who is severely beating regularly (and even feeling gratitude *for* the beatings) is having a virtuous reaction, the most excellent expression of her humanity. (Although, of course, there would hopefully not be judgment either, rather an appreciation that this may be what she needs to do to survive.) The example here is deliberately extreme, although this process likely occurs very regularly for many people at a less extreme level. Although most people in most societies are not in extremely abusive relationships, many (if not most) people have some unhealthy relationships in their personal or occupational lives, and everyone will routinely encounter others acting inappropriately toward them and with ill-intent if only on a very superficial level (e.g., the person cutting in line, the snappy person in the shop, etc.). To the extent that people are feeling harmful gratitude toward these people they will likely behave nonoptimally. Harmful gratitude, in these types of situations, can also prevent individuals from giving those misbehaving the feedback they need to appropriately alter their behavior. Thus, gratitude can be damaging not only to individuals who bear the brunt of misbehavior, but also to those who sorely need corrective feedback with regard to their damaging behavior. To the extent that people commonly feel such inappropriate emotions toward others with whom they regularly interact, then they will likely create relationship problems, if only through a lack of healthy boundaries.

Extending the sociocognitive model of gratitude (Wood, Maltby, Stewart, Linley, & Joseph, 2008), the beneficial gratitude in this situation is that which is based on appraisals of cost, benefit, and altruism that are *accurate* readings of the situation. Based on the relative model of gratitude (Wood, Brown, & Maltby, 2011), in order to make accurate judgments people would also have to have an accurate idea of the distribution of amounts of help that people normally get. This offers a framework with which to begin analyzing individual cases of when transactional gratitude is beneficial or harmful. The interventional approach of Froh et al. (2014) may offer a way toward promoting this healthy transactional gratitude.

The assumption that accurate readings of the situation are the most beneficial is in line with Aristotelean perspectives and clinical perspectives such as Beck et al. (1979). Part of the motivation for this assumption is that people can make more rational decisions about their life if they can more accurately read the objective situation. However, others (e.g., Taylor & Brown, 1988) have suggested that a slightly rosy view of the world may be positively related to well-being, which here would be a slightly generous interpretation of help received. The implications of this for the promotion of gratitude is discussed by Watkins (2013, Watkins, in press). However, the general literature on positive illusions is controversial (e.g., Joiner, Kistner, Stellrecht, & Merrill, 2006) and the pervasiveness of the illusions has been challenged (Harris & Hahn, 2011). Nevertheless, it is a complex individual and clinical decision if and when to challenge moderately rosy views of the world if they are maintaining well-being perhaps whilst an individual is challenging their appraisals in another domain.

It is also a separate question as to whether beneficial gratitude could still be experienced in even in abusive situations. For example, keeping in mind things for which it is appropriate to be grateful (e.g., outside the abusive relationship) may be important to the individual's recovery. It is possible that such gratitude, quite distinct from the form described above, may be adaptive for the individual. Making these kinds of distinction is a wide open and much needed area for future research. In discussions of gratitude in abusive relationships there needs to be a much clearer distinction between the form of "gratitude" being referred to; talking about the harmful gratitude in this context to critique the beneficial or virtuous form of gratitude may lead to misleading conclusions.

The Systems Justification Problem

Eibach, Wilmot, and Libby (2015) discuss a potential maladaptive form of gratitude that is fostered by social systems to avoid people challenging the system itself. They discuss extensive, although indirect, evidence that this may be occurring (e.g., parents higher on social systems justification of valuing "good manners" in children more). They discuss, for example, that cultural outpourings of gratitude during times of war may increase support for the military actions. This is probably closest to the opening quote from Stalin. It is a version of what Nobel

Prize winner Amartya Sen described as "the happy peasant problem." Here he was referring to the general problem of using subjective measures of states and quality of life (specifically life satisfaction) to assess the person's objective quality of life or the situation in which they are living. In the first author's experience, some of the most apparently grateful people are living in countries in which people are the least free (as judged by corruption and low political and human rights, including the systematic subjugation of women). Further, it is possible that some people in some of these states may be grateful *to* the state *for* the treatment (a group version of the abusive relationship problem). Indeed, it was the first author's perception in one such state that, when talking to the locals about the aggressive behavior of the border guards in the airport (who were shouting at people to get in line), the locals cheerfully, unanimously, and apparently sincerely said they were grateful *to* the guards *for* this behavior, which they said had been explained to them on many occasions as necessary to keep them safe and free. He saw the scene as somewhat reminiscent of Huxley's (1931) fictional *Brave New World*, in which a despotic state without the population's best interests at heart focused on increasing positive moods as a way to keep the people in line.

Indeed, given the ubiquity with which organized religion has promoted feeling gratitude as a moral obligation (Emmons & Crumpler, 2000), and as organized religion has at least partially operated in league with unhealthy states as an agent of social control, then it seems likely that the promotion of gratitude for the purposes of state subjugation has been widespread throughout history. There is, however, no direct research on this, and much is needed that interacts subjective gratitude with objective living conditions at the individual and group (national) level. The prediction would be that people feeling more harmful gratitude toward those in control and also those that are less free would be more likely to put up with their lot and be less likely to take appropriate action to assert their human rights. Such phenomena, of course, may also manifest in all countries in the form of a contentment that leads to a lack of striving for change. But it should again be noted that these are examples of harmful not beneficial gratitude, which would not meet the definition of gratitude in a virtues framework. It may very well be that even in such states there may be situationally appropriate experiences of beneficial gratitude, for example, to the state for genuinely beneficial provisions, and if not toward the state, then toward sources not connected to the state (e.g., family members). Even were there increased gratitude in such states, it would be important to separate out whether this is beneficial or harmful gratitude as well as its source; whether it is harmful gratitude toward the state or beneficial gratitude emerging out of other positive aspects of the culture (such as stronger communities). There also needs to be consideration of whether any evidence for the "happy peasant" problem is due uniquely to harmful gratitude or the shared variance between gratitude and life satisfaction (Wood, Joseph, & Maltby, 2008), given that the latter is normally what is considered in this context. Nevertheless, this does highlight concern about how gratitude interventions could potentially be misused in some settings by those in control, as well as the care with which large-scale interventions have to be delivered in order to promote beneficial rather than harmful gratitude.

The Nonidentity Problem

From a pure philosophical viewpoint, and for one specific type of gratitude, Smilansky (in press) describes the "nonidentity" problem, how gratitude for being alive necessitates gratitude for the whole chain of events that lead to one's existence. For example, in many Western societies the Second World War caused such great loss of life and population movement that people with families traced to this period would almost certainly not have been born had the Second World War not occurred. How, then, Smilansky asks, can one feel gratitude for one's existence without also being grateful that the war (and antecedent atrocities) occurred? There are perhaps answers, such as from a Stoic (Epictetus, 2008) or Buddhist (Sangharakshita, 1990) viewpoint that one should simply accept the universe as a vast causal entity and be glad that all transpires as it does because this is how it is meant to be, as well as the only way that it could ever have turned out (in secular terms, following the Big Bang, everything may have been predetermined through the interaction of atoms set in chain by that event). This is also likely the view of many of the major religious thinkers, although here there is a danger that this is motivated by the systems justification noted above. It is also a rather radical solution and not one that has been explicitly been adopted by the psychological research into gratitude. Smilansky's criticisms are very early and much more philosophical work is needed to consider his challenge in more depth including its tenability. The scientific method of psychology is unlikely to add much to these ethical considerations of whether a person should feel grateful, although could do much to establish a moral under-standing of whether people generally believe that they should feel grateful in these situations. Survey data would be useful here, as well as experiments in which the saliency of this problem is manipulated to see whether gratitude differs when people are more aware of nonidentity problem barrier to gratitude. However, such work would more likely develop a much needed better understanding of types of harmful gratitude rather than show that beneficial gratitude cannot exist. The direct relevance of the nonidentity problem to the practicing positive clinical psychologist is perhaps less than some of the other considerations in this chapter, and the rele-vance is perhaps more towards those interested in the philosophy and ethics underpinning clinical practice.

The Slave–Foreman Problem

As discussed in Carr (in press) there are ethical problems with feeling gratitude toward people who are themselves giving aid that is costly, valuable, and altruistic, but who are cogs within an oppressive regime. For example, is it appropriate for a slave to feel gratitude toward a foreman who treats him or her kindly, with good intent, and going beyond what is expected of their position? (Critically, in this example it is beyond the authority of the foreman to release the slave, although one assumes within their physical capability, if even at the cost of their own life.) It is an ethically difficult question as to whether the slave should feel gratitude to this captor (many would say not, although based on the social-cognitive model the person would be expected to do so). Despite the foreman acting in a way that is costly, valuable, and altruistic, the system could not exist without foremen, and, as such, they are as much of the problem as the (pitifully inadequate) solution. Again, an extreme example is presented, partially due to a philosophical epistemology in which a theory is expected to hold at the extremes, and should be tested with thought experiments at these extremes (where it is perhaps most saliently not going to hold). However, everyday examples of this will regularly occur; for example, should one feel grateful in the situation where, when faced with mistreatment by an organization (e.g., cold-calling or pro-vision of substandard products by unethical companies), an employee of that organization goes beyond what is expected of their role to lessen the harm in a way that is costly, valuable, and altruistic? In many ways, this is a version of the systems justification problem, but differs in moral complexity as here it is not those that are in charge of the system (e.g., the slave owner) that are the focus of the thought experiment, but rather those who in a sense victim themselves to it whilst simultaneously allowing it to continue to exist. A concern would be that gratitude expressed to these people would make them less likely to stop supporting the system, which if done in sufficient numbers, would cause system change. More philosophical work is needed into these issues, as well as experimental work to see how people do behave in these situations and survey data to quantify people's moral understanding of how people should react in these situations. Practicing clinical psychologists need to be aware of these ethical complexities when promoting gratitude in specific cases.

The Other Personality Characteristics Problem

So far the examples have considered the situations in which gratitude is likely to be problematic. Increasingly, the social sciences are focusing on how individual personality characteristics interact with the objective environment to determine the person's reaction (e.g., Boyce, Wood & Brown, 2010; Boyce & Wood, 2011a,b). Applying this approach to gratitude suggests that there may be some people for whom the situations highlighted above may be particularly problematic. The personality theory underlying Schema Therapy (Young, Klosko, & Weishaar, 2003; van Vreeswijk, Broersen, & Nadort, 2015; see Taylor and Arntz, Chapter 30, this volume) is especially helpful in this regard. Eighteen ways of viewing the world (each ranging from maladaptive to adaptive) (Lockwood & Perris, 2015) are identified, which in turn arise from particular parenting conditions (themselves ranging from maladaptive to adaptive). Several are particularly relevant: (1) people with maladaptive self-sacrifice schemas believe that they have to put others needs before their own or they will suffer terrible consequences; (2) those with subjugation schemas believe that it is unsafe to have even expressed their preferences and needs in the first place; and (3) people with dependency schemas believe that they cannot function autonomously in the world without deferring to more powerful others. Each of these (all on continua, continuous with adaptive counterparts) are pervasive, long-term ways of viewing the world, involving selective attention toward confirmatory information, selective ease of encoding for confirmatory information, and greater ease of recall of confirmatory information (with the opposite processes for disconfirming information). They have emerged from chronic negative environments or acute negative events (normally the former, and normally involving the primary care givers during childhood). Particular configurations of the eighteen schemas (and whether people are acting in line with them, trying to avoid the triggering situation, or overcompensating by trying to do the opposite) provide the underlying psychological process of what manifests externally as a categorical personality disorder. It is possible (and a testable hypothesis) that maladaptive gratitude may be particularly seen in these individuals, who may mislabel it as beneficial gratitude. This would be consistent with Watkins et al.'s (2006) findings that grateful emotion is associated with yielding to others. In therapy, clinicians may consider carefully questioning what clients are labeling gratitude and helping them to explore whether it is beneficial gratitude or a harmful form. It may be that the gratitude that such individuals feel is well placed, not linked to subjugation, but rather the genuinely costly, valuable, and altruistic things that, for example, the partner provides, or it may be misplaced and related to self-sacrifice, subjugation, and dependency schemas. Given the majority of clients in clinical therapy have some maladaptive functioning on the eighteen schemas, this underscores the importance in clinical practice of distinguishing between beneficial and harmful gratitude, as well as the care with which any gratitude intervention is presented to such clients to ensure that it is beneficial gratitude that is being fostered rather than a deepening of their schemas.

Bringing Together the Positive and Negative Sides of Gratitude

Whereas the psychological literature (Wood, Froh, & Geraghty, 2010) has focused almost exclusively on the benefits of gratitude, the philosophical literature (Carr, in press) has focused more on ethical issues and special cases where gratitude may not be appropriate, tending if anything toward focusing on when it is problematic. Partially this is due to psychology focusing on the impact of gratitude in general in people's lives, rather than situation-specific effects, and through focusing on looking at the impact of gratitude in general irrespective of the other traits of the individual. The philosophical literature has generally focused on ethics, when *should* an individual feel gratitude, whereas the psychological literature has focused more on what happens *when* an individual feels gratitude. A lack of integration between these literatures is harming research efforts, with some of the philosophical literature speculating on falsifiable statements of fact on which there are already answers provided by psychology, and psychology not sufficiently reflecting on underlying conceptual and philosophical challenges to gratitude that would lead to testable predictions about when the concept is beneficial and when it is harmful. Moving the study of gratitude forward will require: (a) a better integration between the philosophical and psychological literatures, and (b) movement away from looking at the general ("on average") impact of gratitude on well-being irrespective of other personality characteristics or the specific situations in which a person is living. It will also involve movement toward testing whether the impact of gratitude is beneficial or harmful depending on dynamic interactions between gratitude, other personality traits, and the objective environment. Within clinical therapy, it is important that: (a) gratitude is considered, given its strong, unique, and possibly causal impact on well-being; but that (b) in case conceptualization, the role of gratitude in people's lives and in specific relationships is considered in light of other characteristics of the individual and the exact situations which a person is facing; and (c) that any attempt to increase gratitude therapeutically is done carefully based on clinician judgment in collaboration with the client. This, until more research is conducted, is the best way to ensure that beneficial rather than harmful gratitude is being promoted, and that it will have a positive rather than negative impact on a person's life.

Note

1 Aristotle did not specifically consider gratitude in *Nicomachean Ethics*. From his other work it seems that he considered gratitude to not be a characteristic for which the situationally appropriate usage would be socially considered an excellent expression of humanity (failing his test for inclusion). He saw gratitude as generally aversive as it reflected an imbalance in what one is giving and receiving. This is perhaps closer to indebtedness, which has since been shown by research to be a separate emotion caused by different appraisals and leading to different thought action tendencies (Watkins, Scheer, Ovnicek, & Kolts, 2006). Difficulty of translation from classical sources (including different concepts of emotions) can make it unclear whether the same topic is being discussed in ancient and contemporary work. Aristotle seems focused on transactional gratitude (or perhaps indebtedness), whereas (at least in later Stoic accounts) the wide sense of gratitude representing a general sense of appreciation for what one has was revered. In this chapter we aim to use Aristotle's wider conceptualization of virtue and apply it to contemporary conceptions of gratitude, rather than present the Aristotelean view of the emotion (which is discussed extensively in Carr, in press). Given that he explicitly chose to apply his framework to characteristics *within his own time and culture* that were considered excellent, we consider it legitimate to apply a virtues ethics framework analysis to characteristics valued in our time and place. We stress, however, that we are applying a loosely Aristotelean framework rather than representing Aristotle's views.

References

Algoe, S. B. (2012). Find, remind, and bind: The functions of gratitude in everyday relationships. *Social and Personality Psychology Compass, 6*, 455–469.

Algoe, S. B., Haidt, J., & Gable, S. L. (2008). Beyond reciprocity: Gratitude and relationships in everyday life. *Emotion, 8*, 425–429.

Algoe, S. B. & Stanton, A. L. (2012). Gratitude when it is needed most: Social functions of gratitude in women with metastatic breast cancer. *Emotion, 12*, 163–168.

American Psychiatric Association. (2013). *Diagnostic and statistical manual of mental disorders*, 5th edn. Washington, DC: APA.

Aristotle ([305 BC] 1999). *Nicomachean ethics*, trans. T. Irwine. Indianapolis, IN: Hackett.

Beck, A., Rush, A., Shaw, B., & Emery, G. (1979). *Cognitive therapy for depression*. New York: Guildford Press.

Bono, G., Emmons, R. A., & McCullough, M. E. (2004). Gratitude in practice and the practice of gratitude. In: P. A. Linley & S. Joseph (Eds.), *Positive psychology in practice* (pp. 464–481). Hoboken, NJ: John Wiley.

Boyce, C. J. & Wood, A. M. (2011a). Personality prior to disability determines adaptation: Agreeable individuals recover lost life satisfaction faster and more completely. *Psychological Science, 22,* 1397–1402.

Boyce, C. J., & Wood, A. M. (2011b). Personality and the marginal utility of income: Personality interacts with increases in household income to determine life satisfaction. *Journal of Economic Behavior & Organization, 78,* 183–191.

Boyce, C. J., Wood, A. M., & Brown, G. D. A. (2010). The dark side of conscientiousness: Conscientious people experience greater drops in life satisfaction following unemployment. *Journal of Research in Personality, 44,* 535–539.

Card, ?. (in press). Chapter title. In: D. Carr (Ed.), *Perspectives on gratitude: An interdisciplinary approach* (pp. 00–00). London: Routledge.

Carr, D. (Ed.). (in press). *Perspectives on gratitude: An interdisciplinary approach.* London: Routledge.

Cohen, S., Gottlieb, B., & Underwood, L. (2000). Social relationships and health. In: S. Cohen, L. Underwood, & B. Gottlieb (Eds.), *Measuring and intervening in social support* (pp. 3–25). New York: Oxford University Press.

Davidson, A. & Wood, A. M. (in press). The state of the psychological research into gratitude and the need for more interdisciplinary collaboration. In: D. Carr (Ed.), *Perspectives on gratitude: An interdisciplinary approach.* London: Routledge.

Eibach, R. P., Wilmot, M. O., & Libby, L. K. (2015). The system-justifying function of gratitude norms. *Social and Personality Psychology Compass, 9,* 348–358.

Emmons, R. A. & Crumpler, C. A. (2000). Gratitude as a human strength: Appraising the evidence. *Journal of Social and Clinical Psychology, 19,* 56–69.

Emmons, R. A. & McCullough, M. E. (2003). Counting blessings versus burdens: An experimental investigation of gratitude and subjective well-being in daily life. *Journal of Personality and Social Psychology, 84,* 377–389.

Epictetus ([180 AD] 2008). *Discourses and selected writings,* trans. R. Dobbin. London: Penguin.

Froh, J. J., Bono, G., Fan, J., Emmons, R. A., Henderson, K., Harris, C., Leggio, H., & Wood, A. M. (in press). Nice thinking! An educational intervention that teaches children how to think gratefully. *School Psychology Review (Special Issue), 43,* 132–152.

Froh, J. J., Kashdan, T. B., Ozimkowski, K. M., & Miller, N. (2009). Who benefits the most from a gratitude intervention in children and adolescents? Examining positive affect as a moderator. *Journal of Positive Psychology, 4,* 408–422.

Froh, J. J., Sefick, W. J., & Emmons, R. A. (2008). Counting blessings in early adolescents: An experimental study of gratitude and subjective well-being. *Journal of School Psychology, 46,* 213–233.

Froh, J. J., Yurkewicz, C., & Kashdan, T.B. (2009). Gratitude and subjective well-being in early adolescence: Examining gender differences. *Journal of Adolescence, 32,* 633–650.

Geraghty, A. W. A., Wood, A. M., & Hyland, M. E. (2010a). Attrition from self-directed interventions: Investigating the relationship between psychological predictors, intervention content and dropout from a body dissatisfaction intervention. *Social Science & Medicine, 71,* 31–37.

Geraghty, A. W. A., Wood, A. M., & Hyland, M. E. (2010b). Dissociating the facets of hope: Agency and pathways predict dropout from unguided self-help therapy in opposite directions. *Journal of Research in Personality, 44,* 155–158.

Harris, A. J. L. & Hahn, U. (2011). Unrealistic optimism about future life events: A cautionary note. *Psychological Review, 118,* 135–154.

Huxley, A. (1932). *Brave New World.* London: Chatto & Windus.

Joiner, T. E., Kistner, J. A., Stellrecht, N. E., Merrill, K. A. (2006). On seeing clearly and thriving: interpersonal perspicacity as adaptive (not depressive) realism (or where three theories meet). *Journal of Social and Clinical Psychology, 25,* 542–556.

Lambert, N. M., Clarke, M. S., Durtschi, J. A., Fincham, F. D., & Graham, S. M. (2010). Benefits of expressing gratitude: Expressing gratitude to a partner changes one's views of the relationship. *Psychological Science, 21,* 574–580.

Lambert, N. M. & Fincham, F. D. (2011). Expressing gratitude to a partner leads to more relationship maintenance behavior. *Emotion, 11,* 52–60.

Lambert, N. M., Fincham, F. D., & Stillman, T. F. (2012). Gratitude and depressive symptoms: The role of positive reframing and positive emotion. *Cognition and Emotion, 26,* 602–614.

Lazarus, R. S. (1993). From psychological stress to the emotions: A history of changing outlooks. *Annual Review of Psychology, 44,* 1–21.

Lockwood, G. & Perris, P. (2015). A new look at core emotional needs. In: M. van Vreeswijk, J. Broersen, & M. Nadort (Eds.), *The Wiley-Blackwell handbook of schema therapy: Theory, research and practice* (pp. 41–66). Chichester: Wiley-Blackwell.

McCullough, M. E., Emmons, R. A., & Tsang, J. A. (2002). The grateful disposition: A conceptual and empirical topography. *Journal of Personality and Social Psychology, 82*, 112–127.

McCullough, M. E., Kilpatrick, S. D., Emmons, R. A., & Larson, D. B. (2001). Is gratitude a moral affect? *Psychological Bulletin, 127*, 249–266.

Peterson, C. & Seligman, M. E. P. (2004). *Character strengths and virtues: A handbook and classification.* Washington, DC: American Psychological Association.

Rodriguez, M. C. & Cohen, S. (1998). Social support. In: H. Friedman (Ed.), *Encyclopedia of mental health.* New York: Academic Press.

Sangharakshita (1990). *A guide to the Buddhist path.* Cambridge: Windhorse Publications.

Seligman, M. E. P., Steen, T. A., Park, N., & Peterson, C. (2005). Positive psychology progress: Empirical validation of interventions. *American Psychologist, 60*, 410–421.

Shelton, C. M. (2010). *The gratitude factor: Enhancing your life through grateful living.* New Jersey: Hidden Spring (Paulist Press).

Sin, N. L., Della Porta, M. D., & Lyubomirsky, S. (2011). Tailoring positive psychology interventions to treat depressed individuals. In: S. I. Donaldson, M. Csikszentmihalyi, & J. Nakamura (Eds.), *Applied positive psychology: Improving everyday life, health, schools, work, and society* (pp. 79–96). New York: Routledge.

Smilansky, S. (in press). Gratitude: The dark side. In: D. Carr (Ed.), *Perspectives on gratitude: An interdisciplinary approach* (pp. 00–00). London: Routledge.

Taylor, S. E. & Brown, J. (1988). Illusion and well-being: A social psychological perspective on mental health. *Psychological Bulletin, 103*, 193–210.

van Vreeswijk, M., Broersen, J., & Nadort, M. (Eds.). (2015). *The Wiley-Blackwell handbook of schema therapy: Theory, research and practice.* Chichester: Wiley-Blackwell.

Watkins, P. C. (2013). *Gratitude and the good life: Toward a psychology of appreciation.* Dordrecht: Springer.

Watkins, P. C. (in press). Chapter title: In: D. Carr (Ed.), *Perspectives on gratitude: An interdisciplinary approach* (pp. 00–00). London: Routledge.

Watkins, P. C., Scheer, J., Ovnicek, M., & Kolts, R. (2006). The debt of gratitude: Dissociating gratitude from indebtedness. *Cognition and Emotion, 20*, 217–241.

Wood, A. M., Brown, G. D. A., & Maltby, J. (2011). Thanks, but I'm used to better: A relative rank model of gratitude. *Emotion, 11*, 175–180

Wood, A. M., Froh, J. J., & Geraghty, A. W. A. (2010). Gratitude and well-being: A review and theoretical integration. *Clinical Psychology Review, 30*, 890–905.

Wood, A. M., Joseph, S., & Linley, P. A. (2007a). Coping style as a psychological resource of grateful people. *Journal of Social and Clinical Psychology, 26*, 1076–109.

Wood, A. M., Joseph, S., & Linley, P. A. (2007b). Gratitude: Parent of all virtues. *The Psychologist, 20*, 18–21.

Wood, A. M, Joseph, S., Lloyd, J., & Atkins, S. (2009). Gratitude influences sleep through the mechanism of pre-sleep cognitions. *Journal of Psychosomatic Research, 66*, 43–48.

Wood, A. M., Joseph, S., & Maltby, J. (2008). Gratitude uniquely predicts satisfaction with life: Incremental validity above the domains and facets of the five factor model. *Personality and Individual Differences, 15*, 49–54.

Wood, A. M, Joseph, S., & Maltby, J. (2009). Gratitude predicts psychological well-being above the Big Five facets. *Personality and Individual Differences, 46*, 443–447.

Wood, A. M., Maltby, J., Gillett, R., Linley, P. A., & Joseph, S. (2008). The role of gratitude in the development of social support, stress, and depression: Two longitudinal studies. *Journal of Research in Personality, 42*, 854–871.

Wood, A. M., Maltby, J., Stewart, N., & Joseph, S. (2008). Conceptualizing gratitude and appreciation as a unitary personality trait. *Personality and Individual Differences, 44*, 619–630.

Wood, A. M., Maltby, J., Stewart, N., Linley, P. A., & Joseph, S. (2008). A social-cognitive model of trait and state levels of gratitude. *Emotion, 8*, 281–290.

Wood, A. M. & Tarrier, N. (2010). Positive Clinical Psychology: A new vision and strategy for integrated research and practice. *Clinical Psychology Review, 30*, 819–829.

Young, J. E., Klosko, J. S., & Weishaar, M. E. (2003). *Schema therapy: A practitioner's guide.* New York: Guilford Press.

11

Using Eudaimonic Well-being to Improve Lives

Chiara Ruini and Carol D. Ryff

Introduction

This *Handbook on Positive Clinical Psychology* signals a sea change in mental health research and practice. A central premise is that understanding and treatment of psychological disorders requires a combined focus on positive and negative psychological experience. We submit that efforts to promote good psychological health in the general public also require a prevention focus built on knowledge of psychological strengths and vulnerabilities. In this chapter, we give primary emphasis to a eudaimonic conception of psychological well-being, arguing that it is richly suited to the tasks at hand given its inherent emphasis on achieving wellness vis-à-vis the existential challenges of living. In the first section below, we review philosophical foundations of the eudaimonic approach, and along the way note its distinctiveness from hedonic conceptions of psychological well-being. We then review the psychological foundations of the eudaimonic approach, which were built on the integration of multiple conceptions of positive functioning from clinical, development, existential, and humanistic psychology. We briefly highlight growing evidence of the protective value of eudaimonic well-being for physical health, and then turn our attention to the relevance of eudaimonia for mental health. A first topic therein summarizes findings that have linked traditional indicators of mental illness (depression, anxiety) to eudaimonic well-being. Evidence from across the life course shows that those who suffer from psychological disorders are less likely to experience eudaimonia, which underscores the importance of well-being as a target for treatment. We then review evidence of interventions to promote eudaimonic, both in clinical contexts (treating psychological disorders) and in educational contexts (preventing psychological disorders via promotion of eudaimonic well-being). A main message is that efforts to facilitate experiences of purposeful engagement, self-realization, and growth are vital avenues for improving human lives.

Distant Philosophical Foundations of Eudaimonia

In *Nichomachean Ethics*, written in 350 BC, Aristotle asserted that highest of all goods achievable by human action was "eudaimonia." He used the term not to refer to things like pleasure, worth, or honor, but instead to activities of the soul in accordance with virtue. His conception of virtue had two parts. The first, involved aiming for balance or that which is intermediate. Those of virtuous character thus engage in deliberate actions chosen to avoid excess or

The Wiley Handbook of Positive Clinical Psychology, First Edition. Edited by Alex M. Wood and Judith Johnson.
© 2016 John Wiley & Sons, Ltd. Published 2016 by John Wiley & Sons, Ltd.

deficiency, whether they are extremes of pleasure or pain, fear or confidence, vanity or humility. Beyond striving for the mean in modes of conduct, Aristotle's deeper message about virtue was that it involves achieving the best that is within us, each according his or her unique talents and capacities. Eudaimonia is thus growth toward realization of one's true and best nature. Although Aristotle's *Ethics* described multiple virtues, it is important to emphasize that he considered eudaimonia (realization of one's best self) the highest and most important virtue. In contemporary scholarship (Norton, 1976), Hellenic eudaimonism is characterized as an ethical doctrine in which each person is obliged to know and live in truth to his *daimon* (a kind of spirit given to all persons at birth), thereby progressively actualizing an excellence (from the Greek "arête"). Eudaimonia is meaningful living conditioned upon self-truth and personal responsibility. As such, it embodies the two great Greek imperatives, to "know thyself" and to "become what you are" (Ryff & Singer, 2008).

It is important to note that other ancient Greeks, such as Aristippus and Epicuris, emphasized a different approach to the highest human good. For them, experiences of pleasure and contentment – distilled as hedonia – were primary. These two contrasting approaches have been described as key distinctions in contemporary research (Ryan & Deci, 2001) on well-being, one concerned with human potentials and the other with human happiness. Empirical investigations have documented that the two approaches are related but distinct (Keyes, Shmotkin, & Ryff, 2002). Our focus is on the tradition of well-being that began with Aristotle's eudiamonia.

Contemporary Psychological Perspectives on Eudaimonia

Many subfields of psychology have addressed the task of defining positive functioning. Some articulate its meaning with an emphasis on human growth and development (Bühler, 1935; Erikson, 1959; Bühler & Massarik, 1968; Neugarten, 1968, 1973), exemplified by tasks and challenges individuals at different life stages. Others have drawn on existential and humanistic formulations (Allport, 1961; Rogers, 1962; Maslow, 1968; Frankl,1992), which emphasize finding meaning and purpose in life, sometimes in a world that makes no sense (e.g., times of war). Others from clinical psychology sought to define mental health in positive terms rather than to focus on dysfunction (Jung, 1933; Jahoda, 1958).

These diverse perspectives reveal points of convergence and recurrent themes, which were integrated into a multidimensional formulation of psychological well-being (Ryff, 1989). The six key dimensions resulting from the integration are briefly described below. Subsequent sections will demonstrate their utilization in empirical research, clinical practice, and educational programs.

Self-Acceptance

The Greeks admonished that we know ourselves – that is, strive to accurately perceive our own actions, motivations, and feelings. Subsequent psychological formulations emphasized the importance of positive self-regard, as a central feature of mental health (Jahoda) and a characteristic of self-actualization (Maslow), optimal functioning (Rogers), and maturity (Allport). Life-span theories further emphasized acceptance of self, including one's past life (Erikson, Neugarten). The process of individuation (Jung) underscored the need to come to terms with the dark side of one's self (the shadow). Thus, both ego integrity (Erikson) and individuation (Jung) emphasized a kind of self-acceptance that goes beyond standard self-esteem. It is a more long-term self-evaluation that involves awareness and acceptance of personal strengths and weaknesses.

Positive Relations With Others

All the above perspectives emphasize interpersonal ties as central to a positive, well-lived life. Aristotle's *Ethics* included lengthy sections on friendship and love. Jahoda considered the ability to love a central component of mental health, while Maslow described self-actualizers as having strong feelings of empathy and affection for others and a capacity for great love and deep friendship. Warm relating to others was a key criterion of maturity for Allport. Erikson's view of adult development emphasized the achievement of close unions with others (intimacy) as well as the guidance and direction of others (generativity). Contemporary philosophical accounts of the "criterial goods" of a well-lived life (Becker, 1992) also underscored the primacy of love, empathy, and affection.

Personal Growth

This aspect of well-being comes closest in meaning to Aristotle's eudiamonia, as it is explicitly concerned with realization of potential as seen from the vantage point of internal self-evaluation. Personal growth involves a dynamic, continual process of becoming. Maslow's self-actualization was centrally concerned with realization of one's personal potential, as was Jahoda's positive formulation of mental health. Rogers described the fully functioning person as having openness to experience in which he or she is continually developing and becoming, rather than achieving a fixed state wherein problems are solved. Life-span theories (Buhler, Erikson, Neugarten, Jung) also gave explicit emphasis to continued growth and the confronting of new challenges at different periods of life.

Purpose in Life

This dimension of well-being draws heavily on existential perspectives, especially Frankl's *search for meaning* in the face of adversity. Creating meaning and direction in life is fundamental to living authentically as emphasized in existential perspectives. Themes of purpose are also evident in Russell's emphasis on zest and Jahoda's definition of mental health. Allport's conception of maturity included having a clear comprehension of life's purpose, which included a sense of directedness and intentionality. Life-span developmental theories, in turn, referred to the changing purposes or goals that characterize different life stages, such as being productive in midlife, and turning toward emotional integration in later life.

Environmental Mastery

Jahoda defined the individual's ability to choose or create environments suitable to his or her psychological needs as a key characteristic of mental health. Life-span theories emphasized the importance of being able to manipulate and control complex environments, particularly in midlife, as well as the capacity to act on and change the surrounding world through mental and physical activities. Allport's criteria of maturity included the capacity to participate in significant spheres of endeavor that go beyond the self. This area of well-being parallels other psychological constructs, such as sense of control and self-efficacy, although the emphasis on creating a surrounding context that suits one's personal capacities is unique to environmental mastery.

Autonomy

Many conceptual frameworks of well-being emphasize qualities such as self-determination, independence, and the regulation of behavior from within. Self-actualizers are described as showing autonomous functioning and resistance to enculturation (Maslow). The fully functioning person has an internal locus of evaluation, whereby one does not look to others for approval, but evaluates oneself by personal standards (Rogers). Individuation is described in terms of a "deliverance from convention" (Jung), in which one no longer belongs to the collective beliefs, fears, and laws of the masses. The existential idea of living in "bad faith" similarly conveys the importance of self-determination and living authentically, rather than following the dogma or dictates of others. Finally, life-span perspectives emphasized gaining a sense of freedom from the norms governing everyday life in the later years.

The above six dimensions were operationalized with structured, self-report scales to allow for empirical assessment of the extent to which individuals see themselves as having or lacking various aspects of well-being. In the 25 years since they were created, more than 400 publications using them have been generated. Many inquiries have examined how well-being changes with aging, and how it is linked with experiences in work and family life. For present purposes, we briefly review scientific findings that have linked well-being to physical and mental health.

Eudaimonia and Physical Health

Numerous studies, as reviewed by Ryff (2014), have linked eudaimonia to physical health outcomes. Some have shown diminished well-being when people are dealing with health problems (e.g., frailty, disability, fibromyalgia, Parkinson's), but others have examined possible protective benefits of higher well-being, measured in terms of having fewer chronic conditions, greater productivity, and lower use of health care. Cancer survivors have been studied with findings revealing their psychological strengths and vulnerabilities relative to non-cancer comparison groups. Engaging in better health behaviors (exercising, not smoking) has been shown to predict higher eudaimonic well-being as well as good sleep. Together, these investigators underscore the likely reciprocal relationships between eudaimonic well-being and health.

Other studies have linked eudaimonic well-being to multiple physiological systems in an effort to evaluate whether qualities such as purposeful life engagement and personal growth are beneficial. Findings have shown those with higher well-being have lower levels of daily salivary cortisol, lower pro-inflammatory cytokines, and lower cardiovascular risk (Lindfors & Lundberg, 2002; Hayney et al., 2003; Ryff, Singer, & Love, 2004). Eudaimonic well-being has also been examined as a possible moderator of links between life challenges and biological risk factors. Research on social inequalities has documented that those with lower levels of educational standing have higher levels of interleukin-6 (IL-6), after adjusting for numerous factors (Morozink, Friedman, Coe, & Ryff, 2010). IL-6 is implicated in the etiology of cardiovascular and rheumatological disease as well as osteoporosis and Alzheimer's disease. However, among those with a high-school education or less, higher eudaimonic well-being (multiple dimensions) was associated with lower IL-6, thus revealing a possible protective influence. Shifting to the challenges of aging, eudaimonic well-being has been found to moderate the relationships between later life comorbidity and inflammation (Friedman & Ryff, 2012). That is, many older adults live with multiple chronic conditions known to fuel further inflammatory processes that can contribute to functional decline. Although IL-6 and C reactive protein (CRP) were higher among those with higher levels of chronic conditions, these effects were buffered by levels of eudaimonic well-being. Older adults with higher levels of purpose in life and positive relations with others had levels of inflammation comparable with those with fewer chronic conditions. Gene expression profiles related to inflammation have also been linked to eudaimonic well-being (Fredrickson et al., 2013), with findings showing that those high in eudaimonic well-being showed decreased expression of pro-inflammatory genes and increased expression of antibody synthesis genes. Notably, these health-related benefits for gene expression were not apparent for hedonic well-being.

Particular interest has been shown in purpose in life, a key existential aspect of eudaimonia. Longitudinal inquiries have shown that those higher in purpose in life had decreased risk for mortality, after adjusting for numerous potential confounds (Boyle, Barnes, Buchman, & Bennett, 2009; Hill & Turiano, 2014). Higher levels of purpose in life also predict reduced risk for incident Alzheimer's disease and mild cognitive impairment (Boyle, Buchman, Barnes, & Bennett, 2010), even in the presence of organic pathology in the brain (Boyle et al., 2012). Higher levels of purpose in also predict reduced risk of stroke and myocardial infarction (Kim, Sun, Park, & Peterson, 2013; Kim, Sun, Park, Kubzansky, & Peterson, 2013), as well as better preventive healthcare practices (Kim, Strecher, & Ryff, 2014).

The neural correlates of eudaimonic well-being have also been studied. Using functional magnetic resonance imaging, those who were faster to evaluate negative emotional stimuli showed increased amygdala activation by the effects varied by reported levels of eudaimonic well-being (van Reekum et al., 2007). Those with higher levels of well-being were slower to evaluate negative information and they showed reduced amygdala activation. Another study documented that higher eudaimonic well-being was linked with sustained activity in reward circuitry (e.g., ventral striatum), while viewing positive stimuli as well as with lower cortisol output (Heller et al., 2013). Finally, eudaimonic well-being has been linked with insular cortex volume, which is involved in higher-order functions. Those with higher levels of personal growth, positive relations with others, and purpose in life showed greater right insular cortex great matter volume (Lewis, Kanai, Rees, & Bates, 2014).

In summary, growing evidence indicates that well-being is compromised in those with physical illnesses and disabilities, but also that it appears to play a protective role in the face of disease risk and earlier mortality. Further benefits have linked with higher eudaimonic well-being with lower stress hormones and lower inflammatory markers, including in contexts of adversity or challenge, as well as better gene expression profiles. Eudaimonic well-being has also been connected to various brain-based processes involved in emotion regulation and high-order cognitive functions. Given these salubrious connections, it is all the more important to examine whether eudaimonic well-being can be promoted, both among those who suffer from depression and anxiety as well as among mentally healthy individuals in early and later life. These possibilities are examined in the next section.

Eudaimonia and Mental Health

In this section, we first review evidence, largely from population-based epidemiological studies, on the linkages of traditional indicators of mental health (e.g., depression, anxiety) with eudaimonic well-being. Such findings underscore an important point: namely, that the absence of eudaimonic well-being may be a vulnerability factor contributing to, or resulting from, other psychological disorders. We examine evidence of these linkages both in adulthood and later life as well as in early life, particularly the period of adolescence. A central question in linking mental illness to positive mental health is whether eudaimonia is modifiable. We examine this question via evidence of longitudinal studies of change in well-being across time as well as via studies that have linked eudaimonia to personality traits. An overarching message of this section is that eudaimonic well-being is critical for good mental health throughout the life course.

Epidemiological Findings on Well-Being and Mental Illness

In his complete model of mental health, Keyes (2002, 2006) used data from the Midlife in the US (MIDUS) national study to describe the condition of *flourishing*, which referred to the presence of high levels of hedonic, eudaimonic, and social well-being. Alternatively, *languishing* referred to impaired levels of these aspects of well-being, albeit without suffering from anxiety, depression, panic disorder, or alcohol dependence. Keyes suggested that a state of languishing could characterize both the prodromal (early symptom stage), or the residual phase of having experienced mental disorders. Further probing of the interplay between well-being and mental health incorporated longitudinal data from MIDUS. Findings showed that cross-time gains in well-being predicted cross-time declines in mental illness, and alternatively that losses in well-being over time predicted increases in mental illness (Keyes, Dhingra, & Simoes, 2010). The absence of well-being was also linked with increased the probability of all-cause mortality (Keyes & Simoes, 2012). Such work, based on samples of adults, underscored that mental health involves a complex balance of positive and negative psychological characteristics, and, importantly, emphasized that impaired levels of well-being may constitute risk for psychological distress, including relapse and recurrence in psychiatric disorders (Wood & Joseph, 2010).

Studies with adult clinical samples strengthened these observations. In an investigation that included comparison with mentally healthy control samples, Rafanelli et al. (2000) studied twenty remitted patients with mood and anxiety disorders. They presented with significant impairments in well-being compared with healthy control subjects. Similarly, Fava et al. (2001) evaluated eudaimonic well-being in thirty remitted patients with panic disorder and thirty matched controls, and also found impairments for patients in some specific areas, but not in others. Importantly, these patients were judged to be in the remission phase of their disorders, and not in need for further therapies. The treatments they received were thus effective in improving psychological symptoms, but left dimensions of well-being impaired compared with those of healthy controls. That aspects of eudaimonic well-being were impaired in such patients suggested vulnerability for recurrence of the prior disorder. In this formulation, experiences of eudaimonia can thus be construed as a key component of what is required to prevent relapse (Fava, Ruini, & Belaise, 2007).

The above ideas, built around research on adults, are also relevant for earlier periods in the life course. In pioneering work on a population-based sample of American adolescents (aged 12–18), Keyes (2006) found that only a small proportion (around 25%) were actually flourishing (following above definition) and, further, that levels of mental health declined with age. That is, there was a 10% loss of flourishing between middle school and high school. Subsequent analysis confirmed age differences in flourishing, with the lowest prevalence in the youngest age cohorts (Keyes 2006, 2007; Keyes & Westerhof, 2012).

Other studies have further documented the high prevalence of psychological difficulties in children and adolescents. Currently available epidemiological data suggest a worldwide prevalence of child and adolescent mental disorders of approximately 20%. (World Health Organization, 2001). An international meta-analysis of population-based studies found that in all cultures depressive disorders were higher for adolescents than for children, and for adolescent girls than for boys (Costello, Erkanli, & Angold, 2006). Such work shows increases in prevalence of depression with age, which more than doubles at puberty. Impaired school performance, the absence or paucity of positive interpersonal relationships, and low self-esteem are some of the most common problems associated with poor mental health in early development (Tao, Emslie, Mayes, Nakonezny, & Kennard, 2010). Further, these problems can be considered as factors predicting future episodes of anxiety or depressive disorders (Emslie et al., 2008). Of particular relevance to the present chapter, indicators of poor psychosocial functioning in children and adolescents may reflect the lack of eudaimonic well-being in areas described by Ryff's model (1989), such as environmental mastery, personal growth, positive relation with other, self-acceptance, purpose in life and autonomy.

Longitudinal Change in Eudaimonic Well-Being

If eudaimonic well-being is implicated in the prevention of, or recovery from psychological disorders, a primary question is whether well-being itself is largely stable, or shows variability and change over time. Strong evidence of stability might suggest that aspects of eudaimonic well-being are not easily modifiable. With regard to adulthood and later life, multiple initial investigations, based on cross-sectional designs, documented age differences in particular aspects of eudaimonic well-being. Specifically, that older persons in several studies were found to have notably lower profiles on purpose in life and personal growth compared with midlife adults (e.g., Ryff, 1989; Ryff & Keyes, 1995; Clarke, Marshall, Ryff & Rosenthal, 2000). These findings suggested possible vulnerabilities that come with aging, possibly linked with loss of roles and significant relationships as well as physical health decline. Subsequent findings from multiple longitudinal studies, including those based on large national samples (Springer, Pudrovska, & Hauser, 2011), confirmed these age declines in the strongly existential aspects of well-being (purpose, self-realization, and growth). While conveying a disconcerting message that growing old may entail losses in aspects of eudaimonia, such findings nonetheless clarified that well-being is neither stable nor fixed over the life course, but rather appears to be responsive to events and experiences of people's lives.

Such age-related declines in eudaimonia may be implicated in findings from other investigations showing an increasing trend of depressive disorders in late life (around 75 years) (Haynie, Berg, Johannson, Gatz, & Zarit, 2001; Steffens, Fisher, Langa, Potter, & Plassman, 2009). Speaking directly to this possibility, Wood & Joseph (2010) documented that adults and older adults with low levels of eudaimonic well-being were over seven times more likely to be depressed ten years later, and twice as likely to be depressed, even after controlling for personality, negative functioning, prior depression, demographic, economic and physical health status. Other longitudinal inquiries have addressed links between early personality profiles (age 16) and midlife well-being, finding that teenage females who were more extraverted had higher well-being in all PWB dimensions in midlife (Abbott et al., 2008). Teenage neuroticism, in contrast, predicted lower well-being on all dimensions, with the effects mediated through emotional adjustment.

Thus, eudaimonia has a relevant role in human development and along the life course. As described in the previous section, both ancient and modern philosophers have underlined the importance of living according to personal values and of pursuing meaningful life goals that involve developing one's potential across the life-span. Because the relationship between eudaimonia and mental illness seems appears to be particularly significant across the life-span, it heightens the importance of developing specific interventions designed to foster eudaimonic well-being, both to reduce mental illness and psychological distress at diverse ages as well as to promote optimal functioning outside the clinical context.

Clinical and Educational Interventions for Promoting Eudaimonia

Our focus on intervention first addresses treating emotional disorders in the clinical context via promotion of well-being. Second, we shift to an emphasis on prevention of emotional disorders in educational contexts also built on the promotion of eudaimonia. The investigations described in the previous section indicated that the absence of well-being creates conditions of vulnerability to possible future adversities. Following Ryff and Singer (1996), we thus advocate for the implementation of interventions designed not only and exclusively to alleviate the negative, but also to engender the positive.

Clinical Interventions for Promoting Eudaimonia

Persistent impairment of well-being can occur even after a successful treatment of affective disorders (Rafanelli et al., 2000; Fava et al., 2001). This realization calls for a reframing of the concept of "effective treatment" in clinical psychology and psychiatry to encompass a broader clinical vision that sees the restoration of well-being as a specific endpoint of an effective therapy

(Fava et al., 2007). Such a perspective has led to the development of new therapeutic techniques with the aims of increasing patient's personal comfort, and improving quality of life and eudaimonia (Seligman, Rashid, & Parks, 2006; Wood & Tarrier, 2010; Ruini & Fava, 2012; Bolier et al., 2013). One such positive psychotherapeutic strategy –Well-being Therapy (WBT) – adopted Ryff's model of eudaimonia and was tested in a number of controlled investigations with patients with mood and anxiety disorders (Ruini & Fava, 2012). WBT was found to be a protective factor for recurrent depression up to six-year follow-up (Fava et al., 2004).

In this investigation, patients with recurrent major depression, who had been successfully treated by pharmacotherapy, were randomly assigned to either WBT or clinical management (CM) and followed up for six years. During this period no antidepressant drugs were used unless a relapse ensued. This happened in eight (40%) of the twenty patients in the WBT group, compared with eighteen (90%) in the CM group. The WBT group had a total of twelve depressive episodes during the follow-up, compared with thirty-four of the CM group. Importantly, in the WBT group patients tended to relapse four years after treatment, whereas patients in the CM conditions relapsed after two years. Thus, WBT had a highly significant effect in decreasing and delaying the number of relapses into depression (Fava et al., 2004). Another example of the protective role of WBT in depression comes from a clinical case illustration. Ruini, Albieri, & Vescovelli (2014) described the case of a woman with a severe depressive episode following a marital crisis who was treated by WBT over one year. She had no relapses up to two years after treatment, even when she faced another marital crisis that led to divorce. The clinical story of this patient illustrates how improved levels of eudaimonic well-being buffered against relapse, which is usually triggered by psychosocial stressor.

Further, WBT was found to be particularly effective in treating anxiety disorders (Fava et al., 2005; Ruini & Fava, 2009; Ruini et al., 2014) with long-lasting effects. Twenty patients with generalized anxiety disorders (GAD) were randomly assigned to eight sessions of cognitive-behavioral therapy (CBT) or the sequential administration of four sessions of CBT followed by another four sessions of WBT. A one-year follow-up was undertaken. In both groups, eudaimonic well-being, particularly impaired in self-acceptance and environmental mastery, was impaired before treatment. These dimensions, together with anxiety symptoms, greatly improved after treatment, however. Further, the CBT–WBT approach displayed significant advantages over CBT only, and these improvements were maintained at follow-up. Ruini and Fava (2009) provided subsequent clinical evidence for the efficacy of WBT in treating anxious patients. They described a case of a woman with GAD, perfectionism, and obsessive compulsive personality traits, who was treated with a sequential combination of CBT and WBT. CBT was particularly effective in providing cognitive restructuring to worries and catastrophic thinking style, whereas WBT was particularly valuable in addressing perfectionism by promoting self-acceptance. Improvements in environmental mastery and interpersonal relationships were also observed. These gains were maintained in the long term and provided protection to the patients when she faced major life changes (work relocation, death of her father-in-law) (Ruini and Fava, 2009).

In light of these promising outcomes, Albieri et al. (2009, 2011) applied a modified WBT protocol (Child-WBT) in a group of clinically distressed children, reporting emotional and behavioral disorders. Even though it was an open trial, the results were encouraging and children significantly improved in symptom and well-being dimensions after eight sessions of Child-WBT (Albieri et al., 2009, 2011).

Educational Interventions for Promoting Eudaimonia

Beyond clinical populations, the promotion of eudaimonia may have an important role in preventing mental illness and psychological distress in the broader population. This potential may be of crucial importance in vulnerable phases of life, such as adolescence or later life.

Preventive interventions in adolescence find a natural context in schools and educational settings. In fact, schools are increasingly recognized as not only an ideal setting for learning and education, but also as forums for building skills that promote resilience and psychological well-being (Caffo, Belaise, & Forresi, 2008). Further, the philosophical foundation of eudaimonia, as described earlier, emphasizes that fact that ancient philosophers used to teach and discuss these existential issues with their pupils. Eudaimonia thus appears, across the wide sweep of time, to be particularly feasible in educational settings.

In a pilot work, a modified form of WBT was developed and applied in school settings (Well-Being Therapy-School Program protocol, Ruini, Belaise, Brombin, Caffo, & Fava, 2006). In this School WBT protocol, which encompassed four class sessions, middle school students were randomly assigned to either (a) a protocol using theories and techniques derived from cognitive-behavioral therapy, or (b) a protocol derived from WBT. Both school-based interventions resulted in a comparable improvement in symptoms and psychological well-being (Ruini et al., 2006), thereby documenting the feasibility of WBT techniques in younger populations. However, the number of sessions was low (four) and the first two sessions were shared by the same treatments.

The differential effects of WBT and CBT approaches were subsequently explored in another controlled school investigation, involving longer interventions and an adequate follow-up. In this investigation (Tomba et al., 2010). 162 students were randomly assigned to either (a) a protocol derived from WBT, or (b) an anxiety-management protocol (AM). The aim of this study was to test whether each strategy would yield better results for its specific target (well-being/distress) relative to the other. Compared with the pilot study (Ruini et al., 2006), the number of sessions was increased to six. The results of this new investigation showed that the school-based WBT intervention produced significant improvements in autonomy and friendliness, whereas the school-based Anxiety Management (AM) intervention ameliorated psychological distress (anxious and depressive symptoms). When the two interventions were compared using the covariance analyses for baseline measurements, the AM intervention produced a significant decrease in anxiety and depression, whereas WBT showed a significant positive effect in improving students' interpersonal functioning and also physiological symptoms of anxiety. These findings suggest that improvement in psychological well-being may also yield a decrease in anxiety, within the complex balance of positive and negative affect. However, an important aspect to be noted is that both intervention strategies maintained their effects at a six-month follow-up.

Considering the promising results obtained with middle school students (Ruini et al., 2006; Tomba et al., 2010), the WBT school intervention has been extended to high school students, who are considered a more "at risk population" for mood and anxiety disorders (Clarke et al., 1995). School interventions were performed on a sample of 227 students. The classes were randomly assigned to (a) a protocol derived from WBT (five classes) or (b) attention-placebo protocol (four classes). Also in this case both school-based interventions consisted of six, two-hour sessions. WBT school intervention was found to be effective in promoting psychological well-being, with particular reference to personal growth compared with the attention placebo group (Ruini et al., 2009). Further, it was found to be effective in decreasing distress, in particular anxiety and somatization. Such data confirm results obtained in the preliminary investigations on the WBT school program performed on middle school schools (Ruini et al., 2006; Tomba et al., 2010) where the intervention yielded significant improvement in physical well-being and somatization. Overall, the findings suggest that school-based WBT has important clinical implications in light of the documented high prevalence of somatic symptoms in children and adolescents (Ginsburg, Riddle, & Davies, 2006; Muris, Vermeer, & Horselenberg, 2008). In the latter study, the beneficial effect of a WBT school protocol in decreasing anxiety was also maintained at the follow-up, whereas in the attention placebo group improvements faded and disappeared. With young populations, promoting positive functioning and building individual strengths thus appears to be more beneficial in the long term than simply addressing depressive or anxious symptoms.

Building on these promising results, a group intervention for promoting eudemonia in older people in the community was recently developed (Friedman et al., 2015). Later life comes with many challenges (loss of roles and significant others, health changes), and longitudinal studies have documented decline occurs in certain aspects of well-being, such as purpose in life and personal growth (see Ryff, 2014). With these vulnerabilities in mind, the WBT school protocol was adapted for older adults, including the addition of age-appropriate exercises such as life review (Serrano, Latorre, Gatz, & Montanes, 2004). The program consists of 90-minute classes meeting once per week in community settings (e.g., senior centers; public libraries) with sharing of positive memories and discussion on the characteristics and role of eudemonia in later life. A combination of CBT techniques with specific exercises for promoting eudaimonia in later life characterized the program. It was delivered to a sample of 103 men and women aged 60 or over. At the end of the eight weeks, participants reported significantly increased eudaimonic well-being, life satisfaction, and social well-being along with lower levels of depression and fewer physical symptoms and sleep complaints. Interestingly, these gains were particularly robust for individuals with lower pre-program levels of eudaimonic well-being. Similarly, those presenting initial higher levels of depression benefited the most from the intervention. The results are preliminary, but suggest the feasibility and effectiveness of a preventive group intervention for enhancing positive functioning in older adults in the community.

Summary and Conclusions

This chapter aimed at describing eudaimonia and its crucial role in human life. We illustrated how eudaimonia is deeply embedded in our cultural history by providing an overview of philosophical and psychological theories that date back to ancient Greek philosophers. These perspectives and subsequent formulations in modern times clearly emphasize the importance of possessing life goals and virtues, meaningful relationships, and realizing one's true potential across the life course. These positive characteristics have been maintained as core values across centuries, thus making it clear that eudaimonia encompasses the essential characteristics of what defines optimal human functioning.

A recent and large body of research has documented the benefits of these positive psychological characteristics for physical and mental health. This chapter summarized the growing evidence, which documents the protective role of such eudaimonic characteristics as purposeful engagement, positive interpersonal relationships, and personal growth in the face of life challenges. People possessing high levels of well-being displayed lower levels of biological risk factors associated with chronic metabolic and degenerative disorders. The protective role of eudaimonia appears to be particularly crucial during later life, in which aging individuals who maintaining high levels of well-being have reduced risk for cognitive impairments, fewer comorbidities, and they tend to live longer.

Beside physical health benefits, we emphasized how eudaimonia is deeply linked to mental health, which we argue involves a complex balance of positive and negative psychological characteristics. People with low levels of well-being (eudaimonic, hedonic, eudaimonic, social) may characterize the prodromal (early) or the residual phase of mental disorders. We summarized a large body of epidemiological and clinical research showing that impaired well-being constitutes risk for psychological distress, including relapse and recurrence in psychiatric disorders. The association between eudaimonia and mental health was also examined in therapeutic settings, where the restoration of well-being has been recently included as a criterion of recovery in depressive disorders. This observation translated to psychotherapeutic interventions designed specifically to improve patients' well-being.

One such positive intervention, known as WBT, adopted Ryff's model of well-being. We described the benefits reported by patients with mood and anxiety disorders, both after treatment and on the long term. Importantly, this technique was recently modified for use with child clinical populations, which also displayed improvement in symptoms and well-being after treatment.

Building on such clinical work, we then described more recent efforts to translate such interventions to preventive practices. These were illustrated with a series of school interventions seeking to improve eudaimonia in children and adolescents. Scientific findings showed important benefits in reducing anxiety and psychological distress. Finally, because later life constitutes a vulnerable stage in the human journey, we reported on promising results from a group intervention aiming to promote eudaimonia in older individuals living in the community.

In conclusion, this chapter contributes to the *Handbook of Positive Clinical Psychology* by underscoring the importance of eudaimonic well-being for improving lives from early development in adolescence to adulthood and later life. Perhaps our most important message is that eudaimonia, which has a long tradition of being valued from the ancient Greeks until the present, can be promoted in ways that are feasible, cost-effective, and fundamentally worthwhile. We see great potential in expanding such work for vulnerable individuals, such as those who are socioeconomically disadvantaged or who are facing stressful life situations. Targeted clinical and educational interventions, such as those described herein, that seek to preserve, restore, or improve eudaimonic well-being for such individuals could prevent them from falling into a state of languishing, or developing physical or mental illnesses. Eudaimonia is, in our view, an opportunity that each human being deserves.

References

Abbott, R. A., Croudace, T. J., Ploubidis, G. B., Kuh, D., Richards, M., & Huppert, F. A. (2008). The relationship between early personality and midlife psychological well-being: Evidence from a UK birth cohort study. *Social Psychiatry and Psychiatric Epidemiology*, 43(9), 679–687. doi.10.1007/s00127-008-0355-8.

Albieri, E., Visani, D., Offidani, E., Ottolini, F., & Ruini, C. (2009). Well-being therapy in children with emotional and behavioral disturbances: A pilot investigation. *Psychotherapy and Psychosomatics*, 78(6), 387–390. doi.10.1159/000235983.

Albieri, E., Visani, D., Ottolini, F., Vescovelli, F., & Ruini, C. (2011). L'applicazione della Well-Being Therapy nell'infanzia: Esemplificazioni cliniche. (The application of Well-Being Therapy in childhood: Clinical cases presentation). *Rivista di Psichiatria*, 46(4), 265–272.

Allport, G. W. (1961). *Pattern and growth in personality*. New York: Holt, Rinehart & Winston.

Aristotle. (1925). *The Nicomachean ethics*, trans. D. Ross. New York: Oxford University Press.

Becker, L. C. (1992). Good lives: Prolegomena. *Social Philosophy & Policy*, 9, 15–37. doi.10.1017/S0265052500001382.

Bolier, L., Haverman, M., Kramer, J., Westerhof, G. J., Riper, H., Walburg, J. A., & Bohlmeijer, E. (2013). An internet-based intervention to promote mental fitness for mildly depressed adults: Randomized controlled trial. *Journal of Medical Internet Research*, 15(9), 209–226. doi.10.2196/jmir.2603.

Boyle, P. A., Barnes, L. L., Buchman, A. S., & Bennett, D. A. (2009). Purpose in life is associated with mortality among community-dwelling older persons. *Psychosomatic Medicine*, 71(5), 574–579. doi.10.1097/PSY.0b013e3181a5a7c0.

Boyle, P. A., Buchman, A. S., Barnes, L. L., & Bennett, D. A. (2010). Effect of a purpose in life on risk of incident Alzheimer disease and mild cognitive impairment in community-dwelling older persons. *Archives of General Psychiatry*, 67(3), 304–310. doi.10.1001/archgenpsychiatry.2009.208.

Boyle, P. A., Buchman, A. S., Wilson, R. S., Yu, L., Schneider, J. A., & Bennett, D. A. (2012). Effect of purpose in life on the relation between Alzheimer disease pathologic changes on cognitive function in advanced age. *JAMA Psychiatry*, 69(5), 499–506. doi.10.1001/archgenpsychiatry.2011.1487.

Bühler, C. (1935). The curve of life as studied in biographies. *Journal of Applied Psychology*, 43, 653–673. doi.10.1037/h0054778.

Bühler, C. & Massarik, F. (Eds.). (1968). *The course of human life*. New York: Springer.

Caffo, E., Belaise, C., & Forresi, B. (2008). Promoting resilience and psychological well-being in vulnerable life stages. *Psychotherapy and Psychosomatics, 77*(6), 331–336. doi.10.1159/000151386.

Clarke, G. N., Hawkins, W., Murphy, M., Sheeber, L. B., Lewinsohn, P. M., & Seeley, J. R. (1995). Targeted prevention of unipolar depressive disorder in an at-risk sample of high school adolescents: A randomized trial of group cognitive intervention. *Journal of the American Academy of Child & Adolescent Psychiatry, 34*(3), 312–321. doi.10.1097/00004583-199503000-00016.

Clarke, P. J., Marshall, V. W., Ryff, C. D., & Rosenthal, C. J. (2000). Well being in Canadian seniors: Findings from the Canadian Study of Health and Aging. *Canadian Journal on Aging, 19*(2), 139–159. doi.10.1017/S0714980800013982.

Costello, E. J., Erkanli, A., & Angold, A. (2006). Is there an epidemic of child or adolescent depression? *Journal of Child Psychology and Psychiatry, 47*(12), 1263–1271. doi.10.1111/j.1469-7610.2006.01682.x.

Emslie, G. J., Kennard, B. D., Mayes, T. L., Nightingale-Teresi, J., Carmody, T., Hughes, C. W., & Rintelmann, J. W. (2008). Fluoxetine versus placebo in preventing relapse of major depression in children and adolescents. *American Journal of Psychiatry, 165*(4), 459–467. doi.10.1176/appi.ajp.2007.07091453.

Erikson, E. H. (1959). Identity and the life cycle: Selected papers. *Psychological Issues, 1*, 1–171.

Fava, G. A., Rafanelli, C., Ottolini, F., Ruini, C., Cazzaro, M., & Grandi, S. (2001). Psychological well-being and residual symptoms in remitted patients with panic disorder and agoraphobia. *Journal of Affective Disorders, 65*(2), 185–190. doi.10.1016/S0165-0327(00)00267-6.

Fava, G. A., Ruini, C., & Belaise, C. (2007). The concept of recovery in major depression. *Psychological Medicine, 37*(3), 307–317. doi.10.1017/s0033291706008981.

Fava, G. A., Ruini, C., Rafanelli, C., Finos, L., Conti, S., & Grandi, S. (2004). Six-year outcome of cognitive behavior therapy for prevention of recurrent depression. *American Journal of Psychiatry, 161*(10), 1872–1876.

Fava, G. A., Ruini, C., Rafanelli, C., Finos, L., Salmaso, L., Mangelli, L., & Sirigatti, S. (2005). Well-being therapy of generalized anxiety disorder. *Psychotherapy and Psychosomatics, 74*(1), 26–30. doi.10.1159/000082023.

Frankl, V. E. & Lasch, I. ([1959] 1992). *Man's search for meaning: An introduction to logotherapy*. Boston, MA: Beacon Press.

Fredrickson, B. L., Grewen, K. M., Coffey, K. A., Algoe, S. B., Firestine, A. M., Arevalo, J. M. G., & Cole, S. W. (2013). A functional genomic perspective on human well-being. *Proceedings of the National Academy of Sciences, 110*(33), 13684–13689. doi.10.1073/pnas.1305419110.

Friedman, E. M. & Ryff, C. D. (2012). Living well with medical comorbidities: A biopsychosocial perspective. *Journals of Gerontology. Series B, Psychological Sciences and Social Sciences, 67*(5), 535–544. doi.10.1093/geronb/gbr152.

Friedman, E. M., Ruini, C., Foy, C. R., Jaros, L., Sampson, H. & Ryff, C. D. (2015). Lighten UP! A community-based group intervention to promote psychological well-being in older adults. *Aging and Mental Health*, submitted

Ginsburg, G. S., Riddle, M. A., & Davies, M. (2006). Somatic symptoms in children and adolescents with anxiety disorders. *Journal of the American Academy of Child & Adolescent Psychiatry, 45*(10), 1179–1187. doi.10.1097/01.chi.0000231974.43966.6e.

Hayney, M. S., Parm, D., Love, G. D., Buck, J. M., Ryff, C. D., Singer, B. H., & Muller, D. (2003). The association between psychosocial factors and vaccine-induced cytokine production. *Vaccine, 21*, 2428–2432. doi.10.1016/S0264-410X(03)00057-4.

Haynie, D. A., Berg, S., Johansson, B., Gatz, M., & Zarit, S. H. (2001). Symptoms of depression in the oldest old: A longitudinal study. *Journal of Gerontology: Series B: Psychological Sciences and Social Sciences, 56B*(2), P111–P118. doi.10.1093/geronb/56.2.P111.

Heller, A. S., van Reekum, C. M., Schaefer, S. M., Lapate, R. C., Radler, B. T., Ryff, C. D., & Davidson, R. J. (2013). Sustained ventral striatal activity predicts eudaimonic well-being and cortisol output. *Psychological Science, 24*(11), 2191–2200. doi.10.1177/0956797613490744.

Hill, P. L. & Turiano, N. A. (2014). Purpose in life as a predictor of mortality across adulthood. *Psychological Science, 25*(7), 1482–1486. doi.10.1177/0956797614531799.

Jahoda, M. (1958). *Current concepts of positive mental health*. New York: Basic Books.

Jung, C. G. (1933). *Modern man in search of a soul*, trans. W. S. Dell & C. F. Baynes. New York: Harcourt, Brace & World.

Keyes, C. L. M. (2002). The mental health continuum: From languishing to flourishing in life. *Journal of Health & Social Behavior, 43*(2), 207–222.

Keyes, C. L. M. (2006). Mental health in adolescence: Is America's youth flourishing? *American Journal of Orthopsychiatry, 76*(3), 395–402. doi.10.1037/t05317-000.

Keyes, C. L. M. (2007). Promoting and protecting mental health as flourishing. *American Psychologist, 62*(2), 95–108. doi.10.1037/0003-066X.62.2.95.

Keyes, C. L., Dhingra, S. S., & Simoes, E. J. (2010). Change in level of positive mental health as a predictor of future risk of mental illness. *American Journal of Public Health, 100*, 2366–2371.

Keyes, C. L. M., Shmotkin, D., & Ryff, C. D. (2002). Optimizing well-being: The empirical encounter of two traditions. *Journal of Personality & Social Psychology, 82*(6), 1007–1022. doi.10.1037/0022-3514.82.6.1007.

Keyes, C. L. & Simoes, E. J. (2012). To flourish or not: positive mental health and all-cause mortality. *American Journal of Public Health, 102*, 2164–2172.

Keyes, C. L. M. & Westerhof, G. J. (2012). Chronological and subjective age differences in flourishing mental health and major depressive episode. *Aging & Mental Health, 16*(1), 67–74. doi.10.1080/13607863.2011.596811.

Kim, E. S., Strecher, V. J., & Ryff, C. D. (2014). Purpose in life and use of preventive health care services. *Proceedings of the National Academy of Sciences of the United States of America, 111*(46), 16331–16336. doi.10.1073/pnas.1414826111.

Kim, E. S., Sun, J. K., Park, N., & Peterson, C. (2013). Purpose in life and reduced stroke in older adults: The health and retirement study. *Journal of Psychosomatic Research, 74*(5), 427–432. doi.10.1016/j.jpsychores.2013.01.013.

Kim, E. S., Sun, J. K., Park, N., Kubzansky, L. D., & Peterson, C. (2013). Purpose in life and reduced risk of myocardial infarction among older US. Adults with coronary heart disease: A two-year follow-up. *Journal of Behavioral Medicine, 36*(2), 124–133. doi.10.1007/s10865-012-9406-4.

Lewis, G. J., Kanai, R., Rees, G., & Bates, T. C. (2014). Neural correlates of the "good life": Eudaimonic well-being is associated with insular cortex volume. *Social Cognitive and Affective Neuroscience, 9*(5), 615–618. doi.10.1093/scan/nst032.

Lindfors, P. & Lundberg, U. (2002). Is low cortisol release an indicator of positive health? *Stress and Health, 18*(4), 153–160. doi.10.1002/smi.942.

Maslow, A. H. (1968). *Toward a psychology of being*, 2nd edn. New York: Van Nostrand.

Morozink, J. A., Friedman, E. M., Coe, C. L., & Ryff, C. D. (2010). Socioeconomic and psychosocial predictors of interleukin-6 in the MIDUS national sample. *Health Psychology, 29*(6), 626–635. doi.10.1037/a0021360.

Muris, P., Vermeer, E., & Horselenberg, R. (2008). Cognitive development and the interpretation of anxiety-related physical symptoms in 4–13-year-old non-clinical children. *Journal of Behavior Therapy and Experimental Psychiatry, 39*(1), 73–86. doi.10.1016/j.jbtep.2006.10.014.

Neugarten, B. L. (1968). *Middle age and aging*. Chicago: University of Chicago Press.

Neugarten, B. L. (1973). Personality change in late life: A developmental perspective. In: C. Eisodorfer & M. P. Lawton (Eds.), *The psychology of adult development and aging* (pp. 311–335). Washington, DC: American Psychological Association.

Norton, D. L. (1976). *Personal destinies: A philosophy of ethical individualism*. Princeton, NJ: Princeton University Press.

Rafanelli, C., Park, S. K., Ruini, C., Ottolini, F., Cazzaro, M., & Fava, G. A. (2000). Rating well-being and distress. *Stress Medicine, 16*, 55–61. doi.10.1002/(SICI)1099-1700(200001)16:1<55::AID-SMI832>3.0.CO;2-M.

Rogers, C. R. (1962). The interpersonal relationship: The core of guidance. *Harvard Educational Review, 32*(4), 416–429.

Ruini, C., Albieri, E., & Vescovelli, F. (2014). Well-Being Therapy: State of the art and clinical exemplifications. *Journal of Contemporary Psychotherapy*. Advance online publication. doi.10.1007/s10879-014-9290-z.

Ruini, C., Belaise, C., Brombin, C., Caffo, E., & Fava, G. A. (2006). Well-being therapy in school settings: A pilot study. *Psychotherapy and Psychosomatics, 75*(6), 331–336. doi.10.1159/000095438.

Ruini, C. & Fava, G. A. (2009). Well-being therapy for generalized anxiety disorder. *Journal of Clinical Psychology, 65*(5), 510–519. doi.10.1002/jclp.20592

Ruini, C. & Fava, G. A. (2012). Role of well-being therapy in achieving a balanced and individualized path to optimal functioning. *Clinical Psychology & Psychotherapy, 19*(4), 291–304. doi.10.1002/cpp.1796.

Ruini, C., Ottolini, F., Tomba, E., Belaise, C., Albieri, E., Visani, D., & Fava, G. A. (2009). School intervention for promoting psychological well-being in adolescence. *Journal of Behavior Therapy and Experimental Psychiatry, 40*(4), 522–532. doi.10.1016/j.jbtep.2009.07.002.

Ryan, R. M. & Deci, E. L. (2001). On happiness and human potentials: A review of research on hedonic and eudaimonic well-being. *Annual Review of Psychology, 52,* 141–166. doi.10.1146/annurev.psych.52.1.141.

Ryff, C. D. (1989). Happiness is everything, or is it? Explorations on the meaning of psychological well-being. *Journal of Personality and Social Psychology, 57*(6), 1069–1081. doi.10.1037/0022-3514.57.6.1069.

Ryff, C. D. (2014). Psychological well-being revisited: Advances in the science and practice of eudaimonia. *Psychotherapy and Psychosomatics, 83*(1), 10–28. doi.10.1159/000353263.

Ryff, C. D. & Keyes, C. L. M. (1995). The structure of psychological well-being revisited. *Journal of Personality & Social Psychology, 69*(4), 719–727. doi.10.1037/0022-3514.69.4.719.

Ryff, C. D. & Singer, B. H. (1996). Psychological well-being: Meaning, measurement, and implications for psychotherapy research. *Psychotherapy & Psychosomatics, 65,* 14–23. doi.10.1159/000289026.

Ryff, C. D. & Singer, B. H. (2008). Know thyself and become what you are: A eudaimonic approach to psychological well-being. *Journal of Happiness Studies, 9*(1), 13–39. doi.10.1007/s10902-006-9019-0.

Ryff, C. D., Singer, B. H., & Love, G. D. (2004). Positive health: Connecting well-being with biology. *Philosophical Transactions of the Royal Society of London. Series B, Biological Sciences, 359,* 1383–1394. doi.10.1098/rstb.2004.1521.

Seligman, M. E. P., Rashid, T., & Parks, A. C. (2006). Positive psychotherapy. *American Psychologist, 61*(8), 774–788. doi.10.1037/0003-066X.61.8.774.

Serrano, J. P., Latorre, J. M., Gatz, M., & Montanes, J. (2004). Life review therapy using autobiographical retrieval practice for older adults with depressive symptomatology. *Psychology and Aging, 19*(2), 272–277.

Springer, K. W., Pudrovska, T., & Hauser, R. M. (2011). Does psychological well-being change with age? Longitudinal tests of age variations and further exploration of the multidimensionality of Ryff's model of psychological well-being. *Social Science Research, 40*(1), 392–398. doi.10.1016/j.ssresearch.2010.05.008.

Steffens, D. C., Fisher, G. C., Langa, K. M., Potter, G. G., & Plassman, B. L. (2009). Prevalence of depression among older Americans: The aging, demographics and memory study. *International Psychogeriatrics, 21*(5), 879–888. doi.10.1017/S1041610209990044.

Tao, R., Emslie, G. J., Mayes, T. L., Nakonezny, P. A., & Kennard, B. D. (2010). Symptom improvement and residual symptoms during acute antidepressant treatment in pediatric major depressive disorder. *Journal of Child and Adolescent Psychopharmacology, 20,* 423–430. doi.10.1089/cap.2009.0116.

Tomba, E., Belaise, C., Ottolini, F., Ruini, C., Bravi, A., Albieri, E., & Fava, G. A. (2010). Differential effects of well-being promoting and anxiety-management strategies in a non-clinical school setting. *Journal of Anxiety Disorders, 24*(3), 326–333. doi.10.1016/j.janxdis.2010.01.005.

van Reekum, C. M., Urry, H. L., Johnstone, T., Thurow, M. E., Frye, C. J., Jackson, C. A., & Davidson, R. J. (2007). Individual differences in amygdala and ventromedial prefrontal cortex activity are associated with evaluation speed and psychological well-being. *Journal of Cognitive Neuroscience, 19*(2), 237–248. doi.10.1162/jocn.2007.19.2.237.

Wood, A. M. & Joseph, S. (2010). The absence of positive psychological (eudemonic) well-being as a risk factor for depression: A ten-year cohort study. *Journal of Affective Disorders, 122*(3), 213–217. doi.1016/j.jad.2009.06.032.

Wood, A. M. & Tarrier, N. (2010). Positive clinical psychology: A new vision and strategy for integrated research and practice. *Clinical Psychology Review, 30*(7), 819-829. doi:10.1016/j.cpr.2010.06.003

World Health Organization (2001). *The World health report 2001: Mental health: new understanding, new hope.* Available at: http://www.who.int/whr/2001/en/whr01_en.pdf.

12

Positive Clinical Gerontology
Integrating "Positive" and "Negative" Perspectives on Aging
Adam Davidson and George Vaillant

Biographies are not Written in Black and White

Rejected for military service during the Second World War and later judged occupationally feckless, Charles Boatwright had difficulty establishing a career. In his early fifties his alcoholic wife left him for another man, and he had become estranged from his children. Yet time and again in questionnaires he exclaimed his good fortune and optimism. At 83 years of age, Boatwright enjoyed working 28 hours a week for his nonprofit organization. At 85 he was an exemplar of wisdom, and at 89 he still exercised for two hours at day. At 91 Boatwright had been happily married for 35 years, and was totally devoted to his stepchildren (Vaillant, 2012c).

Could we have predicted Boatwright's seemingly successful aging? What should we expect of our old age: happiness and wisdom or loneliness and ill health? Surely such a black-and-white distinction between extreme positive and negative expectations is naive. The tangled tapestry of human life is woven in many directions: good, bad, ambivalence, and apathy are assured for us all. Every biography of human life has ups and downs, twists and turns, opportunities and challenges. All "simple facts" conceal a story that is more subtle and sophisticated. Clear-cut "positive" or "negative" statements simply cannot convey the nuances of reality. This is as applicable to science as it is to people. (The irony of stating this as a "simple fact" is not lost on the authors.)

However, "simple facts" seize attention, especially when seasoned with shock and sensationalism. Ezikiel Emanuel, a leading American bioethicist and one of the architects of the Affordable HealthCare Plan, says he hopes to die at 75 (Emanuel, 2014). He contends Fries' (1980) "compression of morbidity," which argues that people are living longer and healthier, instead believing in a prolonged period of incapability and physical frailty at the end of life.

The Ambivalence Of Aging

Many aspects of aging can appear threatening to independence and competency. Negative stereotypes of disease, disability, dependency, and depression are rife (Scheidt, Humpherys, & Yorgason, 1999; Kite, Stockdale, Whitley, & Johnston, 2005). As we age, chronic diseases become more prevalent (Department of Health, 1992), and physical and cognitive deterioration seems inevitable. The elderly generally experience a reduction in physical strength (Larsson,

The Wiley Handbook of Positive Clinical Psychology, First Edition. Edited by Alex M. Wood and Judith Johnson.
© 2016 John Wiley & Sons, Ltd. Published 2016 by John Wiley & Sons, Ltd.

Grimby, & Karlsson, 1979; Andrews, Thomas, & Bohannon, 1996; Bohannon, 1997), an increase in body fat (Jackson et al., 2002), and sensory impairment (Doty, Shaman, Applebaum, Giberson, Siksorski, & Rosenberg, 1984; Woodruff-Pak, 1997), as well as a decline in mental processing speed (Kail & Salthouse, 1994), verbal fluency (Light & Burke, 1993), and mathematical abilities (Schaie, 1988).

However, this need not be the case. Hardman and Stensel (2009) argue that this decline is caused, at least in part, by a lack of activity and could be largely reversed by activities like high-resistance exercise (Vandervoort, 1992). Various empirical studies have shown the reversal of strength loss (Fiatarone, Marks, Ryan, Meredith, Lipsitz, & Evans, 1990; Skelton, Young, Greig & Malbut, 1995; Melov, Tarnopolsky, Beckman, Felkey, & Hubbard, 2007). Furthermore, encouraging activity in older people may have somatopsychic benefits, such as reducing the decline in cognitive function (Hertzog, Kramer, Wilson, & Lindenberger, 2008; Aichberger, Busch, Reischies, Ströhle, Heinz, & Rapp, 2010).

Although some cognitive abilities may decline with age, most retirees consider themselves cognitive impairment-free (Sauvaget, Jagger, & Arthur, 2001), and they are less likely to suffer mental disorders (Drentea, 2002; Mein, Martikainen, Hemingway, Stansfeld, & Marmot, 2003). The minds of the elderly are more content, more capable of emotional complexity, experience fewer negative emotions (whilst maintaining similar levels of positive emotions), retain emotionally important memories, comprehend multiple points of view, and derive greater satisfaction from relationships (Carstensen & Charles, 2003; Helmuth, 2003; Vaillant, 2012a).

We need not fear old age, even with regard to our physical health. Nearly 90% of 65–74 year olds, and nearly 75% of 75–84 year olds have no disabling conditions, and these percentages are rising (Manton, Corder, & Stallard, 1997). Although neurons are lost from the brain with age, new neurons continue to develop (Shingo et al., 2003), and judicious pruning continues to develop throughout the life-span (Vaillant, 2012c). The average 5-year-old has twice as many neurons as a 21-year-old. Evidence shows most people maintain a sense of well-being until the very ends of their lives (Rowe & Kahn, 1998; Mayer & Baltes, 1999).

Indeed, we *should* not fear old age, as the experiences of the elderly are susceptible to expectation bias. Negative stereotypes of aging can reduce performance on tasks, whilst positive stereotypes improve it (Levy, 1996, 2009). Having a positive self-perception at the age of 50 can increase life-span by over seven years (Levy, Hausdorff, Hencke, & Wei, 2000; Levy, Slade, Kunkel, & Kasl, 2002).

Although surviving to an old age is necessary for "successful" aging, it is not a sufficient condition. The aim is to "add more life to years, not just years to life" (Vaillant, 2004, p. 561). This chapter begins with the issues of quantifying "positive" health, then summarizes the factors that predict "positive" aging, both those that are commonly thought of as "positive," and those considered "negative." An examination of how to describe, prescribe, and facilitate flourishing in later years follows, including a consideration of the complexities introduced by separation of "positive" and "negative."

Dilemmas of Dialectics

Gerontology is complicated by the heterogeneity of the elderly population. The longer our lives, the further they can diverge from the norm. For some, each passing year increases the probability that accidents, disease, or poor self-care will take their toll. For others, the passing of time presents the opportunity to mature, build success, and grow social circles.

Before it is possible to analyze antecedents of "successful" aging, the term must be defined. What indicators of "success" reveal a life well lived? Clearly, survival and the lack of illnesses are factors, but they are not sufficient. Health is not simply the absence of illness (World Health

Organization (WHO), 1952). Physical health can be measured by blood pressure or the step test (Brouha, 1943), but mental health is subjective; it requires cultural sensitivity and caution over value judgments. Vaillant (2003, 2012b) suggests the following possibilities.

Above Normal Functioning

Supporters of the disease model may define mental health as a global assessment of functioning (GAF) (American Psychiatric Association (APA), 1994) score of above 80 (Vaillant, 2012b, p. 94). However, although the GAF has been empirically validated across countries and languages (Armelius, Gerin, Luborsky, & Alexander, 1991), it seems to be based upon Freud's view that "mental health is an ideal fiction" (Valliant, 2003, p. 1374), as even the highest scores describe "minimal symptoms" (APA, 1994, p. 34). The WHO Disability Assessment Schedule replaces it in the *DSM-5* (APA, 2013), but the new tool remains a measure of mental illness rather than health; all 36 questions contain the words "difficulty," "problem," "drain," or "health condition" (pp. 747–748).

Presence of Multiple Strengths

Positive psychologists may prefer to discount weaknesses and define mental health as the presence of strengths. In an attempt to resolve the controversy of what could (or should) be considered a "strength," Dahlsgaard, Peterson, and Seligman (2005) identified six "core virtues" they believe are universal across history, culture, religion, and philosophy, and created the Values in Action Inventory of Strengths (VIA-IS) (Peterson & Seligman, 2004). However, subsequent statistical analysis has questioned these six core virtues, with three-, four-, and five-factor models being proposed (Shryack, Steger, Krueger, & Kallie, 2010).

The VIA-IS is a self-report measure, which may reveal only what people consider socially desirable (Crowne & Marlowe, 1960), or incorrectly believe they possess (Kristjánsson, 2013). It may simply measure what virtues they subjectively value, although the word "values" implies beliefs that are prioritized over others, so perhaps this is the definition of a character strength. Criticized as being a "bag of virtues" (Kristjánsson, 2012), wisdom is required to choose when and how to apply the VIA strengths (Aspinwall & Staudinger, 2003; Schwartz & Hill, 2006). Of course, possession does not guarantee use, and Seligman, Steen, Park, and Peterson (2005) found those not using their strengths were no different from those who did not possess them. Perhaps a more objective measurement of strength application is required to judge mental health.

Subjective Well-being

Who better to ask about well-being than the person who experiences it? There are many concerns with self-reporting (Nisbett & Ross, 1980), but if a deluded person believes they have a good life, it is matter of ontological debate to argue with them. Of course, should the delusion end, their answer may change, and this is the main problem with this measure; it is a temporary measure of state rather than a longer-term judgment of living well. Events change our circumstances and new information alters our point-of-view. Had Vincent Van Gogh known what was to become of his art, would his subjective well-being have been different?

Positive Emotions

Using the prevalence of positive emotions as a proxy for quality of life has attracted much criticism (King, 2001), often because positive psychologists are guilty of an *a priori* appraisal of valence (Held, 2004). For Lazarus (2003), there are three reasons to decide emotions are "positive": they subjectively feel good, they arise from favorable circumstances, or they bring about desired outcomes. All three reasons are subjective, depending on personal experience and social context. An objective measurement of valance may one day come from neuroscience (Panksepp, 1998), but Barrett (2006) argues that emotions are features of the mind, not the brain, experienced differently and are not objectively observable. Biology could classify emotion depending on whether it activates the sympathetic nervous system, causing a fight or flight response, or the parasympathetic nervous system, causing relaxation. This is consistent with Fredrickson's (2001) broaden-and-build theory: negative emotions narrow our focus to immediate dangers, whilst positive emotions broaden our awareness, encouraging exploration and play. However, the sympathetic nervous system can also be stimulated by "positive" emotions, such as the excitement of going on a rollercoaster. The authors disagree as to whether or not this is "positive," so the question of contextualizing valance remains.

High Socioemotional Intelligence

Context is key. Negative emotions can be crucial for survival; a feeling of contented joy would be a hindrance if a lion attacked you, and society would judge too much happiness mania (Wood & Tarrier, 2010). Like character strengths, wise application of emotions determines if they are adaptive or maladaptive. High socioemotional intelligence is the accurate perception of emotions, the appropriate emotional response to situations, and the management of emotion to nurture relationships and achieve goals (Goleman, 2006). A person high in socioemotional intelligence would appreciate the value of both positive and negative emotions. Negative emotions are protective, positive emotions are social and empathic. Either could be an appropriate response, and both could be applied strategically in the pursuit of goals.

Involuntary Coping Mechanisms

Socioemotional intelligence assumes that responses to conflict can be voluntary choices. A different conceptualization of mental health considers involuntary coping mechanisms that alter the perception of reality to protect us from painful stressors (Vaillant, 1977, 1992, 2000). Just as our body maintains homeostasis through involuntary heart rate and temperature control, what Freud called "ego defense mechanisms" are usually unconscious, certainly involuntary. Although unconscious processes are unpopular with positivist cognitive psychologists (Vaillant, 2012a), these ontologically subjective concepts are epistemologically objective (Searle, 1995) and they are returning to fashion under the monikers of grit (Duckworth, Peterson, Matthews, & Kelly, 2007), defensive pessimism (Norem & Chang, 2002), and "the marshmallow test" (Mischel, 2014). Involuntary alteration of perception may not seem mentally healthy, but these mechanisms can be ordered by magnitude of reality distortion from "psychotic" to "mature" (Vaillant, 1971; APA, 1994). "Psychotic defenses," such as delusional projection, psychotic denial, and psychotic distortion, are common in young children and the mentally ill. "Immature defenses," such as passive aggression, projection, and acting out, are common in adolescents, those with personality disorders, and substance abusers. "Neurotic defenses," including displacement and isolation, are common among many adults, especially those with phobias and compulsions. The "mature defenses" of humor, altruism, and sublimation alter the perception of reality least, and are generally considered virtuous and adaptive.

This continuum spans the realms of both the maladaptive covered by clinical psychology and the adaptive of positive psychology. "Mature defenses" are associated with self-reported happiness, physical health, job satisfaction, and good relationships (Vaillant, 1977; Malone,

Cohen, Liu, Vaillant, & Waldinger, 2013); whereas more distorting defenses are associated with poor adjustment, marital problems, sick days, and poor friendships. Individuals who suffer brain injuries or prolonged substance abuse typically descend to lower levels (Vaillant, 2000). However, psychotherapy has been shown to aid a person in moving from maladaptive coping mechanisms to more adaptive ones, a transformation associated with clinical change (Bond, 2004; Bond & Perry, 2004; Perry & Bond, 2012). Coping mechanisms are independent of socioeconomic class and levels of education, and generally become more adaptive with age (Vaillant, 2000).

Maturity

This leads to our final definition of mental health, maturity. Drawing on Erikson's (1951) stages of human development, and two additional stages (Vaillant, 1995), longitudinal studies have provided empirical evidence that mastery of developmental tasks is associated with mental health (Vaillant & Milofsky, 1980; Vaillant, 2002, 2012c), whilst being independent of gender, socioeconomic class, and level of education (Vaillant, 2012b).

The first adult stage is "identity," separating our values and beliefs from those of the family and culture of childhood. The second is "intimacy," reciprocally and interdependently committing to a person or community. "Career consolidation" involves committing to a career we enjoy, are competent at, and for which we are compensated. "Generativity" is the fourth task, when caring for others and guiding the community become valued more than personal achievements. Becoming a "keeper of the meaning" or guardian usually occurs in late midlife and involves preserving history, culture, and principles with impartiality. Finally "integrity" is the acceptance of death, past events and decisions, and being at peace with the world.

Each of these stages represents personal growth, wrestling with changes that often hard to bear. We make compromises and commitments, sever attachments, and limit options, usually with excitement for opportunities to come and sorrow for those that will not. Often unaware, protected by our involuntary coping strategies, this process of growing, of living, of aging involves all three aspects of mind – affective, cognitive and conative – in both "positive" and "negative" ways. As we struggle and ascend through these stages, should guidance come from clinical psychology, positive psychology, or both disciplines?

Quantifying Positive Aging

Which definition of mental health is superior? It depends on context: the words "adaption" and "fitness" imply conformity to some external standard. When selecting roles for Navy recruits, paranoid personalities are a poor fit for submarines, but well adapted to airplane spotting (Vaillant, 2012b, p. 93). Positive emotions can appear important in individualist cultures, but there is evidence that optimism is not suited to collectivist cultures (Chang, 1996). All the suggested definitions need cross-cultural examination.

An analogy for these different types of mental health can be found in athletes, because the antonym of physical illness is not the absence of illness, but the presence of fitness. Again, the word "fit" implies a purpose, and there is no commonly agreed answer to what people are "for." Humans are capable of many diverse tasks, a ballet dancer is very different to a power-lifter, and both are impressive demonstrations of human potential.

There are many ways to flourish. It is imperative that scientists do not impose personal ideals of the "good" life (King, 2001; Held, 2004; Becker & Marecek, 2008), and run the risk of creating a "myth of mental illness" for those who do not fit (Szasz, 1960).

Predicting Positive Aging

The antecedents of successful aging can best be determined by prospective longitudinal studies of people's lives (Vaillant, 2012c, p. 95), although cross-sectional and retrospective studies can provide information of interest, both have severe limitations. A cross-sectional study of aging is limited to contrasting groups of people at a single point in time. The between-groups comparison can examine only averages, not life stories. The old and young under comparison are not the same people; they come from different periods in history, experiencing differing technologies, educational standards, qualities of healthcare, and culture. A cross-sectional study captures a single point in time, measuring states not traits. On a single measure, it can be difficult to distinguish an athlete with the flu from a chronically ill patient having a good day, whereas longitudinal studies expose the participants "normal."

Retrospective studies discuss the past in the present, a very different process to recording a life as it happens because history is often forgotten, embellished, or modified. Even a retrospective analysis of objective facts is subject to selection bias and limited solely to measurements taken and preserved to the present day. Prospective longitudinal studies go beyond "rosy retrospection" to reveal the truth; butterflies were born from caterpillars, tadpoles turned into toads – warts and all.

One such study is the Harvard Study of Adult Development (affectionately known as "The Grant Study"), described in detail in previous reports (Vaillant, 2002, 2012c). It began in 1938 with the intention of studying the lives of successful, high-achieving, healthy men – a Positive Psychology endeavor 60 years before Seligman's and Csikszentmihalyi's (2000) seminal introductory paper. The original purposive sample contained a few hundred Harvard students, each subjected to physical examinations, psychiatric interviews, psychometric testing, home interviews with family members, and even EEG and Rorschach tests (Vaillant, 2012c, p. 74). After combat experience for many in the Second World War, the men were debriefed. Psychological testing and interviews, including with the men's wives, continued. The men have been re-interviewed a further three times since reaching the age of 45, and continue to undertake biennial questionnaires and physical examinations every five years.

Although not a perfect prospective study (information about childhood was collected when the men were in college, and information about girlfriends after many were married in 1955), the surviving men are now over 90, and have been measured at least every two years (with a few very minor exceptions) their entire adult lives (Vaillant, 2012c, p. 83). These multiple data points allow contextualization of the sample, distinguish between states and traits, and protect against the alteration of history to determine causation from correlation.

To enable comparisons between socioeconomic backgrounds, levels of education, and gender, data for a cohort of nondelinquent inner-city men from the Glueck Study of Juvenile Delinquency and for a cohort of gifted women, originally part of the Stanford (Terman) Study, have also been collected (Vaillant, 2012c)

The Happy-Well and the Sad-Sick

Vaillant (2004) quantified "successful aging" by considering both the subjective and objective forms of physical and mental health. Thus, the "happy-well" could be contrasted to the "sad-sick." These groups were differentiated by six factors, each assessed blind to the outcome variables (Vaillant & Mukamal, 2001).

1   Objective physical health as assessed by an internist. At age 75 for the college men and 65 for the inner-city men, their medical reports, which had been taken every five years, were rated on a four-point scale; 1 – no irreversible illness present; 2 – irreversible illness present,

but neither disabling nor life shortening; 3 – chronically ill, but not yet disabled; 4 – irreversible illness and significant disability (Vaillant, 1979).

2   Self-reported subjective physical health as measured by a fifteen-point scale called "Instrumental Activities of Daily Living" (Vaillant, 2002) at age 75, which contains items questioning beliefs in capabilities.

3   Years of life before 80 living without objective or subjective disability.

4   Objective mental health was assessed at age 65 using evidence of competence in work, relationships, play, and the absence psychiatric problems with good inter-rater reliability (Vaillant & Vaillant, 1990).

5   Objective assessment of social support, by two independent assessors reviewing interviews and questionnaires, including questionnaires from family members (Vaillant, Meyer, Mukamal, & Soldz, 1998).

6   Subjective life satisfaction, from self-report questionnaires assessing nine aspects of live over the past 20 years.

Using these categorizations for the college cohort ($N = 237$), 62 were classified as "happy-well," 40 as "sad-sick," and 60 as "prematurely dead" (died between 50 and 75). Similarly for the inner-city cohort ($N - 332$), 95 were classified as "happy-well," 48 "sad-sick," and 75 "prematurely dead" (before age 65). "Successful aging" was coded for each participant, on a scale of "1" for the "happy-well" to "4" for the "prematurely dead." The two cohorts allow for the comparison between groups who were measured to differ in IQ, socioeconomic status, and levels of education, whilst controlling variables such as gender, race and nationality.

Predictors of Positive Aging

Flourishing is associated with longevity. Previous studies have demonstrated happy people live longer (Friedman, Tucker, Tomlinson-Keasey, Schwartz, Wingard, & Criqui, 1993; Danner, Snowdon, & Friesen, 2001). Vaillant and Mukamal (2001) showed no exception. The mean age of death or impairment through disability for "sad-sick" college men was 71.4 years old, and for "sad-sick" inner-city men it was 62.3 years old. In contrast, the "happy-well" were, on average, still alive at ages 80 and 70 for the college and inner city men, respectively. Interestingly, the health decline of inner-city men who completed more than 15 years of education was similar to the college men, suggesting education is more important than socioeconomic status in predicting future health. The mediating variable here is not so much education per se; it is the belief that you have a future and the capacity to postpone present gratification for future gain. Duckworth calls this coping mechanism "Grit" (Duckworth et al., 2007).

The most important antecedent for successful aging was the avoidance of nicotine and alcohol abuse (Vaillant & Mukamal, 2001). The number of pack years (packs per day multiplied by years smoking) correlated with a lack of successful aging (lower scores representing healthier and happier) for both the college men ($r = .35$, $p < 0.001$) and inner-city men ($r = .31$, $p < 0.001$). This may be due to the physical health risks associated with smoking; the correlations with subjective life satisfaction were not significant, but the correlations with length of active life were (college men $r = -.30$, $p < 0.001$; inner-city men $r = -.31$, $p < 0.001$). Alcohol abuse was also detrimental to successful aging (college men $r = .42$, $p < 0.001$; inner-city men $r = .19$, $p < 0.001$) and reduced the length of active life (college men $r = -.38$, $p < 0.001$; inner-city men $r = -.18$, $p < 0.001$) for the inner-city men. It should be noted that smoking and alcohol are often confounding variables that occur simultaneously and difficult to separate (DiFranza & Guerrera, 1990).

The most important factor in predicting mental health, subjectively or objectively, was the use of mature coping mechanisms (Vaillant & Mukamal, 2001). The men were assessed from interviews at age 47 using a nine-point scale similar to the *DSM-IV* Defensive Functioning Scale

(Vaillant, 1992). The scores were coded "1" when mature defenses (coping mechanisms) were deemed present (a score of 1–3 on the nine-point scale) and "2" if deemed absent when the men scored 4–9 on the scale). Maturity of defenses explained a great deal of variance in the objective mental health of both the college men ($r = .41$, $p < 0.001$) and the inner-city men ($r = .46$, $p < 0.001$). The correlation between maturity of coping mechanisms and subjective life satisfaction was significant for both the college men ($r = .34$, $p < 0.001$) and inner-city men ($r = .28$, $p < 0.001$), further supporting the argument for the use of involuntary coping mechanisms as a measure of mental health as discussed above.

Vaillant and Mukamal (2001) also coded a body mass index (BMI) between 21 and 29 at age 50 as "1" and other values as "2," and found healthy weight was correlated with successful aging (college men $r = .14$, $p < 0.05$; inner-city men $r = .11$, $p < 0.05$). Stability of marriage, coded "1" if the participant was married without divorce, separation, or serious problems at age 50, "2" otherwise, was another very significant factor (college men $r = .27$, $p < 0.001$; inner-city men $r = .22$, $p < 0.001$). Exercise that burned over 500 kilocalories per week was coded as "1," and little or no exercise as "2" (for the college men only), and this was also found to predict successful aging ($r = .22$, $p < 0.001$).

Comparing the college men to the inner-city cohort suggests the privileged are better at self-care (Vaillant, 2012c). Diseases that can be the result of lifestyle choices, such as lung cancer and Type II diabetes were far more prevalent in the inner-city men, whilst illnesses independent of self-care, such as cancer and arthritis, occurred in similar numbers. However, this increased risk was not seen in inner-city men with postgraduate education, who were similar to the Harvard sample, suggesting education leads to successful aging through improved self-care.

It should be noted that both the college and inner-city groups were all white, all male, all American born between 1915 and 1935. The small size (total $N = 569$) and limited variability of the sample limits generalization of these findings. However, longitudinal studies that span entire adult lifetimes are not easily replicable, so these findings are offered as a heuristic guide to focus future nomothetic research.

Simple Strategies are not Sufficient

It is apparent that gerontology spans the domains of positive psychology and clinical psychology. Some predictors of successful aging could be separated into "positive" (such as exercise and education) and "negative" (such as not being a smoker and not abusing alcohol), but other predictive factors (such as mature involuntary coping mechanisms and healthy weight) could belong to either school of thought. Stability of marriage is a more complex issue; divorce is usually considered "negative," but it would be maladaptive to remain in a "bad" relationship.

Vaillant (2002), describes successful aging as a minefield, and advises that we follow the footprints. But some paths vanish (do not follow those) and some footprints appear as if from nowhere; the trampled grass distinguishing significant variables from dead-ends changes with time (Melström, 1993). Again, the length of the Grant Study reveals the complexities of predictors across the life-span. Vaillant (2012c) summarizes three studies that span ages 55 to over 90, separating factors that are important to health decline at different age periods (p. 245). Of the six mental health variables (such as high use of drugs, major depression, immature defenses) that were important to health before age 55, none are significant over that age. Levels of education appear to be unimportant before age 55, important between 55 and 80, and then not significant after the age of 80. Alcohol abuse and Type II diabetes have similar patterns, appearing significant for a time then not significant after, but this could be explained by the mortality rates of those diseases and the attrition of the affected in the sample.

These sleeper effects, variables with changing correlations throughout the life-span, highlight the difficulty in predicting "positive" aging. Both "positive" and "negative" variables can predict both "positive" and "negative" outcomes, confounding others in a many-to-many relationship, which changes over time.

Concluding Complexities, and Contradictions

Every aspect of gerontology requires an insight into "positive" and "negative," from describing successful aging and quantification of measurement, to prediction, prescription, and facilitation. Segregating life improvement techniques into clinical treatments, which solely reduce the negative, or PPIs, which solely improve the positive, overlooks the multifaceted nature of life. Most clinical psychologists would not consider simply advising alcoholics "to quit" to be sufficient treatment. Fostering social support (Vaillant, 2014) and the development of mature coping mechanisms (Vaillant, 2000) are also required. Likewise, a positive psychologist advocating the benefits of exercise is unlikely to ignore the dangers of smoking. Both positive and negative issues are addressed by "positive" and "business as usual" psychologists alike, "in the positive hope of better living" (Held, 2004, p. 39). So why not just call them all "psychologists"?

Any treatment of aging is a simplification. We all tell many stories, our lives are multifaceted, and multidimensional; work, play, relationships are just some of the many tapestries we weave simultaneously. Psychologists tend to prefer nomothetic methods to make "blanket" statements about large groups, to generalize into "good" or "bad." We are all guilty of oversimplification and overgeneralization. (Yes, those statements are simple generalizations.) Idiographic data starts to reveal some subtleties of reality. Under the right conditions, with the right choices, some people do mature and flourish. Others do not.

Psychology will mature with time. The field is but a sum of the idiographic narratives of the academics within it. Each idea is a thread in the tapestry of psychology. Untangling the truth requires an appreciation of the twists and turns, the opportunities and challenges of this fascinating subject. We all work together to weave that rich tapestry of understanding human life, and the process of aging well.

References

Aichberger, M. C., Busch, M. A., Reischies, F. M., Ströhle, A., Heinz, A., & Rapp, M. A. (2010). Effect of physical inactivity on cognitive performance after 2.5 years of follow-up: Longitudinal results from the Survey of Health, Ageing, and Retirement. *Journal of Gerontopsychology and Geriatric Psychiatry*, 23(1), 7. doi.org/10.1024/1662-9647/a000003.

American Psychiatric Association. (1994). *Diagnostic and statistical manual of mental disorders: DSM-4*. Washington, DC: APA.

American Psychiatric Association. (2013). *DSM-5*. Washington, DC: APA.

Andrews, A. W., Thomas, M. W., & Bohannon, R. W. (1996). Normative values for isometric muscle force measurements obtained with hand-held dynamometers. *Physical Therapy*, 76(3), 248–259.

Armelius, B. Å., Gerin, P., Luborsky, L., & Alexander, L. (1991). Clinicians' judgment of mental health: An international validation of HSRS. *Psychotherapy Research*, 1(1), 31–38. doi.org/10.1080/105033091 12331334051.

Aspinwall, L. G. & Staudinger, U. M. (2003). A psychology of human strengths: Some central issues of an emerging field. In: L. G. Aspinwall & U. M. Staudinger (Eds.), *A psychology of human strengths: Fundamental questions and future directions for a positive psychology* (pp. 9–22). Washington, DC: American Psychological Association. doi.org/10.1037/10566-001.

Barrett, L. F. (2006). Are emotions natural kinds? *Perspectives on Psychological Science*, 1(1), 28–58. doi.org/10.1111/j.1745-6916.2006.00003.x.

Becker, D. & Marecek, J. (2008). Positive psychology history in the remaking? *Theory & Psychology, 18*(5), 591–604. doi.org/10.1177/0959354308093397.

Bohannon, R. W. (1997). Comfortable and maximum walking speed of adults aged 20–79 years: Reference values and determinants. *Age and Ageing, 26*(1), 15–19. doi.org/10.1093/ageing/26.1.15.

Bond, M. (2004). Empirical studies of defense style: Relationships with psychopathology and change. *Harvard Review of Psychiatry, 12*(5), 263–278. doi.org/10.1080/10673220490886167.

Bond, M. & Perry, J. C. (2004). Long-term changes in defense styles with psychodynamic psychotherapy for depressive, anxiety, and personality disorders. *American Journal of Psychiatry, 161*(9), 1665–1671. doi.org/10.1176/appi.ajp.161.9.1665.

Brouha, L. (1943). The step test: A simple method of measuring physical fitness for muscular work in young men. *Research Quarterly. American Association for Health, Physical Education and Recreation, 14*(1), 31–37.

Carstensen, L. L. & Charles, S. T. (2003). Human aging: Why is even good news taken as bad? In: L. G. Aspinwall & U. M. Staudinger (Eds.). *A psychology of human strengths: Fundamental questions and future directions for a positive psychology.* Washington, DC: American Psychological Association. doi.org/10.1037/10566-006.

Chang, E. C. (1996). Evidence for the cultural specificity of pessimism in Asians vs Caucasians: A test of a general negativity hypothesis. *Personality and Individual Differences, 21*(5), 819–822. doi.org/10.1016/0191-8869(96)00110-9.

Crowne, D. P. & Marlowe, D. (1960). A new scale of social desirability independent of psychopathology. *Journal of Consulting Psychology, 24*(4), 349. doi.org/10.1037/h0047358.

Dahlsgaard, K., Peterson, C., & Seligman, M. E. (2005). Shared virtue: The convergence of valued human strengths across culture and history. *Review of General Psychology, 9*(3), 203. doi.org/10.1037/1089-2680.9.3.203.

Danner, D. D., Snowdon, D. A., & Friesen, W. V. (2001). Positive emotions in early life and longevity: Findings from the nun study. *Journal of Personality and Social Psychology, 80*, 804–813. doi.org/10.1037/0022-3514.80.5.804.

Department of Health. (1992). *The health of elderly people: An Epidemiological overview.* London: Central Health Monitoring Unit, HMSO.

DiFranza, J. R. & Guerrera, M. P. (1990). Alcoholism and smoking. *Journal of Studies on Alcohol and Drugs, 51*(2), 130.

Doty, R. L., Shaman, P., Applebaum, S. L., Giberson, R., Siksorski, L., & Rosenberg, L. (1984). Smell identification ability: changes with age. *Science, 226*(4681), 1441–1443. doi.org/10.1126/science.6505700.

Drentea, P. (2002). Retirement and mental health. *Journal of Aging and Health, 14*(2), 167–194. doi.org/10.1177/089826430201400201.

Duckworth, A. L., Peterson, C., Matthews, M. D., & Kelly, D. R. (2007). Grit: Perseverance and passion for long-term goals. *Journal of Personality and Social Psychology, 92*(6), 1087. doi.org/10.1037/0022-3514.92.6.1087.

Emanuel, E. J. (2014). Why I hope to die at 75: An argument that society and families – and you – will be better off if nature takes its course swiftly and promptly. *The Atlantic*, September 17.

Erikson, E. (1951). *Childhood and society.* Albury: Imago.

Fiatarone, M. A., Marks, E. C., Ryan, N. D., Meredith, C. N., Lipsitz, L. A., & Evans, W. J. (1990). High-intensity strength training in nonagenarians: effects on skeletal muscle. *Jama, 263*(22), 3029–3034. doi.org/10.1001/jama.1990.03440220053029.

Fredrickson, B. L. (2001). The role of positive emotions in positive psychology: The broaden-and-build theory of positive emotions. *American Psychologist, 56*(3), 218. doi.org/10.1037/0003-066X.56.3.218.

Friedman, H. S., Tucker, J. S., Tomlinson-Keasey, C., Schwartz, J. E., Wingard, D. L., & Criqui, M. H. (1993). Does childhood personality predict longevity? *Journal of Personality and Social Psychology, 65*, 176–185. doi.org/10.1037/0022-3514.65.1.176.

Fries, J. F. (1980). Aging, natural death, and the compression of morbidity. *New England Journal of Medicine, 303*(23), 1369–1370. doi.org/10.1056/NEJM198012043032317.

Goleman, D. (2006). *Emotional intelligence.* Bantam: New York.

Hardman, A. E. & Stensel, D. J. (2009). *Physical activity and health: The evidence explained.* London: Routledge.

Held, B. S. (2004). The negative side of positive psychology. *Journal of Humanistic Psychology, 44*(1), 9–46. doi.org/10.1177/0022167803259645.

Helmuth, L. (2003). The wisdom of the wizened. *Science, 299*(5611), 1300–1302. doi.org/10.1126/science.299.5611.1300.

Hertzog, C., Kramer, A. F., Wilson, R. S., & Lindenberger, U. (2008). Enrichment effects on adult cognitive development can the functional capacity of older adults be preserved and enhanced? *Psychological Science in the Public Interest, 9*(1), 1–65.

Jackson, A. S., Stanforth, P. R., Gagnon, J., Rankinen, T., Leon, A. S., Rao, D. C., Skinner, J. S., Bouchard, C., & Wilmore, J. H. (2002). The effect of sex, age and race on estimating percentage body fat from body mass index: The Heritage Family Study. *International Journal of Obesity and Related Metabolic Disorders, 26*(6), 789–796.

Kail, R. & Salthouse, T. A. (1994). Processing speed as a mental capacity. *Acta Psychologica, 86*(2), 199–225. doi.org/10.1016/0001-6918(94)90003-5.

King, L. A. (2001). The hard road to the good life: The happy, mature person. *Journal of Humanistic Psychology, 41*(1), 51–72. doi.org/10.1177/0022167801411005.

Kite, M. E., Stockdale, G. D., Whitley, B. E., & Johnson, B. T. (2005). Attitudes toward younger and older adults: An updated meta-analytic review. *Journal of Social Issues, 61*(2), 241–266. doi.org/10.1111/j.1540-4560.2005.00404.x.

Kristjánsson, K. (2012). Positive psychology and positive education: Old wine in new bottles?. *Educational Psychologist, 47*(2), 86–105. doi.org/10.1080/00461520.2011.610678.

Kristjánsson, K. (2013). Ten myths about character, virtue and virtue education – Plus three well-founded misgivings. *British Journal of Educational Studies, 61*(3), 269–287. doi.org/10.1080/00071005.2013.778386.

Larsson, L., Grimby, G., & Karlsson, J. (1979). Muscle strength and speed of movement in relation to age and muscle morphology. *Journal of Applied Physiology, 46*(3), 451–456.

Lazarus, R. S. (2003). Does the positive psychology movement have legs? *Psychological Inquiry, 14*(2), 93–109. doi.org/10.1207/S15327965PLI1402_02.

Levy, B. (1996). Improving memory in old age through implicit self-stereotyping. *Journal of Personality and Social Psychology, 71*(6), 1092. doi.org/10.1037/0022-3514.71.6.1092.

Levy, B. (2009). Stereotype embodiment a psychosocial approach to aging. *Current Directions in Psychological Science, 18*(6), 332–336. doi.org/10.1111/j.1467-8721.2009.01662.x.

Levy, B. R., Hausdorff, J. M., Hencke, R., & Wei, J. Y. (2000). Reducing cardiovascular stress with positive self-stereotypes of aging. *Journals of Gerontology Series B: Psychological Sciences and Social Sciences, 55*(4), P205–P213. doi.org/10.1093/geronb/55.4.P205.

Levy, B. R., Slade, M. D., Kunkel, S. R., & Kasl, S. V. (2002). Longevity increased by positive self-perceptions of aging. *Journal of Personality and Social Psychology, 83*(2), 261. doi.org/10.1037/0022-3514.83.2.261.

Light, L. L. & Burke, D. M. (Eds.). (1993). *Language, memory, and aging.* Cambridge: Cambridge University Press.

Malone, J. C., Cohen, S., Liu, S. R., Vaillant, G. E., & Waldinger, R. J. (2013). Adaptive midlife defense mechanisms and late-life health. *Personality and Individual Differences, 55*(2), 85–89. doi.org/10.1016/j.paid.2013.01.025.

Manton, K. G., Corder, L., & Stallard, E. (1997). Chronic disability trends in elderly United States populations: 1982–1994. *Proceedings of the National Academy of Sciences, 94*(6), 2593–2598. doi.org/10.1073/pnas.94.6.2593.

Mayer, K. U. & Baltes, P. B. (1999). *The Berlin Aging Study: Aging from 70 to 100.* Cambridge: Cambridge University Press.

Mein, G., Martikainen, P., Hemingway, H., Stansfeld, S., & Marmot, M. (2003). Is retirement good or bad for mental and physical health functioning? Whitehall II longitudinal study of civil servants. *Journal of Epidemiology and Community Health, 57*(1), 46–49.doi.org/10.1136/jech.57.1.46.

Melov, S., Tarnopolsky, M. A., Beckman, K., Felkey, K., & Hubbard, A. (2007). Resistance exercise reverses aging in human skeletal muscle. *PLoS One, 2*(5), e465. doi.org/10.1371/journal.pone.0000465.

Melström, D. (1993). A longitudinal and cross-sectional gerontological population study in Gothenburg. In: J. J. F. Schroots (Ed.), *Aging, health and competence: The next generation of longitudinal research* (pp. 127–141). Amsterdam: Elsevier.

Mischel, W. (2014). *The marshmallow test: Understanding self-control and how to master it.* London: Random House.

Nisbett, R. E. & Ross, L. (1980). *Human inference: Strategies and short-comings of social judgment.* Englewood Cliffs, NJ: Prentice Hall.

Norem, J. K. & Chang, E. C. (2002). The positive psychology of negative thinking. *Journal of Clinical Psychology, 58*(9), 993–1001. doi.org/10.1002/jclp.10094.

Panksepp, J. (1998). *Affective neuroscience: The foundations of human and animal emotions.* Oxford: Oxford University Press.

Perry, J. C. & Bond, M. (2012). Change in defense mechanisms during long-term dynamic psychotherapy and five-year outcome. *American Journal of Psychiatry, 169*(9), 916–925. doi.org/10.1176/appi. ajp.2012.11091403.

Peterson, C. & Seligman, M. E. P. (2004). *Character strengths and virtues: A handbook and classification.* New York and Washington, DC: Oxford University Press and American Psychological Association.

Rowe, J. W. & Kahn, R. L. (1998). *Successful aging: The MacArthur Foundation Study.* New York: Pantheon.

Sauvaget, C., Jagger, C., & Arthur, A. J. (2001). Active and cognitive impairment-free life expectancies: results from the Melton Mowbray 75+ health checks. *Age and Ageing, 30*(6), 509–515. doi.org/10.1093/ageing/30.6.509.

Schaie, K. W. (1988). Variability in cognitive function in the elderly: Implications for societal participation. *Phenotypic Variation in Populations* (pp. 191–211). New York: Springer. doi.org/10.1007/978-1-46 84-5460-4_20.

Scheidt, R. J., Humpherys, D. R., & Yorgason, J. B. (1999). Successful aging: What's not to like? *Journal of Applied Gerontology, 18*(3), 277–282. doi.org/10.1177/073346489901800301.

Schwartz, B. & Hill, K. E. (2006). Practical wisdom: Aristotle meets positive psychology. *Journal of Happiness Studies, 7*, 377–395. doi.org/10.1007/s10902-005-3651-y.

Searle, J. R. (1995). *The construction of social reality.* New York: Simon & Schuster.

Seligman, M. E. & Csikszentmihalyi, M. (2000). Positive psychology: An introduction. *American Psychologist, 55*(1), 5. doi.org/10.1037/0003-066X.55.1.5.

Seligman, M. E., Steen, T. A., Park, N., & Peterson, C. (2005). Positive psychology progress: Empirical validation of interventions. *American Psychologist, 60*(5), 410. doi.org/10.1037/ 0003-066X.60.5.410.

Shingo, T., Gregg, C., Enwere, E., Fujikawa, H., Hassam, R., Geary, C., Cross, J. C., & Weiss, S. (2003). Pregnancy-stimulated neurogenesis in the adult female forebrain mediated by prolactin. *Science, 299*, 117–120. doi.org/10.1126/science.1076647.

Shryack, J., Steger, M. F., Krueger, R. F., & Kallie, C. S. (2010). The structure of virtue: An empirical investigation of the dimensionality of the virtues in action inventory of strengths. *Personality and Individual Differences, 48*(6), 714–719. doi.org/10.1016/j.paid.2010.01.007.

Skelton, D. A., Young, A., Greig, C. A., & Malbut, K. E. (1995). Effects of resistance training on strength, power, and selected functional abilities of women aged 75 and older. *Journal of the American Geriatrics Society, 43*(10), 1081–1087.

Szasz, T. S. (1960). The myth of mental illness. *American Psychologist, 15*(2), 113. doi.org/10.1037/ h0046535.

Vaillant, G. E. (1971). Theoretical hierarchy of adaptive ego mechanisms. *Archives of General Psychiatry, 24*, 107–118. doi.org/10.1001/archpsyc.1971.01750080011003.

Vaillant, G. E. (1977). *Adaptation to life.* Boston, MA: Little Brown.

Vaillant, G. E. (1979). Natural history of male psychological health: Effects of mental health on physical health. *New England Journal of Medicine, 301*, 1249–1254. doi.org/10.1056/ NEJM197912063012302.

Vaillant, G. E. (1992). *Ego mechanisms of defense.* Washington, DC: APA.

Vaillant, G. E. (1995). *The wisdom of the ego.* Cambridge, MA: Harvard University Press.

Vaillant, G. E. (2000). Adaptive mental mechanisms: Their role in a positive psychology. *American Psychologist, 55*(1), 89. doi.org/10.1037/0003-066X.55.1.89.

Vaillant, G. E. (2002). *Aging well: Surprising guideposts to a happier life.* Boston, MA: Little, Brown.

Vaillant, G. E. (2003). Reviews and overviews: Mental health. *American Journal of Psychiatry, 160*(8), 1373–1384. doi.org/10.1176/appi.ajp.160.8.1373.

Vaillant, G. E. (2004). Positive aging. In: P. A. Linley & S. Joseph (Eds.). *Positive Psychology in Practice.* (pp. 561–578). Hoboken, NJ: John Wiley.

Vaillant, G. E. (2012a). Lifting the Field's "repression" of defenses. *American Journal of Psychiatry*, *169*(9), 885–887. doi.org/10.1176/appi.ajp.2012.12050703.

Vaillant, G. E. (2012b). Positive mental health: Is there a cross-cultural definition? *World Psychiatry*, *11*(2), 93–99. doi.org/10.1016/j.wpsyc.2012.05.006.

Vaillant, G. E. (2012c). *Triumphs of experience: The men of the Harvard Grant Study*. Cambridge, MA: Harvard University Press. doi.org/10.4159/harvard.9780674067424.

Vaillant, G. E. (2014). Positive emotions and the success of Alcoholics Anonymous. *Alcoholism Treatment Quarterly*, *32*(2/3), 214–224. doi.org/10.1080/07347324.2014.907032.

Vaillant, G. E. & Milofsky, E. (1980). Natural history of male psychological health: IX. Empirical evidence for Erikson's model of the life cycle. *American Journal of Psychiatry*, *137*(11), 1348–1359. doi.org/10.1176/ajp.137.11.1348.

Vaillant, G. E. & Mukamal, K. (2001). Successful aging. *American Journal of Psychiatry*, *158*(6), 839–847. doi.org/10.1176/appi.ajp.158.6.839.

Vaillant, G. E. & Vaillant, C. O. (1990). Natural history of male psychological health: XII. A 45-year study of predictors of successful aging at age 65. *American Journal of Psychiatry*, *147*(1), 31–37.

Vaillant, G. E., Meyer, S. E., Mukamal, K., & Soldz, S. (1998). Are social supports in late midlife a cause or a result of successful physical aging. *Psychological Medicine*, *28*, 1159–1168. doi.org/10.1017/S0033291798007211.

Vandervoort, A. A. (1992). Effects of ageing on human neuromuscular function: implications for exercise. *Canadian Journal of Sport Sciences (Journal Canadien des Sciences du Sport)*, *17*(3), 178–184.

Wood, A. M. & Tarrier, N. (2010). Positive clinical psychology: A new vision and strategy for integrated research and practice. *Clinical Psychology Review*, *30*(7), 819–829. doi.org/10.1016/j.cpr.2010.06.003.

Woodruff-Pak, D. S. (1997). *The neuropsychology of aging*. Oxford: Blackwell.

World Health Organization. (1952). Constitution of the World Health Organization. In: *World Health Organization handbook of basic documents*, 5th edn. Geneva: WHO.

Part III
Disorders

13

Improving the Capacity to Treat Depression using Talking Therapies

Setting a Positive Clinical Psychology Agenda

Barnaby D. Dunn and Henrietta Roberts

Depression is a debilitating, chronically recurring, and common condition with a lifetime prevalence of 16% (Judd, 1997). At any one time approximately 2.5% of the UK population (1.6 million people) are depressed, accounting for 17% of UK disability, serving as a significant risk factor for poor physical health, and placing a major burden on the economy (Layard et al., 2006). By 2020, depression is predicted to become the leading worldwide contributor to disability (Ustun, Ayuso-Mateos, Chatterji, Mathers, & Murray, 2004). Depression is suboptimally treated by current interventions. For example, the talking treatment with the strongest evidence of efficacy is cognitive behavior therapy (CBT) (Beck, Rush, Shaw, & Emery, 1979; see Butler, Chapman, Forman, & Beck, 2006, for a review of meta-analyses). However, at best only two-thirds of individuals will respond (i.e., show at least a 50% drop in symptoms) during CBT and, of those who no longer meet diagnostic criteria for depression at the end of treatment, over half will relapse within two years. This parallels similarly poor outcomes for other psychosocial interventions for depression (Vittengl, Clark, Dunn, & Jarret, 2007; Cuijpers, van Straten, Andersson, & van Oppen, 2008; Fournier et al., 2010). Similarly mixed acute treatment and relapse prevention outcomes are observed following anti-depressant treatment – currently by far the most widely utilized intervention despite increasing availability of psychosocial approaches (e.g., Spence, Roberts, Ariti, & Bardsley, 2014). For example, 55–65% of individuals treated with antidepressants experience significant continuing symptoms (Anderson et al., 2008). Relapse rates are particularly high if individuals cease ongoing maintenance treatment once they are no longer acutely depressed. Indeed, there is ongoing debate as to whether active treatments for depression lead to clinically significant gains in comparison with control/placebo conditions (Kirsch, Deacon, Huedo-Medina, Scoboria, Moore, & Johnson, 2008; Cuijpers, Karyotaki, Weitz, Andersson, Hollon, & Streets, 2014; Cuijpers et al., 2014). There is a pressing need to improve clinical outcomes. However, despite considerable effort and investment, there have not been stepwise gains in the capacity to treat acute depression. One way forward is to target prognostically important but clinically neglected features of depression.

Anhedonia (a loss of interest and pleasure in previously enjoyable activities and a general deficit in positive affect) is one such core feature of depression. It is one of the two cardinal symptoms of depression required to gain a diagnosis of depression and yet has been neglected in treatment to date. For example, of UK National Institute for Health and Care Excellence (NICE) recommended acute depression treatments, CBT emphasizes changing negative cognitions to reduce negative mood (Beck et al., 1979) and interpersonal psychotherapy (IPT) attends to resolving difficulties in

The Wiley Handbook of Positive Clinical Psychology, First Edition. Edited by Alex M. Wood and Judith Johnson.
© 2016 John Wiley & Sons, Ltd. Published 2016 by John Wiley & Sons, Ltd.

a core relationship domain (Weissman, Markowitz, & Klerman, 2000). Neither extensively prioritizes repairing anhedonia. Behavioral activation (BA) (e.g., Martell, Dimidjian, & Hermann-Dunn, 2010) does systematically schedule potentially rewarding activities and there is some evidence that it can foster well-being (Mazzucchelli, Kane, & Rees, 2010). However, BA concentrates on psychological barriers blocking engagement with positive activities (e.g., avoidance), but neglects mechanisms that may reduce pleasure once an individual is engaged. NICE recommended anti-depressants (see NICE, 2009) target neurotransmitters predominantly linked to negative affect (e.g., selective serotonin reuptake inhibitors) and neglect neurotransmitters linked to positive affect (e.g., dopamine). The underlying mechanisms driving positive affect are partially independent from those driving negative affect (Watson, Weise, Vaidya, & Tellegen, 1999). Therefore, current treatments targeting negative affect will not necessarily build positive affect (Dunn, 2012).

The scope of the anhedonia problem and the extent to which it contributes to depression prognosis are challenging to assess conclusively, since existing psychosocial and pharmacological treatment trials do not typically report anhedonia outcomes. However, there is evidence from a large-scale evaluation of mood disorder treatments in outpatient care that treatment successfully lowered negative affect, but failed to raise positive affect (Brown, 2007), suggesting routine outpatient treatment may leave individuals with residual anhedonia.

This chapter will build the case that there is a need to develop integrated treatments that simultaneously reduce negative affect and build positive affect in order to maximize depression treatment outcomes. Standard depression interventions targeting reducing negative affect should be combined with emerging positive psychology techniques and other approaches that aim to bolster positive affect, to create a cohesive, unified treatment framework (i.e., a positive clinical psychology agenda) (Wood & Tarrier, 2010). Such an approach has potential both to alleviate depression symptoms and to build well-being. First, the chapter will propose an opera-tional definition of what we mean by anhedonia and positive affect. Second, we will review the evidence that anhedonia is a core and prognostically important feature of depression that should be an explicit treatment focus. Third, we will discuss emerging intervention work from positive psychology (and related fields), demonstrating its proven efficacy in repairing anhedonia in moderately depressed populations. Fourth, we will consider the possible pitfalls of introducing a positive psychology focus into depression interventions (the "Pollyanna problem") (Dunn, 2012), and propose approaches to overcome these. Finally, we will propose an agenda for positive clinical psychology in depression. We argue there is a need to: (1) agree standard measures of positivity to use in treatment trials; (2) better characterize positivity disturbances in depression; (3) better understand underlying mechanisms driving positivity deficits in depression; (4) place a greater emphasis on motivation and adopt a more nuanced approach to goal-setting; (5) fully harness the potential of digital technology in novel positive clinical psychology inter-ventions; and (6) utilize implementation science to maximize application of positive clinical psychology within routine mental health care settings.

The chapter will focus on how to build positive affect in depression. This is not to say that we do not think it is equally important to reduce negative affect. In our view, existing treatment approaches already emphasize targeting mechanisms associated with negative affect (e.g., BA, CBT, IPT), and these treatments have been extensively reviewed elsewhere (see Beck, 2005; Dimidjian, Barrera, Martell, Munoz, & Lewinsohn, 2011, Markowitz & Weissman, 2012), so for the sake of brevity we do not consider them in detail further here.

A Working Definition of Anhedonia

To improve the capacity to treat anhedonia, it is first important for the field to agree on a standard definition that can integrate psychological and neurobiological accounts. As discussed above (and following Dunn, 2012), at the psychological level of explanation anhedonia is defined as a loss of interest and pleasure in previously enjoyable activities and can be contextualized as a deficient positive affect system. Positive affect can be viewed as a loose constellation of subjective positive feeling states (e.g., happiness, joy, contentment), positive appraisals (judging a stimulus as rewarding), positive action tendencies (e.g., approach behavior toward rewarding stimuli), and physiological responses (e.g., calm or excited bodily response) (see Dillon & Pizzagalli, 2010). State positive affect can be short-lived in response to a particular internal or external trigger (i.e., an emotion) or relatively longer lasting and less clearly linked to a particular trigger (i.e., a mood) (Rottenberg, 2005). Dispositional (trait) positivity is the tendency to experience stronger and longer-than-average lasting positive mood/emotions across a range of different triggering events and contexts (Dunn, 2012). Psychological and pharmacological treatments primarily focus on addressing the subjective feeling component, but to do so it is often necessary to manipulate appraisals, action tendencies, and physiological responses.

Anhedonia is intrinsically linked to reward system function in the brain, predominantly involving dopamine and opioid neurotransmitter pathways (Treadway & Zald, 2011). Reward system functioning is implicated in a range of (particularly high arousal) positive affective responses across all four domains of the positive affect system (emotional states, appraisals, action tendencies, and physiological responses). Neuroscience has fractionated the reward system into at least three partly dissociable components: wanting (the willingness to work to gain reward); liking (subjective pleasure experience when attaining a reward); and learning (changing associations/behaviors following reward attainment) (Kringelbach & Berridge, 2009). Until recently, there has been relatively little integration between clinical operationalizations of anhedonia and basic science fractionation of reward system function. However, with the advent of the Research Domains Criteria framework (RdoC) (Insel et al., 2010), there is now an increasing movement to contextualize anhedonia (across disorders) with reference to deficiencies in positive affect system function.

For the remainder of this chapter the term anhedonia will be used as a short-hand to refer to deficiencies in positive affect system functioning, including associated dysfunction in the reward system.

The Centrality of Anhedonia to Depression

A range of recent narrative reviews extensively evaluate psychological and neuroscience evidence that anhedonia is a core component of depression (e.g., Treadway & Zald, 2011; Watson & Naragon-Gainey, 2011; Dunn, 2012). Depressed individuals report significant anhedonia on a range of self-report scales, including the Snaith–Hamilton Pleasure Scale (Snaith, Hamilton, Morley, Hurmayan, Hargreaves, & Trigwell, 1995; see Nakozeny, Carmody, Morris, Kurian, & Trivedi, 2010) and the Positive Affect Negative Affect Schedule (Watson, Clark, & Tellegen, 1988). Anhedonia symptoms remain constant despite considerable fluctuation in overall depression severity in chronically depressed groups (Schrader, 1997). Depressed individuals report experiencing less happiness and pleasure when processing positive images and video clips in the laboratory (e.g., Dunn, Dalgleish, Lawrence, Cusack, & Ogilvie, 2004; see meta-analysis by Bylsma, Morris, & Rottenberg, 2008). Experience-sampling method (ESM) studies tracking emotional experience across multiple time points in everyday life also reveal clear evidence of reduced absolute levels of positive affect in depression (see review by Telford, McCarthy-Jones, Corcoran, & Rowse, 2012). However, when depressed individuals do report engaging with positive activities in ESM, there is surprisingly little clear-cut evidence of reduced positive reactivity (e.g., Bylsma, Taylor-Clift, & Rottenberg, 2010). Therefore, reduced overall levels of positivity may be a by-product of lower engagement with potentially rewarding situations.

Moreover, depressed individuals exhibit reduced positive cognitive biases in some domains, for example, showing a reduced tendency to overevaluate their own performance (Dunn, Dalgleish, Lawrence, & Ogilvie, 2007a; Dunn, Stefanovitch, Buchan, Lawrence, & Dalgleish, 2009), less of an attentional bias to positive stimuli (Gotlib, McLachlan, & Katz, 1988), and a less positive autobiographical memory structure (Dalgleish, Hill, Golden, Morant, & Dunn, 2011), compared with nondepressed groups. Further, depressed individuals are less willing to expend effort to gain a monetary reward (Treadway, Bossaller, Shelton, & Zald, 2012), consistent with reduced reward motivation (or "wanting"). Depressed individuals also show reduced acquisition of a response bias to frequently rewarded stimuli (Pizzagalli, Iosifescu, Hallett, Ratner, & Fava, 2008; Vrieze et al., 2013), interpreted as a deficit in reward learning.

Neuroimaging studies show clear dysfunction in brain reward circuitry in depression (Keedwell, Andrew, Williams, Brammer, & Phillips, 2005; Epstein et al., 2006; Heller et al., 2009; Pizzagalli et al., 2008; Smoski et al., 2009). A recent review concludes that the reward pathway connecting the ventraltegmental area to the nucleus accumbens (involving glutamatergic, dopaminergic, and GABAergic neurotransmission) is particularly important in depression (Russo & Nestler, 2013). In summary, there is good evidence (albeit not universally observed) that anhedonia and positive affect system deficiencies are central to depression.

The Prognostic Importance of Anhedonia

There is now increasing evidence that anhedonia predicts a pernicious depression course. High levels of anhedonia predict ongoing depression at one-year follow-up in community depressed samples (Spijker, Bijl, de Graaf, & Nolen, 2001). Baseline elevations in anhedonia predict a poor response to anti-depressants/CBT (Geschwind, Nicolson, Peeters, van Os, Barge-Schaapveld, & Wichers, 2011; McMakin et al., 2012; Uher et al., 2012). Recovery from depression during anti-depressant treatment is more reliably connected to increased reward experience than to reduced stress sensitivity (Wichers et al., 2009). In a large treatment-seeking sample ($N = 826$), stable reductions in positive mood uniquely predicted improvement in depression symptoms over time, even when taking into account initial symptom levels (Naragon-Gainey, Gallagher, & Brown, 2013).

Positive affect has been shown to foster resilience and adaptive coping. For example, Fredrickson's broaden-and-build framework details how positive emotion diverts attention to the external world, bolsters creativity, and makes people more prosocial, in turn building that individual's personal resources to cope with potential future setbacks (see Garland, Fredrickson, Kring, Johnson, Meyer, & Penn, 2010). It is therefore possible that residual anhedonia may constitute an important vulnerability factor for relapse following recovery from a depressive episode. Consistent with this proposition, low levels of well-being predict 10-year depression levels (Wood & Joseph, 2010) and self-reported anhedonia has been associated with depression symptoms over a 20-year period (Shankman, Nelson, Harrow, & Full, 2010). Moreover, mindfulness-based cognitive therapy (MBCT) (Segal, Williams, & Teasdale, 2002) – a group intervention with proven efficacy to reduce relapse rates in depression vulnerable individuals (see meta-analysis by Piet & Hougaard, 2011) – may in part work by bolstering positive affective experience (Geschwind Peeters, Drukker, van Os, & Wichers, 2011; Batink, Peeters, Geschwind, Van Os, & Wichers, 2013).

Can Positive Interventions Bolster Well-being and Reduce Depression?

We now review evidence examining whether psychological techniques that aim to bolster positivity can be effectively used in depression. The earliest evidence in support of recognizably "positive psychology" approaches emerged from work of Seligman and colleagues. The use of self-guided positive psychology exercises were shown to have beneficial effects in reducing dysphoria (Seligman, Steen, Park, & Peterson, 2005). Mildly depressed volunteers ($N = 411$) were randomized to complete one of five positive psychology techniques (gratitude letter, writing about three good things, writing about a time they were at their best, identifying signature strengths, and using strengths in a new way) or to a placebo condition (writing about an early memory). Participants in all activities received a boost in happiness and a reduction in depression symptoms. However, in the placebo condition this effect had dissipated one week later, whereas in the positive conditions the effects persisted. Moreover, the "three good things" and "using signature strengths in a new way" exercises continued to confer benefits at six month follow up.

Later studies found these approaches can work in individuals with more significant depression. Mildly to moderately depressed young adults showed a benefit from participating in group positive psychotherapy (PPT), which involves using different positive psychology exercises over six weeks (Seligman, Rashid, & Parks, 2006, Study 1). PPT ($N = 19$), relative to a no-treatment control ($N = 21$), lowered depression symptoms and raised life satisfaction. These benefits to some extent persisted at one-year follow-up. An adapted form of PPT (delivered in individual format and targeting both bolstering positivity and reducing negativity) was evaluated in adults with a diagnosis of major depressive disorder (Seligman et al., 2006, Study 2). PPT ($N = 13$) produced greater increase in happiness, reduction in sadness, and elevated remission rates, compared with treatment as usual (TAU) ($N = 15$) or treatment as usual with medication ($N = 17$). However, the TAU condition in this study consisted of an integrative and eclectic approach rather than a proven active intervention, the study was only partially randomized, and a small sample size was used. An interesting recent study suggests that use of these positive psychology exercises is feasible and leads to short-term gains in building optimism and reduced hopelessness in suicidal inpatients (Huffman et al., 2014). However, not all the positive psychology exercises were well received. For example, writing a "forgiveness letter" often led to a resurgence of sadness or anger in this severely depressed sample.

Another good example of a positive psychology intervention is well-being therapy (WBT), developed by Fava and colleagues. This aims to bolster well-being in depressed or other clinical populations by building a sense of balance and development in Ryff's six areas of eudaimonic well-being (autonomy, environmental mastery, personal growth, purpose in life, self-acceptance, and positive interpersonal relationships) (Ryff & Singer, 1996; see review by Ruini & Fava, 2012). There is encouraging preliminary evidence of the efficacy of WBT, although more research is needed. For example, WBT can effectively treat residual symptoms in those with mood disorders who had partially responded to previous pharmacological or behavioral interventions, with some hints of superiority over standard CBT as a residual intervention (Fava, Rafanelli, Grandi, Canestrari, & Morphy, 1998a). A combination of standard CBT with well-being therapy has been shown to reduce depressive relapse in those with a history of three or more episodes of depression who are currently well, compared to standard clinical management (Fava, Rafanelli, Grandi, Conti, & Belluardo, 1998b).

Two additional positive psychology approaches that also show promise are broad minded affective coping (BMAC) (Tarrier, 2010) and goal-setting and planning (GAP) (MacLeod, Coates, & Hetherton, 2008). BMAC is a positive emotion induction technique (intended to be used in conjunction with other psychological therapies) that encourages individuals to recall and relive positive autobiographical memories using imagery techniques (Tarrier, 2010). BMAC has been shown to bolster positivity in PTSD (Panagioti, Gooding, & Tarrier, 2012) and psychosis (Johnson, Gooding, Wood, Fair, & Tarrier, 2013), although it has yet to be extensively validated in depression. GAP is a well-being intervention that encourages individuals to set, and work toward realizing, positive goals that are self-concordant (i.e., are intrinsically rewarding and aligned with a person's self-identity) (see Sheldon, 1999). GAP has been shown to be effective at bolstering well-being and reducing depression symptoms in both nonclinical and clinical samples (MacLeod et al., 2008; Ferguson, Conway, Endersby, & MacLeod, 2009; Coote & MacLeod, 2012; Farquharson & MacLeod, 2014).

A recent meta-analysis examined how well these positive psychology techniques bolster well-being and decrease depressive symptoms, combining fifty-one studies with a total sample of 4,266 individuals (Sin & Lyubomirsky, 2009). These studies had a mixture of nonclinical and clinical (predominantly depressed) samples. In general, positive psychology approaches were effective at both reducing depression symptoms (pooled $r = .31$) and promoting well-being (pooled $r = .29$), compared with control conditions. However, there was considerable heterogeneity between studies (well-being effect sizes ranged from $-.31$ to $.84$; depression effect sizes ranged from $-.28$ to $.81$). Interestingly, there was some evidence that beneficial effects became *more* marked with increasing depression severity, potentially indicating positive psychology techniques may be of particular benefit to those who are depressed.

In general, this provides support for the possible efficacy of positivity techniques in depression. However, there are important limitations to note with this meta-analysis. First, very few of the studies included in the meta-analyses included significantly clinically depressed participants and it is unclear if these beneficial effects found in mild dysphoria will always transfer to more severe depression presentations. Second, the finding that interventions were more effective with increasing depression symptoms was significant only in fixed effects analyses and not random effects analyses (arguably a more appropriate model given the heterogeneity in interventions included in the meta-analysis). Third, a lack of methodological stringency may have led to an inflated estimate of the effects of these positive psychology techniques. Indeed, a more recent meta-analysis that included only studies that used a randomized controlled trial design) found a far smaller overall beneficial effect (0.3 effect size points lower) (Bolier, Haverman, Westerhof, Riper, Smit, & Bohlmeijer, 2013).

Notwithstanding these caveats, there is promising support for positive psychology treatments of depression. However, what is needed is more definitive randomized controlled trial evaluation of these approaches in significantly depressed populations. Further, the possibility that these positive techniques may also be helpful in preventing subsequent relapse in depression vulnerable individuals needs to be satisfactorily evaluated. It is plausible that positive psychology approaches may be particularly helpful in preventing relapse because these techniques continue to be relevant to the individual even when they are no longer experiencing a depressive episode.

It is also important to point out that, even assuming that exactly the same effect sizes emerge in more definitive trials, these interventions are highly unlikely to be satisfactory standalone treatments for depression. Blunted positivity is only one half of the depression picture and it continues to be important to help clients reduce elevated negativity. What is needed now is a systematic integration of positive- and negative-oriented approaches into a unified treatment package that simultaneously reduces negativity and builds positivity – a positive clinical psychology agenda. Such approaches are likely to have the greatest chance of treating acute depression and protecting individuals from subsequent relapse.

The Pitfalls of Positive Psychology Approaches in Depression: The "Pollyanna Problem"

Having so far presented the possible benefits of a positive psychology agenda, it is also important to consider some of the pitfalls inherent in this approach. A focus on positivity can seem naively optimistic about the world and this can invalidate individuals' suffering and distress. These concerns seem particularly pertinent in the context of depression, where discussing positive objectives can seem entirely out of reach and irrelevant in the midst of an acute depressive episode. This has previously been referred to as the "Pollyanna problem" (Dunn, 2012). For example, asking a depressed client to engage in gratitude or kindness exercises when they are feeling suicidal and potentially resentful to the world is, if not sensitively and skillfully executed, likely to be experienced as invalidating.

There is evidence that positive psychology interventions work best in those who apply high effort and are intrinsically motivated to perform them (e.g., Sheldon & Lyubomirsky, 2006), and these characteristics are unlikely to match the severely depressed state. More worryingly (and contradicting findings from the Sin and Lyubomirsky meta-analysis), there is emerging evidence of positive psychology techniques backfiring in those with low mood. For example, the use of positive self-statements (e.g., saying to self "I'm a successful person") while helpful in those with high self-esteem, *lowered* positive mood in those with low self-esteem (Wood, Perunovic, & Lee, 2009). The practice of gratitude led to a *drop* in well-being in dysphoric students (Sin, Della Porta, & Lyubomirsky, 2011). As discussed earlier, forgiveness letters also generated sadness and anger in suicidally depressed inpatient populations (Huffman et al., 2014).

Why might depressed clients be reluctant to engage with a positive agenda and why might these approaches sometimes backfire in depressed populations? There is a long (albeit controversial) tradition arguing that depressed individuals exhibit "depressive realism," whereby they lose the positive information-processing biases that lead to nondepressed individuals seeing the world in an overly optimistic light (Alloy & Abramson, 1979; see Moore & Fresco, 2012). Moreover, it has been proposed that adopting a position of "defensive pessimism" can protect individuals from experiencing hurt when life does not live up to hopes and expectations (Norem & Cantor, 1986). Therefore, depressed individuals may be understandably reluctant to contemplate engaging with a positive agenda if they subscribe to the "realism" or "defensive pessimism" viewpoint.

Moreover, depressed clients can be actively afraid of experiencing positive emotions (Werner-Seidler, Banks, Dunn, & Moulds, 2013; Gilbert, McEwan, Catarino, Baiao, & Palmeira, 2014), and so will go to some lengths to avoid being put in touch with pleasure. Anecdotally, many depressed individuals report that there is an inevitable "fall back to earth" following fleeting moments of pleasure. The contrast between feeling good and the default depressed state is highly aversive, meaning individuals sometimes would rather never enjoy anything at all than experience this contrast. This is similar to contrast avoidance models of worry (e.g., Newman & Llera, 2011; Cooper, Miranda, & Mennin, 2013), but as far as we are aware this framework has yet to be empirically validated in depression in the context of positive experience. If this does turn out to be the case for depression, simply suggesting that depressed individuals engage in positive psychology exercises is unlikely to be constructive until this fear of positive affect has been worked through.

Related to this, depressed individuals frequently report chronic feelings of guilt and shame and the belief that they do not deserve happiness (Gilbert, 2009). There is evidence that beliefs about deserving bad outcomes result in self-defeating behaviors and self-handicapping (Callan, Kay, & Dawtry, 2014) and that a sense of personal deservingness increases anticipatory depressed mood and self-blame when contemplating rejection (Major, Kaiser, & McCoy, 2003). Moreover, feelings of guilt and shame can cause the intentional self-denial of pleasurable experience and engagement in self-punishment (Nelissen & Zeelenberg, 2009; Bastian, Jetten, & Fasoli, 2011; Inbar, Pizarro, Gilovich, & Ariely, 2012; Nelissen, 2012; Watanabe & Ohtsubo, 2012). In this context, positive psychology approaches may be experienced as being at odds with a sense of deserving bad outcomes, and engaging in gratitude exercises may result in paradoxical increases in feelings of guilt and subsequent self-punishment if such beliefs have not been addressed.

Some have also argued that if individuals exhibit certain expectations and behaviors, the quest for happiness can be actively unhelpful (Ford & Mauss, 2013). For example, if individuals set unreasonably high standards for happiness (i.e., expect to enjoy things perfectly), engage in counterproductive action to attain happiness (e.g., chasing status, money, or promotion, rather than seeking social connection), and constantly monitor their own emotional state, then this can lead to potentially positive experiences becoming actively aversive. It is noteworthy that a number of basic science studies report that depressed individuals show a paradoxical increase in sadness to positive stimuli (e.g., Rottenberg, Kasch, Gross, & Gotlib, 2002; Dunn et al., 2004), which may in part relate to these characteristics.

So how should positive clinical psychology approaches deal with the "Pollyanna problem"? One approach is to tailor existing positive psychology interventions for depressed clients (see Sin et al., 2011). For example, it is important to provide more individualized interventions with greater therapeutic guidance and greater treatment duration in acutely depressed participants. Further, it should be ensured that the client is committed to the treatment and believes it will be helpful rather than it being assigned to them (e.g., Sin & Lyubomirsky, 2009). Moreover, it is useful to play to an individual's strengths by ensuring there is a good fit between them and the activity. For example, a sociable individual may benefit more from social activities (e.g., acts of kindness) than those who are solitary (e.g., reflective journal about personal positive traits). Likewise, process-focused activities tend to be more beneficial to well-being than performance-focused ones, and are more likely to promote engagement with unfolding positive experience (Elliott & Dweck, 1988).

Moreover, it is necessary to be realistic about the scope of positive change for each individual client. It has been argued that individuals have a genetic "setpoint" for happiness which determines their capacity to experience positive emotions in life (Lyubomirsky, Sheldon, & Schkade, 2005). Depression vulnerable individuals are likely to have a dispositionally low happiness setpoint, setting a ceiling on the potential for growth in positivity. If individuals are encouraged to push for a level of positivity significantly above this setpoint, this could gradually alienate them over the course of treatment.

The "Pollyanna problem" is not the only risk associated with positive psychology approaches. Chasing positive mood may also be problematic in individuals with manic features. These features are often not detected during clinical assessment and individuals are treated as though they have unipolar rather than bipolar depression (e.g., see Hirschfield, Lewis, & Vornik, 2003). Positive psychology techniques could promote an unhelpful ascent into mania in these individuals (see Mansell, 2006; Johnson, Gooding, Wood, Fair, & Tarrier, 2013).

An Agenda for Positive Clinical Psychology Approaches to Depression

Despite these caveats around the "Pollyanna problem," there is still a strong case for focusing more explicitly on building positivity in depression interventions. The final part of this chapter will comment on what we see as sensible areas on which positive clinical psychology approaches to depression might focus in the future.

Agreeing Universal Measures of Anhedonia to Incorporate into Treatment Trials

It is accepted that rigorous evaluation of positive clinical psychology approaches will be required (see Wood & Tarrier, 2010). However, this is currently thwarted by the lack of "gold standard" well-validated self-report and interview measures of anhedonic symptoms that can be routinely incorporated into randomized controlled trials. In addition to leading to more robust evaluation of each particular intervention, this would also aid comparison between them. For example, existing meta-analyses of positive psychology approaches typically have to aggregate very diverse measures of outcome (see Sin & Lyubomirsky, 2009; Bolier et al., 2013), minimizing conviction in the conclusions drawn.

Clinical interviews like the Structured Clinical Interview for Diagnosis (SCID-I) (First, Spitzer, Gibbon, & Williams, 1997) and the Hamilton Depression Rating Scale (HDRS) (Hamilton, 1960), and self-report scales like the Beck Depression Inventory (BDI-II) (Beck, Steer, & Brown, 1996) and the Patient Health Questionnaire (PHQ-9) (Kroenke, Spitzer, & Williams, 2001) are widely deployed in research, and frequently in routine clinical, settings. While these scales do include some items measuring anhedonia, they make a very small contribution to the overall scale (e.g., on the BDI-II only two out of twenty-one items index anhedonia) and suffer from range restriction if considered as separate anhedonia factors. Research trials and routine clinical practice need instead to deploy bespoke anhedonia measures.

Candidate self-report measures of anhedonia include the Snaith–Hamilton Pleasure Scale (Snaith et al., 1995; Nakozeny et al., 2010), indexing consummatory pleasure – a measure well validated in depressed populations. A good measure of positive and negative mood is the Positive Affect Negative Affect Schedule (PANAS) (Watson et al., 1988), which has been used extensively in state and trait forms, including in depression studies. The Mood and Anxiety Symptom Questionnaire (MASQ) (Watson & Clark, 1991) includes factors measuring depression-specific anhedonia symptoms, anxiety-specific bodily arousal symptoms, and elevations in negative affect ("general distress") common to both anxiety and depression.

No single depression-validated measure satisfactorily captures the broad range of different forms of positive affect (in particular, including levels of positivity at high, medium and low levels of arousal) and so there is a need for further scale development. Given the emergence of the Research Domains Criteria framework (RdoC) (see Insel et al., 2010), it also makes sense for a battery of self-report measures to be established that captures the various distinctions in the positive affect system (e.g., facets of reward system functioning: reward valuation, willingness to work for reward, reward expectancy, action selection, initial and sustained responsiveness to reward, reward learning; regulation of the social engagement system) (see Porges, 2007).

Better Characterizing Anhedonia Deficits in Depression

It is also important to improve characterization of the nature of anhedonia in depression. While clinicians tend to have sensitively nuanced vocabulary to differentiate different flavors and blends of negative emotions (e.g., fractionating disgust, shame, and guilt), a somewhat impoverished vocabulary exists for positive experience (e.g., focusing solely on activity "pleasantness" in CBT). Clearly there are multiple forms of positive affect (e.g., joy, excitement, contentment, love) and we need a better clinical vocabulary to describe them and a taxonomy to classify them. Basic science laboratory work can help to identify which of these positive states are most likely to be affected in depression. For example, in preliminary work, depression has been linked to more marked deficits in pride relative to happiness and amusement (Gruber, Oveis, Keltner, & Johnson, 2011). Existing research has tended to focus on high arousal positive affect states such as excitement and amusement, and it will be important also to look at low arousal positive affect states like contentment and tranquility. In particular, individuals with depression and related forms of psychopathology may especially struggle with activating affect systems that promote contentment, soothing, and safeness in situations where there is no threat and sufficient physical and socioemotional resources are available (Gilbert, 2009, 2014).

Additionally, the field has typically viewed positive emotion experience as a static phenomenon, but it is now apparent that positive affect unfolds over time ("affective chronometry") (Davidson, 1998). For example, we feel pleasure when anticipating an event, when experiencing it, and when recalling it. Moreover, during an event we can distinguish between our baseline mood at the start (likely to be a habitual "setpoint"), how much mood increases during the activity ("emotion reactivity"), and how long this mood increase is sustained after the activity ("emotion regulation") (see Dyn Affect framework) (Kuppens, Oravecz, & Tuerlinckx, 2010). There is emerging evidence that depression may be associated with deficits, particularly in sustaining positive emotion experience (Heller et al., 2009), but more work is needed to characterize fully the temporal profile of positive affect in the disorder.

It is also important to note that disturbances in positivity in depression extend beyond positive affect experience. There is strong evidence of a reduction or reversal of typically held positive information-processing biases when depressed (i.e., deficits in positive cognition). For example, depressed individuals do not judge their performance as better than it actually is (Dunn, 2007a); rather, they estimate that fewer positive events will happen to them than do nondepressed individuals (MacLeod & Byrne, 1996); they do not preferentially attend to and recall positive information over negative information (e.g., Matt, Vazquez, & Campbell, 1992; McCabe & Gotlib, 2005); and they show a less richly elaborated positive (relative to negative) auto-biographical memory structure (Dalgleish et al., 2011).

Moreover, as discussed earlier, neuroscience has identified how the reward system fractionates into "wanting" (motivation to work toward reward), "liking" (pleasure experienced when attaining awards), and "learning" (changes in behavior/thinking following rewards) components (Kringelbach & Berridge, 2009). Depression has been associated with disturbances in all three systems, each predicting a poor depression course (see Bylsma et al., 2008; Treadway et al., 2012; Vrieze et al., 2013). However, possible interactions between these different systems (and how they map onto the psychological experience of anhedonia) are poorly understood and need to be examined in future research.

We also need to recognize that depression may vary in its presentation over its life course. For example, there may be important similarities and differences in positivity deficits (or pockets of preserved function) that predict vulnerability to first onset, early episodes of depression, episodes of depression in a more chronic course, and pockets of recovery/residual symptoms between episodes. It is largely unknown how positivity changes across these phases. Longitudinal cohort designs (where the same individuals are tested at multiple time points) could be deployed to explore these issues.

Identifying Mechanisms Maintaining Anhedonia in Depression

A majority of positive psychology interventions to date are "mechanism neutral." In other words, a practice is evaluated as being helpful in building positivity without much explicit consideration of what underlying positivity blocking or bolstering mechanism is being manipulated. Considerable gains in the anxiety disorder field have been made by identifying, and then explicitly targeting, anxiety maintenance mechanisms, including in PTSD (e.g., Ehlers, Clark, Hackmann, McManus, & Fennell, 2005), social phobia (Clark et al., 2003), and panic disorder (Clark, Salkovis, Hackmann, Middleton, Anastasiades, & Gelder, 1994). Such an approach could also lead to stepwise gains in our capacity to repair anhedonia in depression.

A range of promising anhedonia maintenance mechanisms are starting to emerge from the basic science literature, but more work is needed. Here we will briefly discuss three promising candidate mechanisms, linked to reduced pleasure experience, on which our research group is currently focusing: positive appraisal style, mind-wandering, and a disconnection from the body.

There is now good evidence that depressed individuals differ in how they appraise their own positive emotion experience. In particular, depressed individuals are more likely to utilize "dampening" appraisals (e.g., think "this is too good to last" or "I don't deserve this"), reducing happiness and increasing negative emotional experience (Feldman, Joormann, & Johnson, 2008). Similarly, depressed individuals show reduced use of amplifying appraisals that can increase or sustain happiness experience, for example, they are less likely to think "I am living up to my potential" (self-focus) or to dwell on how positive they feel (emotion-focus). In cross-sectional studies, greater dampening and lesser emotion focus are linked to depression (Feldman et al., 2008; Raes, Smets, Nelis, & Schoofs, 2012; Raes et al., 2014). The anhedonic symptoms of depression are cross-sectionally related to elevated dampening and reduced emotion-focus appraisals, even when controlling for the other symptoms of depression (Werner-Seidler et al., 2013). What is required now is evidence that causally manipulating positive appraisal style can increase or decrease reactivity to positive material and alter positive mood.

Another promising anhedonia maintenance mechanism is that depressed individuals struggle to keep their attention in the moment during positive activities and instead their mind can "wander." A large experience-sampling study in the general population found that mind-wandering reduced pleasure during everyday life, particularly if the mind wandered to negative or neutral themes (Killingsworth & Gilbert, 2010). There is now good evidence that depressed individuals show elevated mind-wandering. Self-reported mind-wandering has been shown to correlate with depression severity (Smallwood, O'Connor, & Heim, 2005; Smallwood, O'Connor, Sudbury, & Obonsawin, 2007; Stawarczyk, Majerus, Van der Linden, & D'Argembeau 2012; Murphy, Macpherson, Jeyabalasingham, Manly, & Dunn 2013). It seems plausible that this elevated mind-wandering could in part drive anhedonia, blocking experiential engagement with potentially rewarding activities. Studies are now needed examining whether elevated mind-wandering does indeed partly mediate the relationship between depression and reduced happiness during everyday pleasant activities. A key question to resolve is whether all forms of mind-wandering are unhelpful or if it depends on the nature of the mind-wandering. For example, the mind-wandering to an anticipated positive future occurrence during a routine task could actually bolster positive mood.

A third plausible candidate anhedonia mechanism is that depressed individuals are disconnected from the bodily feedback processes that amplify affect. The collection of processes by which physiological signals in the body are transmitted back to the brain is referred to as "interoception" (see Cameron, 2001, p. 534; Craig, 2009). There is now reasonable evidence that interoception impacts on a wide range of cognitive-affective processes, including emotion-experience and decision-making (Dunn et al., 2010b; Dunn, Evans, Makarova, White, & Clark, 2012). These results are consistent with frameworks arguing that the body has a causal role in how we think (e.g., Somatic Marker Hypothesis, Damasio, 1994; for a review, see Dunn, Dalgleish, & Lawrence, 2006) and feel (e.g., James–Lange theory of emotion, James, 1894; for a review, see Dalgleish, Dunn, & Mobbs, 2009). Interoceptive awareness (measured by the capacity to monitor the heart accurately) has been shown to be impaired in depression (Dunn et al., 2007; Dunn, Stefanovitch, Evans, Oliver, Hawkins, & Dalgleish, 2010a; Furman, Waugh, Bhattacharjee, Thompson, & Gotlib, 2013), and preliminary evidence suggests that relates particularly to anhedonic symptoms of the disorder (Dunn et al., 2009; Furman et al., 2013; see Harshaw, in press).

There is increasing acknowledgement of the potential potency of working with the body (Farb et al., submitted). However, in order to harness this potential to bolster positivity, it is likely to be necessary to move to a more fine-grained level of analysis of how the interoception system works. It has recently been argued that interoception needs to be subdivided into at least three components: (1) the nature of the bodily response (i.e., signal); (2) how accurately the bodily response is perceived (i.e., perception); and (3) how the bodily response is appraised (i.e., appraisal) (Verdejo-Garcia, Clark, & Dunn, 2012). It is conceivable that different intervention techniques could act on each of these systems to alter positive affect function. For example, bodily meditation practices may increase the ability to perceive and label changes in the body (see Mirams, Poliakoff, Brown, & Lloyd, 2013; although see Parkin et al., 2014). Certain kinds of relaxation exercises may promote para-sympathetic nervous system activation linked with contentment and calm (cf. Polyvagal theory) (Porges, 2007; see Gilbert, 2009). Finally, certain kinds of appraisal training could alter how individuals make sense of internal bodily responses (analogous to internal appraisal focus in bipolar and panic disorder cognitive models) (e.g., Mansell, 2006).

What is needed next is delineation of further mechanisms driving anhedonia. Moreover, systematic and careful evaluation is required of how these mechanisms interact with each other to impact on the various components of the positive affect system (e.g., reward wanting versus liking versus learning; reward anticipation versus direct experience versus recall). Experimental and naturalistic manipulation designs that increase or decrease candidate mechanisms need to be used to evaluate if these mechanisms causally drive changes in positive affect. These manipulation techniques, if successful, can serve as the building blocks for subsequent clinical interventions. It has already been illustrated that this kind of translational research pathway can deliver concrete outcomes. For example, work showing that depressed individuals struggle to recall specific positive autobiographical memories (Williams et al., 2007) has now led to emerging memory specificity (Neshat-Doost et al., 2013) and memory recall (method of loci approach) (Dalgleish, Navrady, Bird, Hill, Dunn, & Golden, 2013) training.

We also need to develop clinically appropriate (and sufficiently brief) measures for assessing these constructs, to be able to tell how effective our treatments are at targeting these mechanisms and if changes in these mechanisms are associated with superior treatment outcomes. This could help lead to a more 'personalized medicine' approach, where we adapt our interventions for the needs of a particular client (similar to successful interventions emerging in the cancer domain) (see Mendelsohn, Tursz, Schilsky, & Lazar, 2011). For example, if mind-wandering does cause anhedonia, then mindfulness training techniques to help individuals "stay in the moment" may be particularly helpful for those individuals who exhibit mind-wandering difficulties at assessment.

Focusing on Building Client Motivation

A major stumbling block with positive psychology interventions is that clients may lack motivation to engage with them in the first place. Rather than assuming depressed individuals want to feel more positive, it will be critical for intervention approaches explicitly to formulate and overcome motivational obstacles for each client. This process can be facilitated by utilizing insights from basic science research into goal setting in depression. Personal goal difficulties are common in depression (Hadley & MacLeod, 2010), with depressed individuals perceiving their goals to be unattainable, uncontrollable, and in conflict with each other (Dickson & Moberly, 2010; Dickson, Moberly, & Kinderman, 2011). Depression is also associated with holding fewer approach goals (goals motivated by working to move toward desired outcomes), and making less specific and more avoidant plans for goal pursuit (Dickson & MacLeod, 2004). Pursuing avoidance goals (working to move away from feared outcomes) may be unhelpful, and is linked with reduced progress and satisfaction with the goal and poorer coping (Elliot & Sheldon, 1997; Elliot, Thrash, & Murayama, 2011). It is beneficial to pursue intrinsically motivated goals (i.e., "doing something because it is inherently interesting or enjoyable") (Ryan & Deci, 2000, p. 55), and this is central in supporting individuals to develop a sense of autonomy, competence, and relatedness (core psychological needs), which is beneficial to mental health (Sheldon & Elliott, 1999; Deci & Ryan, 2000, 2002; Neimiec, Ryan, & Deci, 2009). In contrast, goals that are extrinsically motivated (i.e., "doing something because it leads to a separable outcome"; Ryan & Deci, 2000, p. 55), are associated with poorer mental health and are not beneficial to well-being (Deci & Ryan, 2002; Neimiec et al., 2009). It can also be helpful to set goals with learning rather than performance objectives, as when an individual is low in confidence this is more likely to lead to effective problem-solving (Elliott & Dweck, 1988).

Harnessing Digital Technology

There has been an explosion of availability and use of mobile computing technology in recent years. This digital technology can be harnessed to help achieve widespread (and affordable) access to positive clinical psychology approaches – a key issue given that a vast majority of depression goes undetected and untreated by clinical services (Gilbody, Whitty, Grimshaw, & Thomas, 2003). The positive psychology movement has been an early adopter of digital approaches (e.g., see Schueller & Parks, 2014) with some success. There is potential to use experience-sampling applications to provide individuals with personalized feedback about their engagement with reward in everyday life (e.g., Kramer et al., 2014), and also to bolster information-processing styles that maximize pleasure experience (e.g., train a positive facial recognition bias) (Penton-Voak, Bate, Lewis, & Munafo, 2013).

It is important to ensure that these digital applications are not perceived as "Pollyannaish," In the absence of the right kind of support, there is potential for internet treatments to backfire (see Rozental et al., 2014, for a discussion of negative effects of internet interventions). One possible way forward is to consider embedding these positive psychology digital applications within standard one-to-one therapies (e.g., as homework or practice between sessions).

Tapping the Potential of Implementation Science

Essential in the design of positive clinical psychology interventions for depressed populations will be ensuring that they are fit for purpose for end users (clinicians administering them, commissioners funding them, and, most importantly, the depressed clients undergoing them). This could be achieved by tapping into the emerging field of implementation science, which focuses on maximizing the integration of research findings and evidence into healthcare policy and routine practice (e.g., see Schillinger, 2010). Historically, implementation has been thought of as something to consider only after an intervention has been shown to be effective in an "ivory tower" randomized controlled trial. Often, however, it is then too late to make substantive amendments to a treatment protocol. In a worst-case scenario, an effective treatment developed in the ivory tower may not be adopted in the health care system because it is not fit for that real-world context. Therefore, it makes good scientific and economic sense to consider implementation from the outset (e.g., see Medical Research Council, 2008).

One example of a proven framework is the intervention mapping procedure (Bartholomew, Parcel, Kok, Gottlieb, & Fernandez, 2011). This has shown utility both for developing novel interventions (e.g., a schools-based program for obesity) (Lloyd, Logan, Greaves, & Wyatt, 2011) and adapting existing interventions for novel contexts (e.g., a return to work program for stress-related mental health problems) (van Oostrom, Anema, Terluin, Venema, de Vet, & van Mechelen, 2007). Service-user consultation may be particularly important to help minimize the "Pollyanna problem" discussed earlier in this chapter.

Another useful conceptual framework from implementation is May's work on normalization. This is defined as the routine embedding of a technique or organizational practice in everyday life, whereby individuals work individually and collectively to implement new approaches (May et al., 2007; May & Finch, 2009). Successful normalization critically relies on building a sense of coherence about what the practice entails; ensuring cognitive participation of key stakeholders in the practice; building a system that supports and organizes involvement in the practice, and encouraging reflexive monitoring of the value and success of the practice.

Conclusion

This chapter has made the case that by simultaneously targeting reducing negativity *and* building positivity, outcomes following depression treatment are likely to improve (i.e., a greater acute treatment response, reduced likelihood of subsequent relapse, and enhanced subjective well-being). Such advances are most likely to come about by integrating existing depression-focused clinical interventions with elements drawn from positive psychology, adapting these positive elements carefully to minimize the "Pollyanna problem" and maximize the potential for therapeutic gains. An agenda has been proposed to help facilitate the development of effective positive clinical psychology interventions that work toward this goal, including recommendations for how to measure positive changes in treatment evaluations; how better to characterize positivity disturbances and the mechanisms that maintain them; how best to support and enhance client motivation; the harnessing of digital technology, and capitalization on insights from implementation science. Such an agenda offers exciting opportunities to capitalize on recent insights from the fields of clinical and positive psychology to develop innovative new approaches to depression. We believe there is potential to deliver stepwise gains in depression treatment outcomes through the movement to a positive clinical psychology framework.

Acknowledgments

Thanks to Sophie Dunn, Leigh-Anne Burr, Grace Fisher, and Harriet Bunker-Smith for helpful feedback on earlier drafts of this chapter.

References

Alloy, L. & Abramson, L. (1979). Judgment of contingency in depressed and nondepressed students: Sadder but wiser? *Journal of Experimental Psychology: General, 108*, 441–485. doi.org/10.1037/0096-3445.108.4.441.

Anderson, I. M., Ferrier, I. N., Balwin, R. C., Cowen, P. J., Howard, L., Lewis, G., & Tylee, A. (2008). Evidence-based guidelines for treating depressive disorders with antidepressants: A revision of the 2000 British Association for Psychopharmacology guidelines. *Journal of Psychopharmacology, 22*, 343–396. doi.org/10.1177/0269881107088441.

Bartholomew, L. K., Parcel, G. S., Kok, G., Gottlieb, N. H., & Fernandez, M. E. (2011). *Planning health promotion programs: An intervention mapping approach.* San Francisco: John Wiley.

Bastian, B., Jetten, J., & Fasoli, F. (2011). Cleansing the soul by hurting the flesh: The guilt-reducing effect of pain. *Psychological Science, 22*, 334–335. doi.org/10.1177/0956797610397058.

Batink, T., Peeters, F., Geschwind, N., Van Os, J., & Wichers, M. (2013). How does MBCT for depression work? Studying cognitive and affective mediation pathways. *PLosONE, 8*, e72778. doi.org/10.1371/journal.pone.0072778.

Beck, A. T. (2005). The current state of cognitive therapy: A 40-year retrospective. *Archives of General Psychiatry, 62*, 953–959. doi.org/10.1001/archpsyc.62.9.953.

Beck, A. T., Rush, A. J., Shaw, B. F., & Emery, G. (1979). *Cognitive therapy of depression.* New York: Guilford.

Beck, A. T., Steer, R. A., & Brown, G. K. (1996). *BDI-II, Beck depression inventory: Manual.* San Antonio, TX: Psychological Corporation.

Bolier, L., Haverman, M., Westerhof, G. J., Riper, H., Smit, F., & Bohlmeijer, E. (2013). Positive psychology interventions: A meta-analysis of randomized controlled studies. *BMC Public Health, 13*, 119. doi.org/10.1186/1471-2458-13-119.

Brown, T. A. (2007). Temporal course and structural relationships among dimensions of temperament and DSM-IV anxiety and mood disorder constructs. *Journal of Abnormal Psychology, 116*, 313–328. doi.org/10.1037/0021-843X.116.2.313.

Butler, A. C., Chapman, J. E., Forman, E. M., & Beck, A. T. (2006). The empirical status of cognitive-behavioral therapy: A review of meta-analyses. *Clinical Psychology Review, 26*, 17–31. doi.org/10.1016/j.cpr.2005.07.003.

Bylsma, L. M., Morris, B. H., & Rottenberg, J. (2008). A meta-analysis of emotional reactivity in major depressive disorder. *Clinical Psychology Review, 28*, 676–691. doi.org/10.1016/j.cpr.2007.10.001.

Bylsma, L. M., Taylor-Clift, A., & Rottenberg, J. (2011). Emotional reactivity to daily events in major and minor depression. *Journal of Abnormal Psychology, 120*, 155–167. doi.org/10.1037/a0021662.

Callan, M. J., Kay, A. C., & Dawtry, R. J. (2014). Making sense of misfortune: Deservingness, self-esteem, and patterns of self-defeat. *Journal of Personality and Social Psychology, 107*, 142–162. doi.org/10.1037/a0036640.

Cameron, O. G. (2001). Interoception: The inside story – a model of psychosomatic processes. *Psychosomatic Medicine, 63*, 697–710. doi.org/10.1097/00006842-200109000-00001.

Clark, D. M., Ehlers, A., McManus, F., Hackmann, A., Fennell, M., Campbell, H., Flower, T., Davenport, C., & Louis, B. (2003). Cognitive therapy versus fluoxetine in generalized social phobia: A randomized placebo-controlled trial. *Journal of Consulting and Clinical Psychology, 71*, 1058–1067. doi.org/10.1037/0022-006X.71.6.1058.

Clark, D. M., Salkovis, P. M., Hackmann, A., Middleton, H., Anastasiades, P., & Gelder, M. (1994). A comparison of cognitive therapy, applied relaxation and imipramine in the treatment of panic disorder. *British Journal of Psychiatry, 164*, 759–769. doi.org/10.1192/bjp.164.6.759.

Cooper, S. E., Miranda, R., & Mennin, D. S. (2013). Behavioral indicators of emotion avoidance and subsequent worry in generalized anxiety disorder and depression. *Journal of Experimental Psychopathology, 5*, 566–583.

Coote, H. & MacLeod, A. (2012). A self-help, positive goal-focused intervention to increase well-being in people with depression. *Clinical Psychology and Psychotherapy, 19*, 305–315. doi.org/10.1002/cpp.1797.

Craig, A. D. (2009). How do you feel – now? The anterior insula and human awareness. *Nature Reviews Neuroscience, 10*, 59–70. doi.org/10.1038/nrn2555.

Cuijpers, P., Karyotaki, E., Weitz, E., Andersson, G., Hollon, S. D., & Streets, A. (2014). The effects of psychotherapies for major depression in adults on remission, recovery and improvement: A meta-analysis. *Journal of Affective Disorders, 159*, 118–126, doi.org/10.1016/j.jad.2014.02.026.

Cuijpers, P., Turner, L. H., Mohr, D. C., Hofmann, S. G., Andersson, G., Berking, M., & Coyne, J. (2014). Comparison of psychotherapies for adult depression to pill placebo control groups: a meta-analysis. *Psychological Medicine, 44*, 685–695. doi.org/10.1017/S0033291713000457.

Cuijpers, P., van Straten, A., Andersson, G., & van Oppen, P. (2008). Psychotherapy for depression in adults: A meta-analysis of comparative outcome studies. *Journal of Consulting and Clinical Psychology, 76*, 909–922. doi.org/10.1037/a0013075.

Dalgleish, T., Dunn, B. D., & Mobbs, D. (2009). Affective neuroscience: Past, present and future. *Emotion Review, 1*, 355–368. doi.org/10.1177/1754073909338307.

Dalgleish, T., Hill, E., Golden, A. M., Morant, N., & Dunn, B. D. (2011). The structure of past and future lives in depression. *Journal of Abnormal Psychology, 120*, 1–15. doi.org/10.1037/a0020797.

Dalgleish, T., Navrady, L., Bird, L., Hill, E., Dunn, B. D., & Golden, A. M. (2013). Method-of-loci as a mnemonic device to facilitate access to self-affirming personal memories for individuals with depression. *Clinical Psychological Science, 1*, 156–162. doi.org/10.1177/2167702612468111.

Damasio, A. R. (1994). *Descartes' error: Emotion, reason, and the human brain.* New York: Avon Books. See at: https://bdgrdemocracy.files.wordpress.com/2014/04/descartes-error_antonio-damasio.pdf.

Davidson, R. J. (1998). Affective style and affective disorders: Perspectives from affective neuroscience. *Cognition and Emotion, 12*(3), 307–330. doi.org/10.1080/026999398379628.

Deci, E. L. & Ryan, R. M. (2000). The "what" and "why" of goal pursuits: Human needs and the self-determination of behavior. *Psychological Inquiry, 11*, 227–268. doi.org/10.1207/S15327965PLI1104_01.

Deci, E. L. & Ryan, R. M. (2002). *Handbook of self-determination research.* New York: University of Rochester Press.

Dickson, J. M. & MacLeod, A. K. (2004) Approach and avoidance goals and plans: Their relationship to anxiety and depression. *Cognitive Therapy and Research, 28*, 415–432. doi.org/10.1023/B:COTR.0000031809.20488.ee.

Dickson, J. M. & Moberly, N. J. (2010). Depression, anxiety, and reduced facilitation in adolescents' personal goal systems. *Cognitive Therapy and Research, 34*, 576–581. doi.org/10.1007/s10608-010-9307-1.

Dickson, J. M., Moberly, N. J., & Kinderman, P. (2011). Depressed people are not less motivated by personal goals but are more pessimistic about attaining them. *Journal of Abnormal Psychology, 120*, 975–980. doi.org/10.1037/a0023665.

Dillon, D. G. & Pizzagalli, D.A. (2010). Maximizing positive emotions: A translational, transdiagnostic look at positive emotion regulation. In: A. M. Kring and D. M. Sloan (Eds.), *Emotion Regulation and Psychopathology* (pp. 229–252). New York: Guilford.

Dimidjian, S., Barrera Jr., M., Martell, C., Munoz, R., & Lewinsohn, P. (2011): The origins and current status of behavioral activation treatments for depression. *Annual Review of Clinical Psychology, 7*, 1–38. doi.org/10.1146/annurev-clinpsy-032210-104535.

Dunn, B. D. (2012). Helping depressed clients reconnect to positive emotion experience: Current insights and future directions. *Clinical Psychology & Psychotherapy, 19*, 326–340. doi.org/10.1002/cpp.1799.

Dunn, B. D., Dalgleish, T., & Lawrence, A. D. (2006). The somatic marker hypothesis: a critical evaluation. *Neuroscience and BioBehavioral Reviews, 30,* 239–271. doi.org/10.1016/j.neubiorev.2005.07.001.

Dunn, B. D., Dalgleish, T., Lawrence, A. D., Cusack, R., & Ogilvie, A. D. (2004). Categorical and dimensional reports of experienced affect to emotion-inducing pictures in depression. *Journal of Abnormal Psychology, 113,* 654–660. doi.org/10.1037/0021-843X.113.4.654.

Dunn, B. D., Dalgleish, T., Lawrence, A. D., & Ogilvie, A. D. (2007a). The accuracy of self-monitoring and its relationship to self-focused attention in dysphoria and clinical depression. *Journal of Abnormal Psychology, 116,* 1–15. doi.org/10.1037/0021-843X.116.1.1.

Dunn, B. D., Dalgleish, T., Ogilvie, A. D., & Lawrence, A. D. (2007b). Heartbeat perception in depression. *Behaviour Research and Therapy, 45,* 1921–1930. doi.org/10.1016/j.brat.2006.09.008.

Dunn, B. D., Evans, D., Makarova, D., White, J., & Clark, L. (2012). Gut feelings and the reaction to perceived inequity: The interplay between bodily responses, regulation, and perception shapes the rejection of unfair offers on the ultimatum game. *Cognitive, Affective and Behavioral Neuroscience, 12,* 419–429. doi.org/10.3758/s13415-012-0092-z.

Dunn, B. D., Stefanovitch, I., Buchan, K., Lawrence, A. D., & Dalgleish, T. (2009). A reduction in positive self-judgment bias is uniquely related to the anhedonic symptoms of depression. *Behaviour Research and Therapy, 47,* 374–381. doi.org/10.1016/j.brat.2009.01.016.

Dunn, B. D., Stefanovitch, I., Evans, D., Oliver, C., Hawkins, A., & Dalgleish, T. (2010a). Can you feel the beat? Interoceptive awareness is an interactive function of anxiety- and depression-specific symptom dimensions. *Behaviour Research and Therapy, 48,* 1133–1138. doi.org/10.1016/j.brat.2010.07.006.

Dunn, B. D., Galton, H. C., Morgan, R., Evans, D., Oliver, C., Meyer, M., Cusack, R., Lawrence, A. D., & Dalgleish, T. (2010b). Listening to your heart: How interoception shapes emotion experience and intuitive decision-making. *Psychological Science, 21,* 1835–1844. doi.org/10.1177/0956797610389191.

Ehlers, A., Clark, D. M., Hackmann, A., McManus, F., & Fennell, M. (2005). Cognitive therapy for PTSD: Development and evaluation. *Behaviour Research and Therapy, 43,* 413–431. doi.org/10.1016/j.brat.2004.03.006.

Elliot, A. J. & Sheldon, K. M. (1997). Avoidance achievement motivation: A personal goals analysis. *Journal of Personality and Social Psychology, 3,* 171–185. doi.org/10.1037/0022-3514.73.1.171.

Elliot, A. J., Thrash, T. M., & Murayama, K. (2011). A longitudinal analysis of self-regulation and well-being: Avoidance personal goals, avoidance coping, stress generation, and subjective well-being. *Journal of Personality, 79,* 643–674. doi.org/10.1111/j.1467-6494.2011.00694.x.

Elliott, E. S. & Dweck, C. S. (1988). Goals: An approach to motivation and achievement. *Journal of Personality and Social Psychology, 54,* 5–12. doi.org/10.1037/0022-3514.54.1.5.

Epstein, J., Pan, H., Kocsis, J. H., Yang, Y., Butler, T., Chusid, J., & Silbersweig, D. A. (2006). Lack of ventral striatal response to positive stimuli in depressed versus normal subjects. *American Journal of Psychiatry, 163,* 1784–1790. doi.org/10.1176/ajp.2006.163.10.1784.

Farb, N., Daubenmier, J., Price, C., Gard, T., Kerr, C., Dunn, B. D., Klein, A., Paulus, M., Mehling, W. (submitted). Interoception, contemplative practice and health. *Frontiers in Human Neuroscience.*

Farquharson, L. & Macleod, A. (2014). A brief goal-setting and planning intervention to improve well-being for people with psychiatric disorders. *Psychotherapy and Psychosomatics, 83,* 122–124. doi.org/10.1159/000356332.

Fava, G. A., Rafanelli, C., Grandi, S., Canestrari, R., & Morphy, M. A. (1998a). Six-year outcome for cognitive behavioral treatment of residual symptoms in major depression. *American Journal of Psychiatry, 155,* 1443–1445. doi.org/10.1176/ajp.155.10.1443.

Fava, G. A., Rafanelli, C., Grandi, S., Conti, S., & Belluardo, P. (1998b). Prevention of recurrent depression with cognitive behavioral therapy: preliminary findings. *Archives of General Psychiatry, 55,* 816–820. doi.org/10.1001/archpsyc.55.9.816.

Feldman, G. C., Joormann, J., & Johnson, S. L. (2008). Responses to positive affect: A self-report measure of rumination and dampening. *Cognitive Therapy and Research, 32,* 507–525. doi.org/10.1007/s10608-006-9083-0.

Ferguson, G., Conway, C., Endersby, L., & MacLeod, A. K. (2009). Increasing subjective well-being in long-term forensic rehabilitation: Evaluation of well-being therapy. *Journal of Forensic Psychiatry and Psychology, 20,* 906–918. doi.org/10.1080/14789940903174121.

First, M. B., Spitzer, M., Gibbon, M., & Williams, J. B. W. (1997). *Structured Clinical Interview for DSM-IV Axis I Disorders: Clinician version.* Washington, DC: American Psychiatric Association.

Ford, B. Q. & Mauss, I. B. (2013). The paradoxical effects of pursuing positive emotion: When and why wanting to feel happy backfires. In: J. Gruber & J. Moskowitz (Eds.), *The light and dark sides of positive emotion* (pp. 363–381). New York: Oxford University Press.

Fournier, J. C., DeRubeis, R. J., Hollon, S. D., Dimijian, S., Amsterdam, J. D., Shelton, R. C., & Fawcett, J. (2010). Antidepressant drug effects and depression severity: A patient level meta-analysis. *Journal of American Medical Association*, *303*, 47–53. doi.org/10.1001/jama.2009.1943.

Furman, D. J., Waugh, C. E., Bhattacharjee, K., Thompson, R. J., & Gotlib, I. H. (2013). Interoceptive awareness, positive affect, and decision making in major depressive disorder. *Journal of Affective Disorders*, *151*, 780–785. doi.org/10.1016/j.jad.2013.06.044.

Garland, E. L., Fredrickson, B., Kring, A. M., Johnson, D. P., Meyer, P. S., & Penn, D. L. (2010). Upward spirals of positive emotions counter downward spirals of negativity: Insights from the broaden-and-build theory and affective neuroscience in the treatment of emotion dysfunction and deficits in psychopathology. *Clinical Psychology Review*, *30*, 849–864. doi.org/10.1016/j.cpr.2010.03.002.

Geschwind, N., Nicolson, N. A., Peeters, F., van Os, J., Barge-Schaapveld, D., & Wichers, M. (2011). Early improvement in positive rather than negative emotion predicts remission from depression after pharmacotherapy. *European Neuropsychopharmacology*, *21*, 241–247. doi.org/10.1016/j.euroneuro.2010.11.004.

Geschwind, N., Peeters, F., Drukker, M., van Os, J., & Wichers, M. (2011). Mindfulness training increases momentary positive emotions and reward experience in adults vulnerable to depression: A randomized controlled trial. *Journal of Consulting & Clinical Psychology*, *79*, 618–626. doi.org/10.1037/a0024595.

Gilbert, P. (2009). Introducing compassion-focused therapy. *Advances in Psychiatric Treatment*, *15*, 199–208. doi.org/10.1192/apt.bp.107.005264.

Gilbert, P. (2014). Attachment theory and compassion focused therapy for depression. In: A. N. Danquah and K. Berry (Eds.), *Attachment theory in adult mental health: A guide to clinical practice* (pp. 35–48). New York: Routledge.

Gilbert, P., McEwan, K., Catarino, F., Baiao, R., & Palmeira, L. (2014). Fears of happiness and compassion in relationship with depression, alexithymia, and attachment security in a depressed sample. *British Journal of Clinical Psychology*, *53*, 228–244. doi.org/10.1111/bjc.12037.

Gilbody, S., Whitty, P., Grimshaw, J., & Thomas, RE. (2003). Educational and organizational interventions to improve the management of depression in primary care. A systematic review. *Journal of the American Medical Association*, *289*, 3145–3151. doi.org/10.1001/jama.289.23.3145.

Gotlib, I. H., McLachlan, A. L., & Katz, A. N. (1988). Biases in visual attention in depressed and non-depressed individuals. *Cognition & Emotion*, *2*, 185–200. doi.org/10.1080/02699938808410923.

Gruber, J., Oveis, C., Keltner, D., & Johnson, S. L. (2011). A discrete emotions approach to positive emotion disturbance in depression. *Cognition and Emotion*, *25*, 40–52. doi.org/10.1080/02699931003615984.

Hadley, S. & MacLeod, A. K. (2010). Conditional goal-setting, personal goals and hopelessness about the future. *Cognition and Emotion*, *24*, 1191–1198. doi.org/10.1080/02699930903122521.

Hamilton, M. (1960). A rating scale for depression. *Journal of Neurology, Neurosurgery and Psychiatry*, *12*, 56–62. doi.org/10.1136/jnnp.23.1.56.

Harshaw, C. (in press). Interoceptive dysfunction: Toward an integrated framework for understanding somatic and affective disturbance in depression. *Psychological Bulletin*.

Heller, A. S., Johnstone, T., Shackman, A. J., Light, S. N., Peterson, M. J., Kolden, G. G., Kalin, N. H., & Davidson, R. J. (2009). Reduced capacity to sustain positive emotion in major depression reflects diminished maintenance of fronto-striatal brain activation. *Proceedings of the National Academy of Sciences*, *106*, 22445–22450. doi.org/10.1073/pnas.0910651106.

Hirschfield, R. M., Lewis, L., & Vornik, L. A. (2003). Perceptions and impact of bipolar disorder: how far have we really come? Results of the national depressive and manic depressive association 2000 survey of individuals with bipolar disorder. *Journal of Clinical Psychiatry*, *64*, 161–74. doi.org/10.4088/JCP.v64n0209.

Huffman, J. C., DuBois, C. M., Healy, B. C., Boehm, J. K., Kashdan, T. B., Celano, C. M., Denninger, J. W., & Lyubomirsky, S. (2014). Feasibility and utility of positive psychology exercises for suicidal inpatients. *General Hospital Psychiatry*, *36*, 88–94. doi.org/10.1016/j.genhosppsych.2013.10.006.

Inbar, Y., Pizarro, D. A., Gilovich, T., & Ariely, D. (2012). Moral masochism: On the connection between guilt and self-punishment. *Emotion*, *13*, 14–18. doi.org/10.1037/a0029749.

Insel, T., Cuthbert, B., Garvey, M., Heinssen, R., Pine, D. S., Quinn, K., Sanislow, C., & Wang, P. (2010). Research domain criteria (RDoc): Toward a new classification framework for research on mental disorders. *American Journal of Psychiatry, 167*, 748–751.

James, W. (1894). The physical bases of emotion. *Psychological Review, 1*, 516–529.

Johnson, J., Gooding, P. A., Wood, A. M., Fair, K. L. & Tarrier, N. (2013). A therapeutic tool for boosting mood: The broad minded affective coping procedure. *Cognitive Therapy and Research, 37*, 61–70. doi.org/10.1007/s10608-012-9453-8.

Johnson, S. L., Edge, M. D., Holmes, M. K., & Carver, C. S. (2012). The behavioral activation system and mania. *Annual Review of Clinical Psychology, 8*, 243–267. doi.org/10.1146/annurev-clinpsy-032511-143148.

Judd, L. L. (1997). The clinical course of major depressive disorders. *Archives of General Psychiatry, 54*, 989–991. doi.org/10.1001/archpsyc.1997.01830230015002.

Keedwell, P. A., Andrew, C., Williams, S. C. R., Brammer, M. J., & Phillips, M. L. (2005). The neural correlates of anhedonia in major depressive disorder. *Biological Psychiatry, 58*, 843–853. doi.org/10.1016/j.biopsych.2005.05.019.

Killingsworth, M. A. & Gilbert, D. T. (2010). A wandering mind is an unhappy mind. *Science, 330*, 932. doi.org/10.1126/science.1192439.

Kirsch, I., Deacon, B. J., Huedo-Medina, T. B., Scoboria, A., Moore, T. J., & Johnson, B. T. (2008). Initial severity and antidepressant benefits: A meta-analysis of data submitted to the Food and Drug Administration. *PLOS Medicine, 5*, e45. doi.org/10.1371/journal.pmed.0050045.

Kramer, I., Simons, C. J. P., Hartmann, J. A., Menne-Lothmann, C., Viechtbauer, W., Peeters, F., & Wichers, M. (2014). A therapeutic application of the experience sampling method in the treatment of depression: A randomized controlled trial. *World Psychiatry, 13*(1), 68–77. doi.org/10.1002/wps.20090.

Kringelbach, M. L. & Berridge, K. C. (2009). Towards a functional neuroanatomy of pleasure and happiness. *Trends in Cognitive Science, 13*, 479–487

Kroenke, K., Spitzer, R. L., & Williams, J. B. (2001). The PHQ-9: Validity of a brief depression severity measure. *Journal of General Internal Medicine, 16*, 606–613. doi.org/10.1046/j.1525-1497.2001.016009606.x.

Kuppens, P., Oravecz, Z., & Tuerlinckx, F. (2010). Feelings change: Accounting for individual differences in the temporal dynamics of affect. *Journal of Personality and Social Psychology, 99*, 1042–1060. doi.org/10.1037/a0020962.

Layard, R., Clark, D., Bell, S., Knapp, M., Meacher, B., Priebe, S., Turnberg, L., Thornicroft. G., & Wright, B. (2006). *The depression report: A new deal for depression and anxiety disorders.* London: Centre for Economic Performance's Mental Health Policy Group, LSE.

Lloyd, J. J., Logan, S., Greaves, C. J., & Wyatt, K. M. (2011). Evidence, theory and context: Using intervention mapping to develop a school-based intervention to prevent obesity in children. *International Journal of Behavioral Nutrition and Physical Activity, 8*, 17. doi.org/10.1186/1479-5868-8-73.

Lyubomirsky, S., Sheldon, K. M., & Schkade, D. (2005). Pursuing happiness: The architecture of sustainable change. *Review of General Psychology, 9*, 111–131. doi.org/10.1037/1089-2680.9.2.111.

MacLeod, A. & Byrne, A. (1996). Anxiety, depression and the anticipation of future positive and negative experiences. *Journal of Abnormal Psychology, 105*, 286–289. doi.org/10.1037/0021-843X.105.2.286.

MacLeod, A. K., Coates, E., & Hetherton, J. (2008). Increasing well-being through teaching goal setting and planning skills: Results of a brief intervention. *Journal of Happiness Studies, 9*(2), 185–196. doi.org/10.1007/s10902-007-9057-2.

Major, B., Kaiser, C. R., & McCoy, S. K. (2003). It's not my fault: When and why attributions to prejudice protect well-being. *Personality and Social Psychology Bulletin, 29*, 772–781. doi.org/10.1177/0146167203029006009.

Mansell, W. (2006). The Hypomanic Attitudes and Positive Predictions Inventory (HAPPI): A pilot study to identify items that are elevated in individuals with bipolar affective disorder compared to non-clinical controls. *Behavioural and Cognitive Psychotherapy, 34*, 467–476. doi.org/10.1017/S1352465806003109.

Markowitz, J. & Weissman, M. (2012). Interpersonal psychotherapy: Past, present and future. *Clinical Psychology & Psychotherapy, 19*, 99–105. doi.org/10.1002/cpp.1774.

Martell, C. R., Dimidjian, S., & Hermann-Dunn, R. (2010). *Behavioral activation for depression: A clinician's guide.* New York: Guilford.

Matt, G., Vazquez, C., & Campbell, W. (1992). Mood-congruent recall of affectively toned stimuli: A meta-analysis review. *Clinical Psychology Review, 12,* 227–255. doi.org/10.1016/0272-7358(92)90116-P.

May, C. & Finch, T. (2009). Implementing, embedding, and integrating practices: An outline of normalization process theory. *Sociology, 43,* 535–554. doi.org/10.1177/0038038509103208.

May, C., Finch, T., Mair, F., Ballini, L., Dowrick, C., Eccles, M., & Heaven, B. (2007). Understanding the implementation of complex interventions in health care: The normalization process model. *BMC Health Services Research, 7,* 148. doi.org/10.1186/1472-6963-7-148.

McCabe, S. B. & Gotlib, I. H. (1995). Selective attention and clinical depression: Performance on a deployment-of-attention task. *Journal of Abnormal Psychology, 104,* 241–245. doi.org/10.1037/0021-843X.104.1.241.

Mazzucchelli, T., Kane, R., & Rees, C. (2010). Behavioral activation treatments for well-being: A meta-analysis. *Journal of Positive Psychology, 5*(2), 105–121. doi.org/10.1080/17439760903569154.

McMakin, D. L., Olino, T. M., Porta, G., Dietz, L. J., Emslie, G., Clarke, G., & Brent, D. A. (2012). Anhedonia predicts poorer recovery among youth with selective serotonin reuptake inhibitor treatment-resistant depression. *Journal of the American Academy of Child and Adolescent Psychiatry, 51,* 404–411. doi.org/10.1016/j.jaac.2012.01.011.

Medical Research Council. (2008). *Developing and evaluating complex interventions: New guidance MRC Complex Intervention Framework.* London: Medical Research Council.

Mendelsohn, J., Tursz, T., Schilsky, R., & Lazar, V. (2011). WIN Consortium. Challenges and advances. *Nature Reviews Clinical Oncology, 8,* 133–134. doi.org/10.1038/nrclinonc.2010.230.

Mirams, L., Poliakoff, E., Brown, R. J., & Lloyd, D.M. (2013). Brief body-scan meditation practice improves somatosensory perceptual decision making. *Consciousness and Cognition, 22,* 348–359. doi.org/10.1016/j.concog.2012.07.009.

Moore, M. & Fresco, D. (2012). Depressive realism: A meta-analytic review. *Clinical Psychology Review, 32,* 496–509. doi.org/10.1016/j.cpr.2012.05.004.

Murphy, F., Macpherson, K., Jeyabalasingham, T., Manly, T., & Dunn, B. (2013). Modulating mind-wandering in dysphoria. *Frontiers in Psychology, 4,* 888. doi.org/10.3389/fpsyg.2013.00888.

National Institute for Helath and Care Excellence (NICE). (2009). NICE guidance CG90. Available at: https://www.nice.org.uk/guidance/cg90.

Naragon-Gainey, K., Gallagher, M. W., & Brown, T. A. (2013). Stable "trait" variance of temperament as a predictor of the temporal course of depression and social phobia. *Journal of Abnormal Psychology, 122,* 611–623. doi.org/10.1037/a0032997.

Nakozeny, P. A., Carmody, T. J., Morris, D. W., Kurian, B. T., & Trevedi, M. H. (2010). Psychometric evaluation of the Snaith–Hamilton Pleasure Scale (SHAPS) in adult outpatients with major depressive disorder. *International Clinical Psychopharmacology, 25,* 328–333. doi.org/10.1097/YIC.0b013e32833eb5ee.

Neimiec, C. P., Ryan, R. M., & Deci, E. L. (2009). The path taken: Consequences of attaining intrinsic and extrinsic aspirations in post-college life. *Journal of Research in Personality, 43,* 291–306. doi.org/10.1016/j.jrp.2008.09.001.

Nelissen, R. M. A. (2012). Guilt induced self-punishment as a sign of remorse. *Social Psychological and Personality Science, 3,* 139–144. doi.org/10.1177/1948550611411520.

Nelissen, R. M. & Zeelenberg, M. (2009). When guilt evokes self-punishment: Evidence for the existence of a Dobby effect. *Emotion, 9,* 118–122. doi.org/10.1037/a0014540.

Neshat-Doost, H. T., Dalgleish, T., Yule, W., Kalantari, M., Ahmadi, S. J., Dyregov, A., & Jobson, L. (2013). Enhancing autobiographical memory specificity through cognitive training: An intervention for depression translated from basic science. *Clinical Psychological Science, 1,* 84–92. doi.org/10.1177/2167702612454613.

Newman, M. G. & Llera, S. J. (2011). A new theory of experiential avoidance in generalized anxiety disorder: A review and synthesis of research supporting an avoidance of a negative emotional contrast. *Clinical Psychology Review, 31,* 371–382. doi.org/10.1016/j.cpr.2011.01.008.

Norem, J. & Cantor, N. (1986). Defensive pessimism: Harnessing anxiety as motivation. *Journal of Personality and Social Psychology, 51,* 1208–1217. doi.org/10.1037/0022-3514.51.6.1208.

Panagioti, M., Gooding, P., & Tarrier, N. (2012). An empirical investigation of the effectiveness of the broad-minded affective coping procedure (BMAC) to boost mood among individuals with post-traumatic stress disorder (PTSD). *Behaviour Research and Therapy, 50,* 589–595. doi.org/10.1016/j.brat.2012.06.005.

Parkin, L., Morgan, L., Rosselli, A., Howard, M., Sheppard, A., Evans, D., Hawkins, A., Martinelli, M., Golden, A., Dalgleish, T., & Dunn, B. D. (2014). Exploring the relationship between mindfulness and cardiac perception. *Mindfulness, 5*, 298–313. doi.org/10.1007/s12671-012-0181-7.

Penton-Voak, I. S., Bate, H., Lewis, G. H., & Munafo, M.R. (2012). Effects of emotion perception training on mood in undergraduate students: A randomized controlled trial. *British Journal of Psychiatry, 201*, 71–77. doi.org/10.1192/bjp.bp.111.107086.

Piet, J. & Hougaard, E. (2011). The effect of mindfulness-based cognitive therapy for prevention of relapse in recurrent major depressive disorder: A systematic review and meta-analysis. *Clinical Psychology Review, 31*, 1032–1040. doi.org/10.1016/j.cpr.2011.05.002.

Pizzagalli, D. A., Iosifescu, D., Hallett, L. A., Ratner, K. G., & Fava, M. (2008). Reduced hedonic capacity in major depressive disorder: Evidence from a probabilistic reward task. *Journal of Psychiatric Research, 43*, 76–87. doi.org/10.1016/j.jpsychires.2008.03.001.

Porges, S. W. (2007). The polyvagal perspective. *Biological Psychology, 74*, 116–143. doi.org/10.1016/j.biopsycho.2006.06.009.

Raes, F., Smets, J., Nelis, S., & Schoofs, H. (2012). Dampening of positive affect prospectively predicts depressive symptoms in non-clinical samples. *Cognition & Emotion, 26*, 75–82. doi.org/10.1080/02699931.2011.555474.

Raes, F., Smets, J., Wessel, I., Van Den Eede, F., Nelis, S., Franck, E., Jacquemyn, Y., & Hanssens, M. (2014). Turning the pink cloud grey: Dampening of positive affect predicts postpartum depressive symptoms. *Journal of Psychosomatic Research, 77*, 64–69. doi.org/10.1016/j.jpsychores.2014.04.003.

Rottenberg, J. (2005). Mood and emotion in major depression. *Current Directions in Psychological Science, 14*, 167–170. doi.org/10.1111/j.0963-7214.2005.00354.x.

Rottenberg, J., Kasch, K. L., Gross, J. J., & Gotlib, I. H. (2002). Sadness and amusement reactivity differentially predict concurrent and prospective functioning in major depressive disorder. *Emotion, 2*, 135–146.

Rozental, A., Andersson, G., Boettcher, J., Ebert, D., Cuijpers, P., Knaevelsrud, C., & Carlbring, P. (2014). Consensus statement on defining and measuring negative effects of Internet interventions. *Internet Interventions, 1*, 12–19. doi.org/10.1016/j.invent.2014.02.001.

Ruini, C. & Fava, G. A. (2012). Role of well-being therapy in achieving a balanced and individualized path to optimal functioning. *Clinical Psychology and Psychotherapy, 19*, 291–304. doi.org/10.1002/cpp.1796.

Russo, S. J. & Nestler, E. J. (2013). The brain reward circuitry in mood disorders. *Nature Reviews Neuroscience, 14*, 609–625. doi.org/10.1038/nrn3381.

Ryan, R. M. & Deci, E. L. (2000). Intrinsic and extrinsic motivations: Classic definitions and new directions. *Contemporary Educational Psychology, 25*, 54–67. doi.org/10.1006/ceps.1999.1020.

Ryff, C. D. & Singer, B. (1996). Psychological well-being: Meaning, measurement, and implications for psychotherapy research. *Psychotherapy and psychosomatics, 65*, 14–23. doi.org/10.1159/000289026.

Schillinger, D. (2010). *An introduction to effectiveness, dissemination and implementation research.* Eds. P. Fleisher & E. Goldstein. San Francisco, CA: Clinical Translational Science Institute Community Engagement Program, University of California.

Schrader, G. D. (1997). Does anhedonia correlate with depression severity in chronic depression? *Comprehensive Psychiatry, 38*, 260–263. doi.org/10.1016/S0010-440X(97)90057-2.

Schueller, S. M. & Parks, A. C. (2014). The science of self-help: Translating positive psychology research into increased individual happiness. *European Psychologist, 19*(2), 145–155. doi.org/10.1027/1016-9040/a000181.

Segal, Z. V., Williams, J. M. G., & Teasdale, J. D. (2002). *Mindfulness-based cognitive therapy for depression.* New York: Guildford.

Seligman, M. E. P., Rashid, T., & Parks, A. C. (2006). Positive psychotherapy. *American Psychologist, 61*, 774–788. doi.org/10.1037/0003-066X.61.8.774.

Seligman, M. E., Steen, T., Park, N., & Peterson, C. (2005). Positive psychology progress: Empirical validation of interventions. *American Psychologist, 60*, 410–421. doi.org/10.1037/0003-066X.60.5.410.

Shankman, S., Nelson, B., Harrow, M., & Faull, R. (2010). Does physical anhedonia play a role in depression? A 20-year longitudinal study. *Journal of Affective Disorders, 120*, 170–176. doi.org/10.1016/j.jad.2009.05.002.

Sheldon, K. M. & Elliot, A. J. (1999). Goal striving, need-satisfaction, and longitudinal well-being: The self-concordance model. *Journal of Personality and Social Psychology, 76*, 482–497. doi.org/10.1037/0022-3514.76.3.482.

Sheldon, K. M. & Lyubomirsky, S. (2006). How to increase and sustain positive emotion: The effects of expressing gratitude and visualizing best possible selves. *Journal of Positive Psychology*, *1*, 73–82. doi.org/10.1080/17439760500510676.

Sheldon, K. M. & Elliot, A. J. (1999). Goal striving, need satisfaction, and longitudinal well-being: The self-concordance model. *Journal of Personality and Social Psychology*, *76*, 482–497.

Sin, N. L., Della Porta, M. D., & Lyubomirsky, S. (2011). Tailoring positive psychology interventions to treat depressed individuals. In: S. I. Donaldson, M. Csikszentmihalyi, & J. Nakamura (Eds.), *Applied positive psychology: Improving everyday life, health, schools, work, and society* (pp. 79–96). New York: Routledge.

Sin, N. L. & Lyubomirsky, S. (2009). Enhancing well-being and alleviating depressive symptoms with positive psychology interventions: A practice-friendly meta-analysis. *Journal of Clinical Psychology*, *65*, 467–487. doi.org/10.1002/jclp.20593.

Smallwood, J., O'Connor, R. C., & Heim, D. (2005). Rumination, dysphoria, and subjective experience. *Imagination, Cognition, and Personality*, *24*, 355–367. doi.org/10.2190/AE18-AD1V-YF7L-EKBX.

Smallwood, J., O'Connor, R. C., Sudbery, M. V., & Obonsawin, M. (2007). Mind-wandering and dysphoria. *Cognition and Emotion*, *21*, 816–842. doi.org/10.1080/02699930600911531.

Smoski, M. J., Felder, J., Bizzell, J., Green, S. R., Ernst, M., Lynch, T. R., & Dichter, G. S. (2009). fMRI of alterations in reward selection, anticipation, and feedback in major depressive disorder. *Journal of Affective Disorders*, *118*, 69–78. doi.org/10.1016/j.jad.2009.01.034.

Snaith, R. P., Hamilton, M., Morley, S., Hurmayan, A., Hargreaves, D., & Trigwell, P. (1995). A scale for the assessment of hedonic tone: The Snaith–Hamilton Pleasure Scale. *British Journal of Psychiatry*, *167*, 99–103. doi.org/10.1192/bjp.167.1.99.

Spence, R., Roberts, A., Ariti, C. & Bardsley, M. (2014). Focus on antidepressant prescribing: Trends in the prescribing of antidepressants in primary care. Available at: http://www.nuffieldtrust.org.uk/publications/focus-antidepressant-prescribing.

Spijker, J., Bijl, R. V., de Graaf, R., & Nolen, W. A. (2001). Care utilization and outcome of DSM-III-R major depression in the general population. Results from the Netherlands Mental Health Survey and Incidence Study (NEMESIS). *Acta Psychiatrica Scandinavica*, *104*, 19–24. doi.org/10.1034/j.1600-0447.2001.00363.x.

Stawarczyk, D., Majerus, S., Van der Linden, M., & D'Argembeau, A. (2012). Using the daydreaming frequency scale to investigate the relationships between mind-wandering, psychological well-being and present-moment awareness. *Frontiers in Psychology*, *3*, 363. doi.org/10.3389/fpsyg.2012.00363.

Tarrier, N. (2010). Broad minded affective coping (BMAC): A "positive" CBT approach to facilitating positive emotions. *International Journal of Cognitive Therapy*, *3*, 64–76. doi.org/10.1521/ijct.2010.3.1.64.

Telford, C., McCarthy-Jones, S., Corcoran, R., & Rowse, G. (2012). Experience sampling methodology studies of depression: The state of the art. *Psychological Medicine*, *42*, 1119–1129. doi.org/10.1017/S0033291711002200.

Treadway, M. T., Bossaller, N. A., Shelton, R. C., & Zald, D. H. (2012). Effort-based decision-making in major depressive disorder: A translational model of motivational anhedonia. *Journal of Abnormal Psychology*, *121*, 553–558. doi.org/10.1037/a0028813.

Treadway, M. T. & Zald, D. H. (2011). Reconsidering anhedonia in depression: Lessons from translational neuroscience. *Neuroscience and BioBehavioral Reviews*, *35*, 537–555. doi.org/10.1016/j.neubiorev.2010.06.006.

Uher, R., Perlis, R. H., Henigsberg, N., Zobel, A., Rietschel, M., Mors, O., & McGuffin P. (2012). Depression symptom dimensions as predictors of antidepressant treatment outcome: replicable evidence for interest-activity findings. *Psychological Medicine*, *42*, 967–980. doi.org/10.1017/S0033291711001905.

Ustun, T.B., Ayuso-Mateos, J. L., Chatterji, S., Mathers, C., & Murray, C. J. L. (2004). Global burden of depressive disorders in the year 2000. *British Journal of Psychiatry*, *184*, 386–392. doi.org/10.1192/bjp.184.5.386.

Van Oostrom, S. H., Anema, J. R., Terluin, B., Venema, A., de Vet, H. C. W., & van Mechelen, W. (2007). Development of a workplace intervention for sick-listed employees with stress-related mental disorders: Intervention mapping as a useful tool. *BMC Health Services Research*, *7*, 127. doi.org/10.1186/1472-6963-7-127.

Verdejo-Garcia, A., Clark, L., & Dunn, B. D. (2012). The role of interoception in addiction: A critical review. *Neuroscience & Biobehavioural Reviews, 36*, 1857–1869.

Vittengl, J. R., Clark, L. A., Dunn, T. W., & Jarrett, R. B. (2007). Reducing relapse and recurrence in unipolar depression: A comparative meta-analysis of cognitive-behavioral therapy's effects. *Journal of Consulting and Clinical Psychology, 75*, 475–488. doi.org/10.1037/0022-006X.75.3.475.

Vrieze, E., Pizzagalli, D. A., Demyttenaere, K., Hompes, T., Sienaert, P., de Boer, P., Schmidt, M., & Claes, S. (2013). Reduced reward learning predicts outcome in major depressive disorder. *Biological Psychiatry, 73*, 639–645. doi.org/10.1016/j.biopsych.2012.10.014.

Watanabe, E. & Ohtsubo, Y. (2012). Costly apology and self-punishment after an unintentional transgression. *Journal of Evolutionary Psychology, 10*(3), 87–105. doi.org/10.1556/JEP.10.2012.3.1.

Watson, D. & Clark, L. A. (1991). The mood and anxiety symptom questionnaire, unpublished manuscript, University of Iowa City.

Watson, D., Clark, L. A., & Tellegen, A. (1988). Development and validation of brief measures of positive and negative affect: The PANAS scales. *Journal of Personality and Social Psychology, 54*, 1063–1070. doi.org/10.1037/0022-3514.54.6.1063.

Watson, D. & Naragon-Gainey, K. (2011). On the specificity of positive emotional dysfunction in psychopathology: Evidence from the mood and anxiety disorders and schizophrenia/schizotypy. *Clinical Psychology Review, 30*, 839–848. doi.org/10.1016/j.cpr.2009.11.002.

Watson, D., Weise, D., Vaidya, J., & Tellegen, A. (1999). The two general activation systems of affect: Structural findings, evolutionary considerations, and psychobiological evidence. *Journal of Personality and Social Psychology, 76*, 820–838. doi.org/10.1037/0022-3514.76.5.820.

Weissman, M. M., Markowitz, J. C., & Klerman, G. L. (2000). *Comprehensive guide to interpersonal psychotherapy.* New York: Basic Books.

Werner-Seidler, A., Banks, R., Dunn, B. D., & Moulds, M. L. (2013). An investigation of the relationship between positive affect regulation and depression. *Behaviour Research and Therapy, 51*, 46–56. doi.org/10.1016/j.brat.2012.11.001.

Wichers M. C., Barge-Schaapveld D. Q., Nicolson N. A., Peeters F., de Vries M., Mengelers R., & van Os J. (2009). Reduced stress-sensitivity or increased reward experience: The psychological mechanism of response to antidepressant medication. *Neuropsychopharmacology, 34*, 923–931. doi.org/10.1038/npp.2008.66.

Williams, J. M., Barnhofer, T., Crane, C., Herman, D., Raes, F., Watkins, E., & Dalgleish, T. (2007). Autobiographical memory specificity and emotional disorder. *Psychological Bulletin, 133*, 122–148. doi.org/10.1037/0033-2909.133.1.122.

Wood, A. M. & Joseph, S. (2010). The absence of positive psychological (eudemonic) well-being as a risk factor for depression: A ten-year cohort study. *Journal of Affective Disorders, 122*, 213–217. doi.org/10.1016/j.jad.2009.06.032.

Wood, A. M. & Tarrier, N. (2010). Positive Clinical Psychology: A new vision and strategy for integrated research and practice. *Clinical Psychology Review, 30*, 819–829. doi.org/10.1016/j.cpr.2010.06.003.

Wood, J. V., Perunovic, W. Q., & Lee, J. W. (2009). Positive self-statements: Power for some, peril for others. *Psychological Science, 20*, 860–866. doi.org/10.1111/j.1467-9280.2009.02370.x.

14

Don't Worry, Be Happy
Toward a Positive Clinical Psychology for Anxiety Disorders
Philip C. Watkins and Andrew Pereira

Don't Worry, Be Happy: A Positive Clinical Psychology for Anxiety Disorders

During a recent vacation to Kauai, Hawaii, the first author was driving with his wife toward Waimea Canyon, often referred to as the Grand Canyon of the Pacific. As they were approaching their destination, the driver noticed some flashing lights, saw a car rushing toward them in their lane, and calmly pulled to the shoulder. While waiting on the side of the road the car sped past them closely followed by three Hawaii State Patrol cars. It was at this point the first author realized that this was a high-speed chase, and they had narrowly missed a head-on collision. Consequent to this realization, all the effects of the activation of the sympathetic nervous system ensued and he asked his wife, "I wonder how long it will take all the beauty around us to calm us down and forget about this incident?" This anecdote brings out one of the main themes of this chapter: can positive emotions and positive activities counteract the effects of fear and anxiety? The purpose of this chapter is to explore the potential of positive clinical psychology for intervening with anxiety disorders.

At first glance, it might appear that positive interventions have more to offer depressive than anxiety disorders. Indeed, some have argued that unipolar depression distinguishes itself from the other emotional disorders in that deficits in positive emotion are reliable indicators of depression (Watson, Clark & Carey, 1988; Clark & Watson, 1991; Watson & Naragon-Gainey, 2010). In our work we have found that low trait gratitude is more characteristic of depression than anxiety, and that gratitude is significantly correlated with depression after controlling for anxiety (e.g., McComb, Watkins, & Kolts, 2005). Moreover, gratitude seems to counteract negative memory biases in depression, and we have found that gratitude interventions reliably decrease depressive symptoms (e.g., Watkins, Uhder, & Pichinevskiy, 2015). Positive clinical psychology would seem to offer a lot to depression, but what does it have to offer anxiety disorders?

Both theoretical and empirical work suggests that positive interventions and activities may be effective in the treatment of anxiety disorders. For example, there are now several transdiagnostic approaches to psychopathology that emphasize common mechanisms of anxiety and depressive disorders (e.g., Nolen-Hoeksema & Watkins, 2011). We believe the approach of Barlow and colleagues to be very compelling. They propose that the mood and anxiety disorders comprise a broader category they call the "negative affective ayndrome" (NAS) (Barlow, Allen, & Choate, 2004; Moses & Barlow, 2006). They argue that all of these disorders share common distal vulnerability

---

The Wiley Handbook of Positive Clinical Psychology, First Edition. Edited by Alex M. Wood and Judith Johnson.
© 2016 John Wiley & Sons, Ltd. Published 2016 by John Wiley & Sons, Ltd.

factors: neuroticism (or negative affectivity) and a lack of a sense of controllability. Furthermore, all of the disorders of the NAS are characterized by maladaptive emotion regulation. Thus, it is quite possible that treatments that impact dysfunctional mechanisms in depression will also be effective with similar dysfunctions in anxiety disorders.

Second, although deficits in positive affect seem to be particularly characteristic of depression, there is now evidence that a lack of positive affect is characteristic of anxiety disorders as well (Watson & Naragon-Gainey, 2010). Deficits of positive affect seem to be more characteristic of social anxiety than other anxiety disorders, but in the study referred to above (McComb et al., 2005), we found that trait gratitude was inversely correlated with anxiety symptoms after controlling for depression symptoms. Thus, gratitude appears to be independently related to both depression and anxiety. Taken together, there appear to be deficits in positive affect and trait gratitude in dysfunctional anxiety, and this would seem to call for research investigating the effectiveness of interventions that attempt to increase these positive facets.

The third reason that positive interventions should be considered in the treatment of anxiety disorders is that there are now at least two experimental treatment outcome studies showing that positive well-being interventions can significantly decrease anxiety symptoms (Fava et al., 2005; Geraghty, Wood, & Hyland, 2010). Because of the importance of these studies we will discuss them in more detail below, but the point we would like to make here is that there are now sufficient reasons to suggest that positive interventions and activities may have something to offer for the treatment of anxiety disorders, as well as depressive disorders.

Instead of taking a disorder-by-disorder approach, we believe it is more helpful to consider common dysfunctional processes in anxiety disorders, and then consider positive activities and interventions that might contravene these mechanisms. A dysfunction is simply a psychological mechanism that is not functioning adaptively. For example, emotion regulation mechanisms should function to help individuals live well, but when one consistently deals with negative events by amplifying their importance and frequency, this should magnify the negative affect associated with these events, and thus this emotion regulation strategy is likely to be maladaptive. In other words, emotion regulation in this case is *dys*functional.

In the body of this chapter we will describe important dysfunctional mechanisms that are common in the anxiety disorders, along with specific positive interventions that research and theory suggest would be effective in counteracting these mechanisms. We will describe a number of mechanisms organized by five more general categories: emotional dysfunctions, cognitive dysfunctions, coping dysfunctions, dysfunctional self-preoccupation, and dysfunctional world-view. We believe that the final category may be foundational to the other dysfunctions that we will cover, and so we will use this section in an attempt to summarize and integrate the information that we have covered.

How Positive Activities might Counteract Dysfunctional Mechanisms in Anxiety Disorders

Emotional Dysfunctions

In this section we discuss several specific emotional dysfunctions that have been found in the anxiety disorders, and suggest specific positive clinical psychology treatments that might target these mechanisms. Although these dysfunctions likely interact with – and may even be caused by – other dysfunctions (such as cognitive dysfunctions), we believe it is helpful to consider emotional mechanisms in their own right. In this section we will consider three types of emotional dysfunctions: dysfunctional negative experiences, dysfunctional positive experiences, and emotional avoidance.

Negative affect Perhaps the most obvious emotional dysfunction that seems to run across the anxiety disorders has to do with excess negative affect in response to negative events (Clark & Watson, 1991; Watson et al., 1988). How might positive interventions and activities counteract these dysfunctions of negative affect? First, there is now experimental evidence suggesting that positive emotions can "undo" the impact of negative emotions such as fear and anxiety. In a test of her broaden-and-build theory of positive affect (Fredrickson, 1998, 2001), Fredrickson and collaborators investigated the power of positive emotions to undo the effect of negative emotions, including fear (Fredrickson & Levinson, 1998). In Study 1, participants viewed a film designed to induce fear. Following this induction, participants were randomly assigned to one of four different emotion induction conditions: contentment, amusement, sadness, or neutral. Cardiovascular measures were recorded, and they found that those in the positive emotion induction conditions returned to baseline cardiovascular functioning faster than those in the neutral or sadness conditions. Thus, positive emotions appear to have the ability to undo some of the physiological consequences of fear. Subsequent studies suggested that this effect was not simply due to positive emotions replacing negative emotions (Fredrickson, Mancuso, Branigan, & Tugade, 2000).

These findings suggest that clinicians may be able to help their clients "undo" maladaptive negative affective responses by inducing positive emotion. It is certainly incumbent on future researchers to demonstrate that inductions of positive emotion will be effective in undoing maladaptive fear seen in the clinic, and clinicians should also explore effective ways to induce positive emotion in the course of treatment. We suggest that clinicians use creative ways of inducing positive emotion that can be used by their clients outside the clinical setting. This is because the induction of positive emotion is most likely to be effective if actively used by clients as an emotion regulation technique, much as clients have been found to use relaxation procedures. For us, the important message of this research for clinicians is that their clients may use positive emotions to undo the deleterious effects of anxiety in their life, and this approach seems to be better than distraction or neutral emotional states. Thus, an effective means of decreasing negative affectivity would be to increase positive affect.

"Positive reappraisal" also has the potential to decrease the anxiety and fear that people may experience in response to negative events. To exemplify this approach, we describe a study in which we used grateful reappraisal to help bring closure to troubling memories (Watkins, Cruz, Holben, & Kolts, 2008). Although this study is also relevant to dysfunctional avoidance and coping, we will describe the study here because of the potential for grateful reappraisal to reduce the negative affect associated with painful memories. When designing this study we reasoned that much of the impact of negative events in one's life is through the influence of the memory of the event, rather than the event itself. In this study we asked students to recall an "unpleasant open memory." Briefly, an open memory is an emotional memory that has "unfinished business" associated with the event, the event is poorly understood, and it often intrudes into consciousness at unwelcome times. After recalling this event, our participants evaluated the memory on a number of variables. We then had all our subjects engage in a journaling exercise for the next three days. Some participants wrote about something irrelevant to their painful memory (the control condition), others were instructed to write about the painful event in the emotional disclosure technique prescribed by Pennebaker (1997), and others were assigned to a grateful reappraisal writing condition. In the reappraisal condition, participants were asked to write about consequences of this difficult event that they can now feel grateful for. Briefly, we found that compared with the two control conditions, individuals in the grateful reappraisal condition showed more psychological closure of their painful memory, and in a real-time assessment we found that the memory was less intrusive. More important for our discussion here, we found that grateful reappraisal decreased the negative emotional impact of the memory. Thus, positive interventions such as grateful reappraisal can decrease the negative emotions that are produced when recalling difficult events from one's past.

Positive affect   When treating patients with anxiety disorders, it may be just as important to target dysfunctional positive experiences as negative experiences. Just because one decreases excess negative affectivity does not necessarily mean that this will increase positive affectivity (Diener & Emmons, 1985). We submit that, particularly in the case of social anxiety disorder (SAD), deficits in positive experiences should be targeted in treatment. Research has now demonstrated several different dysfunctions in positive experiences that are associated with anxiety. Although these deficits appear to apply more to SAD than to other anxiety disorders, it is likely that individuals with other anxiety disorders (e.g., GAD) might also show deficits in positive experiences. Research has demonstrated that socially anxious individuals show less enjoyment of positive activities, have a lower frequency of positive events (Kashdan, 2007), have a lowered expectation of the frequency of positive events, anticipate more negative reactions and consequences to positive events (Gilboa-Schechtman, Franklin, & Foa, 2000), show decreased maintenance of positive emotions, and increased downregulation of positive emotions (for a review, see Carl, Soskin, Kerns, & Barlow, 2013). All these aspects likely lead to the avoidance of potentially rewarding events.

What positive activities might be effective interventions for these dysfunctions? Clearly, inductions that increase the frequency of positive affect would be effective in this regard, and in this sense inductions of positive affect should decrease negative affectivity as well as increase positive affectivity. In addition to the positive affect inductions suggested earlier, research suggests several other positive activities that might intervene with these dysfunctions. First, research suggests that gratitude interventions might enhance positive experiences. Elsewhere, we have argued that gratitude encourages flourishing because it amplifies the good in one's life (Watkins, 2008, 2011, 2014). If this is the case, positive affect should be enhanced if one experiences a positive event with gratitude. To date, there is very little research that speaks directly to this hypothesis (but see Watkins, Sparrow, Pereira, & Suominen, 2013), but research with grateful recounting exercises certainly is consistent with this suggestion. For example, in the initial "counting blessings" studies, Emmons and McCullough (2003) found that the activity of recording up to five things that one is thankful for enhanced positive affect relative to comparison conditions. Moreover, because Geraghty et al. (2010) found that grateful recounting decreased anxiety compared with wait-list controls, it is possible that one reason they found this effect was because the exercise increased positive affect which helped "undo" anxiety. We have also found that grateful reflection (reflecting on someone that one is grateful for) enhances positive affect (Watkins, Woodward, Stone, & Kolts, 2003). Taken together, there is good evidence that gratitude exercises may enhance positive affect in one's day-to-day experience, and thus may prove effective in countering the dysfunctions in positive experiences seen in anxiety disorders.

It is also possible that grateful expressions such as the "gratitude visit" designed by Seligman, Steen, Park, and Peterson (2005) may be effective in enhancing positive experiences for those with anxiety disorders. We submit that this may be particularly true with SAD, but it is possible that one may first need to intervene with the hesitancy to express positive emotions that has been found in these individuals, and we will discuss this issue in more depth later. Enhancing the positive affect that these individuals experience in social encounters would seem to be an important target in treatment. Not only should grateful expression improve positive affect in social situations, we submit that Fredrickson and collaborators' "loving-kindness meditation" (LKM) should be similarly effective (Fredrickson, Cohn, Coffey, Pek, & Finkel, 2008). Briefly, "LKM is a technique used to increase feelings of warmth and caring for self and others" (Fredrickson et al., 2008, p. 1046). Fredrickson was particularly interested in this meditation practice because it was specifically developed to enhance positive emotions one experiences for one's self as well as others. There is now good evidence to suggest that LKM enhances well-being through these mechanisms (Fredrickson et al., 2008; Garland, Fredrickson, Kring, Johnson, Meyer, & Penn, 2010). Thus, we propose that LKM is a good candidate for enhancing positive affect in those suffering from anxiety disorders.

Recent evidence suggests that "acts of kindness" may also enhance positive affect. In an experimental design, Alden and Trew (2013) showed that having socially anxious individuals participate in acts of kindness over a four-week period increased positive affect, but those in comparison treatments (behavioral experiments or activity monitoring), showed no change. Participants in the acts of kindness treatment were asked to do three "kind acts" for each of two days during the week (following Lyubomirsky, Sheldon, & Schkade, 2005). Moreover, those in the kindness condition revealed increased relationship satisfaction and decreased goals of social avoidance. Like LKM and gratitude treatments, this is another other-oriented intervention that has the potential to enhance current treatments of social anxiety.

Emotional avoidance   There is now good evidence that emotional avoidance characterizes the anxiety disorders. For example, the agoraphobic tendencies of many panic disorder patients are due to their avoidance of panic symptoms. Furthermore, there is also evidence to suggest that those high in social anxiety may avoid both positive and negative emotions that are associated with social situations (Kashdan, 2007; Kashdan, Weeks, & Savostyanova, 2011). There is also evidence of muted expressions of positive emotions in socially anxious individuals. Taken together, these findings would seem to recommend mindfulness and acceptance treatment approaches (e.g., Hayes, Luoma, Bond, Masuda, & Lillis, 2006). Clearly, if a person cannot accept his or her positive emotional responses in social situations, this would debilitate his or her ability to enjoy these settings. The inability to accept positive emotions is an interesting phenomenon and is quite different from the more typical tendency for individuals to have trouble accepting negative emotional responses. Acceptance therapies tend to be oriented toward helping individuals accept unpleasant emotional states, so it will be interesting to see how this might translate to positive emotional states. While we await more research concerning this issue, we see real potential for the effectiveness of mindfulness and acceptance based therapies for treating the emotional avoidance often seen in anxiety disorders.

In sum, there is now considerable evidence for both negative and positive emotional dysfunctions in the anxiety disorders. Research suggests that several positive activities may be effective in intervening with these dysfunctions. We believe that LKM, acts of kindness, and gratitude interventions may be particularly effective in this regard, but we wait for more research that investigates these treatments with clinically anxious populations. We turn now to dysfunctional cognitive mechanisms that are common to the anxiety disorders.

Cognitive Dysfunctions

Attention bias   Attention to threat appears to be one of the most reliable information processing biases found in the anxiety disorders (e.g., MacLeod, Mathews, & Tata; for a review, see Mathews & MacLeod, 2005). Although there is some question as to whether threatening information automatically grabs the attention of anxious individuals or anxious people have trouble disengaging their attention from threat (see Fox, 2004), a host of studies have shown that anxious individuals allocate attention resources toward threating information. Furthermore, there is now evidence that the attention bias to threat is not a mere consequence of anxiety, but that it actually contributes to negative affectivity. The so-called "cognitive bias modification" movement has shown through a number of studies that when one's attention is experimentally trained toward threat, this has maladaptive emotional consequences (for a review, see Hertel & Mathews, 2011). Moreover, studies have found beneficial effects when one's attention is trained away from threat (e.g., Hayes, Hirsch, & Mathews, 2010; Hertel & Mathews, 2011). More recent work has shown that training individuals to attend to positive information decreases negative emotion and maintains positive emotion in response to a stressful task (Taylor, Bomyea, & Amir, 2011; Grafton, Ang, & MacLeod, 2012). Taken together, we believe this research makes a strong case for the training of positive attention (as well as training away from threat) in individuals with anxiety disorders. Because these are computer tasks and are even available over the Internet, these attention training methods could be easily integrated into an anxiety treatment regimen.

We should highlight an important caveat however. In the Taylor et al. study (2011), they had difficulty training a positive attention bias in socially anxious individuals. This could be because these individuals have such an ingrained negative attention bias that a positive attention bias is more difficult to establish. Because this was a one-session training, the authors suggested that a more thorough training over multiple sessions might be needed with these individuals. Because of the potential utility of training positive attention biases in anxious individuals, this is clearly an issue in need of further research. Nonetheless, we submit that positive attention training procedures show real promise in the treatment of anxiety disorders.

We believe that there are other positive activities that might promote a positive attention bias that could be useful in treating anxiety. In both the Seligman et al. (2005), and the Watkins et al. (2015) three-blessings studies, they found that the well-being of the participants in the critical intervention continued to climb after the treatment phase. These results stand in stark contrast to the typical treatment outcomes seen in clinical studies, where the greatest improvement is seen immediately after treatment, after which the treatment gains decline. Why did the well-being of those in the three-blessings treatment continue to grow after the conclusion of treatment? We have argued that the continued improvement is because these treatments train cognitive processes that are salubrious to well-being (Watkins, Pereira, & Mathews, 2013). Because the three-blessings treatment requires individuals to identify three things that have gone well recently, it is quite possible that individuals begin looking for the good in their life, and thus their attention is trained to the positive. Indeed, this is often what individuals have reported to us in post-experiment interviews. Although future research needs to more specifically investigate this cognitive mechanism, this might have advantages of ecological validity over the computer-based techniques that have been used with attention bias training in the past. This is because the three-blessings treatments might be training individuals to "look for" real world benefits in their ongoing experience, whereas with computer attention training procedures they are being trained to attend to positive words. On the other hand, one could argue that these procedures might even compliment each other, and thus might best be used in concert when treating anxiety. In sum, attention bias to threat and the lack of a bias toward positive information seems to be an important dysfunctional mechanism to target in those with anxiety disorders. Positive interventions such as positive attention training and grateful recounting exercises may specifically counteract these dysfunctions.

Interpretation bias   Many situations are somewhat ambiguous and require interpretations for individuals to adequately understand their meaning. For some, a situation may suggest that the glass is half empty, for others it is half full. Thus, how one interprets situations is an important determinant to how well they will deal with that situation. Researchers have consistently found that interpretation biases are associated with anxiety – particularly in social anxiety. For example, when provided with an ambiguous scenario, socially anxious individuals have been found to provide negative interpretations of the situation, whereas nonanxious controls tend to provide positive interpretations (e.g., Hirsch & Mathews, 2000; Amir, Beard, & Bower, 2005; for a review, see Hertel & Mathews, 2011). Does positive clinical psychology have anything to offer to counteract these dysfunctional cognitive mechanisms?

There are now several different methods that have been shown to be effective in modifying interpretation biases. Moreover, when interpretation biases are modified, research has shown that this has important emotional consequences (e.g., Grey & Mathews, 2000; Mathews & Mackintosh, 2000; Mackintosh, Mathews, Yiend, Ridgeway, & Cook, 2006; Salemink, van den Hout, & Kindt, 2010; for a review, see Hertel & Mathews, 2011). Furthermore, research has now shown that interpretation biases can be modified in analog and clinical generalized anxiety disorder participants (Hirsch, Hayes, & Mathews, 2009; Hayes, Hirsch, Krebs, & Mathews, 2010) and in those with social anxiety (Beard & Amir, 2008). In both cases, the modification of interpretation biases led to more adaptive emotional responses. Thus, benign interpretation bias training may have utility in the treatment of anxiety disorders. We submit that this kind of interpretation training falls nicely within the domain of positive clinical psychology. It is important to note that often the interpretation "bias" that has been found in those with anxiety disorders is not a preference for threatening interpretations, but rather the lack of a positive interpretation bias that is typically found in nonanxious participants. Moreover, these training procedures are not simply training participants to avoid making negative interpretations of ambiguous situations, but usually they are training people to replace negative interpretations with positive interpretations. For us, this is clearly a positive intervention.

There is also suggestive evidence that other more traditional positive psychology exercises induce positive interpretation biases. Earlier we raised the question as to why the gratitude three-blessing treatment produces a growth in well-being after the treatment phase. We propose that not only does the three-blessings procedure promote well-being by training a positive attention bias, it may also do so by training a positive interpretation bias (Watkins et al., 2013). Recall that in our gratitude three-blessings intervention participants not listed only three blessings, but they also wrote about how each benefit made them feel grateful. If the enhancements in well-being were purely from training individuals to look for the good in their life, then we should have seen no differences between the gratitude and the pride three-blessings treatments. The gratitude treatment, however, significantly outperformed the pride treatment. Thus, something besides shifting participants' attention must have taken place, and we submit that it is likely that individuals also developed the cognitive habit of interpreting positive events in a more grateful manner. This suggestion is admittedly quite speculative at this point, and it calls for more research that investigates the cognitive mechanisms involved with the three-blessings intervention. In sum, we submit that interpretation bias modification techniques and the gratitude three-blessings treatment are promising interventions for the interpretation biases that are associated with anxiety.

Memory bias   Although the finding is not as robust as that found in depression, there is some evidence that anxiety is associated with a negativistic memory bias (for a review, see Hertel & Mathews, 2011). It is important to note, however, that this memory "bias" tends to be better characterized as a lack of a positive bias, rather than excess negative bias. Thus, individuals with anxiety disorders are less likely to remember positive experiences, and consequently may avoid situations that typically enhance well-being. For example, when considering an invitation to a party, research suggests that whereas nonanxious individuals will tend to remember positive experiences with past parties, socially anxious individuals will not remember these positive experiences so clearly, or if they do, they have a tendency to discount these experiences (Vassilopoulos & Banerjee, 2010). More than likely, it is biased attention and interpretation processes that produce these memory biases (Hertel, Brozovich, Joorman, & Gotlib, 2008; Tran, Hertel, & Joorman, 2011), but there is still some room to speculate that retrieval processes may be involved. Perhaps positive training procedures could be developed to help modify the way individuals retrieve information from their past. If dysfunctional retrieval processes are involved in anxiety disorders, then it seems reasonable to propose that positive activities such as the three-blessings intervention would target these dysfunctional mechanisms (Seligman et al., 2005; Watkins et al., 2015). In our study we found that the gratitude three-blessings treatment increased the accessibility of memories of positive events from the previous week, and in another study we found that recalling grateful memories reduced the recall of negative events compared with a control recall treatment (Watkins, Neal, & Thomas, 2004). Moreover, positive reminiscing treatments have been shown to increase well-being in experimental studies (Bryant, Smart, & King,

2005). In another study, students who were instructed to recall past successes before a test were found to have more positive affect and less test anxiety than those who wrote about their typical morning (Nelson & Knight, 2010). Most importantly, they scored better on the test. Thus, there is suggestive evidence that positive recall techniques might be beneficial to those with anxiety disorders, and they may do so by intervening with the positive memory deficits that have been found in anxiety disorders.

Cognitive avoidance   Thus far we have seen that cognitive dysfunctions of attention, interpretation, and memory may be contravened by positive interventions. Anxiety disorders are also characterized by cognitive avoidance. In this section we describe two forms: worry and memory avoidance. Borkovec and colleagues have defined worry as "a chain of thoughts and images, negatively affect-laden and relatively uncontrollable" (Borkovec, Robinson, Pruzinsky, & Depree, 1983, p. 10). How can this be seen as a process of cognitive avoidance? Borkovec argues that the linguistically intense process of worry serves to help individuals avoid emotion-laden imagery that is associated with future threat (Borkovec, Alcaine, & Behar, 2004). Thus, although worry is unpleasant, it does not arouse the more intense negative emotions caused by the images of threat, and therefore worry is negatively reinforced. Although individuals who worry believe they are solving problems associated with the upcoming threat, worry in fact turns out to be a poor coping style because clear concrete solutions to the problem are avoided. Indeed, research has found that threat imagery tends to be more concrete whereas pathological worry is abstract (Hirsch & Mathews, 2012). How might positive activities help intervene with this dysfunctional mechanism?

Previously we described two studies showing that positive psychology interventions significantly decreased worry (Fava et al., 2005; Geraghty et al., 2010). Because the well-being therapy of Fava involves multiple components, it is difficult to determine how this approach specifically intervenes with worry. However, the grateful recounting technique used in Geraghty and colleagues is more specific, therefore it may lend itself to identifying how it contravenes worry. Both procedures emphasize identifying and elaborating on positive aspects of one's life. We submit that this might be how these techniques are effective in reducing worry. Because both of these approaches require individuals to identify positive things in their life, this should enhance the cognitive habit of looking for the good. If one's attention is more chronically directed to positive aspects of their life, one may gain a more positive view of the future. One of the notable aspects of pathological worriers is that they seem to have a chronic expectation that bad things will happen in the future, and their way of coping with this is to engage in the more passive problem solving technique of worry. If, however, one can be trained to look for the good in their life, their expectations for the future should improve, thus counteracting their negative expectations. Moreover, if one's attention shifts to more positive aspects of their life, this may give them more confidence to pursue active and concrete problem solving approaches to an upcoming threat. We submit that in this way grateful recounting and other positive activities that focus an individual on specific positive aspects of their life should counteract worry.

If Borkovec is right that pathological worry is borne out of the avoidance of threat imagery, then techniques that help individuals approach those images (and subsequently engage in concrete problem solving) should be effective. In this regard, we believe that mindfulness and acceptance therapies should prove to be useful. If one can accept the unpleasant emotions that arise when thinking about an image of threat, they should be less likely to avoid this image, and should be better able to engage in concrete problem solving. Positive reappraisal techniques might be useful too. Although these techniques are usually applied to incidents from one's past (see our discussion below), it seems that clinicians could easily adapt this technique to threats in the future. For example, clinicians could encourage individuals to write about potential positive consequences of the upcoming threat that one might eventually feel grateful for (Watkins et al., 2008). Research with those prone to worry has shown that activating threatening images proves to be more adaptive than worry (Hirsch & Mathews, 2011). If grateful reappraisal can assist individuals in approaching these threat images, then this treatment might prove useful. Clearly, these suggestions need more research to recommend their use in clinical settings, but the fact that two positive interventions have demonstrated significant reductions in worry is encouraging.

Many anxiety disorders, most notably PTSD, involve the avoidance of troubling memories, and this seems to be a dysfunctional mechanism that helps maintain these disorders. How can individuals approach these painful memories in a way that brings closure? Although this intervention needs to be tested in clinical populations, our grateful reappraisal intervention described earlier brought closure to unpleasant open memories, decreased the negative affect aroused by the memories, and decreased the intrusiveness of these memories (Watkins et al., 2008). In subsequent analyses, we found that individuals in the grateful reappraisal condition reported more positive affect and less negative affect after each journaling session than was reported in the emotional control condition (Watkins, Xiong, & Kolts, 2008). Thus, reappraising their troubling memory in a grateful manner was more pleasant than simply writing about the emotional incident. We believe that this intervention was effective in part because it provided a means of approach to the open memory, which allowed individuals to process the memory in a way that brought closure. It is certainly possible that the stressful memories our students recalled in this study are qualitatively different from the memories that individuals with anxiety disorders are avoiding, but our results would seem to call for more research using this intervention with clinical populations.

Memory avoidance is often associated with thought suppression (Watkins et al., 2008), and thus procedures similar to our grateful reappraisal treatment might contravene maladaptive thought suppression. Indeed, we have found that trait gratitude is inversely associated with the tendency to engage in thought suppression (Neal, Watkins, & Kolts, 2005). Although highly speculative at this point, interventions designed to enhance gratitude might be effective in reducing the tendency of thought suppression, thus reducing the intrusive thoughts that are a disturbing aspect of many anxiety disorders. Paradoxically, one reason that individuals engage in thought suppression is that they have difficulty suppressing thoughts, and this appears to be a quality common to emotional disorders. However, some research suggests that positive thoughts and memories can serve as an effective distractor so that individuals can successfully inhibit unwanted thoughts (e.g., Wenzlaff & Bates, 2000). Thus, positive interventions that increase the accessibility of positive cognitions may be useful for helping individuals avoid disturbing thoughts.

In sum, a number of cognitive dysfunctions are evident in the anxiety disorders and we believe that it is clinically useful to target specific cognitive dysfunctions with specific interventions. In this section we have seen how positive interventions such as mindfulness/acceptance treatments, gratitude treatments, and LKM can specifically target these dysfunctions. We turn now to exploring how emotional and cognitive dysfunctions result in rigid coping styles that may promote vicious cycles.

Dysfunctional Coping and Vicious Cycles

Although it is beyond the scope of this chapter to review all of the dysfunctional coping styles in the anxiety disorders, there seems to be one common theme to these coping problems: people with anxiety disorders engage in rigid coping styles. Stated differently, individuals with anxiety disorders seem to take one or a few coping approaches, regardless of the problem they are faced with. For example, although thought suppression is undoubtedly functional in some situations, if one invariably uses this coping method when unpleasant thoughts arise, this is bound to be dysfunctional. Moreover, when these coping methods are used rigidly, they often result in vicious cycles. For example, GAD patients invariably use pathological worry in an attempt to deal with upcoming threats. One of the reasons they tend to use this coping approach is because of negative outcome expectations of future threats. This pattern of using passive worry to avoid clear images of the upcoming challenge and hence the avoidance of active problem solving, results in individuals failing to adequately cope with the threat. Because they have not adequately prepared for the threat, unwanted consequences result. This then encourages the individual's propensity for worry, and the cycle continues. The student with test anxiety worries about the worst possible outcomes of the test and so avoids adequately preparing for the test. This then results in a poor test grade and in turn enhances the student's expectations about poor test results in the future. This negative expectation then encourages pathological worry about future tests. These examples illustrate how individuals with anxiety disorders appear to engage in rigid coping styles that result in dysfunctional vicious cycles.

How might positive clinical psychology provide a unique perspective for the treatment of these vicious cycles? Kashdan and Rottenberg (2010) have made a compelling case that "psychological flexibility" should be a strength that is a target for positive interventions. Although we believe their construct of psychological flexibility involves too many psychological processes to direct treatment at this point, they have pointed the way for the development of this idea. It stands to reason that individuals who can be taught flexibility in their coping approach will be better at dealing with life's challenges because each situation demands different solutions. The individual who is able to be flexible in this way should be better at dealing with the changing stressors that one encounters. Research dating back to Isen's work (e.g., Isen, Daubman, & Nowicki, 1987) shows that the induction of mild positive affect enhances cognitive flexibility in problem solving. Thus, interventions that target enhancing positive affect should be effective in supporting psychological flexibility.

Not only should positive affect be instrumental in the midst of stress, Fredrickson and collaborators have argued that it should also be an important factor that builds cognitive flexibility in preparation for dealing effectively with challenging situations (Garland et al., 2010). Indeed, they have shown that their LKM treatment may be effective at least in part because it encourages positive emotions which then support ego resiliency (a construct closely related to psychological flexibility). Ego resiliency then promotes positive affect in the midst of stress (Fredrickson et al., 2008; Kok & Fredrickson, 2010). Thus, positive interventions such as LKM and gratitude interventions may be effective because they encourage resiliency which creates upward spirals that directly counter the downward spirals (or vicious cycles) that we have seen to characterize the anxiety disorders (Fredrickson & Joiner, 2002; Fredrickson, Tugade, Waugh, & Larkin, 2003). Indeed, one of the reasons that gratitude appears to be adaptive is because grateful individuals seem to be very good at coping with difficult situations (e.g., Wood, Joseph, & Linley, 2007; Wood, Maltby, Gillett, Linley, & Joseph, 2008). Clearly, however, there are a number of missing empirical components before we can confidently conclude that positive affect enhancing procedures directly contravene the vicious cycles seen in anxiety disorders. Nonetheless, we believe that the initial results are encouraging, and future research could more specifically investigate these possibilities.

Dysfunctional Self-Preoccupation

One of the more prominent characteristics of the emotional disorders is maladaptive self-focus (Ingram, 1990). Individuals with anxiety and depressive disorders appear to exhibit excessive self-preoccupation. Whereas the cognitive dysfunctions reviewed previously have been more specific, this dysfunction appears to be rather broad and likely involves a number of psychological dysfunctions. There is evidence, however, that this excessive self-awareness depletes cognitive resources that in turn adversely affects performance (Kashdan 2007;

Kashdan et al., 2011). An argument could be made that treatments oriented toward others might effectively counteract maladaptive self-preoccupation, and it strikes us that many of the positive interventions we have described thus far are other-oriented treatments. Acts of kindness, LKM, and gratitude treatments all appear to be focused on others, and thus might be effective antidotes to maladaptive self-preoccupation. Perhaps even procedures such as positive attention and interpretation training could be adapted to promote a more other-oriented perspective.

We believe that the egosystem versus ecosystem theory of Crocker (2008, 2011; Crocker & Canevello, 2011) effectively speaks to the issue of dysfunctional self-preoccupation. She has argued that when dealing with others we typically are in one of two motivational orientations: *egosystem* or *ecosystem*. When the egosystem dominates, one is self-focused, and one's own needs and desires are amplified. The egosystem is typically activated when one is convinced that their needs will not be met by cooperating with others, and therefore one must look out for one's own interests. When the egosystem is activated people "try to meet their needs and achieve their goals by influencing how other people view them. They focus on proving themselves, demonstrating their desired qualities, validating their worth, and establishing their deservingness" (Crocker, 2011, p. 260).

On the other hand, when the ecosystem mindset is activated the individual's concerns transcend themselves: "Like a camera lens zooming out from them, in the ecosystem people focus on what they care about beyond their own needs and desires" (Crocker, 2011, p. 261). In contrast to the egosystem, the ecosystem motivational orientation is activated when one is confident that their needs can be met by collaborating with others in pursuing a greater good for the whole ecosystem. We submit that treatments activating the ecosystem should be effective in counteracting dysfunctional self-preoccupation. Activities such as acts of kindness, LKM, grateful recounting, grateful reflection, and grateful expression seem to fit the bill. We believe that Crocker's theory provides helpful guidance for researchers investigating the mechanisms of these interventions.

Dysfunctional Worldview

Why would individuals with anxiety disorders seem to have the egosystem chronically activated? We submit that it is because there is a dysfunctional worldview shared across anxiety disorders. We find it interesting that diverse theories that have emphasized constructs such as insecure attachment, maladaptive relational mental models, dysfunctional schemata, a lack of a sense of control, and lack of basic trust, all seem to converge on one theme: the anxious person has a malevolent view of their world. Individuals with anxiety disorders seem to share a view of their world that lacks the benign bias that nonanxious individuals demonstrate. For anxious people, the future cannot be trusted (GAD), others cannot be trusted (SAD), the past has been cruel (PTSD), events seem out of control and thus one must control them (OCD), and so on. People are often overly anxious because they believe that they cannot trust people and events to support their well-being. On the other hand, nonanxious individuals seem much more confident that their circumstances and future will help them flourish. How might positive interventions and activities help to replace this malevolent worldview with a more benevolent worldview?

We believe that over time, many of the positive activities we have described may help change the dysfunctional worldview that seems to characterize maladaptive anxiety. Indeed, we present this issue here because we believe it helps summarize the many dysfunctions and interventions we have discussed heretofore. First, treatments that redirect one's attention to the positive in one's life should create a more positive worldview over time. Because of the psychological impact of negative events, it is very easy for the negative to drown out the positive in one's life (Baumeister, Bratslavsky, Finkenauer, & Vohs, 2001). But treatments that help shift one's attention to the positive should counteract this negative bias. And when one is more aware of the positive they should be more inclined to believe that the world might even help them flourish rather than flounder. Thus, treatments such as positive attention training and grateful recounting may well counteract the malevolent worldview of anxious individuals.

Second, interventions that target more positive interpretations of events should also create a more benevolent worldview. We submit that cognitive bias modification procedures such as positive interpretation training should counter malevolent schemas. Because we believe that the three-blessings gratitude treatment may train individuals to interpret situations in a more positive manner, this may also create a more trusting view of the world. In the same way, LKM should improve one's view of others. One would think that acts of kindness might be effective in the same way.

It could also be argued that if positive interventions help create more adaptive coping patterns this would assist in creating a more positive worldview. By more effectively coping with life's challenges, individuals should come to believe that even when bad things happen to them, they can deal with them effectively. Indeed, they may even come to believe that good consequences can emerge from difficult events. In this regard, one can see how interventions such as grateful reappraisal might help create a more benevolent worldview by helping individuals see their life as a good story, even when bad events occur. If treatments such as LKM help enhance the positive emotions that serve to deal effectively with stress, this might be another route whereby positive interventions can improve one's view of their world. It should be highlighted that it is unlikely short-term applications of these procedures would result in permanent changes in worldview, but we suggest that targeting malevolent worldviews may be the important end-goal of treatment. Here again, these questions call out for more research. Taken together, however, there is promising evidence to suggest that positive interventions have the potential to create a more benevolent worldview in anxious individuals.

Summary and Conclusions

Research with positive interventions such as LKM, cognitive bias modification, and gratitude treatments, provide promise for enhancing current treatments of anxiety disorders. Although the research described in this chapter offers some hope, it must be said that we are still early in the game. There are many issues that remain to be resolved before we can confidently assert that positive interventions should be used with anxiety disorders. First, there is clearly a need for more RCTs using these treatments with clinical anxiety disorders. Although using normal or analog populations for testing these interventions is a promising start, research should now focus on clinical populations. Second, there is a need to demonstrate the incremental validity of these treatments. Do these positive activities really add anything to current evidence-based treatments? It is important that those interested in positive clinical psychology not neglect traditional clinical psychology interventions that have been shown to be effective with anxiety disorders.

Third, we recommend conducting experimental research that investigates the effectiveness of positive activities on specific dysfunctional mechanisms. We believe that when researchers can show that a particular positive intervention specifically contravenes a specific dysfunction, the intervention will have a wider applicability to the treatment of anxiety disorders. For example, in our grateful reappraisal study (Watkins et al., 2008), we specifically targeted whether gratefully reappraising unpleasant open memories could bring closure and thus reduce the negative emotional impact and intrusiveness of those memories. Outcome studies that investigate treatment packages that include a number of different components aimed at intervening with a number of different mechanisms, tell us little about the effective mechanisms of treatment. We believe that targeting specific dysfunctional mechanisms with specific treatments is a promising direction for clinical research.

Fourth, future research should look more carefully at potential moderators such as cultural and gender variables. In our recent three-blessings gratitude treatment, we found that women enjoyed the treatment more than men, but men benefitted more from the treatment (Watkins et al., 2015). It is also possible that issues such as individualistic versus collectivist cultures may prove to be important treatment moderators.

Finally, we believe that it is very important to begin considering the importance of the therapeutic alliance in delivering positive interventions. Most of the positive intervention studies described in this chapter were not delivered in a clinical context, and thus the relationship of the client and therapist in administering these treatments needs to be considered. It is possible that when delivered in the context of an accepting warm therapist–client relationship, the effectiveness of these interventions would be enhanced. On the other hand, it is quite possible that these positive activities might enhance the therapeutic alliance. Clearly these are issues that call for more research, and we look forward to the promising potential of applying these positive activities with clinical populations in the context of more traditional clinical settings.

In summary, there appear to be several positive interventions that show promise for intervening with anxiety disorders. In our view, interventions that enhance positive affect such as LKM and gratitude have the potential to add something meaningful to our current treatments of anxiety disorders. Moreover, we see that cognitive bias modification procedures such as positive attention and positive interpretation training fit well with the approach of positive clinical psychology, and have the potential to contravene important cognitive dysfunctions that are evident in anxiety disorders. In this regard we believe that the gratitude three-blessings treatment may also shift one's attention and interpretations toward the positive. Finally, we see potential in positive reappraisal interventions to help individuals more effectively cope with stressful events.

Let us conclude this chapter with what we believe to be the most important "take home message" from this chapter. First, it strikes us that there is a malevolent worldview that seems to be common across the anxiety disorders. In this regard we believe that positive interventions that enhance positive affect, positive attention, and positive interpretations, should help transform one's view of the world into a more benevolent place. Second, we would like to highlight the maladaptive self-preoccupation that seems to characterize the anxiety disorders. This excessive self-focus seems to call for treatments that help individuals focus more on others. While clinicians often argue that individuals with emotional disorders need to fix their own issues and self-esteem before they can focus on reaching out to others, this is an assumption that remains to be tested by research. Here again we would like to highlight Crocker's egosystem versus ecosystem approach (2008, 2011). We believe that her theory has much to offer a positive clinical psychology, and treatments such as acts of kindness, LKM, and gratitude interventions are other-oriented treatments that should help move individuals "from egosystem to ecosystem."

Although the positive clinical psychology approach to anxiety disorders is still in its infancy, we believe that there is great potential here. We now conclude with the question that we opened this chapter with: can positive emotions and positive activities counteract the effects of fear and anxiety? We believe that the studies described in this chapter provide a promising answer to this question, but we look forward to more research. Did the beauty of Kauai calm the fear that the first author experienced when he perceived the danger of a car rushing at him in his lane? As the first author and his wife turned off of the highway to explore Waimea Canyon, this frightening episode was soon forgotten, seemingly drowned out by the beauty of the Grand Canyon of the Pacific. Indeed, the first author and his wife forgot to tell their harrowing highway story to their family until over a week after their vacation. Research has now provided hopeful hints that indeed, positive emotions and activities may help contravene dysfunctional fear and anxiety.

References

Alden, L. E. & Trew, J. L. (2013). If it makes you happy: Engaging in kind acts increases positive affect in socially anxious individuals. *Emotion, 13*, 64–75. doi.10.1037/a0027761.

Amir, N., Beard, C., & Bower, E. (2005). Interpretation bias and social anxiety. *Cognitive Therapy and Research, 29*, 433–443. doi.10.1007/s10608-005-2834-5.

Barlow, D. H., Allen, L. B., & Choate, M. L. (2004). Toward a unified treatment for the emotional disorders. *Behavior Therapy, 35*, 205–230. doi.10.1016/S0005-7894(04)80036-4.

Baumeister, R. F., Bratslavsky, E., Finkenauer, C., & Vohs, K. D. (2001). Bad is stronger than good. *Review of General Psychology, 5*, 323–370. doi.10.1037/1089-2680.5.4.323.

Beard, C. & Amir, N. (2008). A multi-session interpretation modification program: Changes in interpretation and social anxiety. *Behaviour Research and Therapy, 46*, 1135–1141. doi.10.1016/j.brat.2008.05.012.

Borkovec, T. D., Alcaine, O., & Behar, E. (2004). Avoidance theory of worry and generalized anxiety disorder. In: R. G. Heimberg, C. L. Turk, & D. S. Mennin (Eds.), *Generalized anxiety disorder: Advances in research and practice* (pp. 77–108). New York: Guilford.

Borkovec, T. D., Robinson, E., Pruzinsky, T., & Depress, J. A. (1983). Preliminary exploration of worry: Some characteristics and processes. *Behaviour Research and Therapy, 21*, 9–16. doi.10.1016/0005-7967(83)90121-3.

Bryant, F. B., Smart, C. M., & King, S. P. (2005). Using the past to enhance the present: Boosting happiness through positive reminiscence. *Journal of Happiness Studies, 6*, 227–260. doi.10.1007/s10902-005-3889-4.

Carl, J. R., Soskin, D. P., Kerns, C., & Barlow, D. H. (2013). Positive emotion regulation in emotional disorders: A theoretical review. *Clinical Psychology Review, 33*, 343–360. doi.10.1016/j.cpr.2013.01.003.

Clark, L. A. & Watson, D. A. (1991). Tripartite model of anxiety and depression: Psychometric evidence and taxonomic implications. *Journal of Abnormal Psychology, 100*, 316–336. doi.10.1037/0021-843X.100.3.316.

Crocker, J. (2008). From egosystem to ecosystem: Implications for learning, relationships, and well-being. In: H. A. Wayment & J. J. Brauer (Eds.), *Transcending self-interest: Psychological explorations of the quiet ego* (pp. 63–72). Washington, DC: American Psychological Association. doi.10.1037/11771-006.

Crocker, J. (2011). Safety in numbers: Shifting from egosystem to ecosystem. *Psychological Inquiry, 22*, 259–264. doi.10.1080/1047840X.2011.624978.

Crocker, J. & Canevello, A. (2011). Egosystem and ecosystem: Motivational perspectives on caregiving. In: S. E. Brown, M. Brown, & L. A. Penner (Eds.), *Moving beyond self-interest: Perspectives from evolutionary biology, neuroscience, and the social sciences* (pp. 211–223). Oxford: Oxford University Press.

Diener, E. & Emmons, R. A. (1985). The independence of positive and negative affect. *Journal of Personality and Social Psychology, 47*, 1105–1117. doi.10.1037/0022-3514.47.5.1105.

Emmons, R. A. & McCullough, M. E. (2003). Counting blessings versus burdens: An empirical investigation of gratitude and subjective well-being in daily life. *Journal of Personality and Social Psychology, 84*, 377–389. doi.10.1037/0022-3514.84.2.377.

Fava, G. A., Ruini, C., Rafanelli, C., Finos, L., Salmaso, L., Mangelli, L. et al. (2005). Well-being therapy of generalized anxiety disorder. *Psychotherapy and Psychosomatics, 74*, 26–30. doi.10.1159/000082023.

Fox, E. (2004). Maintenance or capture of attention in anxiety-related biases? In: J. Yiend (Ed.), *Cognition, emotion, and psychopathology: Theoretical, empirical, and clinical directions*. New York: Cambridge University Press.

Fredrickson, B. L. (1998). What good are positive emotions? *Review of General Psychology, 2*, 300–319. doi.10.1037/1089-2680.2.3.300.

Fredrickson, B. L. (2001). The role of positive emotions in positive psychology: The broaden-and-build theory of positive emotions. *American Psychologist, 56*, 218–226. doi.10.1037/0003-066X.56.3.218.

Fredrickson, B. L. & Joiner, T. (2002). Positive emotions trigger upward spirals toward emotional well-being. *Psychological Science, 13*, 172–175. doi.10.1111/1467-9280.00431.

Fredrickson, B. L. & Levinson, R. W. (1998). Positive emotions speed recovery from the cardiovascular sequelae of negative emotions. *Cognition and Emotion, 12*, 191–220. doi.10.1080/026999398379718.

Fredrickson, B. L., Cohn, M. A., Coffey, K. A., Pek, L. & Finkel, S. M. (2008). Open hearts build lives: Positive emotions, induced through Loving-kindness meditation, build consequential personal resources. *Journal of Personality and Social Psychology, 95*, 1045–1062. doi.10.1037/a0013262.

Fredrickson, B. L., Mancuso, R. A., Branigan, C., & Tugade, M. M. (2000). The undoing effect of positive emotions. *Motivation and Emotion, 24*, 237–258. doi.10.1023/A:1010796329158.

Fredrickson, B. L., Tugade, M. M., Waugh, C. E., & Larkin, G. R. (2003). What good are positive emotions in crises? A prospective study of resilience and emotions following the terrorist attacks on the United States on September 11, 2001. *Journal of Personality and Social Psychology, 84*, 365–376. doi.10.1037/0022-3514.84.2.365.

Garland, E. L., Fredrickson, B. L., Kring, A. M., Johnson, D. P., Meyer, P. S., & Penn, D. L. (2010). Upward spirals of positive emotions counter downward spirals of negativity: insights from the broaden-and-build theory and affective neuroscience on the treatment of emotion dysfunctions and deficits in psychopathology. *Clinical Psychology Review, 30*, 849–864. doi.10.1016/j.cpr.2010.03.002.

Geraghty, A. W. A., Wood, A. M., & Hyland, M. E. (2010). Dissociating the facets of hope: Agency and pathways predict drop out from unguided self-help therapy in opposite directions. *Journal of Research in Personality, 44*, 155–158. doi.10.1016/j.jrp.2009.12.003.

Gilboa-Schechtman, E., Franklin, M. E., & Foa, E. B. (2000). Anticipated reactions to social events: Differences among individuals with generalized social phobia, obsessive compulsive disorder, and non-anxious controls. *Cognitive Therapy and Research, 24*, 731–746. doi.10.1023/A:1005595513315.

Grafton, B., Ang, C., & MacLeod, C. (2012). Always look at the bright side of life: The attentional basis of positive affectivity. *European Journal of Personality, 26*, 133–144. doi.10.1002/per.1842.

Grey, S. & Mathews, A. (2000). Effects of training on interpretation of emotional ambiguity. *Quarterly Journal of Experimental Psychology, 53*, 1143–1162. doi.10.1080/02724980050156335.

Hayes, S., Hirsch, C. R., Krebs, G., & Mathews, A. (2010). The effects of modifying interpretation bias on worry in generalized anxiety disorder. *Behaviour Research and Therapy, 48*, 171–178. doi.10.1016/j.brat.2009.10.006.

Hayes, S., Hirsch, C. R., & Mathews, A. (2010). Facilitating a benign attentional bias reduces thought intrusions. *Journal of Abnormal Psychology, 119*, 235–240. doi.10.1037/a0018264.

Hayes, S. C., Luoma, J. B., Bond, F. W., Masuda, A., & Lillis, J. (2006). Acceptance and commitment therapy: Model, processes, and outcomes. *Behaviour Research and Therapy, 44*, 1–25. doi.10.1016/j.brat.2005.06.006.

Hertel, P. T., Brozovich, F., Joorman, J., & Gotlib, I. H. (2008). Biases in interpretation and memory in generalized social phobia. *Journal of Abnormal Psychology, 117*, 278–288. doi.10.1037/0021-843X.117.2.278.

Hertel, P. T. & Mathews, A. (2011). Cognitive bias modification: Past perspectives, current findings, and future applications. *Perspectives on Psychological Science, 6*, 521–536. doi.10.1177/1745691611421205.

Hirsch, C. R. & Mathews, A. (2012). A cognitive model of pathological worry. *Behaviour Research and Therapy, 50*, 636–646. doi.10.1016/j.brat.2012.06.007.

Hirsch, C. R., Hayes, S., & Mathews, A. (2009). Looking on the bright side: Accessing benign meanings reduces worry. *Journal of Abnormal Psychology, 118*, 44–54. doi.10.1037/a0013473.

Ingram, R. E. (1990). Self-focused attention in clinical disorders: Review and a conceptual model. *Psychological Bulletin, 107*, 156–176. doi.10.1037/0033-2909.107.2.156.

Isen, A. M., Daubman, K. A., & Nowicki, G. P. (1987). Positive affect facilitates creative problem solving. *Journal of Personality and Social Psychology, 52*, 122–1131. doi.10.1037/0022-3514.52.6.1122.

Kashdan, T. B. (2007). Social anxiety spectrum and diminished positive experiences: Theoretical synthesis and meta-analysis. *Clinical Psychology Review, 27*, 348–365. doi.10.1016/j.cpr.2006.12.003.

Kashdan, T. B. & Rottenberg, J. (2010). Psychological flexibility as a fundamental aspect of health. *Clinical Psychology Review, 30*, 865–878.

Kashdan, T. B., Weeks, J. W., & Savostyanova, A. A. (2011). Whether, how, and when social anxiety shapes positive experiences and events: A self-regulatory framework and treatment implications. *Clinical Psychology Review, 31*, 786–799. doi.10.1016/j.cpr.2011.03.012.

Kok, B. E. & Fredrickson, B. L. (2010). Upward spirals of the heart: Autonomic flexibility, as indexed by vagal tone, reciprocally and prospectively predicts positive emotions and social connectedness. *Biological Psychology, 85*, 432–436. doi.10.1016/j.biopsycho.2010.09.005.

Lyubomirsky, S., Sheldon, K. M., & Schkade, D. (2005). Pursuing happiness: The architecture of sustainable change. *Review of General Psychology, 9*, 111–131. doi.10.1037/1089-2680.9.2.111.

Mackintosh, B., Mathews, A., Yiend, J., Ridgeway, V., & Cook, E. (2006). Induced biases in emotional interpretation influence stress vulnerability and endure despite changes in context. *Behavior Therapy, 37*, 209–222. doi.10.1016/j.beth.2006.03.001.

MacLeod, C., Mathews, A., & Tata, P. (1986). Attentional bias in emotional disorders. *Journal of Abnormal Psychology*, *95*, 15–20. doi.10.1037/0021-843X.95.1.15.

Mathews, A. & Mackintosh, B. (2000). Induced emotional interpretation bias and anxiety. *Journal of Abnormal Psychology*, *109*, 602–615. doi.10.1037/0021-843X.109.4.602.

Mathews, A. & MacLeod, C. (2005). Cognitive vulnerability to emotional disorders. *Annual Review of Clinical Psychology*, *1*, 167–195. doi.10.1146/annurev.clinpsy.1.102803.143916.

McComb, D., Watkins, P., & Kolts, R. (2005, April). *The relationship between gratitude, depression, and anxiety*. Presentation to the 85th Annual Convention of the Western Psychological Association, Portland, OR.

Moses, E. B. & Barlow, D. H. (2006). A new unified treatment approach for emotional disorders based on emotion science. *Current Directions in Psychological Science*, *15*, 146–150. doi.10.1111/j.0963-7214.2006.00425.x.

Neal. M., Watkins, P. C., & Kolts, R. (2005). *Does gratitude inhibit intrusive memories?* Presentation to the Annual Convention of the American Psychological Association, Washington, DC, August.

Nelson, D. W. & Knight, A. E. (2010). The power of positive recollections: Reducing test anxiety and enhancing college student efficiency and performance. *Journal of Applied Social Psychology*, *40*, 732–745. doi.10.1111/j.1559-1816.2010.00595.x.

Nolen-Hoeksema, S. & Watkins, E. R. (2011). A heuristic for developing transdiagnostic models of psychopathology: Explaining multifinality and divergent trajectories. *Perspectives on Psychological Science*, *6*, 589–609. doi.10.1177/1745691611419672.

Pennebaker, J. W. (1997). *Opening up: The healing power of expressing emotions*. New York: Guilford.

Salemink, E., van den Hout, M., & Kindt, M. (2010). Generalization of modified interpretation bias across tasks and domains. *Cognition & Emotion*, *24*, 453–464. doi.10.1080/02699930802692053.

Seligman, M. E. P., Steen, T. A., Park, N., & Peterson, C. (2005). Positive psychology progress: Empirical validation of interventions. *American Psychologist*, *60*, 410–421. doi.10.1037/0003-066X.60.5.410.

Taylor, C. T., Bomyea, J., & Amir, N. (2011). Malleability of attentional bias for positive emotional information and anxiety vulnerability. *Emotion*, *11*, 127–138. doi.10.1037/a0021301.

Tran, T., Hertel, P. T., & Joorman, J. (2011). Cognitive bias modification: Induced interpretive biases affect memory. *Emotion*, *11*, 145–152. doi.10.1037/a0021754.

Vassilopoulos, S. P. & Banerjee, R. (2010). Social interaction anxiety and the discounting of positive interpersonal events. *Behavioural and Cognitive Psychotherapy*, *38*, 597–609. doi.10.1017/S1352465810000433.

Watkins, P. C. (2008). Gratitude: The amplifier of blessing. In: A. Przepiorka (Ed.), *Closer to emotions II*. Lublin, Poland: Publishing House of Catholic University of Lublin.

Watkins, P. C. (2011). Gratitude and well-being. In: C. Martin-Kumm & C. Tarquinio (Eds.), *Traité de psychologie positive: Théories et implications pratiques* (pp. 519–537). Brussels: De Boeck.

Watkins, P. C. (2014). *Gratitude and the good life: Toward a psychology of appreciation*. Dordrecht: Springer.

Watkins, P. C., Cruz, L., Holben, H., & Kolts, R. L. (2008). Taking care of business? Grateful processing of unpleasant memories. *Journal of Positive Psychology*, *3*, 87–99. doi.10.1080/17439760701760567.

Watkins, P. C., Neal, M., & Thomas, M. (2004). *Grateful recall and positive memory bias: Relationships to subjective well-being*. Presentation to the Annual Convention of the American Psychological Association, Honolulu, HI, July.

Watkins, P. C., Pereira, A., & Mathews, A. (2013). Exploring how gratitude impacts cognitive processes that enhance well-being. In: R. A. Emmons & M. McMinn (Chairs), *Mechanisms of gratitude: Exploring how gratitude enhances well-being*. Symposium presented at the Annual Convention of the American Psychological Association, Honolulu, HI, August.

Watkins, P. C., Sparrow, A., Pereira, A., & Suominen, S. (2013). *Are gifts better than goods? Benefits are better when experienced with gratitude*. Poster presented to the Annual Convention of the American Psychological Association, Honolulu, HI, August.

Watkins, P. C., Uhder, J., & Pichinevskiy, S. (2015). Grateful recounting enhances subjective well-being: The importance of grateful processing. *Journal of Positive Psychology*, *2*, 91–98. doi.10.1080/17439760.2014.927909.

Watkins, P. C., Woodward, K., Stone, T., & Kolts, R. (2003). Gratitude and happiness: Development of a measure of gratitude, and relationships with subjective well-being. *Social Behavior and Personality*, *31*, 431–452. doi.10.2224/sbp.2003.31.5.431.

Watkins, P. C., Xiong, I., & Kolts, R. L. (2008). *How grateful processing brings closure to troubling memories.* Presentation at the 20th Annual Convention of the Association for Psychological Science, Chicago, IL, May.

Watson, D. & Naragon-Gainey, K (2010). On the specificity of positive emotional dysfunction in psycho-pathology: Evidence from the mood and anxiety disorders and schizophrenia/schizotypy. *Clinical Psychology Review, 30,* 839–848. doi.10.1016/j.cpr.2009.11.002.

Watson, D., Clark, L. A., & Carey, G. (1988). Positive and negative affectivity and their relation to anxiety and depressive disorders. *Journal of Abnormal Psychology, 97,* 346–353. doi.10.1037/0021-843X.97.3.346.

Wenzlaff, R. M. & Bates, D. E. (2000). The relative efficacy of concentration and suppression strategies of mental control. *Personality and Social Psychology Bulletin, 26,* 1200–1212. doi.10.1177/0146167200262003.

Wood, A. M., Joseph, S., & Linley, P. A. (2007). Coping style as a psychological resource of grateful people. *Journal of Social and Clinical Psychology, 26,* 1076–1093. doi.10.1521/jscp.2007.26.9.1076.

Wood, A. M., Maltby, J., Gillett, R., Linley, P. A., & Joseph, S. (2008). The role of gratitude in the development of social support, stress, and depression: Two longitudinal studies. *Journal of Research in Personality, 42,* 854–871. doi.10.1016/j.jrp.2007.11.003.

15

A Growth Perspective on Post-traumatic Stress

Elizabeth L. Addington, Richard G. Tedeschi, and Lawrence G. Calhoun

A Growth Perspective on Post-traumatic Stress

Since it was incorporated into the third edition of the *Diagnostic and Statistical Manual* (American Psychiatric Association, 1980) as post-traumatic stress disorder (PTSD), post-traumatic stress responses have been viewed in light of specific symptoms. In the fifth edition of that manual this approach continues, and these symptoms include mental intrusions, avoidance, negative thoughts and mood, and hyperarousal (American Psychiatric Association, 2013). Some have suggested additional elements to this post-traumatic response, including the idea that PTSD can include an aspect of moral injury, that is, a disruption in an individual's sense of personal morality and ability to act in a moral and just manner (Drescher, Foy, Kelly, Leshner, Schutz, & Litz, 2011). The concept of PTSD as moral injury fits within a broader framework of understanding the impact of trauma as a disruptive cognitive and emotional experience.

The symptoms seen in PTSD can be considered to be expressions of a disruption of the system of core beliefs and concepts that are used by people to understand the world and their place in it. These understandings have been referred to as the assumptive world (Janoff-Bulman, 1992), working models (Epstein, 1991), and theories of reality (Parkes, 1971). This approach is essentially cognitive, and it is built on the assumption that personal constructs or schemas provide a guide to events in the environment and responses to these events. Trauma can be understood as a set of circumstances that not only produces immediate physiological challenges to the systems that help people avoid or deal with danger and survive, but also challenge or violate people's views of the world and their place in it. Somewhat paradoxically, these challenges to the system of core beliefs can also provide an opportunity to reconsider those beliefs, and to fashion a new understanding of oneself, the world, and the future. In this reconsideration there may emerge a perspective that is more adaptive, and perhaps more profound, in the recognition of new possibilities for living. When these changes to core beliefs hold more value than the prior system, the result can be described as post-traumatic growth (PTG): *positive changes that result from the struggle with highly stressful and demanding life events* (Calhoun & Tedeschi, 1999). Therefore, for a more complete understanding of the experience of traumatized people, and to consider their possibilities for their futures, it is important to consider positive outcomes as well as negative outcomes of trauma. Clinicians who take into account this more complete and accurate picture of the experiences and possibilities for trauma survivors need to ask explicitly about this variety of experiences, and recognize positive and negative outcomes are not mutually exclusive.

The Wiley Handbook of Positive Clinical Psychology, First Edition. Edited by Alex M. Wood and Judith Johnson.
© 2016 John Wiley & Sons, Ltd. Published 2016 by John Wiley & Sons, Ltd.

PTG has been documented in people from diverse places and cultures, dealing with a wide a variety of highly stressful events, including the following: earthquake survivors in China (Xu & Liao, 2011); first responders in the United States, Australia, and eastern and western Europe (Shakespeare-Finch, Gow, & Smith, 2005; Chopko & Schwartz, 2009; Kehl, Knuth, Holubová, Hulse, & Schmidt, 2014); military veterans and active duty service members (Lee, Luxton, Reger, & Gahm, 2010; Kaler, Erbes, Tedeschi, Arbisi, & Polusny, 2011; Palmer, Graca, & Occhietti, 2012); patients with severe or chronic illness (Silva, Crespo, & Canavarro, 2012a; Bluvstein, Moravchick, Sheps, Schreiber, & Bloch, 2013; Danhauer et al., 2013), as well as their family and professional caregivers (Cadell, Regehr, & Hemsworth, 2003; Şenol-Durak & Ayvaşik, 2010; Taku, 2014), and a variety of other life crises (Calhoun & Tedeschi, 2013).

Levels of PTG may vary with the specific circumstances. For example, sexual abuse survivors have reported lower levels of PTG than bereaved persons and survivors of motor vehicle accidents (Shakespeare-Finch & Armstrong, 2010). Survivors of different types of cancer also report differing amounts of PTG, with breast cancer survivors having the highest PTG scores (Morris & Shakespeare-Finch, 2011a). This is consistent with the trend toward higher PTG among women than men, regardless of event type (Vishnevsky, Cann, Calhoun, Tedeschi, & Demakis, 2010).

The Development of PTG

PTG develops as a result of the encounter with a seismic event; one that challenges or shatters core beliefs, or that brings to light the necessity for a more complete and complex perspective. The event is like a psychological earthquake, significantly challenging, or perhaps even bringing down, the schema system and setting off a process of reconstruction. What is important is that the circumstances are of a kind and intensity that lead a person to question what they have believed in a fundamental way. In this process, new schemas may develop that can provide increased meaning in life and more resilience to future shocks. Thus, the event is disruptive and distressing, at least initially, and it may never be viewed as completely positive. Still, positive elements can emerge through the processes described below, with positive and negative responses at times existing alongside and interacting with one another to influence long-term outcomes.

In the aftermath of a seismic event, rebuilding the worldview can be time-consuming and emotionally laden. To let go of what was once thought to be true can cause great distress. The emotional distress may be associated with the destruction of the assumptive world and not the process of going through the event itself. Intrusive thoughts and images are common post-traumatic reactions and may represent an attempt to come to terms with what has happened. The questions about what happened, how it happened, and why it happened provide many opportunities for rumination. For PTG to occur, this rumination must transition from a type that is unproductive and intrusive, to a type that is more deliberate and reflective. In order for this transition to more deliberate and reflective rumination to occur, the survivor of highly stressful events will need to organize this thinking, and gain a sense of control over it. With this organization and control, the questions about what happened and what to believe about oneself, the world, and the future can be considered more constructively.

Moving toward deliberate reflective thinking can be assisted by appropriate self-disclosure. Revealing thought processes to someone else can encourage an attempt at organization and articulation, shaping the thought processes into something that can be grasped by others. The disclosure can occur within conversations or in written accounts (Stockton, Joseph, & Hunt, 2014). The conversations may be in the form of prayer, adaptive writing, psychotherapy, or by telling the story of what happened and its aftermath to a caring and attentive listener who is a friend or acquaintance. We have called the person who is willing to listen attentively, to help trauma survivors create a coherent narrative out of their experiences, and to respond with humility and respect to the trauma survivor, an *expert companion* (Tedeschi & Calhoun, 2006; Calhoun & Tedeschi, 2013).

Studies of social support and of the influence of social and cultural context suggest that this kind of expert companionship can be crucial in the process of trauma recovery in a way that promotes PTG. For example, a review of terror management theory concluded that, among people who faced a threat of death, active engagement with social support and greater cognitive coping could facilitate positive outcomes such as PTG (Vail, Juhl, Arndt, Vess, Routledge, & Rutjens, 2012). In a longitudinal study of women with breast cancer, greater social support seeking and cognitive coping at the time of surgery were associated with greater PTG five months later (Silva et al., 2012a). Similarly, in structural equation models designed to test the PTG theoretical model, examining core beliefs, rumination, and social support have predicted higher levels of PTG (Morris & Shakespeare-Finch, 2011b; Wilson, Morris, & Chambers, 2014). However, typical conceptualizations of social support and their measures may miss the subtle ways of communicating and especially listening that expert companions provide.

The process of PTG leads to several possible changes in core beliefs: changes in relationships with others; a recognition of new possibilities for life paths; spiritual development or greater understanding of existential matters; greater appreciation of life; and a recognition of personal strength. These domains of PTG have been frequently identified in evaluations of the Post-traumatic Growth Inventory (PTGI), a measure that was developed out of qualitative analyses of reports of persons dealing with major life crises and from a review of the literature on responses to traumatic events (Tedeschi & Calhoun, 1996; Taku, Cann, Calhoun, & Tedeschi, 2008). In most cases, PTG is measured using the PTGI, although other measures of similar constructs are sometimes utilized (Joseph & Linley, 2008).

PTG also results in a narrative that encompasses the life prior to the event, the event itself, the aftermath, and the possible positive future, in a way that can guide the trauma survivor forward into constructive choices. There appears to be a wisdom that accrues in this process of considering the lesson from the struggle, and it is characterized by an appreciation of paradox or dialectical thinking, and an understanding that is not merely intellectual, but salient in an emotional way (Calhoun & Tedeschi, 2013). PTG may also promote resilience, such that greater post-traumatic growth after an initial trauma may protect against negative consequences of later events (Janoff-Bulman, 2006). This may be particularly relevant in the context of traumas involving repeated exposure, such as ongoing military conflict or interpersonal violence. For example, a Dutch study of survivors of interpersonal crimes supported this notion. Those who were revictimized reported an increase in PTSD symptoms if they experienced low levels of PTG after their initial trauma, whereas symptoms did not significantly increase among those with greater PTG (Kunst, Winkel, & Bogaerts, 2010).

PTG and PTSD

Post-traumatic distress and post-traumatic growth are not opposite ends of the same spectrum. They are best viewed as distinct constructs that may co-occur in some and may independently influence adjustment (Baker, Kelly, Calhoun, Cann, & Tedeschi, 2008; Barskova & Oesterreich, 2009; Cann, Calhoun, Tedeschi, & Solomon, 2010; Morris & Shakespeare-Finch, 2011b; Palmer et al., 2012; Barrington & Shakespeare-Finch, 2013). For example, post-traumatic distress is associated with poorer quality of life and less meaning in life, while PTG is associated with higher levels on these measures of well-being (Cann et al., 2010).

Viewing an event as central to one's identity or life narrative can be associated with both PTSD and PTG (Boals & Schuettler, 2011; Schuettler & Boals, 2011; Groleau, Calhoun, Cann,

& Tedeschi, 2012). However, the paths by which these differing outcomes develop vary. Intrusive rumination contributes strongly to PTSD, while deliberate rumination and social support play a key role in developing PTG (Prati & Pietrantoni, 2009; Calhoun, Cann, & Tedeschi, 2010; Morris & Shakespeare-Finch, 2011b; Groleau et al., 2012). Moreover, avoidance coping remains a significant component of PTSD but not PTG (Boals & Schuettler, 2011; Schuettler & Boals, 2011).

Thus, attending to themes and processes related to both distress and growth can provide the most comprehensive approach to treating PTSD. Clinicians may be especially helpful to trauma survivors by recognizing clients who view traumas as pivotal events in life and then facilitating more intentional, constructive processing of the events and their effects. Working with survivors and their communities to enhance social support can additionally ameliorate post-traumatic outcomes.

To better understand the relationship between PTG and PTSD, a recent meta-analysis examined data from studies including participants with a variety of traumatic experiences. While linear and quadratic terms were both significant, the quadratic relationship was significantly stronger (Shakespeare-Finch & Lurie-Beck, 2014). The curve formed an inverted U-shape, such that PTG increased among people with greater PTSD symptoms – but only to a point; at the highest levels of PTSD symptom severity, PTG became less likely. The relationship appeared to differ by event type, with weaker or nonsignificant associations between PTG and PTSD among survivors of serious illness or sexual abuse, or their caregivers. While small sample size may have limited the power to detect effects in these populations (Shakespeare-Finch & Lurie-Beck, 2014), a review of PTSD and PTG in breast cancer survivors similarly concluded that the two were not related in a systematic way (Koutrouli, Anagnostopoulos, & Potamianos, 2012). Nonetheless, PTG may co-exist with symptoms of PTSD in some people (Barskova & Oesterreich, 2009).

The relationship between post-traumatic distress and PTG may depend more specifically on which category of PTSD symptoms is considered. For example, studies have found positive associations between PTG and intrusion (Barskova & Oesterreich, 2009), while post-traumatic avoidance may be negatively associated with PTG (Knaevelsrud, Liedl, & Maercker, 2010). This more nuanced view is consistent with the PTG model (Calhoun et al., 2010). As described above, PTG is more likely to develop when an experience is stressful enough to initially prompt some disruptive thoughts about the event and its implications for one's life – if those intrusions eventually give way to more deliberate cognitive processing (Calhoun et al., 2010; Cann et al., 2011). A previous review supported this *impact-engagement* model (Stanton, Bower, & Low, 2006). PTSD symptoms of intrusions may represent the impact of the event that is first required to catalyze the process, while avoidance would preclude the cognitive engagement that is necessary to advance the development of PTG. Thus, clinicians who recognize intrusions as not only a sign of distress, but also as a potential gateway to more constructive processes may seize this opportunity to facilitate PTG.

PTG as Buffer

When both PTG and PTSD symptoms are present, PTG may protect against some of the negative psychological outcomes normally associated with PTSD. For example, a study of cardiovascular patients found that PTG buffered the harmful effects of post-traumatic stress on mental well-being (Bluvstein et al., 2013). Respondents with more PTSD symptoms had poorer psychological health, as measured by multiple scales, if they also reported lower levels of PTG. However, those with greater PTSD symptoms *and* PTG had higher psychological well-being, higher mental quality of life, and less distress. Similar results have been reported among women with breast cancer (Silva, Moreira, & Canavarro, 2012). Among women who perceived more negative consequences of cancer, those with higher PTG had better psychological and social quality of life, as well as less depression. PTG several months after breast cancer diagnosis predicts less depression and better psychological quality of life at one-year post-diagnosis (Silva et al., 2012a). A meta-analysis of cancer and HIV/AIDS research further established links between PTG and better mental health (more positive and less negative), as well as better self-reported physical health (Sawyer, Ayers, & Field, 2010).

PTG's role as a stress buffer is not unique to medical samples. Analyses of mixed trauma samples have found significant links between PTG and meaning in life, which additionally contributes to life satisfaction (Groleau et al., 2012; Triplett, Tedeschi, Cann, Calhoun, & Reeve, 2012). In a study of individuals who had experienced a variety of stressful events, including violent crimes and military deployment, quality of life was better among respondents reporting negative effects of their trauma – if they also reported higher PTG (Cann et al., 2010). Outcomes of traumatic events may therefore depend on the combination of positive and negative responses, and addressing both may provide the most useful approach to understanding trauma responses and improving survivors' well-being.

In clinical practice, combat veterans have described positive experiences stemming from the struggle with service-related trauma. The US military has increasingly recognized the importance and potential for PTG and other strengths-based outcomes, in addition to targeting decreased PTSD symptoms. The US Army's Comprehensive Soldier and Family Fitness program (csf2.army.mil) includes an approach to cultivating PTG (Tedeschi & McNally, 2011). Consistent with the PTG model, which notes the importance of appropriate social support for developing PTG, veterans with more supportive or cohesive units also reported higher levels of PTG (Pietrzak et al., 2010; Mitchell, Gallaway, Millikan, & Bell, 2013). Although causality has not been established, greater PTG in previously deployed US service members has been associated with lower suicidal ideation (Bush, Skopp, McCann, & Luxton, 2011; Gallaway, Millikan, & Bell, 2011), along with less emotional lability and fewer symptoms of PTSD, depression, and substance abuse (Bush et al., 2011).

PTG as Secondary Outcome of Trauma-focused Treatment

PTG occurs spontaneously in some, while in others it can result secondarily from trauma-focused therapies. In a study of trauma survivors receiving outpatient prolonged exposure therapy for PTSD, post-traumatic growth – particularly relating to others, new possibilities, and personal strength – increased from pre- to post-treatment (Hagenaars & van Minnen, 2010). Furthermore, these increases in PTG were associated with decreases in PTSD symptoms. This study showed an additional protective effect of PTG, in that higher pre-treatment scores on the Appreciation of Life subscale predicted lower post-treatment PTSD severity (Hagenaars & van Minnen, 2010). A cognitive-behavioral writing intervention delivered online to survivors of various traumas also reported pre- to post-treatment increases in PTG (Knaevelsrud et al., 2010). Post-treatment PTG was associated with decreased intrusion symptoms, providing further support for the role of deliberate cognitive processing in development of PTG and for the potential for PTG to moderate post-traumatic distress.

Reminders and Recommendations

Now that post-traumatic growth is widely known and researched, reminders about the basic assumptions of the concept may be unnecessary. However, we have found that, given the occasional misunderstanding that some may have, reminders about PTG may still be useful.

To reiterate what the research summarized above has indicated, post-traumatic symptoms and psychological distress, on the one hand, and PTG, on the other, are best viewed as independent dimensions. Although in some contexts they can be related, the general indication is that they tend to be independent; when they are related, PTG seems to buffer distress and facilitate well-being. Although there is some intuitive appeal in assuming that if people grow from their struggle with a major life crisis they will experience a commensurate reduction in feelings of loss, grief, and general distress, that is not necessarily so. Individuals and organizations working with survivors of highly stressful events are therefore reminded not to lose sight of either positive or negative reactions; instead, attending to signs of both distress and growth will provide the most valid and comprehensive response.

In addition, the potential relationship between post-traumatic growth and post-traumatic well-being is clearly dependent on how well-being is assessed. Often well-being is assessed narrowly, using measures that focus on symptoms or positive or negative emotional states. We argue that well-being needs to be assessed more broadly, and from our point of view more deeply, with inclusion of elements that can be described as *eudemonic* (Ryan & Deci, 2001). Thinking of well-being in this way may be one avenue to pursue to further clarify how PTG and distress/well-being are related. If well-being is viewed as including components such as meaningful connections to other human beings, a well thought out and well-developed sense of life priorities, a sense of life purpose, the ability to live mindfully in the moment, and to appreciate the life one does have, then we might anticipate that PTG may well be connected consistently and strongly with those elements. In part, we might expect such relationships between *eudemonic* well-being and PTG simply because much of that broader conceptualization of well-being reflects the experience of PTG itself.

It is very clear that for some the experience of PTG comes at a very high price, and the price may include post-traumatic symptoms that are serious and that may be difficult to treat. Some scholars have reasonably cautioned both researchers and practitioners not to add to the burden of those struggling with the aftermath of trauma, tragedy, and loss by creating the general expectation that PTG is universal and is to be expected (Wortman, 2004). Here we state the obvious, but it is worth a reminder nevertheless. *PTG is neither inevitable, nor universal.* Scholars and practitioners need to be conscious of that truth, and to speak, work, and practice in ways that do not add to the difficult burdens already carried by those touched by traumatic events by suggesting that people who do not experience growth are somehow deficient.

Finally, a brief word about the validity of reports of post-traumatic growth. The data tend to offer very good support for the validity and reliability of inventories that assess PTG (see Calhoun & Tedeschi, 2013, for a more extended discussion). But, as with any self-report, there is always the possibility that distortion may result from trying to recall the past or from self-enhancing biases. However, among some quarters skepticism about reports of post-traumatic growth persist; extreme versions of this skepticism tend to regard all reports of PTG with suspicion at best and derision at worst. What should clinicians do when their clients seem to be reporting the experience of post-traumatic growth? Our suggestion is to accept it as the client's understanding of what has happened, and work within that framework. It is, indeed, curious that some of the few professionals who have great skepticism about reports of growth appear to readily accept reports of post-traumatic symptoms. As the counselor might ask a client - why do you think that is? Something to think about.

References

American Psychiatric Association. (1980). *DSM III: Diagnostic and statistical manual of mental disorders.* Washington, DC: American Psychiatric.

American Psychiatric Association. (2013). *Diagnostic and Statistical Manual of Mental Disorders: DSM-5.* Washington, DC: American Psychiatric Association.

Baker, J. M., Kelly, C., Calhoun, L. G., Cann, A., & Tedeschi, R. G. (2008). An examination of post-traumatic growth and post-traumatic depreciation: Two exploratory studies. *Journal of Loss and Trauma, 13,* 450–465. doi.10.1080/15325020802171367.

Barrington, A. & Shakespeare-Finch, J. (2013). Post-traumatic growth and post-traumatic depreciation as predictors of psychological adjustment. *Journal of Loss and Trauma, 18,* 429–443. doi.10.1080/15325024.2012.714210.

Barskova, T. & Oesterreich, R. (2009). Post-traumatic growth in people living with a serious medical condition and its relations to physical and mental health: A systematic review. *Disability and Rehabilitation, 31,* 1709–1733. doi.10.1080/09638280902738441.

Bluvstein, I., Moravchick, L., Sheps, D., Schreiber, S., & Bloch, M. (2013). Post-traumatic growth, post-traumatic stress symptoms and mental health among coronary heart disease survivors. *Journal of Clinical Psychology in Medical Settings, 20,* 164–172. doi.10.1007/s10880-012-9318-z.

Boals, A. & Schuettler, D. (2011). A double-edged sword: Event centrality, PTSD and post-traumatic growth. *Applied Cognitive Psychology, 25,* 817–822. doi.10.1002/acp.1753.

Bush, N. E., Skopp, N. A., McCann, R., & Luxton, D. D. (2011). Post-traumatic growth as protection against suicidal ideation after deployment and combat exposure. *Military Medicine, 176,* 1215–1222.

Cadell, S., Regehr, C., & Hemsworth, D. (2003). Factors contributing to post-traumatic growth: A proposed structural equation model. *American Journal of Orthopsychiatry, 73,* 279–287. doi.10.1037/0002-9432.73.3.279.

Calhoun, L. G. & Tedeschi, R. G. (1999). *Facilitating post-traumatic growth: A clinician's guide.* New York: Routledge.

Calhoun L.G. & Tedeschi, R.G. (2013) *Post-traumatic growth in clinical practice.* New York: Routledge.

Calhoun, L. G., Cann, A., & Tedeschi, R. G. (2010). The post-traumatic growth model: Sociocultural considerations. In: T. Weiss & R. Berger (Eds.), *Post-traumatic growth and culturally competent practice* (pp. 1–14). Hoboken, NJ: John Wiley.

Cann, A., Calhoun, L. G., Tedeschi, R. G., & Solomon, D. T. (2010). Post-traumatic growth and depreciation as independent experiences and predictors of well-being. *Journal of Loss and Trauma, 15,* 151–166. doi.10.1080/15325020903375826.

Cann, A., Calhoun, L. G., Tedeschi, R. G., Triplett, K. N., Vishnevsky, T., & Lindstrom, C. M. (2011). Assessing post-traumatic cognitive processes: The Event Related Rumination Inventory. *Anxiety, Stress & Coping, 24,* 137–156. doi:10.1080/10615806.2010.529901.

Chopko, B. A. & Schwartz, R. C. (2009). The relation between mindfulness and post-traumatic growth: A study of first responders to trauma-inducing incidents. *Journal of Mental Health Counseling, 31,* 363–376.

Danhauer, S. C., Russell, G. B., Tedeschi, R. G., Jesse, M. T., Vishnevsky, T., Daley, K., & Powell, B. L. (2013). A longitudinal investigation of post-traumatic growth in adult patients undergoing treatment for acute leukemia. *Journal of Clinical Psychology in Medical Settings, 20,* 13–24. doi.10.1007/s10880-012-9304-5.

Drescher, K. D., Foy, D. W., Kelly, C. M., Leshner, A., Schutz, K. E., & Litz, B. T. (2011). An exploration of the viability and usefulness of the construct of moral injury in war veterans. *Traumatology, 17,* 8–13. doi.org/10.1177/1534765610395615.

Epstein, S. (1991). The self-concept, the traumatic neurosis, and the structure of personality. In: D. Ozer, J. M. Healy, & A. J. Stewart (Eds.), *Perspectives in personality* (pp. 63–98) London: Jessica Kingsley.

Gallaway, M. S., Millikan, A. M., & Bell, M. R. (2011). The association between deployment-related post-traumatic growth among US Army soldiers and negative behavioral health conditions. *Journal of Clinical Psychology, 67,* 1151–1160. doi.10.1002/jclp.20837.

Groleau, J. M., Calhoun, L. G., Cann, A., & Tedeschi, R. G. (2012). The role of centrality of events in post-traumatic distress and post-traumatic growth. *Psychological Trauma: Theory, Research, Practice, and Policy, 5,* 477–483. doi.10.1037/a0028809.

Hagenaars, M. A. & van Minnen, A. (2010). Post-traumatic growth in exposure therapy for PTSD. *Journal of Traumatic Stress, 23,* 504–508. doi.10.1002/jts.20551.

Janoff-Bulman, R. (1992). *Shattered assumptions: Towards a new psychology of trauma.* New York: Free Press.

Janoff-Bulman, R. (2006). Schema change perspectives on post-traumatic growth. In: L. G. Calhoun & R. G. Tedeschi (Eds.), *The Handbook of Post-traumatic Growth* (pp. 81–99). New York: Routledge.

Joseph, S. & Linley, P. (2008). Psychological assessment of growth following adversity: A review. In: S. Joseph & P. Linley (Eds.), *Trauma, recovery, and growth: Positive psychological perspectives on post-traumatic stress* (pp. 21–36). Hoboken, NJ: John Wiley.

Kaler, M. E., Erbes, C. R., Tedeschi, R. G., Arbisi, P. A., & Polusny, M. A. (2011). Factor structure and concurrent validity of the Post-traumatic Growth Inventory-Short Form among veterans from the Iraq War. *Journal of Traumatic Stress, 24,* 200–207. doi.10.1002/jts.20623.

Kehl, D., Knuth, D., Holubová, M., Hulse, L., & Schmidt, S. (2014). Relationships between firefighters' postevent distress and growth at different times after distressing incidents. *Traumatology, 20,* 253–261. doi:10.1037/h0099832.

Knaevelsrud, C., Liedl, A., & Maercker, A. (2010). Post-traumatic growth, optimism and openness as outcomes of a cognitive-behavioural intervention for post-traumatic stress reactions. *Journal of Health Psychology, 15,* 1030–1038. doi. 10.1177/1359105309360073.

Koutrouli, N., Anagnostopoulos, F., & Potamianos, G. (2012). Post-traumatic stress disorder and post-traumatic growth in breast cancer patients: A systematic review. *Women & Health, 52,* 503–516. doi.10.1080/03630242.2012.679337.

Kunst, M. J. J., Winkel, F. W., & Bogaerts, S. (2010). Post-traumatic growth moderates the association between violent revictimization and persisting PTSD symptoms in victims of interpersonal violence: A six-month follow-up study. *Journal of Social and Clinical Psychology, 29,* 527–545. doi.10.1521/jscp.2010.29.5.527.

Lee, J. A., Luxton, D. D., Reger, G. M., & Gahm, G. A. (2010). Confirmatory factor analysis of the Post-traumatic Growth Inventory with a sample of soldiers previously deployed in support of the Iraq and Afghanistan wars. *Journal of Clinical Psychology, 66,* 813–819. doi:10.1002/jclp.20692.

Mitchell, M. M., Gallaway, M. S., Millikan, A. M., & Bell, M. R. (2013). Combat exposure, unit cohesion, and demographic characteristics of soldiers reporting post-traumatic growth. *Journal of Loss and Trauma, 18,* 383–395. doi. 10.1080/15325024.2013.768847.

Morris, B. A. & Shakespeare-Finch, J. (2011a). Cancer diagnostic group differences in post-traumatic growth: Accounting for age, gender, trauma severity, and distress. *Journal of Loss and Trauma, 16,* 229–242. doi.10.1080/15325024.2010.519292.

Morris, B. A. & Shakespeare-Finch, J. (2011b). Rumination, post-traumatic growth, and distress: Structural equation modelling with cancer survivors. *Psycho-Oncology, 20,* 1176–1183. doi.10.1002/pon.1827.

Palmer, G. A., Graca, J. J., & Occhietti, K. E. (2012). Confirmatory factor analysis of the Post-traumatic Growth Inventory in a veteran sample with post-traumatic stress disorder. *Journal of Loss and Trauma, 17,* 545–556.

Parkes, C. M. (1971). Psycho-social transitions: A field for study. *Social Science and Medicine, 5,* 101–115.

Pietrzak, R. H., Goldstein, M. B., Malley, J. C., Rivers, A. J., Johnson, D. C., Morgan, C. A. I., & Southwick, S. M. (2010). Post-traumatic growth in veterans of Operations Enduring Freedom and Iraqi Freedom. *Journal of Affective Disorders, 126*(1/2), 230–235. doi.10.1016/j.jad.2010.03.021.

Prati, G. & Pietrantoni, L. (2009). Optimism, social support, and coping strategies as factors contributing to post-traumatic growth: A meta-analysis. *Journal of Loss and Trauma, 14,* 364–388. doi.10.1080/15325020902724271.

Ryan, R. M. & Deci, E. L. (2001). On happiness and human potentials: A review of research on hedonic and eudaimonic well-being.*Annual Review of Psychology, 52,* 141–166. Doi.10.1146/annurev.psych.52.1.141.

Sawyer, A., Ayers, S., & Field, A. P. (2010). Post-traumatic growth and adjustment among individuals with cancer or HIV/AIDS: A meta-analysis. *Clinical Psychology Review, 30,* 436–447. doi.10.1016/j.cpr.2010.02.004.

Schuettler, D. & Boals, A. (2011). The path to post-traumatic growth versus post-traumatic stress disorder: Contributions of event centrality and coping. *Journal of Loss and Trauma, 16,* 180–194. doi.10.1080/15325024.2010.519273.

Şenol-Durak, E. & Ayvaşik, H. B. (2010). Factors associated with post-traumatic growth among the spouses of myocardial infarction patients. *Journal of Health Psychology, 15,* 85–95. doi.10.1177/1359105309342472.

Shakespeare-Finch, J. & Armstrong, D. (2010). Trauma type and post-trauma outcomes: Differences between survivors of motor vehicle accidents, sexual assault, and bereavement. *Journal of Loss and Trauma, 15,* 69–82. doi.10.1080/15325020903373151.

Shakespeare-Finch, J. & Lurie-Beck, J. (2014). A meta-analytic clarification of the relationship between post-traumatic growth and symptoms of post-traumatic distress disorder. *Journal of Anxiety Disorders*, 28, 223–229. doi.10.1016/j.janxdis.2013.10.005.

Shakespeare-Finch, J., Gow, K., & Smith, S. (2005). Personality, coping and post-traumatic growth in emergency ambulance personnel. *Traumatology*, 11, 325–334. doi.10.1177/153476560501100410.

Silva, S. M., Crespo, C., & Canavarro, M. C. (2012a). Pathways for psychological adjustment in breast cancer: A longitudinal study on coping strategies and post-traumatic growth. *Psychology & Health*, 27, 1323–1341. doi.10.1080/08870446.2012.676644.

Silva, S. M., Moreira, H. C., & Canavarro, M. C. (2012b). Examining the links between perceived impact of breast cancer and psychosocial adjustment: The buffering role of post-traumatic growth. *Psycho-Oncology*, 21, 409–418. doi.10.1002/pon.1913.

Stanton, A. L., Bower, J. E., & Low, C. A. (2006). Post-traumatic growth after cancer. In: L. G. Calhoun & R. G. Tedeschi (Eds.), *Handbook of post-traumatic growth: Research & practice.* (pp. 138–175). Mahwah, NJ: Lawrence Erlbaum.

Stockton, H., Joseph, S., & Hunt, N. (2014). Expressive writing and post-traumatic growth. An Internet-based study. *Traumatology*, 20, 75–83. doi.10.1037/h0099377.

Taku, K. (2014). Relationships among perceived psychological growth, resilience and burnout in physicians. *Personality and Individual Differences*, 59, 120–123. doi.10.1016/j.paid.2013.11.003.

Taku, K., Cann, A., Calhoun, L. G., & Tedeschi, R. G. (2008). The factor structure of the post-traumatic growth inventory: A comparison of five models using confirmatory factor analysis. *Journal of Traumatic Stress*, 21, 158–164. doi.10.1002/jts.20305.

Tedeschi, R. G., & Calhoun, L. G. (1995). *Trauma & transformation: Growing in the aftermath of suffering.* Thousand Oaks, CA, US: Sage Publications, Inc.

Tedeschi, R. G. & Calhoun, L. G. (1996). The Post-traumatic Growth Inventory: Measuring the positive legacy of trauma. *Journal of Traumatic Stress*, 9, 455–472. doi.10.1007/BF02103658.

Tedeschi, R. G. & Calhoun, L. G. (2006). Expert companions: Post-traumatic growth in clinical practice. In: L. G. Calhoun and R. G. Tedeschi (Eds.), *Handbook of post-traumatic growth: Research and practice.* (pp. 291–310). Mahwah, NJ: Lawrence Erlbaum.

Tedeschi, R. G. & McNally, R. J. (2011). Can we facilitate post-traumatic growth in combat veterans? *American Psychologist*, 66(1), 19–24. doi.10.1037/a0021896.

Triplett, K. N., Tedeschi, R. G., Cann, A., Calhoun, L. G., & Reeve, C. L. (2012). Post-traumatic growth, meaning in life, and life satisfaction in response to trauma. *Psychological Trauma: Theory, Research, Practice, and Policy*, 4, 400–410. doi.10.1037/a0024204.

Vail, K. E. I., Juhl, J., Arndt, J., Vess, M., Routledge, C., & Rutjens, B. T. (2012). When death is good for life: Considering the positive trajectories of terror management. *Personality and Social Psychology Review*, 16, 303–329. doi.10.1177/1088868312440046.

Vishnevsky, T., Cann, A., Calhoun, L. G., Tedeschi, R. G., & Demakis, G. J. (2010). Gender differences in self-reported post-traumatic growth: A meta-analysis. *Psychology of Women Quarterly*, 34, 110–120. doi.10.1111/j.1471-6402.2009.01546.x.

Wilson, B., Morris, B. A., & Chambers, S. (2014). A structural equation model of post-traumatic growth after prostate cancer: Post-traumatic growth after prostate cancer *Psycho-Oncology*, 23, 1212–1219. doi.10.1002/pon.3546.

Wortman, C. (2004). Post-traumatic growth: Progress and problems. *Psychological Inquiry*, 15, 81–90.

Xu, J. & Liao, Q. (2011). Prevalence and predictors of post-traumatic growth among adult survivors one year following 2008 Sichuan earthquake. *Journal of Affective Disorders*, 133, 274–280. doi.10.1016/j.jad.2011.03.034.

16

"A Positive Mood Cannot be too Positive"

How to Utilize Positive and Negative Clinical Psychology in Bipolar Disorder

Warren Mansell

Introduction

Bipolar disorder is regarded as a severe mental illness, characterized by a history of extreme highs (called *hypomania* or *mania*) and extreme lows of clinical depression (APA, 2013). During hypomania or mania, people are often much more confident than usual, sleep a maximum of few hours per night, speak, think and act more quickly, and become involved in projects and pleasurable activities that can be highly risky (e.g., spending money they do not have; promiscuous sex).

The received wisdom about bipolar disorder is that mania represents a period of mood and associated features that are *so* positive that they cause severe clinical problems (e.g., Gruber, Johnson, Oveis, & Keltner, 2008; Gruber, 2011; Giovanelli, Hoerger, Johnson, & Gruber, 2013). Interestingly, there is also a view that bipolar disorder itself can be a positive experience that forms a key part of people's identity (Jamison, Gerner, Hammen, & Padesky, 1980; Lobban, Taylor, Murray, & Jones, 2013). I will present a contrary view to both accounts, which I believe results from a lack of clear distinction between: (1) *hypomanic experiences*, which I propose are relatively common in the general population and within diverse mental health conditions other than bipolar disorder, to various degrees; and (2) bipolar disorders themselves, which are *defined* by their dysfunction.

I will review evidence that many people appear "vulnerable" to bipolar disorder because of their hypomanic experiences yet never develop it; these people are "red herrings" in the research literature because they are expressing an apparently normal personality trait. Likewise, studies that attempt to identify what is distinctive in people with bipolar disorder from other psychological disorders are chasing the same red herring – a personality trait rather than a dysfunctional process. And it is no surprise that people with bipolar disorder appreciate this underlying personality trait with its qualities of creativity, optimism, and sociability.

I will propose that the hypomanic trait is not what maintains the disorder. It is the processes that all disorders share in common – transdiagnostic processes (Harvey, Watkins, Mansell, & Shafran, 2004) – that make them a disorder, not the features that discriminate between disorders. This take on bipolar disorder frees us up to appreciate how positive psychology can help people with bipolar disorders to flexibly pursue positive experiences and life values without the

The Wiley Handbook of Positive Clinical Psychology, First Edition. Edited by Alex M. Wood and Judith Johnson.

risk that the mood will be "too good." There are other risks, of course, that will be discussed. Yet I propose that it is often the fear of feeling too good that maintains the disorder, especially the persistent feelings of helplessness and alienation that build up from the chronic disengagement from life goals. The work on building the positive can take place in tandem with equally valid work on addressing "negative psychology" that is manifested in processes such as persistent self-criticism, aggression, catastrophic thinking, and long-standing suppression of emotional and interpersonal problems from awareness. Through weaving together these strands of positive and negative psychology, people with bipolar disorder can rejoin the road to recovery by accepting and utilizing the wide range of adaptive positive *and* negative moods that the human condition has to offer.

In order to elaborate on the above account, this chapter will first use the metaphor of Icarus to characterize different ways of thinking about bipolar disorder. Then, I will make a clear statement of the assumptions behind the mainstream account of bipolar disorder and behind that of our group – the Think Effectively About Mood Swings (TEAMS) group (Mansell, Morrison, Reid, Lowens, & Tai, 2007; Searson, Mansell, Lowens, & Tai, 2012) – and operationalize these in a diagram. We will then cover the wide range of evidence that there is indeed a "phenotype" or set of "hypomanic traits" that are associated with bipolar disorder and could be considered to be an exaggerated form of processing positive mood states. We then critique the view that this process is the most important feature of what makes bipolar disorder a *disorder*. Instead, we provide evidence of the normality and utility of hypomanic traits, and then evidence for the relatively greater importance of "negative psychology" in the problematic aspects of possessing these traits. This conclusion is then used to clarify recommendations for psychological therapies. This adaptation of TEAMS typically places prudent pharmaceutical interventions within a psychological context that has the capacity to promote positive change and limit negative outcomes.

The Myth of Icarus

Many people are familiar with the Greek myth of Icarus: the boy with wings who flew too close to the sun. I hope to illustrate that there is both a superficial reading of this myth and a deeper reading when more details of the story of Icarus are uncovered. These parallel a simpler take on the highs in bipolar disorder (the "too much of a good thing" view) with one that considers the function and context of these highs in a person's life.

The familiar part of the myth typically involves the description of Icarus as having wings that were glued on with wax and that he needed to fly away to safety. Therefore, he needed to make sure that he did not fly too close to the sun or his wings would melt. As the familiar story goes, he was tempted by the warmth of the sun so much that he flew closer and closer. The wax holding his wings melted, and he plummeted into the sea below and drowned. The message of this metaphor is clear: do not give in to your temptations to experience a very positive mood or you will pay the price! The same metaphor is often used to generally warn people of *hubris*: the quashed pride after a fall in the eyes of others.

The simple reading of the Icarus myth fits well with the view that people with bipolar disorder may have a tendency to be more influenced and affected by positive mood states, and that this may be underpinned by their biology and brain functioning. However, what is the real story of Icarus? In particular, why was Icarus flying in the first place? Why did he find the sun so beguiling?

The story of Icarus actually begins where the myth of the Minotaur in the labyrinth in Crete ends. The father of Icarus was Daedalus, who had designed the labyrinth for King Minos. When Theseus, the Greek hero, was trapped in the labyrinth, Daedalus had helped him to escape. As punishment, King Minos entrapped Daedalus *and his son* in the labyrinth that, of course,

Daedalus had designed himself – thus he became a victim of his own creative design and his son paid the consequences, even though his son had no role in helping Theseus escape. Icarus then proceeded to grow up with his father in the labyrinth, *never seeing the sun*, for the remainder of his childhood. The scheme with the wings, another creative idea by Daedalus, was the chance for Icarus to escape and for Daedalus to try to recompense his son for what he had been through. Daedalus even instructed Icarus, "Do not fly too close to the sun!" Yet, as we know, Icarus did not follow his father's advice. But imagine you are Icarus. Would you keep away from a warm feeling you dimly remembered and longed to experience again and take the advice of a father whom you resented for a decision to help a different young man (Theseus) that cost you your own freedom?

   The full context of Icarus gives us another take on why positive moods may be so difficult to manage for people with bipolar disorder (Stott, Mansell, Salkovskis, Lavender, & Cartwright-Hatton, 2010). They may be the one way that a person believes will get them out of a perplexing "labyrinth" of depressed mood. They may be one way that the person can express their dismay at how their life has been determined by the mistakes of other people. And yet, at the same time, the positive moods do appear to cause catastrophe – often being admitted to a psychiatric hospital, or looming down to depression, or, at its worst, death from suicide or recklessness. But is this true of positive moods in general? Going back to the metaphor. What if Icarus' feathers had been fixed with wire rather than wax? They would they still have melted. What if Icarus had learned to swim? He would not have drowned. Each of these alternatives question whether a positive mood can be too positive, or whether it is other factors such as one's own way of responding to this mood and its consequences that is the problem. The TEAMS model proposes that swings into and out of positive moods are normal, and the problem in fact lies in how those moods are understood, managed, and appraised. These strategies have their roots in early experiences of emotion regulation that have a strong interpersonal context, often revealing strategies to try to cope with adversity, trauma, and overcontrolling social environments, much like our (real) story of Icarus. I will now state the differences in more explicit terms.

Two Contrasting Models of Vulnerability to Bipolar Disorder

We will shortly cover the extensive evidence of an *endophenotype* of bipolar disorder. This refers to a constellation of personality and behavioral traits with a largely genetic basis that confer a vulnerability to a disorder. Figure 16.1 illustrates that contemporary researchers consider this to be the most important marker of bipolar disorder and then carry out research on the negative and positive qualities of bipolar disorder itself. They do not seem to consider several other possibilities that are made explicit in the TEAMS approach (e.g., Mansell et al., 2007; Mansell & Pedley, 2008). These are illustrated in Figure 16.2. In this diagram, the same hypomanic endophenotype can express itself in a way that does not become bipolar disorder, and this can be the source of what people say are the "positive qualities" of bipolar disorder. In other words, this endophenotype may have a functional counterpart that we can *cultivate* – rather than try to restrict – within positive psychology interventions. Furthermore, and importantly for interventions, the source of what makes bipolar disorder so problematic is proposed to be a whole range of *other* factors such as past trauma, early childhood experiences, and a host of psychological processes such as pervasive self-criticism, worry, and emotion suppression. The key difference here is that the prevailing view sees as disorder as something internal to the individual that is later expressed, whereas our view sees a disorder as the emergent consequence of multiple factors that exists only when the dysfunction is apparent (see also Mansell, 2012).

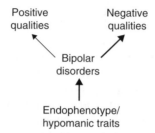

Figure 16.1 The prevailing model of bipolar disorder whereby the endophenotype is closely associated with the disorder, which is in turn associated with mainly negative, but also some positive, qualities. (Thick arrows denote strong links or influences and thin arrows denote weak links or influences.)

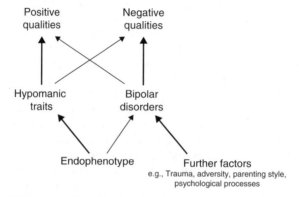

Figure 16.2 The TEAMS approach to bipolar disorder in which the endophenotype is considered to manifest itself as hypomanic traits in both bipolar disorder and to varying degrees in the general population, yet it does not play the most important role in what makes bipolar disorder a *disorder.*

Is the Hypomanic Endophenotype Reliably Associated with Bipolar Disorder?

There is a wide range of evidence that a personality style with biological correlates can be identified, and that people with this trait are more likely to develop bipolar disorder. This evidence is clearly reviewed elsewhere (e.g., Depue, Slater, Wolfstetter-Kausch, Klein, Goplerud, & Farr, 1981; Kwapil, Miller, Zinser, Chapman, Chapman, & Eckblad, 2000; Hasler, Drevets, Gould, Gottesman, & Manji, 2006; Balanzá-Martínez et al., 2008). In sum, individuals with the endophenotype show some evidence of the neuropsychological features of people with bipolar disorder, but to a much smaller degree, and they do develop bipolar disorder at higher rates than the rest of the population. But we shall see that the rates of conversion are modest, even over long periods.

There are several strands of evidence that the hypomanic endophenotype does not in fact determine the development of bipolar disorder. This section is consistent with the report, *Understanding Bipolar Disorder*, published by the British Psychological Society (Jones et al., 2011). The main points will be covered in turn.

First, the "symptoms" of hypomania are far too common to be restricted only to people who are at genuine risk for bipolar disorder. Bipolar disorder, according to recent definitions, is present in only 1% of the population (Merikangas et al., 2011). Yet studies indicate that some hypomanic experiences are reported by the *majority* of certain nonclinical samples (Jones, Mansell, & Waller, 2006; Udachina & Mansell, 2008). For example, a study of 167 undergraduates used the self-report Mood Disorders Questionnaire (Hirschfield et al., 2000) to assess diagnostic symptoms of hypomania and had somewhat astounding findings (Udachina & Mansell, 2008). Only six out of the 167 participants reported no history of hypomanic experiences, the modal number of experiences was nine, and nearly *half* of the sample qualified as "moderately likely" to achieve caseness for bipolar spectrum disorder according to published clinical criteria (Isometsae et al., 2003). This proportion of individuals as achieving caseness is clearly a vast overestimate, leading into question the validity of considering a history of hypomanic experiences as an indicator of bipolar disorder.

The evidence also indicates that the *majority* of people with hypomanic traits do *not* develop bipolar disorder within the time frame of the studies that have been published. This applies even with large studies that use long follow-up periods. For example, only eight out of 36 individuals identified as high risk from an original total of 1,500 students developed a bipolar disorder over a follow-up period of 13 years (Kwapil et al., 2000). Within a community study of adults past the peak age of onset of bipolar disorder (28–30 years), 4% of their cohort in Zurich had experienced at least one day of a hypomanic episode and yet over half of these did not report any impairment, distress, or need for treatment (Wicki & Angst, 1991).

Third, people who have had hypomanic experiences (and not bipolar disorder) report a range of positive, functional qualities of these experiences. This suggests that the experiences themselves may not be the key problem. One study interviewed 12 adults over 30 years of age who had a history of hypomanic experiences, nine of whom had experienced a diagnosed hypomanic episode of four days or more (Seal, Mansell, & Mannion, 2008). None of them had been depressed or sought treatment, and they were working or currently engaged in higher education. They explained to the interviewer that their hypomanic experiences were a positive way of remaining confident, coping, and that they were largely in control of the experiences. They considered their experiences to be somewhat similar to many other people they knew. Although they were aware that sometimes other people reacted negatively to their highs, generally they could ensure that they did not cross social boundaries. Moreover, they reported that their hypomanic experiences fulfilled a social role, such as socializing more or working more efficiently.

Fourth, the notion of an endophenotype of a disorder that is present to a large degree in nonclinical samples and even has functional properties is not unique to bipolar disorder. Indirect support is found from the existence of these parallel nonclinical traits in other domains. For example, schizotypy, an indicator of psychosis-proneness is found widely in the nonclinical population and is associated with measures of creativity and openness to experience (Nelson & Rawlings, 2010).

In sum, whilst the hypomanic traits indicative of an endophenotype are clearly measurable, their high prevalence, limited capacity to predict clinical diagnosis, and the evidence that they have functional properties, each challenge a suggestion of a close relationship with bipolar disorder. This leaves the question open of what actually constitutes the disorder.

What Makes Hypomanic Experiences a Problem?

The TEAMS approach proposes that a hypomanic endophenotype would need to be combined with other factors to lead to a clinical problem. These additional factors are largely common to all mental health problems – transdiagnostic – and are more clearly "negative." They include facets of negative affect during mania, comorbidities, past trauma and aversive experiences, genetics, and a range of psychological processes that indicate inflexible and/or impulsive ways of coping with stress. The evidence for such an account is described below.

Across a number of studies, a history of trauma has been reported by up to a half of participants with bipolar disorder (Hammersley, Dias, Todd, Bowen-Jones, Reilly, & Bentall, 2003; Garno,

Goldberg, Ramirez, & Ritzler, 2005; Kauer-Sant'Anna et al., 2007). These studies may provide an underestimate as they did not assess the prevalence of other aversive childhood experiences identified in other disorders, such as experiences of humiliation and social rejection (Hackmann, Clark, & McManus, 2000). Furthermore, a history of trauma is linked to a number of indicators of greater problems, such as severe childhood abuse associated with auditory hallucinations (Hammersley et al., 2003) and suicidal attempts (Garno et al., 2005), and a history of any trauma has been associated with more comorbid anxiety disorders and substance abuse (Kauer-Sant'Anna et al., 2007). These kind of life events are not unique to bipolar disorder, but raise the risk of psychopathology as a whole.

Research on the genetics of bipolar disorder actually complements the research on trauma. Even though there are indications that some genes may be linked with certain manic symptoms (Backlund et al., 2011), there is convincing evidence that a transdiagnostic factor appears to be key to bipolar disorder. For example, a recent large-scale collaborative study found that bipolar disorder shared a high level of genetic variance with schizophrenia and a moderate level of genetic variance with major depressive disorder (Cross-Disorder Group of the Psychiatric Genomics Consortium, 2013).

Consistent with the evidence on distal factors associated with bipolar disorder, diagnostic evidence also points to the importance of negative affect. A review of seven factor analyses of mania concluded that the factor that accounts for most of the symptoms of mania is dysphoria, not elevated mood (Mansell & Pedley, 2008). In addition, these studies identified a range of other negative affective states in mania, such as panic, anxiety, aggression, and irritability. In a related point, the rates of psychiatric comorbidity in bipolar disorder are huge. For example, over half of patients in a study of 500 patients in a treatment trial had at least one anxiety disorder, and this comorbidity was consistently associated with more serious clinical profile, including poorer quality of life and greater likelihood of attempted suicide (Simon et al., 2004). Overall rates of Axis 1 (nonpersonality) psychiatric comorbidity can be as high as two-thirds of the sample (McElroy et al., 2004) and the estimated rates of comorbid personality disorder vary widely but can be up to 50% (Üçok, Karaveli, Kundakçi, & Yazici, 1998). Consistently across multiple studies, these comorbidities are associated with a more severe and chronic illness. These robust findings indicate a rarely considered possibility – that it is the features of these comorbidities (e.g., impulsivity, aggression, panic) that create and maintain the majority problems for people with bipolar disorder, rather than the hypomanic experiences that are unique to the bipolar diagnosis itself.

In support of the above account, there is evidence that transdiagnostic processes, known to maintain a range of psychological disorders, are elevated in people with bipolar disorder (of whom we have established that the majority may experience comorbidity). These processes include negative rumination (Johnson, McKenzie, & McMurrich, 2008), thought suppression (Miklowitz, Alatiq, Geddes, Goodwin, & Williams, 2010), overgeneral memory (Mansell & Lam, 2004), and attempts to suppress intrusive imagery and memories (Gregory, Brewin, Mansell, & Donaldson, 2010). Indeed, there is evidence from prospective studies that trans-diagnostic constructs such as impulsive nonconformity and critical perfectionism predict bipolar symptomology over time. Specifically, impulsive nonconformity combined with hypomanic personality to predict the development of bipolar disorder (Kwapil et al., 2000) and critical perfectionism interacted with life events to predict mood symptoms (Francis-Raniere, Alloy, & Abramson, 2006). Across a number of studies, these "negative" processes are associated with negative mood states and have been shown to be distinct from the processes associated with hypomanic traits (Johnson et al., 2008; Carver & Johnson, 2009; Dempsey, Gooding, & Jones, 2011; Kelly, Mansell, Sadhnani, & Wood, 2012).

To take these conclusions further, there is specific evidence that it is *negative* thinking *about* high moods that is elevated in bipolar disorder. For example, people may report that they are afraid that they will lose control when they are excited, or that they will be criticized or rejected by other people when they are more agitated than usual. Indirect evidence can be derived from an examination of the nature of the items that assess proneness to bipolar symptoms. For example, a measure of "positive urgency" shows strong correlations with an index of risk for bipolar disorder describe earlier – the hypomanic personality scale (Giovanelli, Hoerger, Johnson, & Gruber, 2013). Many of the items on this scale explicitly require the participant to report on their perceived negative consequences of high moods, for example, "When I am very happy, I cannot seem to stop myself from doing things that can have bad consequences."

In our work on the TEAMS model, we have specifically assessed this negative thinking about high mood states and found that it is elevated in bipolar disorder compared with nonclinical controls (Mansell, 2006; Alatiq, Crane, Williams, & Goodwin, 2010; Mansell et al., 2011), compared with remitted unipolar depression (Alatiq et al., 2010; Mansell et al., 2011), and compared with individuals who have had hypomanic experiences, but have no psychological disorders (Mansell et al., 2011). Moreover, negative thinking about high moods predict mood symptoms in people with bipolar disorder over the period of a month (Dodd, Mansell, Morrison, & Tai, 2011) and over six months (Gilbert, Nolen Hoeksema, & Gruber, 2013). Complementing these findings, a key study found that while positive thinking did differentiate people with bipolar disorder from nonclinical controls, positive thinking about high moods did *not* differentiate bipolar disorder from people who had a history of hypomanic moods but no evidence of a clinical disorder (Mansell et al., 2011).

Some of the most intriguing evidence for the importance of negative cognitive styles came from a study comparing three samples on positive and negative appraisals: 171 individuals with bipolar disorder, 42 with unipolar depression, and 64 nonclinical controls (Kelly et al., 2011). In the absence of negative thinking about high moods, those who endorsed more positive views of high moods actually had a *lesser* likelihood of having bipolar disorder (10%). Yet this effect *reversed* when negative thinking was combined with the positive thinking about high moods, with a staggering 97% of this subsample having bipolar disorder. This study suggests that positive thinking about high moods is a problem only when it is combined with negative thinking about the same mood states – that is, the person is in conflict. A classic example of this conflict would be to see an agitated state as the only way to rise out of depression but to fear that any feelings of agitation are a sign of going "mad" and ending up in hospital.

Taken together, the above literature indicates that high mood alone is not the problem in bipolar disorder. For the positive mood to be detrimental, it needs to be combined with other, more pernicious, factors that are known to commonly associated with most mental health problems. The important clinical message from this is that patients, professionals and family members need not be fearful of good moods in bipolar disorder per se. In fact, to be a human being with a sense of purpose in life, good moods need to be accepted, cherished, and built upon. Many patients in recovery have developed this insight. For example, in a recent qualitative study, four patients with bipolar disorder were clearly able to separate the destruction and chaos of manic symptoms from the self-acceptance and positive connection with others experienced during normal positive mood (Russell & Moss, 2012). Furthermore, given the evidence that hypomania is not uncommon in the general population, we also need to help patients, professionals, and family members to accept some of the activated states of hypomania and the associated negative moods such as irritability, anxiety, anger, and paranoia as potentially understandable experiences. It is from this basis, whereby both positive and negative moods are understood to have a functional and normal explanation, that TEAMS builds an intervention. TEAMS helps people to simply manage these moods in way that can maintain a good quality of life and fulfill life goals.

Positive and Negative Psychology Interventions in TEAMS

TEAMS openly blends the virtues of both "positive" and "negative" psychology. We are most concerned with helping people to pursue their most important and long-term life goals, which often involves pursuing a certain state of themselves in the world and upholding certain principles and values. These often involve needs around both autonomy/mastery and connectedness to others. Our model proposes that people's attempts to control their internal states (mood, physiology, thought processes, and felt actions) interferes with these goals. For example, they may feel that as soon as they feel excited, other people will criticize them for their outrageous behavior, and this conflicts with their goal to be liked by other people. Paradoxically, they may believe that an excited state is the only way they can escape the depths of depression and the only way that they can achieve things and feel worthwhile. Thus, rather than seeing having goals as a risk for relapse, TEAMS regards a certain range of internal states that people often think signal relapse as a normal part of goal attainment; it is the *appraisal* of these states and the way that people try to *suppress* or *enhance* them that is problematic.

Thus, we propose that people with bipolar disorder are in *conflict* over particular internal states, and it is this conflict that prevents them from being in control of their life as a whole. The internal states and the endophenotype underlying them are not the problem in themselves – it is\ how these states are appraised and controlled that are key. Indeed, the internal states people try to control – anger, fear, sadness, excitement – are the emotions that all of us need to function in a social environment. For example, fear keeps us alert to real dangers and communicates a need for support.

In particular, it seems that what makes internal states a problem is when people are focused on only one goal at a time (e.g., "to suppress my excitement at all costs"), rather than to see the balanced picture. This reflexive mindset of focusing on one goal to the expense of others may be associated with perseverance, decisiveness, and single-mindedness in some contexts, but can also lead to impulsive and rigid ways of coping that further exaggerate the conflict. We tend to find that when emotion suppression, self-criticism, and rumination is applied in this inflexible manner, it maintains and exacerbates distress. Thus, the "positive" process of normal living is being limited by the "negative" side effects of inflexible ways of trying to control emotions and their associated memories, images and thoughts.

One of the main strategies we use in TEAMS is to help clients to bring these opposing ways of regulating their mood into awareness at the same time, in order help them to see this paradox and think of alternative ways to improve their well-being. In this reflective mindset people may feel indecisive and uncertain, and yet it allows them to weigh up the pros and cons of their actions and their goals, allows them to see the self-defeating nature of some of their ways of coping, and allows them to select from a range of alternatives. We also help clients to take an active role in dealing with threat. For example, to complement the "negative" strategy of trying to avoid relapse, we encourage clients to develop an image of their "healthy self," of how they want to see themselves in the future, and to notice when they approach this state. In this way, they have a middle ground to head toward when they are afraid of relapsing, rather than escaping from depression into mania (manic defense), and from mania into depression (depressive defense). Indeed, our model proposes that mood swings are maintained by this dichotomous and extreme way of understanding high and low mood, and we use a continuum to help clients to carefully and fully differentiate the states in between, many of which, if sustained, would be less damaging to their lives as a whole.

In this way we see the ideal intervention as one that, at the same time, brings together "positive" and "negative" components of psychology. Both immediate rewards and threats are seen in the light of long-term goals and ideals such that "good decisions" can be made. Maybe this intervention is neither positive nor negative, but is the essence of *functionality* that needs to consider both. We would anticipate that such an approach is facilitated when patients feel able and safe enough to talk freely and allow previously suppressed emotions, memories, and thoughts into their awareness. This may account for why active listening, a sense of containment, empathy, compassion, and warmth can facilitate change across different therapies and presentations (Carey, Kelly, Mansell, & Tai, 2012).

We have been encouraged that TEAMS has led to successful outcomes in an initial case series (Searson et al., 2012), and the therapy is currently being evaluated in a randomized controlled trial (Mansell et al., 2014). Furthermore, the targets of TEAMS match well with patients' own views of what aids recovery. We interviewed 11 people with bipolar disorder who had remained without relapse for an average of 10 years about what had kept them well (Mansell, Powell, Pedley, Thomas, & Jones, 2010). Our analysis generated two themes: ambivalent strategies and universal strategies, each with four subthemes. The ambivalence reflected the central role of conflict in the model; they were in two minds over the degree to which medication, looking for warning signs for relapse, and accepting their diagnosis had helped them, which made them unsure whether they were currently "well" or not. Yet they identified four approaches that were universally helpful: lifestyle fundamentals (balanced sleep and activities), receiving social support, increased understanding and information, and overcoming their social anxiety to express their basic needs to others.

By listening closely to peoples goals at the start, and throughout therapy, and using these to drive TEAMS interventions, we aim to facilitate people's ways of coping in an integrative way. For example, one client with a range of comorbid anxiety disorders was afraid of being criticized and rejected by her care team whenever she talked about returning to work and having a "normal" day-to-day social life when she recovered. The therapist worked with her on identifying the sources of this fear of criticism in early childhood experiences of care and loss, examined its functions, and worked through alternative, more compassionate, imagery around what to expect when expressing needs to others. She seemed to benefit greatly not only from these experiential exercises, but by becoming better informed about recovery by reading personal accounts.

Systemic, Cultural, and Medical Issues

Potentially some of the greatest challenges to using "positive" psychology with patients come from the wider systems – families, clinical services, and employers. Many of them hold assumptions about bipolar disorder, and mental health problems in general, that conflict with the approach we are describing here. There is an assumption that people with bipolar disorder are a distinct class of people who have a life-long condition that requires life-long medication.

On the contrary, TEAMS considers bipolar disorder as a label applied to a range of people that reach a certain threshold on a normal continuum such that their mood swings interfere with their lives. We accept that the extremes of this continuum involve states of mind that are extremely hard to control (i.e., mania and depression) and therefore medication can often be used to successfully reduce risk and to shift mood to a state that is more manageable. We also accept that the severe nature and huge impact of mania and depression builds hopelessness and a sense of fate within services and families. Yet, as supported by evidence, we anticipate that many patients can return to a more "normal" life, and some of these people can do so with reduced medication or without medication in some cases. This simply represents the commonly held viewpoint toward many other mental health problems that are well treated by psychological interventions that include positive psychology interventions (e.g., anxiety disorders, depression).

Our main strategy for addressing systems is to share the evidence of our work at all levels from summary reports of patients, service user involvement in workshops and training, and disseminating the findings of research. However, our aim is to be able to work within a multisystemic framework using a shared TEAMS model in the future.

Summary

The TEAMS approach attempts to question the dichotomous assumptions about bipolar disorder that it is either an untreatable life-long illness or that it is the source of powers of creativity and success. It does this by regarding the endophenotype underlying risk of bipolar disorder as a normal personality trait that can be nurtured in through "positive psychology" to be productive and not undermine one's life goals. At the same time TEAMS uses insights from "negative psychology" to address the pernicious factors such as traumatization, self-criticism, worry, rumination, catastrophizing, and cognitive rigidity that it proposes are the key cause of psychological distress and dysfunction in people with bipolar disorder. In doing so, our model shares much in common with familiar cognitive approaches to treating other mental health problems, but contrasts to therapies for bipolar disorder that unquestioningly accept the view of bipolar disorder as a life-long medical illness. Our theoretical model is well supported, and initial findings for the intervention are promising, but there is considerable work on research and dissemination required to provide this novel outlook to services within everyday practice.

References

Alatiq, Y., Crane, C., Williams, J. M. G., & Goodwin, G. M. (2010). Dysfunctional beliefs in bipolar disorder: Hypomanic vs. depressive attitudes. *Journal of Affective Disorders, 122,* 294–300. doi.10.1016/j.jad.2009.08.021.

American Psychiatric Association (APA). (2013). *Diagnostic and Statistical Manual of Mental Disorders,* 5th edn. Washington, DC: American Psychiatric Association.

Backlund, L., Nikamo, P., Hukic, D. S., Ek, I. R., Träskman-Bendz, L., Landén, M., et al. (2011). Cognitive manic symptoms associated with the P2RX7 gene in bipolar disorder. *Bipolar Disorders, 13,* 500–508. doi.10.1111/j.1399-5618.2011.00952.x.

Balanzá-Martínez, V., Rubio, C., Selva-Vera, G., Martinez-Aran, A., Sanchez-Moreno, J., Salazar-Fraile, J., et al. (2008). Neurocognitive endophenotypes (endophenocognitypes) from studies of relatives of bipolar disorder subjects: a systematic review. *Neuroscience & Biobehavioral Reviews, 32,* 1426–1438. doi.10.1016/j.neubiorev.2008.05.019.

Carey, T. A., Kelly, R. A., Mansell, W., & Tai, S. J. (2012). What's therapeutic about the therapeutic relationship? A hypothesis for practice informed by Perceptual Control Theory. *The Cognitive Behavioural Therapist, 5,* 47–59. doi.org/10.1017/S1754470X12000037.

Carver, C. S. & Johnson, S. L. (2009). Tendencies toward mania and tendencies toward depression have distinct motivational, affective, and cognitive correlates. *Cognitive Therapy and Research, 33,* 552–569. doi.10.1007/s10608-008-9213-y.

Cross-Disorder Group of the Psychiatric Genomics Consortium (2013). Genetic relationship between five psychiatric disorders estimated from genome-wide SNPs. *Nature Genetics, 45,* 984–994. doi.10.1038/ng.2711.

Dempsey, R. C., Gooding, P. A., & Jones, S. H. (2011). Positive and negative cognitive style correlates of the vulnerability to hypomania. *Journal of Clinical Psychology, 67,* 673–690. doi.10.1002/jclp.20789.

Depue, R. A., Slater, J. F., Wolfstetter-Kausch, H., Klein, D., Goplerud, E., & Farr, D. (1981). A behavioral paradigm for identifying persons at risk for bipolar depressive disorder: A conceptual framework and five validation studies. *Journal of Abnormal Psychology, 90,* 381–437. doi.org/10.1037/0021-843X.90.5.381.

Dodd, A. L., Mansell, W., Morrison, A. P., & Tai, S. J. (2011). Extreme appraisals of internal states and bipolar symptoms: The Hypomanic Attitudes and Positive Predictions Inventory. *Psychological Assessment, 23,* 635–645. doi.org/10.1037/a0022972.

Francis-Raniere, E. L., Alloy, L. B., & Abramson, L. Y. (2006). Depressive personality styles and bipolar spectrum disorders: Prospective tests of the event congruency hypothesis. *Bipolar Disorders, 8,* 382–399. doi.10.1111/j.1399-5618.2006.00337.x.

Garno, J. L., Goldberg, J. F., Ramirez, P. M., & Ritzler, B. A. (2005). Impact of childhood abuse on the clinical course of bipolar disorder. *British Journal of Psychiatry, 186,* 121–125. doi.10.1192/bjp.186.2.121.

Giovanelli, A., Hoerger, M., Johnson, S. L., & Gruber, J. (2013). Impulsive responses to positive mood and reward are related to mania risk. *Cognition & Emotion, 27,* 1091–1104. doi.10.1080/02699931.2013.772048.

Gregory, J. D., Brewin, C. R., Mansell, W., & Donaldson, C. (2010). Intrusive memories and images in bipolar disorder. *Behaviour Research and Therapy, 48*, 698–703. doi.10.1016/j.brat.2010.04.005.

Gruber, J. (2011). Can feeling too good be bad? Positive emotion persistence (PEP) in bipolar disorder. *Current Directions in Psychological Science, 20*, 217–221. doi. 10.1177/0963721411414632.

Gruber, J., Johnson, S. L., Oveis, C., & Keltner, D. (2008). Risk for mania and positive emotional responding: Too much of a good thing? *Emotion, 8*, 23–33. doi.org/10.1037/1528-3542.8.1.23.

Gilbert, K. E., Nolen-Hoeksema, S., & Gruber, J. (2013). Positive emotion dysregulation across mood disorders: How amplifying versus dampening predicts emotional reactivity and illness course. *Behaviour Research and Therapy, 51*, 736–741.

Hackmann, A., Clark, D. M., & McManus, F. (2000). Recurrent images and early memories in social phobia. *Behaviour Research and Therapy, 38*, 601–610. doi.10.1016/S0005-7967(99)00161-8.

Hammersley, P., Dias, A., Todd, G., Bowen-Jones, K., Reilly, B., & Bentall, R. P. (2003). Childhood trauma and hallucinations in bipolar affective disorder: preliminary investigation. *British Journal of Psychiatry, 182*, 543–547. doi.10.1192/bjp.182.6.543.

Harvey, A. G., Watkins, E., Mansell, W., & Shafran, R. (2004). *Cognitive behavioural processes across psychological disorders: A transdiagnostic approach to research and treatment.* Oxford: Oxford University Press.

Hasler, G., Drevets, W. C., Gould, T. D., Gottesman, I. I., & Manji, H. K. (2006). Toward constructing an endophenotype strategy for bipolar disorders. *Biological Psychiatry, 60*, 93–105. doi.10.1016/j.biopsych.2005.11.006.

Hirschfield, R. M., Williams, J. B., Spitzer, R. L., Calabrese, J., Flynn, L., Keck, P. E., et al. (2000). Development and validation of a screening instrument for bipolar spectrum disorder: The Mood Disorder Questionnaire. *American Journal of Psychiatry, 157*, 1873–1875. doi.org/10.1176/appi. ajp.157.11.1873.

Isometsae, E., Suominen, K., Mantere, O., Valtonen, H., Leppämäki, S., Pippingsköld, M., & Arvilommi, P. (2003). The Mood Disorder Questionnaire improves recognition of bipolar disorder in psychiatric care. *BMC Psychiatry, 3*, 8. doi.10.1186/1471-244X-3-8.

Jamison, K. R., Gerner, R. H., Hammen, C., & Padesky, C. (1980). Clouds and silver linings: Positive experiences associated with primary affective disorders. *American Journal of Psychiatry, 137*, 198–202.

Johnson, S. L., McKenzie, G., & McMurrich, S. (2008). Ruminative responses to negative and positive affect among students diagnosed with bipolar disorder and major depressive disorder. *Cognitive Therapy and Research, 32*, 702–713. doi.10.1007/s10608-007-9158-6.

Jones, S., Lobban, F., Cooke, A., Hemmingfield, J., Kinderman, P., Mansell, W., et al. (2010). *Understanding bipolar disorder: Why some people experience extreme mood states and what can help.* British Psychological Society, available at: shop.bps.org.uk/understanding-bipolar-disorder.html.

Jones, S. H., Mansell, W., & Waller, L. (2006). Appraisal of hypomania relevant experiences: Development of a questionnaire to assess positive self dispositional appraisals in bipolar and behavioural high risk samples. *Journal of Affective Disorders, 93*,19–28. doi.10.1016/j.jad.2006.01.017.

Kauer-Sant'Anna, M., Tramontina, J., Andreazza, A. C., Cereser, K., Costa, S. D., Santin, A., & Kapczinski, F. (2007). Traumatic life events in bipolar disorder: impact on BDNF levels and psychopathology. *Bipolar Disorders, 9*(s1), 128–135. doi.10.1111/j.1399-5618.2007.00478.x.

Kelly, R. E., Mansell, W., Sadhnani, V., & Wood, A. M. (2012). Positive and negative appraisals of the consequences of activated states uniquely relate to symptoms of hypomania and depression. *Cognition & Emotion, 26*, 899–906. doi.10.1080/02699931.2011.613918.

Kelly, R. E., Mansell, W., Wood, A. M., Alatiq, Y., Dodd, A., & Searson, R. (2011). Extreme positive and negative appraisals of activated states interact to discriminate bipolar disorder from unipolar depression and non-clinical controls. *Journal of Affective Disorders, 134*, 438–443. doi.10.1016/j.jad.2011.05.042.

Kwapil, T. R., Miller, M. B., Zinser, M. C., Chapman, L. J., Chapman, J., & Eckblad, M. (2000). A longitudinal study of high scorers on the Hypomanic Personality Scale. *Journal of Abnormal Psychology, 109*, 222–226.doi.org/10.1037/0021-843X.109.2.222.

Lobban, F., Taylor, K., Murray, C., & Jones, S. (2012). Bipolar disorder is a two-edged sword: A qualitative study to understand the positive edge. *Journal of Affective Disorders, 141*, 204–212. doi.10.1016/j.jad.2012.03.001.

Mansell, W. (2006). The Hypomanic Attitudes and Positive Predictions Inventory (HAPPI): A pilot study to select cognitions that are elevated in individuals with bipolar disorder compared to non-clinical controls. *Behavioural and Cognitive Psychotherapy, 34*, 467–476. doi.org/10.1017/S1352465806003109.

Mansell, W. (2012). Working with comorbidity in CBT. In: W. Dryden & R. Branch (Eds.), *The CBT Handbook.* London: Sage.

Mansell, W. & Lam D. (2004). A preliminary study of autobiographical memory in remitted bipolar and unipolar depression and the role of imagery in the specificity of memory. *Memory, 12*, 437–46. doi.10.1080/09658210444000052.

Mansell, W. & Pedley, R. (2008). The ascent into mania: a review of psychological processes associated with manic symptoms. *Clinical Psychology Review, 28*, 494–520. doi.10.1016/j.cpr.2007.07.010.

Mansell, W., Morrison, A. P., Reid. G., Lowens, I., & Tai, S. (2007). The interpretation of and responses to changes in internal states: an integrative cognitive model of mood swings and bipolar disorder. *Behavioural and Cognitive Psychotherapy, 35*, 515–541. doi.org/10.1017/S1352465807003827.

Mansell, W., Paszek, G., Seal, K., Pedley, R., Jones, S., Thomas, N., et al. (2011). Extreme appraisals of internal states in bipolar I disorder: A multiple control group study. *Cognitive Therapy and Research, 35*, 87–97. doi.10.1007/s10608-009-9287-1.

Mansell W., Powell, S., Pedley, R., Thomas, N., & Jones, S. A. (2010). The process of recovery from Bipolar I Disorder: A qualitative analysis of personal accounts in relation to an integrative cognitive model. *British Journal of Clinical Psychology, 49*, 193-215. DOI: 10.1348/014466509X451447.

Mansell, W., Tai, S., Clark, A., Akgonul, S., Dunn, G., Davies, L., & Morrison, A. P. (2014). A novel cognitive behaviour therapy for bipolar disorders (Think Effectively About Mood Swings or TEAMS): study protocol for a randomized controlled trial. *Trials, 15*, 405. doi. 10.1186/1745-6215-15-405.

McElroy, S. L., Altshuler, L. L., Suppes, T., Keck Jr., P. E., Frye, M. A., Denicoff, K. D., & Post, R. M. (2001). Axis I psychiatric comorbidity and its relationship to historical illness variables in 288 patients with bipolar disorder. *American Journal of Psychiatry, 158*, 420–426. doi.org/10.1176/appi.ajp.158.3.420.

Merikangas, K. R., Jin, R., He, J. P., Kessler, R. C., Lee, S., Sampson, N. A., et al. (2011). Prevalence and correlates of bipolar spectrum disorder in the world mental health survey initiative. *Archives of General Psychiatry, 68*, 241–251. doi.10.1001/archgenpsychiatry.2011.12.

Miklowitz, D. J., Alatiq, Y., Geddes, J. R., Goodwin, G. M., & Williams, J. M. G. (2010). Thought suppression in patients with bipolar disorder. *Journal of Abnormal Psychology, 119*, 355–365. doi.org/10.1037/a0018613.

Nelson, B. & Rawlings, D. (2010). Relating schizotypy and personality to the phenomenology of creativity. *Schizophrenia Bulletin, 36*, 388–399. doi.10.1093/schbul/sbn098.

Russell, L. & Moss, D. (2013). High and happy? Exploring the experience of positive states of mind in people who have been given a diagnosis of bipolar disorder. *Psychology and Psychotherapy: Theory, Research and Practice.* doi.10.1111/j.2044-8341.2012.02064.x.

Seal, K., Mansell, W., & Mannion, H. (2008). What lies between hypomania and bipolar disorder? A qualitative analysis of 12 non-treatment-seeking people with a history of hypomanic experiences and no history of depression. *Psychology and Psychotherapy: Theory, Research and Practice, 81*, 33–54. doi. 10.1348/147608307X209896.

Searson, R., Mansell, W., Lowens, I., & Tai, S. J. (2012). Think Effectively About Mood Swings (TEAMS): A case series of cognitive behavioural therapy for bipolar disorders. *Journal of Behavior Therapy and Experimental Psychiatry, 43*, 770–779. doi.10.1016/j.jbtep.2011.10.001.

Simon, N. M., Otto, M. W., Wisniewski, S. R., Fossey, M., Sagduyu, K., Frank, E., & Pollack, M. H. (2004). Anxiety disorder comorbidity in bipolar disorder patients: Data from the first 500 participants in the Systematic Treatment Enhancement Program for bipolar disorder (STEP-BD). *American Journal of Psychiatry, 161*, 2222–2229. doi.10.1176/appi.ajp.161.12.2222.

Stott, R., Mansell, W., Salkovskis, P. M., Lavender, A., & Cartwright-Hatton, S. (2010). *The Oxford guide to metaphors in CBT: Building cognitive bridges.* Oxford: Oxford University Press.

Üçok, A., Karaveli, D., Kundakçi, T., & Yazici, O. (1998). Comorbidity of personality disorders with bipolar mood disorders. *Comprehensive Psychiatry, 39*, 72–74. doi.10.1016/S0010-440X(98)90081-5.

Udachina, A. & Mansell W. (2007). Cross-validation of the Mood Disorders Questionnaire, the Internal State Scale, and the Hypomanic Personality Scale. *Personality and Individual Differences, 42*, 1539–1549. doi.10.1016/j.paid.2006.10.028.

Wicki, W. & Angst, J. (1991). The Zurich study: X. Hypomania in a 28–30 year-old cohort. *European Archives of Psychiatry and Clinical Neuroscience, 240*, 339–348. doi.10.1007/BF02279764.

17

Positive Clinical Psychology and the Promotion of Happiness, Compassion, and Autonomy in People with Psychosis

Paul Hutton

Although there have been notable advances in our understanding of psychosis in the last 20 years (BPS, 2014), the effectiveness of existing medical and psychological treatments remains limited. A change in thinking may be required if mental health services want to make a more substantial contribution to improving the lives of people with this condition. This chapter will start with a brief overview of existing treatments for psychosis, both pharmacological and psychological, before examining the potential contribution positive clinical psychology might make to improving our understanding of this condition.

The Effectiveness of Existing Treatments for Psychosis

There is much room for improving the effectiveness, acceptability, and safety of treatments offered to people with a diagnosis of nonaffective psychosis. There is also much room for improving the quality of the available evidence. Much of it is unreliable or indirect (Miyar & Adams, 2012), which limits the ability of service users, carers, or professionals to make informed decisions regarding care. Frustratingly few studies of mainstream interventions have examined their effectiveness on domains such as quality of life or subjective recovery, with many focused primarily on symptom reduction.

Medication

The effect of antipsychotic medication on the symptoms of psychosis ranges from minimal to large, depending on the particular drug (Leucht et al., 2013). The average effect is small to moderate, and those antipsychotics that have larger benefits are also more likely to have more adverse effects such as weight gain, sedation, and movement disorder (Leucht, et al., 2013). Although there is very good evidence that people who respond to antipsychotics are much more likely to relapse in the short to medium term if they stop taking them (Leucht et al., 2012), recent evidence suggests that discontinuation may be associated with longer-term improvements in functioning and recovery (Harrow, Jobe, & Faull, 2012; Wunderink, Nieboer, Wiersma,

The Wiley Handbook of Positive Clinical Psychology, First Edition. Edited by Alex M. Wood and Judith Johnson.
© 2016 John Wiley & Sons, Ltd. Published 2016 by John Wiley & Sons, Ltd.

Sytema, & Nienhuis, 2013). For reasons that remain unclear, antipsychotic-attributable effects are becoming smaller over time, with modern drug trials often failing to replicate the more promising results of older trials (Agid et al., 2013). Many question the external validity of industry-sponsored trials, noting the questionable representativeness of the people who take part in them (Leucht, Heres, Hamann, & Kane, 2008).

Service users are often ambivalent about taking antipsychotics, in part due to the unpleasant dampening effect they may have on motivation and volition (Moncrieff, Cohen, & Mason, 2009). Although promoting 100% adherence through use of long-lasting injectable antipsychotics may lead to increased adverse effects (Rosenheck et al., 2011), surprisingly it has no clear benefits on outcomes when compared with traditional pills (Kishimoto et al., 2013; Stroup, 2014). We have recently argued that decisions to not take antipsychotic medication may in many cases reflect an informed choice based on a balanced appraisal of costs and benefits (Morrison, Hutton, Shiers, & Turkington, 2012).

Psychological Treatments

Psychological treatments are popular with service users, with relatively low rates of drop-out being observed in clinical trials (Villeneuve, Potvin, Lesage, & Nicole, 2010). Cognitive behavioral therapy (CBT), one of the more heavily researched interventions, appears to have small effects on reducing residual positive symptoms such as hallucinations and delusions, whereas social skills training appears to have comparable benefits for negative symptoms (Turner, van der Gaag, Karyotaki, & Cuijpers, 2014). Another well-researched treatment, family therapy, has been shown to reduce the risk of relapse in a number of studies (National Institute for Clinical Excellence, 2009), and cognitive remediation therapy (CRT), a form of intensive cognitive training, appears to have moderate effects on cognitive functioning according to a meta-analysis of available trials (Wykes, Huddy, Cellard, McGurk, & Czobor, 2011), although whether these benefits translate to the real world is not clear. The evidence for art and music therapy is promising (National Institute for Clinical Excellence, 2009), but better quality trials may be required before firm conclusions can be drawn.

It should be noted that most research on psychological interventions has been carried out with people who have antipsychotic-resistant residual difficulties, which might help to account for the small to moderate effects observed. On the other hand, one of the biggest moderators of treatment effectiveness appears to be study quality, with promising findings from small poor quality trials very often failing to replicate when examined in larger, more rigorous ones (Wykes, Steel, Everitt, & Tarrier, 2008; Jauhar et al., 2014). Existing psychological interventions are generally assumed to be safe, but few trials have assessed this in sufficient depth, with notable exceptions (Klingberg et al., 2012).

Psychological Models of Psychosis

A number of influential psychological models of psychosis have been published over the last 15 to 20 years (Chadwick & Birchwood, 1994; Bentall, Corcoran, Howard, Blackwood, & Kinderman, 2001; Garety, Kuipers, Fowler, Freeman, & Bebbington, 2001; Morrison, 2001; Freeman, Garety, Kuipers, Fowler, & Bebbington, 2002). Each has found considerable empirical support from observational, experimental, and longitudinal studies, but the effectiveness of CBT approaches derived from these models is, as outlined above, limited. Of course, this may reflect a difficulty in changing the proposed mechanisms of change, but it may also suggest the models specifying these mechanisms are incomplete or inaccurate. Most assume that modification of appraisals, beliefs, and counterproductive safety-seeking behavior should lead to a reduction in distress and/or symptoms. Understanding and building upon existing strengths and capacities have not traditionally been the central focus of these models, which has generally been to explain the positive symptoms of psychosis (hallucinations, delusions) and associated distress.

Cognitive accounts of negative symptoms and impaired functioning have also been developed and tested in recent years (Rector, Beck, & Stolar, 2005). Like preceding models of positive symptoms, these also posit a central role for appraisals and safety-seeking behavior, and also benefit from empirical support from observational studies (Beck & Grant, 2008; Grant & Beck, 2009; Beck, Grant, Huh, Perivoliotis, & Chang, 2013). Unfortunately, treatments based on these models have produced mixed results, with promising results from a recent trial (Grant, Huh, Perivoliotis, Stolar, & Beck, 2012) tempered by a failure to demonstrate advantages over cognitive remediation in a larger high quality trial (Klingberg et al., 2011).

There is now a growing awareness of the limited gains that can be made by focusing on symptom reduction, with recent authors highlighting the importance of promoting positive emotional experience (J. Johnson, Gooding, Wood, Fair, & Tarrier, 2013), interpersonal recovery, compassion, acceptance (Gumley, Braehler, Laithwaite, MacBeth, & Gilbert, 2010), and kindness (D. P. Johnson et al., 2009; D. P. Johnson et al., 2011). Such developments fit well with recent calls for clinical psychology to broaden its focus to include the study of strengths, resilience, and the promotion of well-being (Wood & Tarrier, 2010).

Positive Clinical Psychology and Psychosis

Wood and Tarrier (2010) define Positive Clinical Psychology as an approach to understanding and treating psychological distress that is characterized by a "balanced and equally weighted focus on the positive and negative aspects of life" (Wood & Tarrier, 2010, p. 820), the argument being that clinical psychology has to date been overly focused on understanding the negative. They outline a number of benefits of this emphasis on the positive, including an improved ability to "predict, explain and conceptualize disorder" (p. 820), develop and foster protective factors which buffer against distress in clinical populations, and develop resilience in non-clinical groups (Wood & Tarrier, 2010). Their approach is influenced by positive psychology research, which in turn has been influenced by the positive psychology movement. Wood and Tarrier caution against repeating the separatism that has characterized this movement, however, and call instead for integration of positive psychology ideas within the existing clinical psychology discipline. In short, they call for clinical psychology to expand its focus to include the full range of human behavior and experience, which includes positive experience, strengths, and capacities, as well as negative experiences, deficits, and impairments (Wood & Tarrier, 2010).

Clinical psychologists working within the field of psychosis may be particularly receptive to this call. The influential British Psychological Society report *Recent Advances in Understanding Mental Illness and Psychotic Experiences*, first published in 2000 and recently updated (2014), endorsed very much service-user conceptions of recovery, and argued forcefully for a shift away from "illness management" to promotion of hope and empowerment (BPS, 2000, 2014). The 2000 report quotes Dr. Rufus May, a former service user and clinical psychologist specializing in psychosis:

> Psychiatry and psychology have to ask themselves why despite the millions of pounds spent on researching psychosis, we have neglected to look at those who manage to rebuild their lives and live with their difficulties, who have positive outcomes. This neglect has the consequence of perpetuating a learned hopelessness.... Although I am very critical of the medical treatment I received, from a positive perspective I can see psychiatric hospitals as acting for my family and me as a safety net. My main complaint was the lack of 'springiness' in the net to allow me to get back on the tightrope. (BPS, 2000, p. 69)

One of the contributors to the BPS report was Professor Mike Slade, an international expert in recovery-focused approaches to mental healthcare. Professor Slade has long championed the use of positive psychology approaches in mental healthcare, noting that they may be well-placed to provide the empirical grounding necessary to further the goals of the service user-led recovery movement (Slade, 2010). He notes both approaches share an emphasis on moving beyond illness management toward the promotion of human flourishing, autonomy and well-being. Where the recovery movement draws attention to the importance of individual testimony and recovery-focused goals, the positive psychology tradition may, he argues, help to generate a "clinically credible" evidence base about what is actually effective in promoting recovery (Slade, 2010).

This echoes an earlier call for collaboration by psychiatric researchers Sandra Resnick and Robert Rosenheck, who also suggest the recovery movement would benefit from an alliance with academic researchers who share their vision of empowerment and well-being (Resnick & Rosenheck, 2006). As an example, Resnick and Rosenheck outline their use of the Values in Action Inventory of Strengths (VIA-IS) (Peterson & Seligman, 2004) with veterans with severe mental illness, describing how this assessment, developed by positive psychology researchers as a way of profiling strengths and virtues, may have positive therapeutic effects:

> When at the conclusion the computer returns the "official" signature strengths report, most participants report feelings of pride and expansiveness, with the discovery of a self that is invariably better than expected. (Resnick & Rosenheck, 2006, p. 21)

Slade, in a report for UK mental health charity Rethink, also recommends that staff use the VIA-IS with people with psychosis, arguing that this and other strength-focused measures can help service users to develop a more positive identity (Slade, 2009a). Although research examining the reliability, validity and sensitivity to change of the VIA-IS in psychosis has yet to be completed, a recent uncontrolled study of 29 young people with early psychosis found completion was associated with moderate improvements in positive affect and cognitive performance (Sims, Barker, Price, & Fornells-Ambrojo, 2014). No improvements in state self-esteem or self-efficacy were detected, however, and a number of participants (34%) reported they lacked confidence that they actually had the strengths the measure said they have (Sims et al., 2014), which may suggest a single session is not enough to counteract the high levels of self-criticism observed in people with psychosis (Hutton, Kelly, Lowens, Taylor, & Tai, 2013).

Interest in the development and application of positive psychotherapy to psychosis has been growing over the last few years, paralleled by increased investigation of concepts which are relevant to a more positive clinical psychology. An overview of recent research into understanding and improving happiness, compassion, mindfulness, and treatment-related empowerment will be outlined here, but it should be noted that attention has also been given to improving our understanding of other positive phenomena, including recovery (Slade, 2009b; Hamm, Hasson-Ohayon, Kukla, & Lysaker, 2013), improved functioning (Hodgekins & Fowler, 2010; Penn et al., 2011), spirituality (Wagner & King, 2005; Huguelet et al., 2011; McCarthy-Jones, Waegeli, & Watkins, 2013; Brownell, Schrank, Jakaite, Larkin, & Slade, 2014), hope (McCann, 2002; Noh, Choe, & Yang, 2008), gratitude (Brownell et al., 2014; Bussing et al., 2014), resilience (J. Johnson, Gooding, Wood, Taylor, Pratt, & Tarrier, 2010; Torgalsboen, 2012; Henderson & Cock, 2014), love and attachment (Berry, Barrowclough, & Wearden, 2008; Redmond, Larkin, & Harrop, 2010; McCarthy-Jones & Davidson, 2013; Gumley, Taylor, Schwannauer, & MacBeth, 2014).

Happiness

The view that those with psychosis are continuously unhappy has been challenged by recent research. Although psychosis is thought to be characterized by a reduced capacity to experience or anticipate pleasure, Agid and colleagues found that their sample of 31 remitted first-episode psychosis patients had comparable levels of happiness, satisfaction with life, and perceived success to a matched sample of healthy individuals, despite having greatly reduced functioning and independence (Agid et al., 2012). Agid and colleagues caution against researchers and clinicians making assumptions about the levels of well-being and happiness of people who have recovered from early psychosis, arguing that their sample appeared to demonstrate a preserved capacity for this positive human experience. These results may have been specific to this population, however, and another study of people with longer-term chronic symptoms found they were significantly less happy than matched healthy controls (Palmer, Martin, Depp, Glorioso, & Jeste, 2014). However, even in this group almost 38% reported high levels of happiness, suggesting well-being in severe mental illness is not only possible, but also quite common and potentially malleable. A further study found that young people with psychosis defined happiness in terms of relations with others, self and spirituality, their health (mental and physical), and material happiness (experiences, possessions) (Buckland, Schepp, & Crusoe, 2013). Adverse effects of antipsychotic medication, isolation, not feeling normal, and fear – both in relation to losing mental control and of engaging with the environment around them – were identified as challenges to happiness (Buckland et al., 2013).

There is some encouraging early evidence that it may be possible to directly improve happiness and well-being in psychosis using psychological therapies. One such approach is positive psychotherapy (PPT), a useful description of which is provided by Shrank and colleagues (Schrank, Brownell, Tylee, & Slade, 2014):

> Positive psychotherapy broadens the client's perspective by encouraging him to undertake exercises which can elicit positive emotions, help generate new ideas, and frame difficult situations more positively ... help clients think about negative situations by conducting careful positive reappraisals ... focus on clients' identification and development of key strengths to increase their confidence and motivation ... (teach) clients to actively think about their positive qualities and helping them realise they can use these to solve their problems. Finally, PPT helps clients by re-educating their attention, memory, and expectations away from the negative and towards a more positive mindset. (Schrank et al., 2014, pp. 98–99)

A small uncontrolled study found that 10 sessions of group PPT was associated with improvements in psychological well-being in 15 people with psychosis (Meyer, Johnson, Parks, Iwanski, & Penn, 2011). Complementing these findings, a recent qualitative assessment of the experiences of 37 people who received 11 group sessions of PPT suggested they found it helpful in reducing negative rumination and focusing on positive aspects of life, as well recognizing their individual strengths (Brownell et al., 2014). Although exercises focused on promoting forgiveness and gratitude were positively received, it was noted that some participants also found these tasks challenging and distressing (Brownell et al., 2014), emphasizing the importance of not assuming that psychological interventions are adverse-effect free.

Also supporting the view that happiness can be increased in psychosis, a randomized study of 50 participants diagnosed with schizophrenia found that a 20-minute exercise designed to increase positive affect led to large increases in self-rated happiness over the short term when compared with listening to music alone (J. Johnson et al., 2013). A trial of a therapeutic approach designed to directly improve positive self-esteem in people struggling with distressing voices reported moderate improvements in mood for the 39 participants who received two months of this new treatment, when compared with 38 who received only their usual care (van der Gaag, van Oosterhout, Daalman, Sommer, & Korrelboom, 2012). Another very recent pilot trial found that a new type of cognitive therapy for clinical paranoia, which explicitly incorporated techniques and ideas from PPT, had more success at increasing positive self-cognitions than reducing negative ones (Freeman et al., 2014). This small single-blind study also reported large improvements in paranoid thoughts and overall delusions, but notably even larger benefits were observed for psychological well-being.

Importantly, all these innovations share a focus on enhancing positive emotions and appraisals, with a relatively reduced focused on modifying negative appraisals, cognitive biases, cognitive deficits, or symptoms. Although we will not know the true efficacy and safety of positive psycho-therapy until rigorous controlled studies are completed, these early investigations provide some provide proof of concept that improving well-being, subjective recovery, and happiness may indeed be possible without first attempting to improve residual symptoms, rectify cognitive deficits or modify negative self-concepts.

Compassion and Mindfulness

The benefits of psychosis researchers adopting a more positive clinical psychology approach is also illustrated by the growth in recent years of our understanding of psychological flexibility, mindfulness, and compassion, and how these strengths might be promoted in people with psychosis. A recent review and meta-analysis found several controlled studies suggesting mind-fulness can be successfully taught to people with psychosis, and that this may be associated with reductions in positive and negative symptoms (Khoury, Lecomte, Gaudiano, & Paquin, 2013). However, this did not seem to translate to improvements in functioning, quality of life or acceptance. These mixed findings suggest reducing symptoms alone may not be sufficient for meaningful change, and lend support to the arguments of positive clinical psychology that we need to invest more resources in understanding and promoting well-being, recovery and strengths (Wood & Tarrier, 2010). Indeed, one surprising finding to emerge over the last few years is that psychiatric raters and service users actually require quite considerable symptomatic reduction to notice even minimal clinical improvement (Leucht, Kane, Etschel, Kissling, Hamann, & Engel, 2006; Hermes, Sokoloff, Stroup, & Rosenheck, 2012), suggesting that trying to improve symptoms may not be an efficient way of achieving changes that are of value to service users and clinicians.

There have also been advances in our understanding of the role of compassion in people with psychosis, particularly in relation to recovery. For example, building on previous research (Boyd & Gumley, 2007; Mills, Gilbert, Bellew, McEwan, & Gale, 2007), we found elevated rates of self-criticism and reduced self-compassion in people with persecutory delusions, when compared with healthy participants (Hutton et al., 2013), and Mayhew and Gilbert found those who experience critical voices also struggle to experience self-compassion (Mayhew & Gilbert, 2008). Andrew Gumley and colleagues recently published a comprehensive compassion-focused model of recovery from psychosis, highlighting the importance of self-soothing, forgiveness, and acceptance of self-imperfection in continued well-being in this group (Gumley et al., 2010). They argue that:

> one of the major therapeutic goals [of compassion-focused therapy] is to help individuals cultivate a compassionate self-reflective stance toward their own experiences, in understanding self-other interactions, and in their approach to solving emotional and interpersonal problems. (Gumley et al., 2010, p. 196)

The therapeutic approach of these authors has found early support from a randomized controlled trial, suggesting it is effective at preventing recurrence of psychosis (Gumley et al., 2003), although the non-blind nature of the assessments limits the conclusions that could be drawn (McKenna, 2003). A more explicitly compassion-focused approach, based on the model outlined by Gumley and colleagues (Gumley et al., 2010), also found success in a recent pilot randomized trial, with 20 patients in a high-secure setting being more likely to experience global improvement and increases in compassion, in comparison with 20 patients receiving usual care only (Braehler, Gumley, Harper, Wallace, Norrie, & Gilbert, 2013). Importantly no adverse effects were observed and acceptability was high in this single-blind trial, supporting the findings of preceding case series work (Mayhew & Gilbert, 2008; Laithwaite et al., 2009). Finally an uncontrolled study of group loving-kindness meditation (focused on promoting compassion and kindness to self and others) found that six sessions was associated with improvements in positive emotions, satisfaction with life, consummatory pleasure, and anhedonia in 18 patients, although no improvements in anticipatory pleasure or purpose in life were observed (D. P. Johnson et al., 2011).

Treatment-related Autonomy and Empowerment

Working clinically with people with psychosis who had decided not to take antipsychotic medication (Hutton, Morrison, & Taylor, 2012; Morrison et al., 2012; Morrison et al., 2014) emphasized to me the importance of at least three developments in the services we provide. First, that we need to improve our understanding of those factors which help or hinder the ability of people with psychosis to make autonomous decisions about their care and experience a greater sense of treatment-related empowerment (Grealish, Tai, Hunter, & Morrison, 2011); second, that we need to provide people with psychosis with real choices in relation to the type of care available to them (Howes, 2014), investing resources to develop a range of effective and safe nonpharmacological interventions; third, that prescribers should be encouraged to use shared decision-making when discussing treatment options with those with psychosis (Hamann, Leucht, & Kissling, 2003).

The ideals of positive clinical psychology are particularly relevant to furthering these autonomy-related goals (Slade, 2010). Traditional clinical psychology and psychiatry has provided us with useful concepts relating to impaired decision making, allowing us to begin to understand those factors which lead to deficits in this area (Grisso & Appelbaum, 1995; Grisso, Appelbaum, & Hill-Fotouhi, 1997; Okai, Owen, McGuire, Singh, Churchill, & Hotopf, 2007; Owens, Richardson, David, Szmukler, Hayward, & Hotopf, 2008). Positive clinical psychology, however, might encourage us to be bolder, stimulating us to understand how superior or excellent treatment decision-making ability can develop, or how some people with psychosis have found the capacity to become highly empowered in relation to their care and treatment. Recovery-focused research has already led the way in this area, allowing us insight into the detailed narratives of those who have survived traumatic experiences of the psychiatric system (Romme, 2009). A substantial body of empirical research on subjective empowerment in psychosis now exists, thanks in no small part to the contributions of researchers such as Mike Slade (Slade, 2009a,b), Mary Ellen Copeland (Cook et al., 2013), Patrick Corrigan (Vauth, Kleim, Wirtz, & Corrigan, 2007), David Penn (Penn et al., 2011), Marius Romme (Romme, Honig, Noorthoorn, & Escher, 1992; Romme, 2009), Diana Rose (Rose, Evans, Sweeney, & Wykes, 2011) and Tony Morrison (Neil et al., 2009; Grealish et al., 2011).

Studying enhanced decision-making ability and subjective empowerment may help us learn what services need to do to preserve and promote autonomy (Owen, Freyenhagen, Richardson, & Hotopf, 2009). At present, services seem to focus on reducing symptoms and restoring functioning (Seale, Chaplin, Lelliott, & Quirk, 2006), and it is unusual to hear autonomy being explicitly considered as a goal of psychiatric treatment, although many recognize its intrinsic value (Owen et al., 2009). Indeed, some of the disagreement and controversy in mental health-care may have its roots in differing conceptions of autonomy (Owen et al., 2009; Radden, 2012), with service users regarding the interventions and treatments provided by services to support and enhance their autonomy as instead posing a threat to it (Hamann, Mendel, Fink, Pfeiffer, Cohen, & Kissling, 2008; Owen, David, Hayward, Richardson, Szmukler, & Hotopf, 2009; Grealish et al., 2011; Moritz et al., 2013).

It is interesting to consider what the impact on ethical and legal practice might be of a more positively focused mental health system. Current systems, even those based explicitly on concepts of capacity, are more concerned with assessing whether or not service users have intact or "good enough" capacity, or with meeting the needs of those who do not. However it would be interesting to see whether systems that also place obligations on clinicians to help service users develop *enhanced* autonomy and empowerment in relation to their care could reduce the risk of them experiencing significant loss of autonomy in the future, thus minimizing the risk of traumatizing compulsory care (Lu et al., 2011).

Perhaps promoting and enhancing autonomy beyond the basic requirement to seek consent is something that many clinicians feel they are providing already? It may be that psychiatrists, for example, believe antipsychotic medication empowers their patients and enhances their decision-making capacity, or it may be that psychologists view cognitive remediation, cognitive behavior therapy or family therapy as intrinsically autonomy-promoting. At present, however, we lack sufficient evidence to know either way, and it is clear that mental health services continue to rely on coercion and persuasion in their day-to-day running (Seale et al., 2006; Burns et al., 2011; Canvin, Rugkasa, Sinclair, & Burns, 2013). A group that may be particularly well placed to improve autonomy and empowerment are those service users who have been through their own recovery journey, and several studies have now examined the benefits of training them to provide other service users with mutual or peer support (Lloyd-Evans et al., 2014).

Encouraging prescribers to adopt a shared decision-making (SDM) approach to treatment may also enhance empowerment (Beitinger, Kissling, & Hamann, 2014), or at least reduce disempowerment. SDM involves encouraging clinicians and service users to engage in a collaborative, person-centered dialogue about the benefits and costs of treatments, and the benefits and costs of the alternatives, with explicit consideration of the service user's goals and priorities. We recently reviewed the evidence on SDM in psychosis, and found some small benefits on indices of subjective empowerment and patient–clinician relationships, but no clear benefits on decision-making capacity or use of compulsory treatment (Stovell, Morrison, & Hutton, submitted). More sophisticated interventions may be required if we want to achieve more substantial change, particularly for those who have experienced a lifetime of defeat and social exclusion (Gard et al., 2014). We may also need to better understand the goals of people with psychosis, which may sometimes be more about seeking relatedness, or social contact (Gard et al., 2014), or guidance (Hamann et al., 2011), than about exploration and empowerment.

Summary and some Methodological Recommendations

Positive clinical psychology encourages researchers and clinicians to give more attention to understanding and promoting more positive aspects of human experience, rather than simply trying to alleviate the negative. These goals mirror those of the grass-roots recovery movement, who have long pointed out that symptom reduction is not necessary or sufficient for people with psychosis to experience meaningful recovery. Many researchers and clinicians working in psychosis have identified closely with these goals, meaning that a body of research into concepts such as happiness, compassion, mindfulness, and empowerment already exists. This is encouraging for the application of positive clinical psychology in this area, and there is growing interest in whether new forms of psychotherapy developed by positive psychology researchers may have benefits on these important outcomes. Although the last two decades have seen much progress in our understanding of psychosis, existing treatment approaches, whether pharmacological or psychological, are not as effective as many proponents would have us believe. Although sophisticated cognitive models have been developed, the interventions derived from these have not been as impressive as hoped. To avoid repeating this cycle, positive clinical psychology researchers might consider introducing several methodological innovations in their research.

First, "pre-registration" of all empirical work and basic research should be strongly encouraged (Chambers & Munafo, 2013). Large expensive trials of new psychological treatments for psychosis come at the end of a costly and lengthy development pipeline, yet far too many have failed at this late stage (Lewis et al., 2002; Garety, Fowler, Freeman, Bebbington, Dunn, & Kuipers, 2008; Barrowclough et al., 2010; Klingberg et al., 2011; Crawford et al., 2012). To reduce this, research in positive clinical psychology needs to minimize the risk of publication and selective reporting bias at the very earliest phase – that is, during theory development and intervention component testing. Pre-registration, where hypotheses and methods (including sample-size calculations) are specified *a priori* and in a publicly accessible database, could help with this (Chambers & Munafo, 2013).

Second, positive clinical psychology research should not rely on previous research findings to compute sample sizes. Such calculations should instead be based on providing studies with adequate statistical power to detect effects that are of theoretical and/or practical significance, not simply "what has been observed before." Much existing published clinical psychology research in psychosis is, like neuroscience research (Button et al., 2013), probably underpowered and heavily distorted by nonpublication of small negative studies. Studies lacking statistical power will still be required to provide proof-of-concept and establish feasibility, but these should be clearly labeled as pilot studies.

Third, masked assessments should be used much more widely when researching and developing psychological models of psychosis. We are currently reviewing studies of the "jumping to conclusions" cognitive bias in psychosis (Taylor, Hutton, & Dudley, 2014), and we have found that only a fraction of the controlled studies kept their experimenters masked as to whether participants being assessed had psychosis or not. This is despite clear evidence that experimenter expectation and allegiance can distort results (Schulz, Chalmers, Hayes, & Altman, 1995; Day & Altman, 2000; Schulz & Grimes, 2002), whether consciously or unconsciously. Failure to recognize and minimize this risk delay the development of effective treatments, as researchers try to figure out which findings are robust and which are artifacts of researcher bias.

Finally, the trialing of positive psychotherapeutic interventions for psychosis should include the careful analysis of potential adverse effects. Unfortunately, existing approaches have not been subject to such analysis, largely because researchers have to date *assumed* they are safe – a widespread albeit unjustified assumption in psychotherapy research (Jonsson, Alaie, Parling, & Arnberg, 2014, Vaughan, Goldstein, Alikakos, Cohen, & Serby, 2014). Strategies that can be used in clinical trials to assess safety in a more comprehensive way include qualitative assessment of participant experience, reporting of serious adverse events and rates of significant deterioration, administration of psychotherapy-specific adverse effect questionnaires, and careful analysis of reasons for treatment discontinuation.

Conclusion

The development of better psychological treatments for people with psychosis is essential, and positive clinical psychology has much to offer in this regard. Progress has already been made in understanding happiness, compassion, mindfulness, autonomy and other positive phenomena in psychosis, and the promising initial findings have been outlined here. As argued above, the development of a reliable and robust evidence base on what works to improve such outcomes may benefit from parallel advances in methodological rigor, including the widespread implementation of pre-registration, improved justification of sample sizes, expanded use of blind assessments and much more careful consideration of the adverse effects of new treatments.

References

Agid, O., McDonald, K., Siu, C., Tsoutsoulas, C., Wass, C., Zipursky, R. B., & Remington, G. (2012). Happiness in first-episode schizophrenia. *Schizophrenia Research*, *141*(1), 98–103. doi.10.1016/j.schr es.2012.07.012S0920-9964(12)00406-9 [pii].

Agid, O., Siu, C. O., Potkin, S. G., Kapur, S., Watsky, E., Vanderburg, D., Remington, G., et al. (2013). Meta-regression analysis of placebo response in antipsychotic trials, 1970–2010. *American Journal of Psychiatry*. doi.10.1176/appi.ajp.2013.120303151722041 [pii].

Barrowclough, C., Haddock, G., Wykes, T., Beardmore, R., Conrod, P., Craig, T., Tarrier, N., et al. (2010). Integrated motivational interviewing and cognitive behavioural therapy for people with psychosis and comorbid substance misuse: randomised controlled trial. *British Medical Journal*, *341*, c6325. doi.10.1136/bmj.c6325bmj.c6325 [pii].

Beck, A. T. & Grant, P. M. (2008). Negative self-defeating attitudes: Factors that influence everyday impairment in individuals with schizophrenia. *American Journal of Psychiatry*, *165*(6), 772; author reply 772. doi.10.1176/appi.ajp.2008.08020229165/6/772 [pii].

Beck, A. T., Grant, P. M., Huh, G. A., Perivoliotis, D., & Chang, N. A. (2013). Dysfunctional attitudes and expectancies in deficit syndrome schizophrenia. *Schizophrenia Bulletin*, *39*(1), 43–51. doi.sbr040 [pii] 10.1093/schbul/sbr040.

Beitinger, R., Kissling, W., & Hamann, J. (2014). Trends and perspectives of shared decision-making in schizophrenia and related disorders. *Current Opinion in Psychiatry*, *27*(3), 222–229. doi.10.1097/YCO.0000000000000057.

Bentall, R. P., Corcoran, R., Howard, R., Blackwood, R., & Kinderman, P. (2001). Persecutory delusions: A review and theoretical integration. *Clinical Psychology Review*, *22*, 1–50.

Berry, K., Barrowclough, C., & Wearden, A. (2008). Attachment theory: a framework for understanding symptoms and interpersonal relationships in psychosis. *Behaviour Research and Therapy*, *46*(12), 1275–1282. doi.10.1016/j.brat.2008.08.009S0005-7967(08)00186-1 [pii].

Boyd, T. & Gumley, A. (2007). An experiential perspective on persecutory paranoia: A grounded theory construction. *Psychology and Psychotherapy: Theory, Research and Practice 80*(1), 1–22. doi.10.1348/147608306X100536.

BPS. (2000). *Recent advances in understanding mental illness and psychotic experiences*. Leicester: British Psychological Society.

BPS. (2014). Understanding psychosis and schizophrenia: Why people sometimes hear voices, believe things that others find strange, or appear out of touch with reality … and what can help. In: A. Cooke (Ed.), *Division of Clinical Psychology*. London: British Psychological Society.

Braehler, C., Gumley, A., Harper, J., Wallace, S., Norrie, J., & Gilbert, P. (2013). Exploring change processes in compassion focused therapy in psychosis: Results of a feasibility randomized controlled trial. *British Journal of Clinical Psychology*, *52*(2), 199–214. doi.10.1111/bjc.12009.

Brownell, T., Schrank, B., Jakaite, Z., Larkin, C., & Slade, M. (2014). Mental health service user experience of positive psychotherapy. *Journal of Clinical Psychology*. doi.10.1002/jclp.22118.

Buckland, H. T., Schepp, K. G., & Crusoe, K. (2013). Defining happiness for young adults with schizophrenia: A building block for recovery. *Archives of Psychiatric Nursing*, *27*(5), 235–240. doi.10.1016/j.apnu.2013.07.002S0883-9417(13)00091-5 [pii].

Burns, T., Yeeles, K., Molodynski, A., Nightingale, H., Vazquez-Montes, M., Sheehan, K., & Linsell, L. (2011). Pressures to adhere to treatment ("leverage") in English mental healthcare. *British Journal of Psychiatry*, *199*(2), 145–150. doi.199/2/145 [pii]10.1192/bjp.bp.110.086827.

Bussing, A., Wirth, A. G., Reiser, F., Zahn, A., Humbroich, K., Gerbershagen, K., Baumann, K., et al. (2014). Experience of gratitude, awe and beauty in life among patients with multiple sclerosis and psychiatric disorders. *Health Quality of Life Outcomes*, *12*, 63. doi.10.1186/1477-7525-12-631477-752 5-12-63 [pii].

Button, K. S., Ioannidis, J. P., Mokrysz, C., Nosek, B. A., Flint, J., Robinson, E. S., & Munafo, M. R. (2013). Power failure: Why small sample size undermines the reliability of neuroscience. *Nature Reviews Neuroscience*, *14*(5), 365–376. doi.10.1038/nrn3475nrn3475 [pii].

Canvin, K., Rugkasa, J., Sinclair, J., & Burns, T. (2013). Leverage and other informal pressures in community psychiatry in England. *International Journal of Law and Psychiatry*, *36*(2), 100–106. doi.10.1016/j.ijlp.2013.01.002S0160-2527(13)00003-4 [pii].

Chadwick, P. & Birchwood, M. (1994). The omnipotence of voices: A cognitive approach to auditory hallucinations. *British Journal of Psychiatry*, *164*, 190–201.

Chambers, C. & Munafo, M. R. (2013). Trust in science would be improved by study pre-registration: We must encourage scientific journals to accept studies before the results are in, *The Guardian*. Available at: http://www.theguardian.com/science/blog/2013/jun/05/trust-in-science-study-pre-registration, last accessed June 5, 2013.

Cook, J. A., Jonikas, J. A., Hamilton, M. M., Goldrick, V., Steigman, P. J., Grey, D. D., Copeland, M. E., et al. (2013). Impact of Wellness Recovery Action Planning on service utilization and need in a randomized controlled trial. *Psychiatric Rehabilitation Journal*, *36*(4), 250–257. doi.10.1037/prj00000282013-42745-004 [pii].

Crawford, M. J., Killaspy, H., Barnes, T. R., Barrett, B., Byford, S., Clayton, K., Waller, D., et al. (2012). Group art therapy as an adjunctive treatment for people with schizophrenia: a randomised controlled trial (MATISSE). *Health Technology Assess*, *16*(8), iii–iv, 1–76. doi.10.3310/hta16080.

Day, S. J. & Altman, D. G. (2000). Statistics notes: Blinding in clinical trials and other studies. *British Medical Journal*, *321*(7259), 504.

Freeman, D., Garety, P. A., Kuipers, E., Fowler, D., & Bebbington, P. E. (2002). A cognitive model of persecutory delusions. *British Journal of Clinical Psychology*, *41*(4), 331–347.

Freeman, D., Pugh, K., Dunn, G., Evans, N., Sheaves, B., Waite, F., Fowler, D., et al. (2014). An early Phase II randomised controlled trial testing the effect on persecutory delusions of using CBT to reduce negative cognitions about the self: The potential benefits of enhancing self confidence. *Schizophrenia Research*, *160*(1/3), 186–192. doi.10.1016/j.schres.2014.10.038S0920-9964(14)00607-0 [pii].

Gard, D. E., Sanchez, A. H., Starr, J., Cooper, S., Fisher, M., Rowlands, A., & Vinogradov, S. (2014). Using self-determination theory to understand motivation deficits in schizophrenia: the "why" of motivated behavior. *Schizophrenia Research*, *156*(2/3), 217–222. doi.10.1016/j.schres.2014.04.027S0920-9964(14)00199-6 [pii].

Garety, P. A., Fowler, D. G., Freeman, D., Bebbington, P., Dunn, G., & Kuipers, E. (2008). Cognitive-behavioural therapy and family intervention for relapse prevention and symptom reduction in psychosis: randomised controlled trial. *British Journal of Psychiatry*, *192*(6), 412–423. doi.10.1192/bjp.bp.107.043570192/6/412 [pii].

Garety, P. A., Kuipers, E., Fowler, D., Freeman, D., & Bebbington, P. E. (2001). A cognitive model of the positive symptoms of psychosis. *Psychological Medicine*, *31*, 189–195.

Grant, P. M. & Beck, A. T. (2009). Defeatist beliefs as a mediator of cognitive impairment, negative symptoms, and functioning in schizophrenia. *Schizophrenia Bulletin*, *35*(4), 798–806.

Grant, P. M., Huh, G. A., Perivoliotis, D., Stolar, N. M., & Beck, A. T. (2012). Randomized trial to evaluate the efficacy of cognitive therapy for low-functioning patients with schizophrenia. *Archives of General Psychiatry*, *69*(2), 121–127. doi.10.1001/archgenpsychiatry.2011.129archgenpsychiatry.2011.129 [pii].

Grealish, A., Tai, S., Hunter, A., & Morrison, A. P. (2011). Qualitative exploration of empowerment from the perspective of young people with psychosis. *Clinical Psychology and Psychotherapy*. doi.10.1002/cpp.785.

Grisso, T. & Appelbaum, P. S. (1995). The MacArthur Treatment Competence Study. III: Abilities of patients to consent to psychiatric and medical treatments. *Law and Human Behavior*, *19*(2), 149–174.

Grisso, T., Appelbaum, P. S., & Hill-Fotouhi, C. (1997). The MacCAT-T: A clinical tool to assess patients' capacities to make treatment decisions. *Psychiatry Services*, *48*(11), 1415–1419.

Gumley, A., Braehler, C., Laithwaite, H., MacBeth, A., & Gilbert, P. (2010). A compassion focused model of recovery after psychosis. *International Journal of Cognitive Therapy*, *3*(2), 186–201.

Gumley, A. I., O'Grady, M., McNay, L., Reilly, J., Power, K., & Norrie, J. (2003). Early intervention for relapse in schizophrenia: results of a 12-month randomised controlled trial of cognitive behaviour therapy. *Psychological Medicine*, *33*, 419–431.

Gumley, A. I., Taylor, H. E., Schwannauer, M., & MacBeth, A. (2014). A systematic review of attachment and psychosis: measurement, construct validity and outcomes. *Acta Psychiatrica Scandinavica, 129*(4), 257–274. doi.10.1111/acps.12172.

Hamann, J., Leucht, S., & Kissling, W. (2003). Shared decision making in psychiatry. *Acta Psychiatrica Scandinavica, 107*(6), 403–409. doi.130 [pii].

Hamann, J., Mendel, R., Reiter, S., Cohen, R., Buhner, M., Schebitz, M., Berthele, A., et al. (2011). Why do some patients with schizophrenia want to be engaged in medical decision making and others do not? *Journal of Clinical Psychiatry, 72*(12), 1636–1643. doi.10.4088/JCP.10m06119yel.

Hamann, J., Mendel, R. T., Fink, B., Pfeiffer, H., Cohen, R., & Kissling, W. (2008). Patients' and psychiatrists' perceptions of clinical decisions during schizophrenia treatment. *Journal of Nervous and Mental Disease, 196*(4), 329–332. doi.10.1097/NMD.0b013e31816a62a000005053-200804000-00010 [pii].

Hamm, J. A., Hasson-Ohayon, I., Kukla, M., & Lysaker, P. H. (2013). Individual psychotherapy for schizophrenia: Trends and developments in the wake of the recovery movement. *Psychology Research and Behavior Management, 6*, 45–54. doi.10.2147/PRBM.S47891prbm-6-045 [pii].

Harrow, M., Jobe, T. H., & Faull, R. N. (2012). Do all schizophrenia patients need antipsychotic treatment continuously throughout their lifetime? A 20-year longitudinal study. *Psychological Medicine, 42*(10), 2145–2155. doi.10.1017/S0033291712000220S0033291712000220 [pii].

Henderson, A. R. & Cock, A. (2014). The responses of young people to their experiences of first-episode psychosis: harnessing resilience. *Community Mental Health Journal.* doi.10.1007/s10597-014-9769-9.

Hermes, E. D., Sokoloff, D., Stroup, T. S., & Rosenheck, R. A. (2012). Minimum clinically important difference in the Positive and Negative Syndrome Scale with data from the Clinical Antipsychotic Trials of Intervention Effectiveness (CATIE). *Journal of Clinical Psychiatry, 73*(4), 526–532. doi.10.4088/JCP.11m07162.

Hodgekins, J. & Fowler, D. (2010). CBT and recovery from psychosis in the ISREP trial: Mediating effects of hope and positive beliefs on activity. *Psychiatry Services, 61*(3), 321–324. doi.61/3/321 [pii] 10.1176/appi.ps.61.3.321.

Howes, O. (2014). Cognitive therapy: at last an alternative to antipsychotics? *Lancet, 383*(9926), 1364–1366. doi.10.1016/S0140-6736(13)62569-6S0140-6736(13)62569-6 [pii].

Huguelet, P., Mohr, S., Betrisey, C., Borras, L., Gillieron, C., Marie, A. M., Brandt, P. Y., et al. (2011). A randomized trial of spiritual assessment of outpatients with schizophrenia: Patients' and clinicians' experience. *Psychiatry Services, 62*(1), 79–86. doi.10.1176/appi.ps.62.1.7962/1/79 [pii].

Hutton, P., Kelly, J., Lowens, I., Taylor, P. J., & Tai, S. (2013). Self-attacking and self-reassurance in persecutory delusions: a comparison of healthy, depressed and paranoid individuals. *Psychiatry Research, 205*(1/2), 127–136. doi.10.1016/j.psychres.2012.08.010S0165-1781(12)00442-8 [pii].

Hutton, P., Morrison, A. P., & Taylor, H. (2012). Brief cognitive-behavioural therapy for hallucinations: Can it help people who decide not to take antipsychotic medication? A case report. *Behavioural and Cognitive Psychotherapy, 40*, 111–116.

Jauhar, S., McKenna, P. J., Radua, J., Fung, E., Salvador, R., & Laws, K. R. (2014). Cognitive-behavioural therapy for the symptoms of schizophrenia: Systematic review and meta-analysis with examination of potential bias. *British Journal of Psychiatry, 204*, 20–29. doi.10.1192/bjp.bp.112.116285204/1/20 [pii].

Johnson, D. P., Penn, D. L., Fredrickson, B. L., Kring, A. M., Meyer, P. S., Catalino, L. I., & Brantley, M. (2011). A pilot study of loving-kindness meditation for the negative symptoms of schizophrenia. *Schizophrenia Research, 129*(2/3), 137–140. doi.10.1016/j.schres.2011.02.015S0920-9964(11)00098-3 [pii].

Johnson, D. P., Penn, D. L., Fredrickson, B. L., Meyer, P. S., Kring, A. M., & Brantley, M. (2009). Loving-kindness meditation to enhance recovery from negative symptoms of schizophrenia. *Journal of Clinical Psychology, 65*(5), 499–509. doi.10.1002/jclp.20591.

Johnson, J., Gooding, P. A., Wood, A. M., Fair, K. L., & Tarrier, N. (2013). A therapeutic tool for boosting mood: The broad-minded affective coping procedure (BMAC). *Cognitive Therapy and Research, 37*(1), 61–70.

Johnson, J., Gooding, P. A., Wood, A. M., Taylor, P. J., Pratt, D., & Tarrier, N. (2010). Resilience to suicidal ideation in psychosis: Positive self-appraisals buffer the impact of hopelessness. *Behaviour Research and Therapy, 48*(9), 883–889. doi.10.1016/j.brat.2010.05.013S0005-7967(10)00109-9 [pii].

Jonsson, U., Alaie, I., Parling, T., & Arnberg, F. K. (2014). Reporting of harms in randomized controlled trials of psychological interventions for mental and behavioral disorders: A review of current practice. *Contemporary Clinical Trials, 38*(1), 1–8. doi.10.1016/j.cct.2014.02.005S1551-7144(14)00025-1 [pii].

Khoury, B., Lecomte, T., Gaudiano, B. A., & Paquin, K. (2013). Mindfulness interventions for psychosis: A meta-analysis. *Schizophrenia Research, 150*(1), 176–184. doi.10.1016/j.schres.2013.07.055 S0920-9964(13)00433-7 [pii].

Kishimoto, T., Robenzadeh, A., Leucht, C., Leucht, S., Watanabe, K., Mimura, M., Correll, C. U., et al. (2013). Long-acting injectable vs oral antipsychotics for relapse prevention in schizophrenia: A meta-analysis of randomized trials. *Schizophrenia Bulletin.* doi.sbs150 [pii]10.1093/schbul/sbs150.

Klingberg, S., Herrlich, J., Wiedemann, G., Wolwer, W., Meisner, C., Engel, C., Wittorf, A., et al. (2012). Adverse effects of cognitive behavioral therapy and cognitive remediation in schizophrenia: results of the treatment of negative symptoms study. *Journal of Nervous and Mental Disease, 200*(7), 569–576. doi.10.1097/NMD.0b013e31825bfa1d00005053-201207000-00005 [pii].

Klingberg, S., Wolwer, W., Engel, C., Wittorf, A., Herrlich, J., Meisner, C., Wiedemann, G., et al. (2011). Negative symptoms of schizophrenia as primary target of cognitive behavioral therapy: results of the randomized clinical TONES study. *Schizophrenia Bulletin, 37 Suppl* 2, S98–110. doi.sbr073 [pii] 10.1093/schbul/sbr073.

Laithwaite, H., O'Hanlon, M., Collins, P., Doyle, P., Abraham, L., Porter, S., & Gumley, A. (2009). Recovery After Psychosis (RAP) A compassion focused programme for individuals residing in high security settings. *Behavioural and Cognitive Psychotherapy, 37*(5), 511–526. doi.S1352465809990233 [pii]10.1017/S1352465809990233.

Leucht, S., Cipriani, A., Spineli, L., Mavridis, D., Orey, D., Richter, F., & Davis, J. M. (2013). Comparative efficacy and tolerability of 15 antipsychotic drugs in schizophrenia: A multiple-treatments meta-analysis. *Lancet.* doi.S0140-6736(13)60733-3 [pii]10.1016/S0140-6736(13)60733-3.

Leucht, S., Heres, S., Hamann, J., & Kane, J. M. (2008). Methodological issues in current antipsychotic drug trials. *Schizophrenia Bulletin, 34*(2), 275–285. doi.sbm159 [pii]10.1093/schbul/sbm159.

Leucht, S., Kane, J. M., Etschel, E., Kissling, W., Hamann, J., & Engel, R. R. (2006). Linking the PANSS, BPRS, and CGI: Clinical implications. *Neuropsychopharmacology, 31*(10), 2318–2325. doi.1301147 [pii]10.1038/sj.npp.1301147.

Leucht, S., Tardy, M., Komossa, K., Heres, S., Kissling, W., Salanti, G., & Davis, J. M. (2012). Antipsychotic drugs versus placebo for relapse prevention in schizophrenia: A systematic review and meta-analysis. *Lancet.* doi.S0140-6736(12)60239-6 [pii]10.1016/S0140-6736(12)60239-6.

Lewis, S., Tarrier, N., Haddock, G., Bentall, R., Kinderman, P., Kingdon, D., Dunn, G., et al. (2002). Randomised controlled trial of cognitive-behavioural therapy in early schizophrenia: Acute-phase outcomes. *British Journal of Psychiatry: Suppl., 43*, s91–97.

Lloyd-Evans, B., Mayo-Wilson, E., Harrison, B., Istead, H., Brown, E., Pilling, S., Kendall, T., et al. (2014). A systematic review and meta-analysis of randomised controlled trials of peer support for people with severe mental illness. *BMC Psychiatry, 14*, 39. doi.10.1186/1471-244X-14-391471-244X-14-39 [pii].

Lu, W., Mueser, K. T., Shami, A., Siglag, M., Petrides, G., Schoepp, E., Saltz, J., et al. (2011). Post-traumatic reactions to psychosis in people with multiple psychotic episodes. *Schizophrenia Research, 127*(1/3), 66–75. doi.10.1016/j.schres.2011.01.006S0920-9964(11)00017-X [pii].

Mayhew, S. L. & Gilbert, P. (2008). Compassionate mind training with people who hear malevolent voices: A case series report. *Clinical Psychology & Psychotherapy, 15*(2), 113–138. doi.10.1002/cpp.566.

McCann, T. V. (2002). Uncovering hope with clients who have psychotic illness. *Journal of Holistic Nursing, 20*(1), 81–99.

McCarthy-Jones, S. & Davidson, L. (2013). When soft voices die: auditory verbal hallucinations and a four letter word (love). *Mental Health, Religion & Culture, 16*(4), 367–383.

McCarthy-Jones, S., Waegeli, A., & Watkins, J. (2013). Spirituality and hearing voices: Considering the relation. *Psychosis, 5*(3), 247–258. doi.10.1080/17522439.2013.831945.

McKenna, P. J. (2003). Targeted cognitive behavioural therapy may reduce relapse in people with prodromal symptoms of schizophrenia. *Evidence Based Mental Health, 6*(4), 112.

Meyer, P. S., Johnson, D. P., Parks, A., Iwanski, C., & Penn, D. L. (2011). Positive living: A pilot study of group positive psychotherapy for people with schizophrenia. *Journal of Positive Psychology, 7*(3), 239–248.

Mills, A., Gilbert, P., Bellew, R., McEwan, K., & Gale, C. (2007). Paranoid beliefs and self-criticism in students. *Clinical Psychology & Psychotherapy*, *14*, 358–364.

Miyar, J. & Adams, C. E. (2012). Content and quality of 10,000 controlled trials in schizophrenia Over 60 years. *Schizophrenia Bulletin*, *39*(1), 226–229. doi.sbr140 [pii]10.1093/schbul/sbr140.

Moncrieff, J., Cohen, D., & Mason, J. P. (2009). The subjective experience of taking antipsychotic medication: A content analysis of Internet data. *Acta Psychiatrica Scandinavica*, *120*(2), 102–111. doi.ACP1356[pii]10.1111/j.1600-0447.2009.01356.x.

Moritz, S., Favrod, J., Andreou, C., Morrison, A. P., Bohn, F., Veckenstedt, R., Karow, A., et al. (2013). Beyond the usual suspects: positive attitudes towards positive symptoms is associated with medication noncompliance in psychosis. *Schizophrenia Bulletin*, *39*(4), 917–922. doi.10.1093/schbul/sbs005sbs005 [pii].

Morrison, A. P. (2001). The interpretation of intrusions in psychosis: An integrative cognitive approach to hallucinations and delusions. *Behavioural and Cognitive Psychotherapy*, *29*, 257–276.

Morrison, A. P., Hutton, P., Shiers, D., & Turkington, D. (2012). Antipsychotics: Is it time to introduce patient choice? *British Journal of Psychiatry*, *201*, 83–84. doi.10.1192/bjp.bp.112.112110201/2/83 [pii].

Morrison, A. P., Hutton, P., Wardle, M., Spencer, H., Barratt, S., Brabban, A., Turkington, D., et al. (2012). Cognitive therapy for people with a schizophrenia spectrum diagnosis not taking antipsychotic medication: an exploratory trial. *Psychological Medicine*, *42*(5), 1049–1056. doi.S0033291711001899 [pii]10.1017/S0033291711001899.

Morrison, A. P., Turkington, D., Pyle, M., Spencer, H., Brabban, A., Dunn, G., Hutton, P., et al. (2014). Cognitive therapy for people with schizophrenia spectrum disorders not taking antipsychotic drugs: A single-blind randomised controlled trial. *Lancet*, *383*(9926), 1395–1403. doi.10.1016/S0140-6736(13)62246-1S0140-6736(13)62246-1 [pii].

National Institute for Clinical Excellence (NICE). (2009). *Schizophrenia: core interventions in the treatment and management of schizophrenia in primary and secondary care*. London: NICE.

Neil, S. T., Kilbride, M., Pitt, L., Welford, M., Nothard, S., Sellwood, W., & Morrison, A. P. (2009). The Questionnaire about the Process of Recovery (QPR): A research instrument developed in collaboration with service users. *Psychosis*, *1*, 145–155.

Noh, C., Choe, K., & Yang, B. (2008). Hope from the perspective of people with schizophrenia (Korea). *Archives of Psychiatric Nursing*, *22*(2), 69–77. doi.10.1016/j.apnu.2007.10.002S0883-9417(07)00217-8 [pii].

Okai, D., Owen, G., McGuire, H., Singh, S., Churchill, R., & Hotopf, M. (2007). Mental capacity in psychiatric patients: Systematic review. *British Journal of Psychiatry*, *191*, 291–297. doi.191/4/291 [pii]10.1192/bjp.bp.106.035162.

Owen, G. S., David, A. S., Hayward, P., Richardson, G., Szmukler, G., & Hotopf, M. (2009). Retrospective views of psychiatric in-patients regaining mental capacity. *British Journal of Psychiatry*, *195*(5), 403–407. doi.195/5/403 [pii]10.1192/bjp.bp.109.065151.

Owen, G. S., Freyenhagen, F., Richardson, G., & Hotopf, M. (2009). Mental capacity and decisional autonomy: An interdisciplinary challenge. *Inquiry and Interdisciplinary Journal of Philosophy*, *52*(1), 79–107. doi.10.1080/00201740802661502.

Owens, G. S., Richardson, G., David, A. S., Szmukler, G., Hayward, P., & Hotopf, M. (2008). Mental capacity to make decisions on treatment in people admitted to psychiatric hospitals: Cross-sectional study. *British Medical Journal*, *337*, 448.

Palmer, B. W., Martin, A. S., Depp, C. A., Glorioso, D. K., & Jeste, D. V. (2014). Wellness within illness: Happiness in schizophrenia. *Schizophrenia Research*, *159*(1), 151–156. doi.10.1016/j.schres.2014.07.027S0920-9964(14)00384-3 [pii].

Penn, D. L., Uzenoff, S. R., Perkins, D., Mueser, K. T., Hamer, R., Waldheter, E., Cook, L., et al. (2011). A pilot investigation of the Graduated Recovery Intervention Program (GRIP) for first episode psychosis. *Schizophrenia Research*, *125*(2/3), 247–256. doi.10.1016/j.schres.2010.08.006S0920-9964(10)01452-0 [pii].

Peterson, C. F. & Seligman, M. E. P. (2004). *Character strengths and virtues: A handbook and classification*. Washington, DC and Oxford: American Psychological Association and Oxford University Press.

Radden, J. H. (2012). Recognition rights, mental health consumers and reconstructive cultural semantics. *Philosophy, Ethics and Humanities in Medicine*, *7*, 6. doi.10.1186/1747-5341-7-61747-5341-7-6 [pii].

Rector, N. A., Beck, A. T., & Stolar, N. (2005). The negative symptoms of schizophrenia: A cognitive perspective. *Canadian Journal of Psychiatry, 50*, 247–257.

Redmond, C., Larkin, M., & Harrop, C. (2010). The personal meaning of romantic relationships for young people with psychosis. *Clinical Child Psychology and Psychiatry, 15*(2), 151–170. doi.10.1177/13591 04509341447135910450934147 [pii].

Resnick, S. G. & Rosenheck, R. A. (2006). Recovery and positive psychology: parallel themes and potential synergies. *Psychiatric Services, 57*(1), 120–122. doi.57/1/120 [pii]10.1176/appi.ps.57.1.120.

Romme, M. A. J. (2009). *Living with voices: 50 stories of recovery.* Ross-on-Wye: PCCS Books in association with Birmingham City University.

Romme, M. A., Honig, A., Noorthoorn, E. O., & Escher, A. D. (1992). Coping with hearing voices: An emancipatory approach. *British Journal of Psychiatry, 161*, 99–103.

Rose, D., Evans, J., Sweeney, A., & Wykes, T. (2011). A model for developing outcome measures from the perspectives of mental health service users. *International Review of Psychiatry, 23*(1), 41–46. doi.10.3109/09540261.2010.545990.

Rosenheck, R. A., Krystal, J. H., Lew, R., Barnett, P. G., Fiore, L., Valley, D., Liang, M. H., et al. (2011). Long-acting risperidone and oral antipsychotics in unstable schizophrenia. *New England Journal of Medicine, 364*(9), 842–851. doi.10.1056/NEJMoa1005987.

Schrank, B., Brownell, T., Tylee, A., & Slade, M. (2014). Positive psychology: An approach to supporting recovery in mental illness. *East Asian Archives of Psychiatry, 24*(3), 95–103.

Schulz, K. F., Chalmers, I., Hayes, R. J., & Altman, D. G. (1995). Empirical evidence of bias. Dimensions of methodological quality associated with estimates of treatment effects in controlled trials. *Journal of the American Medical Association, 273*(5), 408–412.

Schulz, K. F. & Grimes, D. A. (2002). Blinding in randomised trials: hiding who got what. *Lancet, 359*(9307), 696–700.

Seale, C., Chaplin, R., Lelliott, P., & Quirk, A. (2006). Sharing decisions in consultations involving antipsychotic medication: A qualitative study of psychiatrists' experiences. *Social Science and Medicine, 62*(11), 2861–2873. doi.S0277-9536(05)00584-8 [pii]10.1016/j.socscimed.2005.11.002.

Sims, A., Barker, C., Price, C., & Fornells-Ambrojo, M. (2014). Psychological impact of identifying character strengths in people with psychosis. *Psychosis: Psychological, Social and Integrative Approaches, 7*(2), 179–182

Slade, M. (2009a). *100 ways to support recovery: A guide for mental health professionals.* Rethink recovery series, vol. 1. London: Rethink.

Slade, M. (2009b). *Personal recovery and mental illness: A guide for mental health professionals.* Cambridge: Cambridge University Press.

Slade, M. (2010). Mental illness and well-being: The central importance of positive psychology and recovery approaches. *BMC Health Service Research 10*, 26. doi.10.1186/1472-6963-10-261472-6963-10-26 [pii].

Stovell, D., Morrison, A. P., & Hutton, P. (submitted). The effect of shared decision making interventions on empowerment-related outcomes in psychosis: systematic review and meta-analysis.

Stroup, T. S. (2014). What is the role of long-acting injectable antipsychotics in the treatment of schizophrenia? *Journal of Clinical Psychiatry, 75*(11), 1261–1262. doi.10.4088/JCP.14com09518.

Taylor, P., Hutton, P., & Dudley, R. (2014). Rationale and protocol for a systematic review and meta-analysis on reduced data gathering in people with delusions. *Systematic Reviews, 3*, 44. doi.10.1186/2046-4053-3-442046-4053-3-44 [pii].

Torgalsboen, A. K. (2012). Sustaining full recovery in schizophrenia after 15 years: Does resilience matter? *Clinical Schizophrenia and Related Psychoses, 5*(4), 193–200. doi.10.3371/CSRP.5.4.3YL08017404 N045VW [pii].

Turner, D. T., van der Gaag, M., Karyotaki, E., & Cuijpers, P. (2014). Psychological interventions for psychosis: a meta-analysis of comparative outcome studies. *American Journal of Psychiatry, 171*(5), 523–538. doi.10.1176/appi.ajp.2013.130811591831621 [pii].

van der Gaag, M., van Oosterhout, B., Daalman, K., Sommer, I. E., & Korrelboom, K. (2012). Initial evaluation of the effects of competitive memory training (COMET) on depression in schizophrenia-spectrum patients with persistent auditory verbal hallucinations: A randomized controlled trial. *British Journal of Clinical Psychology, 51*(2), 158–171. doi.10.1111/j.2044-8260.2011.02025.x.

Vaughan, B., Goldstein, M. H., Alikakos, M., Cohen, L. J., & Serby, M. J. (2014). Frequency of reporting of adverse events in randomized controlled trials of psychotherapy vs. psychopharmacotherapy. *Comprehensive Psychiatry*, *55*(4), 849–855. doi.10.1016/j.comppsych.2014.01.001S0010-440X(14) 00006-6 [pii].

Vauth, R., Kleim, B., Wirtz, M., & Corrigan, P. W. (2007). Self-efficacy and empowerment as outcomes of self-stigmatizing and coping in schizophrenia. *Psychiatry Research*, *150*(1), 71–80. doi.S0165-1781(06)00203-4 [pii]10.1016/j.psychres.2006.07.005.

Villeneuve, K., Potvin, S., Lesage, A., & Nicole, L. (2010). Meta-analysis of rates of drop-out from psychosocial treatment among persons with schizophrenia spectrum disorder. *Schizophrenia Research*, *121*(1/3), 266–270. doi.S0920-9964(10)01256-9 [pii]10.1016/j.schres.2010.04.003.

Wagner, L. C. & King, M. (2005). Existential needs of people with psychotic disorders in Porto Alegre, Brazil. *British Journal of Psychiatry*, *186*, 141–145. doi.186/2/141 [pii]10.1192/bjp.186.2.141.

Wood, A. M. & Tarrier, N. (2010). Positive Clinical Psychology: a new vision and strategy for integrated research and practice. *Clinical Psychology Review*, *30*(7), 819–829. doi.10.1016/j.cpr.2010.06. 003S0272-7358(10)00097-8 [pii].

Wunderink, L., Nieboer, R. M., Wiersma, D., Sytema, S., & Nienhuis, F. J. (2013). Recovery in remitted first-episode psychosis at 7 years of follow-up of an early dose reduction/discontinuation or mainte-nance treatment strategy: Long-term follow-up of a 2-year randomized clinical trial. *JAMA Psychiatry*, *70*(9), 913–920. doi.10.1001/jamapsychiatry.2013.191707650 [pii].

Wykes, T., Huddy, V., Cellard, C., McGurk, S. R., & Czobor, P. (2011). A meta-analysis of cognitive remediation for schizophrenia: Methodology and effect sizes. *American Journal of Psychiatry*, *168*(5), 472–485. doi.appi.ajp.2010.10060855 [pii]10.1176/appi.ajp.2010.10060855.

Wykes, T., Steel, C., Everitt, B., & Tarrier, N. (2008). Cognitive behavior therapy for schizophrenia: Effect sizes, clinical models, and methodological rigor. *Schizophrenia Bulletin*, *34*, 523–537.

18

An Integrative Model of Personality Strengths and Weaknesses
Thomas A. Widiger

An Integrative Model of Personality Strengths and Weaknesses

The purpose of this chapter is to present an integrative model of personality strengths and weaknesses. This model highlights the need to move beyond viewing personality traits in simplistic "positive" and "negative" terms, and recognizes the complex, interactional nature of such traits. Furthermore, the chapter suggests that this model can be used not only to better understand general personality traits, but it could also improve approaches to addressing problems in personality, or "personality disorder." The model is focused on integrating the positive and negative, and, as such, is consistent with ideas outlined in positive clinical psychology (Wood & Tarrier, 2010).

Personality is a person's characteristic manner of thinking, feeling, behaving, and relating to others (McCrae & Costa, 2003). The predominant descriptive model of personality structure within psychology is the "five-factor model" (FFM), consisting of the broad domains of extraversion (versus introversion), agreeableness (versus antagonism), conscientiousness (versus disinhibition), neuroticism (versus emotional stability), and openness (versus closedness) (John, Naumann, & Soto, 2008). It is arguably the case that every personality trait falls somewhere within these five domains. Every person can be well described in terms of the five domains, and more specifically by the individual traits that lie within them. For example, the six primary traits of agreeableness (versus antagonism) are trust (versus suspicion), straightforwardness (versus deception), altruism (versus exploitation), compliance (versus opposition), modesty (versus arrogance), and tender-mindedness (versus tough-mindedness).

Adaptive and Maladaptive Traits

Some FFM domains and traits are generally considered to be adaptive, representing personality strengths (e.g., agreeableness), whereas other domains and traits are generally considered to be maladaptive, representing personality weaknesses (e.g., antagonism). However, an integrative model of personality strengths and weaknesses is not as simple as that. Some of the seemingly maladaptive traits can be adaptive strengths within certain situational contexts, and there are as well maladaptive, extreme variants of the usually adaptive traits.

The Wiley Handbook of Positive Clinical Psychology, First Edition. Edited by Alex M. Wood and Judith Johnson.
© 2016 John Wiley & Sons, Ltd. Published 2016 by John Wiley & Sons, Ltd.

Adaptive Strengths of Usually Maladaptive Traits

It is generally considered to be better for a person to be high in extraversion, agreeableness, conscientiousness, openness, and emotional stability, than for a person to be high in introversion, antagonism, disinhibition, closedness, or neuroticism. There is a considerable body of research to indicate better life outcomes for persons high in extraversion, agreeableness, conscientiousness, openness, and/or emotional stability than for persons with the opposite traits (Ozer & Benet-Martinez, 2006). Nevertheless, a truly positive psychology viewpoint will also recognize that there are potential benefits and advantages in being high in introversion, antagonism, disinhibition, closedness, and neuroticism. There are not as many benefits and advantages, but there can be some and they should be acknowledged and recognized.

"Each of the Big Five dimensions of human personality can be seen as the result of a trade-off between different fitness costs and benefits" (Nettle, 2006, p. 622). This helps to explain the genetics of individual differences. "As there is no unconditionally optimal value of these trade-offs, it is to be expected that genetic diversity will be retained in the population" (p. 622). There are certain contexts and situations in which it is advantageous to be introverted, antagonistic, disinhibited, conventional, and/or, to a degree, even neurotic, hence their continued presence within the population.

Antagonism is most often a problem, but it can also be an advantage. There is some truth to the saying that "nice guys finish last." Antagonistic persons can, on average, obtain higher salaries and other workplace advantages because they are more likely to complain and push for their own benefits (Judge, Livingston, & Hurst, 2012). There can be much to be gained, to the regret and detriment of agreeable persons, in being self-centered, deceptive, manipulative, aggressive, and/or exploitative (Nettle, 2006).

There might appear to be little positive to say about being elevated on neuroticism, but that is not in fact the case. Emotional stability is clearly preferable, on average, to emotional instability. However, imagine being incapable of feeling anxious. Neuroticism exists as a universal trait in part because it does have certain benefits for adaptive functioning (Crespi, 2014; Del Giudice & Del Giudice, 2014). For example, anxiety is a useful trait for anticipating negative outcomes and risks. The absence of an ability to feel anxious is analogous to the inability to feel physical pain, as in the case of congenital analgesia, a very debilitating and life-threatening disease. Persons who are very low in anxiousness are unlikely to avoid dangerous activities, or respond to cues of social and physical harm (Nettle, 2006).

Maladaptive Variants of Usually Adaptive Traits

Traits that are usually adaptive strengths will also have maladaptive variants (Widiger, 2011). For example, FFM conscientiousness includes such traits as competence, orderliness, discipline, achievement-striving, and deliberation (Costa & McCrae, 1992). However, there is a considerable body of research to indicate that persons can take these traits to a maladaptive extreme, evidencing a perfectionism, compulsivity, single-minded doggedness, workaholism, and ruminative deliberation (Samuel & Widiger, 2011).

Samuel, Riddell, Lynam, Miller, & Widiger (2012) in fact developed a measure of the obsessive-compulsive personality disorder (OCPD) from the perspective of the FFM, the Five-Factor Obsessive-Compulsive Inventory (FFOCI), which includes six scales that were hypothesized to assess maladaptive variants of conscientiousness: perfectionism, fastidiousness, punctiliousness, doggedness, workaholism, and ruminative deliberation. They reported that all six scales were moderately to strongly related to FFM conscientiousness (as well as measures of OCPD). Crego, Samuel, and Widiger (2015) replicated and extended their findings, including additional measures of conscientiousness, such as the dependability scale from the Inventory of Personal Characteristics (Tellegen & Waller, 1987); activity from the Zuckerman–Kuhlman–Aluja

Personality Questionnaire (Aluja, Kuhlman, & Zuckerman, 2010); conscientiousness from the International Personality Item Pool-NEO (IPIP-NEO) (Goldberg et al., 2006); and orderliness from the 5-Dimensional Personality Test (van Kampen, 2012). All six FFOCI maladaptive conscientiousness scales related robustly with all four alternative measures of conscientiousness. For example, the correlations with IPIP-NEO conscientiousness ranged from .52 (for ruminative deliberation) to .70 (for perfectionism).

FFM agreeableness includes such traits as being compliant, trusting, modest, and altruistic. It is evident that it is typically preferable to be characteristically agreeable than characteristically antagonistic. However, it would also seem evident that some persons can be overly compliant, excessively trusting, inordinately modest, and/or excessively altruistic. Indeed, there are quite a few maladaptive trait terms within high agreeableness, such as gullibility, self-effacement, subservience, submissive, docile, servile, clinging, defenseless, selfless, and acquiescent (Coker, Samuel, & Widiger, 2002); traits that are suggestive of the dependent personality disorder (Gore & Pincus, 2013).

Gore, Presnall, Lynam, Miller, and Widiger (2012) developed a measure of dependent personality disorder (DPD) from the perspective of the FFM: the Five-Factor Dependency Inventory (FFDI). The FFDI includes scales from neuroticism (i.e., separation insecurity, pessimism, shamefulness, and helplessness), but also has a number of scales from agreeableness (i.e., gullibility, selflessness, subservience, and self-effacing). Gore and colleagues (2012) validated the measure not only with respect to its relationship with other measures of DPD, but also with respect to its relationship with the domains of the FFM, as assessed by the NEO Personality Inventory-Revised (NEO PI-R) (Costa & McCrae, 1992), an experimentally manipulated version of the NEO PI-R Agreeableness scale, which consisted of maladaptive variants of the adaptive NEO PI-R items (as well as adaptive variants of the maladaptive items) (Haigler & Widiger, 2001), and the Interpersonal Adjectives Scale-Big Five (Trapnell & Wiggins, 1990).

Taken together, then, this research suggests that understandings of personality traits as either "positive" or "negative" are overly simplistic, and not supported by empirical evidence. Instead, traits must be recognized as containing both the potential for positive and negative outcomes, depending upon the degree to which they are present, and the context of the person expressing them.

Psychiatric Conceptions of Personality Disorder

The American Psychiatric Association's (APA) *Diagnostic and Statistical Manual of Mental Disorders* (*DSM-5*) (APA, 2013) includes a section devoted to the diagnosis of personality disorders. When personality traits result in a significant impairment to social or occupational activity (or personal distress), a personality disorder is considered to be present. The *DSM-5* includes 10 different types of personality disorder: antisocial, avoidant, borderline, histrionic, narcissistic, paranoid, schizoid, and schizotypal, as well as the dependent and obsessive-compulsive.

There is little that is considered to be positive about these mental disorders. However, just as the generally maladaptive personality traits of the FFM can be associated with some personal gain or benefits within a limited environmental context (Nettle, 2006), there can be some occasional advantages for some of the personality disorders. The workaholism of the obsessive-compulsive personality disorder has been associated with some occupational success (Samuels & Costa, 2012). The arrogant self-confidence and acclaim-seeking of the narcissistic personality disorder has had comparable benefits (Ackerman, Witt, Donnellan, Trzesniewski, Robins, & Kashy, 2011; Miller & Campbell, 2011). The willingness of the person with a dependent personality disorder to accommodate can be very helpful in relationship maintenance (Bornstein, 2012). Nevertheless, these successful outcomes have also been controversial (Pincus & Lukowitsky, 2010; Crego & Widiger, in press) because makes a personality disorder a disorder is the predominance of the maladjustment (Livesley, 2007).

In fact, personality disorders are among the more stigmatizing of the mental disorders (Millon, 2011). They are relatively unique in concerning "egosyntonic" aspects of the self (Tyrer, 2009). Other mental disorders, such as the anxiety, mood, and substance use disorders, involve something that happens to the person (i.e., egodystonic). Most persons experience a mental disorder as something that befell them and they want to overcome it, comparable with the experience of developing a physical disease or injury. In contrast, a personality disorder is not typically experienced as something that happens to the person. It is who that person is (Millon, 2011). It is how the person thinks of him- or herself, relates to others, and behaves throughout much of the day and throughout much of his or her life.

As such, few persons actually seek treatment for a personality disorder (Tyrer, 2009). Very few persons seek treatment for their narcissism, their obsessive-compulsive personality, and/or their dependent personality (an exception to this is borderline and avoidant personality disorder, due perhaps to the substantial involvement of negative affectivity) (Widiger, 2009). Persons are generally comfortable with their personality traits, even when these traits are a major reason for their problems in living. Persons with personality disorders will recognize that they have problematic lives, filled with stress, failure, disruption, and conflict, but they will usually place the blame on others, the situation, chance, fate, or most anything else other than themselves (Millon, 2011).

Given the egosyntonic nature of personality disorder, one might then not consider a personality disorder to be stigmatizing, as persons with personality disorders will often fail to recognize the presence of the disorder. However, the diagnosis can be difficult to provide and acknowledge precisely because of its egosyntonic nature. A diagnosis of a personality disorder suggests that who the person is, and essentially always has been, is itself a mental disorder. It is their sense of self, their way of living and relating to others. In sum, it can be quite stigmatizing to suggest that your fundamental sense of yourself, your manner of relating to others, is a mental disorder.

The authors of the fourth edition of the APA diagnostic manual (APA, 1994) were instructed not to state that a person with anorexia (for instance) is an anorexic, that a person with schizophrenia is a schizophrenic, or that a person with bipolar mood disorder is a bipolar (Frances, First, & Pincus, 1995). Persons are not equivalent to their mental disorders. There is a lot more to each person other than having the presence of a mental disorder.

The same reasoning should apply to the diagnosis of a personality disorder. Persons will comfortably state that someone is a narcissist or a psychopath, yet it is evident that persons with a personality disorder are more than just the personality disorder. A personality disorder concerns a person's characteristic manner of thinking, feeling, and relating to others, but it has become readily evident that persons who share the same personality disorder diagnosis can have markedly different personalities (Clark, 2007; Widiger & Trull, 2007). Each DSM-5 personality disorder concerns only a particular subset of maladaptive personality traits. Persons with a DSM-5 personality disorder will have quite a few additional traits, many of which can be adaptive strengths.

In fact, it is now clearly evident that persons who share the same personality disorder diagnosis are unlikely to even share all of the traits of that particular personality disorder (Clark, 2007). DSM-III (APA, 1980) was the first version of the APA diagnostic manual to include specific criterion sets (Spitzer, Williams, & Skodol, 1980). For some of the personality disorders, all of the stated features were required (APA, 1980). These monothetic criterion sets ensured that everyone who was provided the same diagnosis would share all of the features of that personality disorder. However, it quickly became evident that most persons who would be said to have the respective personality disorder would fail to have all of the features. Therefore, DSM-*III-R* (APA, 1987) converted to polythetic criterion sets in which only a subset of features was required (Widiger, Frances, Spitzer, & Williams, 1988). These polythetic criterion sets more accurately reflect the actual personality structure of patients with personality disorders, but they result in a considerable amount of heterogeneity and/or dissimilarity among persons sharing the same diagnosis. For example, there are eight features for the diagnosis of obsessive-compulsive personality disorder (OCPD), any four of which are required (APA, 2013). This means that two persons could share an OCPD diagnosis, yet not have one feature in common (i.e., each has only four features and not the same ones). There are indeed 163 different potential combinations of four or more of eight features (Samuel et al., 2012). As expressed by Skodol (2012), the Chair of the *DSM-5* Personality and Personality Disorders Work Group, referring to the *DSM-IV* diagnostic criteria for borderline personality disorder, "use of the polythetic criteria of DSM, in which a minimum number (e.g., 5) from a list of criteria (e.g., 9) are required, but no single one is necessary, results in extreme heterogeneity among patients receiving the same diagnosis" (p. 36). There are indeed 256 different possible ways to meet criteria for borderline personality disorder (Johansen, Karterud, Pedersen, Gude, & Falkum, 2004). This degree of potential heterogeneity and/or dissimilarity among persons sharing the same diagnosis complicates substantially the effort to identify a specific etiology, pathology, or treatment for the respective personality disorder, but it also accurately reflects the reality that the *DSM-IV* personality disorders are not homogeneous syndromes (Clark, 2007; Widiger & Trull, 2007).

An additional well-established finding is that persons who share the same personality disorder diagnosis will have additional maladaptive (and adaptive) personality traits (Skodol, 2012). Patients rarely meet the diagnostic criteria for just one personality disorder. Multiple diagnoses can be the norm rather than the exception (Trull & Durrett, 2005; Clark, 2007; Widiger & Trull, 2007). Diagnostic co-occurrence was considered to be so problematic by the *DSM-5* Personality and Personality Disorders Work Group that they proposed deleting literally half of the diagnoses to address the problem (Skodol, 2010). This would have been a rather draconian solution to this problem (Widiger, 2011), particularly since lack of adequate coverage is arguably just as troubling (Westen & Arkowitz-Westen, 1998; Verheul & Widiger, 2004). Nevertheless, it is a clear testament as to the magnitude of the problem. Indeed, this co-occurrence becomes even larger when one recognizes subthreshold cases. That is, some persons with narcissistic personality disorder may not meet diagnostic criteria for antisocial personality disorder, but they are likely to have at least some antisocial personality traits.

The heterogeneity among persons sharing the same personality disorder diagnosis along with the presence of additional personality traits from other personality disorders is all a reflection that persons, including those with personality disorders, are not well described by one word, one specific diagnosis, or one specific constellation of personality traits. Like personality, personality disorder cannot be viewed as simply a sum of "negative" traits. Each person will have a relatively unique constellation of personality traits, with both positive and negative possibilities, and this particular constellation will not be shared by the vast majority of other persons. In sum, the complex patterns of personality structure are not well described by diagnostic categories that refer to one particular syndrome. A more accurate descriptive will be dimensional rather than categorical (Widiger, Simonsen, Krueger, Livesley, & Verheul, 2005; Skodol, 2012).

The Five-Factor Model of Personality Disorder

The FFM was derived from a factor analysis of all of the personality trait terms within the language, and thereby provides a reasonably comprehensive description of general personality structure. The FFM is then quite robust in its ability to cover all other models of personality. "One of the great strengths of the Big Five taxonomy is that it can capture, at a broad level of abstraction, the commonalities among most of the existing systems of personality traits, thus providing an integrative descriptive model" (John et al., 2008, p. 139). The FFM has been used effectively in many prior studies and reviews as a basis for comparing, contrasting, and integrating seemingly diverse sets of personality scales (Goldberg, 1993; Ozer & Reise, 1994; Funder, 2001; McCrae & Costa, 2003).

The FFM is comparably robust in its coverage of abnormal as well as normal personality functioning (Widiger & Costa, 1994). A substantial body of research now indicates that the FFM successfully accounts for the symptoms and traits of the *DSM-IV* (now *DSM-5*) personality disorders (Saulsman & Page, 2004; O'Connor, 2005; Clark, 2007; Samuel & Widiger, 2008), as well as additional maladaptive personality functioning not recognized within *DSM-5* (e.g., psychopathy, alexithymia, and prejudice). Livesley (2001) concluded on the basis of his review of the FFM-personality disorder research that "all categorical diagnoses of DSM can be accommodated within the five-factor framework" (p. 24). Markon, Krueger, and Watson (2005) conducted meta-analytic and exploratory hierarchical factor analyses of numerous measures of normal and abnormal personality functioning, and obtained consistently a five-factor solution that they indicated "strongly resembles the Big Five factor structure commonly described in the literature, including neuroticism, agreeableness, extraversion, conscientiousness, and openness factors" (p. 144). As expressed by Clark (2007), "the five-factor model of personality is widely accepted as representing the higher-order structure of both normal and abnormal personality traits" (p. 246).

In other words, the FFM offers the potential to provide an individualized personality profile of a patient, or any other person, in one integrative model of personality structure that includes both adaptive and maladaptive personality traits. There are a number of advantages of such an approach (Widiger, Samuel, Mullins-Sweatt, & Crego, 2012). Rather than force an individual into a category that fails to provide a fully accurate description, fails to capture important personality traits (including adaptive strengths), and includes traits within the diagnostic syndrome that the person does not have, the FFM allows the clinician to provide an individualized profile of precisely the traits that are present, including adaptive personality strengths as well as the maladaptive dysfunction. This type of diagnostic description is considerably more precise and accurate than a diagnostic category, and, as a result, has obvious benefits for treatment, research, insurance, and other clinical decisions.

The ability to recognize a person's personality strengths, as well as the maladaptive, problematic traits, will also help address the potential stigma of a personality disorder assessment and diagnosis. An FFM of personality disorder would help address stigma in two ways. First, it would provide the same descriptive model to persons with personality disorders that is also being provided to persons who do not suffer from a personality disorder. The same language would be used for both persons. Personality disorders would no longer be considered as something that is qualitatively distinct from normal personality functioning, but would instead be understood simply as the presence of maladaptive and/or extreme variants of the same traits that are present in all persons (Widiger & Trull, 2007).

Second, an FFM of personality disorder would recognize the personality strengths that are present in persons currently diagnosed with personality disorders. No longer would a patient "be" a psychopathic, a borderline, or a narcissistic. The patient would indeed have psychopathic, borderline, and/or narcissistic personality traits, but the FFM description would provide a more complete understanding of each person that recognizes and appreciates that the person is more than just the personality disorder and that other aspects of the self might be adaptive, even commendable, despite the presence of some significant maladaptive personality traits.

"Some of these strengths may also be quite relevant to treatment, such as openness to experience indicating an interest in exploratory psychotherapy, agreeableness indicating an engagement in group therapy" (Widiger & Mullins-Sweatt, 2009, p. 203). Sanderson and Clarkin (2013) described the benefits of obtaining an FFM assessment for treatment planning, in particular, the importance of assessing conscientiousness. As they indicated, "elevations on facets of conscientiousness are not usually seen in patients [with borderline personality disorder] but they bode well for a potential responsivity to the rigors and demands of the dialectical behavior therapy program" (p. 342). Dialectical behavior therapy (DBT) is a very demanding treatment regimen, including the attendance at group didactic meetings, the completion of social skills homework assignments, and mindfulness meditation training (Stepp, Whalen, & Smith, 2013).

Persons high in conscientiousness are much more likely to adhere to successfully complete the program. Stone (2002) uses the domains and facets of the FFM to guide treatment decisions for his psychodynamic therapy for patients with borderline personality disorder. "Neuroticism and agreeableness scales picked up on the pathological aspects of the borderline patients (as did the DSM items) but the extraversion, conscientiousness, and openness scales yielded important information about … issues of perseverance at work, social abilities, and openness to new ideas" (p. 412). As Stone (2002) suggested, "these qualities … play a vital role in determining amenability to therapy" (p. 412).

Krueger and Eaton (2010) likewise described how a person who met criteria for borderline personality disorder had high levels of openness and extraversion that had useful treatment implications. "The high openness might … suggest that this person would be open to a therapeutic approach where depth and underling motives for behavior are explored" (Krueger & Eaton, 2010, p. 102). Exploratory psychotherapy requires in interest and ability to self-reflect, exploring alternative perspectives on one's problems in living as well as present and past interpersonal relationships. Persons high in openness are likely to be well suited for this therapeutic approach.

There is, however, relatively little systematic research on the adaptive strengths in persons with personality disorders. A useful focus for future research would indeed be studies exploring empirically the potential contributions of considering additional personality traits in persons diagnosed with personality disorders. There are a few scattered studies on the potential value of FFM traits in predicting treatment outcome for patients with other forms of psychopathology (e.g., Ogrodniczuk, Piper, Joyce, McCallum, & Rosie, 2003; Talbot, Duberstein, Butzel, Cox, & Giles, 2003). Anecdotal clinical experience suggests a potentially important contribution to treatment planning for patients with personality disorder (Stone, 2002; Sanderson & Clarkin, 2013; Stepp et al., 2013), but what would be of most use would be systematical empirical studies in personality disorder samples with respect to treatment outcome and/or other important aspects of social, clinical functioning.

Clinical Utility Research

There have been a number of studies that have directly compared the FFM with the APA diagnostic categories with respect to matters of clinical utility (Mullins-Sweatt & Lengel, 2012). Samuel and Widiger (2006) provided clinicians with brief vignettes of actual cases and asked them to describe each person with respect to the *DSM-IV* personality disorder diagnoses and the five domains and 30 facets of the FFM (as identified by McCrae & Costa, 2003). They reported that the clinicians rated the FFM higher than the *DSM-IV* with respect to its ability to provide a global description of the individual's personality, to communicate information to clients, and to assist the clinician in formulating effective treatment plans.

Mullins-Sweatt and Widiger (2011) asked clinicians to describe one or two of their personality disordered clients in terms of the FFM and the *DSM-IV*. In some instances, the client was someone who met the criteria for one of the 10 *DSM-IV* personality disorders; in others, the client was someone who received a diagnosis of personality disorder not otherwise specified (PDNOS), a waste-basket diagnosis for patients who do have a personality disorder but not one that is well described in terms of the 10 existing categories. Across both cases, the clinicians rated the FFM as significantly more useful than the *DSM-IV* with respect to its ability to provide a global description of the individual's personality, to communicate information to clients, and to encompass all of the individual's important personality difficulties. Notably, for the PDNOS cases, clinicians also indicated the FFM was moderately to very useful in ease of application and professional communication. A complete summary of the FFM clinical utility research is provided by Mullins-Sweatt and Lengel (2012).

DSM-5 and the FFM

It was the initial intention of the authors of the *DSM-5* personality disorders section to include positive, adaptive traits, along with the maladaptive traits (Krueger & Eaton, 2010). This was evident in the "Personality and Personality Disorders" title for the work group (Skodol, 2012). This aspect of the proposal though was soon abandoned.

The final proposal by the *DSM-5* Personality and Personality Disorders Work Group (PPDWG) did include a five-domain dimensional trait model that was aligned with the FFM. As stated in *DSM-5*, "these five broad domains are maladaptive variants of the five domains of the extensively validated and replicated personality model known as the "Big Five," or the "Five-Factor Model of Personality" (APA, 2013, p. 773). However, this proposal did not include any adaptive traits.

The dimensional trait proposal was also embedded within a much more complex set of additional proposals, including the deletion of four diagnoses, the replacement of the specific and explicit criterion sets with a new hybrid model of personality disorder diagnosis that had not yet been subjected to empirical research (Skodol, 2012), and the broadening of the definition of personality disorder to include deficits in the sense of self and interpersonal relatedness drawn from the psychodynamic literature (Bender, Morey, & Skodol, 2011; Kernberg, 2012). All of the proposals were rejected by a Scientific Review Committee (Kendler, 2013).

It is not entirely clear why the proposals were rejected (Gunderson, 2013; Krueger, 2013; Skodol, Morey, Bender, & Oldham, 2013; Widiger, 2013). It is evident that there is considerable opposition to shifting the personality disorders section to a dimensional trait model (e.g., Gunderson, 2010; Shedler et al., 2010). Miller and Lynam (2013) also suggested that the PPDWG might not have done an adequate job compiling the empirical support for the dimensional trait proposal. There is a substantial body of research in support of the FFM of personality disorder (Widiger, Costa, Gore, & Crego, 2013), but very little of this research was cited by the PPDWG. Blashfield and Reynolds (2012) systematically reviewed the reference list for the final proposal and indicated that there was only one citation of an FFM study. As suggested by Lilienfeld, Watts, and Smith (2012) and Livesley (2012), this might have reflected a somewhat ambivalent attitude of PPDWG members toward the FFM. The final proposal was said to be aligned with the FFM, but the initial proposal was for a six-domain model that was explicitly distinguished from the FFM (i.e., Clark & Krueger, 2010). This helped fuel the opposition to the dimensional trait proposal. As argued by Shedler et al. (2010) "the resulting model no longer rests on decades of research, which had been the chief rationale for including it" (p. 1027). As suggested by First (2014), the embracement of the FFM toward the end of the work group deliberations might have represented a last-minute attempt to buttress the empirical support for their proposal. Nevertheless, it is evident that the dimensional trait model proposed for *DSM-5* is generating a considerable body of supportive research (Krueger & Markon, 2014), including research that supports its alignment with the FFM (e.g., Thomas, Yalch, Krueger, Wright, Markon, & Hopwood, 2012; De Fruyt, De Clerq, De Bolle, Willie, Markon, & Krueger, 2013; Gore & Widiger, 2013; Wright & Simms, 2014; Griffin & Samuel, in press).

An Integrative Assessment of Adaptive and Maladaptive Traits

A common criticism of the FFM, at least with respect to providing a description or assessment of personality disorders, has been that existing FFM measures have lacked adequate fidelity for the assessment of its maladaptive variants (e.g., Reynolds & Clark, 2001; Krueger, Eaton, Derringer, Markon, Watson, & Skodol, 2011). It should be acknowledged, however, that the primary measure of the FFM, the NEO Personality Inventory-Revised (NEO PI-R) (Costa & McCrae, 1992), does provide a valid and effective assessment of some of the *DSM-IV* (now *DSM-5*) personality disorders. The NEO PI-R provides an assessment of maladaptive variants of high neuroticism, low extraversion, low openness, high antagonism, and low conscientiousness (Haigler & Widiger, 2001) and these are the poles of the FFM that are primarily involved for most (but not all) of the *DSM-IV* personality disorders (Lynam & Widiger, 2001). It is largely for this reason that the NEO PI-R, a measure of normal (or general) personality functioning, has in fact been quite effective for the assessment of many of the personality disorders (Miller, 2012). The exceptions tend to be the assessment of the dependent, obsessive-compulsive, schizotypal, and histrionic personality disorders (Miller, 2012) as these include significant components of maladaptive agreeableness, conscientiousness, openness, and extraversion, respectively (Lynam & Widiger, 2001; Samuel & Widiger, 2004) and the NEO PI-R is sorely limited in its coverage of the maladaptive variants of these poles of the FFM domains (Haigler & Widiger, 2001).

The concern of inadequate coverage of maladaptive traits within existing FFM instruments no longer applies though, as the field now has a number of alternative measures with which to assess maladaptive variants of the FFM, including the Personality Inventory for *DSM-5* (Krueger, Derringer, Markon, Watson, & Skodol, 2012), the Computerized Adaptive Test-Personality Disorder (CAT-PD) (Simms, Goldberg, Roberts, Watson, Welte, & Rotterman, 2011), and a series of FFM personality disorder scales (Widiger, Lynam, Miller, & Oltmanns, 2012). Of particular interest for this chapter is perhaps the Structured Interview for the Five Factor Model (SIFFM) (Trull et al., 1998). The SIFFM was modeled after the NEO PI-R (Costa & McCrae, 1992), albeit developed in part to increase the coverage of maladaptive variants of low neuroticism, high extraversion, high openness, high agreeableness, and high conscientiousness. The SIFFM first assesses for adaptive variants of many of the facets of the FFM, and then follows this with the more extreme and/or maladaptive variants, thereby providing within one instrument an assessment of normal, adaptive strengths as well as the abnormal variants of respective FFM facets.

De Clercq, De Fruyt, Van Leeuwen, and Mervielde (2006) modeled the development of the Dimensional Personality Symptom Item Pool (DIPSI) after the SIFFM. They constructed items to assess maladaptive variants of facets within the Hierarchical Personality Inventory for Children (HiPIC) (Mervielde & De Fruyt, 2002). The HiPIC provides an assessment of normal, adaptive FFM traits within children and adolescents, comparable with the NEO PI-R. The DIPSI provides an assessment of the maladaptive variants of HiPIC items and scales. Together they provide an integrative assessment of both positive and negative personality functioning in children and adolescents (De Fruyt & De Clercq, 2014).

There are a number of abbreviated measures of the FFM, such as the Five-Factor Model Rating Form (FFMRF) (Mullins-Sweatt, Jamerson, Samuel, Olson, & Widiger, 2006). The FFMRF is a one-page rating form that includes an assessment of all 30 NEO PI-R FFM facets. The FFMRF has been used in studies as a clinician rating form and as a self-report inventory (Samuel, Mullins-Sweatt, & Widiger, 2013). The FFMRF includes adaptive and maladaptive traits within the same measure, albeit they are not explicitly distinguished.

Rojas and Widiger (2014) therefore developed the Five Factor Form (FFF). The FFF is again a one-page scale that can be used as a rating form or as a self-report. It includes all 30 NEO PI-R FFM facets and, unique to this measure, maladaptive and adaptive (or at least less maladaptive) variants for all 60 poles of all 30 facets. For example, for the facet of modesty (from agreeableness), a score of 5 indicates "self-effacing, self-denigrating" (i.e., maladaptive), a score of 4 is "humble, modest, unassuming" (adaptive), 3 is neutral, 2 is "confident, self-assured" (adaptive), and 1 is "boastful, vain, pretentious, arrogant" (maladaptive). For the facet of achievement-striving (from conscientiousness), 5 indicates "workaholic, acclaim-seeking," 4 as "purposeful, diligent, ambitious," 3 is neutral, 2 is "carefree, content," and 1 is "aimless, shiftless, desultory." One can then use the FFF to provide a description of a person with respect to both their adaptive strengths as well as the extreme, maladaptive variants of the adaptive traits. For example, the FFF assesses for the adaptive dispositions to be trusting, honest, giving, cooperative, humble, and empathic,

Table 18.1 Five-Factor form.*

Please write rating in blank on left below →	Maladaptive high (5)	Normal high (4)	Neutral (3)	Normal low (2)	Maladaptive low (1)
NEUROTICISM					
Anxiousness	Fearful, Anxious	Vigilant, worrisome, wary		Relaxed, calm	Oblivious to signs of threat
Angry hostility	Rageful	Brooding, resentful, defiant		Even-tempered	Will not even protest exploitation
Depressiveness	Depressed, suicidal	Pessimistic, discouraged		Not easily discouraged	Unrealistic, overly optimistic
Self-Consciousness	Uncertain of self, ashamed	Self-conscious, embarrassed		Self-assured, charming	Glib, shameless
Impulsivity	Unable to resist impulses	Self-indulgent		Restrained	Overly restrained
Vulnerability	Helpless, overwhelmed	Vulnerable		Resilient	Fearless, feels invincible
EXTRAVERSION					
Warmth	Intense attachments	Affectionate, warm		Formal, reserved	Cold, distant
Gregariousness	Attention-seeking	Sociable, outgoing, personable		Independent	Socially withdrawn, isolated
Assertiveness	Dominant, pushy	Assertive, forceful		Passive	Resigned, uninfluential
Activity	Frantic	Energetic		Slow-paced	Lethargic, sedentary
Excitement-Seeking	Reckless, foolhardy	Adventurous		Cautious	Dull, listless
Positive Emotions	Melodramatic, manic	High-spirited, cheerful, joyful		Placid, sober, serious	Grim, anhedonic
OPENNESS					
Fantasy	Unrealistic, lives in fantasy	Imaginative		Practical, realistic	Concrete
Aesthetics	Bizarre interests	Aesthetic interests		Minimal aesthetic interests	Disinterested
Feelings	Intense, in turmoil	Self-aware, expressive		Constricted, blunted	Alexithymic
Actions	Eccentric	Unconventional		Predictable	Mechanized, stuck in routine
Ideas	Peculiar, weird	Creative, curious		Pragmatic	Closed-minded
Values	Radical	Open, flexible		Traditional	Dogmatic, moralistically intolerant

AGREEABLENESS

Trust	Gullible	Trusting	Cautious, skeptical	Cynical, suspicious
Straightforwardness	Guileless	Honest, forthright	Savvy, cunning, shrewd	Deceptive, dishonest, manipulative
Altruism	Self-sacrificial, selfless	Giving, generous	Frugal, withholding	Greedy, self-centered, exploitative
Compliance	Yielding, subservient, meek	Cooperative, obedient, deferential	Critical, contrary	Combative, aggressive
Modesty	Self-effacing, self-denigrating	Humble, modest, unassuming	Confident, self-assured	Boastful, vain, pretentious, arrogant
Tender-Mindedness	Overly soft-hearted	Empathic, sympathetic, gentle	Strong, tough	Callous, merciless, ruthless

CONSCIENTIOUSNESS

Competence	Perfectionistic	Efficient, resourceful	Casual	Disinclined, lax
Order	Preoccupied w/organization	Organized, methodical	Disorganized	Careless, sloppy, haphazard
Dutifulness	Rigidly principled	Dependable, reliable, responsible	Easy-going, capricious	Irresponsible, undependable, immoral
Achievement	Workaholic, acclaim-seeking	Purposeful, diligent, ambitious	Carefree, content	Aimless, shiftless, desultory
Self-Discipline	Single-minded doggedness	Self-disciplined, willpower	Leisurely	Negligent, hedonistic
Deliberation	Ruminative, indecisive	Thoughtful, reflective, circumspect	Quick to make decisions	Hasty, rash

as well as the maladaptive variants in being gullible, guileless, self-sacrificing, subservient, self-denigrating, and soft-hearted. Similarly, the FFF assesses for the adaptive dispositions to be cautious, savvy, frugal, critical, confident, and strong, as well as the maladaptive variants in being cynical, dishonest, self-centered, aggressive, arrogant, and callous. Rojas and Widiger (2014) provided initial research concerning the validity of the FFF as a measure of the FFM. Table 18.1 provides all of the items of the FFF.

Conclusions

There are many advantages in having an integrative model of normal and abnormal personality functioning, particularly when coordinated with the FFM. The FFM has considerable construct validity as a dimensional model of personality structure, and this body of research concerning childhood antecedents, behavior genetics, course, and life history outcomes can be brought to bear on the understanding of personality disorders (Widiger & Trull, 2007). An integrative dimensional trait model also allows the clinician, and researcher, to provide an individualized description of a particular patient's personality profile, including both his or her personality strengths as well as his or her deficits.

It is possible that some persons have no redeeming traits, that their entire personality is a constellation of problematic deficits, flaws, and dysfunctions. However, research suggests that all personality traits in fact represent continua with positive and negative possibilities, depending upon the degree with which traits are held, and the context in which they are being expressed. As such, most individuals are likely to demonstrate some form of personality strength. Such a view may improve understandings of personality, and even personality disorder, which at present is a poorly defined and implemented construct. Proposed within this chapter was such a model, along with potential measures for its assessment.

References

Ackerman, R. A., Witt, E. A., Donnellan, M. B., Trzesniewski, K. H., Robins, R. W., & Kashy, D. A. (2011). What does the Narcissistic Personality Inventory really measure? *Assessment*, *18*, 67–87. doi.org/10.1177/1073191110382845.

Aluja, A., Kuhlman, M., & Zuckerman, M. (2010). Development of the Zuckerman–Kuhlman–Aluja Personality Questionnaire (ZKA-P): A factor/facet version of the Zuckerman–Kuhlman Personality Questionnaire (ZKPQ). *Journal of Personality Assessment*, *92*(5), 416–431. doi.org/10.1080/00223891.2010.497406.

American Psychiatric Association (APA). (1980). *Diagnostic and statistical manual of mental disorders*, 3rd edn. Washington, DC: APA.

American Psychiatric Association (APA). (1987). *Diagnostic and statistical manual of mental disorders*, 3rd edn., rev. Washington, DC: APA.

American Psychiatric Association (APA). (1994). *Diagnostic and statistical manual of mental disorders*, 4th edn. Washington, DC: APA. doi.10.1176/appi.books.9780890423349.11547.

American Psychiatric Association (APA). (2013). *Diagnostic and statistical manual of mental disorders*. 5th edn. Washington, DC: APA. doi.org/10.1176/appi.books.9780890425596.

Bender, D. S., Morey, L. C,. & Skodol, A. E. (2011). Toward a model for assessing level of personality functioning in DSM-5, Part I: A review of theory and methods. *Journal of Personality Assessment*, *93*, 332–346. doi.org/10.1080/00223891.2011.583808.

Blashfield, R. K. & Reynolds, S. M. (2012). An invisible college view of the DSM-5 personality disorder classification. *Journal of Personality Disorders*, *26*, 821–829. doi.org/10.1521/pedi.2012.26.6.821.

Bornstein, R. F. (2012). Dependent personality disorder. In: T. A. Widiger (Ed.), *Oxford handbook of personality disorder* (pp. 505–526). New York: Oxford University Press. doi.10.1093/oxfordhb/9780199735013.001.0001.

Clark, L. A. (2007). Assessment and diagnosis of personality disorder: Perennial issues and an emerging reconceptualization. *Annual Review of Psychology, 57,* 277–257. doi.org/10.1146/annurev.psych.57.102904.190200.

Clark, L. A. & Krueger, R. F. (2010,). *Rationale for a six-domain trait dimensional diagnostic system for personality disorder.* Available at: http://www.dsm5.org/ProposedRevisions/Pages/RationaleforaSix-DomainTraitDimensionalDiagnosticSystemforPersonalityDisorder.aspx, February 10.

Coker, L. A., Samuel, D. B., & Widiger, T. A. (2002). Maladaptive personality functioning within the Big Five and the FFM. *Journal of Personality Disorders, 16,* 385–401. doi.org/10.1521/pedi.16.5.385.22125.

Costa, P. T. & McCrae, R. R. (1992). *Revised NEO Personality Inventory (NEO PI-R) and NEO Five-Factor Inventory (NEO-FFI) professional manual.* Odessa, FL: Psychological Assessment Resources.

Crego, C., Samuel, D. B., & Widiger, T. A. (2015). The FFOCI and other measures and models of OCPD. *Assessment, 22,* 135–151. doi.org/10.1177/1073191114539382.

Crego, C. & Widiger, T. A. (in press). Psychopathy and the DSM. *Journal of Personality.*

Crespi, B. (2014). An evolutionary framework for psychological maladaptations. *Psychological Inquiry, 25,* 322–324.

De Clercq, B., De Fruyt, F., Van Leeuwen, K., & Mervielde, I. (2006). The structure of maladaptive personality traits in childhood: A step toward an integrative developmental perspective for DSM-V. *Journal of Abnormal Psychology, 115*(4), 639–657. doi.org/10.1037/0021-843X.115.4.639.

De Fruyt, F. & De Clercq, B. (2014). Antecedents of personality disorder in childhood and adolescence: Toward an integrative developmental model. *Annual Review of Clinical Psychology, 10,* 449–476. doi.org/10.1146/annurev-clinpsy-032813-153634.

De Fruyt, F., De Clercq, B., De Bolle, M., Willie, B., Markon, K. E., & Krueger, R. F. (2013). General and maladaptive traits in a five-factor framework for DSM-5 in a university student sample. *Assessment, 20,* 295–307. doi.org/10.1177/1073191113475808.

Del Giudice, M. & Del Giudice, M. (2014). An evolutionary life history framework for psychopathology. *Psychological Inquiry, 25,* 261–300.

First, M. B. (2014). Empirical grounding versus innovation in the DSM-5 revision process: Implications for the future. *Clinical Psychology: Science and Practice, 21,* 262–268. doi.org/10.1111/cpsp.12069.

Frances, A. J., First, M. B., & Pincus, H. A. (1995). *DSM-IV guidebook.* Washington, DC: American Psychiatric Press.

Funder, D. C. (2001). Personality. *Annual Review of Psychology, 52,* 197–221. doi.org/10.1146/annurev.psych.52.1.197.

Goldberg, L. R. (1993). The structure of phenotypic personality traits. *American Psychologist, 48,* 26–34. doi.org/10.1037/0003-066X.48.1.26.

Goldberg, L. R., Johnson, J. A., Eber, H. W., Hogan, R., Ashton, M. C., Cloninger, C., & Gough, H. G. (2006). The international personality item pool and the future of public-domain personality measures. *Journal of Research in Personality, 40,* 84–96. doi.org/10.1016/j.jrp.2005.08.007.

Gore, W. L. & Pincus, A. L. (2013). Dependency and the five factor model. In: T. A. Widiger & P. T. Costa (Eds.), *Personality disorders and the five-factor model of personality,* 3rd edn. (pp. 163–177). Washington, DC: American Psychological Association.

Gore, W. L., Presnall, J. R., Miller, J. D., Lynam, D. R., & Widiger, T. A. (2012). A five-factor measure of dependent personality traits. *Journal of Personality Assessment, 94,* 488–499. doi.org/10.1080/00223891.2012.670681.

Gore, W. L. & Widiger, T. A. (2013). The DSM-5 dimensional trait model and five factor models of general personality, *Journal of Abnormal Psychology, 122,* 816–821. doi.org/10.1037/a0032822.

Griffin, S. A. & Samuel, D. B. (in press). A closer look at the lower-order structure of the Personality Inventory for DSM-5: Comparison with the five-factor model. *Personality Disorders: Theory, Research, and Treatment.*

Gunderson, J. G. (2010). Commentary on "Personality traits and the classification of mental disorders: Toward a more complete integration in DSM-5 and an empirical model of psychopathology." *Personality Disorders: Theory, Research, and Treatment, 1,* 119–122. doi.org/10.1037/a0019974.

Gunderson, J. G. (2013). Seeking clarity for future revisions of the personality disorders in DSM-5. *Personality Disorders: Theory, Research, and Treatment, 4,* 368–378. doi.org/10.1037/per0000026.

Haigler, E. D. & Widiger, T. A. (2001). Experimental manipulation of NEO PI-R items. *Journal of Personality Assessment, 77,* 339–358. doi.org/10.1207/S15327752JPA7702_14.

Johansen, M., Karterud, S., Pedersen, G., Gude T., & Falkum, E. (2004). An investigation of the prototype validity of the borderline DSM-IV construct. *Acta Psychiatrica Scandinavica, 109*, 289–298. doi.org/10.1046/j.1600-0447.2003.00268.x.

John, O. P., Naumann, L. P., & Soto, C. J. (2008). Paradigm shift to the integrative Big Five trait taxonomy: History, measurement, and conceptual issues. In: O. P. John, R. R. Robins, & L. A. Pervin (Eds.), *Handbook of personality. Theory and research*, 3rd. edn. (pp. 114–158). New York: Guilford.

Judge, T. A., Livingston, B. A., & Hurst, C. (2012). Do nice guys – and gals – really finish last? The joint effects of sex and agreeableness on income. *Journal of Personality and Social Psychology, 102*(2), 390–407. doi.org/10.1037/a0026021.

Kendler, K. S. (2013). A history of the DSM-5 scientific review committee. *Psychological Medicine, 43*, 1793–1800. doi.org/10.1017/S0033291713001578.

Kernberg, O. F. (2012). Overview and critique of the classification of personality disorders proposed for DSM-V. *Swiss Archives of Neurology and Psychiatry, 163*, 234–238.

Krueger, R. F. (2013). Personality disorders are the vanguard of the post-DSM-5.0 era. *Personality Disorders: Theory, Research, and Treatment, 4*, 355–362. doi.org/10.1037/per0000028.

Krueger, R. F., Derringer, J., Markon, K. F., Watson, D., & Skodol, A. E. (2012). Initial construction of a maladaptive personality trait model and inventory for DSM-5. *Psychological Medicine, 42*, 1879–1890. doi.org/10.1017/S0033291711002674.

Krueger, R. F. & Eaton, N. R. (2010). Personality traits and the classification of mental disorders: Toward a complete integration in DSM-V and an empirical model of psychopathology. *Personality Disorders: Theory, Research, and Treatment, 1*, 97–118. doi.org/10.1037/a0018990.

Krueger R. F., Eaton, N. R., Derringer, J., Markon, K. E., Watson, D., & Skodol, A. E. (2011). Personality in DSM-5: Helping delineate personality disorder content and framing the meta-structure. *Journal of Personality Assessment, 93*, 325–331. doi.org/10.1080/00223891.2011.577478.

Krueger, R. F. & Markon, K. E. (2014). The role of the DSM-5 personality trait model in moving toward a quantitative and empirically based approach to classifying personality and psychopathology. *Annual Review of Clinical Psychology, 10*, 477–501. doi.org/10.1146/annurev-clinpsy-032813-153732.

Lilienfeld, S. O., Watts A. L., & Smith, S. F. (2012). The DSM revision as a social psychological process: A commentary on Blashfield and Reynolds. *Journal of Personality Disorders, 26*, 830–834. doi.org/10.1521/pedi.2012.26.6.830.

Livesley, W. J. (2001). Conceptual and taxonomic issues. In: W. J. Livesley (Ed.), *Handbook of personality disorders. Theory, research, and treatment* (pp. 3–38). New York: Guilford.

Livesley, W. J. (2007). A framework for integrating dimensional and categorical classifications of personality disorder. *Journal of Personality Disorders, 21*, 199–224. doi.org/10.1521/pedi.2007.21.2.199.

Livesley, W. J. (2012). Tradition versus empiricism in the current DSM-5 proposal for revising the classification of personality disorders. *Criminal Behavior and Mental Health, 22*, 81–90. doi.org/10.1002/cbm.1826.

Lynam, D. R. & Widiger, T. A. (2001). Using the five factor model to represent the DSM-IV personality disorders: An expert consensus approach. *Journal of Abnormal Psychology, 110*, 401–412. doi.org/10.1037/0021-843X.110.3.401

Markon, K. E., Krueger, R. F., & Watson, D. (2005). Delineating the structure of normal and abnormal personality: An integrative hierarchical approach. *Journal of Personality and Social Psychology, 88*, 139–157. doi.org/10.1037/0022-3514.88.1.139.

McCrae, R. R. & Costa, P. T. (2003). *Personality in adulthood. A five-factor theory perspective*, 2nd edn. New York: Guilford.

Mervielde, I. & De Fruyt, F. (2002). Assessing children's traits with the Hierarchical Personality Inventory for Children. In: B. De Raad & M. Perugini (Eds.), *Big Five assessment* (pp. 129–146). Seattle, WA: Hogrefe & Huber.

Miller, J. D. (2012). Five-factor model personality disorder prototypes: A review of their development, validity, and comparison with alternative approaches. *Journal of Personality, 80*, 1565–1591. doi.org/10.1111/j.1467-6494.2012.00773.x.

Miller, J. D. & Campbell, W. K. (2011). Addressing criticisms of the Narcissistic Personality Inventory (NPI). In: W. K. Campbell & J. D. Miller (Eds.), *The handbook of narcissism and narcissistic personality disorder* (pp. 146–152). New York: John Wiley.

Miller, J. D. & Lynam, D. R. (2013). Missed opportunities in the DSM-5 Section III personality disorder model. *Personality Disorders: Theory, Research, and Treatment, 4*, 365–366. doi.org/10.1037/per0000043.

Millon, T. (2011). *Disorders of personality. Introducing a DSM/ICD spectrum from normal to abnormal,* 3rd edn. New York: John Wiley.

Mullins-Sweatt, S. N., Jamerson, J. E., Samuel, D. B., Olson, D. R., & Widiger, T. A. (2006). Psychometric properties of an abbreviated instrument of the Five-Factor Model. *Assessment, 13,* 119–137. doi.org/10.1177/1073191106286748.

Mullins-Sweatt, S. N & Lengel, G. J. (2012). Clinical utility of the five-factor model of personality disorder. *Journal of Personality, 80,* 1615–1639. doi.org/10.1111/j.1467-6494.2012.00774.x.

Mullins-Sweatt, S. N. & Widiger, T. A. (2011). Clinicians' judgments of the utility of the DSM-IV and five-factor models for personality disordered patients. *Journal of Personality Disorders, 25,* 463–477. doi.org/10.1521/pedi.2011.25.4.463.

Nettle, D. (2006). The evolution of personality variation in humans and other animals. *American Psychologist, 61,* 622–631. doi.org/10.1037/0003-066X.61.6.622.

O'Connor, B. P. (2005). A search for consensus on the dimensional structure of personality disorders. *Journal of Clinical Psychology, 61,* 323–345. doi.org/10.1002/jclp.20017.

Ogrodniczuk, J. S., Piper, W. E., Joyce, A. S., McCallum, M., & Rosie, J. S. (2003). NEO-five factor personality traits as predictors of response to two forms of group psychotherapy. *International Journal of Group Psychotherapy, 53*(4), 417–442. doi.org/10.1521/ijgp.53 4 417.42832.

Ozer, D. J. & Benet-Martinez, V. (2006). Personality and the prediction of consequential outcomes. *Annual Review of Psychology, 57,* 401–421. doi.org/10 1146/annurev.psych.57.102904.190127.

Ozer, D. J & Reise, S. P. (1994). Personality assessment. *Annual Review of Psychology, 45,* 357–388. doi.org/10.1146/annurev.ps.45.020194.002041.

Pincus, A. L. & Lukowitsky, M. R. (2010). Pathological narcissism and narcissistic personality disorder. *Annual Review of Clinical Psychology, 6,* 421–446. doi.org/10.1146/annurev. clinpsy.121208.131215.

Reynolds, S. K. & Clark, L.A. (2001). Predicting dimensions of personality disorder from domains and facets of the Five-Factor Model. *Journal of Personality, 69,* 199–222. doi.org/10.1111/1467-6494.00142.

Rojas, S. L. & Widiger, T. A. (2014). The convergent and discriminant validity of the Five Factor Form. *Assessment, 21,* 143–157. doi.org/10.1177/1073191113517260.

Samuel, D. B., Mullins-Sweatt, S. N., & Widiger, T. A. (2013). An investigation of the factor structure and convergent and discriminant validity of the Five Factor Model Rating Form. *Assessment, 20,* 24–35. doi.org/10.1177/1073191112455455.

Samuel, D. B., Riddell, A. D. B., Lynam, D. R., Miller, J. D., & Widiger, T. A. (2012). A five-factor measure of obsessive-compulsive personality traits. *Journal of Personality Assessment, 94,* 456–465. doi.org/10.1080/00223891.2012.677885.

Samuel, D. B. & Widiger, T. A. (2004). Clinicians' descriptions of prototypic personality disorders. *Journal of Personality Disorders, 18,* 286–308. doi.org/10.1521/pedi.18.3.286.35446.

Samuel, D. B. & Widiger, T. A. (2006). Clinicians' judgments of clinical utility: A comparison of the DSM-IV and five factor models. *Journal of Abnormal Psychology, 115,* 298–308. doi.org/10.1037/0021-843X.115.2.298.

Samuel, D. B. & Widiger, T. A. (2008). A meta-analytic review of the relationships between the five-factor model and *DSM-IV-TR* personality disorders: A facet level analysis. *Clinical Psychology Review, 28,* 1326–1342. doi.org/10.1016/j.cpr.2008.07.002.

Samuel, D. B. & Widiger, T. A. (2011). Conscientiousness and obsessive-compulsive personality disorder. *Personality Disorders: Theory, Research, and Treatment, 2,* 161–174. doi.org/10.1037/a0021216.

Samuels, J. & Costa, P. T. (2012). Obsessive-compulsive personality disorder. In: T. A. Widiger (Ed.), *Oxford handbook of personality disorders* (pp. 566–602). New York: Oxford University Press. doi.10.1093/oxfordhb/9780199735013.001.0001.

Sanderson, C. J. & Clarkin, J. F. (2013). Further use of the NEO PI-R personality dimensions in treatment planning. In: T. A. Widiger & P. T. Costa (Eds.), *Personality disorders and the five-factor model of personality* (pp. 325–349). Washington, DC: American Psychological Association.

Saulsman, L. M. & Page, A. C. (2004). The five-factor model and personality disorder empirical literature: a meta-analytic review. *Clinical Psychology Review, 23,* 1055–1085. doi.org/10.1016/j.cpr.2002.09.001.

Shedler, J., Beck, A., Fonagy, P., Gabbard, G. O., Gunderson, J.G., Kernberg, O., Michels, R., & Westen, D. (2010). Personality disorders in DSM-5. *American Journal of Psychiatry, 167,* 1027–1028. doi.org/10.1176/appi.ajp.2010.10050746.

Simms, L. J., Goldberg, L. R., Roberts, J. E., Watson, D., Welte, J., & Rotterman, J. H. (2011). Computerized adaptive assessment of personality disorder: Introducing the CAT-PD project. *Journal of Personality Assessment, 93*, 380–389. doi.org/10.1080/00223891.2011.577475.

Skodol, A. E. (2010, February 10). Rationale for proposing five specific personality types. Available at: http://www.dsm5.org/ProposedRevisions/Pages/RationaleforProposingFiveSpecificPersonalityD isorderTypes.aspx, February 10.

Skodol, A. E. (2012). Diagnosis and DSM-5: Work in progress. In: T. A. Widiger (Ed.), *The Oxford handbook of personality disorders* (pp. 35–57). New York: Oxford University Press. doi. 10.1093/oxfor dhb/9780199735013.001.0001.

Skodol, A. E., Morey, L. C., Bender, D. S., & Oldham, J. M. (2013). The ironic fate of the personality disorders in DSM-5. *Personality Disorders: Theory, Research, & Treatment, 4*, 342–349. doi.org/10.1037/per0000029.

Spitzer, R. L., Williams, J. B. W., & Skodol, A. E. (1980). DSM-III: The major achievements and an overview. *American Journal of Psychiatry, 137*, 151–164. doi.org/10.1176/ajp.137.2.151.

Stepp, S. D., Whalen, D. J., & Smith, T. D. (2013). Dialectical behavior therapy from the five-factor model perspective. In: T. A. Widiger & P. T. Costa (Eds.), *Personality disorders and the five-factor model of personality* (pp. 395–408). Washington, DC: American Psychological Association.

Stone, M. H. (2002). Treatment of personality disorders from the perspective of the five-factor model. In: P. T. Costa & T. A. Widiger (Eds.), *Personality disorders and the five-factor model of personality*, 2nd edn. (pp. 405–430). Washington, DC: American Psychological Association.

Talbot, N. L., Duberstein, P. R., Butzel, J. S., Cox, C., & Giles, D. E. (2003). Personality traits and symptom reduction in a group treatment for women with histories of childhood sexual abuse. *Comprehensive Psychiatry, 44*, 448–453. doi.org/10.1016/S0010-440X(03)00142-1.

Tellegen, A. & Waller, N. G. (1987). *Exploring personality through test construction: Development of the Multidimensional Personality Questionnaire.* Unpublished manuscript, Minneapolis, Minnesota.

Thomas, K. M., Yalch, M. M., Krueger, R. F., Wright, A. G. C., Markon, K. E., & Hopwood, C. J. (2012). The convergent structure of DSM-5 personality trait facets and five-factor model trait domains. *Assessment, 12*, 308–311. doi.org/10.1177/1073191112457589.

Trapnell, P. D. & Wiggins, J. S. (1990). Extension of the interpersonal adjective scales to include the Big Five dimensions of personality. *Journal of Personality and Social Psychology, 59*, 781–790. doi.org/10.1037/0022-3514.59.4.781.

Trull, T. J. & Durrett, C. A. (2005).Categorical and dimensional models of personality disorder. *Annual Review of Clinical Psychology, 1*, 355–380. doi.org/10.1146/annurev.clinpsy.1.102803.144009.

Trull, T. J., Widiger, T. A., Useda, J. D., Holcomb, J., Doan, B-T., Axelrod, S. R., Stern, B. L., & Gershuny, B. S. (1998). A structured interview for the assessment of the five-factor model of personality. *Psychological Assessment, 10*, 229–240. doi.org/10.1037/1040-3590.10.3.229.

Tyrer, P. (2009). Why borderline personality disorder is neither borderline nor a personality disorder. *Personality and Mental Health, 3*(2), 86–95. doi.org/10.1002/pmh.78.

Van Kampen, D. (2012). The 5-Dimensional Personality Test (5DPT): Relationships with two lexically based instruments and the validation of the Absorption scale. *Journal of Personality Assessment, 94*(1), 92–101. doi.org/10.1080/00223891.2011.627966.

Verheul, R. & Widiger, T.A. (2004). A meta-analysis of the prevalence and usage of the personality disorder not otherwise specified (PDNOS) diagnosis. *Journal of Personality Disorders, 18*, 309–319. doi.org/10.1521/pedi.2004.18.4.309.

Westen, D. & Arkowitz-Westen, L. (1998). Limitations of Axis II in diagnosing personality pathology in clinical practice. *American Journal of Psychiatry, 155*, 1767–1771. doi.org/10.1176/ajp.155.12.1767.

Widiger, T. A. (2009). In defense of borderline personality disorder. *Personality and Mental Health, 3*, 120–123. doi.org/10.1002/pmh.74.

Widiger, T. A. (2011). A shaky future for personality disorders. *Personality Disorders: Theory, Research, and Treatment, 2*, 54–67. doi.org/10.1037/a0021855.

Widiger, T. A. (2013). DSM-5 personality disorders: a postmortem and future look. *Personality Disorders: Theory, Research, and Treatment, 4*, 382–387.

Widiger, T. A. & Costa, P. T. (1994). Personality and personality disorders. *Journal of Abnormal Psychology, 103*, 78–91. doi.org/10.1037/0021-843X.103.1.78.

Widiger, T. A., Costa, P. T., Gore, W. L., & Crego, C. (2013). Five factor model personality disorder research. In: T. A. Widiger & P. T. Costa (Eds.), *Personality disorders and the five-factor model of personality*, 3rd edn. (pp. 75–100). Washington, DC: American Psychological Association.

Widiger, T. A., Frances, A. J., Spitzer, R. L., & Williams, J. B. W. (1988). The DSM-III-R personality disorders: An overview. *American Journal of Psychiatry*, *145*, 786–795. doi.org/10.1176/ajp.145.7.786.

Widiger, T. A., Lynam, D. R., Miller, J. D., & Oltmanns, T. F. (2012). Measures to assess maladaptive variants of the five factor model. *Journal of Personality Assessment*, *94*, 450–455. doi.org/10.1080/00223891.2012.677887.

Widiger, T. A. & Mullins-Sweatt, S. N. (2009). Five-factor model of personality disorder: A proposal for DSM-V. *Annual Review of Clinical Psychology*, *5*, 115–138. doi.org/10.1146/annurev.clinpsy.032408.153542.

Widiger, T. A., Samuel, D. B., Mullins-Sweatt, S., Gore, W. L., & Crego, C. (2012). Integrating normal and abnormal personality structure: the five-factor model. In: T. A. Widiger (Ed.), *Oxford handbook of personality disorders* (pp. 82–107). New York: Oxford University Press. doi.10.1093/oxfordhb/9780199735013.001.0001.

Widiger, T. A., Simonsen, E., Krueger, R. F., Livesley, W. J., & Verheul, R. (2005). Personality disorder research agenda for the DSM-V. *Journal of Personality Disorders*, *19*, 317–340. doi.org/10.1521/pedi.2005.19.3.315.

Widiger, T. A. & Trull, T. J. (2007). Plate tectonics in the classification of personality disorder: Shifting to a dimensional model. *American Psychologist*, *62*, 71–83. doi.org/10.1037/0003-066X.62.2.71.

Wood, A. M. & Tarrier, N. (2010). Positive Clinical Psychology: A new vision and strategy for integrated research and practice. *Clinical Psychology Review*, *30*(7), 819–829. doi.org/10.1016/j.cpr.2010.06.003.

Wright, A. G. C. & Simms, L J. (2014). On the structure of personality disorder traits: Conjoint analysis of the CAT-PD, PID-5, and NEO PI-3 trait models. *Personality Disorders: Theory, Research, and Treatment*, *5*, 43–54. doi.org/10.1037/per0000037.

19

Resilience and Protective Factors in Childhood and Adolescence
Peter J. Taylor

The Resilience Framework within Childhood and Adolescence

Within the study of psychological and emotional disorder in children and young people, the importance of considering those positive factors which buffer and protect young people from disorder, alongside adversity and risk factors, has repeatedly been emphasized (Masten, Best, & Garmezy, 1990; Luthar, Cicchetti, & Becker, 2000; Masten, 2001, 2011). Arguably, the focus on protective and positive variables in understanding psychopathology has been more widely studied in the context of childhood and adolescence than in adults. Much of this research has taken place within a conceptual framework of resilience (Luthar & Cicchetti, 2000; Luthar et al., 2000; Masten, 2001, 2011). The aim of the present chapter is to provide an exploration and critical overview of this literature, considering why the concept of resilience may have particular importance for young people, outlining key issues around the use of the concept of resilience, considering how resilience in childhood may differ to how it might be understood in adults, and exploring how this concept may be implemented in clinical practice.

The resiliency framework within child and adolescent research has developed as both a conceptual and methodological framework for guiding the investigation of protective factors in young people (e.g., Luthar et al., 2000; Masten, 2011). Resilience in this context has been defined in terms of the emergence of positive outcomes in the face of adversity and risk factors. An example of resilience may therefore be young people who experience early abuse and neglect, but who nonetheless do not experience psychopathology later in life (Collishaw, Pickles, Messer, Rutter, Shearer, & Maughan, 2007). Within this definition a number of key components can be delineated: there are the risk or adversity factors the young people face, the protective factors that interact with this risk and account for why not all young people in this group experience difficulty and the outcomes against which positive adaptation or coping may be observed. Adopting this framework, an extensive body of research now exists exploring how the interplay of protective factors with adversity or vulnerability account for the difficulties experienced by young people (see reviews by Masten et al., 1990; Luthar & Cicchetti, 2000; Masten, 2001).

Why does Resilience in Childhood and Adolescence Matter?

The preceding chapters of this book have already provided a case for why resilience, and the consideration of both positive, or protective, factors alongside adversity and risk is important in understanding the emergence and maintenance of psychopathology. These variables and

The Wiley Handbook of Positive Clinical Psychology, First Edition. Edited by Alex M. Wood and Judith Johnson.
© 2016 John Wiley & Sons, Ltd. Published 2016 by John Wiley & Sons, Ltd.

processes may, however, be especially important within childhood and adolescence. There are two key reasons for this:

Childhood as the Origin of Adult Disorder

First, there is a growing consensus that in many cases adult psychological difficulties have their origins in childhood. Numerous theoretical frameworks attest to such a link. Attachment theory, for example, argues that early relationships with primary caregivers have a crucial influence on the formation of an individual's interpersonal behavior, emotion regulation and the beliefs and expectations they hold about themselves and others (Cassidy, 1994; Bretherton & Munhollan, 1999; Shaver & Mikulincer, 2007, 2011). Where early parenting is insensitive, inappropriate, or abusive, the internal working models that individuals develop in childhood are believed to leave them vulnerable to psychopathology, both in childhood and subsequent adulthood. Other theories of psychopathology, developed within the context of treatment models like Schema Therapy (Young, Klosko, & Weishaar, 2003) or Cognitive Analytic Therapy (Ryle & Kerr, 2002), similarly adhere to the notion that psychopathology often has its origins in childhood. In support of such theories, it is well established that experiences such as childhood abuse and maltreatment are substantial predictors of a wide range of psychological difficulties both in childhood and adulthood (Gilbert, Widom, Browne, Fergusson, Webb, & Janson, 2009; Maniglio, 2009, 2010; Radford et al., 2011; Varese et al., 2012). Likewise, a variety of neuro-physiological changes, such as altered hypothalamic–pituitary–adrenal (HPA) axis functioning, have been associated with early adversity in children, and are believe to lead to risk of subsequent disorder (Penza, Heim, & Nemeroff, 2003; Elzinga, Spinhoven, Berretty, de Jong, & Roelofs, 2010). Longitudinal studies have shown that difficulties emerging in childhood can often continue into adulthood, including eating disorders (Kotler, Cohen, Davies, Pine, & Walsh, 2001), psychotic symptoms (Poulton Caspi, Moffitt, Cannon, Murray, & Harrington, 2000), and internalizing problems (Fichter, Kohlboeck, Quadflieg, Wyschkon, & Esser, 2009). This continuity of psychopathology highlights the importance of childhood in the longer-term development of psychological difficulty.

These observations suggest that often childhood is the crucible within which adult disorder is forged. From this perspective, understanding the interplay of adversity and protective factors in young people is likely to be important in providing an insight not only into psychopathology emerging in childhood, but also the disorders experienced in adulthood. Relatedly, authors have highlighted the benefits of a shift in focus from fixing a problem that has already become established to enhancing prevention and developing resilience in the face of adversity in young people (Forrest & Riley, 2004; Lynch, Geller, & Schmidt, 2004; Saxena, Jane-Llopis, & Hosman, 2006; Masten, 2011).

Considering Strengths as a Counter to Stigma

A second reason for the importance of focusing on positive characteristics and protective factors in childhood comes from a consideration of the impact of being diagnosed with a mental health or behavioral disorder for this population. It is known that mental health-related diagnoses can carry much more stigma and embarrassment than those associated with physical health conditions (Alonso et al., 2008), although there may be some exceptions, such as the case of Human Immunodeficiency Virus (Neuman, Obermeyer, & The MATCH Study Group, 2013). Moreover, there is evidence that children and young people, as well as adults, experience the shame and stigma associated with such conditions (Mukolo, Heflinger, & Wallston, 2010). Young people diagnosed with a mental health disorder may readily internalize such labels and stigmatized views of themselves, and this may in turn impact on their recovery and well-being

(Link, Struening, Neese-Todd, Asmussen, & Phelan, 2001; Eisenberg, Downs, Golberstein, & Zivin, 2009; Moses, 2009, 2010). Such problems may even emerge where formal diagnoses are not present, such as in the case of young people deemed to be "at-risk" of psychotic disorders (Pyle et al., in press).

Developing mental health services that routinely recognize and emphasize young people's strengths and positive qualities, alongside trying to understand their difficulties, may be one way to buffer against any iatrogenic consequences of labeling and treatment. An example of where this occurs is within therapeutic models such as solution-focused therapy that encourage the use of "non-problem talk," essentially talk focused on the young person's strengths and positive traits, as part of clinical encounters (Young & Holdorf, 2003). A balanced approach to clinical work and research with young people that accommodates adversity, dysfunction, and protective factors or strengths may reduce stigma and help to build optimism.

Form and Character of Protective Factors

Whilst resilience is a popular and informative framework for both understanding and working with the difficulties experienced by children and young people, it is helpful to consider further the form and character of protective factors. Particular issues include the labeling of such factors as bipolar or unipolar continua, the level at which protective variables operate, whether their protective effects are conditional to a certain context, and the consideration that positive characteristics and strengths may be valid and clinically meaningful outcomes in their own right as well as determinants of well-being.

Unipolar or Bipolar Dimensions of Risk and Resilience

Within the resilience framework a distinction is made between positive or protective factors and negative, risk or adversity factors (Luthar & Cicchetti, 2000). However, in many instances these variables represent bipolar dimensions that have both positive and negative poles (Luthar & Cicchetti, 2000; Johnson, Wood, Gooding, Taylor, & Tarrier, 2011). For example, whilst social isolation may be considered a risk factor, social support is often regarded as a protective factor. Likewise, whilst authoritative parenting is related to positive outcomes such as greater empathy, academic competence, and lower internalizing disorder compared with indulgent, authoritarian, or neglectful parenting, these parenting styles sit upon underlying bipolar continua of warmth and firmness (DeVore & Ginsburg, 2005; Steinberg, Blatt-Eisengart, & Cauffman, 2006). Hence, whilst authoritative parenting may be viewed as protective (e.g., DeVore & Ginsberg, 2005), it would be just as accurate to describe these other parenting styles as risk factors. This brings in to question the value and validity of the distinction between protective and risk factors.

There are some contexts where the labels of positive and negative may be more appropriate or useful. One example would be instances where variables could be said to be truly unipolar, and so can readily be labeled as protective or risk factors. For example, not experiencing abuse or neglect as a child might be regarded the norm (although abuse is surprisingly prevalent) (Gilbert et al., 2009), and so would not be regarded a protective factor in itself, meaning that the experience of abuse in childhood could be considered a unipolar risk factor. A similar case could be made for substance use; whilst its presence is a source of adversity, the absence of substance abuse would perhaps be seen as the norm rather than an actively protective factor. A distinction between protective and risk factors may also have some relevance in clinical practice. Certain intervention, such as attempts to modify maladaptive schema within cognitive behavioral therapy, could be said to be reducing vulnerability, whereas other interventions, such as attempts to enhance parenting skills or teach children new coping strategies, could be said to be building protective factors.

Labeling what is essentially a bipolar dimension either as a protective or a risk factor may therefore depend on the demands of the situation, but in many cases may be considered a largely semantic issue. However, such labeling may become problematic when this bipolar dimension is treated as if it is unipolar with the opposing pole of this scale becoming neglected as a consequence. This may occur, for example, in instruments designed to measure bipolar psychological constructs, where emphasis might be placed on one pole with the consequence of neglecting and truncating the other pole of the construct. Shame, for example, is an important emotional experience that is closely linked to psychopathology (Kim, Thibodeau, & Jorgensen, 2011). Shame may be particularly important for children with experiences of abuse, where it may mediate the emergence of later psychopathology (Andrews, 1995, 1997; Murray & Waller, 2002). It has been argued that shame is actually on a continuum of emotional experience with pride occurring at the opposite pole (Weisfeld & Wendorf, 2000). However, many self-report measures of shame do not attempt to also capture positive feelings of pride (e.g., Goss, Gilbert, & Allan, 1994; Andrews, Qian, & Valentine, 2002), and so this pole of the dimension is truncated and not fully captured. A similar issue may emerge with measures of pessimism, which arguably exists on a continuum with the positive experience of optimism (Roysamb & Strype, 2002).

Resilience at Multiple Levels

Within adults, some conceptual frameworks for the study of resilience have specifically focused on variables occurring at the level of the individual (e.g., Johnson et al., 2011).[1] In young people and children, a variety of such individual-level variables, including attachment patterns (Grych & Kinsfogel, 2010), prosocial traits (Griese & Buhs, in press), and empathy (Dallaire & Zeman, 2013), have been identified as factors which interact with adversity to determine negative outcomes such as loneliness and externalizing problems. However, protective factors also often occur at broader interpersonal, institutional, and societal levels (Luthar & Cicchetti, 2000). For example, variables related to good parental care and family structure are predictive of adjustment following childhood maltreatment in both cross-sectional and longitudinal studies (Afifi & MacMillan, 2011). Greater autonomy and relatedness in parent–adolescent interactions has also been shown to reduce internalizing and externalizing symptoms in the face of life stress (Willemen, Schuengel, & Koot, 2011), and adolescent externalizing problems were related to maternal depression only when co-occurring in the context of unavailable or hostile parenting behavior (McCullough & Shaffer, 2013). Brody and colleagues (2001) provide another example of variables interacting across several levels to predict deviant peer group affiliation in 10–11-year-old African American children. Greater collective socialization (the perception that adults in the area would intervene if they saw children misbehaving) and more nurturing and involved parenting were both predictors of a lower level of deviant peer group affiliation, but these effects were strengthened in the context of more disadvantaged communities suggesting these protective factors may yield a stronger effect in the context of greater adversity.

Ecological models such as the work of Bronfenbrenner (1994) have been influential in drawing attention to the wider systems within which young people live. Of course, the importance of protective factors occurring within these wider systems is not unique to children and young people. Similar processes would be expected in adults. However, the consideration of resilience occurring across multiple nested systems may have particular importance for young people whose lives, in particular, are encapsulated and integrated within families and wider institutions (schools, clubs), and whose autonomy is constrained by these systems, arguably to a greater extent than in adults.

Studying resilience at broader interpersonal and societal levels can present difficulties. These include the challenges of sampling broadly enough to capture adequate variation in higher-order constructs. For example, where the protective effect of school culture is the area of interest, sampling will ideally occur across a number of schools, each varying in their particular culture. Similarly, issues of nonindependence may arise from clustered data, requiring more complex analyses than are needed for single-level designs (Snijders & Bosjer, 2012).

Nonetheless, considering resilience at multiple levels has clear benefits in terms of prediction and intervention. Considering prediction of difficulties, higher-order variables associated with young people's wider social, institutional and community context has the capacity to account for additional variance in outcomes beyond what person-level variables can explain (e.g., Brody et al., 2001). In terms of intervention, parents would typically have far greater contact with their child than a therapist is liable to have, so that interventions occurring at the level of parents may be more efficacious than trying to intervene through direct contact with the child alone. Interventions aimed at reducing behavioral difficulties in children through the modification of parenting practices have been shown to be effective (Woolfenden, Williams, & Peat, 2002; Kendrick, Barlow, Hampshire, Stewart-Brown, & Polnay, 2008). Likewise, an intervention directed at parents and parenting behavior was effective in reducing body mass index and weight-related problem behaviors in overweight children (West, Sanders, Cleghorn, & Davies, 2010). Moreover, there is evidence that the level of specific parent-directed interventions employed in a cognitive behavioral intervention for children with anxiety contributed to treatment outcomes in global functioning for the child (Khanna & Kendall, 2009). It would be rare, at least in the United Kingdom, for clinical work to take place with a child without any attempt to also involve the parents or caregivers.

In terms of efficiency, it may also be far more cost effective to implement an intervention at a broader community or school level than to work individually with each child within this school or community. For example, the Triple P parenting intervention employs a tiered structure, starting at broad population-level interventions involving the sharing of information around positive parenting approaches through the media and other channels, before narrowing down, through the use of group seminars and consultation sessions, to more focused interventions involving more active training and support for individual parents (Prinz, Sanders, Shapiro, Whitaker, & Lutzker, 2009). This tiered, multi-level structure is clearly more efficient than attempting to work individually with all children in the population, and ensures that even those individuals with more minor difficulties may still gain some form of support.

Absolute versus Conditional Resilience

It is tempting in studying psychological difficulties in young people to view variables as either being protective or sources of risk and adversity. However, protective factors may not always operate in an absolute way. One example of this is the case of prosociality. Prosociality is conceptualized as a trait-like variable involving the tendency for young people to engage in behaviors that aim to benefit others, such as sharing, cooperating, and supporting others (Eisenberg & Mussen, 1989; Hay, 1994; Chen, Li, Li, Li, & Liu, 2000; Eisenberg et al., 2002). There is evidence that greater levels of prosociality tend to be associated with lower levels of psychopathology and greater self-esteem and functioning in other areas. Moreover, prospective research suggests an effect whereby for individuals already experiencing internalizing problems, prosocial traits are related with fewer internalizing difficulties at follow-up (Chen et al., 2000). However, other researchers have noted that at high levels prosociality may become associated with excessive concerns about the well-being of those close to them, which could in turn lead to anxiety and distress (Hay, 1994; Hay & Pawlby, 2003; Zahn-Waxler, Shirtcliff, & Marceau, 2008). Research has supported this association between prosociality and extreme worry about others in 11-year-old children, with those reporting extreme worry about others also tending to have greater internalizing problems (Hay & Pawlby, 2003). Another study shows that "proactive" prosocial behavior (prosocial behavior specifically motivated by a desired goal or aim, such as sharing with peers in the hope of being invited to a party) is moderately positively correlated with social anxiety (Culotta & Goldstein, 2008).

Some traits may therefore have mixed consequences. It may be that whilst prosociality is associated with lower levels of some forms of difficulties, such as externalizing or behavioral problems, it is also positively associated with other forms such as anxiety (Hay & Pawlby, 2003). As another example, there is evidence that shyness tends to be greater in children with internalizing problems like depression and anxiety. However, at the same time shyness was lower in children with externalizing problems than those without such difficulties (Oldehinkel, Hartman, De Winter, Veenstra, & Ormel, 2004). This may be because shyness is typically associated with inhibiting behavior, particularly behavior liable to draw negative attention from others. Such traits are in contrast to experiences such as child maltreatment, which seem to have a universal negative effect, being associated with a wide range of both physical and psychological problems (Gilbert et al., 2009; Maniglio, 2009, 2010; Radford et al., 2011; Varese et al., 2012).

It is also possible for protective factors to have a quadratic relationship or curvilinear with psychopathology. For example, in a sample of Latino American children attending a day camp there was a quadratic relationship between ego-control (relating to the extent to which individuals control their impulses) and a composite functioning outcome variable, capturing both behavior and social aspects of functioning (Flores, Cicchetti, & Rogosch, 2005). The results suggested that there was an optimal level of ego-control, with excessive over-control or under-control becoming problematic.

In considering whether or not a certain construct has a protective effect, it may also be important to consider from whose perspective this construct is being rated. Within the context of research into child and adolescent mental health, low rates of parent–child agreement on measures of psychopathology are common (Achenbach, McConaughy, & Howell, 1987; De Los Reyes & Kazdin, 2005). It has been demonstrated that the discrepancy between parents' perceptions of their child's prosociality, and the child's self-appraisals regarding this trait is actually predictive of a greater risk of internalizing disorder (i.e., depressive and anxiety disorders) (Taylor & Wood, 2013). Specifically, a higher risk of internalizing problems was associated with lower parental ratings of prosociality occurring in the context of high self-ratings. This finding has important implications for how protective factors are assessed in routine clinical practice. If a clinician is presented with a young person who reports highly on their level of prosocial qualities, the clinician might take this as an indicator of strength and resilience. However, if this young person's self-perception is substantially discrepant with what their parents say, this may actually be an indicator of psychological difficulties.

In summary, the protective or adverse effects of many variables may depend upon the context within which they occur. Whether or not a variable exerts a protective effect may depend on the outcome of interest, on the level of the variable and upon how the variable is measured, as well the wider context within which this process is taking place. As research continues to identify those experiences and characteristics that protect young people from the development of psychopathology it will become important to explore the conditions under which these protective factors operate.

Positive Outcomes

So far in this chapter we have largely looked at strengths and positive factors in terms of those variables which predict the development of or severity of difficulties in young people. The outcomes that have been considered have predominantly been internalizing and externalizing type difficulties. However, resilience research in young people has typically taken a broad approach to outcomes, focusing on the general ability for young people to meet, social, academic and personal milestones (Luthar & Cicchetti, 2000). Within clinical psychology, the development of psychopathology and levels of associated distress and impaired functioning, are often of key interest but a broader approach to outcomes may be advantageous. Many authors have argued for broader conceptualizations of mental health, incorporating not only symptoms and distress but also areas of positive functioning and adaptation as well (Park, 2004; Wood & Tarrier, 2010; Suldo, Thalji, & Ferron, 2011; Lyons, Huebner, Hills, & Shinkareva, 2012).

Subjective well-being (SWB) is one example of an important positive outcome. This is a higher-order construct involving an individual's evaluation of their lives as a whole and encompasses life satisfaction and positive affective elements (Diener, 1994; Diener, Suh, Lucas, & Smith, 1999). In children and adolescents, SWB is predictive of a variety of physical and psychological difficulties (Gilman & Huebner, 2003; Park, 2004; Proctor, Linley, & Maltby, 2009). It has been argued that within clinical settings, work should focus more on the improvement of SWB, and therefore less on symptom reduction as a primary outcome (Pais-Ribeiro, 2004; Swan, Watson, & Nathan, 2009).

The dual-factor model of mental health represents one framework which outlines a multi-dimensional approach to mental health, which has been advocated for use in young people. This model frames mental health in terms of two distinct continua, one capturing psychopathology and the other capturing SWB (Antaramian, Scott Huebner, Hills, & Valois, 2010; Lyons et al., 2012). Within this framework, a young person can present without any symptoms of a particular mental disorder, but nonetheless experience impaired SWB (termed "vulnerable" individuals). There is evidence that such individuals may experience less parental social support, less academic engagement, and poorer academic support than those young people low in psychopathology and high in SWB (Antaramian et al., 2010; Lyons et al., 2012). Likewise, other young people appear to be symptomatic but otherwise have good SWB. Such young people appear to have fewer sources of support and face more adversity than "vulnerable" young people (low SWB, low psychopathology), but are still better off than those young people with low SWB and high psychopathology (Lyons et al., 2012). Such research suggests that there may be meaningful distinctions to be made between young people, not only in terms of symptomatology but also in terms of well-being and positive aspects of functioning.

Resilience in Clinical Practice

The interplay of protective factors or strengths and adversity in determining difficulties in young people has important consequences for intervention and clinical practice. It does not seem to be the case that young people who become involved in clinical services demonstrate a complete lack of resilience and strengths. For example, for families presenting at Child and Adolescent Mental Health Services, parents were able to recognize and identify various strengths, such as being able to seek support from each other, in spite of their presenting problems (Allison, Stacey, Dadds, Roeger, Woode, & Martinf, 2003). Even for young people with apparently substantial internalizing or externalizing difficulties, it may be that positive factors occurring at the individual, interpersonal, or social level played an important role in preventing these problems form becoming even more pronounced.

Seeking information about strengths and positive factors alongside information on adversity and dysfunction is clearly important in providing the full picture of that individual, thus maximizing options for intervention. Where a young person is experiencing problems with depression and anxiety, but demonstrates strengths as well in terms of the capacity to form positive and supportive relationships with others, it may be the therapeutic work focuses on further developing and utilizing this strength rather than trying to modify the cognitive or behavioral processes that underlie the emotional difficulties. Discussing positive factors, or adopting interventions that focus on strengths, may have other benefits, such as improving engagement in the therapeutic process or countering pessimism (e.g., Tedeschi & Kilmer, 2005; Geraghty, Wood, & Hyland, 2010). However, a central tenet of a resilience-based approach to intervention is considering the balance of positive and negative factors, and hence a focus on a young person's strengths or positive characteristics whilst neglecting the adversity they are facing, or dysfunctional processes that are in place, is likely to be as unhelpful as only focusing on the negative. If a child experiences ongoing criticism and hostility from parents, working only to develop the child's coping skills may have limited efficacy when the interpersonal style of the parents is left unchecked.

Another area where a resilience-based approach to intervention may be particularly important may be situations where a young person faces ongoing adversity that is not easy to modify. An example of this may be children who are in the care system. Such "looked after children" (LAC) are at increased risk of psychological difficulties, and face ongoing adversity associated with the challenges and uncertainties of the care system, as well as earlier traumas and separations (Legault, Anawati, & Flynn, 2006; Fernandez, 2007). For such individuals, where it is not possible to remove these challenges and uncertainties, clinical work that emphasizes strengths and works towards building coping resources may be valuable.

It is recommended that clinical psychologists consider protective factors as part of their formulations or case conceptualizations of young people's difficulties (Carr, 2006). However, it can sometimes be difficult to truly integrate protective factors into a formulation, particular as these formulations typically serve to provide a putative explanation of how difficulties have developed and been maintained. One approach to achieving this integration is to draw on the knowledge of a young person's strengths in outlining where in a formulation change is possible (and how it might be achieved). For example, a formulation of a child with separation anxiety might note a maintaining pattern involving negative thoughts about separation (e.g., concerns a parent will come to harm) and subsequent avoidance of separation (e.g., by refusing to attend school). In considering where change can occur a psychologist may note protective factors such as good relationships with a particular school teacher or the child's commitment to achieving well academically as factors that may support a particular intervention (e.g., graded exposure).

A number of interventions and treatment programs have been developed which aim to build a young person's strength and resilience. These include group-based and parenting interventions that aim to develop prosocial traits (Dumas, Prinz, Smith, & Laughlin, 1999; Kim & Leve, 2011). Initial evidence supports the ability of such interventions to foster prosociality in young people (Kim & Leve, 2011). Moreover, an experimental study in a nonclinical group found that a basic prosociality intervention (performing three acts of kindness a week versus visiting three places over a four-week period) led to increases in popularity and positive affect (although improvement in the latter outcome did not vary between intervention groups) (Layous, Nelson, Oberle, Schonert-Reichl, & Lyubomirsky, 2012). Further research is needed to explore the impact of such basic interventions in clinical populations. Whilst these interventions work at the individual level, it has been noted that resilience operates at multiple levels, providing opportunities for interventions at higher levels (see Resilience at Multiple Levels, above).

Conclusions

The case for considering the interplay of adversity and protective factors in understanding psychological difficulties and distress has been made extensively. This approach may be particularly important in the context of children and adolescence where many psychological difficulties may have their origins, and where an overly "dysfunction and adversity" orientated approach may have negative consequences. Nonetheless, there are numerous complications and issues to consider in adopting this resilience approach, including the labeling of bipolar constructs as either positive or negative, the multi-level nature of many relevant protective factors, and the potentially conditional nature in which some protective factors may operate. It is possible to integrate this resilience approach into clinical practice and this may have a number of advantages over an adversity, dysfunction and symptom-reduction dominated approach.

Note

1   It should be noted that developmental resilience researchers have argued strongly against the use of the term "resilience" as an internal characteristic of the young person (i.e., regarding any individual as resilient or not resilient) (Luthar et al., 2000). Those preferring to avoid the use of the term "resilience" as a personal quality have done so partly through concerns about how labeling children as resilient or not may unfairly place the responsibility for negative outcomes with the child. Nonetheless, even where the term "resilience" is not used to refer to internal, individual-level characteristics, such approaches still refer to protective or positive factors that may include internal, individual-level characteristics.

References

Achenbach, T. M., McConaughy, S. H., & Howell, C. T. (1987). Child/adolescent behavioral and emotional problems: Implications of cross-informant correlations for situational specificity. *Psychological Bulletin*, *101*, 213–232. doi.10.1037/0033-2909.101.2.213.

Afifi, T. O. & MacMillan, H. L. (2011). Resilience following child maltreatment: A review of protective factors. *Canadian Journal of Psychiatry*, *56*, 266–272. doi.10.1002/car.2258.

Allison, S., Stacey, K., Dadds, V., Roeger, L., Woode, A., & Martinf, G. (2003). What the family brings: Gathering evidence for strengths-based work. *Journal of Family Therapy*, *25*, 263–284. doi.10.1111/1467-6427.00248.

Alonso, J., Buron, A., Bruffacrts, R., He, Y., Posada-Villa, J., Lepine, J-P., The World Mental Health Consortium, et al. (2008). Association of perceived stigma and mood and anxiety disorders: Results from the World Mental Health Surveys. *Acta Psychiatria Scandinavica*, *118*, 305–314. doi.10.1111/j.1600-0447.2008.01241.x.

Andrews, B. (1995). Bodily shame as a mediator between abusive experiences and depression. *Journal of Abnormal Psychology*, *104*(2), 277–285.

Andrews, B. (1997). Bodily shame in relation to abuse in childhood and bulimia: A preliminary investigation. *British Journal of Clinical Psychology*, *36*(1), 41–49. doi.10.1111/j.2044-8260.1997.tb01229.x.

Andrews, B., Qian, M., & Valentine, J. D. (2002). Predicting depressive symptoms with a new measure of shame: The Experience of Shame Scale. *British Journal of Clinical Psychology*, *41*(1), 29–42. doi.10.1348/014466502163778.

Antaramian, S. P., Scott Huebner, E., Hills, K. J., & Valois, R. F. (2010). A dual-factor model of mental health: Toward a more comprehensive understanding of youth functioning. *American Journal of Orthopsychiatry*, *80*(4), 462–472. doi.10.1111/j.1939-0025.2010.01049.x.

Bretherton, I. & Munhollan, K. A. (1999). Internal working models in attachment relationships: Elaborating a central construct in attachment theory. In: J. Cassidy & P. R. Shaver (Eds.), *Handbook of attachment: Theory, research, and clinical applications* (pp. 89–114). New York: Guilford Press.

Brody, G. H., Xiaojia, G., Conger, R., Gibbons, F. X., Murry, V. M., Gerrard, M., & Simons, R. L. (2001). The influence of neighborhood disadvantage, collective socialization, and parenting on African American children's affiliation with deviant peers. *Child Development*, *72*, 1231–1246. doi.10.1111/1467-8624.00344.

Bronfenbrenner, U. (1994). Ecological models of human development. In: M. Gauvain & M. Cole (Eds.), *Readings on the development of children*, 2nd edn. New York: Freeman.

Carr, A. (2006). *The handbook of child and adolescent clinical psychology: A contextual approach*, 2nd edn. London: Routledge.

Cassidy, J. (1994). Emotion regulation: Influences of attachment relationships. *Monographs of the Society for Research in Child Development, 59*, 228–249. doi.10.2307/1166148.

Chen, X., Li, D., Li, Z., Li, B., & Liu, M. (2000). Sociable and prosocial dimensions of social competence in Chinese children: Common and unique contributions to social, academic, and psychological adjustment. *Developmental Psychology, 36*, 302–314. doi.10.1037//0012-1649.36.3.302.

Collishaw, S., Pickles, A., Messer, J., Rutter, M., Shearer, C., & Maughan, B. (2007). Resilience to adult psychopathology following childhood maltreatment: Evidence from a community sample. *Child Abuse & Neglect, 31*(3), 211–229. doi.10.1016/j.chiabu.2007.02.004.

Culotta, C. M. & Goldstein, S. E. (2008). Adolescents' aggressive and prosocial behavior: Associations with jealousy and social anxiety. *Journal of Genetic Psychology, 169*, 21–33. doi.10.3200/GNTP.169.1.21-33.

Dallaire, D. H. & Zeman, J. L. (2013). Empathy as a protective factor for children with incarcerated parents. *Monographs of the Society for Research in Child Development, 78*, 7–25. doi.10.1111/mono.12018.

De Los Reyes, A. & Kazdin, A. E. (2005). Informant discrepancies in the assessment of childhood psychopathology: A critical review, theoretical framework, and recommendations for further study. *Psychological Bulletin, 131*, 483–509. doi.10.1037/0033-2909.131.4.483.

DeVore, E. R. & Ginsburg, K. R. (2005). The protective effects of good parenting on adolescents. *Current Opinions in Pediatrics, 17*, 460–465. doi.10.1097/01.mop.0000170514.27649.c9.

Diener, E. (1994). Assessing subjective well-being: Progress and opportunities. *Social Indicators Research, 31*(2), 103–157. doi.10.1007/BF01207052.

Diener, E., Suh, E. M., Lucas, R. E., & Smith, H. L. (1999). Subjective well-being: Three decades of progress. *Psychological Bulletin, 125*(2), 276–302. doi.10.1037/0033-2909.125.2.276.

Dumas, J. E., Prinz, R. J., Smith, E. P., & Laughlin, J. (1999). The EARLY ALLIANCE prevention trial: An integrated set of interventions to promote competence and reduce risk for conduct disorder, substance abuse, and school failure. *Clinical Child and Family Psychlogy Review, 2*, 37–53. doi.10.1023/A:1021815408272.

Eisenberg, D., Downs, M. F., Golberstein, E., & Zivin, K. (2009). Stigma and help seeking for mental health among college students. *Medical Care Research and Review, 66*(5), 522–541. doi.10.1177/1077558709335173.

Eisenberg, N., Guthrie, I. K., Cumberland, A., Murphy, B. C., Shepard, S. A., Zhou, Q., & Carlo, G. (2002). Prosocial development in early adulthood: A longitudinal study. *Journal of Personality and Social Psychology, 82*, 993–1006. doi.10.1037/0022-3514.82.6.993.

Eisenberg, N. & Mussen, P. H. (1989). *The roots of prosocial behavior in children*. Cambridge: Cambridge University Press.

Elzinga, B. M., Spinhoven, P., Berretty, E., de Jong, P., & Roelofs, K. (2010). The role of childhood abuse in HPA-axis reactivity in social anxiety disorder: A pilot study. *Biological Psychology, 83*(1), 1–6. doi.10.1016/j.biopsycho.2009.09.006.

Fernandez, E. (2007). How children experience fostering outcomes: Participatory research with children. *Child & Family Social Work, 12*(4), 349–359. doi.10.1111/j.1365-2206.2006.00454.x.

Fichter, M. M., Kohlboeck, G., Quadflieg, N., Wyschkon, A., & Esser, G. (2009). From childhood to adult age: 18-year longitudinal results and prediction of the course of mental disorders in the community. *Social Psychiatry and Psychiatric Epidemiology, 44*(9), 792–803. doi.10.1007/s00127-009-0501-y.

Flores, E., Cicchetti, D., & Rogosch, F. A. (2005). Predictors of resilience in maltreated and nonmaltreated Latino children. *Developmental Psychology, 41*(2), 338–351. doi.10.1037/0012-1649.41.2.338.

Forrest, C. B. & Riley, A. W. (2004). Childhood origins of adult health: A basis for life-course health policy. *Health Affairs, 23*(5), 155–164. doi.10.1377/hlthaff.23.5.155.

Geraghty, A. W. A., Wood, A. M., & Hyland, M. E. (2010). Attrition from self-directed interventions: Investigating the relationship between psychological predictors, intervention content and dropout from a body dissatisfaction intervention. *Social Science & Medicine, 71*, 30–37. doi.10.1016/j.socscimed.2010.03.007.

Gilbert, R., Widom, C. S., Browne, K., Fergusson, D., Webb, E., & Janson, S. (2009). Burden and consequences of child maltreatment in high-income countries. *Lancet, 373*, 68–81. doi.10.1016/S0140-6736(08)61706-7.

Gilman, R. & Huebner, S. (2003). A review of life satisfaction research with children and adolescents. *School Psychology Quarterly, 18*, 192–205. doi.10.1521/scpq.18.2.192.21858.

Goss, K., Gilbert, P., & Allan, S. (1994). An exploration of shame measures – I: The other as Shamer scale. *Personality and Individual Differences*, *17*(5), 713–717. doi.http://dx.doi.org/10.1016/0191-8869(94)90149-X.

Griese, E. R. & Buhs, E. S. (in press). Prosocial behavior as a protective factor for children's peer victimization. *Journal of Youth & Adolescence*. doi.10.1007/s10964-013-0046-y.

Grych, J. H. & Kinsfogel, K. M. (2010). Exploring the role of attachment style in the relation between family aggression and abuse in adolescent dating relationships. *Journal of Aggression, Maltreatment & Trauma*, *19*(6), 624–640. doi.10.1080/10926771.2010.502068.

Hay, D. F. (1994). Prosocial development. *Journal of Child Psychology and Psychiatry*, *35*, 29–71. doi.10.1111/j.1469-7610.1994.tb01132.x.

Hay, D. F. & Pawlby, S. (2003). Prosocial development in relation to children's and mothers' psychological problems. *Child Development*, *74*, 1314–1327. doi.10.1111/1467-8624.00609.

Johnson, J., Wood, A. M., Gooding, P., Taylor, P. J., & Tarrier, N. (2011). Resilience to suicidality: The buffering hypothesis. *Clinical Psychology Review*, *31*(4), 563–591. doi.10.1016/j.cpr.2010.12.007.

Kendrick, D., Barlow, J., Hampshire, A., Stewart-Brown, S. L., & Polnay, L. (2008). Parenting interventions and the prevention of unintentional injuries in childhood: Systematic review and meta-analysis. *Child: Care, Health & Development*, *34*, 682–695. doi.10.1111/j.1365-2214.2008.00849.x.

Khanna, M. S. & Kendall, P. C. (2009). Exploring the role of parent training in the treatment of childhood anxiety. *Journal of Consulting and Clinical Psychology*, *77*(5), 981–986. doi.10.1037/a0016920.

Kim, H. K. & Leve, L. D. (2011). Substance use and delinquency among middle school girls in foster care: A three-year follow-up of a randomized controlled trial. *Journal of Consulting & Clinical Psychology*, *79*(6), 740–750. doi.10.1037/a0025949.

Kim, S., Thibodeau, R., & Jorgensen, R. S. (2011). Shame, guilt, and depressive symptoms: A meta-analytic review. *Psycholoigcal Bulletin*, *137*, 68–96. doi.10.1037/a0021466.

Kotler, L. A., Cohen, P., Davies, M., Pine, D. S., & Walsh, B. T. (2001). Longitudinal relationships between childhood, adolescent, and adult eating disorder. *Journal of the American Academy of Child and Adolescent Psychiatry*, *40*, 1434–1440. doi.10.1097/00004583-200112000-00014.

Layous, K., Nelson, S. K., Oberle, E., Schonert-Reichl, K. A., & Lyubomirsky, S. (2012). Kindness counts: Prompting prosocial behavior in preadolescents boosts peer acceptance and well-being. *PLoS One*, *7*(12), e51380. doi.10.1371/journal.pone.0051380.

Legault, L., Anawati, M., & Flynn, R. (2006). Factors favoring psychological resilience among fostered young people. *Children and Youth Services Review*, *28*(9), 1024–1038. doi.10.1016/j.childyouth.2005.10.006.

Link, B. G., Struening, E. L., Neese-Todd, S., Asmussen, S., & Phelan, J. C. (2001). Stigma as a barrier to recovery: The consequences of stigma for the self-esteem of people with mental illnesses. *Psychiatry Services*, *52*(12), 1621–1626. doi.10.1176/appi.ps.52.12.1621.

Luthar, S. S. & Cicchetti, D. (2000). The construct of resilience: Implications for interventions and social policies. *Developmental Psychopathology*, *12*, 857–885.

Luthar, S. S., Cicchetti, D., & Becker, B. (2000). The construct of resilience: A critical evaluation and guidelines for future work. *Child Development*, *71*, 543–562. doi.10.1111/1467-8624.00164.

Lynch, K. B., Geller, S. R., & Schmidt, M. G. (2004). Multi-year evaluation of the effectiveness of a resilience-based prevention program for young children. *Journal of Primary Prevention*, *24*, 335–353. doi.10.1023/B:JOPP.0000018052.12488.d1.

Lyons, M. D., Huebner, E. S., Hills, K. J., & Shinkareva, S. V. (2012). The dual-factor model of mental health: Further study of the determinants of group differences. *Canadian Journal of School Psychology*, *27*(2), 183–196. doi.10.1177/0829573512443669.

Maniglio, R. (2009). The impact of child sexual abuse on health: A systematic review of reviews. *Clinical Psychology Review*, *29*, 647–657. doi.10.1016/j.cpr.2009.08.003.

Maniglio, R. (2010). Child sexual abuse in the aetiology of depression: A systematic review of reviews. *Depression and Anxiety*, *27*, 631–642. doi.10.1002/da.20687.

Masten, A. S. (2001). Ordinary magic: Resilience processes in development. *American Psychologist*, *56*(3), 227–238. doi.10.1037//0003-066x.56.3.227.

Masten, A. S. (2011). Resilience in children threatened by extreme adversity: Frameworks for research, practice, and translational synergy. *Development and Psychopathology*, *23*(2), 493–506. doi.10.1017/S0954579411000198.

Masten, A. S., Best, K. M., & Garmezy, N. (1990). Resilience and development: Contributions from the study of children who overcome adversity. *Development and Psychopathology*, *2*, 425–444. doi.10.1017/S0954579400005812.

McCullough, C. & Shaffer, A. (2013). Maternal depressive symptoms and child externalizing problems: Moderating effects of emotionally maltreating parenting behaviors. *Journal of Child and Family Studies, 23*(2), 389–398. doi.10.1007/s10826-013-9804-4.

Moses, T. (2009). Stigma and self-concept among adolescents receiving mental health treatment. *American Journal of Orthopsychiatry, 79*(2), 261–274. doi.10.1037/a0015696.

Moses, T. (2010). Being treated differently: Stigma experiences with family, peers, and school staff among adolescents with mental health disorders. *Social Science & Medicine, 70*(7), 985–993. doi.10.1016/j.socscimed.2009.12.022.

Mukolo, A., Heflinger, C. A., & Wallston, K. A. (2010). The stigma of childhood mental disorders: A conceptual framework. *Journal of the American Academy of Child and Adolescent Psychiatry, 49*, 92–103. doi.10.1016/j.jaac.2009.10.011.

Murray, C. & Waller, G. (2002). Reported sexual abuse and bulimic psychopathology among nonclinical women: The mediating role of shame. *International Journal of Eating Disorders, 32*(2), 186–191. doi.10.1002/eat.10062.

Neuman, M., Obermeyer, C. M., & The MATCH Study Group. (2013). Experiences of stigma, discrimination, care and support among people living with HIV: A four country study. *AIDS and Behavior, 17*, 1796–1808. doi.10.1007/s10461-013-0432-1.

Oldehinkel, A. J., Hartman, C. A., De Winter, A. F., Veenstra, R., & Ormel, J. (2004). Temperament profiles associated with internalizing and externalizing problems in preadolescence. *Development and Psychopathology, 16*, 421–440. doi.10.1017S0954579404044591.

Pais-Ribeiro, J. (2004). Quality of life is a primary end-point in clinical settings. *Clinical Nutrition, 23*, 121–130. doi.10.1016/S0261-5614(03)00109-2.

Park, N. (2004). The role of subjective well-being in positive youth development. *Annals of the American Academy of Political and Social Science, 591*, 25–39. doi.10.1177/0002716203260078.

Penza, K. M., Heim, C., & Nemeroff, C. B. (2003). Neurobiological effects of childhood abuse: Implications for the pathophysiology of depression and anxiety. *Archives of Women's Mental Health, 6*(1), 15–22. doi.10.1007/s00737-002-0159-x.

Poulton, R., Caspi, A., Moffitt, T. E., Cannon, M., Murray, R., & Harrington, H. (2000). Children's self-reported psychotic symptoms and adult schizophreniform disorder: A 15-year longitudinal study. *Archives of General Psychiatry, 57*, 1053–1058. doi.10.1001/archpsyc.57.11.1053.

Prinz, R. J., Sanders, M. R., Shapiro, C. J., Whitaker, D. J., & Lutzker, J. R. (2009). Population-based prevention of child maltreatment: The US triple P system population trial. *Prevention Science, 10*, 1–12. doi.10.1007/s11121-009-0123-3.

Proctor, C., Linley, A. P., & Maltby, J. (2009). Youth life satisfaction measures: A review. *Journal of Positive Psychology, 4*(2), 128–144. doi.10.1080/17439760802650816.

Pyle, M., Stewart, S. L. K., French, P., Byrne, R., Patterson, P., Gumley, A., Morrison, A. P., et al. (in press). Internalized stigma, emotional dysfunction and unusual experiences in young people at risk of psychosis. *Early Intervention in Psychiatry*. doi.10.1111/eip.12098.

Radford, L., Corral, S., Bradley, C., Fisher, H., Bassett, C., Howat, N., & Collishaw, S. (2011). Child abuse and neglect in the UK today. Available at: http://www.nspcc.org.uk/Inform/research/findings/child_abuse_neglect_research_wda84173.html.

Roysamb, E. & Strype, J. (2002). Optimism and pessimism: Underlying structure and dimensionality. *Journal of Social and Clinical Psychology, 21*, 1–9. doi.10.1521/jscp.21.1.1.22403.

Ryle, A. & Kerr, I. B. (2002). *Introducing cognitive analytic therapy: Principles and practice*. Oxford: Wiley-Blackwell.

Saxena, S., Jane-Llopis, E., & Hosman, C. (2006). Prevention of mental and behavioural disorders: Implications for policy and practice. *World Psychiatry, 5*, 5–14. doi.http://www.ncbi.nlm.nih.gov/pmc/articles/PMC1472261.

Shaver, P. R. & Mikulincer, M. (2007). Adult attachment strategies and the regulation of emotion. In: J. J. Gross (Ed.), *Handbook of emotion regulation* (pp. 446–465). New York: Guilford Press.

Shaver, P. R. & Mikulincer, M. (2011). An attachment-theory framework for conceptualizing interpersonal behavior. In: L. M. Horowitz & S. Strack (Eds.), *The handbook of interpersonal psychology: Theory, research, assessment and therapeutic intervention* (pp. 17–36). Hoboken, NJ: John Wiley.

Snijders, T. A. B. & Bosjer, R. J. (2012). *Multilevel analysis: An introduction to basic and advanced multilevel modeling*, 2nd edn. London: Sage.

Steinberg, L., Blatt-Eisengart, I., & Cauffman, E. (2006). Patterns of competence and adjustment among adolescents from authoritative, authoritarian, indulgent, and neglectful homes: A replication in a sample of serious juvenile offenders. *Journal of Research on Adolescence*, *16*, 47–58. doi.10.1111/j.1532-7795.2006.00119.x.

Suldo, S., Thalji, A., & Ferron, J. (2011). Longitudinal academic outcomes predicted by early adolescents' subjective well-being, psychopathology, and mental health status yielded from a dual factor model. *Journal of Positive Psychology*, *6*, 17–30. doi.10.1080/17439760.2010.536774.

Swan, A., Watson, H. J., & Nathan, P. R. (2009). Quality of life in depression: An important outcome measure in an outpatient cognitive-behavioural therapy group programme? *Clinical Psychology & Psychotherapy*, *16*(6), 485–496. doi.10.1002/cpp.588.

Taylor, P. J. & Wood, A. M. (2013). Discrepancies in parental and self-appraisals of prosocial characteristics predict emotional problems in adolescents. *British Journal of Clinical Psychology*, *52*, 269–284. doi.10.1111/bjc.12013.

Tedeschi, R. G. & Kilmer, R. P. (2005). Assessing strengths, resilience, and growth to guide clinical interventions. *Professional Psychology: Research and Practice*, *36*, 230–237. doi.10.1037/0735-7028.36.3.230.

Varese, F., Smeets, F., Drukker, M., Lieverse, R., Lataster, T., Viechtbauer, W., et al. (2012). Childhood adversities increase the risk of psychosis: A meta-analysis of patient-control, prospective and cross-sectional cohort studies *Schizophrenia Bulletin*, *38*, 661–671. doi 10.1093/schbul/sbs050.

Weisfeld, G. E. & Wendorf, C. A. (2000). The involuntary defeat strategy and discrete emotions theory. In: L. Sloman & P. Gilbert (Eds.), *Subordination and defeat: An evolutionary approach to mood disorders and their therapy* (pp. 125–150). Mahwah, NJ: Lawrence Erlbaum.

West, F., Sanders, M. R., Cleghorn, G. J., & Davies, P. S. (2010). Randomised clinical trial of a family-based lifestyle intervention for childhood obesity involving parents as the exclusive agents of change. *Behaviour Research & Therapy*, *48*(12), 1170–1179. doi.10.1016/j.brat.2010.08.008.

Willemen, A. M., Schuengel, C., & Koot, H. M. (2011). Observed interactions indicate protective effects of relationships with parents for referred adolescents. *Journal of Research on Adolescence*, *21*(3), 569–575. doi.10.1111/j.1532-7795.2010.00703.x.

Wood, A. M., & Tarrier, N. (2010). Positive Clinical Psychology: A new vision and strategy for integrated research and practice. *Clinical Psychology Review*, *30*, 819–829. doi: 10.1016/j.cpr.2010.06.003.

Woolfenden, S. R., Williams, K., & Peat, J. K. (2002). Family and parenting interventions for conduct disorder and delinquency: A meta-analysis of randomised controlled trials. *Archives of Disease in Childhood*, *86*, 251–256.

Young, J. E., Klosko, J. S., & Weishaar, M. (2003). *Schema therapy: A practitioner's guide*. New York: Guilford Press.

Young, S. & Holdorf, G. (2003). Using solution focused brief therapy in individual referrals for bullying. *Educational Psychology in Practice*, *19*(4), 271–282. doi.10.1080/0266736032000138526.

Zahn-Waxler, C., Shirtcliff, E. A., & Marceau, K. (2008). Disorders of childhood and adolescence: Gender and psychopathology. *Annual Review of Clinical Psychology*, *4*, 275–303. doi.10.1146/annurev.clinpsy.3.022806.091358.

20

Suicidal Behavior
The Power of Prospection
Andrew K. MacLeod

On the face of it nothing could be further away from Positive Psychology than suicide. But that very distance presents several unique opportunities. The first opportunity is scientific and arises because those who are suicidal represent the paradigm case of a state of low well-being. In fact, to be at the point of suicide is perhaps most clearly thought of as a complete absence of well-being. In much the same way that understanding of any typical processes are informed when those processed go awry, viewing suicidal behavior as a definitive absence of well-being can potentially yield valuable information about the nature of well-being that is otherwise difficult to discover.

The second opportunity is clinical. It arises because applying well-being or positive psychological concepts opens up a new way of understanding suicidality, as well as offering potential interventions for what has proven to be a very difficult-to-treat problem. Traditional approaches to clinical problems focus mainly on the presence of unwanted experiences (symptoms) and treatment aims to reduce, eliminate, or minimize the impact of those experiences. Positive psychology, in contrast, has provided many insights into flourishing lives – what is present when people's lives are going well (e.g., Seligman, 2011). The question is whether those insights can be used to help people who patently are not flourishing? Can understanding more about what are the components of a good life be used to elucidate what is missing in the lives of people who are suicidal? Perhaps such an approach can complement traditional views through focusing on building up those components of a life that is good for the person in addition to trying to reduce or manage what it is that makes a life bad (cf, MacLeod, 2012). There are some indications of a well-being approach to suicidality being a fruitful one to pursue. For example, Heisel and Flett (2004) found in a sample of psychiatric patients that lack of a sense of purpose in life predicted suicide ideation over and above depression. Malone, Oquendo, Haas, Ellis, Li, and Mann (2000) found that having more reasons for living distinguished depressed non-attempters from depressed attempters. So, both rationally and empirically, there are reasons to suggest that there is value in conceptualizing suicidality as severe absence of well-being as well as presence of distress.

Research linking positive well-being and suicidality is rare, but there is a key meeting point which is the area of future-directed thinking, or prospection as it has been called recently (Seligman, Railton, Baumeister & Srifada, 2013). This meeting point will be a key focus of this chapter. The overall aim of the chapter is to open up the area for debate and to stimulate thinking about how a more well-being focused approach might provide a useful additional way of thinking about suicidality. The chapter begins with an overview of suicidal behavior, followed by a review of the depression–suicidality link. Prospection (future-directed thinking) is then introduced and its link to well-being in general and suicidal behavior in particular reviewed. Finally, areas where well-being concepts might be applied to interventions for suicidal thoughts and behavior are discussed.

The Wiley Handbook of Positive Clinical Psychology, First Edition. Edited by Alex M. Wood and Judith Johnson.
© 2016 John Wiley & Sons, Ltd. Published 2016 by John Wiley & Sons, Ltd.

Suicidal Behavior

Types, Terminology, and Demographics

The term suicidal behavior covers a wide range of phenomena, from thoughts of suicide through to completed suicide. Completed suicide is fairly straightforward to define, at least in theory, as it is defined by a legal judgment where there is clear evidence that the person intended to take his or her own life. In practice, it is not always that easy because the evidence is not always that clear. Cases where clear evidence is lacking though the suspicion is of suicide are usually recorded in other ways. Thoughts of suicide include passing thoughts of wishing one was dead through to a recurring and active desire to be dead accompanied by plans of how to achieve that. Lying in between suicidal thoughts and completed suicide is the category of deliberate self-harming behavior that is nonfatal. It has been suggested that nonfatal deliberate self-harm falls into two categories: attempted suicide and nonsuicidal self-injury (NSSI) (Klonsky, May and Glenn, 2013). NSSI involves behaviors like cutting, burning, scratching where there is no intent to die and which can be contrasted to attempted suicide where the self-harm is potentially lethal and there is clear intent to die. However, although some acts fall clearly into one of these two categories there are many that do not, often involving taking an overdose which is by far the most common form of deliberate self-harm that comes to the attention of services. People are frequently unaware of the medical lethality of the overdose they have taken, thus rendering it a poor criterion for judging intent, and, when asked, people most commonly say they wanted to escape; they may often not be clear about whether they wanted to die or not (e.g., Bancroft, Hawton, Simkin, Kingston, Cumming, & Whitwell, 1979). Perhaps because of this, many research studies do not distinguish among types of deliberate self-harm. In this chapter the term deliberate self-harm will be used to cover all nonfatal self-harming behavior (which may include serious attempts), and suicide attempt will be used where the study has explicitly identified people based on a high level of intent to die.

Suicide itself is the tenth leading cause of death worldwide, accounting for 1.5% of all deaths (Windfuhr & Kapur, 2011). Deliberate self-harm is much more common than suicide, though data tend to be less reliable due to the even more varied ways they are collected as well as different definitions being used in different places, but is estimated to be about at least ten times the rate of completed suicide (Welch, 2001). Nock et al. (2008), reporting data from a cross-country World Health Organization (WHO) survey, found a 2.7% prevalence for suicide attempts. In a large population survey in the United States, 4.6% reported having made a suicide attempt, with around half saying it was a serious attempt with at least some intent to die (Kessler, Borges, & Walter, 1999). In the same survey, Kessler et al. (1999) found that 13.5% reported having experienced suicidal thoughts at some point in their lives, and Nock et al. (2008) in the WHO survey found a prevalence rate of 9.2% for thoughts.

Repetition of deliberate self-harm is common and represents a serious clinical problem. In the WHO European study, 54% of attempters had a previous attempt and 30% made another attempt during the one-year follow-up (Kerkhof, 2000). Approximately 1% of attempters go on to complete suicide within one year, and studies with a follow-up period of at least five years show rates of between 3% and 13% (Sakinofsky, 2000). The risk is particularly elevated immediately following the attempt and declines thereafter, but still remains significantly higher than average three years later (Qin et al., 2009). Between one-third and two-thirds of those who die by suicide will have made a previous attempt (Sakinofsky, 2000). Much is known about the epidemiology of suicidal behavior, including relationships to gender, age, ethnicity, nationality, and so on – discussion of which is beyond the scope of this book (see, e.g., Windfuhr & Kapur, 2011).

Depression and Suicidal Behavior

Depression merits a special mention when talking about suicidal behavior because of the close relationship between the two. This close relationship means that what is known about depression has a relevance to suicidal behavior, whilst bearing in mind that they are distinct phenomena. The standardized mortality ratio (risk of dying from a particular cause compared with the general population risk of dying by that cause) for suicide in those who have experienced depression is around 20 (Ösby, Brandt, Correia, Ekbom, & Sparén, 2001). This means that the chances of dying by suicide are about 20 times greater in those who have had an episode of major depression compared with the general population rates. However, it must be borne in mind that though the *relative* risk is greatly increased, it is still very much more likely that those who have experienced depression will *not* die by suicide: estimates of the lifetime risk of dying by suicide in those who have experienced an episode of major depression are between 5% and 15% (Bostwick & Pancratz, 2000). Deliberate self-harm occurs somewhere in the region of a third of depressed patients (MacLeod, 2013a) and suicidal thoughts in around 50% (Schaffer et al., 2000). Looked at from the other end, somewhere between one-third and one-half of those who complete suicide are depressed, whereas between a half and three-quarters of attempters are depressed (MacLeod, 2013a).

The link between depression and suicidal behavior means that knowledge of basic processes and intervention effectiveness for depression is relevant to suicidal behavior. However, the distinctiveness of the two phenomena means that there is no simple translation from what is known about depression to understanding suicidality. What has become very clear, though, from the substantial body of research on suicidal behavior and depression is that one particular aspect of depression – hopelessness about the future – is the component of depressive experience that links to suicidal behavior (see Niméus, Träskman-Bendz, & Alsén, 1997). The role of hopelessness in suicidality points to the fundamental importance of thinking and feeling states that are directed toward the future.

Future-directed Thinking (Prospection)

Human beings are future-oriented, reflected in expectancies, plans and goals for the future. This ability to project into the future is shared with other animals (Thom, Clayton & Simons, 2013), but humans are distinctive in the extent to which they are able to think about the future in a way that is not stimulus-dependent and also in a way that extends far into the future (Gilbert, 2006). Moreover, these future-oriented states are often affective – there are things we desire or look forward to and things that we worry about or dread.

The importance of such future-directed thinking to human experience and behavior is increasingly recognized. For example, Seligman et al. (2013) have presented a very plausible argument that prospection is essentially what motivates human behavior. These authors argue that whereas past prevailing theories of motivation have viewed humans as being driven by their history, a prospective account sees behavior as being guided by the representations that people hold in the present about the future. Such an account also clearly sits comfortably with the way people experience their own lives. The importance of prospection has always been recognized within social and personality psychology, often in the form of goal theory (e.g., Carver & Scheier, 1990), with some interesting variations such as Little's Personal Projects Analysis (Little, 1989). Personal Projects represent a person's desires, concerns, and aspirations for the future, which are embedded within a social and environmental context that helps to shape those projects and can also facilitate or impede them.

Goal-based accounts are valuable ways of thinking about how thinking, feeling, and motivation are underpinned by the mental representations we hold about the future. But not all prospection is obviously in the form of goals or personal projects. Much prospection is about expectations or anticipation in a wider sense, one that is not necessarily directly related to goal-directed activity. For example, when someone thinks about meeting up with friends at the weekend, family coming to visit them next week or a trip to the opera next month these are not obviously what would normally be called goals. Of course, it is possible to view these thoughts as part of broader affiliation goals or pleasure goals, but that probably stretches the goal concept in a way that loses much of the sense of what is meant when talking about a goal. Goals are an important part of prospection, but prospection is a wider concept that encompasses all cognitive-affective representations about the future as well as ongoing activity related those representations.

Prospection and Well-being

Theories that see humans as essentially future-oriented organisms assume that well-being, by definition, is inherently linked to prospection. Consequently, many list approaches to well-being (those that draw up a list of "goods" that constitute well-being) have in their list an aspect related to thinking about the future. For example, in Ryff's model of Psychological Well-Being (Ryff, 1989), Purpose in Life – having goals and a sense of directedness – is laid out as one of the six components of a good life.

Alongside simply defining future-directed thinking as a component of well-being, the other way that a link between the two can be looked at is empirically. Much of the literature here has focused on people's goals (see MacLeod, 2013b). Having and progressing toward goals is related to self-reported well-being (e.g., Sheldon & Elliot, 1999; Sheldon et al., 2010), as long as the goals are a good fit with individuals' underlying motivations. Brunstein, Schultheiss, and Grässman (1998) found that well-being benefit was determined by whether people were pursuing goals that were congruent with underlying motivations of agency (effectiveness) or communion (relatedness). Agency-motivated participants did not derive well-being benefit from progressing toward communal goals, but they did derive benefit from agentic goals; communion-motivated participants showed the opposite. Sheldon and Elliot (1999) found that those who pursued goals because of more internal motives (because they enjoyed them or valued them: high self-concordance) showed increases in well-being with goal progress, whereas those who pursued their goals because they felt they ought to or would feel bad if they did not (low self-concordance) did not. Progress needs to be linked to goals that fit with the person's underlying motivation or values, and goals related to external motivations do not appear to be beneficial for well-being. In addition, studies have shown that having more approach goals, where someone is trying to bring something desirable into existence, is related to higher levels of well-being; conversely, having more avoidance goals, which are about trying to prevent something undesirable from coming about, is related to lower well-being. This is true at both a non-clinical (Elliot, Thrash & Murayama, 2011) and a clinical (e.g., Sherratt & MacLeod, 2013) level.

As mentioned earlier, many aspects of thinking about the future are not explicitly in the form of goals. MacLeod and colleagues devised the Future-Thinking Task (FTT) (MacLeod, Rose & Williams, 1993) to assess individuals' positive and negative expectancies about the future more broadly. In the FTT participants are asked to think of things they are looking forward to and not looking forward to for various time periods in the future. The main measure is the number of different responses participants are able to generate within fixed time periods, although additional ratings can be made on the responses. This measure is different from goal-based measures in a number of ways. It assesses future-oriented thoughts that are not necessarily goal-like, for example, someone might say they are looking forward to eating dinner tonight, seeing friends at the weekend, or getting married next year. If prompted for goals such prospective cognitions are unlikely to feature because when asked for goals people give (a) things they see as substantial rather than small scale, and (b) things that they aspire to, but require further effort and the where the outcome is uncertain. But many thoughts about the future are relatively small scale and many are projections into the future of a trajectory that people are already on, that are just perceived as things that are going to happen. Asking for future thoughts in this broader way may also generate goal-like prospection, especially for the longer-term future, but it does capture a broader class of prospective thinking.

There is strong evidence for a link between future-directing thinking in this broader sense and well-being. Within a community sample, MacLeod & Conway (2005) found having more things to look forward to was associated with higher levels of positive affect (PA) and having more things *not* looked forward to was correlated with negative affect (NA), but unrelated to PA. More positive and less negative anticipation were both associated with higher levels of life satisfaction. Evidence also comes from studies looking at clinical and subclinical levels of disturbance, both on disruption to future-directed thinking and also on patterns of specificity of this disruption. Depressed patients have been distinguished from nondepressed controls by reporting fewer things to look forward to, but not differing in the extent of their negative anticipation (MacLeod, Tata, Kentish, Jacobsen, 1997; MacLeod & Salaminiou, 2001; Bjärehed, Sarkohi, & Andersson, 2010). Anxious patients, on the other hand, show increased negative thoughts about the future in the absence of any reduced positive thoughts (MacLeod & Byrne, 1996; MacLeod, Pankhania, Lee, & Mitchell, 1997). Those who meet criteria for both anxiety and depression show increased negative and reduced positive anticipation (MacLeod & Byrne, 1996).

To summarize, having an orientation to the future in terms of purpose, directedness and goals is often included in models of well-being that list or define the constituents of a good life. Furthermore, there is strong evidence from both clinical and nonclinical sources that how people think about the future, whether in terms of goals or expectancies more broadly, is related to well-being. The following section examines the relationship of future-directed thinking to suicidality.

Prospection and Suicidality

It was stated earlier that there is strong evidence that hopelessness is the particular aspect of depression that links to suicidal behavior (Niméus et al., 1997). Studies have found that hopelessness mediates the relationship between depression and suicidal intent within deliberate self-harm populations (Wetzel, Margulies, Davis & Karam, 1980; Salter & Platt, 1990), predicts repetition of deliberate self-harm six months later (Petrie, Chamberlain, & Clarke, 1988), as well as completed suicides up to ten years later (Beck, Brown, & Steer, 1989; Fawcett et al., 1990). Similar links between hopelessness and suicidal behavior have been found in the other two diagnostic groups with highest suicidal risk: individuals with psychosis (e.g., Klonsky, Kotov, Bakst, Rabinowitz, & Bromet, 2012) and those with substance misuse (Weissman, Beck & Kovacs, 1979).

Hopelessness in these studies is characterized as a global negative outlook on the future and has been measured either by a single question or the Beck Hopelessness Scale (Beck, Weissman, Lester & Trexler, 1974), a 20-item yes/no response self-report measure containing questions such as "My future looks dark to me." Hopelessness, operationalized in this way, is a very broad construct. It was in attempting to decompose the broad construct of hopelessness into more specific elements that the FTT was originally devised (MacLeod et al., 1993). MacLeod and colleagues (1993) found that those who were suicidal – had recently taken an overdose and been admitted to hospital – were distinguished from controls through their lack of positive thoughts about the future (things they were looking forward to), and were in fact no different in the number of negative thoughts (things were not looking forward to) that they could generate. MacLeod et al. (1997) replicated these findings, with the additional finding that the lack of positive anticipation was not dependent on the level of depression with the suicidal group – depressed and nondepressed suicidal patients showed the effect equally. Within a large sample of suicidal patients, positive expectancies correlated with self-reported hopelessness, whereas negative expectancies showed no relationship to self-reported hopelessness (MacLeod, Tata, Tyrer, Schmidt, Davidson, & Thompson, 2005), a result replicated by O'Connor, Fraser, Whyte, McHale, and Masterton (2008). Moreover, O'Connor et al. (2008) actually found that lack of positive expectancies was a stronger predictor than self-reported hopelessness of future suicidal ideation. As well as a lack of positivity on the FTT, suicidal individuals also show problems with goal-related thoughts. When asked for personal goals, suicidal patients have been found to be able to provide goals, but showed markedly lower belief in the goals coming about (Vincent, Boddana, & MacLeod, 2004; Danchin, MacLeod, & Tata, 2010) Thus, it appears that the kind of problems those who are suicidal have when thinking about their future are predominantly related to a lack of positive thoughts rather than to a preponderance of negative thoughts about the future. Such a conclusion obviously introduces the potential for understand suicidality in positive psychological terms as well as paving the way for possible new ways of helping those who are suicidal.

Planning and Painful Engagement

An obvious question is: why do some people have fewer things that they are looking forward to? There are probably a number of important contributors, but one plausible candidate is planning ability. Thoughts about a positive future are related to planning. Many of the things that people think about and engage with in the future are dependent on planning and acting on those plans. Consistent with the idea that positive anticipation is dependent on planning, MacLeod et al. (2005) found within a community sample that those who performed best on a planning task for achieving their goals showed highest levels of positive future thinking on the FTT. Planning was measured by presenting participants with their goals and asking them to say how they would get from where they are now to the goal being achieved. This measure was based upon the Means End Problem Solving Task (Platt & Spivack, 1975) but is focused on attaining positively desired goals rather than solving current problems. Various measures can be derived that assess how good those plans are at moving from the person's current situation to the goal being achieved, such as the number of steps in the plan or independent raters' judgments of their effectiveness. Suicidal patients have been found to be significantly poorer at this planning task than matched controls (Vincent et al., 2004).

So, it appears that suicidal individuals do have personal goals, but are unable to see those goals coming about, perhaps in part because they are less good at thinking about effective steps that they could take to bring them about. They are able to describe goals, but are not able to derive well-being benefit in the here and now from those goals due to the lack of sense of progress toward their goals or envisaging their successful outcome. In fact, MacLeod and colleagues (MacLeod & Conway, 2007; Danchin et al., 2010) have argued that this configuration – having goals but not having a sense of them being achievable, what they called "painful engagement" (Danchin et al., 2010, p. 915) – is the kind of goal-related thinking that is most pernicious for well-being, and seems to be characteristic of those who engage in suicidal behavior. This pattern fits with Melges' and Bowlby's (1969) description of hopelessness as a state of having goals, but feeling that these goals are unattainable, at the same time as being unable to relinquish the goals. The lack of relinquishing goals may mean that other goals are not pursued. O'Connor, Fraser, Whyte, MacHale, and Masterton (2009), using a self-report measure of general attitude to goals, found that when faced with goals that were unlikely to succeed, a lack of self-reported effort and commitment to alternative goals predicted suicidal ideation in a group of attempters.

One question that arises from the painful engagement concept is why people persist in holding goals that they do not see as likely to come about. An answer to this puzzle may lie in the concept of conditional goal setting (Street, 2002). Conditional goal-setting is where people link higher-order goals, such as "being happy," to specific lower-order goals, such as "living with Tom." Such linkage reflects the fact that goals are naturally organized hierarchically, but problems can arise when global higher-order goals are linked too closely and in too dependent a way with specific lower-order goals. Hadley and MacLeod (2010) found that within a sample of individuals belonging to a depression self-help group the extent to which people believed their happiness, fulfillment and self-worth were dependent on achieving particular goals was strongly correlated with hopelessness. Danchin et al. (2010) also found that those with a recent suicidal episode showed particularly high levels of conditional goal-setting when compared with non-suicidal depressed/anxious controls or general population controls. The link between conditional goal setting and hopelessness and suicidality may help explain why individuals persist in holding on to goals that they feel are relatively unlikely to come about. Recent studies have shown that the ability to disengage from unproductive goals and engage with alternative goals characterizes healthy functioning and those who are low in well-being are less likely to show this disengagement–re-engagement ability (Wrosch & Miller, 2009). Conditional goal-setting might explain why this happens: if people feel that their happiness is dependent on a particular goal they have little choice but to stick with it even in the face of believing that it is relatively unlikely. This is the state of "painful engagement" described by MacLeod and Conway (2007): having goals, believing that they are unlikely but having little option but to remain attached to them because of believing that future well-being is dependent on them.

Intervention

Suicidal behavior has traditionally proven to be fairly resistant to intervention, but there is now accumulating evidence that psychological therapies are helpful (see Wenzel, Brown, & Beck, 2009; Hawton, Taylor, Saunders, & Mehadevan, 2011, for overviews). A range of psychological treatments, including problem-solving therapy (Salkovskis, Atha, & Storer, 1990), cognitive-behavior therapy (Brown, Have, Henriques, Xie, Hollander, & Beck, 2005), and interpersonal psychodynamic therapy (Guthrie et al., 2001), have shown lower rates of repetition at follow-up when compared with treatment as usual, and Dialectical Behavior Therapy has shown lower rates of repetition for those with a diagnosis of borderline personality disorder (Linehan, Armstrong, Suarez, Allmon, & Heard, 1991). However, where there have been positive results the effects have tended to be small, sometimes disappearing at longer follow-up, and there is clearly a lot of scope for treatments to be more effective. Although it is almost certainly something that clinicians do address, to varying degrees, in routine practice, there have been no systematic applications of well-being focused concepts to treating suicidality. A question that arises is whether a more systematic focus on well-being might enhance treatment of suicidality.

Those who are suicidal often have a complex range of problems and difficulties and any intervention focusing on enhancing positive well-being would need to be located within an overall therapeutic framework that takes account of the complexity, variation, and severity of individuals presenting with suicidal thoughts and behavior. An example of such a therapeutic framework is the Collaborative Assessment and Management of Suicidality (CAMS) framework of Jobes and colleagues (Jobes, Comtois, Brenner, & Gutierrez, 2011). CAMS is a broad framework for targeting suicidality and includes: establishing a strong working alliance with the patient, partly through empathizing (though not endorsing) their suicidal thoughts; assessing and ongoing monitoring of risk; targeting underlying drivers of suicidal thoughts, including hopelessness; and safety and crisis response planning. A final element is developing a sense of purpose and meaning and having positive reasons for living, which Jobes et al. (2011) point out the need to include within any overall treatment package plans and goals for the future in order to foster a sense of hope and instill purpose and meaning, but acknowledge that it is not always easy to do so.

MacLeod and colleagues devised a well-being focused intervention package specifically focused on teaching goal setting and planning (GAP) skills (MacLeod, Coates, & Hetherton, 2008). GAP has been shown to increase subjective well-being in a general population sample (MacLeod et al., 2008), reduce psychiatric symptoms and hopelessness, as well as increasing positive future thinking in long-term, forensic psychiatric patients (Ferguson, Conway, Endersby, & MacLeod, 2009), and reduce depression and negative affect and increase life satisfaction and positive affect in a chronic depression sample (Coote & MacLeod, 2012). There have been no applications of GAP to suicidality, but there is obviously a good fit between a future-oriented goal-setting and planning skills intervention and the future-thinking and planning deficits identified in people who are suicidal. Other future-oriented therapeutic developments are also taking place. For example, Vilhauer and colleagues have developed future-oriented therapy for depression (Vilhauer, Cortes, Moali, Chung, Mirocha, & Ishak, 2013), and Van Beek, Kerkhof, and Beekman (2009) have developed a future-oriented group treatment specifically for suicidality.

A second promising well-being focused approach for suicidality is Well-being Therapy (WBT) developed by Giovanni Fava and colleagues (e.g., Ruini & Fava, 2012). WBT integrates the well-being model of Ryff into a CBT model and structure. Clients are asked to record instances of positive experiences to help them become more aware of experiencing episodes of well-being, even short-lived ones. A second stage then moves to identifying thoughts or behaviors that may (prematurely) terminate the positive experience. For example, someone may interrupt a moment of closeness with their partner by having the thought that they are unlovable, or may lose the feeling of enjoyment after succeeding with something by starting to remember times when they have failed or thinking that it will not last. These experiences are understood within the six dimensions of PWB proposed by Ryff (1989), for example, Positive Relations with Others and Environmental Mastery in the above examples, and deficits in these dimensions are identified and addressed within the therapy. The therapy originally developed as a treatment for residual depression, but has since expanded to other disorders (Ruini & Fava, 2012) and to children (Ruini et al., 2009). There have been no direct applications of WBT to suicidality, but given the link between suicidality and depression it would be an obvious avenue to pursue. Absence of purpose in life (measured by the subscale of the Ryff (1989) measure of the six dimensions) having an additional predictive relationship to ideation over and above that of depression, further reinforces the applicability of this model to suicidality.

A final potential area of application arises from strengths-based models. Padesky and Mooney (2012) describe their strengths-based CBT model, which is a variation of standard CBT that they have developed over a number of years. The model is based around helping clients to identify their strengths, which are then used as the basis to think about how strengths can make a person resilient when things are getting difficult. The person's own identified strengths are then generalized into a personal model of resilience that can be applied to lots of life areas. Padesky and Mooney (2012) helpfully point out that in a clinical context people may well need considerable help in identifying their strengths in the first place due to the pervasive negativity that may be enveloping them. Seligman (2003) developed a model of happiness that had as the central feature the identification and application of individual strengths. The Seligman model is not about resilience per se, but rather is about people enhancing their well-being through exercising their own particular signature strengths in work, relationships and other activities. The models, which have developed in parallel, are different in their emphases, but share the common theme of identifying individuals' strengths and using those strengths to lead a better life, either through greater resilience or through direct enhancement of well-being. Helping those who are suicidal to identify their strengths and then use those strengths in these two ways may help them to deal with obstacles. It may also help them to envisage a future life pathway that is meaningful and enjoyable, as well as engaging because it involves the exercise of their strengths in the present to build that future.

Conclusion

Suicidal behavior, both lethal and nonlethal, is a both serious public health problem and a devastating personal problem. There is strong evidence that the way people think about their own future holds the key for understanding suicidal thinking. The importance of prospection has been recognized in the clinical literature and maps on well to work on the link between general well-being and prospection. Treating suicidal behavior has proven to be difficult and the bringing together of the clinical and nonclinical literatures offers a potential addition to the understanding and treatment of suicidal behavior.

References

Bancroft, J., Hawton, K., Simkin, S., Kingston, B., Cumming, C., & Whitwell, D. (1979). The reasons people give for taking overdoses: A further inquiry. *British Journal of Medical Psychology*, 52(4), 353–365. doi.org/10.1111/j.2044-8341.1979.tb02536.x.

Beck, A. T., Brown, G., & Steer, R. A. (1989). Prediction of eventual suicide in psychiatric inpatients by clinical ratings of hopelessness. *Journal of Consulting and Clinical Psychology*, 57(2), 309–310.

Beck, A. T., Weissman, A., Lester, D., & Trexler, L. (1974). The measurement of pessimism: The Hopelessness Scale. *Journal of Consulting and Clinical Psychology*, 42(6), 861–865.

Bjärehed, J., Sarkohi, A., & Andersson, G. (2010). Less positive or more negative? Future-directed thinking in mild to moderate depression. *Cognitive Behaviour Therapy*, 39(1), 37–45. doi.org/10.1080/16506070902966926.

Bostwick, J. M. & Pankratz, V. S. (2000). Affective disorders and suicide risk: A reexamination. *American Journal of Psychiatry*, 157(12), 1925–1932. doi.org/10.1176/appi.ajp.157.12.1925.

Brown, G. K., Have, T. T., Henriques, G. R., Xie, S. X., Hollander, J. E., & Beck, A. T. (2005). Cognitive therapy for the revention of suicide attempts: A randomized controlled trial. *Journal of the American Medical Association*, 294(5), 563–570. doi.org/10.1001/jama.294.5.563.

Brown, M. Z., Comtois, K. A., & Linehan, M. M. (2002). Reasons for suicide attempts and nonsuicidal self-injury in women with borderline personality disorder. *Journal of Abnormal Psychology*, 111(1), 198–202. doi.org/10.1037/0021-843X.111.1.198.

Brunstein, J. C., Schultheiss, O. C., & Grässman, R. (1998). Personal goals and emotional well-being: The moderating role of motive dispositions. *Journal of Personality and Social Psychology*, 75(2), 494–508. doi.org/10.1037/0022-3514.75.2.494.

Carver, C. S. & Scheier, M. F. (1990). Origins and functions of positive and negative affect: A control-process view. *Psychological Review*, 97(1), 19–35. doi.org/10.1037/0033-295X.97.1.19.

Coote, H. M. J. & MacLeod, A. K. (2012). A self-help, positive goal-focused intervention to increase well-being in people with depression: Self-help, goals, well-being, and depression. *Clinical Psychology & Psychotherapy*, 19(4), 305–315. doi.org/10.1002/cpp.1797.

Danchin, C. L., MacLeod, A. K., & Tata, P. (2010). Painful engagement in deliberate self-harm: The role of conditional goal setting. *Behaviour Research and Therapy*, 48(9), 915–920. doi.org/10.1016/j.brat.2010.05.022.

Elliot, A. J., Thrash, T. M., & Murayama, K. (2011). A longitudinal analysis of self-regulation and well-being: Avoidance personal goals, avoidance coping, stress generation, and subjective well-being. *Journal of Personality*, 79(3), 643–674. doi.org/10.1111/j.1467-6494.2011.00694.x.

Fawcett, J., Scheftner, W. A., Fogg, L., Clark, D. C., Young, M. A., Hedeker, D., & Gibbons, R. (1990). Time-related predictors of suicide in major affective disorder. *American Journal of Psychiatry*, 147(9), 1189–1194.

Ferguson, G., Conway, C., Endersby, L., & MacLeod, A. (2009). Increasing subjective well-being in long-term forensic rehabilitation: evaluation of well-being therapy. *Journal of Forensic Psychiatry & Psychology*, 20(6), 906–918. doi.org/10.1080/14789940903174121.

Gilbert, D. (2006). *Stumbling on Happiness*, new edn. London: Harper Perennial.

Guthrie, E., Kapur, N., Mackway-Jones, K., Chew-Graham, C., Moorey, J., Mendel, E., Tomenson, B., et al. (2001). Randomised controlled trial of brief psychological intervention after deliberate self poisoning. *British Medical Journal*, 323(7305), 135–135. doi.org/10.1136/bmj.323.7305.135.

Hadley, S. A. & MacLeod, A. K. (2010). Conditional goal-setting, personal goals and hopelessness about the future. *Cognition & Emotion*, *24*(7), 1191–1198. doi.org/10.1080/02699930903122521.

Hawton, K., Taylor, T. L, Saunders, K. E. A, & Mehadevan, S. (2011). Clinical care of deliberate self-harm patients: An evidence-based approach. In: R. C. O'Connor, S. Platt, & J. Gordon (Eds.), *International handbook of suicide prevention* (pp. 329–352). Chichester: Wiley-Blackwell.

Heisel, M. J. & Flett, G. L. (2004). Purpose in life, satisfaction with life, and suicide ideation in a clinical sample. *Journal of Psychopathology and Behavioral Assessment*, *26*(2), 127–135. doi.org/10.1023/B:JOBA.0000013660.22413.e0.

Jobes, D, Comtois, K. A., Brenner, L. A., & Gutierrez, P.M. (2011). Clinical trial feasibility studies of the collaborative assessment and management of suicidality. In: R. C. O'Connor, S. Platt, & J. Gordon (Eds.), *International handbook of suicide prevention* (pp. 383–400). Chichester: Wiley-Blackwell.

Kerkhof, A. J. F. M (2000). Attempted suicide: Patterns and trends. In: K. Hawton & K. van Heeringen (Eds.), *The international handbook of suicide and attempted suicide* (pp. 49–64). Chichester: Wiley-Blackwell.

Kessler, R. C., Borges, G., & Walters, E. E. (1999). Prevalence of and risk factors for lifetime suicide attempts in the National Comorbidity Survey. *Archives of General Psychiatry*, *56*(7), 617–626. doi.org/10.1001/archpsyc.56.7.617.

Klonsky, E. D., Kotov, R., Bakst, S., Rabinowitz, J., & Bromet, E. J. (2012). Hopelessness as a predictor of attempted suicide among first admission patients with psychosis: A 10-year cohort study. *Suicide and Life-Threatening Behavior*, *42*(1), 1–10. doi.org/10.1111/j.1943-278X.2011.00066.x.

Klonsky, E. D., May, A. M., & Glenn, C. R. (2013). The relationship between nonsuicidal self-injury and attempted suicide: Converging evidence from four samples. *Journal of Abnormal Psychology*, *122*(1), 231–237. doi.org/10.1037/a0030278.

Linehan, M. M., Armstrong, H. E., Suarez, A., Allmon, D., & Heard, H. L. (1991). Cognitive-behavioral treatment of chronically parasuicidal borderline patients. *Archives of General Psychiatry*, *48*(12), 1060–1064. doi.org/10.1001/archpsyc.1991.01810360024003.

Little, B. R. (1989). Personal projects analysis: Trivial pursuits, magnificent obsessions, and the search for coherence. In: D. Buss & N. Cantor (Eds.), *Personality psychology: Recent trends and emerging directions* (pp. 15–31). New York: Springer.

MacLeod, A. K. (2012). Well-being, positivity and mental health: An introduction to the special issue: well-being positivity and mental health: An introduction. *Clinical Psychology & Psychotherapy*, *19*(4), 279–282. doi.org/10.1002/cpp.1794.

MacLeod, A. K. (2013a). Suicide and attempted suicide. In: M. Power (Ed.), *Mood disorders: A handbook of science and practice*, 2nd edn. (pp. 319–336). Chichester: Wiley-Blackwell.

MacLeod, A. (2013b). Goals and plans: Their relationship to well-being. In: A. Efklides & D. Moraitou (Eds.), *A positive psychology perspective on quality of life*, vol. 51 (pp. 33–50). New York: Springer.

MacLeod, A. K. & Byrne, A. (1996). Anxiety, depression, and the anticipation of future positive and negative experiences. *Journal of Abnormal Psychology*, *105*(2), 286–289.

MacLeod, A. K., Coates, E., & Hetherton, J. (2008). Increasing well-being through teaching goal-setting and planning skills: results of a brief intervention. *Journal of Happiness Studies*, *9*(2), 185–196. doi.org/10.1007/s10902-007-9057-2.

MacLeod, A. K. & Conway, C. (2005). Well-being and the anticipation of future positive experiences: The role of income, social networks, and planning ability. *Cognition & Emotion*, *19*(3), 357–374. doi.org/10.1080/02699930441000247.

MacLeod, A. K. & Conway, C. (2007). Well-being and positive future thinking for the self versus others. *Cognition & Emotion*, *21*(5), 1114–1124. doi.org/10.1080/02699930601109507.

MacLeod, A. K., Pankhania, B., Lee, M., & Mitchell, D. (1997). Parasuicide, depression and the anticipation of positive and negative future experiences. *Psychological Medicine*, *27*(4), 973–977. doi.org/10.1017/S003329179600459X.

MacLeod, A. K. & Salaminiou, E. (2001). Reduced positive future-thinking in depression: Cognitive and affective factors. *Cognition and Emotion*, *15*(1), 99–107.

MacLeod, A. K., Tata, P., Kentish, J., & Jacobsen, H. (1997). Retrospective and prospective cognitions in anxiety and depression. *Cognition and Emotion*, *11*(4), 467–479.

MacLeod, A. K., Tata, P., Tyrer, P., Schmidt, U., Davidson, K., & Thompson, S. (2005). Hopelessness and positive and negative future thinking in parasuicide. *British Journal of Clinical Psychology*, *44*(4), 495–504. doi.org/10.1348/014466505X35704.

MacLeod, A., Rose, G., & Williams, J. M. (1993). Components of hopelessness about the future in parasuicide. *Cognitive Therapy and Research*, 17(5), 441–455. doi.org/10.1007/BF01173056.

Malone, K. M., Oquendo, M. A., Haas, G. L., Ellis, S. P., Li, S., & Mann, J. J. (2000). Protective factors against suicidal acts in major depression: Reasons for living. *American Journal of Psychiatry*, 157(7), 1084–1088. doi.org/10.1176/appi.ajp 157.7.1084.

Melges, F. T. & Bowlby, J. (1969). Types of hopelessness in psychopathological process. *Archives of General Psychiatry*, 20(6), 690–699. doi.org/10.1001/archpsyc.1969.01740180074007.

Niméus, A., Träskman-Bendz, L., & Alsén, M. (1997). Hopelessness and suicidal behavior. *Journal of Affective Disorders*, 42(2/3), 137–144. doi.org/10.1016/S0165-0327(96)01404-8.

Nock, M. K., Borges, G., Bromet, E. J., Alonso, J., Angermeyer, M., Beautrais, A., Williams, D., et al. (2008). Cross-national prevalence and risk factors for suicidal ideation, plans and attempts. *British Journal of Psychiatry*, 192(2), 98–105. doi.org/10.1192/bjp.bp.107.040113.

O'Connor, R. C., Fraser, L., Whyte, M-C., MacHale, S., & Masterton, G. (2008). A comparison of specific positive future expectancies and global hopelessness as predictors of suicidal ideation in a prospective study of repeat self-harmers. *Journal of Affective Disorders*, 110(3), 207–214. doi.org/10.1016/j.jad.2008.01.008.

O'Connor, R. C., Fraser, L., Whyte, M-C., MacHale, S., & Masterton, G. (2009). Self-regulation of unattainable goals in suicide attempters: The relationship between goal disengagement, goal reengagement and suicidal ideation. *Behaviour Research and Therapy*, 47(2), 164–169. doi.org/10.1016/j.brat.2008.11.001.

Ösby, U., Brandt, L., Correia, N., Ekbom, A., & Sparén, P. (2001). Excess mortality in bipolar and unipolar disorder in Sweden. *Archives of General Psychiatry*, 58(9), 844–850. doi.org/10.1001/archpsyc.58.9.844.

Padesky, C. A. & Mooney, K. A. (2012). Strengths-based cognitive-behavioural therapy: A four-step model to build resilience. *Clinical Psychology & Psychotherapy*, 19(4), 283–290. doi.org/10.1002/cpp.1795.

Petrie, K., Chamberlain, K., & Clarke, D. (1988). Psychological predictors of future suicidal behaviour in hospitalized suicide attempters. *British Journal of Clinical Psychology*, 27(3), 247–257.

Platt, J. J. & Spivack, G. (1975). *The means end problem solving procedure manual*. Philadelphia, PA: Hahnemann University.

Qin, P., Jepsen, P., Nørgård, B., Agerbo, E., Mortensen, P. B., Vilstrup, H., & Sørensen, H. T. (2009). Hospital admission for non-fatal poisoning with weak analgesics and risk for subsequent suicide: A population study. *Psychological Medicine*, 39(11), 1867–1873. doi.org/10.1017/S0033291709005741.

Ruini, C. & Fava, G. A. (2012). Role of well-being therapy in achieving a balanced and individualized path to optimal functioning. *Clinical Psychology & Psychotherapy*, 19(4), 291–304.

Ruini, C., Ottolini, F., Tomba, E., Belaise, C., Albieri, E., Visani, D., Fava, G. A., et al. (2009). School intervention for promoting psychological well-being in adolescence. *Journal of Behavior Therapy and Experimental Psychiatry*, 40(4), 522–532. doi.org/10.1016/j.jbtep.2009.07.002.

Ryff, C. D. (1989). Happiness is everything, or is it? Explorations on the meaning of psychological well-being. *Journal of Personality and Social Psychology*, 57(6), 1069–1081. doi.org/10.1037/0022-3514.57.6.1069.

Sakinofsky, I. (2000). Repetition of suicidal behaviour. In: K. Hawton & K. van Heeringen (Eds.), *The international handbook of suicide and attempted suicide* (pp. 385–404). Chichester: Wiley-Blackwell.

Salkovskis, P. M., Atha, C., & Storer, D. (1990). Cognitive-behavioural problem solving in the treatment of patients who repeatedly attempt suicide: A controlled trial. *British Journal of Psychiatry*, 157, 871–876. doi.org/10.1192/bjp.157.6.871.

Salter, D. & Platt, S. (1990). Suicidal intent, hopelessness and depression in a parasuicide population: The influence of social desirability and elapsed time. *British Journal of Clinical Psychology*, 29(4), 361–371.

Schaffer, A., Levitt, A. J., Bagby, R. M., Kennedy, S. H., Levitan, R. D., & Joffe, R. T. (2000). Suicidal ideation in major depression: Sex differences and impact of comorbid anxiety. *Canadian Journal of Psychiatry (La revue Canadienne de psychiatrie)*, 45(9), 822–826.

Seligman, M. E. P. (2011). *Flourish*. London: Nicholas Brealey.

Seligman, M. E. P., Railton, P., Baumeister, R. F., & Sripada, C. (2013). Navigating into the future or driven by the past. *Perspectives on Psychological Science*, 8(2), 119–141. doi.org/10.1177/1745691612474317.

Sheldon, K. M., Abad, N., Ferguson, Y., Gunz, A., Houser-Marko, L., Nichols, C. P., & Lyubomirsky, S. (2010). Persistent pursuit of need-satisfying goals leads to increased happiness: A 6-month experimental longitudinal study. *Motivation and Emotion, 34*(1), 39–48. doi.org/10.1007/s11031-009-9153-1.

Sheldon, K. M. & Elliot, A. J. (1999). Goal striving, need satisfaction, and longitudinal well-being: The self-concordance model. *Journal of Personality and Social Psychology, 76*(3), 482–497. doi.org/10.1037/0022-3514.76.3.482.

Sherratt, K. A. L. & MacLeod, A. K. (2013). Underlying motivation in the approach and avoidance goals of depressed and non-depressed individuals. *Cognition & Emotion, 27*(8), 1432–1440. doi.org/10.1080/02699931.2013.786680.

Street, H. (2002). Exploring relationships between goal setting, goal pursuit and depression: A review. *Australian Psychologist, 37*(2), 95–103. doi.org/10.1080/00050060210001706736.

Thom, J. M., Clayton, N. S., & Simons, J. S. (2013). Imagining the future: A bird's eye view. *The Psychologist, 26*, 418–421.

Van Beek, W., Kerkhof, A., & Beekman, A. (2009). Future oriented group training for suicidal patients: A randomized clinical trial. *BMC Psychiatry, 9*. doi.org/10.1186/1471-244X-9-65.

Vilhauer, J. S., Cortes, J., Moali, N., Chung, S., Mirocha, J., & Ishak, W. W. (2013). Improving quality of life for patients with major depressive disorder by increasing hope and positive expectations with future directed therapy (FDT). *Innovations in Clinical Neuroscience, 10*(3), 12–22.

Vincent, P. J., Boddana, P., & MacLeod, A. K. (2004). Positive life goals and plans in parasuicide. *Clinical Psychology & Psychotherapy, 11*(2), 90–99.

Weissman, A. N., Beck, A. T., & Kovacs, M. (1979). Drug abuse, hopelessness, and suicidal behavior. *International Journal of Addiction, 14*, 451–464.

Welch, S. S. (2001). A review of the literature on the epidemiology of parasuicide in the general population. *Psychiatric Services, 52*(3), 368–375. doi.org/10.1176/appi.ps.52.3.368.

Wenzel, A., Brown, G. K., & Beck, A.T. (2009). *Cognitive therapy for suicidal patients.* Washington, DC: American Psychological Association.

Wetzel, R. D., Margulies, T., Davis, R., & Karam, E. (1980). Hopelessness, depression, and suicide intent. *Journal of Clinical Psychiatry, 41*(5), 159–160.

Windfuhr, K. & Kapur, N. (2011) International perspective on the epidemiology and aetiology of suicide and self-harm. In: R. C. O'Connor, S. Platt, & J. Gordon (Eds.), *International handbook of suicide prevention* (pp. 27–58). Chichester: Wiley-Blackwell.

Wrosch, C. & Miller, G. E. (2009). Depressive symptoms can be useful: Self-regulatory and emotional benefits of dysphoric mood in adolescence. *Journal of Personality and Social Psychology, 96*(6), 1181–1190. doi.org/10.1037/a0015172.

Part IV

Positive Psychology Interventions in Clinical Practice

21

Positive Psychological Interventions
An Overview
Acacia C. Parks and Liudmila Titova

Although positive psychology is a relatively new field, it has created a considerable body of research on how people can learn happiness. Happiness can be pursued via numerous pathways: through sensory experiences, using savoring; through social interactions, using active-constructive responding and gratitude; through cognitive experiences, using optimism activities. Taken together, these types of technique are called Positive Psychological Interventions (PPIs) (Schueller & Parks, 2014), and they have been applied in both nondistressed and clinical populations to promote happiness.

PPIs are fairly new, so there is some inconsistency in the way they are defined by different researchers. For instance, a definition proposed by Sin and Lyubomirsky (2009) stresses two important factors which describe PPIs: concentration on increasing positivity rather than on decreasing negativity; and long-term effects. Bolier, Haverman, Westerhof, Riper, Smit, and Bohlmeijer (2013) took this definition a step further, by adding that these activities need to be intentionally based on theories developed by positive psychology. Thus, following these definitions, certain activities can be excluded from the realm of PPIs. For instance, a brief mood inductions often use for laboratory experiments would not fit the category Although they increase someone's mood in the moment, they are lacking a long-term component. On the other hand, activities such as regular exercise or a healthy diet, although long-term oriented, would not fit either, as they are not based on positive psychology theories.

Although these definitions give a better understanding of PPIs, they are still not completely comprehensive. Parks and Biswas-Diener (2013) proposed the most detailed definition, which expanded on those described earlier, and took it a step further. According to them, an activity has to meet the following criteria to be called a PPI: it needs address a "positive psychology construct" and to have a body of research evidence supporting its effectiveness. Thus, a lot of activities could potentially have qualified as PPIs, but they have not yet obtained enough scientific evidence to support their effectiveness. Parks and Biswas-Diener (2013) emphasize that this addition of evidence-based piece helps to distinguish PPIs from the movement of "positive thinking" and its products such as *The Secret*, which are very well-known and popular, yet have no scientific base behind them.

PPIs are designed to promote positivity in people's everyday life and by doing so they help them to cope with the negative events and moods they might experience (Seligman, Rashid, & Parks, 2006). In this chapter we will examine the theories and research findings that serve as a foundation to the mechanism underlining PPIs. We will look at the different types of activities

The Wiley Handbook of Positive Clinical Psychology, First Edition. Edited by Alex M. Wood and Judith Johnson.

that fall under the PPI "umbrella" and the modalities through which they have been delivered. Further, we will take a look at what applications they have in clinical practice. Finally, we will discuss the limitations and difficulties connected to the PPIs as well as future directions.

Can Happiness be Lastingly Changed?

In order to talk about ways to enhance happiness we need to take a step back and see if happiness levels can actually be changed. Although this used to be a debatable question, recent research suggests that despite genetics and situational circumstances happiness levels can be increased (Lyubomirksy, Sheldon, & Schkade, 2005). Lyubomirsky and colleagues (2005) proposed that despite "happiness set point" (a base-line level that a person bounces back to despite external influences), which all people have set genetically, chosen behaviors play a very important role in the happiness level. A useful analogy is the idea of a weight set point; if a person is predisposed to obesity, they will likely become obese if they do not make an effort to offset the set point. However, with substantial and regular effort, even a person with a strong genetic loading for obesity can reach and maintain a normal BMI. With enough effort, behavior can quite substantially offset genetic predispositions. Similarly, a person who is dispositionally grouchy can work to improve their daily mood, which, with enough sustained practice, eventually amounts to being a "happy person." This theory is supported by empirical evidence, as numerous studies show that people who participate in activities designed to enhance happiness can show lasting increases in well-being (Lyubomirsky et al., 2005).

Even though happiness can be changed, one might wonder whether individuals will get used to the activities they are using to improve their mood, eventually reverting to where they began as the activities lose their potency. The *Hedonic Adaptation Prevention Model*, proposed by Sheldon and Lyubomirsky (2012), explains how to address the problem of hedonic adaptation (a process that allows people to get used to the stimuli and bring them back to their default emotional level) and sustain a long-term increase in happiness. This model stresses two key processes by which adaptation can be prevented. First, it highlights the significance of renewing one's appreciation of both circumstantial changes (such as a new house or job, which can be easy to take for granted as one becomes accustomed) and regularly practiced activities (such as time spent with a loved one, which could become monotonous or be new and interesting every time, depending on one's outlook). It also suggests keeping realistic expectations – not constantly aiming to experience more and more positive emotions than one has experienced previously. Moreover, it stresses that the variety of activities and the element of surprise are essential to progress – so all else being equal (time and effort spent, etc.), it is better to practice a variety of different activities rather than repeat the same activity (reaffirmed by Parks, Della Porta, Pierce, Zilca, & Lyubomirsky, 2012), and to infuse the same activity with new elements (e.g., going out to dinner with one's spouse, but trying somewhere new each time).

People differ in the extent to which they adapt to life events, with personality playing a key role (Boyce & Wood, 2011); it is possible that this may also be true for day-to-day activities. Therefore, some individuals may need to take every possible step to prevent hedonic adaptation, others may avoid hedonic adaptation with little or no effort.

How can Happiness be Increased?

PPIs can be divided into seven main categories: (1) savoring, (2) gratitude, (3) kindness, (4) empathy, (5) optimism, (6) strengths, and (7) meaning (Parks & Layous, in press). Each of these categories is discussed below.

Savoring

The purpose of savoring is to focus attention and awareness on a specific experience and in so doing, prolong its pleasurable effects (Peterson, 2006). Although mindfulness meditation itself does not meet the criteria of a PPI, the underlying principle of savoring is based on its basic activities, which encourage individuals to intentionally and deliberately process of all the parts of an experience (Kabat-Zinn, 2009). Savoring PPIs can have different targets; they can range from sensory experiences, such as those connected to food or smell, to more mental and cognitively-oriented stimuli, such as memories and other emotional experiences (Bryant, Smart, & King, 2005). People who practice savoring show more happiness and life satisfaction, as well as fewer depressive symptoms (Bryant, 2003). There are also several factors that enhance the savoring process, such as concentration on the meaning of the experience, writing about it, doing it in the presence of other people, integrating humor, remembering that the activity has a transient nature, and being aware of counterfactuals (Bryant & Veroff, 2007).

Schueller and Parks (2014) proposed two subcategories of savoring interventions. The first category includes activities that concentrate on general principles of savoring by teaching these principles and encouraging their practice. For instance, in the study done by Schueller (2010), participants were instructed to reflect on two pleasurable experiences for 2–3 minutes every day, as well as to try to make them last as long as they could. As an example, this instruction could be applied to the experience of a favorite food, like a cupcake. A person can concentrate on different parts which cupcake is made of, paying special attention to the texture and taste of each one. The experience can be prolonged by recognizing all these parts separately, and how they combined together. Although the instructions were very simple, participants practicing savoring in this way showed improvements in the level of well-being after a week (Schueller, 2010). This type of activity focuses on savoring as a general skill, which can be practiced in a wide variety of situations.

The second category of savoring activities concentrates on teaching and encouraging to practice a specific skill or activity. For example, in a "mindful photography" intervention (Kurtz, 2012), participants were instructed to take pictures which would have meaning for them, would be creative and beautiful. They did that every day for at least 15 minutes, and after just two weeks they showed more positive emotions tan the participants who did not receive specific instructions regarding their photographs. Another example of a specific savoring skill is active-constructive responding – a series of behaviors that help a friend or loved one to prolong and savor a piece of good news (Gable, Reis, Impett, & Asher, 2004). Both examples are savoring skills, but designed to be used in a very specific set of situations, and to elicit a very specific set of behaviors in response to those situations.

Gratitude

Gratitude activities strive to evoke feeling of gratitude toward someone or something outside of oneself, which is responsible for creating positive events or feelings in a person's life (Schueller & Parks, 2013). Gratitude PPIs can be concentrated solely on reflection or also on the activities motivated by the feeling of gratitude. For example, Emmons' and McCullough's (2003) classic study had people practice gratitude that was reflection-only – they kept a journal, and were asked not to share that journal with anyone. The benefits of gratitude in that study, then, were based only on a person's self-reflection of gratitude – not on sharing or conveying the gratitude to anyone. Other subsequent studies have replicated and extended the effects of gratitude journals, finding benefits of gratitude even compared with robust control groups (Geraghty, Wood, & Hyland, 2010a,b). While some versions of gratitude activities stress the importance of elaboration of the reasons as to why the feeling of gratitude is present in the described situation, some benefits were shown from just naming the grateful event (Emmons & McCullough, 2003; Seligman, Steen, Park, & Peterson, 2005).

Other Gratitude PPIs, however, feature a social component – where gratitude is contemplated, but also *expressed*. In a classic gratitude intervention that is both contemplative and expressive, the "Gratitude Letter," a person is asked to express gratitude to a particular individual in significant depth through a written letter (Seligman, 2002). Most variations of this activity emphasize the importance of delivering the letter to the person it is written about, ideally in person, read aloud. While it does appear that, as discussed above, just writing a detailed account of one's gratitude is beneficial, actually delivering the letter has led to even stronger effects (Boehm, Lyubomirsky, & Sheldon, 2011; Lyubomirsky, Dickerhoof, Boehm, & Sheldon, 2011; Schueller, 2012).

Overall, all these different variations of gratitude PPIs have shown ability to improve well-being by increasing positive emotions, improving health, and decreasing depressive symptoms (Wood, Froh, & Geraghty, 2010). However, it is worth noting that the effects of the more "social" gratitude activities – those that involve delivering a single, powerful expression gratitude – tend to be short-lived, despite their initial often powerful effects. This makes sense, as a single event is subject to hedonic adaptation (see above) and is likely to lose its potency over time. Variations of the Gratitude Letter/Visit that are more sustainable long term have been proposed and used in everyday practice – for example, a person might create a log of the things that a loved one does over a month for which one is grateful, then give a monthly gratitude report. However, such a variation has not yet been tested empirically, to our knowledge.

Kindness

Kindness activities ask their participants to perform deliberate acts of kindness toward other people. The acts can vary greatly from buying small gifts and donations to things which do not involve spending money, such as helping someone carry a heavy bag. It has been noted by research that acting kindly is a common characteristic of happy people, and, moreover, happiness and kindness often coexist in a circular fashion where one reinforces the other (Aknin, Dunn, & Norton, 2012; Dunn, Aknin, & Norton, 2008).

An example of a PPI that falls under the kindness category is "prosocial spending," or spending money on others (Dunn et al., 2008). This activity can include simple things such as buying a sandwich for a homeless person on a street, buying a cup of coffee for a colleague, or donating to charity. Spending money on others, rather than on oneself, leads to increase in well-being (Dunn et al., 2008). This example illustrates an important exception to popular belief that "money does not buy happiness," emphasizing that when it is spent on kindness it actually does (Howell, Pchelin, & Iyer, 2012).

Activities that promote kindness on a more general level also enhance well-being. For example, when participants were asked to do kind acts for other people (not necessarily involving money), participants experienced improved happiness (Lyubomirsky, Tkach, & Sheldon, 2004). However, they found an important dose–response relationship; when five kind acts were performed all in one day as opposed to these acts being spread throughout a week, a significant increase in well-being was found. There was no benefit, however, to doing one kind act per day, five days a week. The likely explanation for this finding is that most people are involved in a small amount of kind activities daily, so in order to notice the effect the number of kind acts has to be increased above and beyond what a person would normally do.

Empathy

Empathy-based activities intend to strengthen social connections by promoting an understanding within the relationship. A great body of research suggests that meaningful social relationships are essential for happiness (Myers & Diener, 1995; Diener & Seligman, 2002; Peterson, 2006).

One of the examples of empathy-based PPIs is loving-kindness mediation. In this activity, by using meditation techniques people create positive feeling and emotions toward someone else or even themselves. Research has found that participating in this activity leads to improvement in life satisfaction, a decrease in depressive symptoms, and also promotes positive emotions and behaviors in general (Fredrickson, Cohn, Coffey, Pek, & Finkel, 2008).

Other empathy-based PPIs that concentrated on perspective-taking, which emphasizes increasing the self–other overlap that exists between two people (Davis et al., 2004). In short, by attempting to see another person's perspective well enough to truly understand how they feel, one might find oneself feeling more similar to the other person (Hodges, Clark, & Myers, 2011). Extensive literature finds that people who experience self–other overlap with a person experience stronger social bonds (Galinsky, Ku, & Wang, 2005) are ultimately able to understand the other person in a way that is more complex and nuanced (Waugh & Fredrickson, 2006). Work on promoting empathy is closely tied with, and can be used to promote, forgiveness (McCullough, Root & Cohen, 2006).

Optimism

Optimism based activities ask people to think about the future in a positive way and create positive expectations. For instance, one such activity asks people in the laboratory to write about how they see themselves in the future in the best possible way for about 10–15 minutes (King, 2001). Although very easy to do, this activity can lead to significant improvements in subjective well-being, and was also connected to less illness (King, 2001). Another activity that is similar, but typically done outside the laboratory, called "Life Summary," was used by Seligman et al. (2006). In Life Summary, participants write a 1–2 page summary of their life as they would like it to be relayed via a biography, assuming they lived a long, fruitful life. They are then asked to examine how they spend their time in everyday life and to consider whether they might adjust their daily routine to more effectively pursue their ideal life.

As both of these activities are one-time, difficult to turn into an ongoing routine, Sheldon and Lyubomirsky (2006) created an optimism activity that is more repeatable. They asked participants to do a similar activity to those described above, writing out some ideas for what their best possible self might look like, and then they asked participants to spend two weeks after that thinking back on a regular basis to what they wrote. They found a robust benefit for this activity both immediately and at follow-up.

Strengths

The activities which fall under the "strengths" category ask people to recognize, and then either use or develop one's strengths (Parks & Biswas-Diener, 2013). A study by Seligman et al. (2005) instructed participants to identify and use their strengths, which resulted in increased happiness and decreased depressive symptoms. However, this approach has been questioned by more recent research, as the "identify and use" strategy raised concerns that this might create an idea of consistency and rigidness of strengths (Biswas-Diener, Kashdan, & Minhas, 2011). Indeed, research evidence suggests that concentrating on developing strengths rather than simply identifying them was found to be more enjoyable by the participants and resulted in them believing that strengths can be changed and developed (Haidt, 2002; Louis, 2011). When using strengths-based PPIs, which call for applying one's strengths, it is important to be careful and make sure that this application is appropriate (Schwartz & Hill, 2006). For instance, if one identifies honesty as a strength, there are other situations when being honest can hurt someone's feelings or stir up a conflict. It is important to also cultivate what Schwartz and Sharpe (2005) call "practical wisdom" – the ability to use one's strengths *when appropriate and beneficial*.

Meaning

Meaning-based PPIs are focused on understanding what brings meaning to one's life and often on actions connected to enhancing or achieving this meaning. Research suggests that having meaning in life is a consistent predictor for happiness and life satisfaction (Steger, Kashdan, & Oishi, 2008; Steger, Oishi, & Kashdan, 2009). There are several ways that meaning can be facilitated through PPIs. These types of PPI include such activities as reflecting on the meaning of one's profession (Grant, 2008), setting a meaningful goal and planning (Linley, Nielson, Gillett, & Biswas-Diener, 2010), or just simply reflecting on one's life in writing (McAdams, Reynolds, Lewis, Patten, & Bowman, 2001). Meaning-making – specifically, writing about the positive events that have come out of a negative event – can also be an important way to cope with negative life events (Folkman & Moskowitz, 2000).

Methods of Disseminating PPIs

The easiness and accessibility of PPIs makes them a very useful tool for therapists and individual happiness seekers alike. Although research suggests that the best results from PPIs were reached in a therapeutic setting (perhaps due to members of clinical populations having greater room to grow due to their distress), self-administered PPIs were still effective in improving well-being (Sin & Lyubomirsky, 2009). Both of these modalities of dissemination will be discussed in turn, but first, below, we will cover more self-administered interventions designed for nonclinical populations, and in the section after, we will discuss clinical uses of PPIs.

Book-based Interventions

One of the most simple and inexpensive methods of self-administered psychological help are self-help books. A substantive self-help book that contains specific techniques for improving one's psychological state has great potential to help the well-being of an entire population. A study by Parks and Szanto (2013) examined the effectiveness of two such self-help books in increasing the well-being of incoming college freshmen. Students were randomly assigned to receive either *The How of Happiness* book by Sonja Lyubomirsky (2008), a positive psychology-based book which describes many of the PPIs discussed above, or *Control Your Depression*, a book based on cognitive-behavioral therapy principles (Lewinsohn, Muñoz, Youngren, & Zeiss, 1992). Both were shown to be effective at decreasing depressive symptoms. However, the positive psychology self-book led to higher levels of life satisfaction, and students reported that they found activities from that book more enjoyable and meaningful. These findings suggest that a book-based mode of dissemination has potential for delivering PPIs to the general public.

Classrooms

Another way of making PPIs accessible is through a course. Recently, more and more college courses on positive psychology either have a component of self-help embedded within the course (Magyar-Moe, 2011) or even concentrate solely on self-help and well-being (Parks, 2013). Even though the main goal of such courses is usually to teach the theoretical prospective behind PPIs, they often have a practical component which teaches the students the skills that can be useful for future self-management of their well-being (Biswas-Diener & Patterson, 2011). An emerging type of widely-accessible free online courses (MOOCs) can be especially valuable for making PPIs more attainable for the general public, as these courses attract a more diverse group of people compared with traditional college courses.

Technology

Self-help books and college courses are effective, but often time-consuming, which could present a problem for a lot of people. Technology-based interventions – another popular and quickly growing method of PPI delivery – addresses this problem. Internet sites and smart phone applications are easy tools to deliver the interventions as well as track the progress they generate (Schueller & Parks, 2013). Some PPI-based websites concentrate just on one activity. For instance, *Gratitude Bucket* by Zach Prager and *Thnk4.org* by the Greater Good Foundation are both designed to promote gratitude. Some other websites, however, include a wide range of different PPIs. One such website – *Daily Challenge* – was also examined by researchers who accessed its efficacy. Cobb and Poirier (2014) found that people who used activities from the website showed more well-being than a control group. Empirical research also supports the effectiveness of cell-phone applications based on PPIs, as users of *Live Happy* iPhone app, based on the works of Sonja Lyubomirsky, experienced benefits in their happiness level (Parks et al., 2012). Other interventions such as *Happify* contain both web- and smartphone-based components, allowing users to choose whichever modality best suits them, or to switch as they like (Ben-Kiki, Leidner, & Parks, 2013).

PPIs in Clinical Practice

Thus far, the use of PPIs has mostly been described amongst healthy individuals in the general population. However, PPIs can also be a useful tool in a process of prevention of some disorders, as well as in helping those already diagnosed in a process of recovery. Well-being becomes of especially high importance and high concern for individuals suffering from mental disorders, and enhancing it can be an essential element on the road to recovery. A more detailed description of how PPIs have been used effectively in clinical settings can be found in Parks et al. (2015) – but an overview of some of those applications is presented below.

A recent study examined a role PPIs can play to help individuals diagnosed with schizophrenia (Meyer, Johnson, Parks, Iwanski, & Penn, 2012). They included PPIs as a part of a larger intervention – Positive Living – which was designed to make psychological improvements for those with schizophrenia. The program was heavily based on Parks' and Seligman's (2007) group PPI, with the addition of a mindfulness activity. The program was shown to be effective in improving well-being, clinical functioning, savoring, and hope. Most impressively, they also reported improvements in symptoms of schizophrenia after completing Positive Living. This improvement was seen right after the intervention, as well as three months later. Implementation of PPIs with more traditional methods for the treatment of schizophrenia (CBT, psychoeducation, social skills training, etc.) could enhance the progress to recovery for diagnosed individuals.

PPIs have been implemented in smoking cessation programs (Kahler et al., 2002). Kahler and colleagues (2002) designed a Positive Psychotherapy for Smoking Cessation (PPT-S), which was based on the original Positive Psychotherapy (PPT) protocol designed by Parks and Seligman (2007). The purpose of PPT-S is to enhance individuals levels of well-being before and during their attempt to quit smoking. Although the results of this study are only preliminary, they give an optimistic view regarding efficacy of PPT-S. The mood of the participants remained stable through the quitting stage, despite the fact that they reported an increase in depressive symptoms right before the intervention. Unfortunately, the absence of a control group in this study does not allow us to heavily rely on these results, but it is still a good start for future research in this area.

In addition to providing a useful adjunct to standard treatments in cases of clinical disorders, PPIs have implications when it comes to physical health related clinical practice as well. A study by Hausmann, Parks, Youk, and Kwoh (2014) found that PPIs lead to a long-term decrease in pain levels. This study was administered online and targeted the general public, and not those suffering from chronic pain. However, it led Hausmann and colleagues to develop a special program for veterans who suffer from chronic pain due to arthritis: Staying Positive with Arthritis. Although research regarding the efficacy of this program is still in progress, it looks promising as it was specifically tailored to suit veterans through feedback from the patients themselves and consideration of previous research regarding PPIs efficacy.

Interestingly, research suggests that use of PPIs can serve as preventive factor in developing mental disorders (Lyubomirsky & Layous, 2013; Layous, Chancellor, & Lyubomirsky, 2014). The combination of enhanced well-being and a number of strategies developed though PPIs could allow for mitigation of risk factors for mental disorders such as rumination and loneliness; moreover, PPIs help to offset other possible environmental triggers through the skills they develop (Layous, Chancellor, & Lyubomirsky, 2014).

Concerns and Limitations

Thus far we have explained the mechanism behind PPIs, and discussed all the main types and methods of delivery. Although PPIs have been shown to be effective and easy to administer, there are certain concerns and limitations as well. They range from concerns regarding motivation and personal fit to broader issues such as valuing happiness and cultural differences. Here we will acknowledge all these caveats in greater detail.

Motivation and Person–Activity Fit

When it comes to self-administered interventions, motivation is always a great concern. Certain events or feelings might push people into downloading a mobile application, buying a book, or signing up for class. However, over time the motivation that got them there in the first place might drop. Indeed, research shows that only a small percentage of those who have downloaded the *Live Happy* app used it enough times for any conclusion to be made regarding improvements in their mood (Parks et al., 2012). Other research also suggests that an immense number of those who sign up for Internet-based interventions drop out without even going through the first assignment (Christensen, Griffiths, Groves, & Korten, 2006). Therefore, if researchers want the interventions they develop to be used by consumers or clients, they must pay attention not only to the quality of the intervention's content, but to the extent to which the intervention will keep people engaged.

One key approach to improving user adherence and motivation is a consideration of *person–activity fit*. In other words: not all PPI-users are the same and different types of user might need different types of approach to benefit optimally. The significance of this issue has been emphasized by many researchers. For instance, Parks et al. (2012) found that happiness seekers (people who actively try to find ways to make them happier) can be divided into two distinct subgroups: one included people who are already fairly happy, and another comprised people whose well-being levels were close to the level of clinically depressed. Lumping everyone together and assuming that all users or clients have uniform needs is not an ideal approach.

Other research also showed that personality differences (Sergeant & Mongrain, 2011; Senf & Liau, 2013), personal preference for activity (Schueller, 2010), and level of motivation (Lyubomirsky et al., 2011) are all very important to the efficacy of PPIs. Moreover, a number of other factors such as culture, age, and opinion about PPIs were recognized as possible moderators of PPI effectiveness (Layous & Lyubomirsky, 2014). It is worthwhile, therefore, to pay careful attention to person–activity fit and to look at whether a given intervention is appropriate for the particular individual considering it.

Expectations and Attitudes

The expectations a person has about completing a PPI can greatly impact on the extent to which they benefit from it. For example, a study by Sheldon and colleagues (2010) found that the extent to which a person values happiness is an important factor in succeeding in becoming happier. They found that people who had more positive view about happiness showed more improvement, and were more likely to sustain the obtained improvement over time. The study suggests that two key components are important for successful intervention: willingness or a desire to become happier, and an appropriate tool to reach that goal. Similarly, Parks and Szanto (2013) found that those who valued happiness tried harder and, as a result, benefited more from a PPI.

But is valuing happiness always good? A recent study raised a new concern for happiness research and the role attitudes toward happiness plays in it. Mauss, Tamir, Anderson, and Savino (2011) found a surprising paradox: people who valued happiness more actually showed less happiness and more depressive symptoms. However, subsequent studies showed that it is actually very important how happiness valuation is measured. While Mauss and colleagues' (2011) scale is worded in a very extreme language, there are other scales which set a more neutral tone. It has been found that the paradoxical effect is not present at all when a different measure of attitudes toward happiness is used (Titova & Parks, 2014). Participants who valued happiness highly on a different scale introduced by Ferguson and Sheldon (2013) showed more positive emotions after a positive mood induction task, than participants who valued happiness less. On the other hand, a completely opposite trend was observed for participants who showed high valuation of happiness according to Mauss and colleagues' (2011) scale. Even more interestingly, even using Mauss' scale, some pilot data in our laboratory has found that valuing happiness is, indeed, problematic if a person is given an ineffective way to become happier. The person becomes frustrated at their inability to achieve their goal and reports more negative affect. However, a person who values happiness and is given an effective way to pursue it benefits *more* than someone who does not value happiness. So context is relevant – valuing happiness is a problem if one does not know how to become happier. If one *does* know how to become happier, valuing happiness is an asset.

Cultural Considerations

Cultural differences play a very important role when it comes to happiness. Understanding of what it is to be happy, for example, varies greatly across cultures. Lu and Gilmour (2004) compared how people in the United States and people in China defined this concept. While Chinese participants found happiness to be more about connecting with other people and the environment, Americans saw it more as the achievement of goals and personal growth. Moreover, hedonistic and material values were highly important for people in the United States in their view of happiness, while people from China did not find them important. Another study looked at beliefs about the controllability of happiness. Oishi, Grahan, Kesebir, and Galinha (2013) found that in many countries happiness is attributed to luck or faith and overall has an accidental characteristic, while in the United States the belief is more common that happiness is within an individual's control. Other research has also pointed out that some cultures exhibit a "fear of happiness" or a certain amount of hesitation toward open pursuit of happiness, for fear that welcoming happiness intentionally might later cause a retaliatory negative event to occur and balance things out (Lyubomirsky, 2000; Joshanloo, 2013).

Having different definitions of well-being is connected to methods of achieving happiness, which in turn has implications when trying to design and administer an effective PPI. To examine cross-cultural differences in the level of happiness in response to positive psychology interventions,

Boehm, Lyubomirsky, and Sheldon (2011) compared two distinct cultural groups: Asian Americans and Anglo-Americans. They found that overall Anglo-Americans had significantly more improvement than Asian Americans regardless of what kind of activity were they assigned to, although no difference was observed in control groups. However, Asian Americans were more susceptible to gratitude rather than optimism activity. These results suggest that cultural mindset plays an important role in the effectiveness of strategies designed to improve happiness.

In a different study, Layous, Lee, Choi, and Lyubomirsky (2013) continued to examine cross-cultural differences in the level of happiness in response to PPIs. However, this time they compared Americans and South Koreans. The activities Layous and colleagues (2013) used were gratitude and kindness. The results indicated that overall Americans showed significantly more improvement than South Koreans from both activities, which could be attributed to the higher level of effort reported by American participants. Both groups showed improvement in their level of well-being from the kindness activity, while Americans benefited more from the gratitude activity than did South Koreans. This difference could be explained by the fact that in Asian cultures positive feelings of gratitude can be accompanied with negative feelings such as guilt (Layous et al., 2013). Moreover, cultural background was also noted to be very important in connection with the effectiveness of PPIs in the meta-analysis of 51 different studies (Sin & Lyubomirsky, 2009).

Most of the research on PPIs that has been done so far has taken place in Western countries and did not assess cultural differences. However, those few studies that did consider these differences, along with other theoretical and empirical knowledge about cultural differences connected to happiness, suggest that while some PPIs work equally well universally, some only suitable for Western cultures.

Closing Remarks

In this chapter, we have defined a PPI, described the different types of PPI, and provided an overview of the modalities by which PPIs have been disseminated, both to the general public and to clinical populations. We have also discussed some key caveats to keep in mind when using PPIs – namely, the person's beliefs about happiness, and their cultural background.

The amount of attention we dedicated to the caveats conveys, we hope, the importance of thinking critically when using PPIs, or any intervention approach, in clinical or coaching practice. Yes, PPIs are appealing to many clients, and, yes, meta-analyses have found them useful on the whole. However, there are subpopulations – certain cultural groups, certain personality types, and so on – for whom certain PPIs are not useful, or may even be harmful. One should not be applying PPIs universally to every person who walks in the door without consideration of who that person is and whether they would benefit. PPIs are useful, but like any technique, have their time and their place.

References

Aknin, L. B., Dunn, E. W., & Norton, M. I. (2012). Happiness runs in a circular motion: Evidence for a positive feedback loop between prosocial spending and happiness. *Journal of Happiness Studies, 13*, 347–355.

Biswas-Diener, R., Kashdan, T.B., & Minhas, G. (2011). A dynamic approach to psychological strength development and intervention. *Journal of Positive Psychology, 6*, 106–118.

Biswas-Diener, R. & Patterson, L. (2011). An experiential approach to teaching positive psychology to undergraduates. *Journal of Positive Psychology, 6*, 477–481.

Boehm, J. K., Lyubomirsky, S., & Sheldon, K. M. (2011). A longitudinal experimental study comparing the effectiveness of happiness-enhancing strategies in Anglo-Americans and Asian Americans. *Cognition & Emotion, 25,* 1263–1272.

Bolier, L., Haverman, M., Westerhof, G. J., Riper, H., Smit, F. & Bohlmeijer, E. (2013). Positive psychology interventions: A meta-analysis of randomized controlled studies. *BMC Public Health, 13,* 119.

Boyce, C. J. & Wood, A.M. (2011). Personality prior to disability determines adaptation: Agreeable individuals recover lost life satisfaction faster and more completely. *Psychological Science, 2011,* 1397–1402.

Bryant, F. B. (2003). Savoring Beliefs Inventory (SBI): A scale for measuring beliefs about savoring. *Journal of Mental Health, 12,* 175–196.

Bryant, F. B., Smart, C. M., & King, S. P. (2005). Using the past to enhance the present: Boosting happiness through positive reminiscence. *Journal of Happiness Studies, 6,* 227–260.

Bryant, F. B. & Veroff, J. (2007). *Savoring: A new model of positive experience.* Mahwah, NJ: Lawrence Erlbaum.

Christensen, H., Griffiths, K., Groves, C., & Korten, A. (2006). Free range users and one hit wonders: Community users of an Internet-based cognitive behaviour therapy program. *Australian and New Zealand Journal of Psychiatry, 40,* 59–62.

Cobb, N. K. & Poirier, J. (2014). Effectiveness of a multimodal online well-being intervention: A randomized controlled trial. *American Journal of Preventive Medicine, 46*(1), 41–48.

Davis, M. H., Soderlund, T., Cole, J., Gadol, E., Kute, M., Myers, M., & Weihing, J. (2004). Cognitions associated with attempts to empathize: how do we imagine the perspective of another? *Personality and Social Psychology Bulletin, 30,* 1625–1635.

Diener, E. & Seligman, M. E. (2002). Very happy people. *Psychological Science, 13,* 81–84.

Dunn, E. W., Aknin, L. B., & Norton, M. I. (2008). Spending money on others promotes happiness. *Science, 319,* 1687–1688.

Emmons, R. A. & McCullough, M. E. (2003). Counting blessings versus burdens: An experimental investigation of gratitude and subjective well-being in daily life. *Journal of Personality and Social Psychology, 84,* 377–389.

Ferguson, Y. L. & Sheldon, K. M. (2013): Trying to be happier really can work: Two experimental studies. *Journal of Positive Psychology, 8*(1), 23–33.

Folkman, S. & Moskowitz, J. T. (2000). Positive affect and the other side of coping. *American Psychologist, 55,* 647–654.

Fredrickson, B. L., Cohn, M. A., Coffey, K. A., Pek, J., & Finkel, S. M. (2008). Open hearts build lives: Positive emotions, induced through loving-kindness meditation, build consequential personal resources. *Journal of Personality and Social Psychology, 95,* 1045–1062.

Gable, S. L., Reis, H. T., Impett, E. A., & Asher, E. R. (2004). What do you do when things go right? The intrapersonal and interpersonal benefits of sharing positive events. *Journal of Personality and Social Psychology, 87*(2), 228–245.

Galinsky, A. D., Ku, G., & Wang, C.S. (2005). Perspective-taking and self-other overlap: Fostering social bonds and facilitating social coordination. *Group Processes Intergroup Relations, 8,* 109–124.

Geraghty, A. W. A., Wood, A. M., & Hyland, M. E. (2010a). Dissociating the facets of hope: Agency and pathways predict dropout from unguided self-help therapy in opposite directions. *Journal of Research in Personality, 44,* 155–158.

Geraghty, A. W. A., Wood, A. M., & Hyland, M. E. (2010b). Attrition from self-directed interventions: Investigating the relationship between psychological predictors, intervention content and dropout from a body dissatisfaction intervention. *Social Science & Medicine, 71,* 30–37.

Grant, A. M. (2008). The significance of task significance: Job performance effects, relational mechanisms, and boundary conditions. *Journal of Applied Psychology, 93*(1), 108–124.

Haidt, J. (2002). It's more fun to work on strengths than weaknesses (but it may not be better for you). Manuscript available at: http://people.virginia.edu/~jdh6n/strengths_analysis.doc.

Hausmann, L. M., Parks, A., Youk, A. O., & Kwoh, C. K. (2014). Reduction of bodily pain in response to an online positive activities intervention. *Journal of Pain, 15*(5), 560–567.

Hodges, S. D., Clark, B., & Myers, M. W. (2011). Better living through perspective taking. In: R. Biswas-Diener (Ed.), *Positive psychology as a mechanism for social change* (pp. 193–218). Dordrecht: Springer.

Howell, R. T., Pchelin, P., & Iyer, R. (2012). The preference for experiences over possessions: Measurement and construct validation of the Experiential Buying Tendency Scale. *Journal of Positive Psychology, 7,* 57–71.

Joshanloo, M. (2013). The influence of fear of happiness beliefs on responses to the satisfaction with life scale. *Personality and Individual Differences, 54*(5), 647–651.

Kabat-Zinn, J. (2009). *Full catastrophe living: Using the wisdom of your body and mind to face stress, pain, and illness.* New York: Random House.

Kahler, C. W., Brown, R. A., Ramsey, S. E., Niaura, R., Abrams, D. B., Goldstein, M. G., Miller, I. W., et al. (2002). Negative mood, depressive symptoms, and major depression after smoking cessation treatment in smokers with a history of major depressive disorder. *Journal of Abnormal Psychology, 111*(4), 670–675.

King, L. A. (2001). The health benefits of writing about life goals. *Personality and Social Psychology Bulletin, 27,* 798–807.

Kurtz, J. L. (2012). *Seeing through new eyes: An experimental investigation of the benefits of photography.* Unpublished manuscript.

Layous, K., Chancellor, J., & Lyubomirsky, S. (2014). Positive activities as protective factors against mental health conditions. *Journal of Abnormal Psychology, 123,* 3–12.

Layous, K., Lee, H., Choi, I., & Lyubomirsky, S. (2013). Culture matters when designing a successful happiness-increasing activity: A comparison of the United States and South Korea. *Journal of Cross-Cultural Psychology, 44*(8), 1294–1303.

Layous, K. & Lyubomirsky, S. (2014). The how, what, when, and why of happiness: Mechanisms underlying the success of positive interventions. In: J. Gruber & J. Moskowitz's (Eds.), *Positive emotion: Integrating the light sides and dark sides* (pp. 473–495). New York: Oxford University Press.

Lewinsohn, P. M., Muñoz, R. F., Youngren, M. A., & Zeiss, A. M. (1992). *Control your depression.* New York: Fireside.

Linley, P. A., Nielsen, K. M., Gillett, R., & Biswas-Diener, R. (2010). Using signature strengths in pursuit of goals: Effects on goal progress, need satisfaction, and well-being, and implications for coaching psychologists. *International Coaching Psychology Review, 5,* 6–15.

Louis, M. (2011). Strengths interventions in higher education: Effects on implicit self-theory. *Journal of Positive Psychology, 6,* 204–215.

Lu, L. & Gilmour, R. (2004). Culture and conceptions of happiness: Individual oriented and social oriented SWB. *Journal of Happiness Studies, 5*(3), 269–291.

Lyubomirsky, S. (2000). In the pursuit of happiness: Comparing the US and Russia. Paper presented at the Annual Meeting of the Society of Experimental Social Psychology, Atlanta, Georgia.

Lyubomirsky, S. (2008). *The how of happiness: A scientific approach to getting the life you want.* New York: Penguin Press.

Lyubomirsky, S., Dickerhoof, R., Boehm, J. K., & Sheldon, K. M. (2011). Becoming happier takes both a will and a proper way: An experimental longitudinal intervention to boost well-being. *Emotion, 11,* 391–402.

Lyubomirsky, S. & Layous, K. (2013). How do simple positive activities increase well-being? *Current Directions in Psychological Science, 22,* 57–62.

Lyubomirsky, S., Sheldon, K. M., & Schkade, D. (2005). Pursuing happiness: The architecture of sustainable change. *Review of General Psychology, 9,* 111–131.

Lyubomirsky, S., Tkach, C., & Sheldon, K. M. (2004). *Pursuing sustained happiness through random act of kindness and counting one's blessings: Tests of two six-week interventions.* Unpublished raw data.

Magyar-Moe, J. L. (2011). Incorporating positive psychology content and applications into various positive psychology courses. *Journal of Positive Psychology, 6,* 451–456.

Mauss, I. B., Tamir, M., Anderson, C. L., & Savino, N. S. (2011). Can seeking happiness make people unhappy? Paradoxical effects of valuing happiness. *Emotion, 11,* 807–815.

McAdams, D. P., Reynolds, J., Lewis, M., Patten, A. H., & Bowman, P. J. (2001). When bad things turn good and good things turn bad: Sequences of redemption and contamination in life narrative and their relation to psychosocial adaptation in midlife adults and in students. *Personality and Social Psychology Bulletin, 27,* 474–485.

McCullough, M.E., Root, L. M., & Cohen, A. D. (2006). Writing about the benefits of an interpersonal transgression facilitates forgiveness. *Journal of Consulting and Clinical Psychology, 74,* 887–897.

Meyer, P., Johnson, D., Parks, A. C., Iwanski, C., & Penn, D. L. (2012). Positive living: A pilot study of group positive psychotherapy for people with severe mental illness. *Journal of Positive Psychology, 7,* 239–248.

Myers, D. G. & Diener, E. (1995). Who is happy? *Psychological Science, 6*, 10–19.

Oishi, S., Graham, J., Kesebir, S., & Galinha, I. (2013). Concepts of happiness across time and cultures. *Personality and Social Psychology Bulletin, 39*(5), 559–577.

Parks, A. C. (2013). *Positive psychology in higher education.* New York: Routledge.

Parks, A. C. & Biswas-Diener, R. (2013). Positive interventions: Past, present and future. In: T. Kashdan & J. Ciarrochi (Eds.), *Mindfulness, acceptance, and positive psychology: The seven foundations of well-being* (pp. 140–165). Oakland, CA: Context Press.

Parks, A. C., Della Porta, M. D., Pierce, R. S., Zilca, R., & Lyubomirsky, S. (2012). Pursuing happiness in everyday life: The characteristics and behaviors of online happiness seekers. *Emotion, 12*, 1222–1234.

Parks, A. C., Kleiman, E. M., Kashdan, T. B., Hausmann, L. R., Meyer, P., Day, A. M., Spillane, N. S., & Kahler, C. W. (2015). Positive psychotherapeutic and behavioral interventions. In: D. V. Jeste & B. W. Palmer (Eds.), *Positive psychiatry: A clinical handbook.* Arlington, VA: American Psychiatric Press.

Parks, A. C. & Layous K. (in press). Positive psychological interventions. In: J. C. Norcross, G. R. VandenBos, & D. K. Freedheim (Eds.), *APA handbook of clinical psychology, vol. III: Applications and methods.* Washington, DC: American Psychological Association.

Parks, A. C. & Seligman, M. E. P. (2007). 8-week group positive psychotherapy (PPT) manual. Unpublished manual, available by request.

Parks, A. C. & Szanto, R. K (2013). Assessing the efficacy and effectiveness of a positive psychology-based self-help book. *Terapia PsicolÓgica, 31*, 141–149.

Peterson, C. (2006). *A primer in positive psychology.* New York: Oxford University Press.

Seligman, M. E. P. (2002). *Authentic happiness: Using the new positive psychology to realize your potential for lasting fulfillment.* New York: Free Press.

Seligman, M. E., Rashid, T., & Parks, A. C. (2006). Positive psychotherapy. *American Psychologist, 61*, 774–788.

Seligman, M. E. P., Steen, T. A., Park, N., & Peterson, C. (2005). Positive psychology progress: Empirical validation of interventions. *American Psychologist, 60*, 410–421.

Senf, K. & Liau, A. K. (2013). The effects of positive interventions on happiness and depressive symptoms, with an examination of personality as a moderator. *Journal of Happiness Studies, 14*, 591–612.

Sergeant, S. & Mongrain, M. (2011). Are positive psychology exercises helpful for people with depressive personality styles? *The Journal of Positive Psychology, 6*, 260–272.

Sheldon, K. M., Abad, N., Ferguson, Y., Gunz, A., Houser-Marko, L., Nichols, C. P., & Lyubomirsky, S. (2010). Persistent pursuit of need-satisfying goals leads to increased happiness: A 6-month experimental longitudinal study. *Motivation and Emotion, 34*(1), 39–48.

Sheldon, K. M. & Lyubomirsky, S. (2006). Achieving sustainable gains in happiness: Change your actions, not your circumstances. *Journal of Happiness Studies, 7*, 55–86.

Sheldon, K. M. & Lyubomirsky, S. (2012). The challenge of staying happier: Testing the Happiness Adaptation Prevention model. *Personality and Social Psychology Bulletin, 38*, 670–680.

Schueller, S. M. (2010). Preferences for positive psychology exercises. *Journal of Positive Psychology, 5*, 192–203.

Schueller, S. M. (2012). Personality fit and positive interventions: Extraverted and introverted individuals benefit from different happiness increasing strategies. *Psychology, 3*, 1166–1173.

Schueller, S. M. & Parks, A. C. (2014). The science of self-help: Translating positive psychology research into individual happiness. *European Psychologist, 19*, 145–155.

Schwartz, B. & Hill, K. E. (2006). Practical wisdom: Aristotle meets positive psychology. *Journal of Happiness Studies, 7*, 377–395.

Schwartz, B. & Sharpe, K.E. (2005). Practical wisdom: Aristotle meets positive psychology. *Journal of Happiness Studies, 1*, 1–19.

Sin, N. L. & Lyubomirsky, S. (2009). Enhancing well-being and alleviating depressive symptoms with positive psychology interventions: A practice-friendly meta-analysis. *Journal of Clinical Psychology: In Session, 65*, 467–487.

Steger, M. F., Kashdan, T. B., & Oishi, S. (2008). Being good by doing good: Daily eudaimonic activity and well-being. *Journal of Research in Personality, 42*, 22–42.

Steger, M. F., Oishi, S., & Kashdan, T. B. (2009). Meaning in life across the life span: Levels and correlates of meaning in life from emerging adulthood to older adulthood. *Journal of Positive Psychology, 4*, 43–52.

Titova, L. & Parks, A. C. (2014). *Valuing happiness: A hindrance or asset to the pursuit of happiness?* Poster presented at the 122nd Annual Convention of the American Psychological Association, August.

Waugh, C. E. & Fredrickson, B.L. (2006). Nice to know you: Positive emotions, self-other overlap, and complex understanding in the formation of a new relationship. *Journal of Positive Psychology*, *1*, 93–106.

Wood, A. M., Froh, J. J., & Geraghty, A. W. (2010). Gratitude and well-being: A review and theoretical integration. *Clinical Psychology Review*, *30*, 890–905.

22

Positive Psychotherapy
Clinical Application of Positive Psychology
Tayyab Rashid and Ryan N. Howes

Introduction

Hundreds, if not thousands of forms of psychotherapies are available to alleviate symptoms and psychological stress. Clinicians can select from empirically updated treatments to anecdotally informed approaches, ways to modify behavior to methods that train the mind to react alternatively. Clients, in addition to these brands, read self-help books, attend retreats, enroll in courses, and utilize alternative health remedies. The focus in these interventions is nearly always on symptoms remittance and habit remediation. This focus is understandable as clients seeking psychotherapy experience and report significantly more negatives than positives (Schwartz, Ward, Monterosso, Lyubomirsky, White, & Lehman, 2002a; Wong, 2012). They enter therapy feeling emotionally fragile, perceiving themselves to be habitually flawed, and mentally fragmented. For clients, psychotherapy is a place where bottled emotions are vented, where troubled relationships are discerned, and dark secrets are disclosed – all in an effort to build or restore tattered self-concept – in the presence of an empathic therapist with expertise to ameliorate the negatives. Therapists, on the other hand, dispense the bulk of their efforts and expertise in making clients less depressed and less anxious by uncovering childhood traumas, untwisting faulty thinking, or adjusting dysfunctional relationships. Clients and psychotherapists focus almost exclusively on negatives for several reasons. First, quintessentially the primary function of psychotherapy is to discern and deal with negatives. Second, irrespective of being a client or psychotherapist, the human mind defaults toward negativity such that it responds more strongly to negatives than to positives (Rozin & Royzman, 2001; Williams, Gatt, Schofield, Olivieri, Peduto, & Gordon, 2009). Negative impressions and stereotypes are quicker to form and harder to undo (Baumeister, Bratslavsky, Finkenauer, & Vohs, 2001). Negative memories stay with us for days, months, or even years, while positive memories tend to be transient (Lyubomirsky, Caldwell, & Nolen-Hoeksema, 1998). Third, focusing on negatives can also be functional and not always counterproductive. People may be motivated to feel negative emotions because they may be more adaptive than positive emotions (Young, Kashdan, & Macatee, 2014). Sadness may inform individuals about the importance of objects, relations, or abilities lost; anxiety may signal impending threat and anger, especially against an injustice or abuse, and may encourage one to take appropriate action. The benefits and pitfalls of negative emotions depend on the context.

Without dismissing, minimizing, or hastily replacing negatives with positives, positive psychotherapy (PPT) dispenses equal effort on positives, because, despite the prevalence, potency, and pull of negatives, most clients seek therapy in order to be less sad, anxious, angry, or ambivalent. They want to be happy, kind, courageous, connected, interested, engaged, optimistic, and creative. Without articulating it explicitly, clients want lives that are engaged and purposeful.

The Wiley Handbook of Positive Clinical Psychology, First Edition. Edited by Alex M. Wood and Judith Johnson.
© 2016 John Wiley & Sons, Ltd. Published 2016 by John Wiley & Sons, Ltd.

It is perhaps not surprising that clients are often heard saying, "Doc, I want to be happy." They are heard, but their plea is not heeded. PPT addresses their desire beyond its rhetoric. It can be defined as a treatment approach that systematically amplifies the positive resources of clients; specifically positive emotions, character strengths, meaning, positive relationships, and intrinsically motivated accomplishments with the aim of undoing psychopathology. Despite the word positive in its title, PPT is not only about positives, nor does it suggest that other treatments are negative. PPT is not aimed at replacing or competing with other well-established treatments. It is a treatment approach based on the premise that psychotherapy presents a unique opportunity for both accentuating the positive aspects of human experience as well as ameliorating the negatives. Focusing exclusively on negatives or positives might be an easier or simpler approach, but the therapeutic challenge is to understand the complexity of clients' experiences, including both negative and positive experiences. Psychotherapy has done well in assessing and intervening with psychopathology (Leykin & DeRubeis, 2009; Castonguay, 2013). Perhaps the next frontier for psychotherapy is to discern clients' distress, deficits, dysfunctions, and disorders in tandem with their assets, abilities, strengths, and skills. This integration, however complex and challenging, will likely open additional therapeutic alleys and avenues that psychotherapists have not yet navigated. PPT is an attempt to translate this integration from abstraction into more concrete therapeutic applications. For example, it engages clients in discussions about, say, an injustice done whilst also getting them to focus on recent acts of kindness. Similarly, along with insults, hubris, and hate, experiences of genuine praise, humility, and harmony are also deliberately elicited. Pain associated with trauma is empathetically attended to, whilst also exploring the potential for growth. The reasons for holding onto grudges are explored, but at the same time a sense of relief is also explored that comes from forgiving. Situations and stressors that produce anxiety are identified, but sources that enable clients to sooth and unwind are also discussed.

It is important to expand the horizons of psychotherapy, especially when its usage is on the decline and psychotropic medications have become the most prescribed class of all medications (Olfson & Marcus, 2010), together with an easily accessible plethora of New-Age and self-help remedies (e.g., books, CDs, websites, artifacts, diets). In the United States alone, these remedies, almost always ineffective beyond placebo, cost an estimated $12 billion in self-help books (Salerno, 2006; Valiunas, 2010). Psychotherapy, on the other hand, has a solid scientific foundation that shows that it is effective and, in most cases, it works equally well as medication or better (Leykin & DeRubeis, 2009; Castonguay, 2013). There is an acute need to make the therapeutic process attractive and accessible. Many do not seek treatment due to stigma (Corrigan, 2004). For the cyber-savvy, urban and culturally diverse millennial generation, psychotherapy needs to be innovative, destigmatizing, focused, short-term, and compatible with mobile and online interfaces. Responding to mind–body integration (Smith & Aaker, 2013), it is connected to multiple outcomes such as symptom remittance, increase in well-being, better physical health, healthier relationships, and civic engagement.

Assumptions

PPT has three assumptions regarding the nature, cause, course, and treatment of specific behavioral patterns. Consistent with the humanistic psychology, PPT's first assumption is that: psychopathology ensues when clients' inherent capacities for growth, fulfillment, and wellbeing are thwarted by prolonged psychosocial distress. Taking genetic influence into account, wellbeing and psychopathology are not entirely endogenous processes, rather, they are a complex interplay between clients' proclivities and environmental factors. Whenever people become "damaged," this interplay becomes unsupportive, halting their growth. Psychotherapy offers as a unique opportunity to initiate or restore human potential through the transformative power of human connection. It presents an unparalleled human interaction in which an empathetic and nonjudgmental therapist is privy to clients' deepest emotions, desires, aspirations, thoughts, beliefs, actions, and habits. If this exclusive access is dispensed mostly to processing the negatives – something that comes naturally to us – and repairing the worst, the opportunity to nurture growth is either overshadowed or often completely lost. Remediation makes clients less vulnerable, whereas growth makes them resilient. Venting anger may be cathartic (and necessary at times), whereas mustering will and finding a way to forgive could be more therapeutic. Deliberate and careful exposure to feared stimuli may be necessary to treat anxiety and avoidance, whereas creating experiences that yield genuine positive emotions could take the edge off anxiety. Therefore, assessing and enhancing strengths toward growth is as important as assessing and alleviating symptoms to ward off psychological distress. Focusing on strengths enables clients to learn specific skills in order to be more spontaneous, playful, creative, and grateful, rather than learning skills of how not to be rigid, boring, conventional, and complaining. Emerging evidence shows that strengths can play a key role in growth even in dire life circumstances. In a multiyear longitudinal study of a national sample, people with a history of some lifetime adversity reported better mental health and well-being outcomes than not only those with a high history of adversity but also those with no history of adversity (Seery, Holman, & Silver, 2010). Likewise, the presence of character strengths such as optimism, appreciation of beauty, and spirituality facilitates recovery from depression (Huta & Hawley, 2008). Linley, Nielsen, Wood, Gillett, and Biswas-Diener (2010) found that individuals who use their strengths were more likely to achieve their goals. Individuals high on positive characteristics are buffered from the impact of negative life events and from psychopathology (Johnson, Wood, Gooding, Taylor, & Tarrier, 2011). Taken together, these lines of research suggest that both resilience to withstand psychological stressors and recovery to adaptively deal with these stressors – two cardinal features of psychological growth and maturity – may not be possible without positive characteristics.

Second, PPT considers that: positive emotions and strengths are authentic and as real as symptoms and disorders, and they are valued in their own right. Strengths are not defenses, nor are they Pollyannaish illusions or by-products of symptom relief that sit idle on the clinical peripheries. If resentment, deception, competition, jealousy, greed, worry, and stress are real, so too are attributes such as honesty, cooperation, contentment, gratitude, compassion, and serenity. Solid lines of research have demonstrated that the absence of symptoms is not the presence of mental well-being (Wood & Joseph, 2010; Keyes & Eduardo, 2012; Fink, 2014). Therefore, it is imperative, especially in therapeutic contexts, that strengths are not considered to be the outcome of an absence of negative traits. When a therapist actively works to restore and nurture courage, kindness, modesty, perseverance, and emotional and social intelligence, the lives of clients are likely to become more fulfilling. In contrast, when a counselor focuses on amelioration of symptoms, clients' lives may become less miserable. Additionally, a focus on symptoms is more likely to overlook strengths, with an underlying assumption that a cluster of symptoms explains a coherently constructed diagnosis. And in doing so, therapy inevitably becomes a process of exploring clients' deep and complicated clinical issues (Boisvert & Faust, 2002). Considering strengths as authentic and active therapeutic ingredients is fundamental in PPT, as distressed clients are likely to accept without many reservations whatever diagnosis a therapist formulates. Some clients may even define themselves through diagnostic labels, "*I am so OCD*) (Obsessive Compulsive Disorder); "*I am ADHD*" (Attention Deficit and Hyperactivity Disorder), "*He has all the features of Narcissist Personality Disorder*". Incorporating strengths along with symptoms expands the self-perception of clients and offers the therapist additional routes of intervening. Cheavens, Strunk, Lazarus, and Goldstein (2012) have recently shown that matching relative strengths of clients in psychotherapy, compared with their weaknesses, leads to a superior outcome. Likewise, Flückiger and Grosse Holtforth (2008) found that focusing on a client's strengths before each therapy session improved therapy outcome. These lines of research demonstrate that strengths are real and have therapeutic potential.

The third, and final, assumption of PPT is that: effective therapeutic relationships can be built on the exploration and analysis of positive personal characteristics and experiences (e.g., positive emotions, strengths, and virtues). This is in contrast to the traditional approach in which the psychotherapist analyzes and explains the constellation of symptoms to the client in the form of a diagnosis. This role of the psychotherapist is further reinforced by the unsophisticated portrayal of psychotherapy in the popular media, which shows the therapeutic relationship as quintessentially marked by talking about troubles, disclosing bottled-up emotions, and recovering lost or tattered self-esteem with the help of a therapist. Clients begin psychotherapy socialized with an underlying assumption that they are somehow deeply flawed or damaged, with the only way "out" being protracted and painful discussions of one's childhood traumas, dissatisfactions, unmet needs, and so forth. These stereotypes are further reinforced when the therapeutic relationship is moderated with empathy, but focused around description and discussion of troubles and weaknesses. The reinforcement of stereotypes may increase the dispositional negative bias among therapists, who have pre-existing knowledge of psychiatric labels and conditions to draw negative inferences about the client's support systems and subsequently overvalue the therapeutic relationship (Boisvert & Faust, 2002). Clients already vulnerable due to psychiatric distress are more likely to adopt a "sick" role consistent with psychiatric labels. To some this role may offer a socially sanctioned relief, but to others it may bring feelings of shame, causing alienation, social distance, and feelings of rejection – all of which may contribute to premature termination of the therapeutic process. Yet a few clients may become fixed at the diagnosis and use diagnoses as an excuse to avoid personal responsibility within their volition. Listening, empathizing, and working actively with clients presenting with mental health issues, make psychotherapists vulnerable to burn-out (Jenaro, Flores, & Arais, 2007). Emerging evidence is challenging this traditional view of therapeutic relationships. Scheel, Davis, and Henderson (2012), through a qualitative study examining therapist's use of client strengths, found that focusing on strengths helped therapists in building trusting relationships and motivated clients by instilling hope. Another study, based on interviews with 26 Brazilian psychotherapists, found that that when therapists derive positive emotions from clients' input in the therapy, it can improve treatment by increasing in-session awareness, resourcefulness, and by cuing efforts to professional development. Furthermore, it enhances involvement in the relationship with the client by prompting compassion and closeness in the dyad (Vandenberghe & Silvestre, 2014).

PPT: From Theory to Application

PPT is based on Seligman's conceptualization of happiness and well-being (Seligman, 2002, 2011). Seligman operationalizes highly subjective and somewhat unwieldy concepts of happiness and well-being into five measurable, manageable, and malleable components: (1) positive emotion; (2) engagement; (3) relationships; (4) meaning; and (5) accomplishment. The first letter of each component adds to the mnemonic PERMA (Seligman, 2011) (Table 22.1). PERMA is a revised version of the authentic happiness theory, which included positive emotions, engagement and meaning (Csikzentmihalyi, 1990; Seligman, 2002). Research has shown that fulfillment in three elements is associated with lower rates of depression and higher life satisfaction (Vella-Brodrick, Park, Peterson, 2008; Sirgy & Wu, 2009; Headey, Schupp, Tucci, & Wagner, 2010; Lamont, 2011; Bertisch, Rath, Long, Ashman, & Rashid, 2014). PPT was originally based on these three elements, but its exercises also encapsulate relationships and accomplishment. The following section describes operationalization of PERMA in concrete PPT exercises and explains the process of conducting these exercises.

Table 22.1 PERMA: the theory of well-being.*

Elements	Description
Positive emotions	Experiencing positive emotions such as contentment, pride, serenity, hope, optimism, trust, confidence, gratitude.
Engagement	Immersing oneself deeply in activities which utilize one's strengths to experience an optimal state marked with razor-sharp concentration, optimal sate of experience with intense focus and intrinsic motivation to further develop.
Relationship	Having positive, secure, and trusting relationships.
Meaning	Belonging to and serving something with a sense of purpose and belief that it is larger than the self.
Accomplishment	Pursuing success, mastery and achievement for its own sake.

*Based on Seligman (2011).

PPT can be divided into initial, middle, and final phases, although the sequence of exercises can be custom tailored to address the presenting problems of clients. The initial phase focuses on establishing rapport and understanding clients' narratives to instill hope and enhance self-efficacy, and by letting clients hear themselves that they are more than the sum of their symptoms. Clients then assess their strengths from multiple resources and set realistic goals connected to their presenting problems as well as toward their well-being. The middle phase focuses on helping clients to apply strengths adaptively, to deal with grudges, crippling negative memories, or traumas. They are also invited to explore potential growth from their adversities. Clients also develop awareness about allocation of their attentional resources and learn skills to simplify their lives and to savor good experiences to improve their day-to-day well-being. The third and final phase of PPT exercises focuses primarily on restoring or fostering positive relationships – intimate and communal – and the search and pursuit of meaning and purpose. Throughout the course of therapy, clients keep a journal on a daily basis about good things, small or big, that happen during the course of the day to offset the impact of negativity-bent. Although PPT exercises may appear well planned in Table 22.2, flexibility in sequence and structure is recommended to accommodate the presenting concerns of clients.

From the onset, the therapist empathically listens to the presenting concerns of clients, to establish and maintain a trusting therapeutic relationship. At the same time, the counselor actively looks for opportunities to help clients identify and own their strengths. Attending to clients' presenting concerns, the counselor encourages clients to discuss events, experiences, and anecdotes which brought out the best of them, such as handling a challenge adaptively, learning constructively from mistakes or missteps, helping others, experiences that establish healthy relationships, accomplish something, despite the odds, everyday acts or habits of doing good things – big or small. The goal of this exercise, known as the Positive Introduction, is to gently expand clients' fractured, fragmented, fragile self-concept, and often perceived as deeply flawed mindset. This exercise is discussed in detail with parallels drawn to the current situation. Without giving any list or descriptors of strengths based on a model or taxonomy, counselors encourage clients to identify strengths illustrated in their Positive Introduction. This narrative, connected meaningfully with the current situation could become a dynamic narrative throughout the course of counseling – an internal positive anchor for clients to start the process of healing and growth. This deeply personal, uplifting, yet authentic, self-representation could enhance the self-efficacy of clients. Most, if not all, clients seek therapy after hearing from others, and themselves, of the many ways in which they are inadequate. Research has shown that recall of positive memories plays an important role in mood regulation (Joormann, Siemer, & Gotlib, 2007). Moreover, the recall of positive memories often generates positive emotions at the onset of the therapeutic process. Fitzpatrick and Stalikas (2008) suggest that facilitating a process of generating positive emotions, especially in the early phase of the therapeutic process, powerfully predicts therapeutic change.

Table 22.2 Session-by-session overview of positive psychotherapy (PPT).

Session & theme	Skill description	Skill practice
1. Orientation to PPT. Positive emotions	• Discussing ground rules, client–clinician role and responsibilities. • Discussing the practicing skills within and after the therapy session is discussed.	*Positive introduction*: client recalls, reflects, and writes a one-page Positive Introduction sharing a story with a beginning, middle, and an positive end, in concrete terms which called for the best in the client.
Gratitude (on going exercise) Positive emotions	• Honing gratitude skills from developing awareness acknowledging and appreciating everyday good events and experiences.	*Gratitude Journal*: client starts an ongoing journal to record three good things every night (big or small) and also write what made these happen.
2. Character strengths Engagement	• Understanding that character strengths are intrinsically valued attributes that can be used, refined, and developed toward self-development. • Understanding that exploring character strengths are as real and authentic as symptoms and weaknesses.	*Character Strengths*: Client compiles his or her client signature strengths profile by collecting information from multiple resources, including self-report, an online measure, a family member, and a friend.
3. Signature strengths action plan (*A Better Version of Me*) Accomplishment	• Integrating character strengths from various perspectives to determine signature strengths. • Learning and practicing skills of practical wisdom skills to use one's signature strengths in a balanced and adaptive way, especially in the context of one's presenting concerns.	*A Better Version of Me*: Client writes a self-development plan "A Better Version of Me" which uses his or her strengths adaptively through specific, measurable and achievable goals.
4. Open vs. closed memories Meaning	• Reflecting and exploring consequences of holding on to open (bitter) memories, including those that perpetuate his psychological distress.	*Positive Cognitive Appraisal*: After practicing relaxation, client writes bitter memories and learns a variety of ways to deal with them adaptively.
5. Forgiveness Positive relationships	• Discerning forgiveness as a process of deceasing negative resentment-based emotions, motivation and thoughts. • Learning how forgiveness can help to heal and empower. • Learning what forgiveness is and is not.	*Forgiveness*: Client learns about REACH – a process of forgiveness and/or writes a letter of forgiveness, but does not necessarily deliver it.
6. Gratitude Positive emotions and relationships	• Attuning awareness toward good. • Exploring gratitude as a process of enduring thankfulness. • Broadening the perspective and building other positive emotions.	*Gratitude Letter and Visit*: Client writes a letter of gratitude to someone whom the client never properly thanked; client polishes the draft and makes arrangements to deliver it in person.

Table 22.2 (*Continued*)

Session & theme	Skill description	Skill practice
Therapeutic progress Accomplishment	• Discussing motivation and therapeutic progress; elicit and offer feedback. • Discussing potential barriers and generate strength-based solutions.	Client completes the Forgiveness and Gratitude exercises. Client discusses his or her experience regarding *A Better Version of Me*.
7. Satisficing vs. maximizing Positive emotions and meaning	• Learning about maximizing, which entails getting the best possible option, decision, or product; while satisficing entails settling for the good enough in most domains of life. • Understanding the cost of maximizing.	*Satisficing*: Client explores in which domains of life he or she maximizes or satisfices. Client drafts a plan to increase satisficing.
8. Hope and optimism Positive emotions	• Developing the ability to see the best possible, yet realistic, side of most things. • Believing that challenges faced are temporary and one is capable of overcoming them. • Hoping that most of my goals are attainable.	*One Door Closed, One Door Opened*: Client reflects and writes of three doors that closed on him or her, but also three that opened.
9. Post-traumatic growth (PTG) Meaning	• Exploring that PTG can potentially occur even after the trauma. • Learning that PTG is often accompanied by a renewed philosophy of life, resolve to prevail, commitment to improve relationships, and prioritizing what really matters.	*Reflection & Writing about PTG*: Client can complete an optional exercise of transporting troubling and traumatic experiences onto a piece of paper with the assurance that writing is only for his or her own eyes and will be kept in a secure place. The exercise is completed after the client develops healthy coping skills and is not overwhelmed by current stressors.
10. Slowness & savoring Positive emotions and engagement	• Learning about the psychological hazards of being fast and about specific applied ways to slow down. • Developing awareness about savoring as an ability that represents the completeness of human experience. • Learning to attend mindfully the positive features of an event, experience or situation.	*Slow & Savor*: Client selects one slowness and one savoring technique that fits his or her personality and life circumstances.
11. Positive relationships Relationships	• Learning that connecting with others is not only a biological need, but motivates us to achieve and maintain well-being. • Learning about capitalization: a process of being seen, felt, and valued – the sum that is greater that its parts.	*Active-Constructive Responding (ACR)*: Client explores strengths of his or her significant other and also practices active-constructive responding.

(Continued)

Table 22.2   (*Continued*)

Session & theme	Skill description	Skill practice
12. Altruism meaning	• Learning about belonging to and serving something larger than oneself can be a potent antidote to psychological distress.	*Gift of Time*: Client plans to give the gift of time by doing something that also uses his or her signature strengths.
13. Positive legacy Meaning and accomplishment	• Integrating elements of well-being together and reflecting on group exercises and ways in which these have, and can be integrated. • Maintaining client therapeutic progress.	*Positive Legacy*: Client writes well, especially personal actions as to how he or she would like to be remembered, what would be the client's positive legacy? would be client positive legacy

A number of positive interventions often select a straightforward strategy of "identify and use your strengths." Participants complete an online measure, typically the Values in Action (VIA) (Peterson & Seligman, 2004; 240 items) and are then coached to use their top five or six strengths more often in their daily lives. In PPT, given that clients are part of complex interpersonal dynamics which contain both resources and risks, they are guided to complete a comprehensive process that incorporates multiple self-report measures, collateral reports from significant others identifying (not ranking) their signature strengths. For self-report, PPT uses a briefer, valid, and reliable 72-item self-report measure, Signature Strength Questionnaire (Rashid et al., 2013), which is based on the Classification of Strengths and Virtues (CSV) (Peterson & Seligman, 2004) model. To keep signature strengths front and center throughout the course of PPT and whenever appropriate, counselors are encouraged to gently nudge clients to share memories, experiences, real-life stories, anecdotes, accomplishments, and skills that illustrate development and use of their signature strengths (Rashid & Ostermann, 2009). Clients are encouraged to share if their signature strengths are an authentic representation of themselves, if they own them self-consciously, and if they feel invigorated while using them, as suggested by Seligman (2002). Collaboratively with therapists, clients set specific, attainable, and behavioral goals, which target their presenting concerns and adaptive use of their signature strengths. It is important that goals are personally meaningful as well as being adaptive in the interpersonal context of clients. For example, if the goal is that clients use their curiosity more, an optimal balance of curiosity through concrete actions is discussed so that it does not become intrusiveness (overuse) or boredom (underuse). Description of 24 character strengths and their under- and over-use is presented in Table 22.3. While setting goals, clients are also taught to use their strengths in a calibrated and flexible way that could adaptively meet situational challenges (Schwartz & Sharpe, 2006; Biswas-Diener, Kashdan, & Minhas, 2011). In doing so, specific actions or habits that may explain symptoms or troubles as either lack or excess of strengths are highlighted. Some illustrations include depressed mood, feeling hopeless or slow, as lack of zest and playfulness; worrying excessively, as lack of gratitude or inability to let go, indecision, as lack of determination; repetitive intrusive thoughts, as lack of mindfulness; narcissism, as lack of modesty; feeling inadequate, as lack of self-efficacy; or difficulty making decision, as excess of prudence. Furthermore, therapists also discuss that sometimes clients get into trouble for overuse of love and forgiveness (being taken for granted), underuse of self-regulation in a specific domain of life (indulgence), or fairness only in few situations or teamwork only with preferred groups (bias and discrimination). Throughout the course of therapy, clients and therapists monitor progress toward goals. Therapists are encouraged to provide and elicit feedback to

Table 22.3 Character strengths: definitions and usage (lacking/excess).*

	Character strengths	Description	Lacking/under use	Excess/over use
1	Appreciation of beauty and excellence	Being moved deeply by beauty in nature, in art (painting, music, theater, etc.), or in excellence in any field of life.	Oblivion	Snobbery
2	Authenticity and honesty	Not pretending to be someone one is not; coming across as a genuine and honest person.	Shallowness, phoniness	Righteousness
3	Bravery and valor	Overcoming fears to do what needs to be done; not give up in the face of hardship or a challenge.	Fears, easily scared	Foolhardiness, risk-taking
4	Creativity & originality	Thinking of new and better ways of doing things; not being content with doing things in conventional ways	Conformity	Eccentricity
5	Curiosity, interest in the world, and openness to experience	Being driven to explore things; asking questions; not tolerating ambiguity easily; being open to different experiences and activities.	Disinterest, boredom	Nosiness
6	Fairness, equity, and justice	Standing up for others when they are treated unfairly, bullied, or ridiculed; day-to-day actions show a sense of fairness.	Prejudice, partisanship	Detachment
7	Forgiveness and mercy	Forgiving easily those who offend; not holding grudges.	Mercilessness	Permissiveness
8	Gratitude	Expressing thankfulness for good things through words and actions; not take things for granted.	Entitlement	Ingratiation
9	Hope, optimism, and future-mindedness	Hoping and believing that more good things will happen than bad ones; recovering from setbacks and taking steps to overcome them.	Present orientation	Panglossism
10	Humor and playfulness.	Being playful, funny and using humor to connect with others.	Humorlessness	Buffoonery
11	Kindness and generosity	Doing kind deeds for others, often without asking; helping others regularly; being known as a kind person.	Indifference	Intrusiveness
12	Leadership	Organizing activities that include others; being someone others like to follow; being often chosen to lead by peers.	Compliance	Despotism
13	Capacity to love and be loved	Having warm and caring relationships with family and friends; showing genuine love and affection through actions regularly.	Isolation, detachment	Emotional promiscuity
14	Love of learning	Loving to learn many things, concepts, ideas, facts in school or on one's own.	Complacency, smugness	"Know-it-all"-ism

(Continued)

Table 22.3 (*Continued*)

	Character strengths	Description	Lacking/under use	Excess/over use
15	Modesty and humility	Not liking to be the center of attention; not acting as being special; admitting shortcomings readily; knowing what one can and cannot do.	Footless self-esteem	Self-depreciation
16	Open-mindedness and critical thinking	Thinking through and examining all sides before deciding; consulting with others; being flexible to change one's mind when necessary.	Unreflective	Cynicism, skepticism
17	Perseverance, diligence, and industry	Finishing most things; being able to refocus when distracted and completing the task without complaining; overcoming challenges to complete the task.	Slackness, laziness	Obsessiveness, fixation, pursuit of unattainable goals
18	Perspective (wisdom)	Putting things together to understand underlying meaning; settling disputes among friends; learning from mistakes.	Superficiality	Ivory tower, arcane, and pedantic thinking
19	Prudence, caution, and discretion	Being careful and cautious; avoid taking undue risks; not easily yielding to external pressures.	Recklessness	Prudishness, stuffiness
20	Religiousness and spirituality	Believing in God or a higher power; liking to participate in religious or spiritual practices, e.g., prayer, meditation, etc.	Anomie	Fanaticism
21	Self-regulation and self-control	Managing feelings and behavior well most of the time; following gladly rules and routines.	Self-indulgence	Inhibition
22	Social intelligence	Easily understanding others' feelings; managing oneself well in social situations; displaying excellent interpersonal skills.	Obtuseness, cluelessness	Psycho-babbling
23	Teamwork, citizenship, and loyalty	Relating well with teammates or group members; contributing to the success of the group.	Selfishness and rebelliousness	Mindless and automatic obedience
24	Zest, enthusiasm, and energy	Being energetic, cheerful and full of life; being liked by others to spend time with.	Passivity, restraint	Hyperactivity

*Rashid (2015) (reproduced with permission of Taylor & Francis).

make necessary changes, as well as continuously explore the nuances and subtleties of strengths, especially about encountering their challenges through strengths. Continuous feedback is shown to critical in therapy outcome (Lambert, 2010). Clients learn to identify their troubling emotions and memories by harnessing their social intelligence, toning down their grudge by accessing positive memories of specific situations, individuals or experiences, and instead of avoiding difficult situations, mustering up courage and self-regulation to face them. The following case scenarios are from clients seen by the author in individual or group therapy at a university counseling center. These depict nuanced, goal-directed use of strengths in overcoming presenting problems:

- A 20-something, Caucasian single client, in with presenting symptoms of emotional dysregulation and a history of unstable relationships, was initially highly skeptical of PPT exercises. In the group setting, the client remained quiet for the most part. While most group members shared parts of their positive introduction, the client was asked to share something related to resilience. The client sarcastically said that my introduction had included severe emotional abuse by my family, alcoholism, and the untreated mental illness of one of my parents. There was nothing good about it. I felt like I had committed a faux pas and could feel the weight of the client's distress. After an uncomfortable and long pause, another group member gently asked the client, "but you are here in this group, every week." Upon hearing this, a stream of tears flowed from client's eyes. "This is my only hope ... something I will never let go." Everyone became silent but was deeply moved.
- An undergraduate university student, despite a solid academic achievement record, expected the worst in the future and believed he would not achieve his goal of getting into a graduate school no matter how hard he tried. This not only precipitated symptoms of depression, but also experimentation with illicit drugs. Through individual PPT the client discovered that his signature strengths were love of learning, spirituality, authenticity, persistence, appreciation of beauty, and kindness. Over the course of the therapy, he started using his strengths, in particular, love of learning and kindness. He read a lot on the science of addictive behavior. After slow progress, he made a breakthrough when he was offered a volunteer position which helped young people to learn healthy coping strategies.
- The signature strength profile of a 20-something, single client from a conservative cultural background showed that kindness, authenticity, humility, social intelligence, and spirituality were core parts of her personality. An introvert by disposition, she presented with symptoms consistent with dysthymic depression disorder. Although PPT exercises helped her to improve her mood somewhat, her interpersonal challenges did not improve. Her family responded negatively when she started using strengths (e.g., expressing her emotions, social intelligence), asking for more gender-based equality (fairness), standing up for her rights (courage), and not being humble and kind when someone violated her right. Although the client felt empowered, at the same time some friction between her and her family increased. The client dealt with this friction with her kindness, but success was moderate.

These brief vignettes show ways in which clients can integrate their character strengths to deal adaptively with their challenges. Inherent bias toward negativity and symptomatic distress may keep these pathways obscure from clients. PPT brings them front and center and offers both therapists and clients multiple avenues to deal with problems. In doing so, PPT never dismisses, avoids, or trivializes negatives nor rushes to point out positives. The adaptive value of emotions depends on the context and situation. By that token, negative emotions in PPT are not inherently undesired. Sadness, anxiety, anger, embarrassment, shame, guilt, jealousy, and envy can be beneficial in social interactions and in maintaining or restoring balance in relationship. Furthermore, negative emotions are valued and expressed differently in different cultures (Parrott, 2014). For example, anger, especially against cruelty, discrimination and injustice, and wrongdoing is preferred over unconditional forgiveness; pessimism is useful if it activates problem-focused coping. Anxiety, if not debilitating, improves our performance and can sometimes prompt us to take precautionary measures (Kashdan & Rottenberg, 2010).

Clinical experience suggests most clients seek therapy to manage their stress as a means of managing the stressors associated with living in fast-paced and highly complex environments. PPT exercises such as *satisficing versus maximizing* (Schwartz et al., 2002b) and *savoring* (Bryant & Veroff, 2007) teach clients to deliberately slow down and enjoy small pleasures experientially (e.g., eating a meal, taking a shower, walking to work). When the experience is over, clients reflect and write down what they did, and how they felt differently compared with when they rushed through it. Similarly, throughout the course of therapy clients are asked to keep a gratitude journal to write three good things that happened to them, and why they happened, during the course of the each day. Most clients find this helpful to direct their attention deliberately to good experiences that are otherwise missed in the hustle and bustle of daily life. These favorable experiences are often embodied by others, fostering a sense of appreciation for others. In the gratitude letter and visit exercise, clients recall someone who has done something good, positive, and supportive for them, recently or remotely, but they have not been able to say thank you properly. Clients recall details and write a draft in the session. After several drafts, clients describe the specifics of their acts of kindness and its positive consequences. Clients are then encouraged to read the letter to the recipient in person or on the phone. When done in person, this exercise often generates powerful positive emotions on both ends – often described by clients as a deeply moving experience with which they were initially reluctant to engage. In group PPT, the exercise on slowness and savoring introduces clients to be aware of how the ways of speed, from instant messaging to drive thru's, and multitasking, is depriving us of appreciation and enjoyment of the good things in life. These exercises are aimed to cultivate positive emotions. According to broaden-and-build theory the goal is to change clients' mindsets, expanding their attention, broadening their behavioral repertoire, and enhancing their creativity. Positive emotions build resilience by "undoing" the effects of negative emotions (Fredrickson, 2001). Positive emotions such as joy, amusement, hope, and awe, if cultivated systematically, intentionally, in a contextually appropriate ways, can buffer against and undo the deleterious effects of psychological distress. Indeed, emerging lines of research on neuroplasticity suggests that positive emotional states may trigger lasting, durable changes in the structure and function of the brain and in gene expression (Garland & Howard, 2009; Fredrickson et al., 2013). It appears that cultivating positive emotions could be a goal of psychotherapy as it is likely to appeal to distressed clients. In PPT, the goal is not to cultivate decontextualized positive emotions, but to help clients learn skills of adaptively using both positive and negative emotions. As noted above, there are times when negative emotions are adaptive. Being upright, sad, or out of sorts does not always impede clients; it may make their decision more accurate (Seligman, 2002).

Notwithstanding the value of positive emotions, clients presenting for therapy are often embittered by negative emotions, holding on to grudges, and brooding over passive and inactive thoughts and emotions. Schwartz and colleagues (2002) have found that depressed clients seeking psychotherapy experience at least twice the negative emotions compared with positive ones They want to break free from these cycles. In the middle phase of PPT, after establishing solid therapeutic rapport and helping clients to explore their strengths to restore their self-efficacy, they are encouraged to write down grudges, bitter memories, or resentment and then discuss in therapy the effects of holding on to them. The notion of positive appraisal, which has been shown to build resilience and healthy coping through specific evidence-based strategies, is used in PPT to help clients to unpack their grudges and resentments (Luyten, Boddez, & Hermans, 2015). The positive appraisal in PPT utilizes the following four specific strategies:

1 Psychological space: clients are asked to write or describe the bitter memory from a third-person perspective, with slight temporal and spatial modifications but keeping the core issue intact (Joormann, Dkane, & Gotlib, 2006; Ayduk & Kross, 2010).

2   Reconsolidation: clients, in a relaxed and safe milieu, are encouraged to recall a troubling memory and look for any positives missed initially due to negativity-bent. Clients learn that each recall of a memory offers an opportunity to revise it or reconsolidate it, especially if they are troubled by the memory. This strategy is based on the research lines that demonstrate that our memories tend to be more plastic than we think and recall; especially in a relaxed milieu that offers us an opportunity to draw new meanings from old memories (Sandler, 2007; Alberini & Ledoux, 2013).
3   Mindful focus: clients are taught to mindfully observe, rather than react to negative memories and gradually develop greater awareness about cues, situations, and experiences that trigger negative memories (Gockel, 2010).
4   Diversion and intentional forgetting: after clients develop awareness about triggers, they are guided to create an inventory of alternative and adaptive behavioral (noncognitive) activities to stop the full recollection of a bitter or negative memory. Densely interconnected, the bitter memories of psychiatrically distressed clients are often trigged by external cues. Engaging in alternative activities that divert clients' attentional resources can help them (diversion), which they can easily employ to stop the downward spiral of bitter memories (Van Dillen & Koole, 2007; Hertel & McDaniel, 2010).

In addition to positive appraisal, clients are also invited to consider the process of forgiveness. Forgiveness in PPT is conceptualized as a process of change, not as an event or exercise, to willingly forsaking one's right (perceived or real) to take revenge (Worthington, Witvliet, Pietrini, & Miller, 2007). Clients are educated that forgiveness is not condoning or pardoning the offender, lowering or loosening the demands for justice through socially acceptable means, forgetting the wrong, or ignoring the natural consequences of the offense. They learn that forgiveness is also not simply replacing the negative thoughts or emotions with neutral or positive ones (Enright & Fitzgibbons, 2014). Some exercises in PPT, like forgiveness, may generate negative and uncomfortable emotions – some of which could be associated with trauma or traumatic memories. Much like any psychotherapy, PPT attends to all varieties of emotional experiences. However, while empathetically attending to pain associated with traumatic experiences, PPT gently encourages clients to also explore meaning and psychological growth (Calhoun & Tedeshi, 2006; McKnight & Kashdan, 2009; Bonanno & Mancini, 2012). An example would be the exercise "One Door Closes, One Door Opens," which focuses on exploring door of growth, exploration, and meaning that might have opened after doors of opportunities, attachments, and expressions closed. In doing so, therapists, however, should avoid pointing out the positive outcomes from trauma, loss, or adversity too quickly. Emphasis is on the integration of strengths with symptoms to help clients learn how to encounter negative experiences with a more positive mindset, and to reframe and label those experiences in ways that are adaptable and helpful.

The third and final phase of PPT exercises (e.g., positive relationships, positive communication, gift of time, positive legacy) continue to use clients' strengths, but focus is placed on using them to belong to and serve something bigger than oneself. One exercise, "positive communication," teaches clients ways to validate and capitalize precious moments when their partners share good news with them (Gable, Reis, Impett, & Asher, 2004). Others such as "Gift of Time," help clients to search and pursue meaning and purpose by using their strengths. Meaning and purpose can be pursued in a number of ways, such as strengthening close interpersonal and communal relationships, pursuing artistic, intellectual or scientific innovations, philosophical or religious contemplation (Frankl, 1963; Wrzesniewski, McCauley, Rozin, & Schwartz, 1997; Hicks & King, 2009; Stillman & Baumeister, 2009). There is solid evidence that having a sense of meaning and purpose helps individuals to recover or rebound quickly from adversity and buffer against feelings of hopelessness and uncontrollability (Lightsey, 2006; Graham, Lobel, Glass, & Lokshina, 2008).

In conducting PPT, some caveats are important to both process and outcome of therapy. First, despite emphasizing strengths, PPT is not a prescriptive. Rather, it is a descriptive approach based on converging scientific evidence indicating that certain benefits accrue when individuals attend to the positive aspects of their experience. With time, specific lines of evidence will also accrue that positives and strengths play a causal role measured by biological and genetic markers. For example, doing well, not simply feeling good, is associated with stronger expression of antibody and antiviral genes (Fredrickson et al., 2013). Public health officials carefully count when heart disease is identified as the underlying cause of death. They also collect meticulous data about possible risk factors, such as rates of smoking, obesity, hypertension, and lack of exercise. This data is available on a county-by-county level in the United States. A research team from the University of Pennsylvania aimed to match this physical epidemiology with their digital Twitter version. Drawing on a set of public tweets made between 2009 and 2010, these researchers used established emotional dictionaries to analyze a random sample of tweets from individuals who had made their locations available. With enough tweets and health data from about 1,300 US counties, which contain 88% of the country's population, they found that after for controlling income and educational level, the expressions of negative emotions such as anger, stress, and fatigue in the tweets from people in a given county were associated with higher heart disease risk in that county. On the other hand, expressions of positive emotions like excitement and optimism were associated with lower risk (Eichstaedt et al., 2015). Therefore, assumptions and assertions of positive psychology and PPT are prescriptive and will increasingly be constrained by evidence. That said, it is important to be cognizant that PPT is beneficial for some psychological concerns and not beneficial for others. For example, PPT was initially validated with adult clients experiencing symptoms of severe depression (Seligman, Rashid, & Parks, 2006). This finding has been replicated in three independent studies (Asgharipoor, Farid, Arshadi, & Sahebi, 2010; Cuadra-Peralta, Veloso-Besio, Pérez, & Zúñiga, 2010; Bay & Csillic, 2012). It has also been found to be affective with symptoms of anxiety (Kahler et al., 2014) and more recently with symptoms of Borderline Personality Disorder (Uliaszek, Rashid, Williams, & Gulamani, 2016) and psychosis (Riches, Schrank, Rashid, & Slade, 2015; Schrank et al., 2015). Since its initial validation study, eight studies of manualized PPT, published in peer-review journals have found it equally effective or better when compared with active treatments such as cognitive-behavior therapy (CBT) and dialectical behavior therapy (DBT). Compared with the baby boomer generation, which experienced several traumas including world wars, social oppression, and relatively less freedom, millennial and post-millennials may find PPT a more congenial approach which addresses their symptoms of depression and anxiety, but also offers them the means and mechanisms for exploring their potential, abilities, capacities and explicitly builds skills based on their strengths. Perhaps the rapid popularity and expansion of positive psychology explains this yearning. That said, it would be clinically imprudent to apply PPT to clients experiencing acute symptoms of panic disorder, selective mutism, or paranoid personality disorder as currently there is no evidence that PPT could be effective for these disorders. Still, some clients may have a strong feeling that their symptoms, not strengths, ought to be the focus of treatment. They may fear that expression or articulation of their weaknesses may invoke judgment by the therapist. Others may have deeply entrenched self-perception of being a victim, which they may be more accustomed to. Yet for others, identification of character strengths may exaggerate narcissistic characteristics. Therefore, it is important that strengths are discussed in specific situational contexts and their nuances are discussed thoroughly. For example, some clients may not benefit from being kind or forgiving in some situations. Likewise, some may feel conflicted between being authentic and socially intelligent. Some may face the dilemma of solving a complex challenge either by being honest or empathic. Similarly, clients with a long-standing history of abuse and with a strengths profile of being humble, kind, and forgiving may not readily benefit from PPT until they develop the strength of perspective and critical thinking skills to understand situations more accurately and realistically. Clients with a history of unresolved trauma and symptoms of post-traumatic stress, may respond better to symptom-focused treatments and may not be ready for PPT exercises on post-traumatic growth. In summary, PPT is not a panacea nor is it completely irrelevant for most clients. Its fit has to be explored and monitored continuously during the course of the treatment.

Second, PPT is not a panacea and will not be appropriate for all clients in all situations. As such, clinical judgment is needed to determine the suitability of PPT for individual clients. For example, a client with an inflated self-perception may use strengths to further support his or her narcissism. Likewise, a client with a deeply entrenched sense of being a victim may feel too comfortable in that role, and may not believe in his or her own strengths. A therapist using PPT also should not expect a linear progression of improvement because the motivation to change long-standing behavioral and emotional patterns fluctuates during the course of therapy. The progress of one client should not bias therapists about the likely progress (or lack of) of another client. The mechanism of change in PPT has not been explored systematically, but inferring from change of mechanism uncovered by Lyubomirsky and Layous (2013) about positive interventions, it can be argued that change brought by positive interventions could be moderated by level of symptoms severity, individual personality variables (motivation, effort), flexibility in completing and practicing the exercises and skills, and overall client–intervention fit. Nonetheless, therapists must also be aware that change is not due to expectancy effect. Finally, it is important to be aware of cultural sensitivities in assessing strengths. An emotive style of communication, interdependence on extended family members, or avoiding direct eye contact may convey zest, love, and respect (Pedrotti, 2011).

Positive psychology has been criticized for not exploring people's troubles deeply enough and steering people quickly to individually based positive notions (Ehrenreich, 2009; Coyne & Tennen, 2010; McNulty & Fincham, 2012). As reiterated throughout this chapter in various ways, the therapeutic arm of PPT does not deny negative emotions, nor does it encourage clients to search for positives all too quickly through rose-colored glasses. PPT is neither a panacea nor does it encourage a Pollyannaish or Panglossian view of happiness and well-being. It is a scientific endeavor to gently encourage clients to explore their intact resources and learn to use them in overcoming their challenges.

Empirical Evidence, Caveats, and Future Directions

PPT's empirical support has been found in several, albeit pilot and feasibility, studies. Initially individual exercises were validated through a randomized control trial (RCT) (Seligman, Steen, Park, & Peterson, 2005) with participants in the positive intervention condition showing a significant decrease in symptoms of depression and an increase in well-being. These findings have since been independently replicated with somewhat similar results (Giannopoulos & Vella-Brodrick, 2011; Mongrain & Anselmo-Matthews, 2012; Senf & Liau, 2013). Subtle aspects such as preference for a specific exercise and its relation to adherence has also been explored (Schueller, 2010). Table 22.4 lists 14 studies which have explicitly used the PPT manual (Seligman et al., 2006; Rashid & Seligman, in press) as a packaged treatment. Mostly group treatments, eight of the 14 are randomized controlled studies, nine published in peer-reviewed journals, and three dissertations. Seven of these studies treated community samples from Canada, China, Chile, France, Iran, and the United States, addressing clinical concerns, including depression, anxiety, borderline personality disorder, psychosis, and nicotine

Table 22.4 Positive psychotherapy: summary of studies.

Authors and publication status	Intervention description & sample characteristics	Primary outcome measures	Key findings
Randomized clinical trials (RCTs)			
1 Seligman, Rashid, & Parks (2006), published	Individual PPT; $N = 11$), 12–14 sessions, with clients diagnosed with Major Depressive Disorder (MDD), compared with Treatment as Usual (TAU; $N = 9$) and Treatment as Usual plus medication (TAUMED; $N = 12$). Clients were undergraduate and graduate students seeking psychotherapy at a university counseling center in the United States.	Depression (*ZDRS* & *Hamilton*), Overall psychiatric distress (*OQ-45*), Life Satisfaction (*SWLS*), and Well-being (*PPTI*).	Clients completing PPT faired significantly better on measures of depressive, overall psychiatric distress, and well-being.
2 Seligman, Rashid, & Parks (2006), published	Group PPT ($N = 21$) with clients at a university counseling center, experiencing mild to moderate depressive symptoms compared with no-treatment control ($N = 21$) in six sessions.	Depression (*BDI-II*) and Life Satisfaction (*SWLS*).	PPT did better on measure of depression at post-treatment, 3-, 6- and 12-month follow-up, with a rate of change that was significantly greater than that of the control group.
3 Parks-Schiener (2009), dissertation	Individual ($N = 52$) completed six PPT exercises online were compared with no treatment control group ($N = 69$).	Depression (*CES-D*), Life Satisfaction (*SWLS*), and Positive and Negative affect (*PANAS*).	Individuals completing PPT exercises reported significantly less depression at post-treatment, 3- and 6-month follow-ups.
4 Lu, Wang, & Liu (2013), published	Group PPT ($N = 16$), (two hours for 16 weekly sessions, with university students in China were compared with a no treatment control group ($N = 18$). The study explored the impact of positive affect on vagal tone in handling environmental challenges.	Positive and negative affect (*PANAS*) and Respiratory Sinus Arrhythmia (*RSA*).	Participants completing PPT exercises reported significantly less depressive symptoms, less negative emotions and more positive emotions.
5 Rashid, et al. (2013), published	Group PPT ($N = 9$), was offered in eight sessions to grade six and seven students at a public school in Canada, and compared with no treatment control ($N = 9$).	Social Skills (*SSRS*), Student Satisfaction (*SLSS*), Well-being (*PPTI-C*), and Depression (*CDI*).	Participants improved on their social skills as rated by their parents and teachers.
6 Reinsch, C. (2012), dissertation	Group PPT ($N = 9$), was compared with a no treatment control group ($N = 8$) with adults seeking psychotherapy through Employee Assistance Program in Canada.	Depression (*CES-D*) and Well-being (*PPTI*).	Compared with the control group, the treatment group showed a significant decrease in depression at a rate of 45%. Therapeutic gains were maintained 1 month post-intervention.

7	Rashid & Uliaszek (2013), presentation	Group PPT ($N = 6$) compared group dialectical behavior therapy (DBT) ($N = 10$) with undergraduate students diagnosed with the symptoms of Borderline Personality Disorder who sought treatment at a university counseling center in Canada.	Depression (*SCID*), Psychiatric Symptoms (*SCL-90*), Emotion Regulation (*DER*), Distress Tolerance (*DTS*), Mindfulness (*KIMS*), Wellbeing (*PPTI*), and Life Satisfaction (*SWLS*).	Participants in both PPT and DBT improved significantly on measures of depression, anxiety, emotional dysregulation, mindfulness, well-being, and life satisfaction. However, the two treatments did differ significantly, with the exception of Distress Tolerance, where DBT show significantly more improvement.
8	Asharipoor et al. (2012), published	Group PPT ($N = 9$) was compared with cognitive-behavior therapy (CBT), for 12 weeks, each group, with Community Adults diagnosed with Major Depressive Disorder, seeking treatment at a hospital affiliated psychological treatment center in Iran.	Depression (*SCID* & *BDI-II*), Happiness (*OTS*), Life Satisfaction (*SWLS*), and Psychological Well-being (*SWS*).	At post-intervention, PPT group showed significantly higher level of happiness, whereas no differences between two treatment were found on measures of depression.
9	Brownwell et al. (2014), published	Group PPT (11 sessions; $N = 94$), adapted for patients diagnosed with psychosis, was compared with treatment as usual in a randomized controlled trial (ISRCTN04199273) in London, UK. While the outcome paper is in submission, qualitative data from 37 clients was included in the study mentioned here.	Wellbeing (*Warwick-Edinburgh Mental Well-Being Scale*); Psychiatric Stress (*Brief Psychiatric Rating Scale*).	Participants who completed PPT exercises, at the post-treatment interview reported that PPT exercises were quite beneficial, especially the savoring, experiencing, identifying, and developing strengths, forgiveness, and gratitude.
Non-Randomized			
10	Cuadra-Peralta et al. (2010), published	Group PPT ($N = 8$) in nine sessions, with clients diagnosed with depression, compared with behavioral therapy ($N = 10$) at a community center in Chile.	Depression (*BDI-II* & *CES-D*), Happiness (*AHI*).	Compared with Behavior Therapy, PPT showed significant increases in happiness, and significant decrease in symptoms of depression.
11	Bay & Callidiac (2012), presentation	Group PPT ($N = 10$) compared with Group cognitive-behavior therapy ($N = 8$) and medication ($N = 8$).	Depression (*BDI-Shortened*), Depression and Anxiety (*HADS*), Happiness (*SHS*), Emotional Inventory (*EQ-I*), Life Satisfaction (*SWLS*), and Positive and Negative Affect (*PANAS*).	PPT faired better than CBT and medication group on measures of depression, optimism, emotional intelligence, and well-being.

(Continued)

Table 22.4 (Continued)

	Authors and publication status	Intervention description & sample characteristics	Primary outcome measures	Key findings
12	Meyer, Johnson, Parks, Iwanski, & Penn (2012), published	Group PPT with two cohorts recruited from a hospital and a community mental health center, with a current diagnosis of schizophrenia or schizoaffective disorder, completed ten sessions.	Psychological Well-being (SWS), Savoring (SBI), Hope (DHS), Recovery (RAS), Symptoms (BSI), and Social Functioning (SFS).	At post-treatment, PPT faired better on measure of depression, happiness, life satisfaction, and optimism. In most cases both PPT and CBT faired better than medication group.
13	Kahler et al. (2014), published	Individual PPT (N = 19), in eight sessions was integrated with smoking cessation counseling and nicotine patch at a community medical center.	Depression (SCID, CES-D), Nicotine Dependence (FTND), Positive and Negative Affect (PANAS), and Client Satisfaction (CSQ-8).	Rate of session attendance and satisfaction with treatment were high with most participants who completed the PPT exercise. Almost one-third (31.6%) of the sample sustained smoking abstinence for six months after their quit date.
14	Goodwin (2010), dissertation	Group PPT (N = 11), in a pre- to post-group design explored relationship satisfaction among anxious and stressed individuals at a community center. In ten sessions explored if treatment increased relationship satisfaction among anxious and stressed individuals with a community sample at a training clinic	Anxiety (BAI), Stress (PSS), relationship adjustment (DAS).	Individuals who experienced a reduction in perceived stress also showed significant improvement in overall relationship functioning. Similarly, participants who experienced a reduction in anxiety also showed significant improvement in relationship satisfaction level of anxiety at post-treatment, while no changes were observed on the on relationship satisfaction

Outcome measures (in alphabetical order): Beck Depression Inventory-II (*BDI-II*) (Beck, Steer, & Brown, 1996); Beck Depression Inventory-II Short Form (*BDI-SF*) (Chibnall & Tait, 1994); Beck Anxiety Inventory (*BAI*) (Beck, Epstein & Steer, 1988); Brief Symptom Inventory (*BSI*) (Derogatis, 1993); Centre for Epidemiological Studies for Depression (*CES-D*) (Radloff, 1977); Children Depression Inventory (*CDI*) (Kovacs, 1992); Client Satisfaction Questionnaire (*CSQ-8*) (Larsen, Attkisson, Hargreaves, & Nguyen, 1979); Difficulties in Emotion Regulation (*DERS*) (Gratz & Roemer, 2004); Distress Tolerance Scale (*DTS*) (Simons & Gaher, 2005); Dyadic Adjustment Scale (*DAS*) (Spanier, 1976); Emotional Quotient inventory (*EQ-I*) (Dawda & Hart, 2000); Fagerstrom Test for Nicotine Dependence (*FTND*) (Heatherton, Kozlowski, Frecker, & Fagerström, 1991); Hamilton Rating Scale for Depression (*HRSD*) (Hamilton, 1960); Hospital Anxiety and Depression Scale (*HADS*) (Bjelland, Dahl, Haug, & Neckelmann, 2002); Kentucky Inventory of Mindfulness Skills (*KIMS*) (Baer, Smith, & Allen, 2004); Orientations to happiness (Peterson, Park, & Seligman, 2005); Life Orientation Test-Revised (*LOT-R*) (Scheier, Carver, & Bridges, 1994); Outcome Questionnaire-45 (*OQ-45*) (Lambert et al., 1996); Positive and Negative Affective Scale (*PANAS*) (Watson, Clark, & Tellegen, 1988); Positive Psychotherapy Inventory (*PPTI*) (Rashid, 2005); Positive Psychotherapy Inventory-Children's Version (*PPTI-C*) (Rashid & Anjum, 2008); Recovery Assessment Scale (*RAS*) (Corrigan, Salzer, Ralph, Sangster, & Keck, 2004); Respiratory sinus arrhythmia (*RSA*) (Berntson et al., 1997), measures the degree of respiration-linked variability in the heart rate; Savoring Beliefs Inventory (*SBI*) (Bryant, 2003); Scales of Well-being (*SWB*) (Ryff, 1989); Social Skills Rating System (*SSRS*) (Gresham & Elliot, 1990); Structured Clinical Interview for DSM-IV-Axis I (*SCID*) (First, Spitzer, Gibbon, & Williams, 2007); Students' Life Satisfaction Scale (*SLSS*) (Huebner, 1991); Social functioning scale (*SFS*) (Birchwood, Smith, Cochrane, & Wetton, 1990); Values in Action (*VIA-Youth*) (Park & Peterson, 2006); Zung Self-Rating Depression Scale (*ZSRS*) (Zung, 1965).

dependence. Of these, the methodologically most rigorous study of PPT has been completed at the Institute of Psychiatry, London. In this randomized study, WELLFOCUS PPT, an adapted version was compared with treatment as usual (Riches at al., 2015). Results showed that compared with treatment as usual, the PPT group showed significant improvement in symptoms of depression, whereas changes in well-being were found on PPT-related measure, but not on second measure of well-being (Schrank et al., 2015). Four of 14 studies listed in Table 22.4, including two randomized controlled trials, have compared PPT directly with two other active manualized treatments: DBT and CBT. Overall, in all these studies, PPT significantly lowered symptoms of distress and enhanced well-being on post-treatment outcome measures when compared with control or pre-treatment scores, with medium- to large-effect sizes (for effect sizes, see Rashid, 2015). When compared with another treatment such as CBT or DBT, PPT performed equally well or better, most notably on well-being measures (e.g., Asgharipoor et al., 2010; Cuadra-Peralta et al., 2010). One important caution in reviewing these studies is the small sample sizes.

The results of these 14 studies are consistent with two meta-analyses done on positive interventions. The first meta-analysis of 51 positive interventions conducted by Sin and Lyubomirsky (2009) found that positive interventions are effective, with moderate effect sizes in significantly decreasing symptoms of depression (mean $r = .31$) and enhancing well-being (mean $r = .29$). Positive interventions, including PPT, are beginning to establish that positives can reduce symptoms and enhance well-being. The second meta-analysis, by Bolier and her colleagues (2013), reviewing 39 randomized published studies totaling 6,139 participants, found that positive interventions reduced depression (mean $r = 0.23$) with small effect size, but enhanced well-being with moderate effect size ($r = 0.34$). Compared with more structured, manualized, sequential PPT, which is used with clinical samples, positive interventions could benefit nonclinical patrons as well-being enhancing strategies that could prevent or reduce risk of future psychological disorders. In a systematic analysis, Hone, Jarden, and Schhofield (2015) reviewed the effectiveness 40 positive psychology interventions in terms of key outcomes, their accessibility, implementation, and acceptance. They found that 73% of positive interventions achieved efficacy score, 84% adoption, and 58% scored on implementation.

Empirical foundations of PPT are critical, but equally essential is establishing a repertoire of case studies, vignettes and illustrations of PPT exercises, conducted as a packaged treatment, stand-alone intervention, and incorporated with established treatments. This will help clinicians to understand the day-to-day implementation of PPT. A few developments in this regard are worth noting. The May 2009 issue of the *Journal of Clinical Psychology* exclusively focused on positive interventions for clinical disorders with rich case illustrations. George Burns (2010) compiled a 27-chapter casebook, written by leading practitioners of positive psychology. Each chapter provides a rich case illustration regarding the clinical use of positive psychology, including PPT exercises with clients in distress. Most of the chapters offer step-by-step strategies. In addition to protocoled treatment packages, single positive interventions have also been applied to examine their effectiveness for specific clinical conditions, such as gratitude in undoing symptoms of depression (Wood, Maltby, Gillett, Linley, & Joseph, 2008), best possible self and three good things for depression (Pietrowsky & Mikutta, 2012), hope as a treatment of post-traumatic stress disorder (Gilman, Schumm, & Chard, 2012), the therapeutic role of spirituality and meaning in psychotherapy (Steger & Shin, 2010), positive psychology interventions to treat drug abuse (Aktar & Boniwell, 2010), cultivation of positive emotions in treating symptoms of schizophrenia (Johnson, Penn, Fredrickson, Meyer, Kring, & Brantley, 2009), and forgiveness as a way of slowly letting go of anger (Harris et al., 2006). The role of positive interventions in complementing and supplementing traditional clinical work is also being explored (e.g., Fava & Ruini, 2003; Frisch, 2006; Karwoski, Garratt & llardi, 2006; Harris, Thoresen, & Lopez, 2007; Ruini & Fava, 2009; Moeenizadeh & Salagame, 2010). Links between specific clinical conditions and strengths and well-being have also been explored, including creativity and bipolar disorder (Murray & Johnson, 2010), positive psychology and brain injury (Evans, 2011), positive emotions and social anxiety (Kashdan, Julian, Merritt, & Uswatte, 2006), social relationships and depression (Oksanen, Kouvonen, Vahtera, Virtanen, & Kivimäki, 2010), various aspects of well-being and psychosis (Schrank, Bird, Tylee, Coggins, Rashid, & Slade, 2013), positive psychology and war trauma (Al-Krenawi, Elbedour, Parsons, Onwuegbuzie, Bart, & Fer, 2011), school-based positive psychology interventions (Waters, 2011), neuroscience (Kapur et al., 2013), and character strengths and well-being (Niemiec, Rashid, & Spinella, 2012). In addition, a number of online studies have effectively used PPT-based interventions with promising results (e.g., Mitchell, Stanimirovic, Klein, & Vella-Brodrick, 2009; Parks, Della Porta, Pierce, Zilca, & Lyubomirsky, 2012; Schueller & Parks, 2012). This could be a relatively cost effective way of offering mental health services to nonclinical patrons as a preventative strategy.

To help psychotherapists to incorporate positive interventions in their clinical practice, a few books also been published (e.g., Linley & Joseph, 2004; Joseph & Linley, 2006; Conoley & Conoley, 2009; Magyar-Moe, 2009; Levak, Siegel, & Nichols, 2011; Bennink, 2012; Proctor & Linley, 2013). Journal articles exploring theoretical advances regarding incorporation of strengths in clinical practice, exploring the application of positive psychology and strengths in various applied settings have also been published (e.g., Lent, 2004; Smith, 2006; Dick-Niederhauser, 2009; Slade, 2010; Wong, 2012). An outcome measure, Positive Psychotherapy Inventory (PPTI) to assess the specific active ingredients of PPT, including positive emotions, engagement, meaning, and relationships, has been devised and validated (Rashid, 2008; Guney, 2011; Bertisch et al., 2014).

Establishing efficacy or effectiveness of interventions takes decades of research, including open trial, case reports, and then moving into controlled pilots and finally multi-site studies. PPT has a long journey to travel in order to establish its efficacy, and still requires the discovery and identification of the mechanism of change. PPT still has to answer sophisticated questions about specific aspects of the treatment, such as mechanism of change and its incremental effectiveness over and beyond a symptoms-focused approach. In the future, longitudinal, and multi-method (e.g., experiential sampling, physiological, and neurological indices) research design may uncover the effectiveness of PPT for specific disorders. There is a dearth of knowledge about the epistemology of well-being, especially in clinical settings. These questions hopefully will be answered through more rigorous, well-defined and refined studies.

References

Al-Krenawi, A., Elbedour, S., Parsons, J. E., Onwuegbuzie, A. J., Bart, W. M., & Ferguson, A. (2011). Trauma and war: Positive psychology/strengths approach. *Arab Journal of Psychiatry*, *22*, 103–112.

Akhtar, M. & Boniwell, I. (2010). Applying positive psychology to alcohol-misusing: A group intervention. *Groupwork*, *20*, 7–23.

Alberini, C. M. & Ledoux, J. E. (2013). Memory reconsolidation. *Current Biology*, *23*, R746–50. doi.10.1016/j.cub.2013.06.046.

American Psychiatric Association (2013). *Diagnostic and Statistical Manual of Mental Disorders (DSM-5)*, 5th edn. Arlington, VA: American Psychiatric Association.

Asgharipoor, N., Farid, A. A., Arshadi, H., & Sahebi, A. (2010). A comparative study on the effectiveness of positive psychotherapy and group cognitive-behavioral therapy for the patients suffering from major depressive disorder. *Iranian Journal of Psychiatry and Behavioral Sciences*, *6*, 33–41.

Ayduk, Ö. & Kross, E. (2010). From a distance: Implications of spontaneous self-distancing for adaptive self-reflection. *Journal of Personality and Social Psychology*, *98*, 809–829. doi.10.1037/a0019205.

Baer, R. A., Smith, G. T., & Allen, K. B. (2004). Assessment of mindfulness by self-report: The Kentucky inventory of mindfulness skills. *Assessment*, *11*, 191–206.

Baumeister, R. F., Bratslavsky, E., Finkenauer, C., & Vohs, K. D. (2001). Bad is stronger than good. *Review of General Psychology*, *5*, 323–370. doi.10.1037/1089-2680.5.4.323.

Bay, M. & Csillic, A (2012). *Comparing Positive Psychotherapy with cognitive behavioral therapy in treating depression.* Unpublished manuscript. Université Paris Ouest Nanterre la Défense, Paris.

Beck, A. T., Steer, R. A., & Brown, G. K. (1996). BDI-II. *Beck Depression Inventory: Manual,* 2nd edn Boston, MA: Harcourt Brace.

Beck A. T., Epstein N., Brown, G., & Steer R. A. (1988). An inventory for measuring clinical anxiety: Psychometric properties. *Journal of Consulting and Clinical Psychology, 56,* 893–897.

Bennink, F, (2012). *Practicing Positive CBT: From reducing distress to building success.* Hoboken. NJ: John Wiley.

Bertisch, H., Rath, J., Long, C., Ashman, T., & Rashid, T. (2014). Positive psychology in rehabilitation medicine: A brief report. *NeuroRehabilitation.* doi.10.3233/NRE-141059.

Birchwood, M., Smith, J., Cochrane, R., & Wetton, S. (1990). The social functioning scale: The development and validation of a new scale of social adjustment for use in family intervention programmes with schizophrenic patients. *British Journal of Psychiatry, 157,* 853–859.

Biswas-Diener, R., Kashdan, T. K., & Minhas, G. (2011). A dynamic approach to psychological strength development and intervention, *Journal of Positive Psychology, 6*(2), 106–118.

Bjelland, I., Dahl, A. A., Haug, T. T., & Neckelmann, D. (2002). The validity of the Hospital Anxiety and Depression Scale. An updated literature review. *Journal of Psychosomatic Research, 52,* 69–77.

Boisvert, C. M. & Faust, D. (2003). Leading researchers' consensus on psychotherapy research findings: Implications for the teaching and conduct of psychotherapy. *Professional Psychology: Research and Practice, 34,* 508 513.

Bolier, L., Haverman, M., Westerhof, G., Riper, H., Smit, F., & Bohlmeijer, E. (2013). Positive psychology interventions: a meta-analysis of randomized controlled studies. *BMC Public Health, 13,* 119.

Bonanno, G. A. & Mancini, A. D. (2012). Beyond resilience and PTSD: Mapping the heterogeneity of responses to potential trauma. *Psychological Trauma: Theory, Research, Practice, and Policy, 4*(1), 74–83. doi.10.1037/a0017829.

Bryant, F. B. (2003). Savoring Beliefs Inventory (SBI): A scale for measuring beliefs about savouring. *Journal of Mental Health, 12,* 175–196.

Bryant, F. B. & Veroff, J. (2007). *Savoring: a new model of positive experience.* Mahwah, NJ: Lawrence Erlbaum.

Burns, G. W. (Ed.). (2010). *Happiness, healing and enhancement.* Chichester: Wiley-Blackwell.

Calhoun, L. G. & Tedeschi, R. G. (Eds.). (2006). *Handbook of posttraumatic growth: Research and practice.* Mahwah, NJ: Lawrence Erlbaum.

Castonguay, L. G. (2013). Psychotherapy outcome: An issue worth re-revisiting 50 years later. *Psychotherapy, 50*(1), 52–67. doi.10.1037/a0030898.

Cheavens, J. S., Strunk, D. S., Lazarus, S. A., & Goldstein, L. A. (2012). The compensation and capitalization models: A test of two approaches to individualizing the treatment of depression. *Behaviour Research and Therapy, 50,* 699–706.

Chibnall, J. T. & Tait, R. C. (1994). The short form of the beck depression inventory: Validity issues with chronic pain patients. *Clinical Journal of Pain, 10,* 261–266.

Conoley, C. W. & Conoley, J. C. (2009). *Positive psychology and family therapy.* Hoboken, NJ: John Wiley.

Corrigan, P. (2004). How stigma interferes with mental health care. *American Psychologist, 59,* 614–625.

Corrigan, P. W., Salzer, M., Ralph, R., Sangster, Y., & Keck, L. (2004). Examining the factor structure of the recovery assessment scale. *Schizophrenia Bulletin, 30,* 1035–1041.

Coyne, J. C. & Tennen, H. (2010). Positive psychology in cancer care: Bad science, exaggerated claims, and unproven medicine. *Annals of Behavioral Medicine, 39,* 16–26. doi.10.1007/s12160-009-9154-z.

Csikszentmihalyi, M. (1990). *Flow: The psychology of optimal experience.* New York: Harper Collins.

Cuadra-Peralta, A., Veloso-Besio, C., Pérez, M., & Zúñiga, M. (2010). Resultados de la psicoterapia positiva en pacientes con depresión (Positive psychotherapy results in patients with depression). *Terapia Psicológica, 28,* 127–134. doi.doi:10.4067/S0718-48082010000100012.

Dawda, D. & Hart, S. D. (2000). Assessing emotional intelligence: Reliability and validity of the bar-on emotional quotient inventory (EQ-i) in university students. *Personality and Individual Differences, 28*(4), 797–812.

Derogatis, L. R. (1993). *Brief symptom inventory (BSI): Administration, scoring, and procedures manual* (3rd ed.). Minneapolis, MN: National Computer Systems.

Dick-Niederhauser, A. (2009). Therapeutic change and the experience of joy: Toward a theory of curative processes. *Journal of Psychotherapy Integration, 19,* 187–211.

Eichstaedt, J. C., Schwartz, H. A., Kern, M. L., Park, G., Labarthe, D. R., Merchant, R. M., Seligman, M. E. P., et al. (2015). Psychological language on Twitter predicts county-level heart disease mortality. *Psychological Science.* doi.10.1177/0956797614557867.

Enright, R. D. & Fitzgibbons, R. P. (2014). *Forgiveness therapy: An empirical guide for resolving anger and restoring hope.* Washington, DC: American Psychological Association.

Ehrenreich, B. (2009). *Bright-sided: How positive thinking is undermining America.* New York: Metropolitan Books.

Evans, J. (2011). Positive psychology and brain injury rehabilitation. *Brain Impairment, 12,* 117–127. doi.10.1375/brim.12.2.117.

Fava, G. A. & Ruini, C. (2003). Development and characteristics of a well-being enhancing psychotherapeutic strategy: Well-being therapy. *Journal of Behavior Therapy and Experimental Psychiatry, 34*(1), 45–63. doi.10.1016/S0005-7916(03)00019-3.

First, M. B., Spitzer, R. L., Gibbon, M., & Williams, J. (2007). *Structured Clinical Interview for DSM-IV-TR Axis I Disorders, Research Version, Patient Edition (SCID-VP).* New York: Biometrics Research, New York State Psychiatric Institute.

Fitzpatrick, M. R. & Stalikas, A. (2008). Integrating positive emotions into theory, research, and practice: A new challenge for psychotherapy. *Journal of Psychotherapy Integration, 18,* 248–258.

Flückiger, C. & Grosse Holtforth, M. (2008). Focusing the therapist's attention on the patient's strengths: A preliminary study to foster a mechanism of change in outpatient psychotherapy. *Journal of Clinical Psychology, 64,* 876–890.

Frankl, V. E. (1963). *Man's search for meaning: An introduction to logotherapy.* New York: Washington Square Press.

Fredrickson, B. L. (2001). The role of positive emotions in positive psychology. *American Psychologist, 56,* 218–226.

Fredrickson, B. L., Grewen, K. M., Coffey, K. A., Algoe, S. B., Firestine, A. M., Arevalo, J. M. G., Cole, S. W., et al. (2013a). A functional genomic perspective on human well-being. *Proceedings of the National Academy of Sciences, 110*(33), 13684–13689. doi.10.1073/pnas.1305419110.

Fink, J. E. (2014). Flourishing: Exploring predictors of mental health within the college environment. *Journal of American College Health, 62,* 380–388. doi.org/10.1080/07448481.2014.917647.

Frisch, M. B. (2006). *Quality of life therapy: Applying a life satisfaction approach to positive psychology and cognitive therapy.* Hoboken, NJ: John Wiley.

Gable, S. L, Reis, H. T., Impett, E. A., & Asher, E. R. (2004). What do you do when things go right? The intrapersonal and interpersonal benefits of sharing positive events. *Journal of Personality and Social Psychology, 87,* 228–245.

Garland, E. L. & Howard, M. O. (2009). Neuroplasticity, psychosocial genomics, and the biopsychosocial paradigm in the 21st century. *Health and Social Work, 34*(3), 191–199.

Giannopoulos, V. L. & Vella-Brodrick, D. (2011). Effects of positive interventions and orientations to happiness on subjective well-being. *Journal of Positive Psychology, 6,* 95–105. doi.http://dx.doi.org/10.1080/17439760.2010.545428.

Gilman, R., Schumm, J. A., & Chard, K. M. (2012). Hope as a change mechanism in the treatment of posttraumatic stress disorder. *Psychological Trauma: Theory, Research, Practice, and Policy, 4,* 270–277. doi.10.1037/a0024252.

Gockel, A. (2010). The promise of mindfulness for clinical practice education. *Smith College Studies in Social Work, 80,* 248–268. doi.10.1080/00377311003784184.

Graham, J. E., Lobel, M., Glass, P., & Lokshina, I. (2008). Effects of written constructive anger expression in chronic pain patients: Making meaning from pain. *Journal of Behavioral Medicine, 31,* 201–212.

Gratz, K. L. & Roemer, L. (2004). Multidimensional assessment of emotion regulation and dysregulation: Development, factor structure, and initial validation of the difficulties in emotion regulation scale. *Journal of Psychopathology and Behavioral Assessment, 26,* 41–54.

Gresham, F. M. & Elliot, S. N. (1990). *Social Skills Rating System Manual.* Circle Pines: American Guidance Service.

Guney, S. (2011). The Positive Psychotherapy Inventory (PPTI): Reliability and validity study in Turkish population. *Social and Behavioral Sciences, 29,* 81–86.

Hamilton, M. (1960). A rating scale for depression. *Journal of Neurology, Neurosurgery, and Psychiatry, 23,* 56–62.

Harris, A. H. S., Luskin, F., Norman, S. B., Standard, S., Bruning, J., Evans, S., & Thoresen, C. E. (2006). Effects of a group forgiveness intervention on forgiveness, perceived stress, and trait-anger. *Journal of Clinical Psychology, 62,* 715–33. doi.10.1002/jclp.20264.

Harris, A. S. H., Thoresen, C. E., & Lopez, S. J. (2007). Integrating positive psychology into counseling: Why and (when appropriate) how. *Journal of Counseling & Development, 85*, 3–13.

Headey, B., Schupp, J., Tucci, I., & Wagner, G. G. (2010). Authentic happiness theory supported by impact of religion on life satisfaction: A longitudinal analysis with data for Germany. *Journal of Positive Psychology, 5*, 73–82.

Heatherton, T. F., Kozlowski, L. T., Frecker, R. C., & Fagerström, K. (1991). The Fagerström test for nicotine dependence: A revision of the Fagerström tolerance questionnaire. *British Journal of Addiction, 86*, 1119–1127. doi.org/10.1111/j.1360-0443.1991.tb01879.x.

Hertel, P. T. & McDaniel, L. (2010). The suppressive power of positive thinking: Aiding suppression-induced forgetting in repressive coping. *Cognition and Emotion, 24*, 1239–1249.

Hicks, J. A. & King, L. A. (2009). Meaning in life as a subjective judgment and lived experience. *Social and Personality Psychology Compass, 3*, 638–658.

Hone, L. C., Jarden, A., & Schofield, G. M. (2015). An evaluation of positive psychology intervention effectiveness trials using the re-aim framework: A practice-friendly review. *Journal of Positive Psychology, 10*(4), 303–322. doi.10.1080/17439760.2014.965267.

Huebner, E. S. (1991). Initial development of the Students' Life Satisfaction Scale. *School Psychology International, 12*, 231–243.

Huta, V. & Hawley, L. (2008). Psychological strengths and cognitive vulnerabilities: Are they two ends of the same continuum or do they have independent relationships with well-being and ill-being? *Journal of Happiness Studies, 11*, 71–93. doi.10.1007/s10902-008-9123-4.

Jenaro, C., Flores, N., & Arias, B. (2007). Burnout and coping in human service practitioners. *Professional Psychology: Research and Practice, 38*, 80–87. doi.10.1037/0735-7028.38.1.80.

Johnson, J., Wood, A. M., Gooding, P., Taylor, P. J., & Tarrier, N. (2011). Resilience to suicidality: The buffering hypothesis. *Clinical Psychology Review*. doi.10.1016/j.cpr.2010.12.007.

Johnson, D. P., Penn, D. L., Fredrickson, B. L., Meyer, P. S., Kring, A. M., & Brantley, M. (2009). Loving-kindness meditation to enhance recovery from negative symptoms of schizophrenia. *Journal of Clinical Psychology, 65*, 499–509. doi.10.1002/jclp.20591.

Joormann, J., Dkane, M., & Gotlib, I. H. (2006). Adaptive and maladaptive components of rumination? Diagnostic specificity and relation to depressive biases. *Behavior Therapy, 37*, 269–280. doi.0.1016/j.beth.2006.01.002.

Joormann, J., Siemer, M., & Gotlib, I. H. (2007). Mood regulation in depression: Differential effects of distraction and recall of happy memories on sad mood. *Journal of Abnormal Psychology, 116*(3), 484–490. doi.10.1037/0021-843X.116.3.484.

Joseph, S. & Linley, A. P. (2006). *Positive Therapy: A meta-theory for positive psychological practice.* New York: Routledge.

Kahler, C. W., Spillane, N. S., Day, A., Clerkin, E. M., Parks, A., Leventhal, A. M., & Brown, R. A. (2013). Positive psychotherapy for smoking cessation: Treatment development, feasibility, and preliminary results. *Journal of Positive Psychology*. doi. 10.1080/17439760 .2013.826716.

Kapur, N., Cole, J., Manly, T., Viskontas, I., Ninteman, A., Hasher, L., & Pascual-Leone, A. (2013). Positive clinical neuroscience: Explorations in positive neurology. *The Neuroscientist, 19*, 354–369. doi. org/10.1177/1073858412470976.

Kashdan, T. B., Julian, T., Merritt, K., & Uswatte, G. (2006). Social anxiety and posttraumatic stress in combat veterans: Relations to well-being and character strengths. *Behaviour Research and Therapy, 44*, 561–583.

Kashdan, T. B. & Rottenberg, J. (2010). Psychological flexibility as a fundamental aspect of health. *Clinical Psychology Review, 30*, 865–878.

Karwoski, L., Garratt, G. M., & Ilardi, S. S. (2006). On the integration of cognitive-behavioral therapy for depression and positive psychology. *Journal of Cognitive Psychotherapy, 20*, 159–170.

Keyes, C. L. M. & Eduardo J. S. (2012). To flourish or not: Level of positive mental health predicts ten-year all-cause mortality. *American Journal of Public Health, 102*, 2164–2172.

Kovacs, M. (1992). *Children depression inventory: Manual.* New York: Multi Health Systems.

Lambert, M. J. (2010). *Prevention of treatment failure: The use of measuring, monitoring, and feedback in clinical practice.* Washington, DC: American Psychological Association.

Lambert, M. J., Burlingame, G. M., Umphress, V. J., Hansen, N. B., Vermeersch, D., Clouse, G., & Yanchar, S. (1996). The reliability and validity of the Outcome Questionnaire. Clinical *Psychology and Psychotherapy, 3*, 106–116.

Lamont, A. (2011). University students' strong experiences of music: Pleasure, engagement, and meaning. *Music and Emotion, 15,* 229–249.

Larsen, D. L., Attkisson, C. C., Hargreaves, W. A., & Nguyen, T. D. (1979). Assessment of client/patient satisfaction: Development of a general scale. *Evaluation and Program Planning, 2,* 197–207.doi.org/10.1016/0149-7189(79)90094-6.

Lent, R. W. (2004). Towards a unifying theoretical and practical perspective on well-being and psychosocial adjustment. *Journal of Counseling Psychology, 5,* 482–509.

Levak, R. W., Siegel, L., & Nichols, S. N. (2011). *Therapeutic feedback with the MMPI-2: A positive psychology approach.* London: Taylor & Francis.

Leykin, Y. & DeRubeis, R. J. (2009). Allegiance in psychotherapy outcome research: Separating association from bias. *Clinical Psychology: Science and Practice, 16,* 54–65. doi.10.1111/j.1468-2850.2009.01143.x.

Lightsey, O. (2006). Resilience, meaning, and well-being. *The Counseling Psychologist, 34,* 96–107. doi.10.1177/0011000005282369.

Linley, P. A. & Joseph, S. (Eds.). (2004). *Positive Psychology in practice.* Hoboken, NJ: John Wiley.

Linley, P. A., Nielsen, K. M., Wood, A. M., Gillett, R., & Biswas-Diener, R., (2010). Using signature strengths in pursuit of goals: Effects on goal progress, need satisfaction, and well-being, and implications for coaching psychologists. *International Coaching Psychology Review, 5,* 8–17.

Lu, W., Wang, Z., & Liu, Y. (2013). A pilot study on changes of cardiac vagal tone in individuals with low trait positive affect: The effect of positive psychotherapy. *International Journal of Psychophysiology, 88,* 213–217. doi.10.1016/j.ijpsycho.2013.04.012.

Luyten, L., Boddez, Y., & Hermans, D. (2015). Positive appraisal style: The mental immune system? *Behavioral and Brain Sciences, 38,* e112. doi.10.1017/S0140525X14001629.

Lyubomirsky, S., Caldwell, N. D., & Nolen-Hoeksema, S. (1998). Effects of ruminative and distracting responses to depressed mood on retrieval of autobiographical memories. *Journal of Personality and Social Psychology, 75,* 166–177.

Lyubomirsky, S. & Layous, K. (2013). How do simple positive activities increase well-being? *Current Directions in Psychological Science, 22,* 57–62. doi.0.1177/0963721412469809.

Magyar-Moe, J. L. (2009). *Therapist's guide to positive psychological interventions.* New York: Elsevier Academic.

McKnight, P. E. & Kashdan, T. B. (2009). Purpose in life as a system that creates and sustains health and well-being: An integrative, testable theory. *Review of General Psychology, 13,* 242–251.

McNulty, J. K. & Fincham, F. D. (2012). Beyond positive psychology? Toward a contextual view of psychological process and well-being. *American Psychologist, 67,* 101–110.

Meyer, P. S., Johnson, D. P., Parks, A., Iwanski, C., & Penn, D. L. (2012). Positive living: A pilot study of group positive psychotherapy for people with schizophrenia. *Journal of Positive Psychology, 7,* 239–248. doi.10.1080/17439760.2012.677467.

Mitchell, J., Stanimirovic, R., Klein, B., & Vella-Brodrick, D. (2009). A randomised controlled trial of a self-guided internet intervention promoting well-being. *Computers in Human Behavior, 25,* 749–760. doi.10.1016/j.chb.2009.02.003.

Moeenizadeh, M. & Salagame, K. K. K. (2010). Well-being therapy (WBT) for depression. *International Journal of Psychological Studies, 2,* 107–115.

Mongrain, M. & Anselmo-Matthews, T. (2012). Do positive psychology exercises work? A replication of Seligman et al. (2005). *Journal of Clinical Psychology, 68,* 382–389.

Murray, G. & Johnson, S. L. (2010). The clinical significance of creativity in bipolar disorder. *Clinical psychology Review, 30,* 721–32. doi.10.1016/j.cpr.2010.05.006.

Niemiec, R. M., Rashid, T., & Spinella, M. (2012). Strong mindfulness: Integrating mindfulness and character strengths. *Journal of Mental Health Counseling, 34,* 240–253.

Oksanen, T., Kouvonen, A., Vahtera, J., Virtanen, M., & Kivimäki, M. (2010). Prospective study of workplace social capital and depression: Are vertical and horizontal components equally important? *Journal of Epidemiology and Community Health, 64,* 684–689. doi.10.1136/jech. 2008.086074.

Olfson, M. & Marcus, S. C. (2010). National trends in outpatient psychotherapy. *American Journal of Psychiatry, 167,* 1456–1463.

Park, N. & Peterson, C. (2006). Values in action (VIA) inventory of character strengths for youth. *Adolescent & Family Health, 4,* 35–40.

Parks, A., Della Porta, M., Pierce, R. S., Zilca, R., & Lyubomirsky, S. (2012). Pursuing happiness in everyday life: The characteristics and behaviors of online happiness seekers. *Emotion, 12,* 1222–1234.

Parrott, W. G. (Ed.). (2014). *The positive side of negative emotions.* New York : Guilford.

Pedrotti, J. T. (2011). Broadening perspectives: Strategies to infuse multiculturalism into a positive psychology course. *Journal of Positive Psychology, 6*(6), 506–513. doi.10.1080/17439760. 2011.634817.

Proctor, C. & Linley, A. (Eds.). (2013). *Research, applications, and interventions for children and adolescents: A positive psychology perspective.* New York: Springer.

Peterson, C. (2006). *A Primer in Positive Psychology.* New York: Oxford University Press.

Peterson, C. (2013). *Pursuing the good life: 100 reflections on positive psychology.* New York: Oxford University Press.

Peterson, C. & Seligman, M. E. P. (2004). *Character strengths and virtues: A handbook and classification.* Oxford and Washington, DC: Oxford University Press and American Psychological Association.

Peterson, C., Park, N., Seligman M. E. P. (2005). Orientations to happiness and life satisfaction: The full life versus the empty life. *Journal of Happiness Studies, 6,* 25–41.

Pietrowsky, R. & Mikutta, J. (2012). Effects of positive psychology interventions in depressive patients: A randomized control study. *Psychology, 3,* 1067–1073.

Radloff, L. (1977). The CES-D Scale. *Applied Psychological Measurement, 1,* 385–401. doi.10.1177/014662167700100306.

Rashid, T. (2005). *Positive Psychotherapy Inventory (PPTI).* Unpublished Manuscript, University of Pennsylvania.

Rashid, T. (2008). Positive psychotherapy. In: S. J. Lopez (Ed.), *Positive psychology, vol. 4: Exploring the best in people* (pp. 188–217). Westport, CT: Praeger.

Rashid, T. (2013). Positive psychology in practice: Positive psychotherapy. *The Oxford handbook of happiness* (pp. 978–993). New York: Oxford University Press.

Rashid, T. (2015). Positive psychotherapy: A strength-based approach. *Journal of Positive Psychology,* doi. 10.1080/17439760.2014.920411.

Rashid, T. & Anjum, A. (2008). Positive psychotherapy for young adults and children. In: J. R. Z. Abela & B. L. Hankin (Eds.), *Depression in children and adolescents: Causes, treatment and prevention* (pp. 250–287). New York: Guilford Press.

Rashid, T. & Ostermann, R. F. O. (2009). Strength-based assessment in clinical practice. *Journal of Clinical Psychology, 65,* 488–498.

Rashid, T. & Seligman, M. E. (in press). *Positive Psychotherapy: A manual.* Oxford: Oxford University Press.

Rashid, T. & Seligman, M. E. P. (2013). Positive psychotherapy. In: D. Wedding & R. J. Corsini (Eds.), *Current psychotherapies.* (pp. 461–498). Belmont, CA: Cengage.

Rashid, T., Anjum, A., Lennex, C., Quinlin, D., Niemiec, R., Mayerson, D., Kazemi, F. (2013). In: C. Proctor & A. Linley (Eds.), *Research, applications, and interventions for children and adolescents: A positive psychology perspective.* New York: Springer.

Reinsch, C. (2012). *Adding science to the mix of business and pleasure: An exploratory study of positive psychology interventions with teachers accessing employee assistance counselling.* Master's thesis, University of Manitoba, Winnipeg, Manitoba, Canada.

Riches, S., Schrank, B., Rashid, T., & Slade, M. (2015). WELLFOCUS PPT: Modifying Positive Psychotherapy for psychosis. *Psychotherapy.* Advance online publication. doi.org/10.1037/pst0000013

Rozin, P. & Royzman, E. (2001). Negativity bias, negativity dominance, and contagion. *Personality and Social Psychology Review, 5,* 296–320.

Ruini C. & Fava G. A. (2009). Well-being therapy for generalized anxiety disorder. *Journal of Clinical Psychology, 65,* 510–519.

Ryff, C. D. (1989). Happiness is everything, or is it? Explorations on the meaning of psychological well-being. *Journal of Personality and Social Psychology, 57,* 1069–1081.

Salerno, S. (2006). A very critical look at the self-help movement. A review of SHAM: How the self-help movement made America helpless. *Psycritiques, 51,* 2.

Sandler, S. (2007). The reunion process: A new focus in short-term dynamic psychotherapy. *Psychotherapy, 44,* 121–36. doi.10.1037/0033-3204.44.2.121.

Scheel, M. J., Davis, C. K., & Henderson, J. D. (2012). Therapist use of client strengths: A qualitative study of Positive processes. *The Counseling Psychologist, 41*(3), 392–427. doi.10.1177/0011000012439427.

Scheier, M. F., Carver, C. S., & Bridges, M. W. (1994). Distinguishing optimism from neuroticism (and trait anxiety, self-mastery, and self-esteem): A reevaluation of the Life Orientation Test. *Journal of Personality and Social Psychology, 67,* 1063–1078. doi.10.1037/0022-3514.67.6.1063.

Schrank, B., Brownell, T., Jakaite, Z., Larkin, C., Pesola, F., Riches, S., Slade, M., et al. (2015). Evaluation of a positive psychotherapy group intervention for people with psychosis: Pilot randomised controlled trial. *Epidemiology and Psychiatric Sciences*, doi.10.1017/S2045796015000141.

Schrank, B., Bird, V., Tylee, A., Coggins, T., Rashid, T., & Slade, M. (2013). Conceptualising and measuring the well-being of people with psychosis: Systematic review and narrative synthesis. *Social Science and Medicine*, 92, 9–21. doi.10.1016/j.socscimed.2013.05.011.

Schueller, S. (2010). Preferences for positive psychology exercises. *Journal of Positive Psychology*, 5, 192–203.

Schueller, S. M. & Parks, A. C. (2012). Disseminating self-help: Positive psychology exercises in an online trial. *Journal of Medical Internet Research*, 14(3), e63. doi.10.2196/jmir.1850.

Schwartz, B. & Sharpe, K. E. (2006). Practical wisdom: Aristotle meets Positive Psychology. *Journal of Happiness Studies*, 7, 377–395.

Schwartz, B., Ward, A., Monterosso, J., Lyubomirsky, S., White, K., & Lehman, D. R. (2002). Maximizing versus satisficing: Happiness is a matter of choice. *Journal of Personality and Social Psychology*, 83, 1178–1197. doi.10.1037/0022-3514.83.5.1178.

Schwartz, R. M., Reynolds III, C. F., Thase, M. E., Frank, E., Fasiczka, A. L., & Haaga, D. A. F. (2002). Optimal and normal affect balance in psychotherapy of major depression: Evaluation of the balanced states of mind model. *Behavioral and Cognitive Psychotherapy*, 30, 439–450.

Seery, M. D., Holman, E. A., & Silver, R. C. (2010). Whatever does not kill us: Cumulative lifetime adversity, vulnerability, and resilience. *Journal of Personality and Social Psychology*, 99(6), 1025–1041. doi.10.1037/a0021344.

Seligman, M. E. P. (2002). *Authentic happiness: Using the new Positive Psychology to realize your potential for lasting fulfillment*. New York: Free Press.

Seligman, M. E. P. (2011). *Flourish: A visionary new understanding of happiness and well-being*. New York: Simon & Schuster.

Seligman, M. E. P., Steen, T. A., Park, N., & Peterson, C. (2005). Positive psychology progress: Empirical validation of interventions. *American Psychologist*, 60, 410–421.

Seligman, M. E., Rashid, T., & Parks, A. C. (2006). Positive psychotherapy. *American Psychologist*, 61, 774–788. doi.10.1037/0003-066X.61.8.774.

Seligman, M. E., Steen, T. A., Park, N., & Peterson, C. (2005). Positive psychology progress: empirical validation of interventions. *American Psychologist*, 60, 410-421. doi.10.1037/0003-066X.60.5.410.

Senf, K. & Liau, A. K. (2013). The effects of positive interventions on happiness and depressive symptoms, with an examination of personality as a moderator. *Journal of Happiness Studies*, 14, 591–612. doi.10.1007/s10902-012-9344-4.

Simons, J. S. & Gaher, R. M. (2005). The distress tolerance scale: Development and validation of a self-report measure. *Motivation and Emotion*, 29, 83–102. doi.http://dx.doi.org/10.1007/s11031-005-7955-3.

Sin, N. L. & Lyubomirsky, S. (2009). Enhancing well-being and alleviating depressive symptoms with positive psychology interventions: A practice-friendly meta-analysis. *Journal of Clinical Psychology*, 65, 467–487. doi.10.1002/jclp.20593.

Sirgy, M. J. & Wu, J. (2009). The pleasant life, the engaged life, and the meaningful life: What about the balanced life? *Journal of Happiness Studies*, 10, 183–196.

Slade, M. (2010). Mental illness and well-being: The central importance of positive psychology and recovery approaches. *BMC Health Services Research*, 10(26).

Smith, E. J. (2006). The strength-based counseling model. *Counseling Psychologist*, 34, 13–79.

Smith, E. E. & Aaker, J. L. (2013). Millennial searchers, Sunday Review, *The New York Times*, November 30, 2013. Available at: http://www.nytimes.com/2013/12/01/opinion/sunday/millennial-searchers.html?_r=0, last accessed June 13, 2015.

Spanier, G. B. (1976). Measuring dyadic adjustment: New scales for assessing the quality of marriage and similar dyads. *Journal of Marriage and the Family*, 38, 15–28.

Steger, M. F. & Shin, J. Y. (2010). The relevance of the meaning in life questionnaire to therapeutic practice: A look at the initial evidence. *International Forum for Logotherapy*, 33, 95–104.

Stillman, T. F. & Baumeister, R. F. (2009). Uncertainty, belongingness, and four needs for meaning. *Psychological Inquiry*, 20, 249–251.

Valiunas, A. (2010). The science of self-help. *The New Atlantis*. Summer.

Van Dillen, L. F. & Koole, S. L. (2007). Clearing the mind: A working memory model of distraction from negative mood. *Emotion, 7,* 715–23. doi.10.1037/1528-3542.7.4.715.

Vandenberghe, L. & Silvestre, R. L. S. (2014). Therapists' positive emotions in-session: Where they come from and what they are good for. *Counselling and Psychotherapy Research, 14,* 119–127.

Vella-Brodrick, D. A., Park, N., & Peterson, C. (2009). Three ways to be happy: Pleasure, engagement, and meaning: Findings from Australian and U.S. samples. *Social Indicators Research, 90,* 165–179.

Uliaszek, A., Rashid, T., Williams, G., & Gulamani, T. (2016). Group therapy for university students: A randomized control trial of dialectical behavior therapy and positive psychotherapy. *Behaviour Research and Therapy, 77,* 78–85.

Waters, L. (2011). A review of school-based positive psychology interventions. *Australian Educational and Developmental Psychologist, 28*(2), 75–90. doi.org/10.1375/aedp.28.2.75.

Watson, D., Clark, L. A. & Tellegen, A. (1988). Development and validation of brief measures of positive and negative affect: The PANAS scales. *Journal of Personality and Social Psychology, 54,* 1063–1070.

Williams, L. M., Gatt, J. M., Schofield, P. R., Olivieri, G., Peduto, A., & Gordon, E. (2009). Negativity bias in risk for depression and anxiety: Brain–body fear circuitry correlates, 5-HTT-LPR and early life stress. *NeuroImage, 47,* 804–814. doi.http://dx.doi.org/10.1016/j.

Wong, W. J. (2012). Strength-centered therapy: A social constructionist, virtue-based psychotherapy. *Psychotherapy, 43,* 133–146.

Wood, A. M. & Joseph, S. (2010). The absence of positive psychological (eudemonic) well-being as a risk factor for depression: a ten year cohort study. *Journal of Affective Disorders, 122,* 213–217. doi.10.1016/j.jad.2009.06.032.

Wood, A. M., Maltby, J., Gillett, R., Linley, P. A., & Joseph, S. (2008). The role of gratitude in the development of social support, stress, and depression: Two longitudinal studies. *Journal of Research in Personality, 42,* 854–871.

Worthington, E. L., Witvliet, C. V. O., Pietrini, P., & Miller, A. J. (2007). Forgiveness, health, and well-being: A review of evidence for emotional versus decisional forgiveness, *Journal of Behavioral Medicine, 30*(4), 291–302. doi.10.1007/s10865-007-9105-8.

Wrzesniewski, A., McCauley, C., Rozin, P., & Schwartz, B. (1997). Jobs, careers, and callings: People's relations to their work. *Journal of Research in Personality, 31,* 21–33.

Young, K. C., Kashdan, T. B., & Macatee, R. (2014). Strength balance and implicit strength measurement: New considerations for research on strengths of character. *Journal of Positive Psychology, 2015,* 1–8. doi.10.1080/17439760.2014.920406.

Zung, W. W. K (1965). A self-rating depression scale. *Archives of General Psychiatry, 12,* 63–70.

23

Positive Activity Interventions for Mental Health Conditions
Basic Research and Clinical Applications

Lilian J. Shin and Sonja Lyubomirsky

Need for Novel Approaches

In the twenty-first century, mental health has come to be increasingly understood as both the absence of mental illness and the presence of positive psychological resources. Accordingly, we expect positive psychological science to play a critical role in treating mental disorders – particularly, mood disorders. Depression is on the rise, affecting over 150 million people worldwide in 2003 and over 350 million people worldwide in 2012 (World Health Organization (WHO), 2003, 2012; Marcus, Yasamy, van Ommeren, Chisholm, & Saxena, 2012). The World Mental Health Survey conducted in 17 countries found that on average about 1 in 20 people reported having an episode of depression in the previous year (Marcus et al., 2012). In the United States, 9.5% of the adult population suffers from a mood disorder, and 45% of these cases are classified as "severe" (Kessler, Chiu, Demler, & Walters, 2005).

The high prevalence and incidence of mood disorders does not mean that they do not cause a great deal of suffering. Depressive disorders often emerge at a young age, substantially reduce people's daily functioning, and are often chronic or recurrent. For these reasons, they are the leading cause of disability worldwide for both males and females in terms of total years lost due to disability (Marcus et al., 2012). Almost 1 million lives are lost yearly due to suicide, which is equivalent to 3,000 suicide deaths per day. Moreover, for every person who completes a suicide, another 20 attempt it (Marcus et al., 2012; Substance Abuse and Mental Health Services Administration (SAMHSA), 2012).

Although there are established effective treatments for depression, such as psychotherapy and pharmacotherapy, fewer than half of individuals with depression in the world, fewer than one-third in most regions, and fewer than 1 in 10 in some countries receive treatment (WHO, 2003, 2012; Marcus et al., 2012). This means that in most regions of the world, two-thirds of *reported* cases of depression go untreated. Even in developed nations, many people who are depressed are not correctly diagnosed. Barriers to effective care include a lack of financial resources, the lack of trained providers, and the stigma associated with mental disorders (Marcus et al., 2012; SAMHSA, 2012; WHO, 2012).

Not being able to afford treatment is the number one reason for not receiving needed mental health care (SAMHSA, 2012). Therapeutic interventions are costly, ranging from $200 for three psychotherapy sessions to upwards of $1,200 for the American Psychological Association's

The Wiley Handbook of Positive Clinical Psychology, First Edition. Edited by Alex M. Wood and Judith Johnson.
© 2016 John Wiley & Sons, Ltd. Published 2016 by John Wiley & Sons, Ltd.

recommended course of treatment of at least 10 psychotherapy sessions combined with antidepressant medication for optimal care of moderate to severe depression (Watkins, Burnam, Orlando, Escarce, Huskamp, & Goldman, 2009). In addition, individuals at high risk of depression – such as those with low economic resources or young adults aged 19–34 years – may be most likely to lack health insurance and be least able to afford treatment (Wang, Schmitz, & Dewa, 2010; SAMHSA, 2012; Smith & Medalia, 2014).

Furthermore, studies have shown that treatment with antidepressants has limited efficacy. Response rates for a single antidepressant have been found to be around 60–70%, with over 80% of the effects accounted for by placebo effects (Kirsch, Moore, Scoboria, & Nicholls, 2002). Among all but "very severely" depressed patients, effect sizes for the difference between medication and placebo are small (i.e., less than .20) (Fournier et al., 2010; Khin, Chen, Yang, Yang, & Laughren, 2011). Furthermore, the onset of treatment action is typically 4–8 weeks (American Psychiatric Association, 2010), and about one-third of patients will not remit even after two to four different pharmacotherapy trials (Rush, 2007). Antidepressants can also be associated with adverse side effects, such as nausea, sexual dysfunction, and weight gain, which can result in premature discontinuation (American Psychiatric Association, 2010). Finally, persons treated with antidepressants are more likely to relapse than those treated with cognitive and behavioral therapies, which appear to teach strategies that help patients to avoid falling back into negative thought patterns and behaviors (Evans et al., 1992; Fava, Ruini, Rafanelli, Finos, Conti, & Grandi, 2004; Dobson et al., 2008).

Why Use Positive Activity Interventions to Alleviate Depression?

Cost-effective, quick-acting, efficacious, and long-lasting treatments are needed to augment traditional drug and psychotherapy treatments. In this chapter, we describe the potential of positive activity interventions (PAIs): that is, simple, self-administered cognitive and behavioral strategies that can increase subjective well-being (i.e., happiness) by promoting positive feelings, positive thoughts, and positive behaviors. Such practices include (but are not limited to) writing letters of gratitude (Seligman, Steen, Park, & Peterson, 2005; Boehm, Lyubomirsky, & Sheldon, 2011; Lyubomirsky, Dickerhoof, Boehm, & Sheldon, 2011; Layous, Lee, Choi, & Lyubomirsky, 2013a); counting one's blessings (Emmons & McCullough, 2003; Lyubomirsky, Sheldon, & Schkade, 2005b; Seligman et al., 2005; Froh, Sefick, & Emmons, 2008; Chancellor, Layous, & Lyubomirsky, 2014); practicing optimism (King, 2001; Sheldon & Lyubomirsky, 2006; Boehm et al., 2011; Lyubomirsky et al., 2011; Layous, Nelson, & Lyubomirsky, 2013b); performing acts of kindness (Lyubomirsky et al., 2005b; Dunn, Aknin, & Norton, 2008; Layous, Nelson, Oberle, Schonert-Reichl, & Lyubomirsky, 2012; Sheldon, Boehm, & Lyubomirsky, 2012; Layous et al., 2013a; Nelson et al., in press); using one's strengths in a new way (Seligman et al., 2005); affirming one's most important values (Nelson, Fuller, Choi, & Lyubomirsky, 2014); and meditating on positive feelings toward oneself and others (Fredrickson, Cohn, Coffey, Pek, & Finkel, 2008).

Traditional therapies have focused on alleviating negative moods and cognitions and have been less concerned with building positive emotions, thoughts, and behaviors (Seligman & Csikszentmihalyi, 2000). However, negative affect and positive affect are independent constructs (Watson & Tellegen, 1985), and the absence of negative feelings is not equivalent to the presence of positive ones. We propose that PAIs could complement traditional drug and psychotherapy treatments by building strengths and working to address the paucity of positive affect, engagement, and life meaning that characterize depression. Historically, conventional treatments have focused on mitigating depressive symptoms, but most people want not only to not be depressed but also to flourish and feel happy.

Because PAIs can be self-administered, or administered in group or individual therapy, they can be highly cost-effective. Most PAIs require little more than self-reflection (gratefulness, optimism, savoring of experiences, goal setting) or the cultivation of current social relationships (Layous, Chancellor, Lyubomirsky, Wang, & Doraiswamy, 2011).

Some evidence also suggests that PAIs can work quickly and durably. Seligman and his colleagues' (2005) study of mildly depressed individuals showed a significant decrease in depressive symptoms after just one week or less of PAIs and those effects lasted at least 6 months. In contrast, placebo group participants experienced a short-term boost in well-being, but returned to their baseline levels of depression after a week. In another study with severely depressed individuals, participants' depressive symptoms declined from severe to mild-to-moderate within just 15 days of practicing a PAI (Seligman, 2002).

A meta-analysis conducted in 2009 of 51 studies of PAIs with 4,266 individuals revealed that, overall, PAIs do indeed significantly enhance well-being (mean r [effect size] = .29) and reduce depressive symptoms (mean r = .31) over controls (Sin & Lyubomirsky, 2009). A more recent meta-analysis of 39 PAIs found similar though somewhat smaller effect sizes: namely, .34 for well-being and .23 for depression (Bolier, Haverman, Westerhof, Riper, Smit, & Bohlmeijer, 2013). These effect sizes are small- to medium-sized, indicating that not only do PAIs work, but they work well in increasing well-being and decreasing depressive symptoms. To gain perspective on the practical significance of the magnitude of these effects, consider that a highly cited meta-analysis of 375 psychotherapy studies (Smith & Glass, 1977) demonstrated that psychotherapy had an average effect size of r = .32 on various psychological outcomes, such as adjustment and self-esteem.

Finally, PAIs have not only been shown to reliably boost well-being, but also to promote other positive outcomes by increasing positive emotions. The value of positive emotions goes beyond just "feeling good." They precede, are associated with, and may even cause enduring positive outcomes in a variety of life domains, including greater marital satisfaction, enhanced social relationships, superior job performance, and higher creativity (Lyubomirsky, King, & Diener, 2005a). As a case in point, the health benefits of positive emotions are especially relevant to those suffering from depression: Positive emotions speed recovery from the cardiovascular effects of negative emotions (Fredrickson & Levenson, 1998; Tugade & Fredrickson, 2004), buffer against relapses (Fava & Ruini, 2003), and build broad-minded coping skills (Fredrickson & Joiner, 2002). According to Fredrickson's (2001) broaden-and-build theory, positive emotions broaden thinking, which leads to novel ideas and actions (i.e., the urge to play and explore) and to the building of long-lasting personal resources (e.g., durable social bonds and attachments). In contrast to the narrowing of attention (Gasper & Clore, 2002) and behavioral inhibition (Kasch, Rottenberg, Arnow, & Gotlib, 2002) characteristic of negative affective states, positive emotions trigger upward spirals towards greater emotional well-being (Fredrickson & Joiner, 2002).

Positive Activity Interventions For Nondepressed Individuals

Most research on PAIs has been conducted on nondepressed, nonclinical populations. As described above, there are many PAIs that can increase well-being, but those involving the practice of gratitude, kindness, and optimism are three of the most empirically supported by randomized controlled experiments.

Gratitude

Gratitude – the practice of attending to, savoring, and being thankful for one's circumstances and close ones – can promote well-being by preventing one from taking things for granted, strengthening connections with others, and providing an effective coping strategy during difficult times. In an oft-cited study conducted by Emmons and McCullough (2003), participants were directed to "count their blessings" by listing five things for which they were grateful.

Those who engaged in this activity weekly for 10 weeks felt better about their lives as a whole, were more optimistic about their expectations for the upcoming week, and reported fewer physical symptoms relative to neutral control groups. Additionally, counting blessings led to more positive moods, better sleep, and a greater sense of social connectedness in a sample of participants with neuromuscular disease.

Similarly, a six-week study found that counting blessings increased well-being; however, it also demonstrated that frequency mattered, such that students who counted blessings once a week became happier compared with those who did so three times a week (Lyubomirsky et al., 2005a). A recent study randomly assigned employees of an engineering firm to either recount three positive events at work or list completed work tasks (control) (Chancellor et al., 2014). Employees who reflected on positive work events not only reported greater happiness, but also physically moved more than did controls.

Grateful thinking has also been manipulated by prompting participants to write gratitude letters to mentors, friends, or family members. In a longitudinal study of Anglo and Asian Americans, all participants conveying gratitude demonstrated larger increases in life satisfaction relative to controls, with the greatest gains demonstrated by the Anglo Americans (Boehm et al., 2011). Similarly, a cross-cultural study found that compared with controls, US participants benefitted more from writing gratitude letters than South Korean participants (Layous et al., 2013a). These results suggest that Americans may place more effort and commitment into trying to become more grateful. For example, one study showed that relatively more motivated students reported relatively greater increases in well-being after writing gratitude letters (Lyubomirsky et al., 2011). Additionally, participants who put more effort into their gratitude letters (as rated by independent coders) showed greater increases in well-being.

Kindness

Kindness, or prosocial behavior, has also been found to correlate with and promote well-being. Otake and colleagues (2006) found that happy people not only desire to be kind, but they also are more attuned to kindness, and more likely to behave in kind ways. Furthermore, these authors showed that people could become happier simply by "counting kindness" for one week: that is, by keeping track of their own kind behavior towards others. Those recalling a greater number of kind behaviors obtained the largest increases in happiness. People who help others are likely to feel good about themselves and more confident in their abilities to enact change. Furthermore, their prosocial behavior likely helps build better relationships and trigger upward spirals of positive emotions and positive interpersonal exchanges (Lyubomirsky, 2005a; Otake et al., 2006).

An intervention study conducted by Lyubomirsky, Sheldon, and Schkade (2005a) asked students to perform (rather than recall) five acts of kindness per week over a period of six weeks. They found that well-being in the kindness group increased compared with the control group when the five acts were performed all in one day, but not when they were spread across the week. A cross-cultural study showed that both US and South Korean students reported increases in well-bring when performing three kind acts once a week over six weeks (Layous et al., 2013a). Finally, children have been shown to benefit from performing kind acts as well. In a field experiment, fourth, fifth, and sixth graders (ages 9–11) who performed kind acts not only improved in well-being, but also increased in peer acceptance (Layous et al., 2012).

Optimism

Another way to reliably increase well-being is by practicing optimistic thinking, for example, by visualizing one's "best possible selves" in the future. A pioneering study conducted by King (2001) instructed participants to "imagine everything has gone as well as it possibly could" once a day for four consecutive days and to write about it for 20 minutes. Individuals who engaged in this activity experienced a greater boost to their positive moods than those who wrote about a trauma or both trauma and their best possible selves. In addition, those who wrote about their best possible selves reported relatively less illness 5 months later. A more recent follow-up study impressively demonstrated that even 2 minutes of writing about "best possible selves" on two consecutive days could result in similar benefits (Burton & King, 2008).

These results were replicated in a four-week study: participants who imagined and wrote about their best possible selves witnessed both immediate and sustained boosts in positive affect compared with those performing a control exercise (Sheldon & Lyubomirsky, 2006). In follow-up studies, students who wrote about their best possible selves for 15 minutes a week over eight weeks (Lyubomirsky et al., 2011) and community-dwelling adults who wrote for 10 minutes a week over six weeks (Boehm et al., 2011) both increased in well-being compared with controls. Notably, the increases in well-being between experimental and control groups remained even six months and one month, respectively, after the interventions ended. Finally, a study asking students to write about their best possible selves once a week for four weeks found that participants who read a persuasive peer testimonial became happier than those who read neutral information or completed a control task, highlighting the beneficial role of social support (Layous et al., 2013b).

In summary, PAIs involving the practice of gratitude, kindness, and optimism have been shown to reliably increase well-being across many different settings in nonclinical samples.

Positive Activity Interventions for Depressed Individuals

A few studies have tested the efficacy of PAIs for clinically depressed individuals. For example, Seligman and colleagues (2005) found that mildly depressed individuals instructed to write and deliver a gratitude letter increased in happiness and decreased in depressive symptoms immediately afterwards and at a one-month follow-up compared with controls. In the same study, participants who used their signature strengths in a new way or kept track of "three good things" in their lives increased in happiness and decreased in depressive symptoms for up to six months relative to controls. In a different experiment, severely depressed individuals instructed to write about three good things every day for two weeks witnessed significant improvements in their depression (from severe to mild-to-moderate) (Seligman, 2002).

Although few studies have investigated the effects of individual PAIs (e.g., only exercising kindness) in clinical populations, researchers have developed and tested several therapy programs that incorporate multiple PAIs (e.g., practicing kindness, savoring happy moments, and thinking optimistically over the course of several weeks). Such programs include pioneering research on positive psychotherapy (PPT) and well-being therapy (WBT).

In a six-week study of PPT, mildly-to-moderately depressed young adults were assigned to participate in group PPT or to a no-treatment control condition (Seligman, Rashid, & Parks, 2006). The PPT consisted of various positive exercises each week, including counting blessings, practicing active and constructive responding to one's partner, using one's strengths, writing a gratitude letter, and savoring everyday activities. During two-hour weekly sessions, participants engaged in group discussions, received guidance on how to carry out the positive exercises, and were assigned homework. Group PPT was indeed efficacious for ameliorating depressive symptoms and increasing life satisfaction. The results for the lasting relief of depression were impressive: on average, PPT participants reported less depression up to a year later, whereas those in the control group remained mildly-to-moderately depressed.

To compare PPT with traditional treatments for depression, Seligman and colleagues (2006) then randomly assigned individuals with major depressive disorder to receive either 14 sessions of PPT, treatment as usual (involving integrative and eclectic "traditional" psychotherapeutic interventions), or both treatment as usual and antidepressant mediation (matched to PPT clients based on the severity of depression). PPT was administered using a manualized protocol with the aim of balancing the overwhelming negatives of depression with the establishment of congenial and empathetic rapport, coaching the client to remember the good in his or her life, identifying and using the client's strengths, and teaching positive social behaviors. Results showed that PPT produced greater happiness, more symptomatic improvement, and higher remission rates than both treatment as usual and treatment as usual plus medication.

Other research suggests that therapies that enhance well-being may confer an advantage over traditional therapies for relieving *residual* symptoms of major depression. One such therapy, WBT, aims to improve six dimensions of psychological well-being: autonomy, personal growth, environmental mastery, purpose in life, positive relations, and self-acceptance (Ryff, 1989; Fava & Ruini, 2003). In WBT, participants are encouraged to self-monitor episodes of well-being, identify and change beliefs that interrupt well-being, and reinforce beliefs that promote well-being (Fava & Ruini, 2003). Indeed, in a study of 20 patients with remitted affective disorders, WBT resulted in greater increases in psychological well-being compared with cognitive-behavioral therapy according to observer-rated methods (Fava, Rafanelli, Cazzaro, Conti, & Grandi, 1998).

Interventions that promote specific positive perspectives (including forgiveness, hope, and mindfulness meditation) have also been shown to enhance mental health and reduce depressive symptoms. For example, a meta-analysis of several controlled forgiveness interventions suggested that willfully giving up resentment and cultivating empathy for an offender can improve emotional health, as measured by scales of depression, anxiety, hope, and self-esteem (Baskin & Enright, 2004).

Hope therapy is designed to help individuals set meaningful goals, identify pathways to pursuing those goals, and strengthen motivation and monitor progress towards those goals (Snyder et al., 1991; Cheavens, Feldman, Gum, Michael, & Snyder, 2006). A randomized, wait-list controlled study of 32 community members – many of whom had previously undergone psychological treatment and met criteria for a mental disorder – demonstrated that hope-based group therapy reduced depression and enhanced self-esteem and meaning in life (Cheavens et al., 2006).

Finally, the practice of mindfulness meditation, which involves intentional, non-judgmental awareness and acceptance of the present moment (Kabat-Zinn, 1990), has benefitted treatment-resistant individuals with depression (Eisendrath, Delucchi, Bitner, Fenimore, Smit, & McLane, 2008), reduced residual depressive symptoms (Kuyken et al., 2008), decreased rumination (Ramel, Goldin, Carmona, & McQuaid, 2004), and prevented relapse in recurrent depression (Kuyken et al., 2008).

How Positive Activities Can Alleviate Clinical Symptoms

By Boosting Well-Being

We argue that PAIs can boost well-being in clinical populations by stimulating increases in positive emotions, positive thoughts, positive behaviors, and need satisfaction, which in turn increase happiness. Evidence for these mediating processes comes from studies conducted with healthy populations. For example, a meditation-based positive activity triggered increases in positive emotions, which, in turn, improved personal resources such as social relationships and physical health. These enhanced personal resources then boosted life satisfaction (Fredrickson et al., 2008). In another study, people who practiced gratitude and optimism reported their life experiences as more satisfying, even though objective raters did not indicate actual improvements in these experiences, highlighting how PAIs can shift people's construals of their life events in a positive direction (Dickerhoof, 2007). Furthermore, positive activities, such as counting blessings, have also led participants to increase time spent exercising (an unrelated positive behavior) (Emmons & McCullough, 2003).

Positive activities may also boost well-being by satisfying basic psychological needs, such as autonomy (control) and connectedness (relatedness) (Deci & Ryan, 2000). A six-week intervention found that expressing gratitude and optimism increased self-reported autonomy and connectedness, which, in turn, increased life satisfaction (Boehm, Lyubomirsky, & Sheldon, 2012). In a study that directly manipulated these hypothesized mediators, people who engaged in autonomy- and connectedness-enhancing activities attained greater well-being than people who focused on their life circumstances (Sheldon et al., 2010).

By Being Implemented Optimally

To achieve maximal well-being effects in depressed individuals, PAIs must also be implemented in optimal ways. To enhance the efficacy of any particular PAI, researchers must consider (and optimize) the fundamental features of the activity, as well as the person practicing it.

Activity features Any positive activity used in an intervention has certain characteristics – for example, its dosage, its duration, the variety with which it is practiced, and the format with which it is presented – that are likely to impact its effectiveness in raising well-being and alleviating depression. For example, in general, interventions longer in duration (and of optimal dosage) tend to be more effective than shorter ones (Sin & Lyubomirsky, 2009). In a six-week experiment, only students who performed five acts of kindness in a single day experienced increases in well-being compared with controls; those who spread them over one week were no happier than controls (Lyubomirsky et al., 2005b). Because the kind acts were small (i.e., cooking dinner for others, babysitting a sibling), performing them in one day may have delivered a salient burst of positive emotion, which then set into motion an upward spiral of psychological well-being, such that feeling joyful and fulfilled on Monday promoted more productivity at work on Tuesday, and led to performing even more kind acts for a friend on Wednesday, and so on (cf. Fredrickson & Joiner, 2002). PAIs, however, can also be overpracticed, which weakens their freshness and meaning for individuals. Lyubomirsky, Sheldon, and Schkade (2005b) instructed participants to cultivate grateful thinking either once or three times a week. Results suggested that frequency (or dosage) mattered: namely, only participants who counted blessings once a week experienced increases in well-being.

Because practitioners can begin to take for granted or lose enthusiasm for a particular PAI as they practice it over a period of time, it is important to consider what factors can slow down this adaptation. One such factor is the variety with which the positive activity is practiced. Supporting this idea, a ten-week intervention revealed that only those who varied their kind acts each week increased in well-being; those who did not actually became less happy midway through the intervention (Sheldon et al., 2012). PAI practitioners can inject variety by changing up particular strategies or by engaging in several different kinds of positive activities – simultaneously or serially.

Finally, intervention format is associated with greater gains in well-being when practicing PAIs, such that PAIs are most effective (as represented by larger effect sizes) when administered one-on-one, followed by group administration and then by self-administration (Sin & Lyubomirsky, 2009).

Person features Additionally, features of the person practicing PAIs – for example, her motivation and effort, her beliefs about the efficacy of the PAI, her baseline affective state, and her social support – also affect the success of the interventions. For instance, among participants who visualized their best possible selves, those who identified with and expected to enjoy the exercise were more likely to put effort into continuing the exercise at home over 4 weeks; as a result, they witnessed increases in positive mood immediately after the intervention, as well as maintenance of these boosts, relative to those who engaged in a control activity (Sheldon & Lyubomirsky, 2006). Likewise, in another study, US participants who reported summoning greater effort when practicing gratitude or kindness experienced significantly larger increases in well-being relative to participants who reported less effort (Layous et al., 2013a). In other words, PAIs boost well-being when people are aware of their purpose, motivated to improve their happiness, and muster effort for this goal.

A person's baseline affective state also moderates the efficacy of PAIs, such that depressed individuals experience more improvements in well-being and greater reductions in depressive symptoms than nondepressed ones (Sin & Lyubomirsky, 2009). Some research has suggested that people low in positive affect or moderately depressed benefit the most from PAIs simply because they have more room to improve (i.e., a floor effect). However, this finding is confounded with treatment format, as clinically depressed individuals tend to be treated with individual or group therapy and nondepressed individuals tend to self-administer. On the other hand, depressed individuals may experience particular emotional, cognitive, or behavioral deficits that prevent them from taking full advantage of some PAIs. In a randomized longitudinal study, practicing gratitude actually *diminished* the well-being of dysphoric (non-clinically depressed) individuals (Sin, Della Porta, & Lyubomirsky, 2011). It is likely that some dysphoric individuals in this study found the exercise of writing a gratitude letter to be highly difficult or burdensome, as lack of energy and motivation are hallmarks of depression. Alternatively, writing a gratitude letter might have backfired if it led depressed individuals to believe they had little to be grateful for (and therefore that they had "failed" at completing their assignment) or if it led them to feel guilty for not reciprocating their benefactor or not thanking him sooner.

Having social support increases the efficacy of many self-improvement goals (e.g., Norcross & Vangarelli, 1989; Wing & Jeffery, 1999), and PAIs are no exception. For example, participants who received autonomy-supporting messages from a peer while performing kind acts saw greater increases in happiness than those who did not receive such social support (Nelson, Della Porta, Jacobs Bao, Lee, Choi, & Lyubomirsky, in press). Similarly, students who read an empathetic peer testimonial about the challenges of an optimism-boosting exercise experienced greater increases in happiness than other groups (Layous et al., 2013b). Close others can provide encouragement, be a source of inspiration for practicing PAIs (e.g., if they are recipients of gratitude letters), or offer feedback and advice regarding progress towards well-being.

Person-activity fit   Finally, a proper "fit" between a person and a particular PAI is likely to impact the PAI's success. After all, people have needs, strengths, preferences, values, and interests that predispose them to benefit more from some positive interventions than others. For example, members of collectivist cultures who are depressed might benefit more from other-oriented PAIs (e.g., doing acts of kindness), whereas individualists might benefit more from self-oriented ones (e.g., practicing optimism) (see Boehm et al., 2011, for suggestive evidence). Moreover, certain PAIs are social-behavioral in nature (e.g., helping others), whereas others are reflective-cognitive (e.g., savoring happy times), potentially benefitting lonely and anxious individuals, respectively.

Closing Remark

Most studies on the mechanisms underlying the success of PAIs have been conducted solely with healthy populations. More research is needed to replicate and extend this work in depressed individuals. Positive psychological scientists presently lack full understanding of why certain PAIs (e.g., writing gratitude letters) backfire in clinical populations, as well as of the mechanisms that operate in PAIs that do benefit such populations. Future research should aim to discover which PAIs are most efficacious for alleviating certain depressive symptoms (e.g., acts of kindness to target rumination or best possible selves to target automatic negative thoughts). Elucidating the critical mechanisms may help both basic researchers and clinicians discover superior interventions for treating clinical populations.

How Positive Activities Can Protect Against Clinical Conditions

Not only can positive activities alleviate preexisting clinical symptoms, but they may also protect against symptoms from arising in the first place. Using Nolen-Hoeksema's and Watkins' (2011) transdiagnostic risk factor framework, we propose that positive activities may serve as protective factors in three ways: by mitigating so-called proximal risk factors (e.g., rumination, loneliness), by mitigating mechanisms linking distal and proximal risk factors (e.g., negative self-view, body dissatisfaction), and by mitigating moderators that act on proximal risk factors to produce disorder (e.g., recent loss, current social stress).

First, positive activities such as gratitude, savoring, and kindness may serve as a toolkit when people are faced with negative patterns of thoughts and behaviors (i.e., proximal risk factors and the mechanisms that trigger them). For example, rumination – or focusing attention on oneself and one's problems without taking action to resolve them (Nolen-Hoeksema, 1991) – has been proposed to be a pivotal transdiagnostic proximal risk factor that predicts multiple disorders, especially mood disorders (Nolen-Hoeksema & Watkins, 2011). By performing acts of kindness, for example, individuals may be distracted from rumination and self-focus, as well as corrected of their negative self-evaluations (i.e., with alternate self-views, such as "I am a caring person") (Layous, Chancellor, & Lyubomirsky, 2014). In another example of how PAIs might mitigate factors that contribute to psychopathology, gratitude has been found to improve body satisfaction among people who obsess about their body size (Geraghty, Wood, & Hyland, 2010). Similarly, the intervention of affirming one's most important values helps improve unfavorable self-views (Steele, 1988; Sherman & Cohen, 2006), which might, in turn, reduce threatening self-doubts that could trigger ruminative episodes. Finally, positive emotions triggered by PAIs can help stimulate the creative thinking necessary to solve the problems one might be ruminating about or to prevent those problems from happening in the first place (Isen, Daubman, & Nowicki, 1987 Fredrickson, 2001).

Loneliness is another proximal risk factor that can be mitigated via increased closeness and connectedness through positive activities. One such positive activity, gratitude, not only boosts feelings of connectedness with others but also promotes relationship maintenance behaviors and satisfaction with existing relationships (Wood, Maltby, Gillett, Linley, & Joseph, 2008; Algoe, Haidt, & Gable, 2008; Algoe, Gable, & Maisel, 2010; Lambert & Fincham, 2011). In one study, for example, when practicing loving-kindness meditation, participant gains in positive emotions during the intervention period predicted increases in perceived social support and fulfilling relationships with others. Moreover, increases in positive emotion were most pronounced when people interacted with others after the activity (Fredrickson et al., 2008). In sum, positive activities foster positive relationships with others, which may mitigate interpersonally relevant risk factors like loneliness, either directly (by reducing feelings of being unloved and alone) or indirectly (by boosting well-being and its associated benefits).

Life stressors can trigger proximal risk factors (e.g., the distal risk factor of childhood trauma can trigger the proximal risk factor of rumination) and also aggravate them (e.g., the death of a loved one might intensify rumination), thus producing psychopathology (Nolen-Hoeksema & Watkins, 2011). Accordingly, positive emotions elicited by PAIs may mitigate such stressful situations by helping people to construe them as more of a challenge than a threat (Folkman & Moskowitz, 2000; Folkman, 2008). Indeed, positive affect is consistently associated with personal growth after traumatic experiences, and studies have shown that positive emotions play an important role in the adaptive coping response of highly resilient people. Gratitude, for example, has been found to relate to adaptive coping: namely, emotional and instrumental support, positive reinterpretation, active coping, and planning (Wood et al., 2008). People prompted to write gratefully about the positive consequences of an unpleasant event report feeling more closure, fewer intrusive thoughts, and less emotional impact from memories of the unpleasant event (Watkins, Cruz, Holben, & Kolts, 2008). This research suggests that people who express gratitude may be able to temper a negative event, decreasing the likelihood of the event triggering or exacerbating proximal risk factors. Practicing gratitude may also stimulate positive emotions, fostering adaptive coping to other ongoing or future stressful life events, and preventing a downward spiral into clinical symptoms.

In sum, positive emotions triggered by PAIs may serve a number of protective roles (e.g., helping individuals distract, counteract, prevent, or reframe) in preventing mental health conditions from developing.

Future Directions

The majority of the clinically relevant research on PAIs described in this chapter has been conducted with depressed individuals. However, preliminary evidence demonstrates that positive interventions may also benefit individuals with other mental health conditions. For example, exploratory work on individuals with generalized anxiety disorder has provided evidence for the efficacy of WBT on ratings of anxiety (Fava et al., 2005). Furthermore, writing optimistically about one's best possible selves (King, 2001), cultivating hope by setting and achieving future goals (Cheavens et al., 2006), and being grateful in the face of difficult life circumstances (Watkins et al., 2008) have implications for the treatment of post-traumatic stress disorder. Another class of disorders that may be treated through positive interventions is eating disorders (i.e., anorexia nervosa and bulimia nervosa). Performing acts of kindness, being grateful for their health, and affirming their most important values may help distract individuals with eating disorders from self-focus and rumination, improve negative body image and increase body satisfaction, and reduce self-doubts and social comparison, respectively, that characterize such disorders (Steele, 1988; Sherman & Cohen, 2006; Geraghty et al., 2010; Layous et al., 2014). All these mental health conditions (and others, such as addictive disorders or personality disorders) and the corresponding PAIs with the best potential fit need more attention in the literature.

Further research is also needed to advance understanding of when and why PAIs might backfire in clinical populations. Some evidence has shown that overburdening depressed individuals with certain interventions can cause more harm than good. For this reason, it is important to determine what mechanisms cause PAIs to backfire (e.g., the difficulty of the exercise, making failures more salient, or guilty feelings) and the subsequent ways future PAIs may be better tailored to depressed individuals. Moreover, not every depressive episode is alike (e.g., due to idiosyncratic differences in personality, bipolar vs. unipolar depression, bereavement-triggered versus neurotic-personality-triggered versus genetically-based depressions, etc.); consequently, PAIs might need to be specifically tailored to these characteristics.

As evident from this chapter, although PAIs have shown promise in the past decade for treating mental health conditions, most researchers who conduct PAIs have focused on normal (nonclinical) samples. As such, a great deal more attention is needed in the coming decade on examining which positive interventions work best in clinically depressed (and other clinical) populations and how to optimize their utility for such populations. Longitudinal research with longer-term follow-ups (i.e., over several years) will be highly informative in establishing the lasting effects of positive activities, as well as their efficacy relative to antidepressant medications.

Summary and Conclusions

Depression is currently the third leading cause of disease burden globally, and predictions forecast that the burden is only growing larger. The World Health Organization predicts that depression will be the second leading cause of disease burden by 2020, and *the* leading cause by 2030 (Murray & Lopez, 1996; WHO, 2008). Positive activity interventions – that is, experimental programs that primarily aim to cultivate positive emotions and personal strengths – hold promise for augmenting traditional drug and psychotherapy treatment with their potential to benefit patients who have not responded to conventional care. In addition, they are economical, relatively less stigmatizing, and carry no side effects. Importantly, PAIs may also serve as protective factors against some forms of mental illness. Empirical research has already established that well-being can be increased via intentional activity, but future work is needed to test and tailor these interventions for clinical populations, such that the ultimate goal of treatment is not only to alleviate distressing symptoms, but also to promote happiness and thriving.

References

Algoe, S. B., Gable, S. L., & Maisel, N. C. (2010). It's the little things: Everyday gratitude as a booster shot for romantic relationships. *Personal Relationships, 17,* 217–233. doi.10.1111/j.1475-6811.2010.01273.x.

Algoe, S. B., Haidt, J., & Gable, S. L. (2008). Beyond reciprocity: Gratitude and relationships in everyday life. *Emotion, 8,* 425–429. doi.10.1037/1528-3542.8.3.425.

American Psychiatric Association. (2010). *Practice guideline for the treatment of patients with major depressive disorder, Third Edition, Part A.* Available at: http://psychiatryonline.org/pb/assets/raw/sitewide/practice_guidelines/guidelines/mdd.pdf.

Baskin, T. W. & Enright, R. D. (2004). Intervention studies on forgiveness: A meta-analysis. *Journal of Counseling and Development, 82,* 79–90. doi.10.1002/j.1556-6678.2004.tb00288.x.

Boehm, J. K., Lyubomirsky, S., & Sheldon, K. M. (2011). A longitudinal experimental study comparing the effectiveness of happiness-enhancing strategies in Anglo Americans and Asian Americans. *Cognition & Emotion, 25,* 1263–1272. doi.10.1080/02699931.2010.541227.

Boehm, J. K., Lyubomirsky, S., & Sheldon, K. M. (2012). The role of need satisfying emotions in a positive activity intervention. Unpublished raw data.

Bolier, L., Haverman, M., Westerhof, G. J., Riper, H., Smit, F., & Bohlmeijer, E. (2013). Positive psychology interventions: a meta-analysis of randomized controlled studies. *BMC Public Health, 13*(1), 119. doi.10.1186/1471-2458-13-119.

Burton, C. M. & King, L. A. (2008). Effects of (very) brief writing on health: The two-minute miracle. *British Journal of Health Psychology, 13,* 9–14. doi.10.1348/135910707X250910.

Chancellor, J., Layous, K., & Lyubomirsky, S. (2014). Recalling positive events at work makes employees feel happier, move more, but interact less: A 6-week randomized controlled intervention at a Japanese workplace. *Journal of Happiness Studies.* doi.10.1007/s10902-014-9538-z.

Cheavens, J. S., Feldman, D. B., Gum, A., Michael, S. T., & Snyder, C. R. (2006). Hope therapy in a community sample: A pilot investigation. *Social Indicators Research, 77,* 61–78. doi.10.1007/s11205-005-5553-0.

Deci, E. L. & Ryan, R. M. (2000). The "what" and "why" of goal pursuits: Human needs and the self-determination theory of behavior. *Psychological Inquiry, 11,* 227–268. doi.10.1207/S15327965PLI1104_01.

Dickerhoof, R. M. (2007). Expressing optimism and gratitude: A longitudinal investigation of cognitive strategies to increase well-being. *Dissertation Abstracts International, 68,* 4174 (UMI No. 3270426).

Dobson, K. S., Hollon, S. D., Dimidjian, S., Schmaling, K. B., Kohlenberg, R. J., Gallop, R. J., Jacobson, N. S., et al. (2008). Randomized trial of behavioral activation, cognitive therapy, and antidepressant medication in the prevention of relapse and recurrence in major depression. *Journal of Consulting and Clinical Psychology, 76*(3), 468–477. doi.10.1037/0022-006X.76.3.468.

Dunn, E. W., Aknin, L. B., & Norton, M. I. (2008). Spending money on others promotes happiness. *Science, 319,* 1687–1688. doi.10.1126/science.1150952.

Eisendrath, S. J., Delucchi, K., Bitner, R., Fenimore, P., Smit, M., & McLane, M. (2008). Mindfulness-based cognitive therapy for treatment-resistant depression: A pilot study. *Psychotherapy and Psychosomatics, 77,* 319–320. doi.10.1159/000142525.

Emmons, R. A. & McCullough, M. E. (2003). Counting blessings versus burdens: An experimental investigation of gratitude and subjective well-being in daily life. *Journal of Personality and Social Psychology, 84,* 377–389. doi.10.1037/0022-3514.84.2.377.

Evans, M. D., Hollon, S. D., DeRubeis, R. J., Piasecki, J. M., Grove, W. M., Garvey, M. J., & Tuason, V. B. (1992). Differential relapse following cognitive therapy and pharmacotherapy for depression. *Archives of General Psychiatry, 49*(10), 802–808. doi.10.1001/archpsyc.1992.01820100046009.

Fava, G., A., Rafanelli, C., Cazzaro, M., Conti, S., & Grandi, S. (1998). Well-being therapy: A novel psycho-therapeutic approach for residual symptoms of affective disorders. *Psychological Medicine, 28,* 475–480. doi.10.1017/S0033291797006363.

Fava, G. A. & Ruini, C. (2003). Development and characteristics of a well-being enhancing psychothera-peutic strategy: Well-being therapy. *Journal of Behavior Therapy and Experimental Psychiatry, 34,* 45–63. doi.10.1016/S0005-7916(03)00019-3.

Fava, G. A., Ruini, C., Rafanelli, C., Finos, L., Conti, S., & Grandi, S. (2004). Six-year outcome of cognitive behavior therapy for prevention of recurrent depression. *American Journal of Psychiatry, 161*(10), 1872–1876. doi.10.1176/appi.ajp.161.10.1872.

Fava, G. A., Ruini, C., Rafanelli, C., Finos, L., Salmaso, L., Mangelli, L., & Sirigatti, S. (2005). Well-being therapy of generalized anxiety disorder. *Psychotherapy and Psychosomatics, 74*(1), 26–30. doi.10.1159/000082023.

Folkman, S. (2008). The case for positive emotions in the stress process. *Anxiety, Stress & Coping, 21,* 3–14. doi.10.1080/10615800701740457.

Folkman, S. & Moskowitz, J. T. (2000). Stress, positive emotion, and coping. *Current Directions in Psychological Science, 9,* 115–118. doi.10.1111/1467-8721.00073.

Fredrickson, B. L. (2001). The role of positive emotions in positive psychology: The broaden-and-build theory of positive emotions.*American Psychologist, 56*(3), 218–226. doi.10.1037/0003-066X.56.3.218.

Fredrickson, B. L., Cohn, M. A., Coffey, K. A., Pek, J., & Finkel, S. M. (2008). Open hearts build lives: Positive emotions, induced through loving-kindness meditation, build consequential personal resources. *Journal of Personality and Social Psychology, 95,* 1045–1062. doi.10.1037/a0013262.

Fredrickson, B. L. & Joiner, T. (2002). Positive emotions trigger upward spirals toward emotional well-being. *Psychological Science, 13,* 172–175. doi.10.1111/1467-9280.00431.

Fredrickson, B. L. & Levenson, R. W. (1998). Positive emotions speed recovery from the cardiovascular sequelae of negative emotions. *Cognition and Emotion, 12,* 191–220. doi.10.1080/026999398379718.

Froh, J. J., Sefick, W. J., & Emmons, R. A. (2008). Counting blessings in early adolescents: An experi-mental study of gratitude and subjective well-being. *Journal of School Psychology, 46*(2), 213–233. doi.10.1016/j.jsp.2007.03.005.

Fournier, J. C., DeRubeis, R. J., Hollon, S. D., Dimidjian, S., Amsterdam, J. D., Shelton, R. C., & Fawcett, J. (2010). Antidepressant drug effects and depression severity: A patient-level meta-analysis. *Journal of the American Medical Association, 303*(1), 47–53. doi.10.1001/jama.2009.1943.

Gasper, K. & Clore, G. L. (2002). Attending to the big picture: Mood and global versus local processing of visual information. *Psychological Science, 13,* 34–40. doi.0.1111/1467-9280.00406.

Geraghty, A. W., Wood, A. M., & Hyland, M. E. (2010). Attrition from self-directed interventions: Investigating the relationship between psychological predictors, intervention content and dropout from a body dissatisfaction intervention. *Social Science & Medicine, 71,* 30–37. doi.10.1016/j.socscimed.2010.03.007.

Isen, A. M., Daubman, K. A., & Nowicki, G. P. (1987). Positive affect facilitates creative problem solving. *Journal of Personality and Social Psychology, 52,* 1122–1131. doi.10.1037/0022-3514.52.6.1122.

Kabat-Zinn, J. (1990). *Full catastrophe living: Using the wisdom of your body and mind to face stress, pain and illness.* New York: Delacourt.

Kasch, K. L., Rottenberg, J., Arnow, B. A., & Gotlib, I. H. (2002). Behavioral activation and inhibition systems and the severity and course of depression. *Journal of Abnormal Psychology, 111,* 589–597. doi.10.1037/0021-843X.111.4.589.

Kessler, R. C., Chiu, W. T., Demler, O., & Walters, E. E. (2005). Prevalence, severity, and comorbidity of 12-month DSM-IV disorders in the national comorbidity survey replication. *Archives of General Psychiatry, 62*(6), 617–627. doi.10.1001/archpsyc.62.6.617.

Khin, N. A., Chen, Y-F., Yang, Y., Yang, P., & Laughren, T. P. (2011). Exploratory analyses of efficacy data from major depressive disorder trials submitted to the US food and drug administration in support of new drug applications. *Journal of Clinical Psychiatry, 72*(04), 464–472. doi.10.4088/JCP.10m06191.

King, L. A. (2001). The health benefits of writing about life goals. *Personality and Social Psychology Bulletin, 27,* 798–807. doi.10.1177/0146167201277003.

Kirsch, I., Moore, T. J., Scoboria, A., & Nicholls, S. S. (2002). The emperor's new drugs: An analysis of antidepressant medication data submitted to the US Food and Drug Administration. *Prevention & Treatment, 5*(1). doi.10.1037/1522-3736.5.1.523a.

Kuyken, W., Byford, S., Taylor, R. S., Watkins, E., Holden, E., White, K., Teasdale, J. D., et al. (2008). Mindfulness-based cognitive therapy to prevent relapse in recurrent depression. *Journal of Consulting and Clinical Psychology, 76*(6), 966–978. doi.10.1037/a0013786.

Lambert, N. M. & Fincham, F. D. (2011). Expressing gratitude to a partner leads to more relationship maintenance behavior. *Emotion, 11,* 52–60. doi.10.1037/a0021557.

Layous, K., Chancellor, J., & Lyubomirsky, S. (2014). Positive activities as protective factors against mental health conditions. *Journal of Abnormal Psychology, 123*(1), 3–12. doi.10.1037/a0034709.

Layous, K., Chancellor, J., Lyubomirsky, S., Wang, L., & Doraiswamy, P. M. (2011). Delivering happiness: Translating positive psychology intervention research for treating major and minor depressive disorders. *Journal of Alternative and Complementary Medicine, 17*(8), 675–683. doi.10.1089/acm.2011.0139.

Layous, K., Lee, H., Choi, I., & Lyubomirsky, S. (2013a). Culture matters when designing a successful happiness-increasing activity: A comparison of the United States and South Korea. *Journal of Cross-Cultural Psychology, 44,* 1294–1303. doi.10.1177/0022022113487591.

Layous, K., Nelson, S. K., & Lyubomirsky, S. (2013b). What is the optimal way to deliver a positive activity intervention? The case of writing about one's best possible selves. *Journal of Happiness Studies, 14,* 635–654. doi.10.1007/s10902-012-9346-2.

Layous, K., Nelson, S. K., Oberle, E., Schonert-Reichl, K. A., & Lyubomirsky, S. (2012). Kindness counts: Prompting prosocial behavior in preadolescents. *PLOS ONE, 7,* e51380. doi.10.1371/journal.pone.0051380.

Lyubomirsky, S., Dickerhoof, R., Boehm, J. K., & Sheldon, K. M. (2011). Becoming happier takes both a will and a proper way: An experimental longitudinal intervention to boost well-being. *Emotion, 11,* 391–402. doi.10.1037/a0022575.

Lyubomirsky, S., King, L., & Diener, E. (2005a). The benefits of frequent positive affect: Does happiness lead to success? *Psychological Bulletin, 31,* 803–855. doi.10.1037/0033-2909.131.6.803.

Lyubomirsky, S., Sheldon, K. M., & Schkade, D. (2005b). Pursuing happiness: The architecture of sustainable change. *Review of General Psychology, 9,* 111–131. doi.10.1037/1089-2680.9.2.111.

Marcus, M., Yasamy, M. T., van Ommeren, M., Chisholm, D., & Saxena, S. (2012). *Depression: A global public health concern.* Available at: http://www.who.int/mental_health/management/depression/who_paper_depression_wfmh_2012.pdf?ua=1.

Murray C. J. L. & Lopez, A. D. (1996). *The global burden of disease: A comprehensive assessment of mortality and disability from diseases, injuries and risk factors in 1990 and projected to 2020.* Cambridge, MA: Harvard University Press.

Nelson, S. K., Della Porta, M. D., Jacobs Bao, K., Lee, H., Choi, I., & Lyubomirsky, S. (in press). "It's up to you": Experimentally manipulated autonomy support for prosocial behaviors improves well-being in two cultures over six weeks. *Journal of Positive Psychology.*

Nelson, S. K., Fuller, J. A. K., Choi, I., & Lyubomirsky, S. (2014). Beyond self-protection: Self-affirmation benefits hedonic and eudaimonic well-being. *Personality and Social Psychology Bulletin, 40,* 998–1011. doi.10.1177/0146167214533389.

Nolen-Hoeksema, S. (1991). Responses to depression and their effects on the duration of depressive episodes. *Journal of Abnormal Psychology, 100,* 569–582. doi.10.1037/0021-843X.100.4.569.

Nolen-Hoeksema, S. & Watkins, E. R. (2011). A heuristic for developing transdiagnostic models of psychopathology explaining multifinality and divergent trajectories. *Perspectives on Psychological Science, 6*(6), 589–609. doi.10.1177/1745691611419672.

Norcross, J. C. & Vangarelli, D. J. (1989). The resolution solution: Longitudinal examination of New Year's change attempts. *Journal of Substance Abuse, 1,* 127–134. doi.10.1016/S0899-3289(88)80016-6.

Otake, K., Shimai, S., Tanaka-Matsumi, J., Otsui, K., & Fredrickson, B. L. (2006). Happy people become happier through kindness: A counting kindness intervention. *Journal of Happiness Studies, 7,* 361–375. doi.10.1007/s10902-005-3650-z.

Ramel, W., Goldin, P. R., Carmona, P. E., & McQuaid, J. R. (2004). The effects of mindfulness meditation on cognitive processes and affect in patients with past depression. *Cognitive Therapy and Research, 28*, 433–455. doi.10.1023/B:COTR.0000045557.15923.96.

Rush, A. J. (2007). STAR*D: What have we learned? *American Journal of Psychiatry, 164*(2), 201–204. doi.10.1176/appi.ajp.164.2.201.

Ryff, C. D. (1989). Happiness is everything, or is it? Explorations on the meaning of psychological well-being. *Journal of Personality and Social Psychology, 57*, 1069–1081. doi.10.1037/0022-3514.57.6.1069.

Seligman, M. E. P. (2002). *Authentic happiness.* New York: Free Press.

Seligman, M. E. P. & Csikszentmihalyi, M. (2000). Positive psychology: An introduction. *American Psychologist, 55*(1), 5–14. doi.10.1037/0003-066X.55.1.5.

Seligman, M. E. P., Rashid, T., & Parks, A. C. (2006). Positive psychotherapy. *American Psychologist, 61*, 774–788. doi.10.1037/0003-066X.61.8.774.

Seligman, M. E. P., Steen, T. A., Park, N., & Peterson, C. (2005). Positive psychology progress: Empirical validation of interventions. *American Psychologist, 6*, 410–421. doi.10.1037/0003-066X.60.5.410.

Sheldon, K. M., Abad, N., Ferguson, Y., Gunz, A., Houser-Marko, L., Nichols, C. P., & Lyubomirsky, S. (2010). Persistent pursuit of need satisfying goals leads to increased happiness: A 6-month experimental longitudinal study. *Motivation & Emotion, 34*, 39–48. doi.10.1007/s11031-009-9153-1.

Sheldon, K. M., Boehm, J. K., & Lyubomirsky, S. (2012). Variety is the spice of happiness: The hedonic adaptation prevention (HAP) model. In: I. Boniwell & S. David (Eds.), *Oxford handbook of happiness* (pp. 901–914). Oxford: Oxford University Press.

Sheldon, K. M. & Lyubomirsky, S. (2006). How to increase and sustain positive emotion: The effects of expressing gratitude and visualizing best possible selves. *Journal of Positive Psychology, 1*, 73–82. doi.10.1080/17439760500510676.

Sherman, D. K. & Cohen, G. L. (2006). The psychology of self-defense: Self-affirmation theory. In: M. P. Zanna (Ed.), *Advances in experimental social psychology*, vol. *38* (pp. 183–242). San Diego, CA: Academic Press.

Sin, N. L., Della Porta, M. D., & Lyubomirsky, S. (2011). Tailoring positive psychology interventions to treat depressed individuals. In: S. I. Donaldson, M. Csikszentmihalyi, & J. Nakamura (Eds.), *Applied positive psychology: Improving everyday life, health, schools, work, and society* (pp. 79–96). New York: Routledge.

Sin, N. L. & Lyubomirsky, S. (2009). Enhancing well-being and alleviating depressive symptoms with positive psychology interventions: A practice friendly meta-analysis. *Journal of Clinical Psychology, 65*, 467–487. doi.10.1002/jclp.20593.

Smith, M. L. & Glass, G. V. (1977). Meta-analysis of psychotherapy outcome studies. *American Psychologist, 32*(9), 752. doi.10.1037/0003-066X.32.9.752.

Smith, J. C. & Medalia, C. (2014). *Health insurance coverage in the United States: 2013.* Available from US Census Bureau website at: http://www.census.gov/content/dam/Census/library/publications/2014/demo/p60-250.pdf.

Snyder, C. R., Harris, C., Anderson, J. R., Holleran, S. A., Irving, L. M., Sigmon, S. T., Harney, P., et al. (1991). The will and the ways: Development and validation of an individual-differences measure of hope. *Journal of Personality and Social Psychology, 60*(4), 570–585. doi.10.1037/0022-3514.60.4.570.

Steele, C. (1988). The psychology of self-affirmation: Sustaining the integrity of the self. In: L. Berkowitz (Ed.), *Advances in experimental social psychology*, vol. *21* (pp. 261–302). New York: Academic Press. doi:10.1016/S0065-2601(08)60229-4.

Substance Abuse and Mental Health Services Administration (SAMHA). (2012). *Results from the 2010 National Survey on Drug Use and Health: Mental health findings.* NSDUH Series H-47, HHS Publication No. (SMA) 13-4805. Available at: http://archive.samhsa.gov/data/NSDUH/2k10MH_Findings/2k10MHResults.htm.

Tugade, M. M. & Fredrickson, B. L. (2004). Resilient individuals use positive emotions to bounce back from negative emotional experiences. *Journal of Personality and Social Psychology, 86*, 320–333. doi.10.1037/0022-3514.86.2.320.

Wang, J. L., Schmitz, N., & Dewa, C. S. (2010). Socioeconomic status and the risk of major depression: The Canadian National Population Health Survey. *Journal of Epidemiology and Community Health, 64*(5), 447–452. doi.10.1136/jech.2009.090910.

Watkins, K. E., Burnam, M. A., Orlando, M., Escarce, J. J., Huskamp, H. A., & Goldman, H. H. (2009). The health value and cost of care for major depression. *Value in Health*, *12*(1), 65–72. doi,10.1111/j.1524-4733.2008.00388.x.

Watkins, P. C., Cruz, L., Holben, H., & Kolts, R. L. (2008). Taking care of business? Grateful processing of unpleasant memories. *The Journal of Positive Psychology*, *3*, 87–99. doi.10.1080/17439760701760567.

Watson, D. & Tellegen, A. (1985). Toward a consensual structure of mood. *Psychological Bulletin*, *98*, 219–235. doi.10.1037/0033-2909.98.2.219.

Wing, R. R. & Jeffery, R. W. (1999). Benefits of recruiting participants with friends and increasing social support for weight loss and maintenance. *Journal of Consulting and Clinical Psychology*, *67*, 132–138. doi.10.1037/0022-006X.67.1.132.

Wood, A. M., Maltby, J., Gillett, R., Linley, P. A., & Joseph, S. (2008). The role of gratitude in the development of social support, stress, and depression: Two longitudinal studies. *Journal of Research in Personality*, *42*, 854–871. doi.10.1016/j.jrp.2007.11.003.

World Health Organization (WHO) (2003). *Investing in mental health*. Available at: http://www.who.int/mental_health/media/investing_mnh.pdf.

World Health Organization (WHO) (2008). *The Global Burden of Disease: 2004 Update*. Available at: http://www.who.int/healthinfo/global_burden_disease/GBD_report_2004update_full.pdf.

World Health Organization (WHO) (2012). *Depression fact sheet*. Available at: http://www.who.int/mediacentre/factsheets/fs369/en, October.

24

Interventions to Promote Forgiveness are Exemplars of Positive Clinical Psychology

Everett L. Worthington, Jr., Brandon J. Griffin, Caroline R. Lavelock, Chelsea M. Hughes, Chelsea L. Greer, Steven J. Sandage, and Mark S. Rye

Interventions to Promote Forgiveness are Exemplars of Positive Clinical Psychology

In this chapter, we argue that forgiveness is an exemplar for positive clinical psychology. Forgiveness straddles the fence with one foot firmly anchored in the positive psychological focus of character strength, virtue, and well-being and the other foot anchored in clinical psychology as a strategy to prevent stress-related physical and mental health problems. Indeed, some psychological disorders are heavily intertwined with maladaptive dynamics that may include interpersonal traumas resulting from sexual and physical abuse and neglect, incest, rape, murder of a loved one, or even natural disasters (in which victims might hold grudges against God or nature). Many personality disorders also have roots in developmental dynamics laden with unforgiveness, such as narcissistic, paranoid, and borderline personality disorders. Insofar as clients harbor chronic unforgiving negative emotions toward others, they risk experiencing a myriad of poor health and relational consequences. Forgiveness interventions can equip victims of destructive dynamics to overcome maladaptive patterns of behavior to promote adjustment and personal development.

At the core of many disorders are feelings of guilt and shame. Those feelings are usually associated with self-condemnation. Thus, self-forgiveness can become an important part of psychotherapy. For example, rumination is a core process in many disorders – notably major depression, persistent depressive (dysthymic) disorder, various anxiety disorders, anger disorders, many obsessive-compulsive disorders, and post-traumatic stress disorder (McCullough, Orsulak, Brandon, & Akers, 2007). Self-forgiveness may facilitate the restoration of positive self-regard and self-acceptance to clients whose therapeutic progress is arrested by ruminative worry and feelings of worthlessness.

Some of these arguments – that unforgiveness is a pivotal problem in mental health disorders, and forgiveness can help such patients – have been made for years. Enright and Fitzgibbons (2014) forcefully argued for forgiveness therapy. They championed many benefits of their process-oriented forgiveness therapy as a treatment, which they commended for clinical application to people who had many psychological disorders. Since then, evidence has accumulated to suggest that forgiveness interventions from many different approaches can help psychotherapy patients (see Table 24.1).

The Wiley Handbook of Positive Clinical Psychology, First Edition. Edited by Alex M. Wood and Judith Johnson.
© 2016 John Wiley & Sons, Ltd. Published 2016 by John Wiley & Sons, Ltd.

Table 24.1 Comparison of intervention studies using clinical, community, and student samples.

Authors	Sample	Model	Forgiveness issue	N (treat. cond.)	Time (hr)	Δ (CI)
	Clinical samples recruited for intervention					
Waltman et al. (2009)	Clinical health	Enright	Myocardial perfusion	10	9	0.97 (0.39, 1.58)
Lin et al. (2004)	Clinical	Enright	Substance abuse	50	12	1.51 (0.57, 2.44)
Coyle & Enright (1997)	Clinical	Enright	Post-abortion partners (men)	64	18	3.33 (1.38, 5.29)
Hart & Shapiro (2002)	Clinical	Enright	Alcohol treatment (men)	34	20	0.58 (0.32, 1.05)
Reed & Enright (2006)	Clinical	Enright	Emotionally abused women	64	32	2.27 (1.22, 3.32)
Freedman & Enright (1996)	Clinical	Enright	Incest survivors	12	57.2	2.66 (1.06, 4.26)
	Community adult samples recruited for intervention					
DiBlasio & Benda (2008)	Couples from community	DiBlasio	Conflicted couples recruited for couple therapy	45	3	0.35 (−0.14, 0.84) ns
DiBlasio & Benda (2008)	Couples from community (Christian)	DiBlasio	Conflicted couples recruited for couple therapy	30	3	0.42 (0.03, 0.82)
Luskin, Ginzburg, & Thoresen (2005)	Community men	Luskin	Angry men at risk for cardio problems	53	6	0.23 (−0.21, 0.68) ns
Harris et al. (2006)	Community health	Luskin	Anger and health	36	9	−0.18 (-0.38, 0.03) ns
Kiefer et al. (2010)	Community parents	Worthington	Parents forgiving children or spouse	35	9	0.34 (-0.23, 0.91) ns
Worthington et al. (2010)	Community church members in Philippines (Christian)	Worthington	Grudges	31	6	0.92
Worthington et al. (2015)	Community newly married couples	Worthington	Most hurtful persistent offense by partner	40	9	0.54 (0.24, 0.85)

Study	Population	Target	Model	N		Effect size
Luskin & Bland (2000)	Community men	Anger and health	Luskin	53	15	0.61 (−0.12, 1.35) ns
Luskin & Bland (2001)	Community men	Anger and health	Luskin	53	15	0.14 (−0.29, 0.56) ns
	Community members, no intervention (control)					
Lampton et al. (2005)	Community of students (Christian)	Identified persistent hurt		23	6	0.26
Stratton et al. (2008)	Community of students (Christian)	Identified persistent hurt		29	6	0.13
Toussaint et al. (in press)	Community of students (Christian)	Identified persistent hurt		36	2.5	0.09 (−0.07, 0.25) ns
	Community members exposed to community awareness-raising intervention, but not individual intervention					
Griffin et al. (under review)	Community of students	Identified persistent hurt		679	2.5	0.05 (0.025-0.075);
	Students (children, high school, young adult) samples recruited for intervention					
Al-Mabuk et al. (1995)	High school students	Love-deprived adolescents	Enright	54	4	1.04 (0.58, 1.50)
Stratton et al. (2008)	College students	Persistent hurt	Worthington	30	5.5	0.42 (0.03, 0.82)
Lampton et al. (2005)	College students	Persistent hurt	Worthington	42	6	0.15 (−.24, 0.54) ns
Wade et al. (2009)	College students	Persistent hurt	Worthington	35	6	0.36 (−0.25, 0.96) ns
Wade et al. (2009)	College students	Persistent hurt	Worthington	30	6	0.28 (0.04, 0.51)
Sandage & Worthington (2010)	College students	Persistent hurt	Worthington	36	6	0.53 (0.15, 0.90)
Lin et al. (2014)	College students (half US and half international)	Persistent hurt	Worthington	88	6	0.33

(Continued)

Table 24.1 (*Continued*)

Authors	Sample	Model	Forgiveness issue	N (treat. cond.)	Time (hr)	Δ (CI)
Toussaint et al. (in press)	College students	Worthington (W); Luskin (L)	Persistent hurt	34 (W); 31 (L)	6	(Mean, SD) TRIM: W (0.43, 0.10); L (0.30, 0.08); C (0.08, 0.08) W>L>C TFS: W (0.26, 0.10); L (0.21, 0.01); C (0.17, 0.05) W=L, W>C, L=C EFS: W (0.48, 0.10); L (0.38, 0.10); C (0.03 (0.07) W=L>C Rye: W (0.25, 0.08), L (0.36, 0.08); C (0.03, 0.05) L>W>C
Gassin (1995)	Students	Enright		38	6.67	−0.05 (−0.78, 0.88) ns
Greer et al. (2014)	Christian college students (workbook)	Worthington	Forgiving fellow Christian in-group members	52	6.7	1.37
Harper et al. (2014)	College students (workbook)	Worthington	Persistent hurt	41	6.7	1.18
McCullough et al. (1997)	College students	Worthington	Persistent hurt	33	8	0.93 (0.44, 1.42)
Freedman & Knupp (2003)	High school students	Enright	Persistent hurt	61	8	0.41 (−.79, 1.62) ns
Goldman & Wade (2012)	College students	Worthington	Persistent hurt	30	9	0.36 (−0.06, 0.77) ns
Klatt & Enright (2009)	High school students	Enright	Persistent hurt	9	9	0.62 (−0.17, 1.40) ns
Hepp-Dax (1996)	Children	Enright	Fifth graders	NA	NA	0.33 (−0.19, 0.86) ns

In this chapter, we define forgiveness and related concepts, summarize forgiveness interventions, and examine the empirical evidence for their efficacy. We examine potential mechanisms by which forgiveness interventions can promote better physical and mental health. We then examine the strength of forgiveness interventions with clinical populations in contrast to community populations and populations who sought forgiveness to enrich their lives rather than repair problems. We suggest one important implication from our analysis: forgiveness treatments can often be used as adjuncts to make psychotherapy more cost-effective. We conclude that psychotherapists might use forgiveness treatments to speed and deepen psychotherapy. That conclusion, as we will see, is tentative and needs scientific investigation.

Understanding Basic and Applied Investigations of Forgiveness

Transgressions are offenses and injuries that violate physical and/or psychological boundaries. They make people feel unsafe. Sometimes they are easily resolvable, but sometimes they linger because the victim feels resentment, bitterness, hatred, hostility, anger, and fear, which is called unforgiveness. Unforgiveness produces or exacerbates anxiety, depression, anger, hopelessness, and demoralization that attend reactive psychological disorders. Furthermore, by eroding hope, they can hinder healing. Forgiveness is a change that can set the patient with psychological problems and unforgiveness on the road toward psychological health.

Definitions

The victim's perspective on forgiveness Forgiveness refers to a victim reducing negative thoughts, emotions, and motivations toward an offender, and perhaps the promotion of positive thoughts, emotions, and motivations (see Worthington, 2005, for a review of definitions). Forgiveness of others has been measured as both a trait (called forgivingness) and as a state. *Forgivingness* refers to the degree to which a person tends to forgive across time and situations, whereas state *forgiveness* refers to a person's forgiveness of a specific offense. *Unforgiveness* is not merely the lack of forgiveness, but can manifest as grudge-holding or vengeful motives and feelings. Unforgiveness is a combination of negative emotions (i.e., resentment, hatred, bitterness, anger, fear) that the working memory labels as feeling unforgiveness toward an offender (with negative motivations often being associated with those negative emotions). In some cases, unforgiveness can result in the victim feeling numb or repressing awareness of feelings of unforgiveness toward an offender. Forgiveness or unforgiveness as a state can also be directed toward a particular person, such as forgiveness of a marriage partner (Paleari, Regalia, & Fincham, 2009).

McCullough and colleagues conceptualize that forgiveness is a change in motivations and emotions over time to more prosocial (or less antagonistic) emotions or motives (McCullough, Fincham, & Tsang, 2003; McCullough & Root, 2005). They argued that amounts of unforgiveness at the time of offense might differ. Person A might hold higher unforgiveness than Person B. If Person A reduced unforgiveness to the same level as Person B and Person B did not change, then Person A forgave (but not Person B). Thus, forgiveness should be considered as a change over time.

Worthington (2006; see also Exline, Worthington, Hill, & McCullough, 2003) argued that there are two related but distinct types of forgiveness. *Decisional forgiveness* is a behavioral intention to forego revenge and to treat the offender as a person of value. One could make a decision to forgive (i.e., a behavioral intention) and still have negative vengeful motives and unforgiving emotions. Accordingly, *emotional forgiveness* is the neutralization of negative unforgiving emotions by positive other-oriented emotions of empathy, sympathy, compassion, and love.

Unforgiveness sometimes relates to religious beliefs. For example, Exline and colleagues studied anger at God. Some find it theologically offensive to say "forgiving God" because it implies that God sits under human judgment (Wood, Froh, & Geraghty, 2010; Exline, Park, Smyth, & Carey, 2011). However, individuals can experience feelings of unforgiveness toward God or the sacred, and some work through these in ways that approximate the dynamics of forgiveness.

The offender's perspective of forgiveness   The little research that has emerged on offenders has focused on variables affecting their seeking of forgiveness. Forgiveness for offenders and victims differs for many obvious reasons. First, the goal is usually different – to forgive as the victim or to seek forgiveness as the offender. Second, the emotional states are different for the offender and victim. The offender's emotional state is usually dominated by feelings of guilt, shame, or self-justification, whereas the victim's emotional state is usually centered on emotions like anger, fear, hurt, resentment, hostility, or hatred. Third, the offender and victim will perceive the event differently simply because they are in different roles.

Recent work has examined the processes of *communicating about transgressions*. For example, Waldron and Kelly (2008) summarized research on social interactions surrounding the forgiveness process (e.g., making reproaches and giving accounts of various types). Self-condemnation may motivate offenders to communicate about a transgression. Self-condemnation might stimulate people to feel guilt or shame due to: (a) doing wrong to another person, or (b) falling short of one's moral standards or personal expectations. As such, one can feel self-condemnation even if no moral wrong has been committed, especially if one's expectations are unrealistic or illogical. Divine forgiveness and self-forgiveness are usually more about being an offender than a victim. *Divine forgiveness* refers to people's sense of feeling forgiven by the deity they consider sacred. *Self-forgiveness* has been conceptualized within a stress-and-coping model (Worthington, 2006). Hall and Fincham (2005) advanced a model of self-forgiveness that involves seeking reconciliation for wrongdoing with a higher purpose or being, making amends, and forgiving the self in light of the relationship with the victim. They tested this model longitudinally (Hall & Fincham, 2008) and found that self-forgiveness increased linearly over time since the offense. Davis et al. (2015) meta-analyzed over 50 studies investigating self-forgiveness and found robust associations between self-forgiveness and clinical health outcomes.

Thus, a variety of processes and constructs are engaged within the interpersonal context in which transgressions happen. Forgiveness as a tool for positive clinical psychology is aimed at helping people (a) deal with troubling reactions to the transgression (regardless of whether they are the victim or offender), (b) enrich their lives and learn to prevent unforgiveness (particularly in extreme or chronic forms), or (c) build coping skills that help them deal with transgressions without needing to seek reparative treatment. Yet the treatment is a virtue – forgiveness – so they are building that virtue regardless of whether they are engaged in repair, prevention, or enrichment. Positive clinical psychological interventions thus involve forgiveness interventions that can be used in any of those three purposes.

Major Forgiveness Interventions

Enright's Psychotherapeutic and Psychoeducational Forgiveness Interventions

Enright's process model of forgiveness (Enright & Fitzgibbons, 2014) has been used to treat people for whom unforgiveness poses serious health and mental health problems and also for psychological enrichment – a good example of positive clinical psychology. Enright's intervention consists of 20 steps that are grouped into four phases, which are briefly described below.

During the Uncovering Phase, people experience both the pain and reality of the injury and how it has affected them. Feeling pain from the recall of the psychological or physical injury motivates some people to see a need for change and to move toward forgiving. In the Decision Phase, the person thinks about forgiving before committing to forgive. In the Work Phase, emotional replacement is at the core. After empathic reframing, people focus on empathy, compassion, and acceptance. In the Deepening Phase, people seek meaning in suffering and forgiveness, realize one has previously needed others' forgiveness, achieve insight that one is not alone, embrace a new purpose in life after forgiving, and become aware of less negative and more positive affect.

Worthington's REACH Forgiveness Model for Psychoeducational Interventions

Worthington's (2006) REACH Forgiveness model has been most often employed in psychoeducational settings, but recently was applied with borderline personality disorder (Sandage et al., in press). The REACH Forgiveness intervention leads people through a decision to forgive and then through five steps for replacing unforgiving emotions with more forgiving emotions. Each step coincides with a letter of the REACH acronym. First, participants recall the hurt (R), which includes recalling the transgression while lessening the blame and emphasizing one's victim status. People are invited to make a decision to forgive the hurt. Second, participants empathize (E) with the offender to promote empathy and positive, other-oriented emotions toward the offender, like sympathy, compassion, or even love. Third, participants give an altruistic (A) gift of forgiveness. To give the altruistic gift of forgiving, the person is engaged in exercises to stimulate (a) empathy, (b) gratitude for having received others' forgiveness in the past, and (c) humility. Fourth, participants commit (C) to the emotional forgiveness they have experienced by making their experience somewhat public. Finally, the intervention helps participants to hold (H) on to forgiveness in the face of doubts through referring back to commitments and planning strategies for dealing with triggers for unforgiving thoughts, emotions, or related behaviors. Leader and participant manuals are available without cost at www.EvWorthington-forgiveness.com.

Other Forgiveness Interventions

While the above interventions represent the most empirically tested forgiveness interventions, several other approaches have been used. Rye and colleagues (Rye & Pargament, 2002; Rye, Pargament, Pan, Yingling, Shogren, & Ito, 2005; Rye et al., 2012) have developed an intervention targeting individuals' experience of anger and bitterness after the breakup of a romantic relationship that is designed to increase forgiveness toward their ex. This treatment contains five steps: (1) discussion of feelings of betrayal; (2) cognitive-behavioral strategies for coping with anger; (3) forgiveness education, obstacles to forgiveness, and strategies for achieving forgiveness; (4) self-care and self-forgiveness; and (5) relapse prevention and closure. Both religious and secular versions have been tested

Luskin's (2001) Forgive-for-Good model primarily uses cognitive-behavioral therapy methods within his approach to forgiving. He summarizes his Forgive-for-Good model in nine steps: (1) survey one's feelings of distress about the offense; (2) commit oneself to feel better; (3) understand the difference between forgiveness and reconciliation, take offenses less personally; (4) recognize that distress comes from hurt feelings, thoughts, and physical upset, not from the injury itself; (5) when one feels upset, practice stress management to soothe sympathetic nervous system activation; (6) stop expecting that others will provide one's needs; (7) put energy into looking for another way to get positive goals met than through the hurtful experience; (8) remember that a life well lived is one's best revenge, do not focus on wounded feelings, and thereby give power to the offender; instead, look for love, beauty, and kindness; and (9) remind oneself of one's heroic choice to forgive.

Several approaches have been tailored to couple treatment. Gordon and colleagues' developed a model for forgiveness in couples in which an affair has occurred (Gordon, Baucom, & Snyder, 2004). Forgiveness consists of three components: (1) a realistic, nondistorted, balanced view of the relationship; (2) a release from being controlled by negative affect toward the partner; and (3) lessened desire to punish the partner. Conceptualizations and couple therapy methods were drawn from CBT and psychodynamic theory.

Worthington's REACH Forgiveness model fits within a larger model called Forgiveness and Reconciliation through Experiencing Empathy (FREE). That model has been tested in several studies with couples (Ripley & Worthington, 2002; Burchard, Yarhouse, Worthington, Berry, Kilian, & Canter, 2003) and parents (Kiefer et al., 2010).

Greenberg, Warwar, and Malcolm (2010) created a specialized emotion-focused therapy treatment that facilitates the resolution of emotional interpersonal injuries through forgiveness. DiBlasio (2000) has also developed a forgiveness intervention for couples who are dealing with some transgression in couple therapy.

Overall, the treatments for forgiveness use methods from a variety of schools of psychotherapy. Few rely solely on CBT methods; many focus on changing emotional reactivity, but the way such change is effected varies widely. Some are employed within couple or family relationships, but the focus is still forgiving. The question arises, though: do they work?

Evidence Supporting Forgiveness Interventions

Forgiveness Treatments Produce Forgiveness

A meta-analysis of forgiveness interventions has shown that individually administered, couple, psychoeducational, and process group interventions are effective at promoting forgiveness (with effect sizes of about 0.1 S.D. per hour of intervention). Wade, Hoyt, Kidwell, and Worthington (2014) conducted a meta-analysis of forgiveness interventions. Most worked, and different interventions were not differentially effective. Enright's (Enright & Fitzgibbons, 2014) Forgiveness Process ($N = 23$) and Worthington's (2006) REACH Forgiveness ($N = 22$) were tested as often as all others combined ($N = 22$). In head-to-head comparisons, Enright versus Worthington, $p = .27$, and Enright versus others, $p = .15$. Efficacy of the intervention was dependent on (a) modality (individual treatment was better than group treatment, $p =.021$, but not couple treatment, $p = .251$), and (b) dosage. Generally, more severe problems (e.g., incest) resulted in both longer treatment and more gains.

Forgiveness Treatments can Positively Affect Health

Forgiveness has been repeatedly and strongly related to better physical, mental, relational, and spiritual health. Reviews have summarized relational (Waldron & Kelly, 2008) and spiritual health (Davis, Worthington, Hook, & Hill, 2013). We focus mostly on and physical and mental health.

Forgiveness is related to better physical health   In qualitative reviews, forgiveness has been consistently found to be related to better physical health. For example, using a national probability survey sample, Toussaint, Williams, Music, and Everson (2001) found that people aged 65 and over had significant correlations between unforgiveness and negative health markers, but people at younger ages did not. Thus, many health problems are due to the nature of unforgiveness as being a stressor, and thus chronic, long-term stress takes a toll on physical health. Problems occur in the cardiovascular system and the immune system (for a review, see Worthington, Witvliet, Pietrini, & Miller, 2007), and throughout many systems due to elevated cortisol (for a review, see Sapolsky, 2004).

Lavelock and colleagues (2015) proposed a conceptual model to account for some mechanisms by which forgiveness can lead to better physical health. First, they suggested that changing emotions from negative to positive supports Harris' and Thoresen's (2003) model of forgiveness and health. Harris and Thoresen speculated that experiencing more positive and fewer negative emotions led to more health-promoting behaviors, more frequent peak physiological functioning, and better vagal tone. In effect, better health outcomes appear when a reduction of unforgiveness, an increase in positive affect, and their effects on behaviors are combined. Second, forgiveness may help maintain one's social support network, which can influence physical health. Forgiveness leads to greater physical health, while social isolation are dangerous for individuals and groups. Third, forgiveness is tied to mental health variables – like negative affect – that may indirectly contribute to physical health outcomes. Trait forgivingness was also correlated with better conflict management, which fully mediated the relationship between forgiveness and health. Fourth, those who forgive others tend to have stronger immune systems (Seybold, Hill, Neumann, & Chi, 2001), less physiological reactivity to stress (Witvliet, Ludwig, & Vander Laan, 2001), lower blood pressure (Lawler, Younger, Piferi, Jobe, Edmondson, & Jones, 2005), and overall fewer physical symptoms (Toussaint et al., 2001). Physiological responses related to forgiveness have regularly been stress-related. Associations between forgiveness and lower levels of cortisol (Berry & Worthington, 2001, Tabak & McCullough, 2011) and oxytocin (Tabak, McCullough, Szeto, Mendez, & McCabe, 2011) have also been found. Many physiological variables mediate between forgiveness and physical health (for reviews, see Toussaint, Worthington, & Williams, 2015), including indirect effects acting through mental health. Short-term anger may be functional in certain situations, but the chronic anger and related emotions of unforgiveness are typically deleterious to physical health.

Forgiveness Treatments can Positively Affect Mental Health Variables

In Wade et al. (2014), forgiveness treatments were related to lower depression and anxiety and higher sense of hope. For example, when studies treated forgiveness but measured both forgiveness and depression ($k = 10$), forgiveness had a larger effect size than did depression, but there were, nevertheless, strong gains in depression, ES = 0.34, 95% CI [0.17, 0.52] as well as forgiveness ES = 0.60, 95% CI [0.26, 0.94] ($p = .09$). Similarly, when treating anxious people for forgiveness ($k = 7$), the aggregate effect size for anxiety was 0.63, 95% CI [0.0003, 1.26] compared with forgiveness ES = 1.34, 95% CI [0.55, 2.12] ($p = .21$). In both cases, without addressing depression or anxiety, the gains were half as much as the gains in forgiveness. Looking at the gains in relationship to the gains that typically occur with cognitive-behavior therapy for depression and anxiety, they were about one-third to one-half as much as full psychotherapy targeted at depression or anxiety. For hope ($k = 6$), the aggregate effect size for hope was 1.00, 95% CI [0.38, 1.62], while, for forgiveness within those same studies, ES = 0.94, 95% CI [0.16, 1.73] ($p = .96$).

Mechanisms by Which Forgiveness Might Positively Affect Mental Health

Several mechanisms potentially link forgiveness with improved mental health. These show once again how forgiveness straddles the fence between clinical psychology and positive psychology, making it an exemplar for positive clinical psychology.

Forgiveness might stimulate clinical repair. For example, rumination about hurtful events often leads to anxiety, depression, and loss of hope. Rumination decreases as unforgiveness abates, and hope mediates the connection between forgiveness intervention and mental health outcomes (Witvliet, DeYoung, Hofelich, & DeYoung, 2011). As such, the intervention increases hope, which causally affects depression and anxiety. Thus, forgiveness interventions might facilitate general psychological and interpersonal strategies that generalize to dealing with conditions that trigger anxious or depressed cognition and emotion. They might also prompt use of relationship-repair methods that improve the affective balance in relationships.

Forgiveness interventions might also open the door to repair ruptures in patients' attachment schemas and thus promote differentiation of self. Sandage and colleagues (for a review, see Worthington & Sandage, 2015) have most consistently investigated forgiveness and its effect on patients', community members', and students' attachment schemas. In a recent clinical application, Sandage et al. (in press) have incorporated the REACH Forgiveness intervention within an ongoing Dialectical Behavior Therapy treatment protocol for people with Borderline Personality Disorder. They found that patients not only embraced the notion of forgiveness, but positive changes in forgiveness were associated with reductions in psychiatric symptoms and attachment anxiety.

Forgiveness interventions might also stimulate growth and other positive psychological processes. They might promote effective coping strategies to deal with interpersonal transgressions, establish a broaden-and-build growth sequence involving other virtues or character strengths, and prompt religious patients to draw on psychological healing resources of their religious values and communities. Rye and Pargament (2002) and Rye et al. (2005) compared secular and explicitly Christian versions of Rye's forgiveness intervention with Christian undergraduate students and divorced individuals from the community. The intervention showed few differences between secular and explicitly Christian versions, and post hoc analyses showed that Christians drew on their religious tradition and employed religious coping strategies even when in the secular condition. There is evidence that interventions that promote forgiveness operate via increased empathy, which is clearly an important relational strength (McCullough et al., 1998; Sandage & Worthington, 2010). Forgiveness interventions might also build virtues or other character strengths, foster resilience, and inspire hope.

In summary, several mechanisms potentially link forgiveness with improved mental health by reducing symptoms. Other mechanisms might accelerate positive psychological states. Forgiveness interventions work on both the clinical and positive psychology aspects, making it an exemplar for positive clinical psychology.

Forgiveness Intervention for Clinical and General Populations

Summary of Studies

We have sought to analyze forgiveness interventions used with both clinical and subclinical populations (see Table 24.1). We consulted a table of studies from Wade and colleagues (2014), who analyzed randomized clinical trials of forgiveness interventions. We selected only treatments that used Enright's, Worthington's, Luskin's, and DiBlasio's interventions because they were the most frequently used. We supplemented the studies from Wade et al. with other studies to which we had access and which addressed other types of interventions. This included examining control groups in settings in which an entire community was receiving a community awareness-raising intervention (e.g., Lampton, Oliver, Worthington, & Berry, 2005; Stratton, Dean, Nooneman, Bode, & Worthington, 2008) where the article reported only the difference between the treatment groups (receiving an additional psychoeducational intervention) and the community awareness-raising control. We summarized the problem (if specifically targeted), duration of treatment, and effect size for clinical studies. Confidence intervals were not available for some studies, so we reported only the means. We ordered the treatments in each category by duration of treatment because Wade et al.'s meta-analysis found a strong dose–response relationship that overshadowed theoretical approach. As we see from Table 24.1, there is indeed a preponderance of nonsignificant findings among the briefer treatments in each category.

More Forgiveness is Experienced in Clinical Patients than in Subclinical Samples

Clinical treatments   In studies with clinical patients, most used Enright's process model. Enright has most often applied his model with patients; others who have promoted forgiveness with patients have typically used Enright's model because it had a positive track record and other approaches had not been studied with those populations. Treatment of clinical samples usually had significant effects. Sample sizes for the treatment conditions were modest, from 12 to 64 with a mean of 39. Six studies were summarized, and all had significant effects. Clinical patients have severe harms to forgive, such as incest, love-deprived troubled adolescence, and the like. As a result, treatment times were very long, ranging from 9 to 57.2 hours, and effect sizes ranged from 0.58 (AA members) to 3.33 (men troubled by a partner's abortion). The downside of this "forgiveness therapy," as it is called, is that clinicians rarely have 9 hours, and virtually never have 57 hours to devote to treating a single problem to achieve forgiveness, so the transfer of these treatments to the clinic is questionable.

Community-based treatments   When samples have been recruited from the community for treatment, sample sizes have been moderate, ranging from 30 to 63 with a mean of 45. The effect sizes have been somewhat reduced relative to those with patients, likely because not all people have major unforgiven events in their lives. In four studies, Harris and colleagues (2006) recruited men who were concerned with the effect of anger on their cardiovascular risk. The focus of those psychoeducational group interventions was on forgiveness in those four studies, but the participants were likely more concerned with their health. Thus, it is not surprising that all four interventions, of 6, 9, 15 and 15 hours did not produce statistically significant results in promoting forgiveness.

Religious communities   DiBlasio and Benda (2008) recruited community couples and introduced couple therapy with a three-hour intervention to promote forgiveness. Three hours of treatment produced a significant effect for Christian couples (but not for those who did not identify as Christians). Similar findings have been demonstrated in international samples; Worthington et al. (2010) reported an effect size of 0.92 from six-hour psychoeducational group interventions in Christian churches in the Philippines. Greer, Worthington, Lin, Lavelock, and Griffin (2014) used forgiveness intervention in workbook form in a sample of Christians who sought to forgive another member of their church (including, for many, a pastor) who had hurt or offended them. The workbook took 6.7 hours on average to complete, and the mean effect size was 1.37. Davis et al. (2013) also reported significant effects in a meta-analysis of over 50 empirical studies, mostly (but not exclusively) on Christians. Thus, in several intervention studies with Christian members of the community, researchers most often found statistically significant effect sizes. Only 4 of 10 studies in our review yielded a significant effect, even though participants from the community were recruited to participate specifically in forgiveness groups.

Control groups from communities   In community samples in which some community-based change was made or some program (like forgiveness groups) was offered to the whole community and a subsample was selected as a control condition, the effect sizes are smaller. Significance is improbable, though confidence intervals were not reported for two of the three studies. In three studies, samples ranged from 23 to 36. Effect sizes were 0.26, 0.13, and 0.09.

Awareness-raising interventions in a large community   In one community forgiveness-awareness-raising study, Griffin et al. (under review) assessed 877 students and other resident directors, resident assistants, and health personnel. They found that the mean reported exposure to forgiveness interventions in such places as chapel talks, class projects, essay contests, posters, advertisements, newspaper articles, etc. was 2.5 hours. The average amount of change was 0.02 per hour of exposure, so the effect size was 0.05. While this does not seem to be a powerful effect, this was spread across over 700 people (who were tested; more experienced the intervention). Thus, estimating the amount of meaningful forgiveness is difficult. Yet if only one of 10 experienced clinically significant change, this amounts to a substantial amount of change across the community.

Forgiveness Treatments and Psychotherapy

We tentatively conclude that psychotherapists might use forgiveness treatments to speed and deepen psychotherapy. That conclusion, however, has not been investigated. We suggest several hypotheses to investigate that proposition.

- Despite the interpersonal nature of many presentations for psychotherapy, forgiveness is rarely the main focus of psychotherapy. Clinical experience suggests (and this needs to be tested) that people rarely seek "forgiveness therapy" as the focal point of psychological treatment. Surveys of practitioners from couple therapists to social workers to psychologists agree that a high frequency of patients have issues with unforgiveness requiring some attention to it during psychotherapy (DiBlasio & Proctor, 1993).
- When unforgiveness is central to psychotherapy, a forgiveness intervention might be integrated into the psychotherapeutic process without disruption.
- When unforgiveness is not central to psychotherapy, incorporating a forgiveness intervention into psychotherapy can obviate psychotherapy. In other words, we suspect that when unforgiveness is not central to psychotherapy, taking a week to focus on forgiveness could derail psychotherapy.
- Some clients may have negative associations with the topic of forgiveness or particular understandings based cultural and religious traditions. Therapists need high levels of cultural competence when using forgiveness interventions, as with all clinical practice.
- Psychoeducational forgiveness groups or self-administered workbooks may serve as appropriate adjuncts to psychotherapy. For example, forgiveness treatment might involve a (six-hour) psychoeducational forgiveness group that could meet on weekends several times per year within a shared counseling practice that draws on patients who have interpersonal concerns. Such groups might be conducted by master's level practitioners and be billed at a group psychotherapy rate, which typically will (a) benefit clients financially; (b) shorten treatment (but still provide income to the practice); (c) accelerate treatment by the concentrated focus on forgiveness and the attendant benefits to reducing anxiety and depression and increasing hope; (d) provide more generalization because it deals with things not the focus of psychotherapy and because it uses the healing factors of the group (Yalom, 1975); and (e) shifts time from an experienced psychotherapist to a group specialist (who might be an intern or new counselor at the agency, or a seasoned group specialist), allowing the psychotherapist to concentrate on the focal problem without having to sidetrack to deal with what might seem a more peripheral issue for some patients. Similarly, patients can be assigned to work through a take-home or web-based workbook to promote forgiveness (Teachman, 2014). These evidence-based workbooks, which in early randomized clinical trials (Greer et al., 2014; Harper et al., 2014) have had positive effects comparable with individual forgiveness therapy, can be monitored by a psychological technician. That can free professional psychotherapy time and thus have large psychological benefits for patients without much professional or patient cost.

Summary

In reviewing selected studies, we conclude that forgiveness interventions are strongly dependent on dose and on level of initial unforgiveness. Even in well-adjusted communities, though, some need for forgiveness is typically experienced – more with each increasing level of treatment. Clinical applications in randomized clinical trials with targeted offenses have shown the starkest improvement. Yet, this is likely because the treatments have been the longest and the degree of unforgiveness the most. On the other hand, the external validity of these studies have yet to be investigated in moving from efficacy to effectiveness and dissemination trials. Further exploration is needed.

Conclusions

We have shown that forgiveness is an exemplar of positive clinical psychology. It is not merely a way to enhance flourishing, but it is an experience that has been promoted by psychoeducational, psychotherapeutic, and community-based public health interventions for preventing and resolving interpersonal concerns that are often integral to presenting problems. We have suggested one important implication: that forgiveness treatments can often be used as adjuncts to make psychotherapy more cost-effective. At present, there is no experimental evidence for the claim, but given our analysis, that is the logical next step. While many forgiveness interventions have been tested, none has specifically examined psychotherapy patients in treatment with and without the forgiveness groups as adjuncts.

References

Al-Mabuk, R. H., Enright, R. D., & Cardis, P. A. (1995). Forgiving education with parentally love-deprived late adolescents. *Journal of Moral Education*, 24, 427–444.

Berry, J. W. & Worthington, E. L., Jr. (2001). Forgiveness, relationship quality, stress while imagining relationship events, and physical and mental health. *Journal of Counseling Psychology*, 48, 447–455. doi.10.1037/0022-0167.48.4.447.

Burchard, G. A, Yarhouse, M. A., Worthington, E. L., Jr., Berry, J. W., Kilian, M. K., & Canter, D. E. (2003). A study of two marital enrichment programs and couples' quality of life. *Journal of Psychology and Theology*, 31, 240–252.

Coyle, C. T. & Enright, R. D. (1997). Forgiveness intervention with post-abortion men. *Journal of Consulting and Clinical Psychology*, 65, 1042–1045.

Davis, D. E., Ho, M. Y., Griffin, B. J., Bell, C., Hook, J. N., Van Tongeren, D. R., Worthington, E. L., Jr., DeBlaere, C., & Westbrook, C. (2015). Forgiving the self and physical and mental health correlates: A meta-analytic review. *Journal of Counseling Psychology*, 62(2), 329–335.

Davis, D. E., Worthington, E. L., Jr., Hook, J. N., & Hill, P. C. (2013). Research on religion/spirituality and forgiveness: A meta-analytic review. *Psychology of Religion and Spirituality*, 5, 233–241. doi.10.1037/a0033637.

DiBlasio, F. A. (2000). Decision-based forgiveness treatment in cases of marital infidelity. *Psychotherapy: Theory, Research, Practice, Training*, 37(2), 149–158. doi.10.1037/h0087834.

DiBlasio, F. A. & Benda, B. B. (2008). Forgiveness intervention with married couples: Two empirical analyses. *Journal of Psychology and Christianity*, 27(2), 150–158.

DiBlasio, F. A. & Proctor, J. H. (1993). Therapists and the clinical use of forgiveness. *American Journal of Family Therapy*, 21, 175–184. doi.10.1080/01926189308250915.

Enright, R. D. & Fitzgibbons, R. P. (2014). *Forgiveness therapy: An empirical guide for resolving anger and restoring hope*. Washington, DC: American Psychological Association. doi. 10.1037/10381-000.

Exline, J. J., Park, C. L., Smyth, J. M., & Carey, M. P. (2011). Anger toward God: Social-cognitive predictors, prevalence, and links with adjustment to bereavement and cancer. *Journal of Personality and Social Psychology*, 100, 129–148. doi.10.1037/a0021716.

Exline, J. J., Worthington, E. L., Jr., Hill, P. C., & McCullough, M. E. (2003). Forgiveness and justice: A research agenda for social and personality psychology. *Personality and Social Psychology Review*, 7, 337–348. doi.10.1207/S15327957PSPR0704_06.

Freedman, S. R. & Enright, R. D. (1996). Forgiveness as an intervention goal with incest survivors. *Journal of Consulting and Clinical Psychology*, 64, 983–992. doi.10.1037/0022-006X.64.5.983.

Freedman, S. & Knupp, A. (2003). The impact of forgiveness on adolescent adjustment to parental divorce. *Journal of Divorce and Remarriage, 39*, 135–164. doi.10.1300/J087v39n01_08.

Gassin, E. A. (1995). *Social cognition and forgiveness in adolescent romance: An intervention study*. Doctoral dissertation. Available from PsychInfo at: 1995-95020-077.

Goldman, D. & Wade, N.G. (2012). Comparison of group interventions to promote forgiveness: A randomized controlled trial. *Psychotherapy Research, 22*, 604–620. doi.10.1080/10503307.2012.692954.

Gordon, K. C., Baucom, D. H., & Snyder, D. K. (2004). An integrative intervention for promoting recovery from extramarital affairs. *Journal of Marital and Family Therapy, 30*, 213–231. doi.10.1111/j.1752-0606.2004.tb01235.x.

Greenberg, L. S., Warwar, S. H., & Malcolm, W. M. (2010). Emotion-focused couples therapy and the facilitation of forgiveness. *Journal of Marital and Family Therapy, 36*, 28–42. doi.10.1111/j.1752-0606.2009.00185.x.

Greer, C. L., Worthington, E. L., Jr., Lin, Y., Lavelock, C. R., & Griffin, B. J. (2014). Efficacy of a self-directed forgiveness workbook for Christian victims of within-congregation offenders. *Spirituality in Clinical Practice, 1*, 218–230. doi.10.1037/scp0000012.

Griffin, B. J., Toussaint, L. L., Worthington, E. L., Jr., Coleman, J. A., Lavelock, C. R., Wade, N. G., Hook, J. N., Sandage, S. J., & Rye, M. S. (under review). Forgiveness blitz: A community-based forgiveness initiative.

Harper, Q., Worthington, E. L., Jr., Griffin, B. J., Lavelock, C. R., Hook, J. N., Vrana, S. R., & Greer, C. L. (2014). Efficacy of a workbook to promote forgiveness: A randomized controlled trial with university students. *Journal of Clinical Psychology, 70*, 1158–1169. doi.10.1002/jclp.22079.

Hall, J. H. & Fincham, F. D. (2005). Self–forgiveness: The stepchild of forgiveness research. *Journal of Social and Clinical Psychology, 24*, 621–637. doi.10.1521/jscp.2005.24.5.621.

Hall, J. H. & Fincham, F. D. (2008). The temporal course of self-forgiveness. *Journal of Social and Clinical Psychology, 27*, 174–202. doi.10.1521/jscp.2008.27.2.174.

Harris, A. H. S. & Thoresen, C. E. (2003). Strength-based health psychology: Counseling for total human health. In: B. Walsh (Ed.), *Counseling psychology and optimal human functioning* (pp. 199–227). Mahwah, NJ: Lawrence Erlbaum.

Harris, A., Luskin, F., Norman, S. B., Standard, S., Bruning, J., Evans, S., & Thoresen, C. E. (2006). Effects of a group forgiveness interventions on forgiveness, perceived stress, and trait-anger. *Journal of Clinical Psychology, 62*, 715–733. doi.10.1002/jclp.20264.

Hart, K. E. & Shapiro, D. A. (2002). *Secular and spiritual forgiveness interventions for recovering alcoholics harboring grudges*. Paper presented at the annual convention of the American Psychological Association, Chicago, IL, August.

Hepp-Dax, S. H. (1996). *Forgiveness as an educational goal with fifth grade inner city children*. Unpublished doctoral dissertation, Fordham University, New York.

Kiefer, R. P., Worthington, E. L., Jr., Myers, B., Kliewer, W. L., Berry, J. W., Davis, D. E., Kilgour, J., Jr., Miller, A. J., Van Tongeren, D. R., & Hunter, J. L. (2010). Training parents in forgiveness and reconciliation. *American Journal of Family Therapy, 38*, 32–49. doi.10.1080/01926180902945723.

Klatt, J. & Enright, R. D. (2009). Investigating the place of forgiveness within the positive youth development paradigm. *Journal of Moral Education, 38*(1), 35–52. doi.10.1080/03057240802601532.

Lampton, C., Oliver, G., Worthington, E. L., Jr., & Berry, J. W. (2005). Helping Christian college students become more forgiving: An intervention study to promote forgiveness as part of a program to shape Christian character. *Journal of Psychology and Theology, 33*, 278–290.

Lavelock, C. R., Snipes, D., Griffin, B. J., Worthington, E. L., Jr., Davis, D. E., Hook, J. N., Benotsch, E. G., & Ritter, J. (2015). Conceptual models of forgiveness and physical health. In: L. Toussaint, E. L. Worthington, Jr., & D. Williams (Eds.), *Forgiveness and health: Scientific evidence and theories relating forgiveness to better health* (pp. 29–42). New York: Springer.

Lawler, K. A., Younger, J. W., Piferi, R. L., Jobe, R. L., Edmondson, K., & Jones, W. H. (2005). The unique effects of forgiveness on health: An exploration of pathways. *Journal of Behavioral Medicine, 28*, 157–167. doi.10.1007/s10865-005-3665-2.

Lin, W. F., Mack, D., Enright, R. D., Krahn, D., & Baskin, T. W. (2004). Effects of forgiveness therapy on anger, mood, and vulnerability to substance use among inpatient substance- dependent clients. *Journal of Consulting and Clinical Psychology, 72*, 1114–1121. doi.10.1037/0022-006X.72.6.1114.

Lin, Y., Worthington, E. L., Jr., Griffin, B. J., Greer, C. L., Opare-Henaku, A., Lavelock, C. R., Hook, J. N., Ho, M. Y., & Muller, H. (2014). Efficacy of REACH Forgiveness across cultures. *Journal of Clinical Psychology, 70*(9), 781–793.

Luskin, F. M. & Bland, B. (2000). Stanford–Northern Ireland HOPE-1 project. Unpublished manuscript, Stanford University, Palo Alto, CA.

Luskin, F. & Bland, B. (2001). Stanford–Northern Ireland HOPE-2 project. Unpublished manuscript, Stanford University, Palo Alto, CA.

Luskin, F. M., Ginzburg, K., & Thoresen, C. E. (2005). The efficacy of forgiveness intervention in college age adults: Randomized controlled study. *Humboldt Journal of Social Relations, 29,* 163–184.

McCullough, M. E., Rachal, K. C., Sandage, S. J., Worthington, E. L., Jr., Brown S. W., & Hight, T. L. (1998). Interpersonal forgiving in close relationships II: Theoretical elaboration and measurement. *Journal of Personality and Social Psychology, 75,* 1586–1603. doi.10.1037/0022-3514.75.6.1586.

McCullough, M. E., Worthington, E. L., Jr., & Rachal, K. C. (1997). Interpersonal forgiving in close relationships. *Journal of Personality and Social Psychology, 73,* 321–336. doi.10.1037/0022-3514.73.2.321.

McCullough, M. E., Orsulak, P., Brandon, A., & Akers, L. (2007). Rumination, fear, and cortisol: An in vivo study of interpersonal transgressions. *Health Psychology, 26*(1), 126–132. doi.10.1037/0278-6133.26.1.126.

McCullough, M. E. & Root, L. M. (2005). Forgiveness as change. In: E. L. Worthington (Ed.), *Handbook of forgiveness* (pp. 91–107). New York: Brunner-Routledge.

McCullough, M. E., Fincham, F. D., & Tsang, J. (2003). Forgiveness, forbearance, and time: The temporal unfolding of transgression-related interpersonal motivations. *Journal of Personality and Social Psychology, 84*(3), 540–557. doi.10.1037/0022-3514.84.3.540.

Paleari, F. G., Regalia, C., & Fincham, F. D. (2009). Measuring offence-specific forgiveness in marriage: The marital offence-specific forgiveness scale (MOFS). *Psychological Assessment, 21*(2), 194–209. doi.10.1037/a0016068.

Reed, G. L. & Enright, R. D. (2006). The effect of forgiveness therapy on depression, anxiety, and post-traumatic stress for women after spousal emotional abuse. *Journal of Consulting and Clinical Psychology, 74,* 920–929. doi.10.1037/0022-006X.74.5.920.

Ripley, J. S. & Worthington, E. L., Jr. (2002). Hope-focused and forgiveness-based group interventions to promote marital enrichment. *Journal of Counseling and Development, 80,* 452–463. doi.10.1002/j.1556-6678.2002.tb00212.x.

Rye, M. S., Fleri, A. M., Moore, C. D., Worthington, E. L. Jr., Wade, N. G., Sandage, S. J., & Cook, K. M. (2012). Evaluation of an intervention designed to help divorced parents forgive their ex-spouse. *Journal of Divorce & Remarriage, 53,* 231–245. doi.10.1080/10502556.2012.663275.

Rye, M. S. & Pargament, K. I. (2002). Forgiveness and romantic relationships in college: Can it heal the wounded heart? *Journal of Clinical Psychology, 58,* 419–441. doi.10.1002/jclp.1153.

Rye, M. S., Pargament, K. I., Pan, W., Yingling, D. W., Shogren, K. A., & Ito, M. (2005). Can group interventions facilitate forgiveness of an ex-spouse? A randomized clinical trial. *Journal of Consulting and Clinical Psychology, 73,* 880–892. doi.10.1037/0022-006X.73.5.880.

Sandage, S. J. & Worthington, E. L., Jr. (2010). Comparison of two group interventions to promote forgiveness: Empathy as a mediator of change. *Journal of Mental Health Counseling. Special Issue: Forgiveness in Therapy, 32,* 35–57. doi.10.1037/t05863-000.

Sandage, S. J., Long, B., Moen, R., Jankowski, P. J., Worthington, E. L., Jr., Rye, M. S., & Wade, N. G. (in press). Forgiveness in the treatment of Borderline Personality Disorder: A quasi-experimental pilot study. *Journal of Clinical Psychology,* in press.

Sapolsky, R. M. (2004). *Why zebras don't get ulcers,* 3rd edn. New York: Henry Holt.

Seybold, K. S., Hill, P. C., Neumann, J. K., & Chi, D. S. (2001). Physiological and psychological correlates of forgiveness. *Journal of Psychology and Christianity, 203*(3), 250–259.

Stratton, S. P., Dean, J. B., Nooneman, A. J., Bode, R. A., & Worthington, E. L., Jr. (2008). Forgiveness interventions as spiritual development strategies: Workshop training, expressive writing about forgiveness, and retested controls. *Journal of Psychology and Christianity, 27,* 347–357. doi.10.1037/t03960-000.

Tabak, B A. & McCullough, M. E. (2011). Perceived transgressor agreeableness decreases cortisol response and increases forgiveness following recent interpersonal transgressions. *Biological Psychology, 87*(3), 386–392. doi.10.1016/j.biopsycho.2011.05.001.

Tabak, B. A., McCullough, M. E., Szeto, A., Mendez, A., & McCabe, P. M. (2011). Oxytocin indexes relational distress following interpersonal harms in women. *Psychoneuroendocrinology, 36*(1), 115–122. doi.10.1016/j.psyneuen.2010.07.004.

Teachman, B. A. (2014). No appointment necessary: Treating mental illness outside the therapist's office. *Perspectives on Psychological Science, 9,* 85–87. doi.10.1177/1745691613512659.

Toussaint, L., Worthington, E. L., Jr., & Williams, D. (Eds.). (2015). *Forgiveness and health: Scientific evidence and theories relating forgiveness to better health.* New York: Springer.

Toussaint, L. L., Williams, D. R., Music, M. A., & Everson, S. A. (2001). Forgiveness and health: Age differences in a US probability sample. *Journal of Adult Development, 8,* 249–257. doi.10.1023/A:1011394629736.

Wade, N. G., Hoyt, W. T., Kidwell, J. E. M., & Worthington, E. L., Jr. (2014). Efficacy of psychotherapeutic interventions to promote forgiveness: A meta-analysis. *Journal of Consulting and Clinical Psychology, 82*(1), 154–170. doi.10.1037/a0035268.

Wade, N. G., Worthington, E. L., Jr., & Haake, S. (2009). Promoting forgiveness: Comparison of explicit forgiveness interventions with an alternative treatment. *Journal of Counseling and Development, 87,* 143–151.

Waldron, V. R. & Kelley, D. L. (2008). *Communicating forgiveness.* Thousand Oaks, CA: Sage.

Waltman, M. A., Russell, D. C., Coyle, C. T., Enright, R. D., Holter, A. C., & Swoboda, C. M. (2009). The effects of a forgiveness intervention on patients with coronary artery disease. *Psychology and Health, 24*(1), 11–27. doi.10.1080/08870440801975127.

Witvliet, C. V. O., DeYoung, N., Hofelich, A. J., & DeYoung, P. (2011). Compassionate reappraisal and emotion suppression as alternatives to offense-focused rumination: Implications for forgiveness and psychophysiological well-being. *Journal of Positive Psychology, 6,* 286–299. doi.10.1080/17439760.2011.577091.

Witvliet, C. V. O., Ludwig, T. E., & Vander Laan, K. L. (2001). Granting forgiveness or harboring grudges: Implications for emotion, physiology, and health. *Psychological Science, 121,* 117–123.

Wood, A. M., Froh, J. J., & Geraghty, A. W. A. (2010). Gratitude and well-being: A review and theoretical integration. *Clinical Psychology Review, 30,* 890–905. doi.10.1016/j.cpr.2010.03.005.

Worthington, E. L., Jr. (Ed.). (2005). *Handbook of forgiveness.* New York: Brunner-Routledge.

Worthington, E. L., Jr. (2006). *Forgiveness and reconciliation: Theory and application.* New York: Brunner-Routledge.

Worthington, E. L., Jr., Berry, J. W., Hook, J. N., Davis, D. E., Scherer, M., Griffin, B. J., Wade, N. G., Yarhouse, M., Ripley, J. S., Miller, A. J., Sharp, C. B, Canter, D. E., & Campana, K. L. (2015). Forgiveness–reconciliation and communication–conflict–resolution interventions versus rested controls in early married couples. *Journal of Counseling Psychology, 62*(1), 14–27.

Worthington, E. L., Jr. & Sandage, S. J. (2015). *Forgiveness and spirituality in psychotherapy: A relational approach.* Washington, DC: American Psychological Association.

Worthington, E. L., Jr., Witvliet, C. V. O., Pietrini, P., & Miller, A. J. (2007). Forgiveness, health, and well-being: A review of evidence for emotional versus decisional forgiveness, dispositional forgivingness, and reduced unforgiveness. *Journal of Behavioral Medicine, 30,* 291–302. doi.10.1007/s10865-007-9105-8.

Worthington, E. L., Jr., Hunter, J. L., Sharp, C. B., Hook, J. N., Van Tongeren, D. R., Davis, D. E., Miller, A. J., Gingrich, F. C., Sandage, S. J., Lao, E., Budbod, L., & Monforte-Milton, M. (2010). A psychoeducational intervention to promote forgiveness in Christians in the Philippines. *Journal of Mental Health Counseling, 32,* 75–93.

Yalom, I. D. (1975). *The theory and practice of group psychotherapy,* 2nd edn. New York: Basic Books.

25

Mindfulness in Positive Clinical Psychology

Shauna Shapiro, Sarah de Sousa, and Carley Hauck

Central to the development and practice of positive clinical psychology is the call for clinicians to embrace a concept of well-being that honors the interdependence of negative and positive emotions, thoughts, and experience (Wood & Tarrier, 2010). The study of mindfulness as a clinical intervention, as well as a theoretical framework, offers much to this emerging focus in clinical work. A deep appreciation of the interconnectedness of all experience is at the very heart of the wisdom traditions that inform our understanding of mindfulness in clinical psychology.

A central tenet of mindfulness is that everything is interdependent; all things are connected. Mindfulness-informed psychotherapy offers the opportunity to approach our clinical work, as well as our empirical research, from the perspective that all of human experience is connected in a complex, mutually interdependent web of cause and effect (Shapiro & Carlson, 2009). From this perspective, studying the path to greater health and human happiness is not distinct from the study of human suffering in all its various forms. In fact, the difficulties of everyday life contain the very seeds of greater wisdom, peace, clarity and well-being.

As we will explore in this chapter, one of the essential seeds of wisdom and mechanisms of healing that mindfulness cultivates is the capacity to be with negative as well as positive thoughts, feelings, and sensations as they arise. Mindfulness accepts both positive and negative experience as equally valid. The invitation is to "welcome" all of our experience and explore it with equanimity, discernment and kindness. As psychotherapist and mindfulness teacher Jack Kornfield (1993) says, it is "in accepting all the songs of our life that we can begin to create for ourselves a much deeper and greater identity in which our heart holds all within a space of boundless compassion" (p. 48). By facilitating this deep compassion toward the full range of our own experience as well as the experience of others mindfulness supports clinical work, both for practitioners and for those seeking our help in living more meaningful and fulfilling lives.

Defining Mindfulness

We begin our exploration of mindfulness in positive clinical psychology by offering an operational definition of mindfulness. We review the clinical applications of mindfulness, dividing this into three categories: (1) diagnostic disorders, (2) prevention and healthy stressed populations, and (3) positive psychological interventions. We then explore the mechanisms underpinning mindfulness, focusing in particular on a shift in perspective that occurs through mindfulness practice, termed *reperceiving*. We explore future directions in research and clinical applications and, lastly, we posit that mindfulness offers something unique and deeply healing to the field of clinical psychology, through its acceptance of negative and positive experiences as equally important and valid.

The Wiley Handbook of Positive Clinical Psychology, First Edition. Edited by Alex M. Wood and Judith Johnson.
© 2016 John Wiley & Sons, Ltd. Published 2016 by John Wiley & Sons, Ltd.

Mindfulness is often referred to as a consciousness discipline. It is a way of training the mind, heart, and body to be fully present with life. Although often associated with meditation, mindfulness is much more than a meditation technique. It is a way of being, a way of living. Mindfulness is about presence – being here, now, completely. This capacity to be fully alive and fully awake is at the heart of being human – and at the heart of working in a healing profession. A mindful clinician is one who is committed to practicing being present and awake, and to listening deeply to their client, moment by moment.

Three Core Elements of Mindfulness

Mindfulness comprises three core elements: intention, attention, and attitude. *Intention* involves knowing *why* we are doing what we are doing: our ultimate aim, our vision, our aspiration. *Attention* involves attending fully to the present moment and the ability to accept experiences without judging them. *Attitude*, or *how* we pay attention, enables us to stay open, kind, and curious. These three elements are not separate – they are interwoven, each informing and feeding back into the others. Mindfulness *is simply sitting still in our experience. We commit to opening rather than closing, being rather than changing, engaging rather than rehearsing. With mindfulness we can meet all of our experience with wisdom and compassion.*

Intention   The first core component of mindfulness is *intention*. Intention is simply knowing why we are doing what we are doing. When we have discerned our intentions and are able to connect with them, our intentions help motivate us, reminding us of what is truly important. Discerning our intention involves inquiring into our deepest hopes, desires, and aspirations. Listen deeply for the answers, allowing them to arise organically. This deep listening, with trust in the process and the timing, allows your truth to emerge at its own pace. Mindful attention to our own intentions helps us begin to bring unconscious values to awareness and decide whether those values are really the ones we want to pursue.

Intention, in the context of mindfulness, is not the same as (and does not include) striving or grasping for certain outcomes for our patients or ourselves. Rather, as Jack Kornfield puts it, "Intention is a direction not a destination" (personal comm., 2012). We step readily in the direction our intention points, but we step lightly, with open eyes, ears, and heart as well as the consciousness that life has its own say in the matter (whatever the matter may be) and that there is much we have yet to learn.

Attention   The second fundamental component of mindfulness is *attention*. Remember, mindfulness is about seeing clearly, and if we want to see clearly, we must be able to pay attention to what is here, now, in this present moment. Paying attention involves observing and experiencing our moment-to-moment experience. And yet this is not so easy. Recent research demonstrates that our mind wanders approximately 47% of the time (Killingsworth & Gilbert, 2010). The human mind is often referred to as a "monkey mind," swinging from thought to thought as a monkey swings from limb to limb. Mindfulness is a tool that helps us tame and train our mind so that our attention becomes stable and focused, and attention is the component of mindfulness that allows this focus.

Often, as we try to pay attention, our attention becomes tense and contracted. This is because we mistakenly think we have to be stressed or vigilant to focus our attention in a rigorous way. However, the meditation traditions teach us of a different kind of attention, a "relaxed alertness" that involves clarity and precision without stress or vigilance (Wallace & Bodhi, 2006). This relaxed alertness is the kind of attention that is essential to mindfulness. Mindful attention is also deep and penetrating; as Bhikkhu Bodhi notes, "Whereas a mind without mindfulness 'floats' on the surface of its object the way a gourd floats on water, mindfulness sinks into its object the way a stone placed on the surface of water sinks to the bottom" (Wallace & Bodhi, 2006, p. 7).

Attitude   Attitude, the third core component of mindfulness, comes into play once we have learned to intentionally pay attention in the present moment. When we do so, we may notice something: our mind is constantly judging. The attitude with which we pay attention is essential to mindfulness. For example, attention can have a cold, critical quality, or an open-hearted, compassionate quality. The latter is what brings out the best of our humanity and enhances our clinical work, and it is what we are talking about when we speak in terms of mindfulness. As the poet Khalil Gibran (n.d.) says, "Your living is determined not so much by what life brings to you as by the attitude you bring to life."

Attending without bringing the attitudinal qualities of curiosity, openness, acceptance, and love (COAL) (Siegel, 2007) into the practice may result in an attention that is condemning or shaming of inner (or outer) experience – yours or your client's. This may well have consequences contrary to the intentions of the practice; for example, we may end up cultivating patterns of criticism and striving instead of equanimity and acceptance.

These attitudes of mindfulness do not alter our experience, but simply contain it. For example, if while we are practicing mindfulness impatience arises, we note the impatience and see if we can bring an energy of acceptance and kindness to the impatience. We do not try to substitute these qualities for the impatience, or use them to make the impatience disappear. The attitudes are not an attempt to make things be a certain way, but an attempt to relate to whatever *is* in a certain way. By intentionally bringing the attitudes of COAL to our awareness of our own experience, we relinquish the habit of striving for pleasant experiences, or of pushing aversive experiences away. Instead, we attend to whatever is here. Doing so within a context of curiosity, openness, acceptance, and love not only makes it much easier to stay present, it can also transform our capacity to foster well-being in those who seek our clinical care.

Cultivating Mindfulness

What we practice becomes stronger. When we practice mindfulness, we strengthen our capacity to be present moment by moment in a curious, accepting, and loving way. Mindful practice can be categorized into *formal* and *informal* practice; each kind of practice supports the other. The formal practice will support the ability to practice mindfulness in day-to-day life, and informal practice is meant to generalize to everyday life what is learned during the formal practice.

Formal practices, like sitting meditation, are geared toward cultivating mindfulness skills in focused and systematic ways. These can involve relatively brief daily meditation woven into one's day, or intensive days- or weeks-long retreats involving many hours of formal sitting and walking meditation based on centuries-old traditions. Informal practice involves intentionally bringing an open, accepting, and discerning attention to whatever we are engaged in – for example, reading, driving, eating, or practicing therapy. As Kabat-Zinn (2005) points out, the beauty of the informal practice is that all it requires is a rotation in consciousness. As we will explore later in this chapter, this rotation in consciousness, while subtle, is significant, and its implications for health care professionals and clinical work is profound.

Both formal and informal practice have a role to play in clinical work. Below, we review research investigating the efficacy of specific mindfulness-based interventions across diverse clinical populations. In varying measure, mindfulness-based interventions incorporate both formal and informal mindfulness practices, ranging from formal sitting meditation (mindfulness based stress reduction, MBSR) to "mindfulness skills" (dialectical behavior therapy, DBT). In addition to the role that mindfulness can play as a specific intervention, it is worth considering that all therapy and clinical work can be approached as informal mindfulness practice. Setting the intention at the beginning of each therapy session, each group, each clinical training or supervision to "intentionally pay attention with kindness, discernment, openness and acceptance" is a powerful and effective practice that can transform the experience.

Clinical Applications

Research investigating the efficacy of mindfulness-based interventions for the treatment of psychological symptoms and disorders is continuing to grow at a fast pace. As it stands, there is solid evidence that mindfulness-based treatments can be successfully applied to the treatment of symptoms of anxiety and depression. Research investigating psychological outcomes in healthy community populations, however, is currently quite minimal, as is research that addresses the possibilities for personal growth and transcendence (Shapiro & Carlson, 2009). Below we review the current and most relevant literature in each of these domains of clinical research and offer suggestions regarding those areas of research that merit significant future attention from the emerging field of positive clinical psychology.

Diagnostic disorders

We begin our review by examining the effects of mindfulness-based interventions across diverse clinical populations. Research spanning the past 30 years has evaluated the effectiveness of mindfulness-based interventions across diverse clinical populations.

One study compared MBSR with the gold-standard treatment of 12 weekly sessions of cognitive-behavioral therapy (CBT) in 53 patients with social anxiety disorder (Koszycki, Benger, Shlik, & Bradwejn, 2007). Both interventions resulted in improved mood, functionality, and quality of life, but CBT proved superior in terms of improving specific measures of the severity of social anxiety.

Weiss, Nordlie, and Siegel (2005) added MBSR training to psychotherapy for a group of outpatients with primarily anxiety and depressive symptoms. When compared with a group that received psychotherapy only, both groups improved similarly on psychological distress, but those in MBSR showed greater gains on a measure of goal achievement and were able to terminate therapy sooner.

MB-EAT is an adapted form of MBSR specifically designed for persons with binge eating disorder. In a recent study, Kristeller, Wolever, & Sheets (2014) reported decreased bingeing frequency and related symptoms at a clinically meaningful level post-intervention when comparing MB-EAT to both a psychoeducational/cognitive-behavioral intervention and a waitlist control across 150 randomly assigned participants, 66% of whom met full DSM-IV-R criteria for binge-eating disorder. Furthermore, improvement in the degree of symptom reduction was related to the degree of mindfulness practice.

Further clinical research has been conducted on adapted applications of MBSR for psychological and behavioral disorders including insomnia, addiction, and ADHD. However, the research base supporting MBSR's efficacy as a psychological intervention is significantly less robust than the research base addressing efficacy in medical populations. There continues to be a need to investigate the efficacy of MBSR compared with other gold-standard treatments for mental health issues, utilizing stringently designed clinical trials.

Mindfulness-based cognitive therapy (MBCT) is a mindfulness-based intervention that has received considerable attention for its efficacy in treating patients with major depressive disorder (MDD) and in preventing relapse. MBCT studies originate from experienced psychotherapy researchers; therefore, MBCT research tends to be quite strong methodologically. Much of this research has been conducted by Teasdale, Williams, and colleagues in the United Kingdom. Multiple studies conducted by this group have documented significantly fewer relapses in depression when comparing MBCT to treatment as usual (TAU) in at-risk populations (Williams, Teasdale, Segal, & Soulsby, 2000; Ma & Teasdale, 2004). Fruitful directions for future research are beginning to emerge through preliminary investigations of additional MBCT applications, including insomnia (Heidenreich, Tuin, Pflug, Michal, & Michalak., 2006), behavioral problems and anxiety in children (Lee, 2006; Semple, Lee, & Miller, 2006), and anger and domestic violence in men (Silva, 2007).

Acceptance and commitment therapy (ACT), another form of mindfulness-based intervention, has produced a number of randomized controlled trials (RCT) evaluating the effect of ACT on a range of psychological disorders, including BPD (Gratz & Gunderson, 2006), opiate dependence (Hayes et al., 2004), smoking cessation (Gifford et al., 2004), math anxiety (Zettle, 2003), and trichotillomania (Woods, Wetterneck, & Flessner, 2006). A 2008 review of RCT's of ACT described 13 RCT's in which ACT, singly or in combination with another treatment, was compared with a control group or another active treatment (Ost, 2008). The overall effect size on a variety of psychosocial and symptom-related outcome measures when combined with a meta-analysis was 0.68. As with other mindfulness-based treatment modalities, this research suggests that mindfulness-based treatments may be applicable across a wide range of clinical populations, though further research is necessary to determine the details of what is effective for whom.

DBT was developed as a therapy to be applied to people with borderline personality disorder (BPD) (Linehan, 1987, 1993), so it is not surprising that the bulk of the evidence supporting its efficacy is from that treatment population. A 2007 review of DBT in BPD summarized seven RCTs for DBT and four RCTs for non-BPD diagnoses (Lynch, Trost, Salsman, & Linehan, 2007). A further review by Ost (2008) identified 13 RCTs of DBT, nine of which were for patients with BPD. The review by Ost (2008) found that the average effect size of the DBT interventions was 0.58, which is considered to be a medium-sized effect and likely clinically significant. DBT has also been adapted and applied to other groups, primarily people with symptoms of depression. In the case of mixed-modality intensive treatments such as DBT, the underlying mechanisms of action have only begun to be explored, and applicability to diverse populations as well as the efficacy of such interventions in treating specific symptoms offer rich opportunities for clinical research

Prevention and Healthy Stressed Populations

Though limited in scope, research on healthy stressed populations suggests that mindfulness training offers a wide range of physical, emotional and psychological benefits. In a group of healthy university students, six individual sessions of mindfulness training were compared with two guided-imagery sessions (Kingston, Chadwick, Meron, & Skinner, 2007). Students who had the mindfulness training showed significant increases pre- to post-treatment in their pain tolerance compared with those in the other condition, although there were no differences on mood or blood pressure.

Carson, Carson, Gil, and Baucom (2004) evaluated the preliminary efficacy of mindfulness-based relationship enhancement using a randomized wait-list trail in a group of relatively happy, nondistressed couples. Couples participating in the intervention reported improvements in their relationship's satisfaction, autonomy, relatedness, and closeness, as well as improvements in their acceptance of each other and a lessening in distress about their relationship. As individuals, they were also more optimistic and relaxed and reported less distress than did those in the wait-list group. Benefits were maintained at a three-month follow-up, and the amount of meditation practice was related to the magnitude of the benefits reported.

Although most mindfulness research has focused on patient benefits, recent research has found that mindfulness training may be particularly useful for clinical professionals as a means of managing stress and promoting self-care (Irving, Dobkin, & Park, 2009; Shapiro & Carlson, 2009). Studies evaluating the effectiveness of MBSR have found decreased anxiety, depression, rumination, and stress, and increased empathy, self-compassion, spirituality, and positive mood states among premedical students, nursing students, and therapists in training after completion of the MBSR program (Shapiro, Schwartz, & Bonner, 1998; Beddoe & Murphy, 2004). Similar findings have been obtained with studies on nurses and doctors.

In a controlled trial of premedical students, Jain and colleagues (2007) determined that students receiving an MBSR intervention experienced increases in positive mood states and significant decreases in rumination and stress, compared with a control group. Notably, effect sizes for mood state increases were moderate to large in the MBSR group, whereas the control group showed no effect. Practicing nurses have reported significant improvements in aspects of burnout (personal accomplishment and emotional exhaustion) after MBSR training (Cohen-Katz, Wiley, Capuano, Baker, & Shapiro, 2004, 2005; Cohen-Katz, Wiley, Capuano, Deitrick, Baker & Shapiro, 2005), and primary care doctors showed improvements in burnout, depersonalization, empathy, total mood disturbance, consciousness, and emotional stability after an eight-week mindfulness course and a 10-month maintenance phase (2.5 hours per month) (Krasner et al., 2009).

Though research investigating psychological outcomes in healthy community populations as well as healthy stressed populations is growing, future research in these areas would be most welcome. The field of positive clinical psychology is uniquely poised to investigate the effects of mindfulness in these populations with a special emphasis on the complex interrelatedness of negative and positive affect and experience.

Cultivation of Positive Psychological States and Well-being

The mission of positive psychology is to understand and foster the factors that allow individuals, communities, and societies to flourish (Seligman & Csikszentmihalyi, 2000). Bringing mindful presence to positive emotions and experiences can serve as markers of flourishing and are therefore worth cultivating (Fredrickson, 2001). When we bring attention to positive emotions such as joy, contentment, love, or compassion we are not focused on negative emotions or experiences. The term "undoing effect" is a term that says enhancing positive emotions might improve one's psychological well-being, and perhaps also one's physical health, by cultivating experiences of positive emotions at opportune moments to cope with negative emotions (Fredrickson, Mancuso, Branigan, & Tugade, 2000). It was found in a subsequent study that two distinct types of positive emotions – mild joy and contentment – share the ability to undo the lingering cardiovascular aftereffects of negative emotions (Fredrickson et al., 2000).

Loving-kindness (LKM) is a core meditation practice that helps to increase positive emotions. This meditation practice, which inclines the mind towards a well wishing for oneself and others, is known as an antidote to judgment. LKM is a technique used to increase feelings of warmth and caring for self and others (Salzberg, 1995). Like other meditation practices, LKM begins with quiet contemplation in a seated posture, often with eyes closed and an initial focus on the breath. LKM then invites one to turn toward warm and tender feelings in an open-hearted way. Individuals are first asked to focus on their heart region and contemplate a person for whom they already feel warm and tender feelings (e.g., their child, a close loved one). They are then asked to extend these warm feelings first to themselves and then towards a benefactor, a neutral person, a difficult person, and then finally to all beings. The phrases of loving-kindness, offered below, can be used as a mantra to help open the heart and calm the nervous system:

> May I, you, all beings be happy.
> May I, you all beings be safe and protected.
> May I, you all beings be healthy and strong.
> May I, you all beings go through life with ease.

LKM involves a range of thoughts and visualizations, and it directly evokes only select positive emotions (i.e., love, contentment, and compassion) and carries some potential to evoke negative emotions. LKM may well cultivate a broadened attention in addition to positive emotions. In a study observing the effects of a nine-week intervention of LKM at work, it was found to increase a variety of personal resources, including mindful attention, self-acceptance, positive relations with others, and good physical health. These gains in personal resources were consequential and enabled people to become more satisfied with their lives and to experience fewer symptoms of depression (Fredrickson, Cohn, Coffey, Pek, & Finkel, 2008).

Loving-kindness is the first in a series of meditations that produce four qualities of love and positive emotions: friendliness or well wishing (loving-kindness), compassion, sympathetic joy, and equanimity. Compassion practice is different than LKM in that it cultivates empathy for one's own suffering and for the suffering of others. This practice has also been studied and has been found to modulate negative affect states and lead to greater awareness of the individual's own suffering, in turn fostering a greater appreciation of the suffering of others (Pennebaker & Traue, 1993). Research has also found compassion to be associated with decreased negative affect and stress responses, and increased positive affect, social connectedness, and kindness towards oneself and others (Fredrickson et al., 2008; Hutcherson, Seppala, Gross, & Phelps, 2008; Lutz, Brefczynski-Lewis, Johnstone, & Davidson, 2008; Pace et al., 2009; Hofmann, Grossman, & Hinton, 2011).

Compassion practice begins with identifying a specific memory of a difficult experience or time of struggle. One is asked consider this struggle and to be present with it in a compassionate and noncritical way. Some typical phrases of compassion practice are shared below:

Let your mind and body calm. Now bring a steadiness and compassion to yourself. Breathing in and out of your heart, repeat:

May I be free from danger
May I be free from sorrow and pain
May I find peace and healing
May I find openness of heart

As in the LKM practice, one directs compassionate attention first toward oneself and is then asked to extend these feelings of compassion toward a benefactor, a neutral person, a difficult person, and then finally to all beings. Compassion is the most precious gift of all gifts. It is what restores us and offers refuge. It is the force of empathy in our own hearts that allows us to reach out and touch the broken heart of another.

Compassion is a cornerstone of effective therapy. The practices offered above are useful both as therapeutic interventions and as training to enhance the qualities and skills associated with effective clinical work. The therapeutic relationship has been shown to be a strong predictor of therapeutic outcomes, with an emphasis on empathy, unconditional positive regard, and congruence between therapist and client (Bohart, Elliot, Greenburg, & Watson, 2002). By strengthening self-attunement and self-compassion through LKM and compassion practice, clinicians strengthen the qualities that enhance the therapeutic alliance. Research shows that therapists who are the most critical of themselves are also the most hostile, controlling, and critical toward their patients (Henry, Schacht, & Strupp, 1990). Thus, practitioner self-acceptance is critical to engaging clients in supportive and accepting relationships.

Mechanisms of Mindfulness

What can mindfulness offer to positive clinical psychology and how does mindfulness as an intervention facilitate the integration of positive and negative experience in clinical work? The mechanisms of mindfulness involve three elements: intention, attention, and attitude.

Our review of the research has increasingly documented and validated mindfulness as an efficacious psychological intervention. The research and controlled trials on this subject should continue and future research must also address the question of how mindfulness leads to psychological transformation. Such research requires a testable theory of mindfulness. Here, we offer such a theory (developed by Shapiro, Carlson, Astin, & Freedman, 2006), which posits that mindfulness practice leads to a shift in perspective, termed *reperceiving*: the capacity to dispassionately observe or witness the contents of one's consciousness (Shapiro & Carlson, 2009).

Through the process of mindfulness, a person is able to disidentify from the contents of consciousness (i.e., one's thoughts, emotions, value judgments) and view his or her moment-by-moment experience with greater clarity and objectivity. We term this process *reperceiving* because it involves a fundamental shift in perspective. Rather than being immersed in the drama of one's personal narrative or life story, a person is able to stand back and simply witness it. As Goleman (1980) suggested, "The first realization in 'meditation' is that the phenomena contemplated are distinct from the mind contemplating them" (p. 146).

Reperceiving is akin to the Western psychological concepts of decentering (Safran & Segal, 1990), de-automatization (Deikman, 1982; Safran & Segal, 1990), and detachment (Bohart, 1983), which share at their core a fundamental shift in perspective. This shift, we believe, is facilitated through mindfulness: the process of intentionally attending moment by moment with openness and nonjudgment. It allows a person to realize that one's "*awareness* of sensations, thoughts, and feelings is different from the sensations, the thoughts and the feelings themselves" (Kabat-Zinn, 1990, p. 297, italics in original). This awareness, this shift from subject to object, allows a deep equanimity and clarity to arise. Equanimity allows one to see life just as it is, regardless of ones wishes for it to be something else. When we are truly present to things just as they are, there is a freedom from our reactive tendencies, a letting go and peace.

This shift from an egocentric to an objective perspective, what we have termed reperceiving, naturally occurs in the developmental process. Developmental psychologists herald this capacity to take the perspective of another (to recognize as "object" what was once "subject") as key to developmental growth across the life span (Kegan, 1982). This developmental process is often illustrated as the difference between a child offering his mother one of his own toys as a gift, and that same child offering his mother a bouquet of flowers instead. As individuals are able to shift their perspective away from the narrow and limiting confines of their own personal points of reference, development occurs; this is the dawning of empathy. We suggest that mindfulness practice continues and accelerates this process by increasing the capacity for objectivity in relation to one's internal and external experience.

Through the process of intentionally focusing nonjudgmental attention on the contents of consciousness, the mindfulness practitioner begins to strengthen what Deikman referred to as "the observing self" (Deikman, 1982). Reperceiving allows the participant to work with whatever arises in the field of experience. This shift facilitates an openness to and a capacity to "be" with both positive and negative emotions, thoughts, and sensations. Whatever arises – pain, depression, excitement, fear, gratitude – reperceiving allows one to observe the whole show from a meta-perspective.

However, it is important to differentiate between what we mean by the term reperceiving and detachment, apathy or numbness. Reperceiving engenders a deep knowing and intimacy with whatever arises moment by moment, without getting completely lost in the personal drama of the experience. Reperceiving does indeed facilitate greater distance in terms of clarity. And yet this does not translate as disconnection or dissociation. Instead, reperceiving allows one to deeply experience each event of the mind and body without identifying with or clinging to it. Through this process, one is actually able to connect more intimately with one's moment-to-moment experience, allowing it to rise and fall naturally with a sense of nonattachment. A person experiences what *is* instead of a commentary or story about what is. Therefore, reperceiving does not create apathy or indifference, but instead allows one to experience greater richness, texture and depth, moment by moment.

We suggest that reperceiving is a significant factor contributing to the transformational effects of mindfulness. As such, we believe that reperceiving is a meta-mechanism of action, which overarches additional direct mechanisms that can lead to change and positive outcome. Here, we highlight two additional mechanisms which are particularly germane to our discussion of integrating the positive and the negative in clinical psychology: (1) self-regulation and self-management; and (2) psychological flexibility.

Self-Regulation and Self-Management

Emotional regulation, also known as "emotional self-regulation," has been defined by Gross (2013) as the set of cognitive processes that influence the type of emotional response, as well as how individuals experience and express these emotions. Through the process of reperceiving, we are able to attend to the information contained in each moment. We gain access to more data, even those data that may have previously been too uncomfortable to examine. As Hayes (2002) asserted, "experiential avoidance becomes less automatic and less necessary" (p. 104). Through this process, dysregulation and subsequent disease can be avoided. In addition, reperceiving interrupts automatic maladaptive habits. People become less controlled by particular emotions and thoughts that arise, and in turn are less likely to automatically follow them with habitual reactive patterns. For example, if anxiety arises, and a person strongly identifies with it, there will be a greater tendency to regulate the anxiety through some unhealthy behavior such as drinking, smoking or overeating. Reperceiving allows a person to step back from the anxiety, to see it clearly as an emotional state that is arising and will in time pass away.

By developing the capacity to stand back and witness emotional states such as anxiety, people increase their "degrees of freedom" in response to such states, effectively freeing themselves from automatic behavioral patterns. Through reperceiving, they are no longer controlled by states such as anxiety or fear, but instead are able to use those states as information. They are then able to self-regulate in ways that foster greater health and well-being. Preliminary support for this hypothesis can be found in a study by Brown and Ryan (2003) in which people who scored higher on a valid and reliable measure of mindfulness reported significantly greater self-regulated emotion and behavior. Further supportive literature suggests the employment of adaptive emotional regulation strategies (e.g., reappraisal) causes a reduction of stress-elicited emotions tied to physical disorders, thereby enhancing overall well-being.

Psychological Flexibility

The skillful responding that results from a clear seeing of each moment as it arises could also be understood as psychological flexibility, one of the fundamental markers of psychological health (Kashdan & Rottenberg, 2010). As Kashdan and Rottenberg (2010) argue, "Although there is substantial research on the value of particular [regulatory] strategies, the ability to modify responses to best match the situation is intuitively of greater importance. Indeed, one might question whether any regulatory strategy provides universal benefits, as opposed to contingent benefits that hinge on the situation and the values and goals we import" (p. 866). Mindfulness offers an opportunity to respond to the situational demands of each new moment in a way that is congruent with our deepest needs, interests and values (Ryan & Deci, 2000; Brown & Ryan, 2003).

Our capacity to respond with grace, equanimity and discernment in each moment depends upon awareness. A common way to understand awareness is to practice an awareness of the breath. Are you breathing right now? How do you know you are breathing? Your knowing can be an intellectual and conceptual knowing, but it can also be a felt sense; a knowing with your whole being. This deep knowing is mindfulness. Try it now: as you breathe in, know with your whole being, "breathing in." As you breathe out, know with your whole being, "breathing out."

Mindfulness depends upon awareness, because how we perceive and frame this moment generates our reality, and in turn impacts how we respond. "Between stimulus and response there is a space," says Viktor Frankl (1984). "In that space is our power to choose our response. In our response lies our growth and our freedom." When we are able to see clearly, we move closer and closer to our authentic center, where we know what is the most skillful response in each moment. When we practice mindfulness, it supports us in remembering who we truly are: that we are more than our reactivity and our ingrained habits of relating. We begin to wake up to our authentic center of knowing and to focus on what is most important. We intentionally choose to be awake to this moment and to see clearly, with curiosity and compassion. This way of being begins to shift our brain circuits toward empathy, understanding, and a felt sense of our own wisdom. As this shift occurs, we find ourselves clinging less to our positive experiences and meeting our negative experiences with less resistance. Our relationship to the positive and negative forces that enter our lives becomes less like a sail blown about by the wind and more like a captain skillfully navigating the changing tides.

Conclusion

Mindfulness recognizes that life is not so simple, that positive experiences do not occur in a clean, separate space and time from negative experiences. Life is complex; our negative and positive emotions arise and intermingle, in a constantly changing, dynamic interplay. If we begin to shut ourselves off from the painful experiences, we simultaneously close down to the positive experiences. What we practice becomes stronger; if we practice numbing and closing off to experience, then we become skilled at this, and regardless of the emotion, sensation or thought that arises, we are closed down. A traditional Zen kōan helps to illustrate this:

There is a man running through the jungle, as a ferocious tiger is chasing him. The man is running for his life from the gnashing teeth and deadly claws of the tiger. Suddenly, he finds himself at the edge of a cliff. The tiger is about to pounce, so he jumps and luckily there is a branch sticking out of the cliff that he grabs before plunging to his death. He looks down and there are raging rapids below; he cannot let go. He looks to his right for help and finds nothing. He looks to his left, and finds a wild strawberry patch growing on the cliff. He picks a strawberry, and mindfully eats it. As he experiences the burst of sensation in his mouth, he thinks, "What a sweet strawberry!" The End.

What is the moral of the story? When we get stressed, we often close down, numb, and distract ourselves. Mindfulness teaches us how to stay open during stress, to not get overwhelmed, so that we can also experience the sweetness that occurs right in the middle of our stressful lives. Life is complex. Sadness and sweetness, gain and loss, pain and pleasure, light and dark, life contains opposites. If we are to experience all that life has to offer, we must learn to stay open to it all.

References

Beddoe, A. E. & Murphy, S. O. (2004). Does mindfulness decreases stress and foster empathy among nursing students? *Journal of Nursing Education, 43,* 305–312.

Bohart, A. (1983). *Detachment: A variable common to many psychotherapies?* Paper presented at the 63rd Annual Convention of the Western Psychological Association, San Francisco, CA.

Bohart, A. C., Elliott, R., Greenberg, L. S., & Watson, J. C. (2002). Empathy. In: J. C. Norcross (Ed.), *Psychotherapy relationships that work: Therapist contributions and responsiveness to patients* (pp. 89–108). New York: Oxford University Press. doi.10.1093/acprof:oso/9780199737208.001.0001.

Brown, K. W. & Ryan, R. M. (2003). The benefits of being present: Mindfulness and its roles in psychological well-being. *Journal of Personality and Social Psychology, 84,* 822–848. doi.10.1037/0022-3514.84.4.822.

Carson, J. W., Carson, K., Gil, K. M., & Baucom, D. H. (2004). Mindfulness-based relationship enhancement. *Behavior Therapy*, 35, 471–494. doi.10.1016/s0005-7894(04)80028-5.

Cohen-Katz, J., Wiley, S., Capuano, T., Baker, D. M., Deitrick, L., & Shapiro, S. (2005). The effects of mindfulness-based stress reduction on nurse stress and burnout: A qualitative and quantitative study. Part III. *Holistic Nursing Practice*, 19, 78–86. doi.10.1097/00004650-200503000-00009.

Cohen-Katz, J., Wiley, S., Capuano, T., Baker, D. M., & Shapiro, S. (2004). The effects of mindfulness-based stress reduction on nurse stress and burnout: A qualitative and quantitative study. *Holistic Nursing Practice*, 18, 302–308. doi.10.1097/00004650-200411000-00006.

Cohen-Katz, J., Wiley, S., Capuano, T., Baker, D. M., & Shapiro, S. (2005). The effects of mindfulness-based stress reduction on nurse stress and burnout: A qualitative and quantitative study. Part II. *Holistic Nursing Practice*, 19, 26–35. doi.10.1097/00004650-200501000-00008.

Deikman, A. J. (1982). *The observing self*. Boston, MA: Beacon Press. doi.10.1525/jung.1.1982.3.4.25.

Frankl, V. (1984). *Man's search for meaning*, rev. edn. Boston, MA: Washington Square Press.

Fredrickson, B. L., Cohn, M. A., Coffey, K. A., Pek, J., & Finkel, S. M. (2008) Open hearts build lives: Positive emotions, induced through loving-kindness meditation, build consequential personal resources. *Journal of Personality and Social Psychology*, 95(5), 1045–1062. doi,10.1037/a0013262.

Fredrickson, B. L. (2001). The role of positive emotions in positive psychology: The broaden-and-build theory of positive emotions. *American Psychologist*, 56(3), 218–226. doi.10.1037/0003-066x.56.3.218.

Fredrickson B. L., Mancuso R. A., Branigan C., & Tugade M. (2000). The undoing effect of positive emotions. *Motivation and Emotion*, 24(4), 237–258. doi.10.1023/a:1010796329158.

Gifford, E. V., Kohlenberg, B. S., Hayes, S. C., Antonuccio, D. O., Piasecki, M. M., Rasmussen-Hall, M. L., et al. (2004). Acceptance based treatment for smoking cessation. *Behavior Therapy*, 35, 689–705. doi.10.1016/s0005-7894(04)80015-7.

Goleman, D. (1980). A map for inner space. In: R. N. Walsh & F. Vaughan (Eds.), *Beyond ego* (pp. 141–150). Los Angeles: Tarcher.

Gratz, K. L. & Gunderson, J. G. (2006). Preliminary data on an acceptance-based emotion regulation group intervention for deliberate self-harm among women with borderline personality disorder. *Behavior Therapy*, 37, 25–35. doi.10.1016/j.beth.2005.03.002.

Gross, J. J. (2013). Emotion regulation: Taking stock and moving forward. *Emotion*, 13(3), 359–365. doi.10.1037/a0032135.

Hayes, S. C. (2002). Acceptance, mindfulness, and science. *Clinical Psychology: Science and Practice*, 9, 101–106. doi.10.1093/clipsy.9.1.101.

Hayes, S. C., Wilson K. G., Gifford, E. V., Bissett, R., Piasecki, M., Batten, S. V., et al. (2004). A preliminary trial of twelve-step facilitation and acceptance and commitment therapy with polysubstance-abusing methadone-maintained opiate addicts. *Behavior Therapy*, 35, 667–688. doi.10.1016/s0005-7894(04)80014-5.

Heidenreich, T., Tuin, I., Pflug, B., Michal, M., & Michalak, J. (2006). Mindfulness-based cognitive therapy for persistent insomnia: A pilot study. *Psychotherapy and Psychosomatics*, 75, 188–189. doi.10.1159/000091778.

Henry, W. P., Schacht, T. E., & Strupp, H. H. (1990). Patient and therapist introject, interpersonal process, and differential psychotherapy outcome. *Journal of Consulting and Clinical Psychology*, 58, 768–774. doi.10.1037/0022-006x.58.6.768.

Hofmann, S. G., Grossman, P., & Hinton, D. E. (2011). Loving-kindness and compassion meditation: Potential for psychological interventions. *Clinical Psychology Review*, 31(7), 1126–1132. doi.10.1016/j.cpr.2011.07.003.

Hutcherson, C. A., Seppala, E. M., Gross, J. J., & Phelps, E. A. (2008). Loving-kindness meditation increases social connectedness. *Emotion*, 8(5), 720–724. doi.0.1037/a0013237.

Irving, J. A., Dobkin, P. L., & Park, J. (2009). Cultivating mindfulness in health care professionals: A review of empirical studies of mindfulness-based stress reduction. *Complementary Therapies in Clinical Practice*, 15, 61–66. doi.10.1016/j.ctcp.2009.01.002.

Jain, S., Shapiro, S. L., Swanick, S., Roesch, S. C., Mills, P. J., Bell, I., & Schwartz, G. (2007). A randomized control trial of mindfulness meditation versus relaxation training: Effects on distress, positive states of mind, rumination, and distraction. *Annals of Behavioral Medicine*, 33, 11–21. doi.10.1207/s15324796abm3301_2.

Kabat-Zinn, J. (1990). *Full catastrophe living: Using the wisdom of your body and mind to face stress, pain and illness*. New York: Delacourt.

Kabat-Zinn, J. (2005). *Coming to our senses: Healing ourselves and the world through mindfulness.* New York: Hyperion.

Kashdan, T. B. & Rottenberg, J. (2010). Psychological flexibility as a fundamental aspect of health. *Clinical Psychology Review, 30*(7), 865–878. doi.10.1016/j.cpr.2010.03.001.

Kegan, R. (1982). *The evolving self: Problem and process in human development.* Cambridge, MA: Harvard University Press.

Killingsworth, M. A. & Gilbert, D. T. (2010). A wandering mind is an unhappy mind. *Science, 12,* 932. doi.10.1126/science.1192439.

Kingston, J., Chadwick, P., Meron, D., & Skinner, T. C. (2007). A pilot randomized control trial investigating the effect of mindfulness practice on pain tolerance, psychological well-being, and physiological activity. *Journal of Psychosomatic Research, 62,* 297–300. doi.10.1016/j.jpsychores.2006.10.007.

Kornfield, J. (1993). *A path with heart: A guide through the perils and promises of spiritual life.* New York: Bantam.

Koszycki, D., Benger, M., Shlik, J., & Bradweijn, J. (2007). Randomized trail of a meditation-based stress reduction program and cognitive behavior therapy in generalized social anxiety disorder. *Behaviour Research and Therapy, 45,* 2518–2526. doi.10.1016/j.brat.2007.04.011.

Krasner, M. S., Epstein, R. M., Beckman, H., Suchman, A. L., Chapman, B., Mooney, C. J., et al. (2009). Association of an educational program in mindful communication with burnout, empathy, and attitudes among primary care physicians. *Journal of the American Medical Association, 302,* 1284–1293. doi.10.1001/jama.2009.1384.

Kristeller, J., Wolever, R., & Sheets, V. (2014). Mindfulness-Based Eating Awareness Training (MB-EAT) for binge eating: A randomized clinical trial. *Mindfulness, 5*(3), 282–297. doi.10.1007/s12671-012-0179-1.

Lee, J. (2006). *Mindfulness-based cognitive therapy for children: Feasibility, acceptability, and effectiveness of a controlled clinical trial.* Unpublished doctoral dissertation. Columbia University, New York.

Linehan, M. M. (1987). Dialectical behavior therapy for borderline personality disorder. Theory and method. *Bulletin of the Menninger Clinic, 51,* 261–276. doi.10.1016/j.cbpra.2007.08.006.

Linehan, M. M. (1993). *Cognitive-behavioral treatment of borderline personality disorder.* New York: Guilford Press.

Lutz, A., Brefczynski-Lewis, J., Johnstone, T., & Davidson, R. J. (2008). Regulation of the neural circuitry of emotion by compassion meditation: Effects of meditative expertise. *Plos ONE, 3*(3), 1–10. doi.10.1371/journal.pone.0001897.

Lynch, T. R., Trost, W. T., Salsman, N., & Linehan, M. M. (2007). Dialectical behavior therapy for borderline personality disorder. *Annual Review of Clinical Psychology, 3,* 181–205. doi.10.1146/annurev.clinpsy.2.022305.095229.

Ma, S. H. & Teasdale, J. D. (2004). Mindfulness-based cognitive therapy for depressions: Replication and exploration of differential relapse prevention effects. *Journal of Consulting and Clinical Psychology, 72,* 31–40. doi.10.1037/0022-006x.72.1.31.

Ost, L. G. (2008). Efficacy of the third wave of behavioral therapies: A systematic review and meta-analysis. *Behaviour Research and Therapy, 46,* 296–321. doi.10.1016/j.brat.2007.12.005.

Pace, T. W. W., Negi, L. T., Adame, D. D., Cole, S. P., Sivilli, T. I., Brown, T. D., Issa, M. J., Raison, C. L. (2009) Effect of compassion meditation on neuroendocrine, innate immune and behavioral responses to psychosocial stress. *Psychoneuroendocrinology, 34*(1), 87–98. doi.10.1016/j.psyneuen.2008.08.011.

Pennebaker J. W. & Traue H. C. (1993). Inhibition and psychosomatic processes. *Emotion, Inhibition, and Health.* Seattle, WA: Hogrefe Hube.

Ryan, R. M. & Deci, E. L. (2000). Self-determination theory and the facilitation of intrinsic motivation, social development, and well-being. *American Psychologist, 55,* 68–78. doi.10.1037/0003-066x.55.1.68.

Safran J. D. & Segal, Z. V. (1990). *Interpersonal process in cognitive therapy.* New York: Basic Books.

Salzberg, S. (1995). *Lovingkindness: The revolutionary art of happiness.* Boston, MA: Shambhala.

Seligman, M. E. P. & Csikszentmihalyi, M. (2000). Positive psychology: An introduction. *American Psychologist, 55,* 5–14. doi.10.1037/0003-066x.55.1.5.

Semple, R. J., Lee, J., & Miller, L. F. (2006). Mindfulness-based cognitive therapy for children. In: R. A. Baer (Ed.), *Mindfulness-based treatment approaches* (pp. 143–166). New York: Academic Press.

Shapiro, S. & Carlson, L. (2009). *The art and science of mindfulness: Integrating mindfulness into psychology and the helping professions.* Washington, DC: American Psychological Association.

Shapiro, S. L., Carlson, L. E., Astin, J. A., & Freedman, B. (2006). Mechanisms of mindfulness. *Journal of Clinical Psychology, 62,* 373–386. doi.10.1002/jclp.20237.

Shapiro, S., Schwartz, G., & Bonner, G. (1998). Effects of mindfulness-based stress reduction on medical and premedical students. *Journal of Behavioral Medicine, 21*(6), 581–599.

Siegel, D. (2007). *The mindful brain.* New York: W. W. Norton.

Silva, J. M. (2007). Mindfulness-based cognitive therapy for the reduction of anger in married men. *Dissertation Abstracts International: Section B: The Sciences and Engineering, 68*(3-B), 1945.

Wallace, A. B. & Bodhi, B. (2006). The nature of mindfulness and its role in Buddhist meditation: A correspondence between B. Alan Wallace and the venerable Bhikkhu Bodhi. Unpublished manuscript, Santa Barbara Institute for Consciousness Studies, Santa Barbara, CA.

Weiss, M., Nordlie, J., & Siegel, E.P. (2005). Mindfulness-based stress reduction as an adjunct to outpatient psychotherapy. *Psychotherapy and Psychosomatics, 74,* 108–112. doi.10.1159/000083169.

Williams, J. M., Teasdale, J. D., Segal, Z. V., & Soulsby, J. (2000). Mindfulness-based cognitive therapy reduces overgeneral autobiographical memory in formerly depressed patients. *Journal of Abnormal Psychology, 109,* 150–155. doi.10.1037/0021-843x.109.1.150.

Wood, A. & Tarrier, N. (2010). Positive clinical psychology: A new vision and strategy for integrated research and practice. *Clinical Psychology Review, 30*(7), 819–829. doi.10.1016/j.cpr.2010.06.003.

Woods, D. W., Wetterneck, C. T., & Flessner, C. A. (2006). A controlled evaluation of acceptance and commitment therapy plus habit reversal for trichotillomania. *Behaviour Research and Therapy, 44,* 639–656. doi.10.1016/j.brat.2005.05.006.

Zettle, R. D. (2003). Acceptance and commitment therapy (ACT) vs. systematic desensitization in treatment of mathematics anxiety. *The Psychological Record, 53*(2), 197–215.

26

Well-being Therapy

Giovanni A. Fava

Introduction

Well-being therapy (Fava, 1999) developed in a clinical setting and originated from the growing awareness that standard treatments for mood and anxiety disorders were not sufficiently effective in determining full recovery. A substantial residual symptomatology has been found to characterize the majority of patients who were judged to be remitted according to standard criteria. These residual symptoms may progress to become prodromes of relapse (Fava, Ruini, & Belaise, 2007). As a result, the challenge of treatment of mood and anxiety disorders appeared to be the prevention of relapse more than the attainment of recovery (Fava & Tomba, 2010; Fava, 2013). The absence of psychological well-being has been found to be a risk factor for depression (Wood & Joseph, 2010). Thunedborg, Black, and Bech (1995) observed that quality of life measurement, and not symptomatic ratings, could predict recurrence of depression. An increase in psychological well-being may thus protect against relapse and recurrence (Wood & Joseph, 2010). Further, many investigations in psychosomatic settings provided confirmation of the protective role of well-being, both for mental and for physical health. Positive emotions and well-being, with the contribution of other factors, can influence the healing process of various diseases (Chida & Steptoe, 2008; Fava & Sonino, 2010; Ryff, 2014).

However, an intervention that targets the positive may address an aspect of functioning and health that is typically left unaddressed in conventional treatments. As early as 1954, Parloff, Kelman, and Frank suggested that the goals of psychotherapy were increased personal comfort and effectiveness, and humanistic psychology suggested concepts such as self-realization and self-actualization as final therapeutic goal. For a long time these latter achievements were viewed only as by-products of the reduction of symptoms or as a luxury that clinical investigators could not afford. This probably is due to the fact that, historically, mental health research has been dramatically weighted on the side of psychological dysfunction, and health was equated with the absence of illness, rather than the presence of wellness (Ryff & Singer, 1996). In 1991, Garamoni and colleagues suggested that healthy functioning is characterized by an optimal balance of positive and negative cognitions or affects, and that psychopathology is marked by deviations from the optimal balance.

Positive interventions, thus, should not be simply aimed to increase happiness and well-being, but should consider the complex balance between psychological well-being and distress (MacLeod & Moore, 2000) and be targeted to specific and individualized needs. Wood and Tarrier (2010) emphasize that positive characteristics such as gratitude and autonomy often exist on a continuum. They are neither "negative" or "positive": their impact depends on the specific situation and on the interaction with concurrent distress and other psychological attitudes.

The Wiley Handbook of Positive Clinical Psychology, First Edition. Edited by Alex M. Wood and Judith Johnson.
© 2016 John Wiley & Sons, Ltd. Published 2016 by John Wiley & Sons, Ltd.

All these elements should be taken into account in the psychotherapy process. Well-being therapy is a psychotherapeutic intervention that takes into consideration the above concepts for achieving a balanced and individualized path to optimal functioning.

The Structure of Well-Being Therapy

Well-being therapy is a short-term psychotherapeutic strategy, that extends over 8–12 sessions, which may take place every week or every other week (Fava, 1999; Fava & Tomba, 2009). The duration of each session may range from 30 to 50 minutes. It is a technique which emphasizes self-observation (Emmelkamp, 1974), with the use of a structured diary, and interaction between patients and therapists. Well-being therapy is based on a cognitive model of psychological well-being that was originally developed by Marie Jahoda in 1958. She outlined six criteria for positive mental health: autonomy (regulation of behavior from within); environmental mastery; satisfactory interactions with other people and the milieu; the individual's style and degree of growth, development, or self-actualization; the attitudes of an individual toward his or her own self (self-perception/acceptance); the individual's balance and integration of psychic forces, which encompasses both outlook on life and resistance to stress. Carol Ryff (1989) further elaborated these 6 dimensions of positive functioning and introduced a method for their assessment, the Psychological Well-being scales (Ryff, 1989, 2014). We will refer to this latter formulation as WBT. The development of sessions is as follows.

Initial Sessions

These sessions are simply concerned with identifying episodes of well-being and setting them into a situational context, no matter how short lived they were. Patients are asked to report in a structured diary the circumstances surrounding their episodes of well-being, rated on a 0–100 scale, with 0 being absence of well-being and 100 the most intense well-being that could be experienced.

Patients are particularly encouraged to search for well-being moments, not only in special hedonic–stimulating situations, but also during their daily activities. Several studies have shown that individuals preferentially invest their attention and psychic resources in activities associated with rewarding and challenging states of consciousness, in particular with optimal experience (Csikszentmihalyi, 1990). This is characterized by the perception of high environmental challenges and environmental mastery, deep concentration, involvement, enjoyment, control of the situation, clear feedback on the course of activity, and intrinsic motivation (Delle Fave, 2013). Cross-sectional studies have demonstrated that optimal experience can occur in any daily context, such as work and leisure (Delle Fave & Massimini, 2003). Patients are thus asked to report when they feel optimal experiences in their daily life and are invited to list the associated activities or situations. This initial phase generally extends over a couple of sessions. Yet its duration depends on the factors that affect any homework assignment, such as resistance and compliance.

Intermediate Sessions

Once the instances of well-being are properly recognized, the patient is encouraged to identify thoughts and beliefs leading to premature interruption of well-being. The similarities with the search for irrational, tension-evoking thoughts in Ellis' and Becker's rational-emotive therapy (1982) and automatic thoughts in cognitive therapy (Beck, Rush, Shaw, & Emery, 1979) are obvious. The trigger for self-observation is, however, different, being based on well-being instead of distress.

This phase is crucial, since it allows the therapist to identify which areas of psychological well-being are unaffected by irrational or automatic thoughts and which are saturated with them. The therapist may also reinforce and encourage activities that are likely to elicit well-being and optimal experiences (for instance, assigning the task of undertaking particular pleasurable activities for a certain time each day). Such reinforcement may also result in graded task assignments (Beck et al., 1979), with special reference to exposure to feared or challenging situations, which the patient is likely to avoid. Over time patients may develop ambivalent attitudes toward well-being. They complain of having lost it, or they long for it, but at the same time they are scared when positive moments actually happen in their lives. These moments trigger specific negative automatic thoughts, usually concerning the fact that they will not last (i.e., it is too good to be true) or that they are not deserved by patients, or that they are attainable only by overcoming difficulties and distress. Encouraging patients in searching and engaging in optimal experiences and pleasant activities is therefore crucial at this stage of WBT. This intermediate phase may extend over two or three sessions, depending on the patient's motivation and ability, and it paves the way for the specific well-being enhancing strategies.

Final Sessions

The monitoring of the course of episodes of well-being allows the therapist to realize specific impairments in well-being dimensions according to the Jahoda–Ryff conceptual framework. Ryff's six dimensions of psychological well-being are progressively introduced to the patients, as long as the material which is recorded lends itself to it. For example, the therapist could explain that autonomy consists of possessing an internal locus of control, independence and self-determination; or that personal growth consists of being open to new experience and considering self as expanding over time, if the patient's attitudes show impairments in these specific areas. Errors in thinking and alternative interpretations are then discussed. At this point in time the patient is expected to be able to readily identify moments of well-being, be aware of interruptions to well-being feelings (cognitions), utilize cognitive-behavioral techniques to address these interruptions, and to pursue optimal experiences. Meeting the challenge that optimal experiences may entail is emphasized, because it is through this challenge that growth and improvement of self can take place.

Clinical Articulation

The goal of the therapist is to lead the patient from an impaired level to an optimal level in the six dimensions of psychological well-being. This means that patients are not simply encouraged pursing the highest possible levels in psychological well-being, in all dimensions, but to obtain a balanced functioning. This optimal-balanced well-being could be different from patient to patient, according to factors, such as personality traits, social roles and cultural and social contexts.

The various dimensions of positive functioning can compensate each other (some being more interpersonally-oriented, some more personal/cognitive) and the aim of WBT, such as other positive interventions, should be the promotion of an optimal-balanced functioning between these dimensions, in order to facilitate individual flourishing (Keyes, 2002). This means that sometimes patients should be encouraged to decrease their level of positive functioning in certain domains. Without this clinical framework, the risk is to lead patients at having too high levels of self-confidence, with unrealistic expectations that may become dysfunctional and/or stressful to individuals.

Environmental Mastery

This is the most frequent impairment that emerges, that is felt by patients as a lack of sense of control. This leads the patients to miss surrounding opportunities, with the possibility of subsequent regret over them. On the other hand, sometimes patients may require help because they are unable to enjoy and savor daily life, as they are too engaged in work or family activities. Their abilities of planning and solving problems may lead others to constantly ask for their help, with the resulting feeling of being exploited and overwhelmed by requests. These extremely high levels of environmental mastery thus become a source of stress and allostatic load to the individual. Environmental mastery can be considered a key mediator or moderator of stressful life experiences (Fava et al., 2010). A positive characterization of protective factors converges with efforts to portray the individual as a psychological activist, capable of proactive and effective problem- solving, rather than passively buffeted by external forces (Ryff & Singer, 1998), but also capable of finding time for rest and relaxing in daily life.

Personal Growth

Patients often tend to emphasize their distance from expected goals much more than the progress that has been made toward goal achievement. A basic impairment that emerges is the inability to identify the similarities between events and situations that were handled successfully in the past and those that are about to come (transfer of experiences). On the other hand, people with levels of personal growth that are too high tend to forget and do not give enough emphasis to past experiences because they are exclusively future-oriented. Negative or traumatic experiences could particularly be under-estimated, as a sort of extreme defense mechanism (denial), that is, "I just need to get over this situation and go on with my life" (Held, 2002; Norem & Chang, 2002). Dysfunctional high personal growth is similar to a cognitive benign illusion, or wishful thinking, which hinders the integration of past (negative) experiences and their related learning process.

Purpose in Life

Patients may perceive a lack of sense of direction and may devalue their function in life. This particularly occurs when environmental mastery and sense of personal growth are impaired. On the other hand, many other conditions worthy of clinical attention may arise from too high levels of purpose in life. First of all individuals with a strong determination in realizing one (or more) life goal(s) could dedicate themselves fully to their activity, thereby allowing them to persist, even in the face of obstacles, and to eventually reach excellence. This again could have a cost in terms of allostatic load and stress. Further, Vallerand and colleagues (2003) have proposed the concept of obsessive passion for describing an activity or goal that becomes a central feature of one's identity and serves to define the person. Individuals with an obsessive passion come to develop ego-invested self-structures (Hodgins & Knee, 2002) and, eventually, display a rigid persistence toward the activity thereby leading to less than optimal functioning. Such persistence is rigid because it not only occurs in the absence of positive emotions and sometimes of positive feedbacks, but even in the face of important personal costs such as damaged relationships, failed commitments, and conflicts with other activities in the person's life (Vallerand et al., 2007). The individual engagement for a certain goal could thus become a form of psychological inflexibility (Kashdan & Rottenberg, 2010) which is more connected with psychopathology, than well-being. Some individuals, in fact, remains attached to their goals even when these seem to be unattainable, and keep believing that they would be happy pending the achievement of these goals. These mechanisms are associated with hopelessness (MacLeod & Conway, 2005;

Hadley & MacLeod, 2010) and parasuicidal behaviors (Vincent, Boddana, & MacLeod, 2004). Further, this confirms the idea that hope, another future-oriented positive emotion, can become paralyzing and hampers facing and accepting negativity and failures (Bohart, 2002; Geraghty, Wood, & Hyland, 2010).

Autonomy

It is a frequent clinical observation that patients may exhibit a pattern whereby a perceived lack of self-worth leads to unassertive behavior. For instance, patients may hide their opinions or preferences, go along with a situation that is not in their best interests, or consistently put their needs behind the needs of others. This pattern undermines environmental mastery and purpose in life and these, in turn, may affect autonomy, since these dimensions are highly correlated in clinical populations. Such attitudes may not be obvious to the patients, who hide their considerable need for social approval. A patient who tries to please everyone is likely to fail to achieve this goal and the unavoidable conflicts that may result in chronic dissatisfaction and frustration. On the other hand, in Western countries particularly, individuals are culturally encouraged to be autonomous and independent. Certain individuals develop the idea that they should rely only on themselves for solving problems and difficulties, and are thus unable to ask for advice or help. Also in this case, an unbalanced high autonomy can become detrimental for social/interpersonal functioning (Seeman, Singer, Ryff, Dienberg Love, & Levy-Storms, 2002). Some patients complain they are not able to get along with other people, or work in team, or maintain intimate relationships because they are constantly fighting for their opinions and independence.

Self-Acceptance

Patients may maintain unrealistically high standards and expectations, driven by perfectionistic attitudes (that reflect lack of self-acceptance) and/or endorsement of external instead of personal standards (that reflect lack of autonomy). As a result, any instance of well-being is neutralized by a chronic dissatisfaction with oneself. A person may set unrealistic standards for her performance. On the other hand, an inflated self-esteem may be a source of distress and clash with reality, as was found to be the case in cyclothymia and bipolar disorder (Garland, Fredrickson, Kring, Johnson, Meyer, & Penn, 2010; Tomba, Rafanelli, Grandi, Guidi, & Fava, 2012).

Positive Relations with Others

Interpersonal relationships may be influenced by strongly held attitudes of perfectionism which the patient may be unaware and which may be dysfunctional. Impairments in self-acceptance (with the resulting belief of being rejectable and unlovable, or others being inferior and unlovable) may also undermine positive relations with others. There is a large body of literature (Uchino, Cacioppo, & Kiecolt-Glaser, 1996) on the buffering effects of social integration, social network properties, and perceived support. On the other hand, little research has been done on the possible negative consequences of an exaggerated social functioning. Characteristics such as empathy, altruism and generosity are usually considered universally positive. However, in clinical practice, patients often report sense of guilt for not being able to help someone, or to forgive an offence. An individual with a strong prosocial attitude can sacrifice his/her needs and well-being for those of others, and this in the long time becomes detrimental and sometimes disappointing. This individual can also become over-concerned and overwhelmed by others' problems and distress and be at risk for burn-out syndrome. Finally, a generalized tendency to forgive others and be grateful toward benefactors could mask low self-esteem and low sense of personal worth.

Validation Studies

Well-being therapy has been employed in several clinical studies. Other studies are currently in progress.

Residual Phase of Affective Disorders

The effectiveness of well-being therapy in the residual phase of affective disorders was first tested in a small controlled investigation (Fava, Rafanelli, Cazzaro, Conti, & Grandi, 1998a). Twenty patients with affective disorders who had been successfully treated by behavioral (anxiety disorders) or pharmacological (mood disorders) methods, were randomly assigned to either a well-being therapy or cognitive-behavioral treatment (CBT) of residual symptoms. Both well-being and cognitive-behavioral therapies were associated with a significant reduction of residual symptoms, as measured by the Clinical Interview for Depression (CID) (Guidi, Fava, Bech, & Paykel, 2011; Paykel, 1985), and in PWB well-being. However, when the residual symptoms of the two groups were compared after treatment, a significant advantage of well-being therapy over cognitive-behavioral strategies was observed with the CID. Well-being therapy was associated also with a significant increase in PWB well-being, particularly in the Personal Growth scale.

The improvement in residual symptoms was explained on the basis of the balance between positive and negative affect (Fava et al., 1998a). If treatment of psychiatric symptoms induces improvement of well-being, and indeed subscales describing well-being are more sensitive to drug effects than subscales describing symptoms (Kellner, 1987; Rafanelli & Ruini, 2012), it is conceivable that changes in well-being may affect the balance of positive and negative affect. In this sense, the higher degree of symptomatic improvement that was observed with well-being therapy in this study is not surprising: in the acute phase of affective illness, removal of symptoms may yield the most substantial changes, but the reverse may be true in its residual phase.

Prevention of Recurrent Depression

Well-being therapy was a specific and innovative part of a cognitive-behavioral package that was applied to recurrent depression (Fava, Rafanelli, Grandi, Conti, & Belluardo, 1998b). This package included also CBT of residual symptoms and lifestyle modification. Forty patients with recurrent major depression, who had been successfully treated with antidepressant drugs, were randomly assigned to either this cognitive-behavioral package including well-being therapy or clinical management. In both groups, antidepressant drugs were tapered and discontinued. The group that received CBT-WBT had a significantly lower level of residual symptoms after drug discontinuation in comparison with the clinical management group. CBT-WBT also resulted in a significantly lower relapse rate (25%) at a two-year follow-up than did clinical management (80%). At a six-year follow-up (Fava, Ruini, Rafanelli, Finos, Conti, & Grandi, 2004) the relapse rate was 40% in the former group and 90% in the latter.

The findings were replicated by three independent studies. In a multi-center trial performed in Germany, 180 patients with three or more episodes of major depression were randomized to a combination of CBT, well-being therapy, and mindfulness-based cognitive therapy or to manualized psychoeducation (Stangier et al., 2013). Even though the follow-up was limited to one year (in our study the most substantial differences emerged later) and medication was continued, there was a significant effect of the experimental condition on relapse rate of the patients with high risk of recurrence. In the United States, Kennard and colleagues (2014) applied the sequential treatment we had introduced in adults (Fava & Tomba, 2009) to 144 children and adolescents with major depression. They were treated with fluoxetine for six weeks and those who displayed an adequate response were randomized to receive continued medication management or CBT to address residual symptoms and WBT in addition to fluoxetine. The CBT-WBT combination was effective in reducing the risk of relapse, a finding that it was quite exceptional in the literature concerned with children and adolescents with major depression. Unfortunately, unlike in our original study (Fava et al., 1998b), medication was continued also in the CBT-WBT group, despite the problems that are related to long-term treatment with antidepressant drugs in that patient population (Leckman, 2013; Offidani, Fava, Tomba, & Baldessarini, 2013). A third confirmation came from Iran by Moeenizadeh and Salagame (2010). Forty high school and university students suffering from depression were randomly assigned to WBT or CBT. The results unequivocally showed that WBT was more effective than CBT in improving symptoms of depression. The severity of the depressive disturbances was not specifically evaluated and the symptomatology was probably mild. Nonetheless, the results were quite impressive.

Loss of Clinical Effect During Drug Treatment

The return of depressive symptoms during maintenance antidepressant treatment is a common and vexing clinical phenomenon (Fava & Offidani, 2011; Carvalho, Berk, Hyphantis, & McIntyre, 2014). Ten patients with recurrent depression who relapsed while taking antidepressant drugs were randomly assigned to dose increase or to a sequential combination of cognitive-behavior and well-being therapy (Fava, Ruini, Rafanelli, & Grandi, 2002). Four out of five patients responded to a larger dose, but all relapsed again on that dose by one-year follow-up. Four out of the five patients responded to psychotherapy and only one relapsed. The data suggest that application of well-being therapy may counteract loss of clinical effect during long-term antidepressant treatment.

Treatment of Generalized Anxiety Disorder

Well-Being therapy has been applied for the treatment of generalized anxiety disorder (Fava et al., 2005). Twenty patients with DSM-IV GAD were randomly assigned to eight sessions of CBT or the sequential administration of four sessions of CBT followed by other four sessions of WBT. Both treatments were associated with a significant reduction of anxiety. However, significant advantages of the WBT-CBT sequential combination over CBT were observed, both in terms of symptom reduction and psychological well-being improvement. These preliminary results suggest the feasibility and clinical advantages of adding WBT to the treatment of GAD. A possible explanation to these findings is that self-monitoring of episodes of well-being may lead to a more comprehensive identification of automatic thoughts than that entailed by the customary monitoring of episodes of distress in cognitive therapy.

Post-Traumatic Stress Disorder

The use of WBT for the treatment of traumatized patients has not yet been tested in controlled investigations. However, two cases were reported (Belaise, Fava, & Marks, 2005) in which patients improved with WBT, even though their central trauma was discussed only in the initial history-taking session. The findings from these two cases should, of course, be interpreted with caution (the patients may have remitted spontaneously), but are of interest because they indicate an alternative route to overcoming trauma and developing resilience and warrant further investigation (Fava & Tomba, 2009).

Cyclothymic Disorder

Well-being therapy was recently applied (Fava, Rafanelli, Tomba, Guidi, & Grandi, 2011) in sequential combination with CBT for the treatment of cyclothymic disorder, that involves mild or moderate fluctuations of mood, thought, and behavior without meeting formal diagnostic criteria for either major depressive disorder or mania (Tomba et al., 2012). Sixty-two patients with DSM-IV cyclothymic disorder were randomly assigned to CBT-WBT ($N = 31$) or clinical management (CM) ($N = 31$). An independent blind evaluator assessed the patients before treatment, after therapy, and at one- and two-year follow-ups. At post treatment, significant differences were found in all outcome measures, with greater improvements after treatment in the CBT-WBT group compared with the CM group. Therapeutic gains were maintained at one- and two-year follow-ups. The results of this investigation suggest that a sequential combination of CBT and WBT, which addresses both polarities of mood swings and comorbid anxiety, was found to yield significant and persistent benefits in cyclothymic disorder.

School Interventions

Nowadays schools are conceived not only as the ideal setting for developing learning and educational processes, but also for promoting mechanisms of resilience and psychological well-being. School interventions based on WBT in class sessions lasting a couple of hours were performed in three randomized controlled studies of middle and high school students populations. WBT-based interventions produced significantly higher benefits compared with clinical management (Ruini et al., 2009) or improvement in symptoms and psychological well-being comparable with CBT (Ruini, Belaise, Brombin, Caffo, & Fava, 2006; Tomba et al., 2010). These investigations suggested that well-being enhancing strategies could play an important role in the prevention of psychological distress and promoting optimal human functioning among children.

Are Psychotherapy-Induced Modifications in Well-being Enduring?

Well-being therapy effectiveness may be based on two distinct yet ostensibly related clinical phenomena. The first has to do with the fact that an increase in psychological well-being may have protective effect in terms of vulnerability to chronic and acute life stresses. The second has to do with the complex balance of positive and negative affects. There is extensive research – reviewed in detail elsewhere (Rafanelli, Park, Ruini, Ottolini, Cazzaro, & Fava, 2000) – which indicates a certain degree of inverse correlation between positive and negative affects. As a result, changes in well-being may induce a decrease in distress, and vice versa. In the acute phase of illness, removal of symptoms may yield the most substantial changes, but the reverse may be true in its residual phase. An increase in psychological well-being may decrease residual symptoms which direct strategies (whether cognitive-behavioral or pharmacological) would be unlikely to affect.

Cloninger (2006) attributes the clinical changes related to well-being therapy to three character traits defined as self-directness (i.e., responsible, purposeful, resourceful), cooperativeness (i.e., tolerant, helpful, compassionate), and self-trascendence (i.e. intuitive, judicious, spiritual). High scores in all these character traits have frequent positive emotions (i.e. happy, joyful, satisfied, optimistic) and infrequent negative emotions (i.e. anxious, sad, angry, pessimistic). The lack of development in any one of the three factors leaves a person vulnerable to the emergence of conflicts that can lead to anxiety and depression (Cloninger, 2006). These character traits can be exercised and developed by interventions that encourage a sense of hope and mastery for self-directedness.

Further, it has been suggested that cognitive-behavioral psychotherapy may work at the molecular level to alter stress-related gene expression and protein synthesis or influence mechanisms implicated in learning and memory acquisition in neuronal structures (Charney, 2004). Research on the neurobiological correlates of resilience has disclosed how different neural circuits (reward, fear conditioning and extinction, social behavior) may involve the same brain structures, and particularly the amygdala, the nucleus accumbens, and the medial prefrontal cortex (Charney, 2004). Singer, Friedman, Seeman, Fava and Ryff (2005), on the basis of preclinical evidence, suggested that WBT may stimulate dendrite networks in the hippocampus and induce spine retraction in the basolateral amygdala (a site of storage for memories of fearful or stressful experiences), leading to a weakening of distress and traumatic memories. The pathophysiological substrates of well-being therapy may thus be different compared with symptom-oriented cognitive-behavioral strategies, to the same extent that well-being and distress are not merely opposites (Rafanelli et al., 2000).

Conclusions

The controlled trials of well-being therapy that we have discussed indicate that psychological well-being may be increased by specific psychotherapeutic methods and that these changes are closely related to decrease in distress and improvement in contentment, friendliness, relaxation and physical well-being. Unlike non-specific interventions aimed at increasing control or social activity which yield short-lived improvement in subjective well-being (Okun, Olding, & Cohn, 1990), changes induced by WBT tend to persist at follow-up (Fava et al., 2002; Fava et al., 2004; Fava et al., 2005; Fava et al., 2011), underlie increased resilience and entail less relapse in the face of current events. In all randomized controlled trials that have been performed in adult populations, WBT was found to entail incremental compared with standard psychotherapeutic and/or pharmacological approaches or clinical management.

WBT was originally developed as a strategy for promoting psychological well-being which was still impaired after standard pharmacological or psychotherapeutic treatments in clinical populations. It was based on the assumption that these impairments may vary from one illness to another, from patient to patient and even from one episode to another of the same illness in the same patient. These impairments represent a vulnerability factor for adversities and relapses (Fava & Tomba, 2009). WBT, thus, can be considered a therapeutic positive intervention developed in clinical psychology, which takes into consideration both well-being and distress in predicting patients' clinical outcomes (Rafanelli & Ruini, 2012). Further, we suggest that the pathway to optimal, balanced well-being can be obtained with highly individualized strategies. In some cases some psychological dimensions need reinforcement and growth. In other cases an excessive or distorted level of certain dimensions needs to be adjusted because they may become dysfunctional and impede flourishing. Individuals may be helped to move up from impaired low levels to optimal, but also to move down from inappropriately high- to optimal-balanced levels. This could be achieved using specific behavioral homework, assignment of pleasurable activities, but also cognitive restructuring aimed at reaching a more balanced positive functioning in these dimensions. Unlike standard cognitive therapy which is based on rigid specific assumptions (e.g., the cognitive triad in depression), WBT is characterized by flexibility (Kashdan & Rottenberg, 2010) and by an individualized approach for addressing psychological issues that other therapies have left unexplored. This diverse feasibility and flexibility of WBT is in line with the positive clinical psychology approach, which calls for a number of different interventions to be selected based on individual specific needs (Wood & Tarrier, 2010).

References

Beck, A. T., Rush, A. J., Shaw, B. F., & Emery, G. (1979). *Cognitive therapy of depression.* New York: Guilford Press. doi.10.1002/9780470479216.corpsy0198.

Belaise, C., Fava, G. A., & Marks, I. M. (2005). Alternatives to debriefing and modifications to cognitive behavior therapy for posttraumatic stress disorder. *Psychotherapy and Psychosomatics*, 74(4), 212–217. doi.10.1159/000085144.

Bohart, A. C. (2002). Focusing on the positive, focusing on the negative: Implications for psychotherapy. *Journal of Clinical Psychology*, 58(9), 1037–1043. doi.10.1002/jclp.10097.

Carvalho, A. F., Berk, M., Hyphantis, T. N., & McIntyre, R. S. (2014). The integrative management of treatment resistant depression. *Psychotherapy and Psychosomatics*, 83(2), 70–88. doi,10.1159/000357500.

Charney, D. S. (2004). Psychobiological mechanisms of resilience and vulnerability: Implications for successful adaptation to extreme stress. *American Journal of Psychiatry*, 161(2), 195–216. doi.10.1176/appi.ajp.161.2.195.

Chida, Y. & Steptoe, A. (2008). Positive psychological well-being and mortality: a quantitative review of prospective observational studies. *Psychosomatic Medicine*, 70(7), 741–756. doi.10.1097/PSY.0b013e31818105ba

Cloninger, C. R. (2006). The science of well-being: an integrated approach to mental health and its disorders. *World Psychiatry*, 5(2), 71–76.

Csikszentmihalyi, M. (1990). *Flow: The psychology of optimal experience.* New York: Harper & Row. doi.10.1007/978-94-017-9088-8.

Delle Fave, A. (2013). Past, present, and future of flow. In: S. A. David, I. Bomwell, & A. Conley Agers (Eds.), *The Oxford handbook of happiness* (pp. 60–72). Oxford: Oxford University Press. doi.10.1093/oxfordhb/9780199557257.001.0001.

Delle Fave, A. & Massimini F. (2003). Optimal experience in work and leisure among teachers and physicians. *Leisure Studies*, 22(4), 323–342. doi.10.1080/02614360310001594122.

Ellis, A. & Becker, I. (1982). *A guide to personal happiness.* Hollywood, CA: Melvin Powers Wilshire.

Emmelkamp, P. M. G. (1974). Self-observation versus flooding in the treatment of agoraphobia. *Behaviour Research and Therapy*, 12(3), 229–237. doi.10.1016/0005-7967(74)90119-3.

Fava, G. A. (1999). Well-being therapy: conceptual and technical issues. *Psychotherapy and Psychosomatics*, 68(4), 171–179. doi.10.1159/000012329.

Fava, G. A. (2013). Modern psychiatric treatment: A tribute to Thomas Detre, MD (1924–2011). *Psychotherapy and Psychosomatics*, 82(1), 1–7. doi.0.1159/000343002.

Fava, G. A. & Offidani, E. (2011). The mechanisms of tolerance in antidepressant action. *Progress in Neuropsychopharmacology & Biological Psychiatry*, 35(7), 1593–1602. doi.10.1016/j.pnpbp.2010.07.026.

Fava, G. A. & Sonino, N. (2010). Psychosomatic medicine. *International Journal of Clinical Practice*, 64(8), 1155–1161. doi.10.1111/j.1742-1241.2009.02266.x.

Fava, G. A. & Tomba, E. (2009). Increasing psychological well-being and resilience by psychotherapeutic methods. *Journal of Personality*, 77(6), 1903–1934. doi.10.1111/j.1467-6494.2009.00604.x.

Fava, G. A. & Tomba, E. (2010). New modalities of assessment and treatment planning in depression. *CNS Drugs*, 24(6), 453–465. doi.10.2165/11531580-000000000-00000.

Fava, G. A., Guidi, J., Semprini, F., Tomba, E., & Sonino, N. (2010). Clinical assessment of allostatic load and clinimetric criteria. *Psychotherapy and Psychosomatics*, 79(5), 280–284. doi.10.1159/000318294.

Fava, G. A., Rafanelli, C., Cazzaro, M., Conti S., & Grandi, S. (1998a). Well-being therapy. A novel psychotherapeutic approach for residual symptoms of affective disorders. *Psychological Medicine*, 28(2), 475–480. doi.10.1017/S0033291797006363.

Fava, G. A., Rafanelli, C., Grandi, S., Conti, S., & Belluardo, P. (1998b). Prevention of recurrent depression with cognitive behavioral therapy: preliminary findings. *Archives of General Psychiatry*, 55(9), 816–820. doi.10.1001/archpsyc.55.9.816.

Fava, G. A., Rafanelli, C., Tomba, E., Guidi, J., & Grandi, S. (2011). The sequential combination of cognitive behavioral treatment and Well-being therapy in cyclothymic disorder. *Psychotherapy and Psychosomatics*, 80(3), 136–143. doi.10.1159/000321575.

Fava, G. A., Ruini, C., & Belaise, C. (2007). The concept of recovery in major depression. *Psychological Medicine*, 37(3), 307–317. doi.10.1017/S0033291706008981.

Fava, G. A., Ruini, C., Rafanelli, C., & Grandi, S. (2002). Cognitive behavior approach to loss of clinical effect during long-term antidepressant treatment. *American Journal of Psychiatry, 159*(12), 2094–2095. doi.10.1176/appi.ajp.159.12.2094.

Fava, G. A, Ruini, C., Rafanelli, C., Finos, L., Conti, S., & Grandi, S. (2004). Six-year outcome of cognitive behavior therapy for prevention of recurrent depression. *American Journal of Psychiatry, 161*(10), 1872–1876. doi.10.1176/appi.ajp.161.10.1872.

Fava, G. A., Ruini, C., Rafanelli, C., Finos, L., Salmaso, L., Mangelli, L., & Sirigatti, S. (2005). Well-being therapy of generalized anxiety disorder. *Psychotherapy and Psychosomatics, 74*(1), 26–30. doi.10.1159/000082023.

Garamoni, G. L., Reynolds, C. F., Thase, M. E., Frank, E., Berman, S-R., & Fasiczska A. L. (1991). The balance of positive and negative affects in major depression. *Psychiatry Research, 39*(2), 99–108. doi. 10.1016/0165-1781(91)90079-5.

Garland, E. L., Fredrickson, B., Kring, A. M., Johnson, D., Meyer, P. S., & Penn, D. L (2010). Upward spirals of positive emotions counter downward spirals of negativity. Insights from the broaden-and-build theory and affective neuroscience on the treatment of emotion dysfunction and deficits in psychopathology. *Clinical Psychology Review, 30*(7), 849–864. doi.10.1016/j.cpr.2010.03.002.

Geraghty, A. W. A., Wood, A. M., & Hyland, M. E. (2010). Dissociating the facets of hope: Agency and pathways predict dropout from unguided self-help therapy in opposite directions. *Journal of Research in Personality, 44*(1), 155–158. doi.10.1016/j.jrp.2009.12.003.

Guidi, J., Fava, G. A., Bech, P., & Paykel, E. S. (2011). The Clinical Interview for Depression: A comprehensive review of studies and clinimetric properties. *Psychotherapy and Psychosomatics, 80*(1), 10–27. doi.10.1159/000317532.

Hadley, S. & Macleod, A.K. (2010). Conditional goal-setting, personal goals and hopelessness about the future. *Cognition and Emotion, 24*(7), 1191–1198. doi.10.1016/j.brat.2010.05.022.

Held, B. S. (2002). The tyranny of positive attitude in America: Observation and speculation. *Journal of Clinical Psychology, 58*(9), 965–992. doi.10.1002/jclp.10093.

Hodgins, H. S. & Knee, R. (2002). The integrating self and conscious experience. In: E. L. Deci & R. M. Ryan (Eds.), *Handbook on self-determination research* (pp. 87–100). Rochester, NY: University of Rochester Press.

Jahoda, M. (1958). *Current concepts of positive mental health.* New York: Basic Books. doi.10.1037/11258-000.

Kashdan, T. B. & Rottenberg, J. (2010). Psychological flexibility as a fundamental aspect of health. *Clinical Psychology Review, 30*(7), 865–878. doi.10.1016/j.cpr.2010.03.001.

Kellner, R. (1987). A symptom questionnaire. *Journal of Clinical Psychiatry, 48*(7), 269–274. Available at: http://www.psychiatrist.com/jcp/Pages/home.aspx.

Kennard, B. D., Emslie, G. J., Mayes, T. L., Nakonezny, P. A., Jones, J. M., Foxwell, A. A., & King, J. (2014). Sequential treatment with fluoxetine and relapse-prevention CBT to improve outcomes in pediatric depression. *American Journal of Psychiatry, 171*(10), 1083–1090. doi.10.1176/appi.ajp.2014.13111460.

Keyes, C. L. (2002). The mental health continuum: from languishing to flourishing in life. *Journal of Health and Social Behavior, 43*(2), 207–222. Available at: http://www.jstor.org/stable/3090197.

Leckman, J. F. (2013). The risks and benefits of antidepressants to treat pediatric-onset depression and anxiety disorders. *Psychotherapy and Psychosomatics, 82*(3), 129–131. doi.10.1159/000345543.

MacLeod, A. K. & Conway, C. (2005). Well-being and the anticipation of future positive experiences: The role of income, social networks and planning ability. *Cognition and Emotion, 19*(3), 357–374. doi.10.1080/02699930441000247.

MacLeod, A. K. & Moore, R. (2000). Positive thinking revisited: positive cognitions, well-being and mental health. *Clinical Psychology and Psychotherapy, 7*(1), 1–10. doi.10.1002/(SICI)1099-0879(200002)7:1<1::AID-CPP228>3.0.CO;2-S.

Moeenizadeh, M. & Salagame, K. K. K. (2010). The impact of well-being therapy on symptoms of depression. *International Journal of Psychological Studies, 2*(2), 223–230. doi.10.5539/ijps.v2n2p223.

Norem, J. K. & Chang, E. C. (2002). The positive psychology of negative thinking. *Journal of Clinical Psychology, 58*(9), 993–1001. doi.10.1002/jclp.10094.

Offidani, E., Fava, G. A., Tomba, E., & Baldessarini, R. J. (2013). Excessive mood elevation and behavioral activation with antidepressant treatment of juvenile depressive and anxiety disorders. *Psychotherapy and Psychosomatics, 82*(3), 132–141. doi.10.1159/000345316.

Okun, M. A., Olding, R. W., & Cohn, C. M. G. (1990). A meta-analysis of subjective well-being interventions among elders. *Psychological Bulletin, 108*(2), 257–266. doi.10.1037//0033-2909.108.2.257.

Parloff, M. B., Kelman, H. C., & Frank, J. D. (1954). Comfort, effectiveness, and self-awareness as criteria of improvement in psychotherapy. *American Journal of Psychiatry, 111*(5), 343–352. doi.10.1176/ajp.111.5.343.

Paykel, E. S. (1985). The clinical Interview for Depression: Development, reliability and validity. *Journal of Affective Disorders, 9*(1), 85–96. doi.10.1016/0165-0327(85)90014-X.

Rafanelli, C., Park, S. K., Ruini, C., Ottolini, F., Cazzaro, M., & Fava, G. A. (2000). Rating well-being and distress. *Stress Medicine, 16*(1), 55–61. doi.10.1002/(SICI)1099-1700(200001)16:1<55::AID-SMI832> 3.0.CO;2-M.

Rafanelli, C. & Ruini, C. (2012). Assessment of psychological well-being in psychosomatic medicine. *Advances in Psychosomatic Medicine, 32*, 182–202. doi.10.1159/000330021.

Ruini, C., Belaise, C., Brombin, C., Caffo, E., & Fava, G. A. (2006). Well-being therapy in school settings. *Psychotherapy and Psychosomatics, 75*(6), 331–336. doi.10.1159/000095438.

Ruini, C., Ottolini, F., Tomba, E., Belaise, C., Albieri, E, Visani, D, Offidani, E., Caffo, E., & Fava, G. A. (2009). School intervention for promoting psychological well-being in adolescence. *Journal of Behavior Therapy and Experimental Psychiatry, 40*(4), 522–532. doi.10.1016/j.jbtep.2009.07.002.

Ryff, C. D. (1989). Happiness is everything, or is it? Explorations on the meaning of psychological well-being. *Journal of Personality and Social Psychology, 57*(6), 1069–1081. doi.10.1037/0022-3 514.57.6.1069.

Ryff, C. D. (2014). Psychological well-being revisited: advances in the science and practice of eudaimonia. *Psychotherapy and Psychosomatics, 83*(1), 10–28. doi.10.1159/000353263.

Ryff, C. D. & Singer, B. H. (1996). Psychological well-being: meaning, measurement, and implications for psychotherapy research. *Psychotherapy and Psychosomatics, 65*(1), 14–23. doi.10.1159/000289026.

Seeman, T. E., Singer, B. H., Ryff, C. D., Dienberg Love, G. & Levy-Storms, L. (2002). Social relationships, gender, and allostatic load across two age cohorts. *Psychosomatic Medicine, 64*(3), 395–406. doi.10.1097/00006842-200205000-00004.

Singer, B., Friedman, E., Seeman, T., Fava, G. A., & Ryff, C. D. (2005). Protective environments and health status: Cross-talk between human and animal studies. *Neurobiology of Aging, 26*(1)S, S113–S118. doi.10.1016/j.neurobiolaging.2005.08.020.

Stangier, U., Hilling, C., Heidenreich, T., Risch, A. K., Barocka, A., Schlosser, R., Kronfeld, K., Ruckes, C., Berger, H., Roschke, J., Weck, F., Volk, S., Hambrecht, M., Sertling, R., Erkwoh, R., Stirn, A., Sobanski, T., & Hautzinger, M. (2013). Maintenance cognitive-behavioral therapy and manualized psychoeducation in the treatment of recurrent depression. *American Journal of Psychiatry, 170*(6), 624–632. doi.10.1176/appi.ajp.2013.12060734.

Thunedborg, K., Black, C. H., & Bech, P. (1995). Beyond the Hamilton depression scores in long-term treatment of manic-melancholic patients: prediction of recurrence of depression by quality of life measurements. *Psychotherapy and Psychosomatics, 64*(3/4), 131–140. doi.10.1159/000289002.

Tomba, E., Belaise, C., Ottolini, F., Ruini, C., Bravi, A., Albieri, E., Rafanelli, C., Caffo, E., & Fava, G. A. (2010). Differential effects of well-being promoting and anxiety-management strategies in a non-clinical school setting. *Journal of Anxiety Disorders, 24*(3), 326–333. doi.10.1016/j.janxdis.2010.01.005.

Tomba, E., Rafanelli, C., Grandi. S., Guidi, J., & Fava, G. A. (2012). Clinical configuration of cyclothymic disturbances. *Journal of Affective Disorders, 139*(3), 244–249. doi.10.1016/j.jad.2012.01.014.

Uchino, B. N., Cacioppo, J. T., & Kiecolt-Glaser, J. K. (1996). The relationship between social support and physiological processes. *Psychological Bulletin, 119*(3), 488–531. doi.10.1037/0033-2909.119.3.488.

Vallerand, R. J., Blanchard, C. M., Mageau, G. A., Koestner, R., Ratelle, C., Leonard, M., Gagne, M., & Marsolais, J. (2003). Les passions de l'ame: On obsessive and harmonious passion. *Journal of Personality and Social Psychology, 85*(4), 756–767. doi.10.1037/0022-3514.85.4.756.

Vallerand, R. J., Salvy, S. J., Mageau, G. A., Elliot, A. J., Denis, P. L., Grouzet, F. M. E., & Blanchard, C. (2007). On the role of passion in performance. *Journal of Personality, 75*(3), 505–533. doi.10.1111/j.1467-6494.2007.00447.x.

Vincent, P. J., Boddana, P., & MacLeod, A.K. (2004). Positive life goals and plans in parasuicide. *Clinical Psychology and Psychotherapy, 11*(2), 90–99. doi.10.1002/cpp.394.

Wood, A. M. & Joseph, S. (2010). The absence of positive psychological (eudemonic) well-being as a risk factor for depression: A ten-year cohort study. *Journal of Affective Disorders, 122*(3), 213–217. doi.10.1016/j.jad.2009.06.032.

Wood, A. M. & Tarrier, N. (2010). Positive clinical psychology: A new vision and strategy for integrated research and practice. *Clinical Psychology Review, 30*(7), 819–829. doi.10.1016/j.cpr.2010.06.003.

27

Quality of Life Therapy
Michael B. Frisch

Introduction

Quality of Life Therapy (QOLT) (also known as Quality of Life Therapy and Coaching) aims to be a comprehensive, manualized (Frisch 2006), and individually-tailored package of positive psychology interventions suitable for both coaching and clinical applications (coaching clients are those devoid of DSM disorders who nevertheless wish to feel and function better in their daily lives). With respect to clients suffering from DSM-5 disorders, QOLT is meant to augment rather than to supplant evidence-based psychotherapies and pharmacotherapies (Land, 2006; Furey, 2007). Adding positive psychology to the treatment plan and thereby activating what Beck and his colleagues call the "constructive," well-being, or happiness mode of emotion is essential to lasting psychotherapeutic change, according to Clark and Beck (1999). QOLT further integrates positive and clinical psychology by including techniques for the control of *negative* affect and feelings in addition to techniques aimed at boosting positive affective experience.

QOLT clients are taught strategies and skills aimed at helping them to identify, pursue, and fulfill their most cherished needs, goals, and wishes in sixteen valued areas of life said to comprise human well-being or happiness; these areas are defined in detail in Table 27.1 and also depicted in Figure 27.1 as part of a well-being assessment.

This theory-based approach offers an individually tailored *package* of well-being interventions to clients instead of single, brief interventions or a standard package of interventions offered to all clients (All of the client "toolbox" exercises in QOLT and mentioned in this chapter are available for download at: http://www.wiley.com/go/frisch.

QOLT uses an individualized assessment, the Quality of Life Inventory (QOLI) (Frisch, Clark, Rouse, Rudd, Paweleck, & Greenstone, 2005; Frisch 2009), to individually tailor interventions to the particular needs of clients, to assess progress and outcome, to fine-tune treatment, and to assess the risk of a well-being or unhappiness "relapse" (Frisch 2006). The QOLT theory that undergirds the approach attempts to integrate the findings from the fields of positive psychology, well-being, happiness, quality of life and social indicators research, coaching, psychotherapy, in general, and Beck's cognitive therapy, in particular (Clark 2006; Diener, 2006).

The present chapter reviews randomized controlled trials of QOLT and proposes the adoption of standards from clinical psychology for "evidence-based" *treatments* and (in the case of coaching clients) *interventions* in positive psychology. The basic theory and steps of QOLT are delineated and illustrated with a case study. Research and service delivery system action steps are also proposed.

The Wiley Handbook of Positive Clinical Psychology, First Edition. Edited by Alex M. Wood and Judith Johnson.
© 2016 John Wiley & Sons, Ltd. Published 2016 by John Wiley & Sons, Ltd.

Table 27.1   The "sweet 16" areas in Quality of Life Therapy and Coaching and the Quality of Life Inventory or QOLI®: Sixteen Areas of Life Which May Constitute a Person's Overall Quality of Life.*

 1   *Health* is being physically fit, not sick, and without pain or disability.
 2   *Self-Esteem* means liking and respecting yourself in light of your strengths and weaknesses, successes and failures, and ability to handle problems.
 3   *Goals-and-Values* (or philosophy of life) are your beliefs about what matters most in life and how you should live, both now and in the future. This includes your goals in life, what you think is right or wrong, and the purpose or meaning of life as you see it. It may or may not include spiritual beliefs.
 4   *Money* (or standard of living) is made of three things. It is the money you earn, the things you own (like a car or furniture), and believing that you will have the money and things that you need in the future.
 5   *Work* means your career or how you spend most of your time. You may work at a job, at home taking care of your family, or at school as a student. *Work* includes your duties on the job, the money you earn (if any), and the people you work with.
 6   *Play* (or recreation) means what you do in your free time to relax, have fun, or improve yourself. This could include watching movies, visiting friends, or pursuing a hobby like sports or gardening.
 7   *Learning* means gaining new skills or information about things that interest you. *Learning* can come from reading books or taking classes on subjects like history, care repair, or using a computer.
 8   *Creativity* is using your imagination to come up with new and clever ways to solve everyday problems or to pursue a hobby such as painting, photography, or needlework. This can include decorating your home, playing the guitar, or finding a new way to solve a problem at work.
 9   *Helping* (social service and civic action) means helping others in need or helping to make your community a better place to live. *Helping* can be done on your own or in a group such as a church, a neighborhood association, or a political party. *Helping* can include doing volunteer work at a school or giving money to a good cause. *Helping* means helping people who are not your friends or relatives.
10   *Love* (or love relationship) is a very close romantic relationship with another person. *Love* usually includes sexual feelings and feeling loved, cared for, and understood.
11   *Friends* (or friendships) are people (not relatives) you know well and care about who have interests and opinions like yours. *Friends* have fun together, talk about personal problems, and help each other out.
12   *Children* means how you get along with your child (or children). Think of how you get along as you care for, visit, or play with your child.
13   *Relatives* means how you get along with your parents, grandparents, brothers, sisters, aunts, uncles, and in-laws. Think about how you get along when you are doing things together, such as visiting, talking on the telephone, or helping each other out.
14   *Home* is where you live. It is your house or apartment and the yard around it. Think about how nice it looks, how big it is, and your rent or house payment.
15   *Neighborhood* is the area around your home. Think about how nice it looks, the amount of crime in the area, and how well you like the people.
16   *Community* is the whole city, town, or rural area where you live (it is not just your neighborhood). *Community* includes how nice the area looks, the amount of crime, and how well you like the people. It also includes places to go for fun like parks, concerts, sporting events, and restaurants. You may also consider the cost of things you need to buy, the availability of jobs, the government, schools, taxes, and pollution.

* © 2006, Michael B. Frisch, all rights reserved.

Randomized Trials of Quality of Life Therapy

James R. Rodrigue of Beth Israel and Harvard Medical centers and his colleagues have conducted two US NIH-grant funded studies of QOLT, with a third NIH-funded trial currently underway. These trials include severely ill patients waiting for lung transplants, waiting for kidney transplants, and using implantable cardioverter defibrillators (ICDs), respectively.

The years it usually takes to obtain a lung transplant are stressful for lung patients and their caregiving spouses. Both the wait of one to three years and the demands of managing this serious and chronic disease contribute to lowered well-being and quality of life, heightened stress, and strained relationships with caregiving spouses, making these patients and their loved ones prime candidates for well-being/positive psychology interventions. In the first trial, patients with severe lung disease awaiting lung transplants were randomly assigned to either QOLT ($N = 17$) or a treatment-as-usual (TAU) ($N = 18$) condition (Rodrigue, Baz, Widows, & Ehlers, 2005).

QOLI® Profile Report   **ID: 1**
01/03/2008, Page 3   **Blacksheep-PreTx**

OVERALL QUALITY OF LIFE CLASSIFICATION

The client's satisfaction with life is Low. This person is generally unhappy and unfulfilled in life. People scoring in this range cannot get their basic needs met and cannot achieve their goals in several important areas of life. However, this person is able to achieve satisfaction in some areas of life, a fact that can be used in treatment to encourage his efforts to change. Although this person may not show obvious signs of distress or psychological disturbance, he may nevertheless be disturbed. Even if this person is not currently impaired, he is at risk for developing physical and mental health disorders, especially clinical depression. This risk remains until the client's score reaches or exceeds the Average range. You may wish to investigate this individual's status with further psychological assessment.

WEIGHTED SATISFACTION PROFILE

The Weighted Satisfaction Profile helps to explain a person's Overall Quality of Life by identifying the specific areas of satisfaction and dissatisfaction that contribute to the QOLI raw score. Clinical experience suggests that any negative weighted satisfaction rating denotes an area of life in which the individual may benefit from treatment; ratings of -6 and -4 are of greatest concern and urgency. Specific reasons for dissatisfaction should be investigated more fully with the client in a clinical interview. The *Manual and Treatment Guide for the Quality of Life Inventory* suggests treatment techniques for improving patient satisfaction in each area of life assessed by the QOLI.

The following weighted satisfaction ratings indicate areas of dissatisfaction for the client:

| | Weighted |
Area	Satisfaction Rating
Health	-6
Love	-4
Self-Esteem	-2
Community	-2
Learning	-1
Helping	-1
Relatives	-1

OMITTED ITEMS

None omitted.

End of Report

Figure 27.1 Quality of Life Inventory Profile. Case of B: Excerpt from client online profile report. Copyright © 1998, 1994, Michael B. Frisch, Ph.D. Reproduced with permission of NCS Pearson, Inc. All rights reserved. "QOLI" is a trademark of Michael B. Frisch, Ph.D.

INTRODUCTION

The Quality of Life Inventory (QOLI) provides a score that indicates a person's overall satisfaction with life. People's life satisfaction is based on how well their needs, goals, and wishes are being met in important areas of life. The information in this report should be used in conjunction with professional judgment, taking into account any other pertinent information concerning the individual.

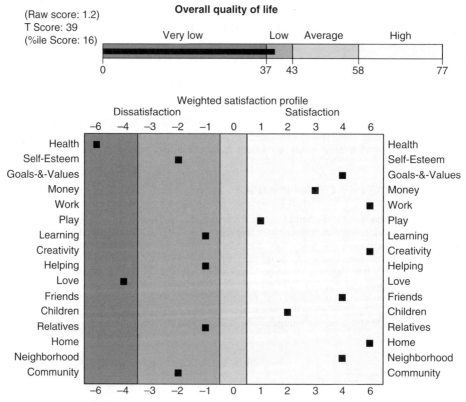

Figure 27.1   (Continued)

The TAU group was designed to mimic the usual treatment for lung patients awaiting transplants, including emotional and educational support, empathic listening to concerns, discussing activities, and encouraging contact with friends, relatives, and other support systems. The mean age of patients was 48.7 years and each received between eight to twelve sessions of treatment. Those collecting data were unaware of patients' treatment condition. QOLT here involved identifying two to five areas of life on the QOLI deemed very important, but also unfulfilling or dis-satisfying that a patient wished to work on. Next, interventions were administered in order to boost client's level of satisfaction with each of these areas of life. For example, relationship skills such as the "Take a Letter Technique" were applied to estranged relationships in order to reestablish contact and closeness. The Five Paths to Happiness exercise was also employed for each area of life, along with emotional control techniques aimed at minimizing negative affect.

While the two groups did not differ significantly at pre-intervention, QOLT patients were significantly more satisfied with their lives than TAU patients at the two follow-up periods of one and three months (post-tests were not conducted). In a measure of clinical or practical significance (Kazdin, 2003) that was also found to be statistically significant, 13 of 17 or 76.47% of the QOLT patients moved to within the normal range on the QOLI for a nonclinical, functional, nationwide standardization sample at the three-month follow-up, compared with only 5 of 18 or 27% of TAU patients. QOLT patients reported significantly greater social intimacy and closeness with their caregiving spouses/partners at the one-month follow-up and significantly less negative affect at the three-month follow up assessment than TAU patients. Changes in health status and therapy-therapist process ratings were comparable for each intervention group at the study's conclusion, making it less likely that these factors affected outcomes.

The caregiving spouses or partners of patients assigned to the two groups took the same assessments at the same times as patients in an effort to see if positive treatment effects might be "contagious" or accrue to spouses or partners not in treatment themselves. These findings are reported in a separate article by Rodrigue, Widows, and Baz (2006). Relative to the caregivers of patients assigned to the TAU condition, caregivers of patients assigned to the QOLT condition reported significantly greater social intimacy at both the one- and three-month follow up assessments, along with greater life satisfaction/quality of life (QOLI) at the one-month follow up and significantly less negative affect at the three-month follow up. This pattern of results for spouse/partners on all three measures directly mirrors that of patients who received QOLT training as reported in Rodrigue et al. (2005). That is, both patients receiving QOLT and the spouse/partner/caregivers that they lived with while receiving QOLT, significantly improved in their quality of life, mood, and social intimacy (relative to those involved in the supportive treatment group) after the QOLT intervention was delivered:

> Caregivers whose patients received Quality of Life Therapy reported vicarious gains in quality of life, mood, and social intimacy, relative to those whose patients received … the usual or standard intervention. These findings suggest that Quality of Life Therapy has beneficial effects that extend beyond the patient to their caregivers … Findings from this study suggest that Quality of Life Therapy provides an opportunity to improve the lives both of patients awaiting a lung transplant and their primary caregivers. Mood disturbance and social intimacy benefits for caregivers may last as long as three months following the patient's completion of psychological treatment. (Rodrigue et al., 2006, p. 341)

The vicarious gains of spouse/partners of QOLT patients may be due to patients sharing and discussing QOLT treatment ideas and homework assignments with their spouse or partner over the course of QOLT. Finally, improvements in patients' quality of life and mood as a result of QOLT predicted higher functioning in their caregiving spouses or partners, thereby helping to maintain a crucial social support system.

The randomized controlled trial with lung patients was replicated in a second NIH grant-funded trial with adults with end-stage renal disease who were awaiting kidney transplantation (Rodrigue, Mandelbrot, & Pavlakis, 2011). Patients were randomly assigned to a no (psychological) treatment control (NTC) group ($N = 20$) or to eight weekly sessions of either QOLT ($N = 22$) or TAU ($N = 20$), which was an elaboration and expansion of the TAU condition present in the lung patient study.

Patients assigned to the QOLT group had significantly higher life satisfaction/quality of life scores than either TAU or NTC patients at both post-treatment and (three-month) follow-up assessments. The QOLT group mean moved from the low to the average range on the QOLI from pre-treatment to post-treatment and follow-up. This move denotes clinically significant change in so far as patients moved to within one standard deviation of the average range for a US nationwide standardization sample of functional, nonclinical adults (Kazdin, 2003). Group means for the other two groups remained in the low or very low range at all times of assessment, indicating an inability to reach the mean (or above) for the functional standardization sample.

Patients assigned to the QOLT group had significantly higher SF-36 Mental Functioning scores than either the TAU or NTC group at the three-month follow up assessment. At follow-up, patients assigned to the QOLT group had significantly higher social intimacy (with caregiver) scores than NTC patients, who failed to differ from TAU patients; the same pattern was found on a measure of negative affect. That is, QOLT patients had significantly lower levels of negative affect, as measured by the Profile of Mood States – Short Form, at follow up than NTC patients who failed to differ from TAU patients. Both QOLT and TAU patients had lower scores than NTC patients at follow up on two symptom measures: the Hopkins Symptom Checklist-25, and the Hopkins' Number of Unhealthy Mental Health Days in the past month.

The two NIH grant-supported studies of QOLT by Rodrigue and his colleagues were replicated in a randomized controlled trial conducted by a different laboratory in a different country, using a heretofore untested population. This third trial involved the often belea-guered parents of children with a challenging DSM psychiatric/mental disorder, that is, obses-sive-compulsive disorder (Abedi & Vostanis, 2010). Forty parents living in Iran were randomly assigned to QOLT ($N = 20$) or a wait list control group ($N = 20$). Training in QOLT was conducted in eight 90-minute group sessions, with ten participants each, over a four-week period. QOLT consisted of strategies for identifying life goals and for increasing happiness and satisfaction in the 16 areas of life said to comprise overall quality of life. As part of the Five Paths intervention, parents also learned to lower expectations, change life priorities, reduce perfectionism, and to adopt a more positive attitude toward their children's symptoms. Parents were also taught time management skills and the need for balance in their lives (Balanced Life Tenet), including time for themselves away from the family. Relative to controls, QOLT parents had higher quality of life or life satisfaction scores (QOLI) at post-test. Indeed, the mean QOLI scores of parents receiving QOLT moved from the very low range (first to tenth percentile scores) to well within the average range of the functional standardization sample, while the mean QOLI scores of parents in the control condition remained in the very low range throughout the study. In a replication of the Rodrigue et al. (2006) "social contagion effect," parents' gains in quality of life generalized to their children even though the children were not exposed to QOLT. Specifically, children of parents in QOLT reported higher overall quality of life and quality of life in three of five specific childhood domains on a measure designed for children. Additionally, children of parents in QOLT reported significant reductions (relative to children of control participants) in general anxiety and OCD symptoms. In contrast to the two Rodrigue studies, this study lacked an active and established treatment/intervention control group.

The Elephant in the Room or What Constitutes an Evidence-based Intervention?

The delineation of evidence-based treatments has become an international movement involving myriad fields and professions, including medicine, dentistry, nursing, clinical psychology, education, social services, and social work (Kazdin, 2006). While touting the pre-eminent importance of using only evidence-based interventions and assessments in their practice, positive psychologists have ignored the proverbial elephant in the room, that is, the lack of agreed-on criteria for reliably designating an intervention "evidence-based" to begin with. Without these criteria or guidelines, it becomes difficult, if not impossible, for practitioners to choose interventions with adequate research support. One solution to this conundrum is for positive psychologists to adopt the rigorous standards developed by clinical psychology (Wood & Tarrier, 2010); this solution is also consonant with QOLT's aim to integrate well-being with existing treatments for DSM disorders. In a review of clinical psychology criteria, Kazdin (2006) summarized the efforts to date, specifying that evidence-based treatments must be:

1 manualized such that the steps in treatment are specified in a written manual or book;
2 compared favorably (statistically significant) to either a no-treatment control group or another established intervention, such as "standard care" or treatment as usual in two or more randomized controlled clinical studies; and
3 found effective in at least one replication study beyond the original investigator or originator of treatment.

With only three randomized controlled trials to date, Quality of Life Therapy clearly needs more research to be an established positive psychology intervention package. Nevertheless (and based on the review of studies herein), Quality of Life Therapy meets the clinical psychology criteria summarized by Kazdin (2006) for an evidence-based intervention. Unfortunately, many positive psychology interventions lack even these three randomized controlled trials; rarer still are studies with active control groups that receive a currently used, standard, or established intervention (Wood & Tarrier, 2010). Established treatment control groups may be especially important when extravagant claims are made that well-being interventions, by themselves, can effectively treat clinical disorders like major depressive disorder or nicotine use disorder. Adopting the criteria used herein or other strict criteria will certainly move the field forward, especially a field that seeks scientific respectability and touts the "empirical validation" of its techniques.

Theory and Therapy

Rationale and Motivation for Intervention

Clients are taught to expect a "trinity" of happiness benefits if they are successful in QOLT: (1) better health and longevity; (2) more rewarding relationships with others; and (3) greater success in work. It is also said that "helping"/altruism/prosocial behavior is positively impacted by greater happiness (the detailed theory of QOLT and supportive references may be found in "the manual" for QOLT) (Frisch 2006; also see Frisch, 2013). This is the rationale for QOLT with nonclinical, *coaching* clients such as the professional groups of lawyers, teachers, businesspeople, physicians, clergy, and police personnel. Clients in treatment for DSM-5 disorders are also taught to expect an increased acute care response when well-being interventions are added to typical psychotherapy and pharmacological regimens; well-being interventions may also prevent clinical relapse (see Fava, Chapter 26, this volume; Kennard et al., 2014; and the Rodrigue studies of QOLT reviewed here).

Clients are next taught the theory of QOLT in summary form (see Frisch 2006, 2013, for detailed theory). After factoring out temperament and so-called "scars of abuse" which may permanently alter baseline mood, 50–80% (Diener and Biswas-Diener 2008) of human happiness and meaning come from efforts to fulfill our most cherished needs, goals, and wishes in the "sweet 16" areas of life found to be related to human happiness (which are defined in detail in the QOLI test booklet and in Table 27.1 here). Our satisfaction with each area of life in the "sweet 16" are, in turn, determined by the area's objective Circumstances, our Attitudes/interpretations about the area, our Standards of fulfillment for the area, and the Importance of and area or the extent to which we value, prize, or prioritize the area relative to others. These four components are combined with a fifth to make up the CASIO or Five Paths to Happiness problem-solving rubric in QOLT. The fifth path or "O" strategy refers to boosting satisfaction in Other areas of the "sweet sixteen" that are not a problem or focus of counseling with the understanding that any increase in satisfaction for a *specific* area will boost satisfaction or quality of life *overall*.

Five Paths is used in QOLT as a general approach to either problem solving or to boosting satisfaction/fulfillment in *any* area of life. A completed example of this exercise is depicted in Figure 27.2.

Besides the general Five Paths strategy, clients are taught to learn and apply area-specific interventions in QOLT. For example, interventions from the Work and Retirement chapter of the manual (Frisch 2006) have been successfully applied to clients' work goals and general work dissatisfaction. Similarly, interventions from the relationship chapter of the manual are designed to help in enhancing relationship satisfaction or in finding a new love relationship or friendship where none presently exists. In fact, QOLT can best be summarized in these terms; that is,

Brainstorm possible solutions under each CASIO strategy, or, in other words, by listing attitudes or actions for managing or solving the problem.				
C	**A**	**S**	**I**	**O**
Changing Circumstances	Changing Attitudes	Changing Goals and Standards	Changing Priorities or What's Important	Boost Satisfaction in Other Areas not Considered Before
Basic Strategy:	Basic Strategy:	Basic Strategy:	Basic Strategy:	Basic Strategy:
Problem solve to improve situation.	Find out what is really happening and what it means for you and your future.	Set realistic goals and experiment with raising and lowering standards. What new goals and standards can you come up with?	Re-evaluate priorities in life and emphasize what is most important and controllable.	Increase satisfaction in any areas you care about for an overall boost to happiness.
I need to decide whether to make peace with Ashley and accept her overtures or keep "blowing" her off.	My folks taught me garbage I don't have to listen to like I'm "no good." I think they were "no good" as parents. No kid is inherently bad!	Try for a B in my class for one week and see if "the sky falls."	Feed my soul with reading a novel, making friends, and going to Temple. Without some Inner Abundance, I'm no good to anybody.	Walking the mall brings me to people and is the best "antidepressant" I got!
	Just 'cause Stan (husband) wants to sit around and "watch" the grass grow, doesn't mean I can't travel to see the kids and grandkids.	Try to just be kind and connect with a "hello" to folks/potential friends as I make a String of Pearls or a "string" of positive connections each day with folks I see.	Quit beating my head against the wall. I can't change Stan (husband). Stop trying and "do your own thing" more.	

Figure 27.2 Five (CASIO) paths to happiness (or problem solving) exercise: excerpt with client examples.

QOLT aims at boosting clients' level of well-being, happiness, meaning in their lives, quality of life, and positive goal success by matching clients' goals with interventions in one of the "sweet 16" areas of life said to comprise human happiness and meaning. In addition, QOLT interventions can be applied to any and all "sweet 16" areas of life that are valued as important to clients, understanding that *overall* happiness and meaning will be increased to the extent that any or all *specific* areas of life are enhanced. QOLT is made more manageable for clients by focusing on only two to five areas of life at a time. Additional areas can be targets for intervention when very small, "doable" changes can boost satisfaction with an area as when a client begins to skype with a distant but dear friend once a month.

Making an Intervention Plan Based on a Well-being Assessment

Once clients are versed in the rationale for QOLT, a domain-based well-being assessment is administered. The QOLI is a measure of satisfaction with life specifically suited for use in QOLT (Frisch et al., 2005; Frisch 2009). The QOLI consists of 16 items selected to include domains of life that have been empirically associated with overall life satisfaction or happiness (see Table 27.1). Respondents rate how important each of the 16 domains is to their overall happiness and satisfaction (0 = not at all important, 1 = important, 2 = very important) followed by rating of how satisfied they are in the area (-3 = very dissatisfied to 3 = very satisfied). The importance and satisfaction ratings for each item are multiplied to form weighted satisfaction ratings ranging from -6 to 6. A "Weighted Satisfaction Profile" akin to an MMPI profile of well-being (versus ill-being) is generated which gives a comprehensive overview of clients satisfaction with life, see Figure 27.1). The overall life satisfaction is computed by averaging all weighted satisfaction ratings with nonzero importance ratings; the total score thus reflects one's satisfaction in only those areas of life one considers important. Respondents can also indicate what problems interfere with their satisfaction in each area on a narrative section of the QOLI test booklet.

The graphic portion of QOLI results for a client are displayed in Figure 27.1. Overall Quality Of Life or well-being is depicted at the top of the page in terms of a nationwide US standardization sample. Results for each of the "sweet 16" areas of life which make up the Overall Quality of Life are depicted in the Weighted Satisfaction Profile in the lower half of Figure 27.1, with areas on right-hand side of the graph denoting strength, fulfillment, and satisfaction and areas on the left-hand side denoting areas of dissatisfaction in which important needs, goals, and wishes are *not* being fulfilled.

Areas of dissatisfaction typically become targets for goal-setting and intervention in QOLT. This is the essence of a case conceptualization and intervention plan shared with clients along with their pre-intervention QOLI results (Frisch 2006). To wit, since their overall contentment is made up of the sum of satisfactions in valued areas of life, interventions will be "prescribed" for their areas of dissatisfaction. According to the theory, boosting satisfaction in specific areas of dissatisfaction will also increase their overall contentment and well-being. Once clients understand and accept this rationale, they collaborate with the therapist/coach in deciding when and how to address their areas of dissatisfaction.

Goal-setting, Self-care, and Making Time for Change Efforts

Next, clients set goals for areas of life they value and put in place some self-care ("Inner Abundance") practices to support their efforts to build a life of greater meaning and happiness. This includes some daily time set aside for relaxation and reflection on their QOLT efforts. Collectively, these steps are called the "Three Pillars" of QOLT.

Controlling Negative Affect and Time Management

QOLT teaches clients basic mood control and life management skills aimed at controlling negative affect and organizing their lives in the service of striving for personal goals in valued areas of life. Since Diener and others (see Diener, Suh, Lucas, & Smith, 1999) defined happiness as a preponderance of positive over negative affective experience, it stands to reason that both coaching and clinical clients must learn skills aimed at controlling negative emotions lest negative affect vitiates or cancels out increases in positive affective experience. Negative emotions are an inevitable part of human experience even for the so-called "chronically" (Lyubomirsky, Sheldon, & Schkade, 2005) or very happy (Diener & Seligman, 2002). For example, when goal pursuits are thwarted, clients may be expected to experience anxiety, depression, and/or anger. Feeling bad is good if it gives us a wake-up call to find a new or different path to getting our needs met, as when unhappy lovers realize their irreconcilable differences and find someone more suitable. Feeling bad often and for long periods of time is not good, however. For this reason, skills in mindfulness, postponement of worry and problem solving, and cognitive restructuring are offered as ways to help clients manage their negative affects constructively, that is, in a way that minimizes their intensity and keeps them active in pursuing positive life goals. Without such skills in "(negative) emotional control" (Frisch, 2006), clients' level of negative affective experience can nullify gains in positive affect, immobilize clients, interfere with relationships, impede advanced social problem solving in postmodern societies, and even lead to addictive or risky behaviors (Witkiewitz & Marlatt, 2004). Clinical clients are especially in need of such skills as they are prone to chronic problems such as "negative affect syndrome" (Barlow, Allen, & Choate, 2004), neuroticism, or negative affectivity.

Matching Goals to Area-specific Interventions in the "Sweet 16"

Aside from use of the generally applicable Five Paths intervention, Quality of Life Therapy intervention consists of matching clients' goals for coaching, therapy, and life with interventions in one of the "sweet 16" areas. The procedure is the same whether the venue is coaching, organizational psychology, mental health, or behavioral medicine. The manual for QOLT (Frisch, 2006) provides step-by-step instruction and case illustrations of assessing well-being, planning and tailoring interventions, and monitoring progress, outcome, and follow-up with the the Quality of Life Inventory. The interventions include a compendium of "state of the art" (Diener, 2006) positive psychology interventions such as gratitude and strengths exercises along with more innovative interventions based upon the integrative theory discussed here, and the author's positive psychology coaching, therapy, and supervision practice of twenty years (Furey, 2007; Sirgy & Wu, 2009). Many of the interventions are summarized in the form of a convenient client checklist, called the "Positive Psychology Practices Questionnaire (P3Q)" in the Appendix.

Reassessment, Fine-tuning, and Follow-up for Relapse Prevention

The Quality of Life Inventory is re-administered every three weeks or so during intervention to gauge progress in areas of life that are targets for intervention. Intervention is fine-tuned or changed when new patterns or problems emerge in assessment results (e.g., see Kazdin, 1993, 2003).

Illustrative Clinical Case: Case of B or "Black Sheep"

As the following case illustrates, adding QOLT to a clinical or therapy practice can be as simple as administering a 10-minute assessment to a client, developing positive life goals for valued areas of life, and applying a few area-specific interventions to accomplish these goals (this is a disguised case history designed to protect the anonymity of the client; B felt rejected by her family of origin who saw her as the "black sheep" in the family).

"Dr. James, this is Jack Sprat. I am in trouble. My supervisor and internship training director (aka B) is "coming on" to me. Our supervision sessions have moved to eight o'clock at night at her apartment with a candlelit dinner! I am afraid to do anything since she is evaluating me and must write a letter of recommendation for any job I get after completing my internship." After an intervention to remove B from any supervisory authority over Jack's work, she was referred to the author for therapy.

B was a 55-year old European-American single woman. B described Jack as "the perfect man" and "God's gift to womanhood." Jack had movie star looks, impeccable manners, and a quick wit. He was a gourmet cook, and loved to discuss "chick" flicks and books. B came to "know and love" Jack during long bus rides to a rural practicum site some distance from the the the medical center in Waco, Texas which served as the primary internship site.

After a successful course of cognitive therapy for major depressive disorder related to the end of her relationship with Jack Sprat, B, while asymptomatic, reported feeling "blah." She no longer felt bad, but did not feel particularly *good*. Specifically, while B's level of negative affect was in the tenth percentile at post-treatment, her level of positive affect experience was also very low (seventh percentile) as measured by the Scale of Positive and Negative Experience (Diener et al., 2010). While her Beck Depression Inventory-II was in the nonclinical or low range at post-treatment, her overall score on the Quality of Life Inventory, was also in the low range, signifying a lack of fulfillment in some highly valued areas of life; B's QOLI test results are presented in Figure 27.1. These assessment results brought to mind David A. Clark's (2006) rationale for adding positive psychology to traditional psychotherapies, to wit:

> In some respects, clinical psychology and psychiatry have exhibited a depressive thinking style in their theories, research, and treatment of psychological disorders. We have tended to focus exclusively on the negative. Our preoccupation has been the relief of suffering, the alleviation of negative emotions, the restructuring of negative cognitions and dysfunctional schemas, and the modification of problematic behavioral responses ... As psychotherapists, we have ignored the "half-full" side of the equation. That is, we rarely address issues of happiness, contentment, and quality of life. At last psychologists like Ed Diener, Martin Seligman, and Michael B. Frisch have begun to readdress this imbalance in our perspective on human emotion ... *Treating negative mood will not automatically lead to happiness and life satisfaction in our patients. Instead a new and expanded therapeutic perspective is needed that directly addresses issues of positive affect, life satisfaction, and contentment.* (Clark, 2006, p. ix, italics added)

Based on this rationale, QOLT was instituted in an effort to boost B's positive affect experience and satisfaction with life (QOLT can also be implemented *concurrently* with a psychotherapy and/or pharmacotherapy; see Furey (2007) and Frisch (2006) for guidelines on how to do this). B was excited and motivated by the prospect of learning ways to be happier and more enthusiastic about her life. She also was intrigued by the part of the rationale that promised a prophylactic effect from QOLT. After five episodes of major depressive disorder, B was eager to learn an approach that would also reduce her risk of relapse.

B's overall quality of life score was broken down into the "Sweet 16" areas of life –see Weighted Satisfaction Profile in Figure 27.1; while satisfied and fulfilled in areas of life such as, money, work, and home, she was *dis*satisfied the areas of health, self-esteem, learning, helping, love, relatives, and community.

Clark and Beck (1999) identify the pursuit of positive goals as key to activating the "constructive mode" of well-being and to "lasting" therapeutic change. Positive goal pursuit is also a core intervention in the QOLT. For example, B identified *positive goals* for each of her six areas of dissatisfaction (i.e., work, relatives, play, creativity, and friends) in contrast to the more negative, symptom-oriented goals characteristic of her first phase of treatment

(These initial goals were aimed at reducing symptoms of sleep and appetite disturbance, suicidal ideation, fatigue, and depressed mood; B also secured services such as adult day care for her frail elderly mother with major neurocognitive disorder due to Alzheimer's disease in this first cognitive therapy phase of treatment). Interventions from the chapters in the QOLT manual corresponding to B's five areas of *dis*satisfaction were discussed with B as a way to plan and prioritize interventions.

In an effort to not overwhelm B, only two of her areas of dissatisfaction were targeted for *sustained* intervention, that is, helping and love. With the help of her therapist and the Five Paths Exercise, B did, however, choose some simple "Happiness Habits" to boost her satisfaction with four additional areas: health, self-esteem, relatives, and community. For example, her concern about health ("I'm overweight and out of shape") was addressed by visiting a local YMCA each weekday morning before work to attend an exercise class where she accrued the added benefit of making new friends and serving or helping the community by supporting a nonprofit agency that she believed in. She pursued the "Do not Ask Path" to self-esteem, by viewing self-esteem as a meaningless abstraction and learning to mindfully ignore self-downing thoughts when they would arise. She also expected a boost in self-esteem as she made progress toward her goals in other areas of life like helping or love (the "Success Path" to self-esteem. With respect to relatives, B set up a weekly time to visit her two estranged sisters from California via Skype or Facetime; they read books together and even bingewatched shows on Netflix contiguously, commenting on an episode via phone as if they were in the same room.

B found helping or altruism/prosocial activities to be her "favorite antidepressant." That is, when feeling down, she called or skyped her two sisters from California or friends from an Alzheimer's support group to visit with them, inquire about how they were doing, and encourage their efforts in dealing with problems. She also sent homemade greeting cards and e-cards to these people. Contacting local people also led to deepening friendships and dates for coffee, lunch, and dinner.

B's most ambitious helping project involved all the steps of establishing a "Helping Routine" in order to form an Alzheimer's disease support group where none existed in her community. Initially, B felt too shy and overwhelmed to consider this project. She spoke with numerous "Expert Friends" in the community about the idea and invoked QOLT skills pertaining to relationship skills and time management to make this dream a reality. For example, B broke down the project into simple, 15-minute tasks such as calling her mother's physician and the US Alzheimer's Association for guidance and advice. Eventually, she asked others take over the leadership roles for this group.

Using QOLT relationship skills such as role-playing and "Making Conversation" and tenets like "Find a Friend, Find a Mate," B found a boyfriend whom she later married, in spite of admonitions from friends that "all the good men are taken or dead" in late middle age. A key for her was an online dating website and meeting men at the "cultural hub" of Waco, that is, a Barnes and Noble bookstore.

In terms of self-care and emotional control, B found a "Relaxation Ritual" helpful when she felt overwhelmed or frustrated in carrying out her "happiness project." Her favorite ritual from the manual consisted of quietly reading over the client handout called "Tenets of Contentment," which summarizes much of the philosophy, attitudes, and skills that make up QOLT. While reading, she gained inspiration from tenets she thought might apply to her "happiness project" as she called it. In her words, "I read the Tenets like a self-help book in a comfortable, quiet place or the bath." B also found it helpful to postpone worries and problem solving to a time of day when she felt calm, centered, and unrushed ("Guide for Worry Warts" exercise). At other times, she would try to distract herself from worries via "Mindful Breathing," which is based on Jon Kabat-Zinn's and the Austin Zen Center's approach to meditation and mindfulness throughout the day.

B's 12 weeks of well-being interventions led to a sense of élan vital and flourishing reflected in increases on the SPANE (Positive Affect subtest score at the eighty-third percentile) and Quality of Life Inventory. The latter score moved to the average range of the standardization sample.

B reported feeling good as if she really "had a reason to get up in the morning," although she would still become upset for days at a time when her goal pursuits were thwarted. At a two-year follow-up, her Quality of Life Inventory scores moved into the high range, according to B, who had taken to assessing her own "emotional temperature" with the Quality of Life Inventory every three or four months (this well-being test and others can be directly obtained and used by clients and laypersons themselves. Periodic self-administration of well-being tests can aid clients like B in preventing relapses into happiness-depleting thoughts, behaviors, and activities.

Future Research and Applications

Research on QOLT and its companion assessment, the Quality of Life Inventory, are still in their infancy. It is hoped that this chapter may inspire talented researchers to further explore the efficacy and effectiveness of QOLT for various populations and disorders as well as its ability to prevent relapse and significantly add to the effects of established treatments for DSM-5 disorders. In one study to date, the QOLI significantly predicted academic retention one to three years in advance in a university setting (Frisch et al., 2005). The theory-based prediction that low QOLI scores may also predict health, work, and relationship problems needs the same rigorous testing, including large cross-validation samples.

The "dismantling strategy" for randomized controlled trials may be employed to establish which components or elements of QOLT are most efficacious. For example, the additive effects of positive versus negative affect interventions on of positive and negative affect as well as satisfaction with life, DSM-5 symptoms and functioning bears scrutiny given the complex interrelationships among these constructs. For example, David Barlow and his colleagues (Carl, Fairholme, Gallagher, Thompson-Hollands, & Barlow, 2014) found that anxiety and depression symptoms decrease positive affect reactivity and increase the downregulation of positive affect. Positive and negative affect are inextricably intertwined like the red and white stripes of a peppermint stick. It is time that we heed the clarion call for simultaneously attending to both constructs in clinical work (Wood and Tarrier, 2010; Gilbert, 2012; Carl, Soskin, Kerns, & Barlow, 2013).

QOLT should also be delivered via the web, including Facebook and smart phone apps, since traditional face to face coaching and clinical delivery systems are not reaching all of those who can benefit from positive psychology intervention and assessment. The use of peer-led support groups emanating from families or groups be they work-, spiritual-, or hobby-based groups can also broaden the exposure of the general public to positive psychology.

QOLT could be tested as a type of training in ethics and emotional competence for health professionals. Fully 50% of ethical lapses are related to unhappiness at the time of the infraction (Frisch, 2006; Koocher & Keith-Spiegel, 2008); this was certainly true in the case of B discussed here. QOLT may prevent burnout and ethical or technical mistakes made by mental health professionals who must learn and practice *emotional* as well as technical competence, according to Pope and Vasquez (2011). How might this be accomplished? Just as Freud and Ellis, tested ideas and techniques on themselves first, clinicians may learn QOLT interventions by first trying them out for themselves. This could boost their well-being at the same time as it schools them in the approach vis-à-vis clients. Professional societies like the British Psychological Society could also offer QOLT training to their members as part of their ethics offerings in continuing education.

In terms of traditional health care, integrated service delivery systems in which well-being assessments and interventions are considered co-equal with and are conducted concurrently with symptom-oriented assessments and interventions should be developed and evaluated. Since it is the goal of all health care interventions is to maintain or enhance well-being and quality of life in addition to effecting a "cure" for a disorder or disease, the addition of routine well being assessment and intervention procedures to psychology and medicine can be expected to improve clients' and patients' well-being and quality of life. An intriguing possibility raised by Diener and Chan (2011) is that well-being intervention packages like QOLT may improve health directly, that is, impact the symptoms of disorder/disease, even when such interventions are not directly related to the disease or disorder (e.g., chronic pain, heart disease).

References

Abedi, M. R. and Vostanis, P. (2010). Evaluation of Quality of Life Therapy for parents of children with obsessive-compulsive disorders in Iran. *European Child and Adolescent Psychiatry.* doi.10.1007/s00787-010-0098-4.

Barlow, D. H., Allen, L. B., & Choate, M. L. (2004). Toward a unified treatment for emotional disorders. *Behavior Therapy, 35,* 205–230.

Carl, J. R., Fairholme, C. P., Gallagher, M. W., Thompson-Hollands, J., & Barlow, D. H. (2014). The effects of anxiety and depressive symptoms on daily positive emotion regulation. *Journal of Psychopathology and Behavioral Assessment, 36*(2), 224–236. doi.10.1007/s10862-013-9387-9.

Carl, J. R., Soskin, D. P., Kerns, C., & Barlow, D. H. (2013). Positive emotion regulation in emotional disorders: A theoretical review. *Clinical Psychology Review, 33*(3), 343–360. doi.10.1016/j.cpr.2013.01.003.

Clark, D. A. (2006). Foreword. In: M. B. Frisch, *Quality of Life Therapy: Applying a life satisfaction approach to positive psychology and cognitive therapy* (pp. xi–x). Hoboken, NJ: John Wiley.

Clark, D. A. & Beck, A. T. (1999). *Scientific foundations of cognitive theory and therapy of depression.* New York: John Wiley.

Diener, E. (2006). Foreword. In: M. B. Frisch, *Quality of Life Therapy.* (pp. vii–viii). Hoboken, NJ: John Wiley.

Diener, E. & Biswas-Diener, R. (2008). *Happiness: Unlocking the mysteries of psychological wealth.* Malden, NJ: Blackwell. doi.10.1002/9781444305159.

Frisch, M. B. (1994). *Quality of Life Inventory Manual and Treatment Guide.* Minneapolis, MN: NCS Pearson & Pearson Assessments.

Diener, E. & Seligman, M. E. P. (2002). Very happy people. *Psychological Science, 13,* 81–84.

Diener, E., Suh, E. M., Lucas, R. E., & Smith, H. L. (1999). Subjective well-being: Three decades of progress. *Psychological Bulletin, 125,* 276–302.

Diener, E., Wirtz, D., Tov, W., Kim-Prieto, C., Choi, D. W., Oishi, S., & Biswas-Diener, R. (2010). New well-being measures: Short scales to assess flourishing and positive and negative feelings. *Social Indicator Research, 97,* 143–156. doi.10.1007/s11205-009-9493-y.

Diener, E. & Chan, M. Y. (2011) Happy people live longer: Subjective well-being contributes to health and longevity. *Applied Psychology: Health and Well-Being, 3*(1), 1–43.

Frisch, M. B. (2006). *Quality of life therapy.* Hoboken, NJ: John Wiley.

Frisch, M. B. (2009). *Quality of life inventory handbook: A guide for laypersons, clients, and coaches.* Minneapolis, MN: NCS Pearson & Pearson Assessments.

Frisch, M. B. (2013). Evidence-based well-being/positive psychology assessment and intervention with quality of life therapy and coaching and the Quality of Life Inventory (QOLI). *Social Indicators Research, 114,* 193–227. doi.10.1007/s11205-012-0140-7.

Frisch, M. B., Clark, M. P., Rouse, S. V., Rudd, M. D., Paweleck, J., & Greenstone, A. (2005). Predictive and treatment validity of life satisfaction and the Quality of Life Inventory. *Assessment, 12*(1), 66–78.

Furcy, R. (2007). Beyond feeling better: Adding happiness to the treatment plan. *PsycCritiques (serial online)* 52(5).

Gilbert, K. E. (2012). The neglected role of positive emotion in adolescent psychopathology. *Clinical Psychology Review, 32*(6), 467–481. doi.10.1016/j.cpr.2012.05.005doi:10.1037/a0006300.

Kazdin, A. E. (1993). Evaluation in clinical practice: Clinically sensitive and systematic methods of treatment delivery. *Behavior Therapy, 24,* 11–45.

Kazdin, A. E. (2003). *Research design in clinical psychology*, 4th edn. Boston, MA: Allyn & Bacon.

Kennard, B. D., Emslie, G. J., Mayes, T. L., Nakonezny, P. A., Jones, J. M., Foxwell, A. A., & King, J. (2014). Sequential treatment with fluoxetine and relapse-prevention CBT to improve outcomes in pediatric depression. *American Journal of Psychiatry*, *171*(10), 1083–1090.

Koocher, G. P. & Keith-Spiegel, P. (2008). *Ethics in psychology: Professional standards and cases*, 3rd edn. New York: Oxford University Press.

Land, K. C. (2006). Quality of life therapy for all!: A review of Frisch's approach to positive psychology, Quality of Life Therapy. *SINET (Social Indicators Network News)*, *85*, 1–4.

Lyubomirsky, S., Sheldon, K. M., & Schkade, D. (2005). Pursuing happiness: The architecture of sustainable change. *Review of General Psychology*, *9*(2), 111–131.

Pope, K. S. & Vasquez, M. T. (2011). *Ethics in psychotherapy and counseling: A practical guide*, 4th edn. Hoboken, NJ: John Wiley.

Rodrigue, J. R., Baz, M. A., Widows, M. R., & Ehlers, S. L. (2005). A randomized evaluation of quality of life therapy with patients awaiting lung transplantation. *American Journal of Transplantation*, *5*(10), 2425–2432.

Rodrigue, J. R. Mandelbrot, D. A., & Pavlakis, M. (2011). A psychological intervention to improve quality of life and reduce psychological distress in adults awaiting kidney transplantation. *Nephrology Dialysis Transplantation*, *26*(2), 709–715. doi.10.1093/ndt/gfq382.

Rodrigue, J. R., Widows, M. R., & Baz, M. A. (2006). Caregivers of patients awaiting lung transplantation: Do they benefit when the patient is receiving psychological services? *Progress in Transplantation*, *16*, 336–342.

Sirgy, M. J. & Wu, J. (2009). The pleasant life, the engaged life, and the meaningful life: what about the balanced life? *Journal of Happiness Studies*, *10*, 183–196.

Wood, A. M. & Tarrier, N. (2010). Positive clinical psychology: A new vision and strategy for integrated research and practice. *Clinical Psychology Review*, *30*(7), 819–829. doi.10.1016/j.cpr.2010.06.003.

Appendix: Positive Psychology Practices Questionnaire (P3Q)

Name:_____   Date: _____   ____

Instructions: This research-supported powerhouse asks you about happiness practices, attitudes, and skills which you can do at any time to build a life of happiness, meaning, and enjoyable feelings. The questionnaire summarizes the major positive psychology techniques for boosting people's happiness or well-being. Experiment with these in your daily life. Activities and attitudes which reliably boost your mood, contentment, and meaning can be made Happiness Habits to maximize their effectiveness. Those items which become "no brainers" that you engage in daily will do the most to enhance your happiness and meaning. Greater happiness will also lead to better health, relationships, work performance, and service to others and the community. Avoid doing things that are illegal, harmful to others, self-defeating, or that get in the way of your long-term goals in life. Each day, make a plan to practice some of these attitudes and skills. Good luck!

CIRCLE each item that applies; "This past month I ... :

1   Visited with friends or loved ones who really love, respect, and believe in me.
2   Asked people who know what they are doing, how to handle a problem situation.
3   Thought about the many things I am thankful for in my life.
4   Made some real progress in achieving my goals in life.
5   Used my strengths, skills, or talents to achieve my goals.
6   Did something that usually makes me feel peaceful, calm, and content.
7   Exercised good self-care or had time to myself to really relax.

8 Did "flow" activities that challenge me, take all my attention, and make me feel great afterwards.

9 Felt inspired or motivated by someone or some activity.

10 Felt a deep sense of awe or wonder at some time.

11 Learned about something that really interests me.

12 Did some things that were really enjoyable, fun, or thrilling.

13 Did yoga, meditation, or prayed.

14 Took pride in someone else's accomplishment.

15 Spent time with friends or loved ones who really love, respect, and believe in me.

16 Took time to really slow down and enjoy a meal or something beautiful.

17 Got seven or eight hours of sleep.

18 Ate healthy but delicious food.

19 Did thirty minutes of brisk physical activity that got my heart rate up.

20 Got thirty minutes or more of aerobic exercise.

21 Gave or received love from someone I care about.

22 Had at least five positive interactions for every stressful or tense encounter with a close loved one, friend, or co-worker.

23 Believed that things will work out for me in life.

24 Felt deeply grateful for the good things in my life.

25 Really "dodged a bullet" or avoided a huge problem or mishap.

26 Bounced back quickly from adversity or something bad that happened.

27 Spent time in nature or a green space.

28 Believed that I will be successful

29 Took some risks to be happier or to try something new.

30 Never gave up on some important life goals and values.

31 Kept trying despite some failures.

32 Believed that I was a good, decent person.

33 Believed in myself as a competent and capable person.

34 Believed in myself as a person who deserves happiness.

35 Believed in myself.

36 Called a friend who is down or struggling.

37 Helped someone else.

38 Did something for another person.

39 Served a cause, group, or person I believe in.

40 "Soldiered on" or persevered through a tough time.

41 Felt optimistic about my future.

42 Felt interested and engaged in my daily activities.

43 Believed that other people really respect me.

44 Told a close friend about problem that I am having.

45 Made a close friend or visited with a close friend.

46 Applied my strengths to a problem I am having or a goal I am pursuing.

47 Spent time with a spiritual community or activity that really gives me comfort and peace.

48 Had times of flow during the day when I was totally engaged, challenged, and unaware of the time.

49 Engaged in Happiness Habits that I know make me a happier person.

50 Made a nice connection with people I saw throughout my day.

51 Affirmed someone and told them what a great person they were or what a great thing that they did.

52 Laughed out loud.

53 Smiled a lot.

54 Thought that I really like my work, a hobby, or retirement pursuit.

55 Took credit for one of my successes.
56 Refused to blame myself entirely for something bad that happened.
57 Had fun with my partner or worked toward finding someone to love.
58 Had fun with two close friends or worked toward making two close friends.
59 Believed that my life had purpose and meaning.
60 Forgave myself or someone else for a mistake.
61 Expressed myself in a creative way.
62 Made something artistic or did something artistic.
63 Distracted myself in a healthy way from anger, depression, or anxiety.
64 Thought about the great things I have accomplished today, this week, and during my life.
65 Believed that I have friends and loved ones who are fun and who really care about me.
66 Was kind or helpful to another person.
67 Journaled about a problem or about a positive future for myself and loved ones.
68 Exercised good sleep hygiene or habits.
69 Exercised good eating habits.
70 Refused to give up on me and my future goals.
71 Smiled at several people throughout the day.
72 Asked many people how they were doing.
73 Greeted many people with a smile throughout the day.
74 Went to a meaningful church/temple/mosque service.
75 Visited some pleasant or beautiful surroundings.
76 Explored some positive part of my home, neighborhood, or community.
77 Did something to make the world a better place.
78 Tackled a problem or task that I was avoiding, but that really needed attention.
79 Distracted myself from regrets about the past.
80 Focused on the present and future instead of the past.
81 Waited before expressing extreme anger toward someone.
82 Was true to my values.
83 Stopped to "smell the flowers" or really luxuriate in a pleasant place or experience.
84 Stood up for my principles, ethics, or personal morals.
85 Refused to act on my extreme anger, depression, or anxiety.
86 Made time for both work and play.
87 Refused to compare myself to others and followed my own standards for what I need and want.
88 Refused to try to "keep up with the Jones'."
89 Organized my time and my life in way that feels good and helps me to get things done.
90 Set some modest goals for the day that I was able to accomplish and feel good about.
91 Thought about WHAT I WANT and HOW CAN I GET IT.
92 Pursued a positive addiction like walking or gardening.
93 Got a "second opinion" about a tough problem from a friend or "expert" in the know.
94 Refused to get down on myself, criticize myself, or give up on myself.
95 Socialized with others whom I enjoy.
96 Shared the hurt behind the anger I feel toward someone.
97 Celebrated a friend or loved one's success.
98 Tried to be kind toward and to connect positively with everyone I interacted with all day.
99 Worked on making a "surrogate" family of friends who love, support me, and really believe in me and in my potential to succeed.
100 Thanked everyone I could for the things that they do for me.
101 Faced a tough problem that I had been "ducking."
102 Told someone that I was proud of them.
103 Focused on my future goals instead of regrets about the past.

Part V
Reinterpreting Existing Therapies

28

Person-Centered Psychology

An Organismic Positive Approach to the Problems of Living and Helping People Flourish[1]

Pete Sanders and Stephen Joseph

This chapter introduces person-centered psychology, founded on the work of Carl R Rogers (1902 1987), as a vibrant, innovative, evidence-based, developing body of work relevant to clinical psychologists, psychotherapists and group workers, and more recently, applied positive psychologists. The theoretical foundations of person-centered therapies began with Rogers' work as a clinical psychologist in the 1930s and 1940s (Rogers, 1939, 1942), and can be traced through both his own later writings, and others' readings of this work (e.g., Rogers, 1951, 1959, 1961; see also Barrett-Lennard, 1998; Mearns & Thorne, 2000, 2007; Sanders, 2006a; Kirschenbaum, 2007). For a thoroughgoing description and analysis of the philosophical underpinnings of contemporary person-centered psychology readers are directed to Tudor and Worrall (2006). While citing Rogers as the seminal source of theory, person-centered psychologists might identify a further subset of theoretical elements to which they subscribe (see Sanders, 2012). Just like variations in other psychological approaches (psychodynamic, cognitive, and behavioral) these variations manifest themselves in practice and everyday theoretical discourse.

This brief summary will look at theory, research and some elements of contemporary practice in a way that aims to facilitate constructive comparison with other contemporary approaches to change; and show how the person-centered approach was the original positive psychology (Joseph, 2015). John Shlien, a Harvard psychologist and one of the early pioneers of person-centered psychology, originally writing in 1956, said:

> In the past, mental health has been a "residual" concept – the absence of disease. We need to do more than describe improvement in terms of say "anxiety reduction." We need to say what the person can *do* as health is achieved. As the emphasis on pathology lessens, there have been a few recent efforts toward positive conceptualizations of mental health. Notable among these are Carl Rogers' "Fully Functioning Person ..." (Shlien, 2003, p. 17)

Traditionally, clinical psychologists have been used to thinking only in terms of symptom reduction. With the advent of positive psychology they have been challenged to consider how to promote positive functioning. It may surprise those unfamiliar with the person-centered approach to know that this was exactly what Rogers' approach to therapy set out to do. His approach to therapy was based on the meta-theoretical assumption that people have

---

an inherent tendency toward growth, development, and becoming fully functioning (Joseph, 2015). But these do not happen automatically. For people to actualize their inherent optimal nature they require the right social environment. Without the right social environment the inherent tendency toward growth can become thwarted and usurped, leading instead to psychological distress and dysfunction. In this way, the person-centered approach conceptualizes a single organismic process underpinning the spectrum of psychological functioning. We will describe Rogers' theory of personality in more detail in the next section and how it provides a unified theory of health and distress.

Personality, Health, and Distress: A Single Organismic Conceptual Framework for the Spectrum of Psychological Functioning

Between the 1930s and the 1960s, person-centered therapy (PCT) developed into a holistic theory, understanding the human being as an integrated whole *organism*. This pulls against the whole idea of dividing being human into "body" and "mind," and further into elements of mind such as "personality." Nevertheless, Rogers followed orthodox psychology conventions and developed a theory of personality in his 1951 and 1959 writings; keen that his ideas, radical as they were, did not alienate academics and professional psychologists at the first turn. A detailed reading of the literature, reveals person-centered psychology constructed as an *organismic* theory which some believe can be translated into more reductionistic framework, but for others this is simply impossible, leading to terminal distortions of the philosophy.

Rogers' chapter 'A theory of personality and behavior' (Rogers, 1951, pp 481–533) is arranged in 19 propositions dealing with the nature of experience; the development and structure of personality; the nature order, disorder and distress, and therapeutic change – ideas refined in 1959 in the seminal chapter in Koch (1959, pp. 184–256). Importantly, the 1951 work positions person-centered psychology as a perceptual theory and phenomenological approach. It is thought of as a "perceptual" theory because in Proposition II (Rogers, 1951, p. 484), Rogers declared that reality as experienced is determined by the perceptual field of the organism: "We live by a perceptual 'map' which is never reality itself" (1951, p. 485). This has implications for change processes, since "That the perceptual field is the reality to which the individual reacts is often strikingly illustrated in therapy … when the perception changes, the reaction of the individual changes."

It is a phenomenological approach because "facts about the world" – the individual's "truth" – is generated by their experience in the moment. With the individual at the center of this experiential world, it is to them that we must turn to engage with and apprehend their world, their story. Clues for understanding the world of an individual client cannot be found in books, theories, frameworks, categories, taxonomies, or systems. Here Rogers builds the rationale for empathy as the keystone for understanding the narrative of the client – the foundation of relationship – but not empathy as an instrument of interrogation.

Many contemporary evidence-based approaches now focus the therapeutic effort on the quality of the relationship, having relegated it to the position of "also ran" after theory-driven interventions and micro-diagnostically indicated techniques. In contraposition to person-centered therapy, the theory and practice of some approaches has empathy as yet another technique to be introduced at the appropriate time, for a designated purpose of, for example, information-gathering or trust-building. Empathy in person-centered psychology is the beginning and end of everything. Carl Rogers was the first to operationalize the therapeutic relationship (Rogers, 1957, 1959), and subsequent developments in PCT have refined and developed understanding of the dynamics.

Having described some of the philosophical background to Rogers' theory we turn to the topic of infant development which describes how experiences early in life determine psychological functioning.

Infant Development

As noted above, the meta-theoretical foundation of the person-centered approach is the view that human beings have a basic propensity and potential toward self-organization, self-regulation, and growth toward the realization of the organisms' full potential. This process is understood to occur naturally when the organism is supported by the right social environmental factors, but easily derailed when the person's context is controlling and coercive. It is this view that makes the person-centered approach a positive psychology because of its assertion that personal growth is intrinsically directed toward constructive and social behavior and the full expression of the individual's potentialities. We first see this taking place in infancy.

The human infant experiences him- or herself as the center of "reality" – the ever-changing world around him or her, *is*, for the infant, reality. The developing organism has an inherent tendency to survive, maintain, and enhance itself, termed "actualization," and is the primary, unitary motivational push (see below). This push to actualize drives the infant to meet the needs he or she experiences by responding to his/her world in an organized way as a whole organism. The actualizing tendency pushes the infant to constantly seek new experiences – curiosity is built in to actualization.

The infant also has an inherent tendency to value experiences which maintain and enhance him or her organism positively; those working against actualization of the organism are valued negatively. "Valuing" can, in the earliest instances in life mean something as simple as "liking," "enjoying," "attractive" (in its literal meaning), or "interesting." This is the organismic valuing process. As he or she develops, the infant is attracted toward and accepts positively valued experiences, whilst avoiding and rejecting negatively valued experiences.

However, as development proceeds, the positive directional force toward the full expression of potentialities becomes thwarted by the social world just as the infant begins to develop a sense of self.

The Development of Self and Personality

Readers should note that Rogers does not specify ages, stages, or sensitive periods. Person-centered psychology presents a number of what, in contrast to, for example, psychoanalytic theory, might appear to be rather loose propositions. It sees development as a unique-to-each-individual process weaving together maturation, learning/adaptation, and innate curiosity driven by the actualizing tendency of the organism.

As development proceeds, at some point the infant differentiates a part of his or her world-as-experienced as having a particular quality; being different and "special." This differentiated portion of experiences comes into awareness as the *self*. The infant then builds up a *concept* of itself (a self-concept) particularly as a result of being with others and being evaluated by others. As the infant becomes aware of its *self*, its general need for satisfaction (originating in the acceptance of actualizing experiences) becomes a particular need for *positive regard* from others. Positive regard from others is so potent (because it is associated with all aspects of the organism; its survival, maintenance, and enhancement) that it becomes more compelling than the organismic valuing process in determining behavior. Such evaluations from others are taken into the self-concept as though they had originated from the organismic valuing process and are called introjected values.

When the infant accepts or avoids a self-experience as a result of conditional positive regard from another, they are said to have developed a "condition of worth." As the self develops into a recognizable entity, it too has a tendency to actualize – to maintain and enhance itself (self-actualization). However, because the self may contain material introjected directly from the evaluations of others, the self may actualize in a different direction to that of the organism. This is a state of potential or actual disharmony or between self and organism. The individual's awareness tends to be filtered through the emerging self, so it is of paramount importance that experiences can be recognized and handled by the self-structure. Ordinarily, however, the typical adult self-structure is in a state of incongruent tension and has a vested interest in avoiding or denying the apprehension of certain experiences, and we will examine this fundamental potential dynamic of human personality below and how it gives rise to distress.

Distress

Psychological distress has a single cause in classical client-centered therapy theory. Whilst other person-centered therapies contribute other possibilities for a person-centered psychopathology (see Sanders, 2012, or Cooper, O'Hara, Schmid, & Bohart, 2013), here we look at Rogers' original work to sketch the origin of psychological distress.

In précis, whereas positive functioning results from congruence in the total personality between self-structure (largely the self-image or the self as perceived) and the lived experience of the person which arises when the social environment has been facilitative of the person's directional tendency towards personal growth, distress is caused by discrepancy or incongruence between the self-structure and the lived experience of the person (Rogers, 1951, pp. 481–533, 1959, pp. 226–227). In classical theory there are likely to be relatively few categories of antecedents to this state of incongruence yet an almost unlimited array of possible consequences (Joseph & Worsley, 2005). So we have a theory effectively positing a unitary cause of functioning, ranging from positive functioning to the infinity of expressions of distress which may arise according to the uniqueness of each individual.

The trajectory of distress is, therefore, absolutely unpredictable in the individual case, and seriously at odds with models of diagnosis, including the medical model. Indeed this renders any taxonomy of symptoms ridiculous and makes person-centered practice the execution of practical phenomenology. Accordingly, person-centered literature is not overburdened with essays on how to treat this problem, or that diagnosis. For professionals who associate highly differentiated diagnostic categories with sophistication, this leaves person-centered theory looking simplistic and naive. To counter this view, it is, however, useful to understand that the so-called psychiatric disorders favored by these professionals can be explained in terms of person-centered theory (see Joseph & Worsley, 2005; Sanders & Hill, 2014). However, Mearns (1997, p. 146) explains, "There is no attempt to use theory to predict the behavior of the individual client … Theory will not give a detailed understanding – only empathy can do that."

Congruence and Positive Functioning

As already noted, when the individual has an experience which fits with his or her self-concept, the experience is in harmony, or congruent with its self-structure, and can be symbolized accurately, resulting in a "fully functioning" person. Rogers used the term fully functioning to describe a state of well-being in which the person is open to experience, present focused, autonomous, and socially harmonious. In this way, the theory provides a developmental understanding of how positive psychological functioning arises and positions person-centered therapy as a potentiality theory rather than a deficiency theory.

In person-centered psychology, symbolization brings an experience into potential awareness.[2] However, since the self-concept contains introjected material, the individual will have experiences which are not in harmony with its self-structure and therefore may not be symbolized accurately. This is incongruence between self and experience and leads to potential or actual psychological tension.

Incongruence and Psychological Tension

The more disharmony there is between self and the organism as a result of introjects, the greater is the likelihood of incongruence between self and experience, and a greater potential for psychological tension. As there is incongruence between self and experience, so incongruence also develops between two sorts of behavior: (1) behaviors consistent with the self-concept (the individual is aware of this behavior); and (2) behaviors consistent with the rest of the organism (the individual may not recognize these behaviors as self-related, i.e., may not "own" them – these behaviors will be out of awareness).

Threat, Defense, Breakdown, and Therapeutic Change

Experiences which are incongruent with the self-concept not only may not be symbolized accurately, but they are also experienced as threatening to the integrity of the self-structure. The experiences would imply that the self-concept was "wrong," and since this is the effective center of the self-structure, the whole of the self would be under threat.

Threatening experiences can be dealt with in two sorts of ways. (1) they can fail to come into full awareness, that is, they are denied symbolization to experience, or (2) they can be changed (distorted) so that they fit into the self-concept without threat.

In a "healthy" individual the self-concept is *flexible* and *adaptable* in the face of new experience. When it is under threat though, the organism protects itself further by making the self-concept rigid and inflexible – the individual retreats into a well-defended rigid set of certainties about themselves. As it becomes more rigid it relies more and more on past experiences – the certainties – therefore, more and more current experiences will be distorted or denied. The processes of defense become entrenched and psychological tension builds up so that under certain circumstances (trauma, or the accumulation of threat), the self-concept effectively "breaks" under the pressure. The resulting state of disorganization will be experienced idiosyncratically by the individual as anxiety, depression, confusion and chaotic thinking, self-criticism, emotional or cognitive overwhelm or pain. These expressions of self-structure tension and collapse can be extremely distressing and might present to observers as symptoms of mental "illnesses" including "psychoses." There is always meaning in these apparently chaotic and disconnected experiences and empathic understanding (below) is the way in to decoding and (re-)making meaning in this confusing, often terrifying world.

The organism will be restored by integration of all experiences into the self-concept by removing threat to the self-concept – resulting in a relaxation of its rigidity and its defenses. This is achieved primarily by embodying unconditional positive regard (below) in a relationship. Newer experiences, previously discrepant with the self-concept may be tentatively admitted and the process of integration begins. This is the process of therapeutic change.

From this we can see the clear theoretical explanation of how this single theoretical framework of personality development explains the spectrum of psychological functioning from distress to fully functioning behavior.[3] As such, person-centered therapists think in terms of the dimension of congruence, or in more recent positive psychology terminology, authenticity (Wood, Linley, Maltby, Baliousis, & Joseph, 2008), rather than using mainstream psychiatric language to describe the ways in which clients experience distress and dysfunction. All manifestations of distress and dysfunction are viewed as ways of relating to the world that arise from incongruence. The person-centered approach does not view positive and negative functioning as separable constructs, but as outcomes of one single developmental process.

As such person-centered therapy which is based on the above theoretical view is always concerned with helping people move toward greater congruence no matter what their presenting issues are. Below the therapeutic mechanism of empathic understanding and unconditional positive regard will be explored in more detail below.

Change and Personality as a Positively Directed Processes

As a consequence of his work with Eugene Gendlin on the "Wisconsin Project" Rogers further developed his interest in the idea that personality and therapeutic change are both *processes* not a state (personality) or an event or procession of changes of state (therapy). Whereas some approaches propose a learning model for change, Rogers included learning as only one of many possible change processes in a growth model for change. This change process has certain features (Rogers, 1961, pp. 125–159) denoted by movement from relative fixity to fluidity. Rogers uses a number of continua to illuminate the nature of the process, including fixity/fluidity of feelings, expressions, personal constructs, attitudes to change, and differentiation and elaboration of experience.

Rogers' interest in process did not stop with the process of change. He extended the idea to include human personality itself. To Rogers, the personality was not a "thing," with "states" (like a computer program or an energy-balancing system in the mind), but simultaneously the form, manner and performance of the experiencing human being. So it would make no sense in person-centered terms to expect a distressed person to be "restored" to a previously nondistressed, pre-morbid state, or to have some faulty mental machinery "repaired." Instead, person-centered theory has the person grow through and with their present moment of experiencing to a new, different one, whilst:

- carrying with them and integrating all previous experience into a more positive and adaptive process;
- embracing the possibilities of "restoration" and "repair" (along with a host of other possible experiences, unique to the trajectory of the individual client's life) along the way; and
- creating new idiosyncratic possibilities for resilience and adaptive functioning.

Intrinsic to this change process is its unpredictability. The therapist is a curious companion, facilitator, and supportive, empowering presence, but brings no expectations of the trajectory of the process, other than to carry a hope for the best outcome. The fate of the process is in the co-created moment between the client (with all their personal and social contextual presses) and the therapist (with their attitudes).

Nature and Conditions for Therapeutic Change

It should be obvious that there are various types of change possible in an organism, not all therapeutic. Of course, "therapeutic" means different things in different contexts or theories, and we are considering the definition in terms of its particular meaning in person-centered theory. We will describe two elements of this therapeutic change, first, what change is (the theory of the nature of change) and, second, what makes change happen (the practice, or conditions for change).

The Nature of Change

When it comes to personality change, there are a few options which are championed by different psychological therapies and can be reported as common-sense explanations in everyday experience. For example, most of us would agree that we can learn to be different and both classical and operant conditioning are pressed into service both in theory and practice in psychotherapy.

Insight is also thought to be an active change agent, that is, simply understanding ourselves and our personal psychology better is accepted as a way to change. Some therapeutic approaches concentrate on methods of getting better insight.

We have described the person-centered theory of change a "growth model" above, but we will begin here from a slightly different place and return to another term – one which might help readers locate these ideas. Person-centered psychology is identified by some as an *organismic theory* and Wikipedia has a straightforward definition:

> Organismic theories in psychology are a family of holistic psychological theories which tend to stress the organization, unity, and integration of human beings expressed through each individual's inherent growth or developmental tendency. (http://en.wikipedia.org/wiki/Organismic_theory, last accessed July 22, 2014)

Person-centered psychology starts with the person as a complete organism, not a machine, computer program or any partial reduction of an organism (like a set of synapses, hormones. or brain structures). Furthermore, the organism is located in a context. Together the person and context create a unique set of opportunities for meaning and action which may or may not be revealed to or be understood by any observer, since each moment of meaning construction is personal and unique. And so it is with change. Any and all possible methods of change can, and will, be pressed into service by the person in pursuit of survival, maintenance, and enhancement. Limiting change-theory horizons to learning, insight, transcendence, or whatever, cannot do justice to the creativity of the person.

Such an expansive set of possibilities is difficult for reductionist systems and practice to accommodate. It is a nonpredictive change-theory that only makes sense in each moment of meaning with each person making it unwieldy for most mental health systems to cope with, with targets, audits, measures, and doses. It also seems to lack the theoretical complexity and sophistication which academics find attractive, offering little or no opportunity to create an elitist art or science, but as the convergence of PCT with self-determination theory shows us, this is not the case (Patterson & Joseph, 2007a). Also, as positive psychology begins to embrace new ways of thinking about functioning that draw on, and are consistent with, the person-centered ambition to help people become more fully functioning, the very targets, audits and measures used may begin to change in ways that do more ably accommodate PCT.

As an organismic change theory it lies alongside other natural science methodologies wrestling with understanding nonlinear dynamical systems – with the practitioner as observer of the system; facilitators of change, not psychotechnicians. Thus, although the person-centered approach is a positive psychology insofar as it is concerned with optimal human functioning, it is grounded in a specific organismic meta-theory that not all positive psychologists would share (Joseph & Murphy, 2013a).

The Conditions for Change

We have seen how Rogers explains the need for a threat-free, empathic relationship to facilitate change, but there is more to the operationalization of the complete relationship necessary for *therapeutic* change. The conditions required for healthy growth are the basis for "the necessary and sufficient conditions for therapeutic personality change" (Rogers, 1957, 1959) – the foundation of the practice of PCT. This 1950s "necessary and sufficient conditions" statement is a set of instructions for a constructive human relationship and is the starting point for Rogers' "if–then" hypothesis-building which characterized the thrust of most research into PCT for the next two decades. *If* the necessary and sufficient conditions are present, *then* therapeutic change will result. No other elements or factors are necessary. Over the years, a consensus across most theoreticians and practitioners suggests that the conditions are indeed *necessary*. That they are *sufficient*, however, was contentious then and remains so today. Rogers presented these conditions in both his 1957 and 1959 writing. Here is the 1959 version (Rogers, 1959, p. 213) with differences in the 1957 version in italics:

1   That two persons are in (*psychological*) contact.
2   That the first person, whom we shall term the client, is in a state of incongruence, being vulnerable, or anxious.
3   That the second person, whom we shall term the therapist, is congruent (*or integrated*) in the relationship.
4   That the therapist is experiencing unconditional positive regard toward the client.
5   That the therapist is experiencing an empathic understanding of the client's internal frame of reference (*and endeavors to communicate this to the client*).
6   That the client perceives, at least to a minimal degree, conditions 4 and 5, the unconditional positive regard of the therapist for him, and the empathic understanding of the therapist. (*The communication to the client of the therapist's empathic understanding and unconditional positive regard is to a minimal degree achieved*).

Detailed attention is paid to conditions 1, 3, 4, 5, and 6 by Bozarth and Wilkins (2001), Haugh and Merry (2001), Wyatt (2001), and Wyatt and Sanders (2002). Joseph and Worsley (2005) edited a collection discussing psychopathology (condition 2), and Tudor and Worrall (2006) present recent a cogent evaluation of the conditions. It is now rare to find person-centered texts using the inappropriate and outdated term "core" conditions – the so-called "therapist-provided" conditions.

Rogers' work firmly established the relationship as an encounter between two persons as the heart of the therapeutic process, not a formulaic "treatment," or the manifest expertise of the therapist, or the implicit or explicit pathology of the client in the form of a diagnosis. In the prevailing therapeutic culture of the 1950s, this was one of Rogers' revolutionary con-tributions, and in the era of the DSM-5, it remains radical today – possibly too radical. In the face of reductionism, competence-based manuals, and atomized practice in the form of micro-interventions, person-centered therapists stubbornly press home the idea that the conditions must be considered as a piece, not one by one. The helping relationship, whilst dissectible in theory, in practice can exist, in person-centered practice, only as an indivisible entity – with all the commonalities and contradictions coexisting in the dynamic tension of the relationship. The conditions, then, are attitudes to be held, not skills to be shuffled, cut and dealt according to diagnosis. These factors further distinguish person-centered practitioners (and their training) from other therapeutic approaches.

Person-centered Therapy and Contemporary Positive Clinical Psychology Themes

In recent years positive psychologists have begun to question the illness ideology and to seek alternative ways of thinking about human experience. There have been attempts to reformulate distress in terms of the absence or excess of positive characteristics (e.g., Rashid, 2015). However, such an approach, although positively oriented, remains grounded in the illness ideology insofar as specific treatments for specific conditions are still thought necessary. In contrast, because the person-centered approach is grounded in the growth model which assumes that distress results from the thwarting of natural impulses toward development, there is no call for specific treatments for specific conditions. As such diag-nosis is unnecessary.

Alternative to Diagnosis

Person-centered therapy has always been set against diagnosis in principle and practice. Since the fully-functioning person has an *essential* active internal locus of evaluation, imposed external judgments are anathema to psychological health and fulfillment. Any psychological treatment that imposes an evaluation, judgment, or diagnosis, is thought to be anti-therapeutic from the start. Only the client's self-diagnosis, story, narrative, or interpretation is acceptable (Rogers, 1951; Shlien, 2001; Sanders, 2006b). Classical PCT makes no distinction between medical diagnoses, therapist interpretations or expert interventions of what would be best. Indeed, rather than seen as benignly ineffective, all are considered *actively injurious* to the client's recovery and building of a congruent, robust self-concept within an autonomous personality.

Moving into the social sphere, person-centered psychology joins with all those who point to the stigmatizing nature of medicalized labels and diagnostic categories (e.g., Rapley, Moncrieff, & Dillon, 2011, Read & Dillon, 2013), being a model for anti-stigmatizing practice. Person-centered practitioners support service-user movements and all efforts to de-stigmatize mental health problems by de-medicalization in both philosophy and vocabulary. Social applications of person-centered approaches echo the insights of Foucault (1965), Illich (1976), and all who see the creep of the iatrogentic medical metaphor in everyday life as the medicalization of diversity and to be resisted at all costs. However, because of its anti-diagnostic stance person-centered therapy has been mistaken as unsuitable for those with serious psychological conditions, but as we shall show below this is not the case. As noted, it is anti-diagnostic because it is based on an alternative paradigm for understanding human experience – organismic, potentiality theory rather than the illness ideology.

Severe and Enduring Distress

As Professor of Psychology and Psychiatry at the University of Wisconsin, Rogers conducted a ground-breaking research project into the use of psychotherapy with people diagnosed with schizophrenia in the 1960s (Rogers, Gendlin, Kiesler, & Truax, 1967).[4] The work with the clients and the results of the study, together with earlier work by Kirtner and Cartwright (1958), all pointed to the importance of the nature of the client's experiencing as a crucial factor in the outcome of therapy. Furthermore, Rogers and his team were pioneers developing methodologies for some of the first outcome research in the field. Since the 1960s, there has been an unbroken line of person-centered practice and innovation in working with people with severe and enduring distress. For a review of some of this work see Traynor, Elliott, and Cooper (2011). Robert Elliott recently presented data from a meta-analysis of person-centered and experiential therapies with people with a diagnosis of psychosis showing an effect size of 1.08, with a .39 effect size improvement over other therapies (Elliott, 2013). Person-centered theory and practice stands comparison with other therapeutic interventions recently developed and favored in the treatment of psychosis.

- The actualizing tendency and inherent human organismic wisdom overlaps with the idea of coping strategy enhancement (Tarrier, 2004). PCT frees the client of constraints, enabling their natural resources to manage their own recovery.
- The actively acceptant, non-judgmental position of PCT chimes with the work of, for example, Romme and Escher (2000) on accepting voices, hallucinations and other unusual ideation. This extends to the clear position in PCT that all experiences, behavior, affect, and ideation have meaning. The person-centered therapist strives to empathically understand the client's experiences (including hallucinations), which in turn often reveal implicit meanings hitherto out of the client's awareness.

- There is no categorization of experience or behavior in PCT and thus no therapist-directed distinction between types or degrees of behavior beyond any that the client applies themselves. This echoes the work of, for example, Bentall (2003) demonstrating the continuity between normal and abnormal experience.
- Loren Mosher (1999, p. 37) described the "treatment" at the original Soteria House as, "24 hour a day application of interpersonal phenomenologic interventions." Since PCT is the premier phenomenological therapy method, Mosher's description is more than a fair approximation to much contemporary PCT practice.
- Rogers (1959) was explicit in his definition of empathy, making a pointed distinction between the actual (client) and the reflected (therapist) experience ("as if" it were the client's, without losing the "as if"). This is analogous to recent ideas in attachment theory and the work of Fonagy (e.g., Allen, Fonagy, & Bateman, 2008) regarding "marked mirroring." The PCT therapeutic relationship as an integrated experience meets the criteria for the type of relationship deemed important for initiating and sustaining mentalizing in clinical practice.

How would person-centered strategies work with, for example, clients who hear voices? The following illustration draws on the work of Rundle (2010).

Hearing voices: possible explanations   The following are ways that hearing voices may be understood with the PCA:

- voices arise because of a childhood event most likely experienced as trauma occurring in an environment which encourages internalization of the trauma;
- voices arise because of adult trauma followed by internalization;
- voices represent internalized aspects of self/others or sub-personalities;
- voices represent dissociated experiences.

Possible PCT strategies   The following are ways that people who hear voices may be helped with PCT:

- offer support and information, witness, and reflect disclosure;
- assist in developing ways of relating to, or coping with, voices;
- engage with and accept voices (including destructive voices) to understand meaning;
- in PCT all strategies are client-determined and self-directed: none are therapist-directed interventions.

Possible outcomes   The following are the outcomes that would be expected if PCT was helpful:

- voice is accepted and integrated into experience;
- client negotiates with voice to be intermittent and/or less threatening;
- voice fades considerably but remains present;
- voice disappears.

Research Evidence

At the University of Chicago Counseling Center, Rogers developed one of the first ever research programs to investigate the effectiveness of psychotherapy – made possible by his pioneering work recording and transcribing complete therapy relationships. The Counseling Center was set up to collect permissions from clients and routinely record client interviews. This steady stream of client data ensured that the research program was well served. In effect, it was the first psychotherapy research clinic.[5] Rogers attracted very large grants and a steady flow of research was published, including developing appropriate methodologies to evaluate psychotherapy in a systematic way. This ensured that first body of empirical research into psychotherapy was almost entirely person/client-centered.

Awarded the first Distinguished Scientific Contribution Award presented by the American Psychological Association in 1955, Carl Rogers was acknowledged as the world's leading psychology and psychotherapy researcher as Howard Kirschenbaum explains:

> As early as 1950 the *Encyclopaedia Britannica* wrote, "These first efforts of Rogers to subject his methods of nondirective therapy to scientific test constituted a landmark for clinical psychology." The *Library Journal* acknowledged that the research project reported in *Psychotherapy and Personality Change* was "the first thoroughly objective study of outcomes of psychotherapy in which adequate controls have been utilized." (Kirschenbaum, 2007, p. 210)

Despite this early pioneering work by Rogers, PCT almost completely disappeared from academic research settings from the 1970s to the 1990s, and today is critically underrepresented in clinical settings, suffering from the assumption that it is not evidence-based. In 2004, Elliott, Greenberg, and Lietaer published a meta-analysis collating person-centered and experiential (PCE) therapy effectiveness, the latest published iteration (Elliott & Freire, 2008) of which included 191 studies. Recently, Elliott (2013) presented the updated cumulative summary with data in the following categories[6]:

1 Pre-post studies
   - "open clinic trials" and & effectiveness studies;
   - 191 studies, 203 research samples;
   - 14,235 clients;
   - conclusion: PCE therapies *do* cause positive client change.
2 Controlled studies
   - versus wait-list or no treatment conditions;
   - 63 research samples, 60 studies, including 31 RCTs;
   - 2,144 clients, 1,958 controls;
   - conclusion: PCE therapies *are* better than waiting list or no treatment, with large effect sizes (overall 0.76, weighted, RCTs only).
3 Comparative studies
   - versus non-PCE therapies (e.g., CBT, treatment as usual, etc.);
   - 135 comparisons, 105 research samples, 100 studies; 91 RCTs;
   - 6,097 clients;
   - conclusion: PCE therapies are as effective as other therapies (main comparisons with CBT) with trivial effect sizes (overall -0.01, weighted, RCTs only).

Elliott and Freire's summary chapter (Elliott & Freire, 2010, pp. 9–11) draws six conclusions most of which require no elaboration:

- conclusion 1: PCE therapies are associated with large pre–post client change;
- conclusion 2: clients' large post-therapy gains are maintained over early and late follow ups;
- conclusion 3: clients in PCE therapies show large gains relative to clients who receive no therapy;
- conclusion 4: PCE therapies in general are clinically and statistically equivalent to other therapies;
- conclusion 5: broadly defined, PCE therapies might be trivially worse that CBT. The conclusion arises because there is a persistent but extremely small difference between PCE

and CBT therapies until the therapeutic orientation of the researcher is controlled for. This is the so-called "researcher allegiance effect" and refers to the effect where the researcher commonly find the most effective treatment is the one to which they favor or have a theoretical allegiance to. When this is removed, there is no difference between PCE and CBT outcomes;

- conclusion 6: so-called "supportive" therapies have slightly worse outcomes than CBT, but other kinds of PCE therapy are as effective, or more effective, than CBT. Further analysis revealed this effect to be due to "supportive" therapies in comparative studies run by non-PCE researchers not being bona-fide person-centered therapy.

Person-centered Therapy in the Twenty-first Century

From the 1970s until the early twenty-first century, person-centered therapy dominated counseling in primary care in the United Kingdom. Around 2005, government initiatives required practice based on particular types of evidence leading to CBT rapidly gaining ground to the exclusion of PCT. However, over the past few years there have been some notable developments in the PCA.

Counseling for Depression

Since 2009, the "Counselling for Depression" project, supported by the British Association for Counselling and Psychotherapy (BACP), led by Head of Research, Andy Hill, has attempted to restore PCT as a recommended choice in UK primary care provision. The aim was to incorporate "counseling for depression" (CfD) as a treatment within the framework of the government's Improving Access to Psychological Therapies (IAPT)[7] program. CfD is a new approach (see Sanders & Hill, 2014), integrating more classical person-centered therapy and some elements of emotion-focused therapy (see Elliott, Watson, Goldman, & Greenberg, 2004). Most importantly, it is approved by the National Institute for Health and Care Excellence (NICE) in its guideline for the treatment of mild to moderate depression.[8] The success of the CfD initiative has been founded on the development of competencies, essentially 'manualizing' a person-centered therapy set of skills and presenting the research evidence of the type reviewed in Elliott (2013).Counselling for depression is not without its critics within the person-centered movement in the UK. The manualiation of person-centered therapy is seen as a philosophical and theoretical offence by some. It is celebrated by others since it gets a foot in the door of the NHS in England ensuring patients will have the choice of person-centered therapy for depression, free as a statutory service; see Sanders and Hill (2014).

Counseling in Schools

A research program evaluating counseling in schools – an integrative person-centered approach specially developed for young people – started in 2002 at the University of Strathclyde, yielded positive results (Cooper, 2006). A further extended project funded by the Welsh Government also received positive evaluation (Pattison et al., 2009) and both of these, together with other research, were reviewed in terms of effectiveness by Cooper (2008). The work to establish a sound evidence base to present to governments continues, with recent developments including further publications and randomized controlled trials, including Cooper et al. (2010).

Building Bridges to Positive Psychology

There has been a massive research effort over the last decade which has begun to (re-)establish the person-centered approach to therapy alongside mainstream cognitive and behavioral approaches. This work has been as a result of the need to re-establish the person-centered approach as way of helping those in distress and as such the research findings reflect this in terms of the questions asked and measures used. However, as should be clear by now, this research is only able to paint a partial picture of the person-centered approach which hypothesizes not only that therapy will lead to a reduction in distress but also the facilitation of positive functioning (Joseph, 2015).

One of the most important recent developments has been the recognition that person-centered personality theory is essentially the same as the more recently developed Self-Determination Theory (SDT), which has proven to be a popular and widely adopted perspective within positive psychology (Patterson & Joseph, 2007a; Joseph & Murphy, 2013b; Sheldon, 2013). As such there is even greater research evidence in support of the person-centered approach than is generally recognized.

There is however the need for new research. Over the years in an attempt to maintain its contemporary relevance person-centered practitioners have often compromised their original positive psychological perspective to accommodate the language of disorder and deficit in order to establish the effectiveness of therapy against medical model constructs, as we have seen above, in order to for example establish statistical equivalence to other therapies, and to establish itself as a treatment for depression. However, now that positive psychology has become more widely accepted, the next generation of research will need to begin to take into account the positive psychological potential of the person-centered approach by introducing theoretically consistent measurement of well-being, authenticity, fully-functioning, and so on (Patterson & Joseph, 2007b; Joseph, 2015; Joseph & Patterson, Chapter 4, this volume).

Finally, one area of research in positive psychology that has advanced considerably over the past decade in a way consistent with the person-centered approach is the field of posttraumatic growth. Rogers spent several years working with and writing about war veterans and the impact of war on psychological functioning – work that came before the introduction of the concept of posttraumatic stress. However, although the person-centered approach predates the literature on psychological trauma that developed following the introduction of the term posttraumatic stress, it nonetheless is theoretically coherent and consistent with the contemporary literature to practice. Joseph (2004) has proposed a person-centered account of posttraumatic stress based in an examination of Rogers (1959) theoretical writings. In his account, posttraumatic stress can be thought of as a particular expression of incongruence. When traumatic events occur people are presented with overwhelming amounts of material that is in a direct conflict with their self-concept. When the self-concept is presented with such extreme dissonance then there is a risk of breakdown and disorganization of the self. Traumatic events can be considered to place such a significant threat to the self-concept that a process of disintegration occurs. An organismic theory would hypothesize that the natural and normal direction of rebuilding of the self-structure that takes place subsequently is posttraumatic growth and that this is a natural and normal process (Joseph & Linley, 2005; Joseph, 2011).

Conclusion

After treading water for decades, person-centered psychology is in much better health in the early twenty-first century. Dogged determination, continuous theory development and a sharpening of the focus of research onto the newer protocols of evidence-based practice have led to resurgence in many fields and recognition that the person-centered approach is an effective approach to developing helping relationships. A further seal of approval can be found in the acknowledgement of the central role of the relationship in therapy, observed and operationalized by Rogers over sixty years ago. The emergence of positive psychology has also led to new interest in the person-centered approach as it becomes recognized that the pioneers of humanistic psychology were the original positive psychologists and that person-centered therapy is an applied positive psychology (Joseph, 2015). Many clinical psychologists will already utilize person-centered helping relationships, but may not have appreciated that in doing so they are engaging in a form of positive clinical psychology. We conclude with a reminder that person-centered psychology is a positive psychology as a result of its core assumption that people are intrinsically motivated towards the personal growth of their potentialities, and that when facilitated in authentic, empathic and unconditionally accepting relationships, this directional force leads to greater positive functioning. As contemporary psychology moves beyond the medical model to look for new ways of thinking and working the person-centered approach offers an alternative positive psychological vision for helping people in distress to flourish.

Notes

1   Adapted from Sanders (2013).
2   Person-centered psychology has a problem with the Freudian concepts of the conscious and unconscious, with some theorists and writers being actively hostile. Rarely will a classical person-centered practitioner use the term, preferring to talk about experiences in awareness or out of awareness. This might sound like nit-picking word play, but the important point is the absolute refutation of the idea of a reservoir of unknown, unknowable, primal urges, revealed only by the interpretation of an expert analyst.
3   As a unified theory of functioning based on the meta-theory that people are intrinsically motivated towards personal development and growth it is almost identical to the self-determination theory (see, Patterson & Joseph, 2007a).
4   Research project at Mendota State Hospital, Wisconsin (Rogers et al., 1967) into the effects of psychotherapy with people diagnosed with schizophrenia.
5   This model is similar to the "research clinic" model currently gaining in popularity in the United Kingdom after being introduced by Robert Elliott at the University of Strathclyde.
6   Throughout, Elliott and his associates use a standard calculation for effect size and make corrections for therapist allegiance.
7   For information, see at: www.iapt.nhs.uk, last accessed June 13, 2013.
8   See at: www.nice.org.uk/nicemedia/pdf/CG90NICEguideline.pdf, last accessed June 13, 2013.

References

Allen, J. G., Fonagy, P., & Bateman, A. W. (2008). *Mentalizing in clinical practice.* Arlington, VA: American Psychiatric Publishing.

Barrett-Lennard, G. T. (1998). *Carl Rogers' helping system: Journey and substance.* London: Sage.

Bentall, R. P. (2003). *Madness explained: Psychosis and human nature.* London: Allen Lane/Penguin.

Bozarth, J. & Wilkins, P. (Eds.). (2001). *Rogers' therapeutic conditions, vol. 2: Unconditional positive regard.* Ross-on-Wye: PCCS Books.

Cooper, M. (2006). *Counselling in Schools Project, Glasgow, Phase II: Evaluation report.* University of Strathclyde: Glasgow.

Cooper, M. (2008). The effectiveness of humanistic counselling in UK secondary schools. In: M. Behr & J. H. D. Cornelius-White (Eds.), *Facilitating young people's development: International perspectives on person-centred theory and practice* (pp. 122–139). Ross-on-Wye: PCCS Books.

Cooper, M., O'Hara, M., Schmid, P. F., & Bohart, A.C. (Eds.). (2013). *The handbook of person-centred psychotherapy and counselling,* 2nd edn. Basingstoke: Palgrave Macmillan.

Cooper, M., Rowland, N., McArthur, K., Pattison, S., Cromarty, K., & Richards, K. (2010). Randomised controlled trial of school-based humanistic counselling for emotional distress in young people: Feasibility study and preliminary indications of efficacy. *Child and Adolescent Psychiatry and Mental Health, 4*(12). doi.10.1186/1753-2000-4-12.

Elliott, R. (2013). *Big data and little data*. Presentation to the British Association for the Person-Centred Approach Research Group, Edge Hill University, June 29, 2013.

Elliott, R. & Freire, B. (2008). *Person-centred experiential therapies are highly effective: Summary of the 2008 meta-analysis*. The British Association for the Person-Centred Approach, available at: http://www.bapca.org.uk/images/files/meta-summary.bapca.pdf, last accessed August 2, 2013.

Elliott, R. & Freire, E. (2010). The effectiveness of person-centred and experiential therapies: A review of the meta-analyses. In: M. Cooper, J. C. Watson, & D. Hölldampf (Eds.), *Person-centred and experiential therapies work: A review of the research on counselling, psychotherapy and related practices* (pp. 1–15). Ross-on-Wye: PCCS Books.

Elliott, R., Greenberg, L. S., & Lietaer, G. (2004). Research on experiential psychotherapies. In: M. J. Lambert (Ed.), *Bergin and Garfield's handbook of psychotherapy and behavior change*, 5th edn. (pp. 493–539). New York: John Wiley.

Elliott, R., Watson, J. C., Goldman, R. S., & Greenberg, L. S. (2004). *Learning emotion-focused therapy: The process-experiential approach to change*. Washington, DC: American Psychological Association.

Foucault, M. (1965). *Madness and civilization: A history of insanity in the age of reason*. Trans. R. Howard. New York: Vintage.

Haugh, S. & Merry, T. (Eds.). (2001). *Rogers' therapeutic conditions, vol. 2: Empathy*. Ross-on-Wye: PCCS Books.

Illich, I. (1976) *Medical nemesis: The expropriation of health*. New York: Pantheon Books.

Joseph, S. (2004). Client-centred therapy, posttraumatic stress disorder and post-traumatic growth: Theory and practice. *Psychology and Psychotherapy: Theory, Research, and Practice, 77*, 101–120.

Joseph, S. (2011). *What doesn't kill us: The new psychology of posttraumatic growth*. New York: Basic Books.

Joseph, S. (2015). *Positive therapy: Building bridges between positive psychology and person-centred psychotherapy*, 2nd edn. Hove: Routledge.

Joseph, S. & Linley, P. A. (2005). Positive adjustment to threatening events: An organismic valuing theory of growth through adversity. *Review of General Psychology, 9*, 262–280. doi.org/10.1037/1089-2680.9.3.262.

Joseph, S. & Murphy, D. (2013a). Person centered approach, positive psychology and relational helping: Building bridges. *Journal of Humanistic Psychology, 53*, 26–51. doi.10.1177/0022167812436426.

Joseph, S. & Murphy, D. (2013b). Person-centered theory encountering mainstream psychology: Building bridges and looking to the future. In: J. H. D. Cornelius-White, R. Motschnig-Pitrik., & M. Lux (Eds.), *Interdisciplinary handbook of the person-centered approach: Research and theory* (pp. 213–226). Springer: New York.

Joseph, S. & Worsley, R. (Eds.). (2005). *Person-centred psychopathology: A positive psychology of mental health*. Ross-on-Wye: PCCS Books.

Kirschenbaum, H. (2007). *The life and work of Carl Rogers*. Ross-on-Wye: PCCS Books.

Kirtner, W. L. & Cartwright, D. S. (1958). Success and failure in client-centred therapy as a function of initial in-therapy behavior. *Journal of Consulting Psychology, 22*(5), 329–333.

Mearns, D. (1997) *Person-centred counselling training*. London: Sage.

Mearns, D. & Thorne, B. (2000). *Person-centred therapy today: New frontiers in theory and practice*. London: Sage.

Mearns, D. & Thorne, B. (2007). *Person-centred counselling in action*, 3rd edn. London: Sage.

Mosher, L. R. (1999). Soteria and other alternatives to acute psychiatric hospitalization: A personal and professional view. *Changes, 17*(1), 35–51.

Patterson, T. G. & Joseph, S. (2007a). Person-centered personality theory: Support from self-determination theory and positive psychology. *Journal of Humanistic Psychology, 47*, 117–139. doi.10.1177/0022167806293008.

Patterson, T. G. & Joseph, S. (2007b). Outcome measurement in person-centred practice. In: R. Worsley & S. Joseph (Eds.), *Person-centred practice: Case studies in positive psychology* (pp. 200–215). Ross-on-Wye: PCCS Books.

Pattison, S., Rowland, N., Cromarty, K., Richards, K., Jenkins, P. L., Cooper, M., & Couchman, A., et al. (2009). *Counselling in schools: A research study into services for children and young people in Wales*. Lutterworth, Leicestershire: BACP.

Rapley, M., Moncrieff, J., & Dillon, J. (2011). *Demedicalising misery: Psychiatry, psychology and the human condition.* Basingstoke: Palgrave Macmillan.

Rashid, T. (2015). Strength-based assessment. In: S. Joseph (Ed.), *Positive psychology in practice: Promoting human flourishing in work, health, education, and everyday life,* 2nd edn. (pp. 519–542). Hoboken, NJ: John Wiley.

Read, J. & Dillon, J. (2013). *Models of madness: Psychological, social and biological approaches to psychosis,* 2nd edn. Hove: Routledge.

Rogers, C. R. (1939). *The clinical treatment of the problem child.* Boston, MA: Houghton Mifflin.

Rogers, C. R. (1942). *Counseling and psychotherapy.* Boston, MA: Houghton Mifflin.

Rogers, C. R. (1951). *Client-centered therapy.* Boston, MA: Houghton Mifflin.

Rogers, C. R. (1957). The necessary and sufficient conditions of therapeutic personality change. *Journal of Consulting Psychology, 21,* 95–103. Reprinted in H. Kirschenbaum & V. L. Henderson (Eds.) (1990) *The Carl Rogers reader* (pp. 219–35). London: Constable.

Rogers, C. R. (1959). A theory of therapy, personality and interpersonal relationships, as developed in the client-centered framework. In: S. Koch (Ed.), *Psychology: A study of science, vol. 3: Formulations of the person and the social context* (pp. 184–256). New York: McGraw-Hill.

Rogers, C. R. (1961). *On becoming a person.* Boston, MA: Houghton Mifflin.

Rogers, C. R., Gendlin, E. T., Kiesler, D. J., & Truax, C.B. (1967). *The therapeutic relationship and its impact: A study of psychotherapy with schizophrenics.* Madison, WI: University of Wisconsin Press.

Romme, M. & Escher, S. (2000). *Making sense of voices: A guide for mental health professionals working with voice-hearers.* London: Mind.

Rundle, K. (2010). *Person-centred therapy and hearing voices.* Presentation at the World Hearing Voices Congress, Nottingham, November 4.

Sanders, P. (2006a). Why person-centred therapists must reject the medicalisation of distress. *Self & Society, 34,* 32–39.

Sanders, P. (2006b). *The person-centred counselling primer.* Ross-on-Wye: PCCS Books.

Sanders, P. (Ed.), (2012). *The tribes of the person-centred nation: An introduction to the schools of therapy related to the person-centred approach,* 2nd edn. Ross-on-Wye: PCCS Books.

Sanders, P. (2013). *Person-centred therapy theory and practice in the 21st century.* Ross-on-Wye: PCCS Books.

Sanders, P. & Hill, A. (2014). *Counselling for depression: A guide for practitioners.* London: Sage.

Sheldon, K. (2013). Self-determination theory, person-centered approaches and personal goals: Exploring the links. In: J. H. D. Cornelius-White, R. Motschnig-Pitrik., & M. Lux (Eds.), *Interdisciplinary handbook of the person-centered approach: research and theory* (pp. 227–244). Springer: New York.

Shlien, J. M. ([1989] 2001) Response to Boy's symposium on psychodiagnosis. *Person-Centered Review, 4*(7), 157–62. Reproduced in D. J. Cain (Ed.). (2002). *Classics in the person-centered approach* (pp. 400–402). Ross-on-Wye: PCCS Books.

Shlien, J. M. (2003). A criterion of psychological health. In: P. Sanders (Ed.), *To lead an honourable life: Invitations to think about Client-Centered Therapy and the Person-Centered Approach* (pp. 15–18). Ross-on-Wye: PCCS Books.

Tarrier, N. (2004). The use of coping strategies in self-regulation in the treatment of psychosis. In: Morrison, A. P. (Ed.), *A casebook of cognitive therapy for psychosis.* Hove: Brunner-Routledge.

Traynor, W., Elliott, R., & Cooper, M. (2011). Helpful factors and outcomes in person-centered therapy with clients who experience psychotic process: Therapists' perspectives. *Person-Centered and Experiential Psychotherapies,10*(2), 89–104.

Tudor, K. & Worrall, M. (2006). *Person-centred therapy: A clinical philosophy.* London: Routledge.

Wood, A. M., Linley, P. A., Maltby, J., Baliousis, M., & Joseph, S. (2008). The authentic personality: A theoretical and empirical conceptualization and the development of the authenticity scale. *Journal of Counselling Psychology, 55,* 385–399. doi.10.1037/0022-0167.55.3.385.

Wyatt, G. (Ed.), (2001). *Rogers' therapeutic conditions, vol. 1: Congruence.* Ross-on-Wye: PCCS Books.

Wyatt, G. & Sanders, P. (Eds.), (2002). *Rogers' therapeutic conditions, vol. 4: Contact and perception.* Ross-on-Wye: PCCS Books.

29

Acceptance and Commitment Therapy

A Contextual View of "Positive" and "Negative" as Applied to Positive Clinical Psychology

Timothy K. Feeney and Steven C. Hayes

Clinical and positive psychology have at times been at odds with one another. Part of the contribution of positive psychology has been to help rein in the excesses of a pathology, in which the promotion of human functioning is reduced in the attempt to eliminate abnormal processes. Neither clinical psychology nor positive psychology are monoliths, however, and it is not by accident that a short chapter on Acceptance and Commitment Therapy (ACT, said as a word, not initials) (Hayes, Strosahl, & Wilson, 2012) is in this volume.

There is a growing body of work in clinical psychology that is based on normal psychological processes, and that balances concerns over what is painful or difficult with a focus on aspirations, strengths, and values. These approaches have dominantly emerged from a more holistic, contextual, or pragmatic worldview, as contrasted to a more mechanistic or reductionistic approach. By attending to the functioning of a whole person, with a history, living in the natural and social environment, what is considered "positive" and "negative" can itself be placed into a larger and more functional context. Sometimes what appears to be horrific can be an unexpected source of thriving, as when people turn illness, death, or loss into sources of growth and or the focus of newfound meaning and purpose. Sometimes what appears to be positive can be an unexpected source of misery, as when people try to grab onto positive experiences as a way of denying the very presence of difficult memories. Thus, while this chapter examines a clinical approach that has been shown to be useful not only for addressing human suffering but also for promoting human growth; it is also based on a set of philosophical assumptions and theoretical principles that help us think more deeply about the context in which positive psychology is pursued. Inside this dialectic we hope ACT can contribute to the maturation and development of Positive Clinical Psychology.

Waves of Behavior Therapy

Behavior therapy is based on a functional and monistic scientific approach that has contributed considerably to our understanding of human action. Although in the history of behavior therapy there has long been an emphasis on a constructional approach to human functioning (e.g., Goldiamond, 1974) the "first order change" focus of behavior therapy undeniably often led to

The Wiley Handbook of Positive Clinical Psychology, First Edition. Edited by Alex M. Wood and Judith Johnson.
© 2016 John Wiley & Sons, Ltd. Published 2016 by John Wiley & Sons, Ltd.

an over emphasis on the reduction of problematic behavior. As behavior therapy has developed, however, it has gone through multiple iterations and in its modern form is increasingly reaching a place that is more obviously consistent with the tenets of Positive Clinical Psychology.

The First Wave

Behavior therapy arose out of a need for the field of clinical psychology to be more closely oriented with other scientific disciplines. The field at the time was predominantly psychoanalytic and humanistic, and largely eschewed experimental science. Behavior therapy provided theories that were more parsimonious and that could take human complexity and relate it to behavioral principles that emerged from the laboratory. A classic example is the case of Little Hans, in which the fantastic theorizing of Freud occasioned by the case ([1928] 1955) could be explained by behavior therapists (e.g., Wolpe & Rachman, 1960) with relatively simple behavioral principles from the laboratory (e.g., Ayllon, Haughton, & Hughes, 1965). Behavior therapy rallied around two basic ideas: services delivered to people should be carefully tested in controlled psychological research; and clinical methods should be based on scientific principles derived from basic knowledge about psychological functioning (Franks & Wilson, 1974). Using basic behavioral principles drawn largely from the animal laboratory, such as reinforcement and stimulus control, a wide variety of new interventions focused on functional classes of behavior were crafted.

Behavior therapy did a large service to the field of clinical psychology by bringing it closer to experimental scientific traditions. The deeper clinical traditions contained both wisdom and nonsense, and the behavior therapy tradition did a service by demanding the highest levels of evidence. What behavior therapy in its earliest forms did not do, however, was to arrive as an approach to human language and cognition that afforded a proper place for human goals, values, and aspirations. This was the very issue that led those with more humanistic leanings to conclude that human psychology demanded a different form of science. For example, when trying to understand such issues, Abraham Maslow wrote "I became interested in certain psychological problems, and found that they could not be answered or managed well by the classical scientific structure of the time (the behavioristic, positivistic, 'scientific,' value free, mechanomorphic psychology). I was raising legitimate questions and had to invent another approach to psychological problems in order to deal with them" (1971, p. 3). Carl Rogers (1964) suggested similarly that the "fundamental discrepancy between the individual's concept and what he is actually experiencing, between the intellectual structure of his values and the valuing process going on unrecognized within – this is a part of the fundamental estrangement of modern man from himself" (p. 163). Behavior therapists themselves soon sensed the same general problems, and tried to do something about it.

The Second Wave

It was not long before behavior therapists themselves felt that basic behavioral principles did not provide an adequate guide for predicting and changing human language and cognition. Seemingly left with no other alternative, clinicians and researchers began developing interventions based on clinical theories of cognition (e.g., Beck, 1976), giving rise to cognitive behavior therapy (CBT).

CBT researchers quickly found that people who experience suffering often do indeed have unusual thought patterns. A central focus of the second wave of the behavior therapy tradition was the idea that distorted and dysfunctional beliefs caused psychopathology, and needed to be directly targeted for change before behavioral change was likely. The label "cognitive-behavior therapy" was an attempt to reconcile the differences between the first and second waves of behavior therapy in an additive fashion. Both behavioral and cognitive techniques would be used, although the unifying model of change quickly became oriented toward cognitive processes and not behavioral principles. The task of traditional "second wave" CBT became and has remained "to help the patient recognize his or her idiosyncratic style of thinking and modify it through the application of evidence and logic" (Leahy, 2003, p. 1) so as "to realign their thinking with reality" (Clark, 1995, p. 155).

The CBT methods generated by this organizing principle were empirically successful, but they tended to be large packages, containing a variety of cognitive and behavioral methods. It took many years before the field at large noticed two disturbing things. First, cognitive techniques generally did not add much to clinical outcomes above and beyond the behavioral components included in these packages. Even major cognitive therapists began to conclude that there is "no additive benefit to providing cognitive interventions in cognitive therapy" (Dobson & Khatri, 2000, p. 913). A comprehensive review of the major studies available (Longmore & Worrell, 2007) concluded that there was "little evidence that specific cognitive interventions significantly increase the effectiveness of the therapy" (p. 173).

The second disturbing finding was that the people who got better in traditional CBT were not necessarily those who changed their thinking. This is normally studied through mediational studies: did a change in a theoretically critical process predict outcome changes? A recent review of the relevant studies (Longmore & Worrell, 2007) found that "there is little empirical support for the role of cognitive change as causal in the symptomatic improvements achieved in CBT" (p. 173). These anomalies set the stage for changes in the CBT tradition.

In the context of the present chapter it is worth noting that although trying to target cognition was a step forward for the field, the focus tended to be negative in nature. The core agenda was often explicitly eliminative in nature (i.e., detecting, challenging, disputing, and changing problematic thoughts). Since reducing problematic thought patterns did not necessarily lead to positive outcome, as the meditational studies revealed, focusing on correcting or reducing problematic thought patterns may have overridden opportunities for growth.

The Third Wave

The third wave of behavior therapy (Hayes, 2004) has shifted the focus from targeting the form of experience (i.e., the topographical characteristics of thoughts or feelings) to targeting the person's relationship to their own experience. The veracity of thoughts or the superficial negativity of feelings began to receive less emphasis, and the persons' openness, acceptance, or awareness of thinking or feeling received more. The development of clinical approaches began to shift focus to the context in which thoughts and feelings occurred, and the functions they served in that context, instead of assuming the importance of an eliminative agenda.

The third wave is comprised of a wide variety of treatment modalities such as Mindfulness-Based Stress Reduction (MBSR) (Kabat-Zinn, 1990), Mindfulness-Based Cognitive Therapy (MBCT) (Segal, Williams, & Teasdale, 2002), Mindfulness-Based Relapse Prevention (MBRP) (Witkiewitz, Marlatt, & Walker, 2005), Metacognitive Therapy (MCT) (Wells, 2000), Integrative Behavioral Couple Therapy (IBCT) (Jacobson & Christensen, 1998), Functional Analytic Psychotherapy (FAP) (Kohlenberg & Tsai, 1991), or Dialectical Behavior Therapy (DBT) (Linehan, 1993), among several others. All of these methods emphasize the importance of openness, awareness, and values-based action (Hayes, Villatte, Levin, & Hildebrandt, 2011) – processes that are more consistent with the Positive Clinical Psychology position and that are central in another third-wave approach that is the focus of this chapter, Acceptance and Commitment Therapy or ACT (Hayes, 2012; by tradition, the term "ACT" is said as one word).

Acceptance and Commitment Therapy

ACT began in the late 1970s and early 1980s after a series of studies on cognitive methods, including an early component analysis of Beck's treatment, uniformly failed to support the cognitive model (see Hayes, 2008, for a summary). In the early 1980s we decided instead to focus on an interesting finding from behavior analysis: if human beings are guided by verbal rules they tend to become insensitive to how their behavior actually relates to outcomes (see Hayes, 1989, for a book length review of this line of research). We developed a set of methods designed to change the way language works so as to undermine excessive rule control and to teach people to relate to their own private experiences in a more accepting and disentangled way. We tested this new approach in an open trial (Hayes, 1987), and then conducted three small studies comparing it with major CBT protocols of the day, in depression, pain, and weight control. All three studies showed different processes of change, and two showed better outcomes. Parts of the depression study were published quickly (Zettle & Hayes, 1986); the pain study was published 16 years later, after our development work on ACT was finished (Hayes et al., 1999); the weight study was never published but instead the protocol was revised and published in recent years (Lillis, Hayes, Bunting, & Masuda, 2009). Having convinced ourselves that an alternative model might succeed, we described it (Hayes, 1984, 1987), and spent nearly 15 years working on the foundations we thought would be needed for such a radical departure to be understood. These foundational matters included development of the basic theory of cognition, Relational Frame Theory (RFT) (Hayes, Barnes-Holmes, & Roche, 2001); explication of the guiding philosophy of science, functional contextualism (Hayes, 1993), development of measures of psychological flexibility (e.g., Hayes et al., 2004), and the development of treatment components. Finally, we described what had been done in book form (Hayes, Strosahl, & Wilson, 1999) and returned to outcome research. At the time of the initial book only two small randomized trials were available. Now, 14 years later, there are 105 randomized trials involving several thousand patients, in addition to scores of component studies (see Levin, Hildebrandt, Lillis, & Hayes, 2012, for a recent meta-analysis), and hundreds of assessment studies, open trials, case studies, and studies on the basic theory of cognition underlying ACT.

The Psychological Flexibility Model

Verbal relations can readily lead to the domination of verbal regulation over behavior, without awareness of the underlying relational process itself: what is termed "cognitive fusion." Even a single word can lead to fusion if the functions of the referents of the word dominate, but the ability of verbal relations to form into networks multiplies this problem exponentially. The human mind looks like a spider's web of stories, beliefs, and assumptions, ready to ensnare the unwary. People often act in a way that is consistent with these verbal networks, regardless of what the current environment affords.

Language is dominantly used for problem solving – not becoming present or taking the perspective of others. In a problem-solving mode of mind, integrating the past and future into a story is strengthened – in part because that is how problems are solved verbally.

People tell stories about who they are and how their life works. As this occurs, we form a "conceptualized self." It is not a big step for people to begin to take themselves to *be* these stories and anything that threatens to violate this conceptualized self becomes emotionally aversive. It becomes more important to defend a verbal view of oneself (e.g., being a victim, never being angry, being broken, being wonderful, etc.) than to learn how to be effective in the world.

Due to the temporal and comparative relations present in human language, private reactions, including so-called "negative" emotions, are verbally predicted and evaluated (e.g., noticing "I'm anxious" carries with it an implicit "and that is bad"). These predictions and evaluations pull for the usual problem solving mode of mind to be applied within. As a result, people tend to focus on how to control emotional and cognitive events as a primary goal and metric of successful living. Experiential avoidance refers to the attempt to alter the form, frequency, or situational sensitivity of private events (Hayes, Wilson, Gifford, Follette, & Strosahl, 1996). It is arguably the single most destructive feature of human psychology (for a summary of data on that point, see Hayes, Luoma, Bond, Masuda, & Lillis, 2006). Attempts to avoid uncomfortable private events tends to narrow behavioral repertoires, and to increase the functional importance of these negative targets. Ironically this can increase their magnitude and frequency. For example when anxiety becomes an object of control it is often verbally linked to conceptualized negative outcomes which tend to elicit anxiety.

Psychological inflexibility is the result of this process, as the long-term desired qualities of life (i.e., values) and committed actions that might lead in that direction take a backseat to more immediate goals of avoiding psychological pain, being right, or defending a conceptualized self. Important positive aspects of human language – contacting a deeper sense of self, making values based choices, linking behavior flexibly to values – are overwhelmed by these negative aspects.

These processes – cognitive fusion, loss of the now, the conceptualized self, experiential avoidance, lack of contact with values, lack of flexible action, and psychological inflexibility – consti tute an analysis of the core of human difficulty from an ACT perspective. Figure 29.1 shows all these processes, now phrased in positive terms. They are meant to serve as middle-level functional terms, bound together into a kind of easily understood "operating system" for clinicians. They are "middle-level" in the sense that they are not common sense or merely clinical terms – but nor are they fully technical terms. Rather, they stand atop the complexity of behavioral principles. Each is described in the following section.

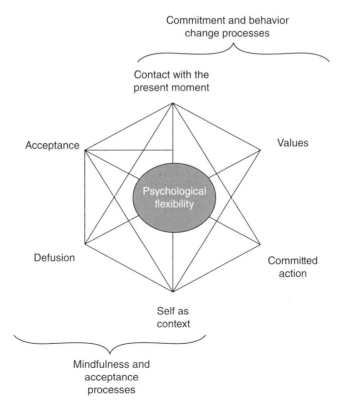

Figure 29.1 The ACT model of psychological flexibility.

Acceptance

Acceptance involves the active and aware embrace of those private events occasioned by one's history and the current circumstance without unnecessary attempts to change their frequency or form, especially when doing so would cause psychological harm. For example, anxiety patients are taught to feel anxiety, as a feeling, with openness and curiosity and without needless defense; pain patients are given methods that encourage them to let go of a struggle with pain, and so on. Acceptance in ACT is not an end in itself. Rather acceptance is fostered as a method of increasing values-based action.

Cognitive Defusion

Cognitive defusion and mindfulness techniques attempt to alter the undesirable functions of thoughts and other private events, rather than trying to alter their form, frequency or situational sensitivity. Said another way, ACT attempts to change the way one *interacts with* or *relates to* thoughts by creating contexts in which their unhelpful functions are diminished. There are scores of such techniques that have been developed for a wide variety of clinical presentations (Hayes & Strosahl, 2005). For example, a negative thought could be watched dispassionately, repeated out loud until only its sound remains, or treated as an externally observed event by giving it a shape, size, color, speed, or form. A person could thank their mind for such an interesting thought, label the process of thinking ("I am having the thought that I am no good"), or examine the historical thoughts, feelings, and memories that occur while they experience that thought. Such procedures attempt to reduce the literal quality of the thought, weakening the tendency to treat the thought as what it refers to ("I am no good") rather than what it is directly experienced to be (e.g., the thought "I am no good"). The result of defusion is usually a decrease in believability of, or attachment to, private events rather than an immediate change in their frequency.

Being Present

ACT promotes ongoing nonjudgmental contact with psychological and environmental events as they occur, with the ability to focus or shift attention in response to task demands. The goal is to have clients experience the world within and without more directly and voluntarily so that behavior can be more flexible and consistent with underlying values.

Self-as-Context (the Noticing Sense of Self)

Because of relational frames such as *I* versus *You*, *Now* versus *Then*, and *Here* versus *There*, human language leads to a sense of self as a locus or perspective, and provides a transcendent, spiritual side to normal verbal humans. This idea was one of the seeds from which both ACT and RFT grew (Hayes, 1984), and there is now growing evidence of its importance to language functions such as empathy, theory of mind, sense of self, and the like (e.g., McHugh, Barnes-Holmes, & Barnes-Holmes, 2004). In brief the idea is that "I" emerges over large sets of exemplars of perspective-taking relations (termed in RFT "deictic relations"), but since this sense of self is a context for verbal knowing, not the content of that knowing, its limits cannot be consciously known. Self as context is important in part because from this standpoint, one can be aware of one's own flow of experiences without attachment to them or an investment in which particular experiences occur. Thus, defusion and acceptance is fostered by this sense of self. Self as context is fostered in ACT by mindfulness exercises, metaphors, and experiential processes.

Together these four processes (acceptance, defusion, the now, a noticing self) provide a working definition of mindfulness within ACT. In an ACT model, mindfulness is not a goal in itself, rather, it allows for a shift in attention to the right in the hexagon, toward commitment and behavior change processes.

Values

Values are chosen qualities of ongoing patterns of action. Valuing in that sense can never be "finished" or obtained as an object but they can be instantiated moment by moment and thus they establish real reinforcers available in the present moment as part of those behavioral patterns. For example, a value of being a loving person can never be finished, but it makes sense of acts of kindness and attention in the moment. ACT uses a variety of exercises to help a client choose life directions in various domains (e.g., family, career, spirituality) while undermining verbal processes that might lead to choices based on avoidance, social compliance, or fusion (e.g., "I should value X" or "A good person would value Y" or "My mother wants me to value Z"). In ACT, acceptance, defusion, being present, and so on are not ends in themselves; rather they clear the path for a more vital, values-consistent life.

Committed Action

Finally, ACT encourages the development of larger and larger patterns of effective action linked to chosen values. In this regard, ACT looks very much like traditional behavior therapy, and almost any behaviorally coherent behavior change method can be fitted into an ACT protocol, including exposure, skills acquisition, shaping methods, goal setting, and the like. Unlike values, which are constantly instantiated but never achieved as an object, concrete goals that are values-consistent can be achieved and ACT protocols almost always involve therapy work and homework linked to short, medium, and long-term behavior change goals. Behavior change efforts in turn lead to contact with psychological barriers that are addressed through other ACT processes (acceptance, defusion, and so on).

Psychological Flexibility as a Whole

Together these six processes define psychological flexibility: the ability as a conscious human being to come into the present, experiencing thoughts and feelings as they are, not as they say they are, and to persist or change in behavior in the service of chosen values.

Psychological Flexibility and Positive Clinical Psychology

Positive psychology has historically been at odds with clinical psychology due to the latter's focus generally being placed on problematic or abnormal psychological processes, to the detriment of giving proper attention and due weight to the promotion of healthy aspects of human functioning. It is important, however, to consider these issues in context rather than taking a more superficial or formal approach. Experiences can be negative in the sense that they are painful or unwelcome, they contribute to life trajectories that are undesired, or that effort is spent trying to get rid of them (i.e., to "negate" them). Each of these scenarios are different and "negative" events function differently based on these different senses and their combinations.

The same is true of the "positive" aspects of one's internal experience. For example, high self-esteem has the potential to restrict learning when mistakes are made (Bond et al., 2011).

High levels of dispositional positive affect have at times been associated with detrimental outcomes such as reduced task performance, biased recall of information, or increased impulsivity (Baron, Hmieleski, & Henry, 2012). Any value or virtue, if pursued in an eliminative or rigid way, has costs. For example, Wood, Perunovic, and Lee (2009) found that despite the fact that positive self-statements are commonly used, generally believed to be useful, and correlate with self-esteem, they tend to be harmful for participants with low baseline levels of low self-esteem. For precisely those who most needed the help, repeating a positive self-statement such as "I'm a lovable person" was actually deleterious, especially if participants believed that these positive self-statements were true. In other words interventions that are formally "positive" may or may not function positively.

The Role of Context

The problem here is a failure to appreciate the role of context. Kashdan (2010) provides multiple exemplars of where "positive" and "negative" ways of behaving and experiencing emotion are context specific. For example, when put into a landlord and tenant role, whether an individual will behave in ways labeled as "negative" or "positive" are dependent on their goal. One is more likely to behave angrily when it is appropriate to collect a debt from a tenant quickly, but more likely to behave with "positive" emotion when the goal is to keep their tenant long term. The utility of any given emotion depends on role and purpose. This appears to be a more general point that deeply resonates with the psychological flexibility model. Striving toward a valued life requires agility: emotionally, cognitively, and behaviorally. There is no universal strategy for happiness or psychological health when we think of experiences in a formal or topographical way.

A study underlining the importance of psychological flexibility was conducted by Bonanno, Papa, Lalande, Westphal, and Coifman (2004) where students were asked to view pictures considered to be emotionally evocative, and were required to either (a) openly communicate their feelings, or (b) attempt to conceal their emotions in a suppressive manner from an observer. What they found was that students who experienced a greater difficulty with expressing emotions in condition (a) and an easier time suppressing their positive emotions in condition (b) experienced elevated levels of distress in one to three months following the tragic events of 9/11. These researchers created a composite score of psychological flexibility based on their tasks and found that those who scored as having higher levels of psychological flexibility had a much easier time adjusting to life over the following two years. A meta-analysis of self-report levels of psychological flexibility show an overall correlation of .42 with beneficial life outcomes such as increased job performance and mental health (Hayes et al., 2006).

Curiosity

Another way to think of emotional and cognitive agility is to focus on how curious people are about their own experiences, and on the world around them. Todd Kashdan defines the construct of curiosity as, "a positive emotional-motivational system associated with the recognition, pursuit, and self-regulation of novel and challenging opportunities" (Kashdan, Rose, & Fincham, 2014). The construct is composed of (a) proclivity toward exploration of new information and experience, and (b) the tendency to become immersed in intrinsically reinforcing activities. Defined that way, curiosity is a malleable behavior that can be promoted. A curious approach to experience is related to a wide variety of positive effects, but it is inherently more flexible. It is not possible to be curious only about positive experiences while attempting to ignore or deny negative ones. That is exactly the kind of judgmental process that interferes with an open posture of curiosity.

Creating an Upside for a Dark Side

There is a phrase that is common in ACT: in your pain you find your values, in your values you find your pain. In other words, psychological pain is the flip side of caring. Love implies loss; depression implies a desire to feel; social anxiety implies a yearning to connect.

This is the sense in which third wave behavior therapy is inherently part of positive psychology. Painful experiences are "negative" in an evaluative sense, but if they are used to connect with values, meaning and purpose, and to increase the capacity to feel without needless avoidance and entanglement, they can contribute to positive life trajectories. Handled properly pain can cast a light into darkness, and help people understand what they most deeply care about. Doing so requires the skills that psychological flexibility recommends: being able to be nonjudgmental, to experience the echoes of one's history without entanglement or needless defense; to be able to mindfully shift attention toward values, and to pursue them in an organized way.

This possibility has been explored empirically. For example, a recent study used ACT to coach patients who were survivors of colorectal cancer (Hawkes et al., 2013). The likelihood of successful long-term health outcomes for patients surviving colorectal cancer is determined in part by positive changes in multiple health behaviors such as exercise, diet, weight management, smoking cessation, and moderation in alcohol consumption, in addition to psychosocial changes such as post-traumatic growth, increased sense of spirituality, or reductions in psychological distress. In this study, 410 colorectal cancer survivors were randomized to 11 sessions of telephone-based ACT health coaching over six months or usual care. In addition to significant differences at a one-year follow up for physical activity, body mass, and fat intake, those in the ACT condition showed higher quality of life, and greater psychological acceptance and mindfulness.

Of most direct relevant for the present argument, ACT participants also showed great post-traumatic growth at six and 12 months. Posttraumatic growth was assessed with the Posttraumatic Growth Inventory (Tedeschi & Calhoun, 1996), which assesses growth in the areas of relating to others, seeing new possibilities, finding personal strengths, spiritual change, and appreciation for life. The differences in the total scores are shown in Figure 29.2; four of the five subscales also showed significant differences. The strongest changes were shown in relating to others (e.g., items describing "a sense of closeness with others"), and new possibilities (e.g., "I developed new interests"). The overall follow up changes in post-traumatic growth were significantly mediated by changes in acceptance and mindfulness.

In the context of the present chapter what this means is that changes produced by an ACT intervention in psychological flexibility processes such as being more mindfully aware of and

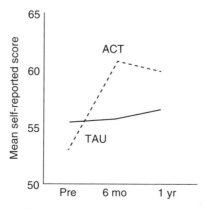

Figure 29.2 Mean Post-Traumatic Growth Inventory Scores (possible range 0–105) in the two conditions from pre- to one-year follow-up.

accepting of painful emotions and difficult thoughts, turned the shock and challenge of a life-threatening disease into positive psychological growth. Instead of trying to eliminate and negate pain, it was integrated into a values-based path of transformation.

Clinical Utility of ACT

The breadth of applicability of psychological flexibility is shown by the breadth of application of ACT. Since publication of the first book, over 100 randomized controlled trials have been published. It is the range of problems addressed that is most stunning. The existing base of controlled studies covers major areas of physical health challenges (e.g., diabetes management, chronic pain, tinnitus, dealing with breast cancer, coping with epilepsy, coping with cerebral palsy); health and wellness challenges (e.g., exercise, worksite stress, weight management, smoking cessation, employee burnout); social problems (e.g., racial prejudice, self-stigma in stigmatized groups, stigma toward people with psychological disorders); learning, playing, and functions (e.g., learning new therapy methods, playing competitive chess, functioning well at work); and mental health or substance use issues of virtually every major type and kind. It is also startling how many different modalities can be used – face to face individual work, groups, books, websites, telephone coaching, smart phone apps –- and from tiny interventions to extended packages. Meta-analyses of randomized trials (e.g., Hayes et al., 2006; Ost, 2008; Powers & Emmelkamp, 2009; A-Tjak, Davis, Morina, Powers, Smits, & Emmelkamp, in press) have shown between group effect sizes in the .5 to 1.0 range, depending on problem and comparison condition.

Benefits of Promoting Psychological Flexibility through ACT

ACT was originally developed to be utilized for individuals experiencing psychological problems, but its underlying theory was based on normal psychological processes. This has made it easy to expand the focus of ACT to be utilized as a preventative intervention or as a way to promote human growth.

The use of psychotherapy methods in prevention is not a unique feature of ACT (e.g., depression prevention programs) (Stice, Shaw, Bohon, & Marti, 2009), but the range of areas that have been addressed make it noteworthy. In studies of selective prevention (i.e., prevention for groups that are at greater risk for some psychopathology than others) ACT has been utilized to prevent stress, burnout, and increase psychological flexibility in nurses (Djordjevic & Frögéli, 2012); to prevent depression in college students (Levin, Pistorello, Seeley, & Hayes 2014); to prevent depression and anxiety in K-12 teachers (Jeffcoat & Hayes, 2012); to prevent burnout and to improve general mental health in social workers (Brinkborg, Michanek, Hesser, & Berglund, 2011); to improve general mental health in a group of employees from a media organization (Bond & Bunce 2000); to decrease stigma and burnout in substance abuse counselors (Hayes et al., 2004); to prevent depression and anxiety in Japanese college students (Muto, Hayes, & Jeffcoat, 2011); to prevent body dissatisfaction and disordered eating behaviors in individuals who had undergone bariatric surgery (Weineland, Hayes, & Dahl, 2012); and to prevent burnout in therapists and other professionals (Bethay, Wilson, Schnetzer, & Nassar, 2013; Lloyd, Bond, & Flaxman, 2013).

In terms of indicated prevention (i.e., prevention for groups that are high risk and showing preliminary signs/symptoms) ACT has been utilized to decrease sick days and lower utilization of medical services in public health service employees (Dahl, Wilson, & Nilsson 2004); to prevent re-hospitalization in patients with psychotic symptoms (Bach & Hayes, 2002); to improve diabetic control in patients with diabetes (Gregg, Callaghan, Hayes, & Glenn-Lawson, 2007); to increase health behaviors in at-risk cardiac patients (Goodwin, Forman, Herbert, Butryn, & Ledley, 2012); to prevent increase in depression and anxiety (Bohlmeijer, Fledderus, Rokx, & Pieterse, 2011); to prevent weight gain in female college students (Katterman, Goldstein, Butryn, Forman, & Lowe, 2014); to prevent disability in patients with chronic headache (Mo'tamedi, Rezaiemaram, & Tavallaie, 2012); and to increase physical activity in women attempting to lose weight (Tapper, Shaw, Ilsley, Hill, Bond, & Moore, 2009).

The extension to human growth and prosperity is somewhat more unusual. For instance, Chase, Houmanfar, Hayes, Ward, Vilardaga, and Follette (2013) utilized an online ACT-based values training with a sample of undergraduate psychology majors. When compared with a goal-setting program and waitlist control, the combination of goal-setting and 15 minutes of ACT-based values work significantly increased students' GPA over the next semester. Butryn, Forman, Hoffman, Shaw, and Juarascio (2011) conducted two two-hour group sessions held two weeks apart that utilized the ACT model and compared that with a psychoeducation group on exercise (e.g., benefits, safety, injury prevention) and found that the ACT group had significantly more visits to a campus athletic center. Luoma and Vilardaga (2013) conducted a two-day ACT workshop for therapists and showed significant increases in psychological flexibility, sense of personal accomplishment, and decreases in therapist burnout with additional gains for those with added six 30-minute ACT-based phone consultations. ACT has also been used to help competitive chess players improve their game, avoid impulsive emotion-driven moves and leading to objective improvements in the international chess ladder for those exposed to the intervention (Ruiz & Luciano, 2009, 2012).

Concluding Remarks

The behavioral and cognitive therapies have not historically been central to positive psychology, but the newest generation of these methods have found a way to address clinical problems in a fashion that can be linked to human thriving. In this brief chapter we focused on ACT as a prime example of these new methods. A growing body of research suggests that people can address negative thoughts and feelings in a non-avoidant and mindful fashion, which in turn actually empowers a behavioral focus on meaning and purpose. The result is a set of methods for human empowerment and prosperity that has application in the clinic and far beyond. "Positive" and "negative" features of human experience need to be defined functionally and contextually. The work on ACT suggests that human thriving is supported by emotional, cognitive, and behavioral agility – human beings can learn to walk through the ups and downs of their own experience, buoyed up by the deeply humanizing lessons in both of these sides of life.

References

A-Tjak, J. G. L., Davis, M. L., Morina, N., Powers, M. B., Smits, J. A. J., & Emmelkamp, P. M. G. (in press). A meta-analysis of the efficacy of Acceptance and Commitment Therapy for clinically relevant mental and physical health problems. *Psychotherapy and Psychosomatics*. doi.10.1159/000365764.

American Psychiatric Association. (2013). *Diagnostic and statistical manual of mental disorders*, 5th edn. Arlington, VA: American Psychiatric Publishing.

Ayllon, T., Haughton, E., & Hughes, H. B. (1965). Interpretation of symptoms: Fact or fiction? *Behaviour Research and Therapy*, 3, 1–7. doi.10.1016/0005-7967(65)90037-9.

Bach, P. & Hayes, S. C. (2002). The use of acceptance and commitment therapy to prevent the rehospitalization of psychotic patients: A randomized controlled trial. *Journal of Consulting and Clinical Psychology*, 70(5), 1129. doi.10.1037/0022-006X.70.5.1129.

Baron, R. A., Hmieleski, K. M., & Henry, R. A. (2012). Entrepreneurs' dispositional positive affect: The potential benefits – and potential costs – of being "up". *Journal of Business Venturing*, *27*, 310–324. doi.10.1016/j.jbusvent.2011.04.002.

Beck, A. T. (1976). *Cognitive therapy and the emotional disorders*. New York: International Universities Press.

Bethay, S., Wilson, K. G., Schnetzer, L., & Nassar, S. (2013). A controlled pilot evaluation of Acceptance and Commitment Training for intellectual disability staff. *Mindfulness*, *4*, 113–121. doi.10.1007/s12671-012-0103-8.

Bohlmeijer, E. T., Fledderus, M., Rokx, T. A. J. J., & Pieterse, M. E. (2011). Efficacy of an early intervention based on acceptance and commitment therapy for adults with depressive symptomatology: Evaluation in a randomized controlled trial. *Behaviour Research and Therapy*, *49*(1), 62–67. doi.10.1016/j.brat.2010.10.003.

Bonanno, G. A., Papa, A., Lalande, K., Westphal, M., & Coifman, K. (2004). The importance of being flexible: The ability to enhance and suppress emotional expression predicts long-term adjustment. *Psychological Science*, *157*, 482–487. doi.10.1111/j.0956-7976.2004.00705.x.

Bond, F. W. & Bunce, D. (2000). Mediators of change in emotion-focused and problem-focused worksite stress management interventions. *Journal of Occupational Health Psychology*, *5*(1), 156. doi.10.1037/1076-8998.5.1.156.

Bond, F. W., Hayes, S. C., Baer, R. A., Carpenter, K. M., Guenole, N., Orcutt, H. K., Zettle, R. D., et al. (2011). Preliminary psychometric properties of the Acceptance and Action Questionnaire – II: A revised measure of psychological inflexibility and experiential avoidance. *Behavior Therapy*, *42*(4), 676–688. doi.10.1016/j.beth.2011.03.007.

Brinkborg, H., Michanek, J., Hesser, H., & Berglund, G. (2011). Acceptance and commitment therapy for the treatment of stress among social workers: A randomized controlled trial. *Behaviour Research and Therapy*, *49*(6), 389–398. doi.10.1016/j.brat.2011.03.009.

Butryn, M. L., Forman, E., Hoffman, K., Shaw, J., & Juarascio, A. (2011). A pilot study of acceptance and commitment therapy for promotion of physical activity. *Journal of Physical Activity & Health*, *8*(4), 516–522.

Chase, J. A., Houmanfar, R., Hayes, S. C., Ward, T. A., Vilardaga, J. P., & Follette, V. (2013). Values are not just goals: Online ACT-based values training adds to goal setting in improving undergraduate college student performance. *Journal of Contextual Behavioral Science*, *2*(3), 79–84.

Clark, D. A. (1995). Perceived limitations of standard cognitive therapy: A reconsideration of efforts to revise Beck's theory and therapy. *Journal of Cognitive Psychotherapy*, *9*, 153–172.

Dahl, J., Wilson, K. G., & Nilsson, A. (2004). Acceptance and Commitment Therapy and the treatment of persons at risk for long-term disability resulting from stress and pain symptoms: A preliminary randomized trial. *Behavior Therapy*, *35*, 785–802. doi.10.1016/S0005-7894(04)80020-0.

Djordjevic, A. & Frögéli, E. (2012). *Mind the gap: Acceptance and Commitment Therapy (ACT) for preventing stress-related ill-health among future nurses. A randomized controlled trial.* Unpublished thesis. Karolinska Institute, Stockholm.

Dobson, K. S. & Khatri, N. (2000). Cognitive therapy: Looking backward, looking forward. *Journal of Clinical Psychology*, *56*, 907–923. doi.10.1002/1097-4679(200007)56:7<907::AID-JCLP9>3.0.CO;2-I.

Franks, C. M. & Wilson, G. T. (1974). *Annual review of behavior therapy: Theory and practice.* New York: Brunner/Mazel.

Goldiamond, I. (1974). Toward a constructional approach to social problems. *Behaviorism*, *2*, 1–79.

Goodwin, C. L., Forman, E. M., Herbert, J. D., Butryn, M. L., & Ledley, G. S. (2012). A pilot study examining the initial effectiveness of a brief acceptance-based behavior therapy for modifying diet and physical activity among cardiac patients. *Behavior Modification*, *36*(2), 199–217. doi.10.1177/0145445511427770.

Gregg, J. A., Callaghan, G. M., Hayes, S. C., & Glenn-Lawson, J. L. (2007). Improving diabetes self-management through acceptance, mindfulness, and values: A randomized controlled trial. *Journal of Consulting and Clinical Psychology*, *75*(2), 336. doi.10.1037/0022-006X.75.2.336.

Hawkes, A. L., Chambers, S. K., Pakenham, K. I., Patrao, T. A., Baade, P. D., Lynch, B. M., Aitken, J. F., Meng, X. Q., & Courneya, K. S. (2013). Effects of a telephone-delivered multiple health behavior change intervention (CanChange) on health and behavioral outcomes in survivors of colorectal cancer: A randomized controlled trial. *Journal of Clinical Oncology*, *31*, 2313–2321. doi.10.1200/JCO.2012.45.5873.

Hayes, S. C. (1984). Making sense of spirituality. *Behaviorism, 12,* 99–110.

Hayes, S. C. (1987). A contextual approach to therapeutic change. In: Jacobson, N. (Ed.), *Psychotherapists in clinical practice: Cognitive and behavioral perspectives* (pp. 327–387). New York: Guilford.

Hayes, S. C. (Ed.). (1989). *Rule-governed behavior: Cognition, contingencies, and instructional control.* New York: Plenum.

Hayes, S. C. (1993). Analytic goals and the varieties of scientific contextualism. In: S. C. Hayes, L. J. Hayes, H. W. Reese, & T. R. Sarbin (Eds.), *Varieties of scientific contextualism* (pp. 11–27). Reno, NV: Context Press.

Hayes, S. C. (2004). Acceptance and commitment therapy, relational frame theory, and the third wave of behavioral cognitive therapies. *Behavior Therapy, 35,* 639–665. doi.10.7202/1023989ar.

Hayes, S. C. (2008). Climbing our hills: A beginning conversation on the comparison of ACT and traditional CBT. *Clinical Psychology: Science and Practice, 15,* 286–295. doi.10.1111/j.1468-2850.2008.00139.x.

Hayes, S. C., Barnes-Holmes, D., & Roche, B. (2001). Relational Frame Theory: A précis. In: S. C. Hayes, D. Barnes Holmes, & B. Roche (Eds.), *Relational Frame Theory: A post-Skinnerian account of human language and cognition* (pp. 141–154). New York: Plenum Press.

Hayes, S. C., Bissett, R. T., Korn, Z., Zettle, R. D., Rosenfarb, I. S., Cooper, L. D., et al. (1999). The impact of acceptance versus control rationales on pain tolerance. *The Psychological Record, 49*(1), 33–47.

Hayes, S. C., Bissett, R., Roget, N., Padilla, M., Kohlenberg, B. S., Fisher, G., & Niccolls, R., et al. (2004). The impact of acceptance and commitment training and multicultural training on the stigmatizing attitudes and professional burnout of substance abuse counselors. *Behavior Therapy, 35*(4), 821–835. doi.10.1016/S0005-7894(04)80022-4.

Hayes, S. C., Luoma, J., Bond, F., Masuda, A., and Lillis, J. (2006). Acceptance and Commitment Therapy: Model, processes, and outcomes. *Behaviour Research and Therapy, 44,* 1–25. doi.10.1016/j.brat.2005.06.006.

Hayes, S. C. & Strosahl, K. D. (Eds.). (2005). *A practical guide to acceptance and commitment therapy.* New York: Springer.

Hayes, S. C., Strosahl, K., & Wilson, K. G. (1999a). *Acceptance and commitment therapy: An experiential approach to behavior change.* New York: Guilford Press.

Hayes, S. C., Strosahl, K. D., Wilson, K. G., Bissett, R. T., Pistorello, J., Toarmino, D., Polusny, M., A., Dykstra, T. A., Batten, S. V., Bergan, J., Stewart, S. H., Zvolensky, M. J., Eifert, G. H , Bond, F. W., Forsyth J. P., Karekla, M., & McCurry, S. M. (2004). Measuring experiential avoidance: A preliminary test of a working model. *The Psychological Record, 54,* 553–578.

Hayes, S. C., Strosahl, K. D., & Wilson, K. G. (2012). *Acceptance and commitment therapy: The process and practice of mindful change,* 2nd edn. New York: Guilford Press.

Hayes, S. C., Villatte, M., Levin, M., & Hildebrandt, M. (2011). Open, aware, and active: Contextual approaches as an emerging trend in the behavioral and cognitive therapies. *Annual Review of Clinical Psychology, 7,*141–168. doi.10.1146/annurev-clinpsy-032210-104449.

Hayes, S. C., Wilson, K. G., Gifford, E. V., Follette, V. M., & Strosahl, K. (1996). Experiential avoidance and behavioral disorders: A functional dimensional approach to diagnosis and treatment. *Journal of Consulting and Clinical Psychology, 64*(6), 1152–1168. doi.10.1037/0022-006X.64.6.1152.

Jacobson, N. S. & Christensen, A. (1998). *Acceptance and change in couple therapy: A therapist's guide to transforming relationships.* New York: W. W. Norton.

Jeffcoat, T. & Hayes, S. C. (2012). A randomized trial of ACT bibliotherapy on the mental health of K-12 teachers and staff. *Behaviour Research and Therapy, 50*(9), 571–579. doi.10.1016/j.brat.2012.05.008.

Kabat-Zinn J. (1990). *Full catastrophe living.* New York: Delacorte.

Kashdan, T. B. (2010) Psychological flexibility as a fundamental aspect of health. *Clinical Psychology Review, 30*(7), 865–878. doi.10.1016/j.cpr.2010.03.001.

Kashdan, T. B., Rose, P., & Fincham, F. D. (2014). Curiosity and exploration: Facilitating positive subjective experiences and personal growth opportunities. *Journal of Personality Assessment, 83*(3), 291–305. doi.10.1207/s15327752jpa8203_05.

Katterman, S. N., Goldstein, S. P., Butryn, M. L., Forman, E. M., & Lowe, M. R. (2014). Efficacy of an acceptance-based behavioral intervention for weight gain prevention in young adult women. *Journal of Contextual Behavioral Science, 3,* 45–50.

Kohlenberg, R. J. & Tsai, M. (1991). *Functional analytic psychotherapy.* New York: Plenum Press.

Leahy, R. L. (2003). *Cognitive therapy techniques: A practitioner's guide.* New York: Guilford Press.

Levin, M. E., Hildebrandt, M. J., Lillis, J., & Hayes, S. C. (2012). The impact of treatment components suggested by the psychological flexibility model: A meta-analysis of laboratory-based component studies. *Behavior Therapy, 43*, 741–756. doi:10.1016/j.beth.2012.05.003.

Levin, M. E., Pistorello, J., Seeley, J., & Hayes, S. C. (2014). Feasibility of a prototype web-based Acceptance and Commitment Therapy prevention program for college students. *Journal of American College Health, 62*(1), 20–30. doi:10.1080/07448481.2013.843533.

Lillis, J., Hayes, S. C., Bunting, K., & Masuda, A. (2009). Teaching acceptance and mindfulness to improve the lives of the obese: A preliminary test of a theoretical model. *Annals of Behavioral Medicine, 37*, 58–69. doi:10.1007/s12160-009-9083-x.

Linehan, M. M. (1993). *Cognitive-behavioral treatment of borderline personality disorder.* New York: Guilford Press.

Lloyd, J., Bond, F. W., & Flaxman, P. E. (2013). Identifying psychological mechanisms underpinning a cognitive behavioural therapy intervention for emotional burnout. *Work & Stress: An International Journal of Work, Health & Organisations, 27*, 181–199.

Longmore, R. J. & Worrell, M. (2007). Do we need to challenge thoughts in cognitive behavior therapy? *Clinical Psychology Review, 27*, 173–187. doi:10.1016/j.cpr.2006.08.001.

Luoma, J. B. & Vilardaga, J. P. (2013). Improving therapist psychological flexibility while training Acceptance and Commitment Therapy: A pilot study. *Cognitive Behaviour Therapy, 42*, 1–8. doi:10.1080/165060 73.2012.701662.

Maslow, A. H. (1971). *The farther reaches of human nature.* New York: Viking Press.

McHugh, L., Barnes-Holmes, Y., & Barnes-Holmes, D. (2004). Perspective-taking as relational responding: A developmental profile. *The Psychological Record, 54*, 115–144.

Mo'tamedi, H., Rezaiemaram, P., & Tavallaie, A. (2012). The effectiveness of a group-based acceptance and commitment additive therapy on rehabilitation of female outpatients with chronic headache: Preliminary findings reducing 3 dimensions of headache impact. *Headache: The Journal of Head and Face Pain, 52*, 1106–1119. doi:10.1111/j.1526-4610.2012.02192.x.

Muto, T., Hayes, S. C., & Jeffcoat, T. (2011). The effectiveness of acceptance and commitment therapy bibliotherapy for enhancing the psychological health of Japanese college students living abroad. *Behavior Therapy, 42*(2), 323–335. doi:10.1016/j.beth.2010.08.009.

Ost, L. G. (2008). Efficacy of the third wave of behavioral therapies: A systematic review and meta-analysis. *Behaviour Research and Therapy, 46*, 296–321. doi:10.1016/j.brat.2007.12.005.

Powers, M. B. & Emmelkamp, P. M. G. (2009). Response to "Is acceptance and commitment therapy superior to established treatment comparisons?". *Psychotherapy and Psychosomatics, 78*. 380–381. doi:10.1159/000235979.

Rogers, C. R. (1964). Toward a modern approach to values: The valuing process in the mature person. *Journal of Abnormal and Social Psychology, 68*, 160–167. doi:10.1037/h0046419.

Ruiz, F. J. & Luciano, C. (2009). Eficacia de la terapia de aceptación y compromiso (ACT) en la mejora del rendimiento ajedrecístico de jóvenes promesas (Acceptance and commitment therapy (ACT) and improving performance in bright youth hope chess-players). *Psicothema, 21*(3), 347–352.

Ruiz, F. J. & Luciano, C. (2012). Improving international-level chess players performance with an acceptance-based protocol: Preliminary findings. *The Psychological Record, 62*, 447–462.

Segal, Z. V., Williams, J. M. G., & Teasdale, J. D. (2002). *Mindfulness-based cognitive therapy for depression: A new approach to preventing relapse.* New York: Guilford Press.

Stice, E., Shaw, H., Bohon, C., Marti, C. N., & Rohde, P. (2009). A meta-analytic review of depression prevention programs for children and adolescents: factors that predict magnitude of intervention effects. *Journal of Consulting and Clinical Psychology, 77*(3), 486–503. doi:10.1037/a0015168.

Tapper, K., Shaw, C., Ilsley, J., Hill, A. J., Bond, F. W., & Moore, L. (2009). Exploratory randomised controlled trial of a mindfulness-based weight loss intervention for women. *Appetite, 52*(2), 396–404. doi:10.1016/j.appet.2008.11.012.

Tedeschi, R. G. & Calhoun, L. G. (1996). The Posttraumatic Growth Inventory: Measuring the positive legacy of trauma. *Journal of Traumatic Stress, 9*, 455–471. doi:10.1002/jts.2490090305.

Wells, A. (2000). *Emotional disorders & metacognition: innovative cognitive therapy.* Chichester: Wiley-Blackwell.

Weineland, S., Hayes, S. C., & Dahl, J. (2012). Psychological flexibility and the gains of acceptance-based treatment for post-bariatric surgery: Six-month follow-up and a test of the underlying model. *Clinical Obesity*, 2(1/2), 15–24.

Witkiewitz, K., Marlatt, G. A., & Walker, D. D. (2005). Mindfulness-based relapse prevention for alcohol use disorders: The meditative tortoise wins the race. *Journal of Cognitive Psychotherapy*, 19, 211 228.

Wolpe, J. & Rachman, S. (1960). Psychoanalytic "evidence": A critique based on Freud's case of little Hans. *Journal of Nervous and Mental Disease*, 131, 135–148.

Wood, J. V., Perunovie, E., & Lee, J. W. (2009). Positive self-statements: Power for some, peril for others. *Journal of Psychological Science*, 20, 860–866. doi.10.1111/j.1467-9280.2009.02370.x.

Zettle, R. D. & Hayes, S. C. (1986). Dysfunctional control by client verbal behavior: The context of reason giving. *Analysis of Verbal Behavior*, 4, 30–38.

30

Schema Therapy
Christopher D. J. Taylor and Arnoud Arntz

Introduction

The integration of clinical psychology with positive psychology approaches has historically been limited in scope (Wood & Tarrier, 2010). Rather than a relentless focus on the reduction of negative aspects of human distress, the boosting of positive strengths and healthy aspects of the self have been gaining increasing attention as psychological therapies develop and refine. Schema therapy is an integrative psychotherapy, which was originally developed for personality disorders, but has increasingly been tailored and applied to other disorders. The model schema therapy is based on proposes that when basic needs are not met in development, this leads to negative beliefs, maladaptive schemas, unhelpful ways of being and, negative/exaggerated responses, and a lack of positive and adaptive schemas and behaviors. The schema therapy model is sometimes seen as being focused on negative beliefs and early maladaptive schemas. However, the schema therapy approach identifies both negative and positive schema modes and uses techniques to boost those which are positive as well as reducing those which are negative. Schema therapy can be delivered as a one to one individual therapy, as couples therapy, and as a group therapy approach. This chapter examines how schema therapy seeks to reduce negative schemas and schema modes but also the significant role of the therapy in seeking to enhance positive schemas and positive schema modes. The aim is to demonstrate how schema therapy could be considered as making a contribution to the development of positive clinical psychology.

Schema Therapy

Schema therapy is an integrative psychotherapy treatment for complex psychological disorders which was first described 25 years ago (Young, 1990). The model and therapeutic techniques draw on a range of theoretical concepts and methods including cognitive-behavioral therapy (CBT), attachment theory, interpersonal ideas, and object relations theory. In addition to some cognitive and behavioral techniques, schema therapy places great emphasis on the use of experiential techniques such as imagery rescripting and chair work.

In brief, the schema therapy model proposes that if individuals have unmet needs in childhood and adolescence, they can develop early maladaptive schema and unhelpful schema coping modes. Early maladaptive schemas have been defined as broad pervasive themes or patterns, which are comprised of memories, emotions, cognitions and bodily sensations (Young, Klosko, & Weishaar, 2003; Rafaeli, Bernstein, & Young, 2011). They can be linked to the self or interpersonal relationships with others, developed through life and tend to be unhelpful to a significant degree. These schemas dominate cognitive processing, leaving little opportunity for

The Wiley Handbook of Positive Clinical Psychology, First Edition. Edited by Alex M. Wood and Judith Johnson.
© 2016 John Wiley & Sons, Ltd. Published 2016 by John Wiley & Sons, Ltd.

positive schemas to influence cognition. Schema modes are the primary emotional state, based on activated schema and coping responses, which are present for an individual at a specific time (Rafaeli et al., 2011). Early maladaptive schemas, dysfunctional coping styles, and dysfunctional schema modes lead to the development of psychopathology which manifest as various mental health disorders. Schema therapy seeks both to weaken maladaptive schemas, coping, and modes, and to strengthen and enhance adaptive schemas and positive schema modes such as the healthy adult mode and happy child mode, very much in the spirit of a positive clinical psychology approach. To date, the strongest evidence for the efficacy of the approach is in the treatment of personality disorders, but there is early stage work on schema therapy being developed and tested in other clinical conditions.

It can be argued that the cognitive concept of early maladaptive schemas has overlap with some psychoanalytic ideas. Horney (1950) outlined a psychoanalytic perspective where negative thinking patterns emerge when basic needs are unmet, and subsequently these thinking patterns become entrenched, which leads to difficulties in later life. Change and therapeutic growth is said to happen when these previous ways of thinking are challenged. This has some similarity to the more cognitive concept of early maladaptive schemas as outlined in schema therapy.

The schema therapist works collaboratively with clients and patients to identify and understand their schemas, schema modes and schema coping responses. A range of cognitive and behavioral techniques are utilized with experiential approaches such as imagery rescripting, chair work and other techniques. The therapeutic relationship is given significant focus with the use of "limited reparenting" and "empathic confrontation." Limited reparenting is utilized when vulnerable child modes have been identified in the assessment and formulation stage. For example, if a client experienced significant trauma as a child, they may often develop vulnerable, abandoned/abused child modes. The aim of limited reparenting is to use the therapeutic relationship to allow a client to feel validated and to allow them to process traumatic memories, feelings and thoughts associated with past experience within the context of a stable and caring therapeutic relationship between client and therapist. This includes clients taking more responsibility with their other interpersonal relationships to ensure that their needs are met in healthy ways. As clients make greater efforts for their needs to be met, there is often a shift, with less reliance on unhelpful ways of coping such as detaching, surrendering or denigrating others.

Evolution of Schema Therapy

Edwards and Arntz (2012) outlined the three stages in development of schema therapy proposed by Jeffrey Young. These include stage one: the development of schema therapy in response to difficult to treat clients, stage two: randomized trials conducted in The Netherlands, and stage three: the development of the group Schema therapy interventions. These will be outlined briefly in turn.

Stage One: Schema Therapy Developed in Response to Difficult to Treat Clients/Patients

Schema therapy originally developed as an adapted version of cognitive therapy for difficult to treat clients who presented with personality disorders (Young, 1990). The main innovations were the development of a model which outlined a wider range of trait like beliefs about the self and others, then later the definition of schema modes, which were more state like experiences, associated with a schema, to explain the flipping of emotions often observed in individuals diagnosed with personality disorders. For example, a client with a failure schema may feel desperate and unhappy due to small mistakes they make. Such a client may then flip into an overcompensation mode, where they boast about their own achievements, overstate things and reject any mistakes. This may also involve activation of avoidance schema coping, to ensure that no situations related to achievement are confronted and thus there is no risk of activating the failure schema.

Early Maladaptive Schemas

Young described the concept of "early maladaptive schemas" (Young, 1990). The term schema originates from information processing theory (Williams, Watts, MacLeod, & Mathews, 1997) highlighting the storage of information in a thematic way. Schema have a variety of definitions within cognitive psychology and cognitive therapy. Schemas can be defined as theoretically hypothesized knowledge structures which are not only verbal, but involve wider knowledge that steer information processes, such as selective attention, interpretation, and retrieval. There are also links with representations, as defined in attachment theory (Bowlby, 1969) and object relation theory.

These schemas can be developed and stored in early life and consist of sensory experience, emotions and the meanings linked with them (Young et al., 2003; van Genderen, Rijkeboer, & Arntz, 2012). Schemas can act as filters with how individuals make sense of the world, in both a negative and a positive ways. Repeated negative experiences can strengthen schemas.

In the context of this chapter, it should be highlighted that although one of the strengths of Young's model was to conceptualize schemas as being wider than core beliefs, encompassing memory, emotion and a more visceral experience when activated, the schemas originally identified were wholly negative in their nature ("early maladaptive"). Little attention was paid at the time to the assessment and formulation of positive schemas or positive beliefs, in line with the prevailing approaches in the early 1990s.

Lockwood and Perris (2012) have proposed contrasting positive early adaptive schemas which are summarized and outlined in Table 30.1 below. Early adaptive schemas are hypothesized to develop when individuals grow up and develop in environments where their core emotional needs are met and could be seen as the equivalent positive schema, in contrast to the early maladaptive schema.

Similar to many psychotherapy models, the schemas described are a clinical heuristic, with mixed research support for the presence or absence of each. Young and colleagues outlined 18 early maladaptive schemas which were developed from clinical experiences and observation. In subsequent empirical research studies investigating them, findings have drawn varied support. For example, a review by Oei and Baranoff (2007) examined psychometric and assessment issues of the Young Schema questionnaire and found that no consistent factor structures emerged.

More recently, a number of detailed studies have been undertaken on the Young Schema Questionnaire (YSQ) and the Schema Mode Inventory (SMI). There have been several versions of the YSQ developed over the past 20 years, including long versions with over 200 items and short versions varying from 75 to 90 items. The most detailed work to date on the YSQ has been conducted by Rijkeboer and colleagues, who summarize findings in their review (Rijkeboer, 2012). The schema questionnaire has also been developed for children (Stallard & Rayner, 2005; Rijkeboer & de Boo, 2010). The YSQ short form version two has been more extensively utilized in research studies and would appear to have good psychometric properties (Stopa, Thorne, Waters, & Preston, 2001).

One of the other widely used therapy specific measures is the Schema Mode Inventory (SMI) (Young et al., 2007). This version gives details regarding specific modes which are linked with specific disorders. Lobbestael and colleagues have examined the Schema Mode Inventory in a number of studies and highlight these in their review (Lobbestael, 2012). The SMI has 118 items, and measures 14 modes on a six-point scale. In addition to the use of the SMI, schema

Table 30.1 Early maladaptive schemas and early adaptive schemas.

Core emotional need	Early maladaptive schema	Early adaptive schema
Stable and predictable emotional attachment figure	Abandonment	Stable attachment
Honesty, trustworthiness, loyalty, and the absence of abuse	Mistrust/abuse	Basic trust
Warmth and affection, empathy, protection guidance and metal sharing of personal experience.	Emotional deprivation	Emotional fulfillment
Significant other who can be playful and spontaneous and who invites the same in you and others – encourages you to express emotions and talk about feelings	Emotional inhibition	Emotional openness/ spontaneity
Unconditional acceptance of private and public self, regular praise, sharing of areas of self-doubt and not keeping secret from others	Defectiveness/ shame	Self-acceptance/ lovability
Inclusion in and acceptance by a community with shared interested and values	Social isolation/ alienation	Social belonging
Support and guidance in developing mastery and competence in chosen areas of achievement	Failure	Success
A reassuring significant other who balances reasonable concern for harm and illness with a sense of manageability of these risks and models taking appropriate action without undue worry or overprotection	Vulnerability to harm	Basic health and safety
Challenge support and guidance in learning to handle day to day decisions tasks and problems on one's own without excessive help from others	Dependence	Healthy self-reliance/ competence
A significant other who promotes and accepts one having a separate identity and direction in life and who respects one's personal boundaries	Enmeshment	Healthy boundaries/ developed self
Freedom to express needs feelings, and opinions in the context of significant relationships without fear of punishment or rejection	Subjugation of needs	Assertiveness/ self-expression
Balance in the importance of each person's needs. Guilt is not used to control expression and consideration of one's needs	Self-sacrifice	Healthy self-interest/ self-care
Guidance in developing appropriate standards and ideals and in balancing performance goals with getting other needs met along with a forgiving attitude toward mistakes or imperfections	Unrelenting standards	Realistic standards and expectations
Guidance and empathic limit setting to learn the consequences for others of actions and to empathize with others perspectives rights and needs. Not made to feel superior to others and limits placed on unrealistic demands	Entitlement/ grandiosity	Emphatic consideration/ respect for others
Guidance and empathic firmness in forgoing short-term pleasure and comfort in order to complete day to day routines, responsibilities and meet longer-term goals. Limits placed on expressing emotions that are out of control, inappropriate or impulsive	Insufficient self-control/ self-discipline	Healthy self-control/ self-discipline

Lockwood & Perris, 2012. Reproduced with permission of Wiley.

modes can also be assessed by identifying with patients problematic experiences and uses these as examples to draw out the salient schema modes and by using experiential techniques (e.g., guided imagery assessment exercises) to explore the origin of modes from early experiences.

Schema Coping Styles

Three broad schema coping styles have been described (schema surrender, schema avoidance and schema overcompensation). For example, if a child's emotional needs are not met in early life, this can result in the development of an emotional deprivation schema. Overcompensation coping style can be activated if as an adult, the schema may be satisfied in those moments by being in a close relationship, but the individual finds it hard to reciprocally express emotions, and seems cut off from the other person. This may be difficult for a partner to cope with, and so they end the relationship, reducing the emotional support and confirming the schema that emotional needs will not be met.

From a negative perspective, where core needs are not met, psychological problems may develop and on a more positive note, where these core needs are met, individuals learn to live and cope with challenges in functional, healthy and positive ways. Arntz and Jacob (2012) highlight that therapists practicing schema therapy may include positive schemas or positive schema modes according to their preferred clinical approach, thus leaving scope for positive interventions to boost positive schemas and healthy and happy schema modes.

Schema Mode Model

The early schema therapy model included an understanding of (1) early maladaptive schemas, (2) how schemas lead to unhelpful coping, (3) developmental origins, (4) ways of being (or modes), (5) impact on life and functioning in relation to work, family and interpersonal relationships, and (6) client–therapist interactions. The schema mode model fits well with a positive psychology approach, in that the therapy seeks to boost the "healthy adult" side of a person, repair damage to the vulnerable child mode (which develops through unfulfilled needs) and to overcome or reduce impact of critical modes and detachment modes (see Table 30.2). As the theory and practice of schema therapy has developed, the model was applied and refined for a range of other clinical disorders. The therapy was no longer seen as a focused form of cognitive therapy but became "Schema Therapy" and was outlined in the first comprehensive manual over ten years ago (Young et al., 2003). Subsequent manuals tailored specifically to individuals with borderline personality disorder based on clinical trials have also been published (Arntz & van Genderen, 2009) and a manual for utilizing the therapy with other disorders (Arntz & Jacob, 2012).

There are some similarities and differences between early maladaptive schemas and schema modes. As a guide, early maladaptive schemas are seen as more trait like, while schema modes focus more on schema states (which could be considered similar to the ego state concept) which are often expressed as intense emotions linked with a specific schema or as an (interpersonal) expression of coping with a schema which may have less emotional content (Arntz & Jacob, 2012).

Early maladaptive schemas can be formulated in several ways to offer the patient a way of making sense of their early experiences, how these have developed into schematic beliefs, schema coping responses and then problematic areas and relationships.

Figure 30.1 offers a schema mode model conceptualization of an individual's borderline personality disorder difficulties. In this example, the interaction between the punitive parent mode and the angry/impulsive child mode and the abandoned/abused child mode can be seen. In addition, also highlighted is the detached protector mode and the underdeveloped healthy adult mode. Parent and child modes are the primary modes while coping modes are more

Table 30.2 Schema modes.

Mode categories	Specific mode	Description
Functional, healthy modes		
	Healthy adult mode	In this mode, the individual is able to engage in healthy adult ways of being including working, parenting, and taking responsibility. They pursue adult activities which they enjoy, such as sex, cultural, aesthetical, and intellectual interests. This also includes looking after one's own health proactively and athletic/exercise activities.
	Happy child mode	In this mode, an individual is able to feel at peace because core emotional needs are currently met. The person feels loved, contented, satisfied, fulfilled, protected, praised, worthwhile, nurtured guided understood, validated, self-confident, competent, appropriately autonomous or self reliant, safe, resilient, strong, in control adaptable, optimistic, and spontaneous.
Child modes	Vulnerable child	The patient believes that there is no one who will fulfill their needs and that all will leave them. A sense that the most important emotional needs of the child have generally not been met, the patient usually feels emotionally empty, alone, socially unaccepted, undeserving of love, unloved, and unlovable.
	Angry child	The patient feels strong anger, rage, and lacks serenity because their basic needs have not been satisfied. They can also feel left alone, embarrassed or let down. Anger can be expressed both in physical and nonphysical means. This has similarities with how children might express their anger.
	Enraged child	This mode is motivated by similar reasons as the angry child mode, but here the patient is unable to control themselves. This can be demonstrated in such ways as hurting people or damaging furniture, possessions, etc.
	Impulsive child	The patient wants to satisfy other wants and needs in a way which is self serving and out of control. Emotions become uncontrolled and rage presents when these other needs are not met.
	Undisciplined child	The patient has limited capacity to cope with challenges when things are tough. Activities of daily living may remain incomplete. Feelings of unhappiness, or unease cannot be tolerated and there is an immaturity to their responses.
Coping modes	Compliant surrender	The patient focuses too much on the needs of others in an attempt to prevent anything bad happening. Emotions are not expressed in healthy ways. Mistreatment from others is tolerated.
	Detached protector	The patient isolates powerful emotions as they have beliefs that such emotions are volatile and cannot be controlled. Recreational activities are avoided and the patient reports feeling unfulfilled, without a real sense of self.

Table 30.2 (*Continued*)

Mode categories	Specific mode	Description
	Detached self-soother	The patient's way of managing is to occupy themselves to avoid any negative feelings. A number of ways of coping are utilized to manage this (e.g., excessive sleep or drug use) or too much activity (e.g., focusing excessively on work or risky intimate relations).
Overcompensator modes	Self-aggrandizer	The patient demonstrates a belief of over importance and entitlement. Following personal desires are prioritized. Dismissing others to make themselves feel better can also be demonstrated in this mode.
	Bully and attack	The patient seeks to avoid bad things happening to them and so their strategy is to attempt to exert influence over others. This is done in a number of ways including dangerous gestures and violence. Being a perceived position of superiority is important and seeking to insult others is common.
Dysfunctional parent modes	Punitive parent	The patient is unkind, denigrating and has little tolerance of errors that they themselves make.
		There is a high level of negative personal assessment and feelings of blame. Patients often have little compassion for themselves and feel they are deserving of punishment in some way.
		The content of this mode is often an internalized voice of an important person from the patient's life who used to say unkind and hurtful things to put them down.
	Demanding parent	The patient has a strong sense that they must behave in a specific way, with little flexibility and a certain black and white thinking. The patient also has a strong unrelenting standard that the work they do is inadequate and not good enough.
		The patient strives for perfection on a regular basis, to the extent that it interferes with rest, social life and interpersonal relationships. Often these standards have been learned from a significant care giver who also holds them the standards in high regard.
	Angry protector	The patient displays anger frequently to keep others who are threatening away. "Outbursts of anger" result in others staying away from the person. This anger can be defined in relation to other modes and is often displayed as having more control than angry child or enraged child.
	Obsessive overcontrollor mode	The patient seeks to avoid and protect themselves from any current or proposed threats. A high level of control is exhibited. Frequent use of repeated behaviors to ensure these standards are met.
	Paranoid	The patient seeks to protect oneself from current or proposed threats by ensuring a high level of control happens. This mode is demonstrated by trying to keep others doing something and then seeking to reveal their true motives.

(*Continued*)

Table 30.2   (*Continued*)

Mode categories	Specific mode	Description
	Conning and manipulative	The patient is dishonest, and self serving in controlling situations for their benefit. Often others are hurt in this process, either by direct impact of their behaviors or by the patient attempting to shift responsibility to someone else.
	Predator mode	The patient removes fears about harm occurring, challenges, and barriers in way which is lacking warmth, and seems manipulative.
	Attention-seeker mode	The patient seeks others positive regard by outlandish actions, possible overly intimate actions, and inflated self statements and actions.

These have been taken from van Genderen, Rijkeboer, & Arntz (2012) and Arntz & Jacob (2012). (Reproduced with permission of Wiley).

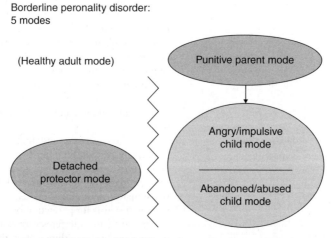

Borderline peronality disorder: 5 modes

(Healthy adult mode)

Punitive parent mode

Angry/impulsive child mode

Detached protector mode

Abandoned/abused child mode

Figure 30.1   Schema Mode Model Formulation (Arntz & van Genderen, 2009. Reproduced with permission of Wiley).

secondary and used to cope with painful experiences (Jacob & Arntz, 2013). Schema therapy uses stages of assessment of schemas, identification of schema, eliminating punitive and demanding schema modes. However, schema therapy also seeks to support individuals develop the healthy adult mode and happy child mode, acknowledging the needs and emotions of the individual and providing positive corrective experiences via therapy.

Positive Schemas and Modes

The schema model tends to focus on negative schemas and a significant number of schema modes are also negative, but with the important inclusion of the healthy adult schema mode and the happy child mode. The mode concept can be integrated with other approaches. Therapists might include positive schemas or positive schema modes. In reviewing all the above schema modes, it is clear that although a large number of negative modes were originally identified, the positive (including healthy adult) modes are those which therapy seeks to strengthen and enhance. In line with the original positive clinical psychology argument put forward by Wood and Tarrier (2010), the schema therapy model and individualized formulations make clear that positive and negative modes interact together, rather than being conceptualized as being isolated. By the end of this initial stage of the development of schema therapy, the approach had garnered significant interest and some case studies of the approach had been published. However, there was a need for rigorous treatment trials testing the efficacy of the therapy.

Stage Two: Randomized Clinical Trials and Schema Mode Model Development

By early 2000, although schema therapy had gained significant attention, the research evidence base supporting the therapy was limited. To address this need for validation, Arntz and colleagues began developing and testing schema therapy for borderline personality disorder in the Netherlands. This was based on some of Young's work of cognitive therapy for personality disorders, but also included an integration of both Young's and Arntz's work on personality disorders, which included the addition of experiential techniques such as imagery rescripting (Arntz & Weertman, 1999). This was then formally tested in a three-year randomized trial ($N = 86$) comparing schema therapy to transference-focused therapy. The results demonstrated that schema therapy was superior to transference focused therapy and that at the end of the study and more of the patients in the schema therapy had recovered from borderline personality disorder compared to the transference focused therapy group (Giesen-Bloo et al., 2006).

A follow up implementation study demonstrated similar effect sizes when used in routine clinical practice and without the out of hours phone support which was a component of the treatment approach of the first trial (Nadort et al., 2009). The schema therapy model has also been adapted for forensic clients diagnosed with psychopathy, with relevant additional modes for this specific client group added (Bernstein, Arntz, & Vos, 2007). The adapted therapy is now being tested in a two-arm randomized trial comparing schema therapy with treatment as usual, with $N = 102$ participants recruited (Bernstein et al., 2012). Chakhssi, Kersten, de Ruiter, and Bernstein (2014) have recently outlined a detailed case study of this approach for a forensic patient with personality disorder over a four year treatment period. The reliable change analysis reported demonstrated improvements in cognitive schemas, psychopathic factors and risk related outcomes. At three-year follow up, the individual had moved to independent living and had not re-offended.

Most recently, schema therapy has been successfully adapted for use with six other personality disorders (Arntz, 2012) and the efficacy of the approach demonstrated in a three-arm randomized controlled trial (Bamelis, Evers, Spinhoven, & Arntz, 2014) where schema therapy was compared with clarification oriented therapy (COT) and treatment as usual (TAU) for cluster C (anxious), paranoid, histrionic or narcissistic personality disorder ($N = 320$). The results demonstrated schema therapy resulted in greater recovery for these patients (81% recovered in schema therapy versus 61% recovered in clarification oriented therapy versus 51% in treatment as usual; Bamelis et al., 2014). Moreover, schema therapy was superior in increasing levels of general, social and societal functioning, including earlier and more return to work in those that were disabled (Bamelis et al., 2014; Bamelis, Arntz, Wetzelaer, Verdoorn, & Evers, in press). These adaptations further demonstrate the use of individual schema therapy as an approach, which can help facilitate positive changes for patients who engage with the therapy.

Stage Three: Group Schema Therapy

The third phase of schema therapy involved the work of Joan Farrell and Ida Shaw, who developed the group schema therapy approach for individuals with borderline personality disorder. This was a group program of 30 weekly sessions of 90 minutes in length over an eight-month period (Farrell, Shaw, & Webber, 2009; Farrell & Shaw, 2012). The treatment approach covers emotional awareness training, borderline personality disorder psychoeducation, distress management training and schema change work.

The goals of group schema therapy incorporate a positive approach from the outset with the initial aim being to (1) develop a positive therapeutic alliance, through therapist validation and helping to offer education to patients about the benefits of engaging in treatment, and (2) to increase their emotional awareness, so that patients can observe times themselves when they are beginning to become distressed and make sense of their emotional experiences. This aspect of the group therapy approach was the first to be developed in the early 1990s as an experiential focusing exercise (Farrell & Shaw, 1994). The content of this group schema therapy approach has some similarities to aspects of the limited re-parenting which was core in the original Young individual schema therapy model.

The schema therapy model and the group treatment approach for borderline personality disorder which Farrell and Shaw had developed matched well with Young schema therapy and they chose to integrate the schema mode model in their protocol. The Farrell and Shaw model draws on positive approaches with a person-centered, collaborative, educational group model, with the therapists in a positive parenting role (Farrell & Shaw, 2012).

In the spirit of positive clinical psychology, the group schema therapy approach utilizes the positive strengths of group therapy work and group therapeutic factors to catalyze change focusing on negative schema change. Two therapists facilitate the group, with specific roles. While the first therapist moves the group forward, the other therapist seeks focuses their efforts on maintaining an emotional connection with the patients participating in the group. The aim is to ensure that patients are seeking to connect to their underdeveloped 'healthy adult' schema mode, in order to strengthen and develop its capacity. It also aims to ensure that participants are only in vulnerable or angry child modes for short periods and are supported in moving into healthy adult modes. Furthermore, group schema therapy aims to reduce the stigma of mental health problems and imagery rescripting exercises are enhanced through the positive benefits of shared experiences. The group format of schema therapy has several features which are in line with a positive schema therapy approach. These include mutual support, validation by other group members, practicing the expression of emotions in a group setting, forming positive attachment bonds with other group members

The efficacy for the approach was demonstrated in a Phase II randomized controlled trial ($N =$ 30) (Farrell, Webber, & Shaw, 2009). The group schema therapy approach is being tested in multi-site group schema therapy clinical trial with a target $N = 448$ participants (Wetzelaer et al., 2014). In summary, schema therapy has developed from a brief model outlining a range of trait early maladaptive schemas, refined with the additional of schema modes, and tested in a number of studies.

Treatment and Techniques

As outlined earlier, schema therapy is an integrative psychotherapy approach and thus draws on numerous techniques and approaches to support the therapeutic process of change for patients. Arntz and van Genderen (2009) outline three areas to focus on when supporting positive change: thinking (in the context of explicit knowledge); feeling (as implicit "felt" knowledge); and doing (as operational representation). The mode model suggests there are key areas to consider in formulation and case conceptualization. In terms of understanding and reducing negative modes, this involves identifying child modes and unhelpful parent modes. The schema coping modes include overcompensation, avoidance, and surrender. The patient and the therapist seek to collaboratively work together to reduce the influence and impact of negative schemas and schema modes and from a positive perspective, to develop and boost the healthy adult and healthy child modes.

Techniques which seek to reduce the influence of negative modes and support the development of positive modes include imagery rescripting (both past and future events), limited reparenting (care and validation of needs and feelings, emotions in therapy), chair work (two-chair technique), role play (to change perspectives and to rescript memories), role modeling (responding in a healthy way), psychoeducation, and cognitive and behavioral techniques where appropriate. Schema therapy has a specific focus on the importance of the therapeutic relationship as a means to offer a model of supportive, boundaried, caring relationship, where the therapist can offer limited "secure base". As therapy progresses, and the impact of negative schemas and negative modes is lessened, the content of sessions can involve supporting the patient to be directed more toward health choices such as engaging in education, work, hobbies, interpersonal relationships with friends and partner, as well as further acquiring healthy views on needs, emotions, and how to develop a fulfilling life. These activities are directed at the healthy adult mode and can be seen as straightforwardly aiming towards the very same goals as positive psychology. Further details of assessment, formulation and schema therapy interventions are outlined in the original comprehensive treatment manual (Young et al., 2003), in a specific borderline personality disorder manual, which was used in the first formal clinical trial (Arntz & van Genderen, 2009) and a schema mode manual written for clinicians interested in using these approaches with a wider range of disorders (Arntz & Jacob, 2012).

Efficacy and Effectiveness Studies

There have been a number of studies to date which have examined the efficacy and effectiveness of schema therapy. There are also studies which have offered some support for the schema therapy empirical model. In this section, we will briefly signpost readers to the existing systematic reviews conducted and highlight specific treatment trials. Two systematic reviews have been published, one by Masley and colleagues (Masley, Gillanders, Simpson, & Taylor, 2012) which identified medium to large effect sizes in the 12 studies included. Bamelis, Bloo, Bernstein, and Arntz (2012) conducted a narrative review which also signposts reviewers to several studies of schema therapy, but did not report a systematic search strategy.

A more recent systematic review in a peer review journal specifically examined the empirical foundations, effectiveness and implementation studies of schema therapy for borderline personality disorder (Sempértegui, Karreman, Arntz, & Bekker, 2013). Thirty-five articles were retrieved and included in the search. The review found three trials of schema therapy: two examining efficacy (Giesen-Bloo et al., 2006; Farrell et al., 2009) and one examining effectiveness in practice (Nadort et al., 2009) with and without therapist phone support. More recently, Bamelis and colleagues (2014) have examined schema therapy adapted for cluster C (anxious) paranoid, histrionic or narcissistic personality disorder (Arntz, 2012) with 323 participants across three arms including clarification oriented therapy (COT) and treatment as usual (TAU). A recent meta-analysis focusing on studies of schema therapy for BPD (Jacob & Arntz, 2013) found a pooled effect size of 2.38 (95% CI 1.70, 3.07; heterogonous variances model).

One of the premises of schema therapy is that psychological disorders develop when early basic needs are not met – the process of therapy allows these experiences to be understood and processed, and allows the individual to develop other ways of meeting their needs, in turn allowing

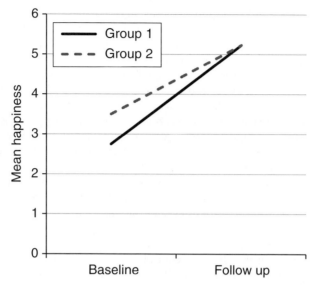

Figure 30.2   Mean Happiness scores (possible range 0–7) in two cohorts receiving group schema therapy from baseline assessment to two-year follow up (following from Dickhaut & Arntz, 2014. Reproduced with permission of Elsevier).

a fulfilling life to be lived. A recent study offers some direct evidence of the positive change which can be experienced for individuals as a result of schema therapy. Dickhaut and Arntz (2014) examined the use of combined group schema therapy and one to one schema therapy in individuals with borderline personality disorder. This was a pilot study with $n=18$ participants across two cohorts. In addition to significant improvements on the Schema Mode Inventory measure, which suggested a lessening of negative schema modes, Dickhaut and Arntz (2014) also measured happiness using the one item happiness question validated in more than 30 countries (Veenhoven, 2008). At baseline, participants with personality disorder mean happiness levels in two groups were 2.75 "very unhappy" and 3.5 "fairly unhappy." At the end of the study, this had increased to 5.23 in both groups, indicating that they were now on average above "fairly happy" (see Figure 30.2). This also compares very favorably with the norms for the ordinary Dutch population using the same measure, which are reported as 5.28, also above "fairly happy" (Veenhoven, 2008). This finding is particularly interesting in light of the Wood and Tarrier (2010) argument that positive and negative emotions can exist on a continuum. In addition to addressing both positive and negative schema modes, this finding suggests that schema therapy can also be effective in both reducing the negative and boosting positive emotion at the same time.

Emerging Areas

Schema therapy has traditionally been known as a psychotherapeutic approach for the treatment of borderline personality disorder. However, in recent years it has been applied to a number of other clinical conditions. Early phase studies have been published utilizing the schema therapy approach with patients who have anorexia nervosa (George, Thornton, Touyz, Waller, & Beumont, 2004), eating disorders more generally (Simpson, Morrow, Vreeswijk, & Reid, 2010), panic or agoraphobia and personality disorders (Hoffart, Versland, & Sexton, 2002), war veterans with post-traumatic stress disorder (Cockram, Drummond, & Lee, 2010) and in chronic depression (Malogiannis et al., 2014). Work has also begun examining the use of schema therapy for individuals who would meet criteria for a diagnosis of dissociative identity disorder (Huntjens, 2014).

There is also emerging work on the use of joy and play within schema therapy, which is very much in line with a positive clinical psychology approach. There are three key aspects to the limited reparenting approach of schema therapy: reducing negative emotions (such as comforting and soothing); increasing positive emotions (such as playfulness and joy); and the management of pushing of boundaries through use of structure and dealing with making clear limits to the therapeutic relationship. Lockwood and Shaw (2012) argue that therapists often do not utilize possible opportunities to put across positive experiences, as the focus in therapy can become too fixated on attempts to relieve pain and suffering (Grawe, 2007). They also highlight work with infants which describes the important role that parents have in infant's early capacities to experience joy and how this links with later development of interpersonal relationships. Lockwood and Shaw also argue that current positive psychology approaches tend to support adults using cognitive and behavioral techniques and have less focus on "the child side" of patients and suggest that some children who develop severe mental health difficulties have gaps in their development including the "early roots of positivity." They argue that capacity for joy is learned (similar to other human capacities, e.g., empathy) and that parents share this capacity with their infants (Schore, 2003) which allows them to internalize this. Lockwood and Shaw (2012) also cite work by Panksepp (1998), which identifies play as one of seven "emotional building blocks" that appear to be common across all mammals. Within schema therapy, absence of play as a child can become apparent during the initial assessment or during imagery exercises linked with the "little self," where if the therapist asks to join in with an activity in an image from the past, if the patient has no memory of parents/adults doing this, it may feel unusual or incongruent to the patient, even if the patient is experienced in imagery work in therapy sessions.

When assessment and case conceptualization stages are complete, if emotional deprivation and more specifically, limited joy and play capacity have been identified, then the schema therapist can utilize a number of positive interventions to support a patient. Lockwood and Shaw (2012) describe "inspired phone calls" where, if agreed within the boundaries of the therapeutic relationship, the therapist might choose to call the patient to reflect on positive progress in therapy and "share happiness" for them in a direct way, which is positively reinforcing. A further approach described suggests that regularly considering the patient and how they would have been as a child, offers opportunities for playful connection, to energize warm and secure attachment in the context of the therapeutic relationship. This approach also allows a chance for the therapist to demonstrate that they enjoy working with the patient, which adds to the caring respect common to psychological therapies, but adds an additional "building block" through which play and positive affect can be boosted. Some might argue that imagery work in itself, involving imagination, is a type of play, which then also holds for other experiential techniques like the empty chair technique and the use of drama therapy.

Within the group schema therapy approach, play can also be successfully utilized. However, for many adults, this can trigger several different beliefs, schemas, and ways of coping. For example, patients with borderline personality disorder who might have a punitive parent mode, might dismiss any suggestion of play as being "childish" or a "waste of time." This could be linked with schemas around not feeling confident about knowing how to play and defectiveness schemas. Lockwood and Shaw (2012) suggest several ways of working with this in the group schema therapy approach. These include "the face game" (using balloons and marker pens to draw how they feel, encouraging discussions with regard to emotions), Olympics (simulated from an inpatient complaining there was nothing but Olympics on TV, and so generating activities around "our own Olympics" and creating banners, flags, costumes, with a patient being the announcer for the opening ceremony, egg and spoon races, etc.).

Playful interventions should be carefully considered in the context of the patient's formulation and their current presenting difficulties. For example, if a patient is struggling with anger or sadness, a playful intervention might be less helpful. In the context of schema therapy modes, the patient's child modes need to be sufficiently settled to engage in the play. It would also be unhelpful if play were to be a distraction from painful feelings or difficult issues. On the other hand, for patients with a weak happy child mode, it might be indicated to integrate in every group schema therapy session a moment of play and joy, to promote the development of this suppressed or underdeveloped mode. Implicit in this is also the importance of therapists ensuring that they take care of themselves, so that they are able to from time to time actively enjoy their work with patients. These examples outlined above demonstrate how a flexible approach to delivering schema therapy can integrate ideas which have more of a focus on play and joy within therapeutic interventions and fit within a positive clinical psychology framework.

Conclusion

Psychological therapies have previously been poorly integrated with positive psychology approaches and focused more on the reduction of negative aspects of human experience, negative aspects of the self, and the reduction of distress. Wood and Tarrier (2010) argued for the development of a positive clinical psychology that needs to become more integrative and focuses on both positive and negative aspects of human experience in research and clinical practice. One of three strengths of schema therapy is the integration of interventions that boost positive modes, as well as seeking to weaken negative modes, which include a more equal balance on positive and negative functioning and highlights how both the positive and negative interact together within a schema therapy formulation. Early evidence would suggest that schema therapy can have a direct impact of individuals reported levels of happiness and well-being, and future work will further explore this. In this chapter, we have outlined how schema therapy can be seen as an example of a psychotherapy which is very much in line with the development of a positive clinical psychology approach.

Acknowledgements

Dr. Christopher Taylor gratefully acknowledges the support of a Research Fellowship Award from the National Institute for Health Research, UK (DRF-2012-05-211). The views expressed in this publication are those of the authors and not necessarily those of the NHS, the National Institute for Health Research, or the Department of Health.

Prof. Arnoud Arntz is supported by the Netherlands Organisation for Health Research and Development (ZonMW; 80-82310-97-12142) and the Netherlands Foundation for Mental Health (2008 6350).

References

Arntz, A. (2012). Schema therapy for cluster C personality disorders. In: J. B. M. van Vreeswijk & M. Nadort (Eds.), *The Wiley-Blackwell Handbook of schema therapy: Theory research and practice* (pp. 397–425). Chichester: Wiley-Blackwell.

Arntz, A. & Jacob, G. (2012). *Schema therapy in practice: An introductory guide to the schema mode approach.* Chichester: Wiley-Blackwell.

Arntz, A. & van Genderen, H. (2009). *Schema therapy for borderline personality disorder.* Chichester: Wiley-Blackwell.

Arntz, A. & Weertman, A. (1999). Treatment of childhood memories: Theory and practice. *Behaviour Research and Therapy*, *37*(8), 715–740.

Bamelis, L. L. M., Arntz, A., Wetzelaer, P., Verdoorn, R., & Evers, S. M. A. A. (in press). Economic evaluation of schema therapy and clarification-oriented psychotherapy for personality disorders: a multicenter randomized trial. *Journal of Clinical Psychiatry*.

Bamelis, L. L., Evers, S. M., Spinhoven, P., & Arntz, A. (2014). Results of a multicenter randomized controlled trial of the clinical effectiveness of schema therapy for personality disorders. *American Journal of Psychiatry*, *171*, 305–322. doi.org/10.1176/appi.ajp.2013.12040518.

Bamelis, L., Giesen-Bloo, J., Bernstein, D., & Arntz, A. (2012). Effectiveness studies of schema therapy. In: M. van Vreeswijk, J. Broersen, & M. Nadort (Eds.), *Handbook of schema therapy: Theory, research and practice*. Chichester: Wiley-Blackwell.

Bernstein, D. P., Arntz, A., & Vos, M. D. (2007). Schema focused therapy in forensic settings: Theoretical model and recommendations for best clinical practice. *International Journal of Forensic Mental Health*, *6*(2), 169–183.

Bernstein, D. P., Nijman, H. L. I., Karos, K., Keulen-de Vos, M., de Vogel, V., & Lucker, T. P. (2012). Schema therapy for forensic patients with personality disorders: Design and preliminary findings of a multicenter randomized clinical trial in the Netherlands. *International Journal of Forensic Mental Health*, *11*(4), 312–324. doi.10.1080/14999013.2012.746757

Bowlby, J. (1969). *Attachment and loss: Attachment*. New York: Basic Books.

Chakhssi, F., Kersten, T., de Ruiter, C., & Bernstein, D. P. (2014). Treating the untreatable: A single case study of a psychopathic inpatient treated with Schema Therapy. *Psychotherapy*, *51*(3), 447–461.

Cockram, D. M., Drummond, P. D., & Lee, C. W. (2010). Role and treatment of early maladaptive schemas in Vietnam veterans with PTSD. *Clinical Psychology & Psychotherapy*, *17*(3), 165–182. doi.10.1002/cpp.690.

Dickhaut, V. & Arntz, A. (2014). Combined group and individual schema therapy for borderline personality disorder: A pilot study. *Journal of Behavior Therapy and Experimental Psychiatry*, *45*(2), 242–251.

Edwards, D. & Arntz, A. (2012). Schema therapy in historical perspective. In: J. B. M. van Vreeswijk & M. Nadort (Eds.), *The Wiley-Blackwell handbook of schema therapy: Theory research and practice* (pp. 3–26). Chichester: Wiley-Blackwell.

Farrell, J. M. & Shaw, I. A. (1994). Emotional awareness training: A prerequisite to effective cognitive-behavioral treatment of borderline personality disorder. *Cognitive and Behavioral Practice*, *1*(1), 71–91.

Farrell, J. M. & Shaw, I. A. (2012). *Group Schema Therapy for borderline personality disorder: A step-by-step treatment manual with patient workbook*. Chichester: Wiley-Blackwell.

Farrell, J. M., Shaw, I. A., & Webber, M. A. (2009). A schema-focused approach to group psychotherapy for outpatients with borderline personality disorder: A randomized controlled trial. *Journal of Behavior Therapy and Experimental Psychiatry*, *40*(2), 317–328. doi.10.1016/j.jbtep.2009.01.002.

George, L., Thornton, C., Touyz, S. W., Waller, G., & Beumont, P. J. V. (2004). Motivational enhancement and schema-focused cognitive behaviour therapy in the treatment of chronic eating disorders. *Clinical Psychologist*, *8*(2), 81–85. doi.10.1080/13284200412331304054.

Giesen-Bloo, J., van Dyck, R., Spinhoven, P., van Tilburg, W., Dirksen, C., van Asselt, T., Arntz, A., et al. (2006). Outpatient psychotherapy for borderline personality disorder: Randomized trial of schema focused therapy vs transference-focused psychotherapy. *Archives of General Psychiatry*, *63*(6), 649–658. doi.org/10.1001/archpsyc.63.6.649.

Grawe, K. (2007). *Neuropsychotherapy: How the neurosciences inform effective psychotherapy*. New York: Psychology Press.

Hoffart, A., Versland, S., & Sexton, H. (2002). Self-understanding, empathy, guided discovery, and schema belief in schema-focused cognitive therapy of personality problems: A process–outcome study. *Cognitive Therapy & Research*, *26*(2), 199–219. doi.10.1023/a:1014521819858.

Horney, K. (1950). *Neurosis and human growth: The struggle towards self-realization*. New York: W. W. Norton.

Huntjens, R. J. C. (2014). Innovation in the treatment of dissociative identity disorder: The application of schema therapy. Available at: http://www.trialregister.nl/trialreg/admin/rctview.asp?TC=4496.

Jacob, G. A. & Arntz, A. (2013). Schema therapy for personality disorders: A review. *International Journal of Cognitive Therapy*, *6*(2), 171–185. doi.org/10.1521/ijct.2013.6.2.171.

Lobbestael, J. (2012). Validation of the Schema Mode Inventory. In: J. B. M. van Vreeswijk & M. Nadort (Eds.), *The Wiley-Blackwell handbook of schema therapy: Theory research and practice* (pp. 541–553). Chichester: Wiley-Blackwell.

Lockwood, G. & Perris, P. (2012). A new look at core emotional needs. In: J. B. M. van Vreeswijk & M. Nadort (Eds.), *The Wiley-Blackwell handbook of schema therapy: Theory research and practice* (pp. 41–66). Chichester: Wiley-Blackwell.

Lockwood, G. & Shaw, I. (2012). Schema therapy and the role of joy and play. In: J. B. M. van Vreeswijk & M. Nadort (Eds.), *The Wiley-Blackwell handbook of schema therapy: Theory research and practice* (pp. 209–227). Chichester: Wiley-Blackwell.

Malogiannis, I. A., Arntz, A., Spyropoulou, A., Tsartsara, E., Aggeli, A., Karveli, S., Zervas, I., et al. (2014). Schema therapy for patients with chronic depression: A single case series study. *Journal of Behavior Therapy and Experimental Psychiatry, 45*(3), 319–329.

Masley, S. A., Gillanders, D. T., Simpson, S. G., & Taylor, M. A. (2012). A systematic review of the evidence base for schema therapy. *Cognitive Behaviour Therapy, 41*(3), 185–202. doi.10.1080/16506 073.2011.614274.

Nadort, M., Arntz, A., Smit, J. H., Giesen-Bloo, J., Eikelenboom, M., Spinhoven, P., van Dyck, R., et al. (2009). Implementation of outpatient schema therapy for borderline personality disorder with versus without crisis support by the therapist outside office hours: A randomized trial. *Behaviour Research and Therapy, 47*(11), 961–973. doi.org/10.1016/j.brat.2009.07.013.

Oei, T. P. S. & Baranoff, J. (2007). Young Schema Questionnaire: Review of psychometric and measurement issues. *Australian Journal of Psychology, 59*(2), 78–86. doi.10.1080/00049530601148397.

Panksepp, J. (1998). *Affective neuroscience: The foundations of human and animal emotions.* Oxford: Oxford University Press.

Rafaeli, E., Bernstein, D. P., & Young, J. E. (2011). *Schema therapy: The CBT distinctive features series.* London: Routledge.

Rijkeboer, M. M. (2012). Validation of the Young Schema Questionnaire. In: J. B. M. van Vreeswijk & M. Nadort (Ed.), *The Wiley-Blackwell handbook of schema therapy: theory research and practice* (pp. 531–541). Chichester: Wiley-Blackwell.

Rijkeboer, M. M. & de Boo, G. M. (2010). Early maladaptive schemas in children: Development and validation of the schema inventory for children. *Journal of Behavior Therapy and Experimental Psychiatry, 41*(2), 102–109. doi.org/10.1016/j.jbtep.2009.11.001.

Schore, A. N. (2003). *Affect dysregulation and disorders of the self.* New York: W. W. Norton.

Sempértegui, G. A., Karreman, A., Arntz, A., & Bekker, M. H. J. (2013). Schema therapy for borderline personality disorder: A comprehensive review of its empirical foundations, effectiveness and implementation possibilities. *Clinical Psychology Review, 33*(3), 426–447. doi.org/10.1016/j.cpr.2012.11.006.

Simpson, S. G., Morrow, E., Vreeswijk, M. V., & Reid, C. (2010). Group schema therapy for eating disorders: A pilot study. *Frontiers in Psychology, 1.* doi.10.3389/fpsyg.2010.00182.

Stallard, P. & Rayner, H. (2005). The development and preliminary evaluation of a Schema Questionnaire for Children (SQC). *Behavioural and Cognitive Psychotherapy, 33*(2), 217–224.

Stopa, L., Thorne, P., Waters, A., & Preston, J. (2001). Are the short and long forms of the Young Schema Questionnaire comparable and how well does each version predict psychopathology scores? *Journal of Cognitive Psychotherapy, 15*(3), 253–272.

van Genderen, H., Rijkeboer, M., & Arntz, A. (2012). Theoretical model: Schemas, coping styles and modes. In: J. B. M. van Vreeswijk & M. Nadort (Eds.), *The Wiley-Blackwell handbook of schema therapy: Theory, research and practice* (pp. 27–40). Chichester: Wiley-Blackwell.

Veenhoven, R. (2008). One item Happiness Question: World Database of Happiness. Available at: http://worlddatabaseofhappiness.eur.nl/hap_quer/hqs_fp.htm, last accessed May 18, 2015.

Wetzelaer, P., Farrell, J., Evers, S. M., Jacob, G. A., Lee, C. W., Brand, O., Harper, R. P., et al. (2014). Design of an international multicentre RCT on group schema therapy for borderline personality disorder. *BMC Psychiatry, 14*(1), 319.

Williams, J., Watts, F., MacLeod, C., & Mathews, A. (1997). *Cognitive psychology and emotional disorders.* Chichester: Wiley-Blackwell.

Wood, A. M. & Tarrier, N. (2010). Positive clinical psychology: A new vision and strategy for integrated research and practice. *Clinical Psychology Review, 30* (7), 819–829. doi.10.1016/j.cpr.2010.06.00.

Young, J. E. (1990). *Schema-focused cognitive therapy for personality disorders: A schema focused approach.* Sarasota, FL: Professional Resource Exchange.

Young, J. E., Arntz, A., Atkinson, T., Lobbestael, J., Weishaar, M. E., & van Vreeswijk, M. F. (2007). *The Schema Mode Inventory (SMI).* New York: Schema Therapy Institute.

Young, J., Klosko, J., & Weishaar, M. (2003). *Schema therapy: A practitioner's guide.* New York: Guilford Press.

Index

The Wiley Handbook of Positive Clinical Psychology, First Edition. Edited by Alex M. Wood and Judith Johnson.
© 2016 John Wiley & Sons, Ltd. Published 2016 by John Wiley & Sons, Ltd.